A BIBLIOGRAPHY OF DESIGN IN BRITAIN 1851~1970

Anthony J. Coulson

Design Council

A Bibliography of Design in Britain 1851-1970

First edition published in the
United Kingdom 1979 by
Design Council Publications
28 Haymarket, London SW1Y 4SU

Designed by Gill Streater

Phototypesetting by
SIOS Ltd
111-115 Salusbury Road, London NW6 6RJ

Printed and bound in the United Kingdom by
Billing & Sons Ltd
Guildford, London and Worcester

Distributed in the United Kingdom by
Heinemann Educational Books Ltd
48 Charles Street, London W1X 8AH

British Library CIP Data

Coulson, Anthony J
A Bibliography of Design in Britain
1851-1970
1. Design – Great Britain – History –
Bibliography
I. Title II. Design Council
016.7454'49'41   Z5956.D5

ISBN 0 85072 091 5

Contents

Introduction

In the past few years the history of design has emerged as a subject for study in its own right. With the setting up of courses in design history at all levels, and of research in many different directions, there is a clear need to pool information about surveys and documents which already exist, but are widely scattered. As a first step, I have chosen to put together this introductory bibliography of the period which has excited the most interest recently – that of the past hundred years or so. By picking the chronological period between 1851 and 1970 I have opted for a convenient envelope for a rich collection of different materials, rather than a historical period standing by itself. Material from earlier and later times is included where it clearly relates to developments in the chosen period. Similarly, my decision to concentrate on British design does not mean that relevant developments elsewhere are excluded. In both cases, however, some kind of limitation is necessary to keep the work within manageable proportions.

Scope and selection

I have described this work as an introductory bibliography for three main reasons. First, anything approaching a comprehensive bibliography is not possible at present, given the enormous span of the subject and the lack of serious historical research and documentation in so many of its areas. Second, I intend this work as an anthology of references to introduce a very wide range of books and articles on many different subjects, including a lot that have scarcely been studied hitherto. In all areas there is scope for an enormous amount of research to produce serious design history, and any interim listing such as this must inevitably be patchy. Third, I have deliberately tried to restrict myself to the more accessible works, which can be used with profit by someone unfamiliar with the intricacies of some of the extremely complex subjects involved.

Apart from monographs, some useful papers and articles from the more generally available journals are included, together with some of the most important exhibitions. Sadly, many original documents and journals may not be readily accessible at present, as they are long out of print, but some are becoming obtainable through reprints and microfilm and microfiche. For this reason reprints and microforms are indicated whenever the information is to hand. Even so, a lot of the older material – particularly in old manuals and handbooks – may never be reprinted, but it would be a mistake to ignore its existence, particularly as it often opens up live issues of its time, which are often remote from current experience.

The core of serious design history writing is still fairly small and growing only slowly, so that a bibliography such as this is bound to include more popular works and surveys as well as the main documentary sources from which the history needs to be constructed. The mix is bound to be uneven, as some subjects are more popular with collectors and enthusiasts than others.

Although I have interpreted design in a broad way, I have had to make some restrictions to keep the work to a reasonable size. I have reluctantly excluded most aspects of architecture, town and country planning, and civil engineering, as these subject areas are already fairly well served by thriving and well organised historical literatures. Furthermore, I have excluded some areas such as toys, musical instruments and photography, where there is a detailed literature which is quite separate from design considerations and which cannot be treated effectively in summary. In the case of other subjects such as transport, stamps and coins, where there is a very large literature catering for the enthusiast and specialist, this bibliography is deliberately very selective. Two other design areas – weapons and military design of all sorts and design for the performing arts – have had to be left out as they would require a consideration of many special factors which cannot be adequately covered in a book of this size.

As regards the actual choice of references, I have deliberately tried to avoid including sources that can be very difficult to obtain or use, such as manuscript material, theses, and trade and specialised literature. Some works that have only a marginal interest in design history have been included, such as company histories, when they are useful in suggesting further sources and plans for research. In the absence of much serious design history writing it has been necessary to detail some marginal sources that provide valuable initial information on which to base further work.

Arrangement

The bibliography has been planned as a collection of sections rather than a continuous narrative to read from cover to cover. Three keys are provided to this mass of information:

1 *Contents page* for an indication of the main sections.
2 *Table of dates* (page 8) for a chronological framework of the period.
3 *Subject finder* (page 292) which provides an index of sections, subjects and some important individuals (but *not* an index of authors or of all individuals named).

The first two sections – 'Fostering Design' and 'Design and Designers' – concern themselves with more general studies, documents and issues. The section on individual designers and theorists includes those who have made a contribution to a number of different activities; their separate listing is in no way exhaustive, but intended to be filled out by later and larger biographical dictionaries.

The most specific information is given in the most specific place with appropriate cross-references – generally in the third section, 'Areas of Design Activity'. In this way, studies of William Morris's designs for wallpaper will be found in the 'Paper' subsection of section three, but more general studies of William Morris are in the earlier 'Design and Designers' section.

Within individual sections the most important introductory references are placed first. In the more detailed elaborations that follow, chronological rather than alphabetical order is preferred. In each case the arrangement of the section tries to reflect the peculiarities and problems of the subject.

Acknowledgements

This work has only been possible through the generous help and advice of a great many people. Although special mention cannot be made of all sources of help and support, I owe a special debt to the following: to the Open University, Mr Simpson and library colleagues for the time, advice and understanding that made the research possible; to Tim and Charlotte Benton, Hazel Conway, Clive Wainwright and other members of the Association of Art Historians Design History Publications Sub-Committee for their advice and guidance; to Roger Newport, Toni del Renzio and many other members of the Design History Research Group (now the Design History Society) for advice and information; to Leela Meineertas, Shirley Bury, Valerie Mendes and other members

of the Victoria and Albert Museum for much useful information; to the librarians of the Design Council Slide Library, Textile Institute, Royal Institute of British Architects, London Library, Royal College of Art, Central School of Art and Design, Kingston Polytechnic, Patent Office, Royal Society of Antiquaries, Middlesex Polytechnic, London School of Fashion, London School of Furniture, London School of Printing, Shoreditch Reference Library, British Library (Reference Division), Royal Society of Arts, and Manchester Polytechnic for unfailing courtesy and valuable assistance; to Terry Bishop, Gill Streater, Nicola Hamilton and others at the Design Council for their patience and care; and above all to my wife for her support and reassurance through the months it took to assemble this book. Any blemishes that remain are my responsibility alone.

Finally, as this is the first attempt to cover this very large and diverse range of subjects, comments and further information will be greatly welcomed by the publishers and myself, as will suggestions for further editions and publications in this area.

Abbreviations

The use of abbreviations and acronyms has been kept to a minimum, but the following have been used to save space:

CoID	Council of Industrial Design
JSA	Journal of the Society of Arts
JRSA	Journal of the Royal Society of Arts
JRIBA	Journal of the Royal Institute of British Architects
bibl.	bibliography
illus.	illustrations
pl.	plates
col.	colour
(ed)	editor
(comp)	compiler
n.d.	no date indicated

Table of Important dates

1836
Mr Ewart's Select Committee report to the Government on 'the best means of extending a knowledge of the arts and principles of design among the people (especially the manufacturing population) of the country'

1837
Normal School of Design established at Somerset House and branch schools 'in order to extend a knowledge of the arts and principles of design among the people'

1839
Designs Copyright Act published 'to secure to proprietors of design for articles of manufacture the copyright of such designs for a limited time'

1841
The True Principles of Pointed or Christian Architecture, by Augustus Welby Northmore Pugin, published

1844
'Exhibition of the Products of National Industry' first held by Society for the Encouragement of Arts, Manufactures and Commerce

1846
Society of Arts first awarded annual prizes to students of design at art schools
Henry Cole (Felix Summerly) awarded silver medal in Society of Arts Competition

1847
Annual exhibition of 'Select Specimens of British Manufactures and Decorative Art'
Society of Arts granted Royal Charter
Summerly's Art Manufactures founded

1851
'Great Exhibition of the Works of Industry of All Nations', London

1851-3
Stones of Venice, by John Ruskin, published

1852
Department of Practical Art established at Marlborough House
Ornamental Art Collection opened at Marlborough House (formed basis of Victoria and Albert Museum)

1853
'Great Industrial Exhibition', Dublin
'World's Fair of the Works of Industry of All Nations', New York
Department of Science and Art moved its museum to South Kensington (formed nucleus of future Royal College of Art and Victoria and Albert Museum)

1855
'Exposition Universelle', Paris

1856
Central Art Training School founded in South Kensington
Grammar of Ornament, by Owen Jones, published

1857
Report on the Present State of Design as Applied to Manufactures, by Richard Redgrave, published

1861
Morris, Marshall and Faulkner, Fine Art Workmen, issued first prospectus

1862
'International Exhibition', London

1865
'International Exhibition of Arts and Manufactures', Dublin

1867
'Exposition Universelle', Paris

1868
Hints on Household Taste, by Charles Eastlake, published

1871
St George's Guild founded by Ruskin
'First Annual International Exhibition', London

1872
'Second Annual International Exhibition', London

1873
'Third Annual International Exhibition', London
'Weltausstellung 1873 Wien', Vienna

1874
'Fourth Annual International Exhibition', London

1875
Arthur Lasenby Liberty opened shop in Regent Street, London

1876
'Centennial Exposition', Philadelphia

1877
Society for the Protection of Ancient Buildings (Anti-Scrape) founded

1878
'Exposition Universelle', Paris

1880
Art Furniture Alliance opened by Christopher Dresser in Bond Street, London

1882
Century Guild formed by Arthur H. Mackmurdo

1884
Art Workers' Guild formed from St George's Art Society and others

Home Art and Industries Association formed

'International Health Exhibition', London

1888
Arts and Crafts Exhibition Society founded by C. R. Ashbee

National Association for Advancement of Art and its Application to Industry founded

Guild and School of Handicraft formed by C. R. Ashbee

1889
'Exposition Universelle', Paris

1890
Kelmscott Press founded by William Morris

Kenton & Co furniture workshops opened by Lethaby, Gimson and Sidney Barnsley

1893
The Studio published

'World's Columbian Exposition', Chicago

1895
L'Art Nouveau shop opened by Samuel Bing in Paris, selling British Arts and Crafts

1896
National Art Training School reconstituted as Royal College of Art

Society of Designers established

Central School of Arts and Crafts opened to encourage the industrial application of decorative art, with Lethaby as joint Principal

Hermann Muthesius sent to German Embassy in London to research British architecture and crafts

1897-9
Glasgow School of Art, first phase, built to the design of Charles Rennie Mackintosh

1898
Heal's first catalogue of Plain Oak Furniture

Northern Art Workers' Guild first exhibition

1899
Darmstadt artistic colony established by Grand Duke of Hesse. Designs for the Ducal Palace by Baillie Scott and Mackintosh

South Kensington Museum became Victoria and Albert Museum

1900
Royal College of Art appoints Lethaby as first Professor of Design

'Exposition Universelle', Paris

1901
'Glasgow International Exhibition'

Die Englische Baukunst der Gegenwart, by Hermann Muthesius, published in Germany

'Ein Dokument Deutscher Kunst' exhibition, Darmstadt

1902
'Esposizione Internazionale D'Arte Decorativa Moderna', Turin

1904
'Louisiana Purchase Exhibition', St Louis

1904-5
Das Englische Haus, by Hermann Muthesius, published in Germany in three volumes

1905
Exhibition of Cheap Cottages at Letchworth, sponsored by *The Spectator*

1906
'Sweated Labour' exhibition

1906-7
Deutsche Werkstätten formed and established at Hellerau, near Dresden

1908
'Franco-British Exhibition', London

1909
Guild and School of Handicrafts dissolved

1910
'Exposition Universelle et Internationale', Brussels

1911
'Esposizione Internazionale D'Industria e De Laboro', Turin

1913
Ministry of Education's Art Examination
introduced in drawing, painting, modelling,
pictorial design and industrial design

1914
Deutscher Werkbund exhibition, Cologne

1915
German industrial design exhibition at
Goldsmiths Hall, London, sponsored by
Board of Trade

'Panama-Pacific Exposition', San Francisco

Design and Industries Association founded

DIA's first exhibition 'Design and
Workmanship in Printing' at Whitechapel
Gallery

1916
'Arts and Crafts' exhibition at Burlington
House

1919
Bauhaus founded

Art and Industry pamphlet published by
Ministry of Reconstruction

1920
British Institute of Industrial Art founded
with gallery in Knightsbridge (but grant
withdrawn in 1921)

Federation of British Industry Industrial
Art Committee formed 'to consider the
question of industrial art in this country',
chairman Charles Tennyson

'Exhibition of Household Things' by DIA at
Whitechapel Gallery

1923
'Industrial Art Today' exhibition

Nonesuch Press founded by Francis Meynell

1924
Designers' Register and Employment
Bureau opened by Industrial Art
Committee
of FBI

Royal Society of Arts annual competitions
for design started

1924-5
'British Empire Exhibition', Wembley

1925
'Exposition Internationale des Arts
Décoratifs et Industriels Modernes', Paris

1927
DIA exhibited at Leipzig Fair

1928
Chermayeff exhibition at Waring & Gillow

Gordon Russell exhibited furniture at
Powell's London showroom

T. S. Tait and Joseph Emberton exhibited
furniture at Shoolbred's

1929
'Industrial Art for the Slender Purse'
exhibition by British Institute of Industrial
Art at Victoria and Albert Museum

'Exposición Internacional de Barcelona'

Report on Design in the Cotton Industry
published by HM Inspectors

1930
Venesta stand in Building Trades
Exhibition designed by Le Corbusier

Society of Industrial Artists founded

Memorandum on State-aided Art Education
published by Industrial Art Committee of
FBI

Report on Handicrafts in Elementary
Schools published by London County
Council

'Stockholm Exhibition'

1931
Exhibition of Swedish Art in London

Committee on Art and Industry appointed
by Board of Trade, Chairman Lord Gorell

1932
Association of Artists in Commerce founded

New British Broadcasting Corporation
building interiors designed by Raymond
McGrath, Wells Coates and Serge
Chermayeff

Import Duties Act imposed 15 per cent duty
on all imported products

Report on Art and Education (in particular
industrial art exhibitions) published by
Gorell Committee

1933
'Design in Modern Life' talks series held by
BBC

Bauhaus closed for political reasons

Ghastly Good Taste, by John Betjeman,
published

'British Industrial Art' exhibition in relation
to the home held in collaboration with DIA,
Dorland Hall, London

Exhibitions of model houses in Manchester
and Welwyn by DIA

Plywood furniture by Aalto on sale in
Britain

1933-4
'Century of Progress International
Exposition', Chicago

1934

Council for Art and Industry established by Board of Trade to encourage good design 'especially in relation to manufacturers', chairman Frank Pick

Small exhibition of silverware held at Victoria and Albert Museum by Pick Council

Second Dorland Hall exhibition

Birmingham exhibition held by DIA

'Exhibition of Modern Living' at Whiteley's

Memorandum on Art Education, with particular reference to the Royal College of Art, sent to Board of Education by DIA

Art and Industry, by Herbert Read, published

1935

'British Art in Industry' exhibition, Burlington House, London

Report on Education for the Consumer, particularly training in design in elementary and secondary schools, published by Council for Art and Industry

FBI Industrial Art Committee Memorandum on industrial art training for management and staff of firms

Industrial Design Partnership founded by Milner Gray, Misha Black and others

'Exposition Universelle et Internationale', Brussels

Nugent Committee Report on Industrial Art to Ministry of Education

1936

Board of Education Committee on Advanced Education in London, chaired by Viscount Hambledon

Board of Trade National Register of Industrial Art Designers formed

Council for Art and Industry Report on The Working Class Home: its Furnishing and Equipment by Mrs C. G. Tomrley

Designers for Industry (from 1937, Royal Designers for Industry) appointed by Royal Society of Arts

'Exhibition of Everyday Things' at Royal Institute of British Architects

Pick Council Exhibition of domestic metalwork

'Seven Architects' exhibition at Heal's, London

1937

BBC Talks on Design by Anthony Bertram concurrent with DIA travelling exhibitions

Council for Art and Industry Report on Design and the Designer in Industry

'Exposition Internationale des Arts et Techniques dans la Vie Moderne', Paris

Institute of Design, Chicago (the new Bauhaus)

An Enquiry into Industrial Art in England, by Nikolaus Pevsner, published

Report on Advanced Art Education in London recommended 'a new orientation should be given to the Royal College of Art'

'Working Class Home' exhibition at Building Centre

Unpublished proposal for Industrial Art Centre by Council for Art and Industry

1938

'British Empire Exhibition', Glasgow

Good Furnishing Group formed by Geoffrey Dunn, Crofton Gane, Gordon Russell and others

Royal Society of Arts Industrial Bursaries Competition started

1939

Central Institute for Art and Design formed to safeguard wartime interests of artists and designers

1939-40

'New York World's Fair'

'Golden Gate International Exposition', San Francisco

1940

Cotton Board Fashion Design and Style Centre opened in Manchester

1942

Board of Trade Utility Furniture Committee, later Design Panel, chaired by Gordon Russell

DIA with Army Bureau of Current Affairs mobile exhibitions

1943

Design Research Unit established with Herbert Read as first manager

Unpublished industrial design and art in industry report by Department of Overseas Trade Post-War Export Trade Committee (recommended a Central Design Council)

1944

Board of Trade and Education Report on Art Training by Meynell-Hoskin Committee (supported idea of a Central Design Council)

Council of Industrial Design (with Scottish Committee) set up 'to promote by all practicable means the improvement of design in the products of British industry'

FBI Industrial Art Committee proposals for a Central Design Council and Industrial Design Centre

The Missing Technician in Industrial Production, by John Gloag, published

Rayon Industry Design Centre opened

1945

'Design for the Home' exhibition held by Council for the Encouragement of Music and the Arts

'Historical and British Wallpapers' exhibition designed by Eric Brown and Stefan Buzas, National Gallery

Institute of Engineering Designers established

National Register of Industrial Art Designers develops to CoID Record of Designers

1946

'Britain Can Make It' exhibition at Victoria and Albert Museum

The Visual Arts report published by Dartington Hall with PEP

Design and Research Centre for Gold, Silver and Jewellery Industries established

National Diploma in Design introduced in art schools

Unpublished CoID report on the Training of the Industrial Designer

1947

'Enterprise Scotland' exhibition by CoID

1948

'Design at Work' exhibition of products by Royal Designers for Industry sponsored by RSA and CoID

International Low-cost Furniture competition at Museum of Modern Art, prize won by Robin Day and Clive Latimer

1949

BBC series 'Looking at Things' for schools

'International Exhibition of Industrial Design', Amsterdam, set up by CoID

1951

Festival of Britain

'Living Traditions of Scotland' exhibition, Edinburgh

Royal College of Art awards first DesRCA

1952

CoID Street Furniture Design competition

'Victorian and Edwardian Decorative Arts' at Victoria and Albert Museum

1953

'Register Your Choice' DIA exhibition at Charing Cross

1954

The Design Centre of British Industries agreed to by Government

Royal Society of Arts Bicentenary Medal for people who 'in a manner other than as industrial designers have exerted an exceptional influence in promoting art and design in British industry' first awarded to Sir Colin Anderson

1955

Design in British Industry, by Michael Farr, published

1956

British Railways Design Panel set up

The Design Centre, Haymarket, London, opened

Management of Design conference by CoID

1957

Committee on Art Examinations report submitted to Minister of Education recommending greater administrative freedom for colleges

Design Centre Awards started

International Council of Societies of Industrial Design (ICSID) established

'Make or Mar' DIA exhibition

Scottish Design Centre opened

1958

'The Design Centre Comes to Newcastle' exhibition, first in a series of promotions in provincial stores

Industrial Design and the Engineering Industries conference by CoID in Birmingham

'Expo 58'. Exposition Universelle et Internationale de Bruxelles

1959

Design Centre labelling scheme begun

Duke of Edinburgh's Prize for Elegant Design first awarded

Gran Premio Internazionale la Rinascente Compasso d'Oro awarded to CoID in Milan

National Advisory Council on Art Education formed under Sir William Coldstream

1960

Coldstream Committee First Report on Art Education submitted, recommending higher standard courses to replace NDD

'Designers of the Future' exhibition at Heal's

Industrial Design (Engineering) Research Unit established at Royal College of Art under Bruce Archer

1961

Design Policy for Corporate Buying international congress organised by CoID

'Modern Jewellery Exhibition', Goldsmiths Hall

National Council for Diplomas in Art and Design established on recommendation of Coldstream Council

'Street Furniture' exhibition by CoID on South Bank

1962

First conference on systematic design methods, Imperial College, London

'Century 21 Exposition', Seattle

Coldstream Council Second Report on vocational courses in colleges and schools of art

1963

Systematic Method for Designers, by L. Bruce Archer, published

Department of Scientific and Industrial Research Report on Engineering Design, chaired by G. B. R. Feilden, to consider present position of mechanical engineering design

First DipAD courses started

International Congress of Graphic Design Associations (ICOGRADA) established

London Transport Design Panel formed

Robbins Report on Higher Education

1964

Coldstream Council Third Report on Post-Diploma Studies in Art and Design

First report of Summerson Council for Diplomas in Art and Design

Grand Prix at Milan Triennale won by Hornsea Mobile Caravan

House of Lords Debate on industrial design

Post-Diploma Studies in Art and Design started

Royal Society of Arts Presidential Awards for Design Management first presented

1965

CoID's first engineering exhibition

FBI Report on Industrial and Engineering Design by committee under G. B. R. Feilden

Society of Industrial Artists renamed Society of Industrial Artists and Designers

1966

A Plan for Polytechnics and Other Colleges published by the Department of Education and Science, recommending absorption of larger art colleges by polytechnics

Diplomas in Art and Design (first degree equivalent) awarded to students at art colleges

Engineering Design Centre established at Loughborough University of Technology

Leverhulme Trust first travelling scholarships in industrial design

Plans first announced for a combined headquarters for ICA, SIAD, and Designers and Art Directors Association at Nash House Terrace

1967

CoID Capital Goods Awards Scheme

Design Centre Awards renamed Council of Industrial Design Awards and broadened to include engineering design

'Expo 67'. Universal and International Exhibition, Montreal

Royal College of Art given university status. MArt and MDes introduced

1968

Institute of Mechanical Engineers working party report to Ministry of Technology advocating a single design council to promote design across the whole span of British industry

Joint Coldstream/Summerson Committee of Inquiry into structure of art and design education

Stedelijk Museum exhibition of industrial design, British representation by Robin Day, Kenneth Grange, David Mellor and Robert Welch

1969

ICSID conference in London

Proposals passed for National Design Council incorporating CoID to cover engineering design as well as industrial design

SIAD and DIA etc move to Nash House Terrace

1970

'Expo 70'. Japan World Exposition, Osaka

Association for Design Education established to promote design in general education

Conway Report on National Design Council

Experimental GCE A-Level design syllabus in Leicestershire schools

Institute for Consumer Ergonomics jointly sponsored by Consumers' Association and Loughborough University of Technology

Joint Coldstream/Summerson Committee of Inquiry into structure of art and design education recommended replacement of vocational courses by new design technician courses

'Modern Chairs' exhibition, Whitechapel Art Gallery

Fostering design

Developments in education

The tangled and often very confusing
history of the development of design
education has never been fully written
up and offers great scope for research.
Some of the fuller histories of art
education offer a useful starting point:

Macdonald, Stuart. *The history and
philosophy of art education.* 1970 London:
University of London Press 400pp

Sutton, George. *Artisan or artist? A history of
the teaching of art and crafts in English
schools.* 1967 Oxford: Pergamon 328pp
illus.

Pevsner, Nikolaus. *Academies of art.* 1940
London: Cambridge University Press
323pp (particularly chapter VI 'The
revival of industrial art and artists'
education today')

Studies of technical and adult education
offer useful background but in practice
have very little information on design:

Kelly, Thomas. *A history of adult education
in Great Britain from the Middle Ages to the
twentieth century.* 1970 second edition
Liverpool University Press 420pp illus.
bibl.

Abbot, A. *Education for industry and
commerce in England.* 1933 London:
Oxford University Press 228pp

Argles, Michael. *South Kensington to Robbins.
An account of English technical and scientific
education since 1851.* 1964 London:
Longmans 178pp bibl.

Documents

There is quite a richness of government
and private material for the history of
design education, but much is difficult to
trace and obtain. However there is a
useful introductory collection of extracts,
ranging from the *Report of the Select
Committee on Arts and Manufactures 1836* to
*Vocational courses in Art and Design (Gann
report) 1974* contained in:

Ashwin, Clive (ed). *Art Education documents
and policies 1768-1975.* 1975 London:
Society for Research into Higher
Education 158pp

and a useful guide to the earlier
documents is provided by the
bibliography:

Argles, Michael. *British government
publications in education during the 19th
century.* 1971 Sheffield: History of
Education Society 20pp

Other reports will be introduced as they
occur in the main phases of historical
development.

Select Committee and the Schools
of Design

To understand the roots and many of the
problems of early design education it is
essential to go back to the 1830s and Mr
Ewart's House of Commons select
committee report on 'the best means of
extending a knowledge of the arts and
principles of design among the people
(especially the manufacturing population)
of the country'. Helpfully, the reports are
available in reprint form:

*Extending a knowledge of the arts and
principles of design among the manufacturing
population. Select committee report with
minutes of evidence and appendix 1835
(598)* vol. V and
*Select committee report with minutes of evidence
and appendix (568)* vol. IX appear in:

*British Parliamentary Papers. Industrial
Design I.* 1968 Shannon: Irish University
Press

As a result the Government established the
Normal School of Design in 1837 'in order
to extend a knowledge of the arts and
principles of design among the people'.
There is a useful introduction to its
unhappy career (and its provincial
branches) in:

Bell, Quentin. *The Schools of Design.* 1963
London: Routledge and Kegan Paul
290pp

Many of the basic documents have been
reprinted in:

*British Parliamentary Papers. Industrial
Revolution. Design 3. Select committee and
other reports on the School of Design and on
foreign schools of Design with Proceedings,
minutes of evidence, appendices and indices
1840-49.* 1971 Shannon: Irish
University Press

which includes:

*Foreign schools of Design. Report from Mr
Dyce to the President of the Board of Trade.*
1840 (98) vol XXIX

Reports from the Council of the School of Design
1841 (65)   vol XIIII
1843 (454) vol XXIX
1844 (566) vol XXXI
1845 (654) vol XXVII
1846 (730) vol XXIV

Report from the special committee on the state and management of the School of Design 1847 (835) vol LXII

Report from the special committee on measures for carrying out the recommendations of the earlier committee 1847 (850) vol LXII

Report from the select committee with proceedings, minutes of evidence 1849 (576) vol XVIII

Furthermore:

Schools of Design, accounts and papers, reports, returns, documents 1850 (730) vol XLII, 1851(1423) vol XLIII have been reprinted in:

British Parliamentary Papers. Industrial Revolution. Design 4. 1970 Shannon: Irish University Press

Manuscript histories of many of the branch schools exist but have never been published since Bell's listing although quite a lot of research is in hand.

Science and Art Department

The transformation and development of design education in the wake of the Great Exhibition and the problems of the Design Schools owed much to Sir Henry Cole who republished a number of his key policy documents in:

Cole, Sir Henry. *Fifty years of public work . . . accounted for in his deeds, speeches and writings.* 1884 London: Bell 2 vols. (volume 1: autobiography, volume 2: speeches and articles)

A further 40 volumes of *Miscellanies and Diaries* are conserved with other unpublished papers in the Victoria and Albert Museum and provide rich material for research. There is a detailed index in the typescript:

The personal papers, manuscripts, pamphlets and other documents left by Sir Henry Cole, first director of the South Kensington Museum, (comp) Vera Kaden. 1973 London: Victoria and Albert Museum Library

In many ways they can be seen as developments of the ideas put forward by Cole and his friends in:

Journal of Design and Manufactures 1849-February 1852
as many of them took posts in the new

organisation. The best sources of information for the official version of the policy of the new constituted Department of Practical Art, later Department of Science and Art, are:

Department of Science and Art. *Annual reports nos 1-46.* 1854-1899 London: HMSO (30th Annual report 1882 contains a short history of the Science and Art Department)

and the:

Addresses of the superintendents of the Department of Practical Art 1853-1858. London: HMSO

particularly:

Redgrave, Richard. *On the necessity of principles in teaching Design.* 1853 reissued as:

The principles of Decorative Art. Published by authority of the Department of Science and Art 1853

The early development of the newer colleges growing at this period can be traced through:

Wallis, George. *Schools of Art; their constitution and management . . . With an introductory chapter on the early progress, constitution and results of Government Schools of Design.* 1857 Birmingham

The documents and directives of the new Department give a fair idea of the centralised control involved:

A list of publications issued by the Science and Art Department for the use of Schools of Art. 1873 London: Chapman and Hall 9pp

Directory (revised to July 1886) with regulations for establishing and conducting Science and Art Schools and Classes. 1886 London: Chapman and Hall

a situation inviting both criticism, as in:

Dresser, Christopher. 'Hindrances to the progress of applied art', *JSA* vol 20 April 12 1872 pp 435-443

Fielding, K. J. 'Charles Dickens and the Department of Practical Art' *Modern Language Review* vol XLVIII July 1953 pp 270-277

further investigation:

Report of the select committee appointed to enquire into the constitution and working, and into the success of the Schools of Art wholly or partially supported by government grants 1864 (466) XII 187 1864 London: HMSO

and surveys:

Art and Industry. Instruction in drawing applied to Industrial and Fine Arts as given in the colleges of agriculture and the mechanic arts and in the public schools and other public educational establishments in the United States by Isaac Edwards Clarke. 1885 Washington: Government Printing Office (appendix F has a very full tabulation and details of 'Governmental Aid to Education in the Industrial and Fine Arts in Great Britain')

Hulme, Frederick Edward. *Art instruction in England.* 1882 London: Longmans 160pp

The impact of these schools on the development of the more technical aspects of education was a subject inviting controversy:

Stephens, W. B. 'Victorian art schools and technical education', *Journal of Educational Administration* December 1969 pp13-19

Report of the Royal Commission on Technical Instruction (chairman Sir B. Samuelson) 1st report 1881 (C.3171) XXVII 153. 1881 London: HMSO
Further reports with evidence and appendix 1884 (C.3981) XXIX, XXX, XXXI, XXXII. 1884 London: HMSO

Part IV of the conclusions of the 1884 report asserts 'your commissioners cannot conceal from themselves the fact that their (Colleges of Art) influence on industrial art in this country is far from being so great as that of similar schools abroad'. Nevertheless the survey of the period 1837-1912 contained in:

Brown, Frank P. *South Kensington and its art training. With a foreword by Commendatore W. Crane.* 1912 London: Longmans Green 66pp

reveals a more optimistic and changing picture.

The whole area of other types of nineteenth-century design education is very complex and most available writing reflects personal preference and experience rather than objective summary:

Hope, Alexander James Beresford. *The Art-Workman's position. A lecture delivered on behalf of the Architectural Museum, at the South Kensington Museum, March 16 1864.* 1864 London

Armstrong, T. 'The condition of applied art in England and the education of the art workman'. *JSA* vol 35 February 4 1887 pp 204-221

Miller, Fred. *The training of a craftsman, illustrated by many workers in the art crafts.* 1898 London: Virtue 249pp

This last reference leads naturally to the ideas of the exponents of the Arts and Crafts movement which are presented in the more general discussion of their work.

See also:
Arts and Crafts Movement *page 70*
Important Designers *page 75*
Art Workers' Guild *page 21*

National Competition

One important and well documented change at the end of the century was the establishment of a national competition and exhibition. A useful barometer of taste and prevailing influences, the exhibitions were lavishly recorded first officially: ·

An illustrated record of the retrospective exhibition held at South Kensington 1896. Compiled and edited by J. Fisher . . . containing two hundred and fifty six illustrations . . . for which gold and silver medals have been awarded by the Department of Science and Art. 1897 London: Chapman and Hall 156pp

National Competitions 1896-7. An illustrated record edited and compiled by John Fisher. 1899 London: Chapman and Hall 101pp illus.

and then primarily through the illustrated pages of *Studio:*

White, Gleeson. 'The National Competition, South Kensington 1898', *Studio* vol 14 1898 pp 263-92 42 illus.

Wood, Esther. 'National Competition at South Kensington', *Studio* vol 17 1899 pp 251-67 45 illus.

Wood, Esther. 'The National Competition 1900', *Studio* vol 20 1900 pp 249-66 45 illus.

Wood, Esther. 'The National Competition 1901', *Studio* vol 23 1901 pp 257-269 34 illus.

Wood, Esther. 'The National Competition of Schools of Art 1902', *Studio* vol 26 1902 pp 268-281 33 illus.

Wood, Esther. 'The National Competition of Schools of Art', *Studio* vol 28 1903 pp 257-274 51 illus.

Vallance, Aymer. 'The National Competition of Schools of Art,' *Studio* vol 32 1904 pp 322-332 21 illus.

Wood, Esther. 'The National Competition of Schools of Art 1905', *Studio* vol 34 1905 pp 316-330 39 illus.

Vallance, Aymer. 'The National Competition of Schools of Art', *Studio* vol 38 1906 pp 309-319 31 illus.

Whitley, W. T. 'National Art Competition at South Kensington 1907', *Studio* vol 41 1908 pp 296-303 10 illus.

Whitley, W. T. 'The National Competition of Schools of Art', *Studio* vol 47 1909 pp 286-294 23 illus.

Whitley, W. T. 'National Competition of Schools of Art 1910', *Studio* vol 50 1910 pp 294-304 33 illus.

Whitley, W. T. 'The National Competition of Schools of Art', *Studio* vol 53 1911 pp 293-303 31 illus.

Whitley, W. T. 'The National Competition of Schools of Art 1912', *Studio* vol 56 1912 pp 298-305 16 illus.

Whitley, W. T. 'The National Competition of Schools of Art 1913', *Studio* vol 59 1913 pp 289-299 21 illus.

Whitley, W. T. 'The National Competition of Schools of Art 1914', *Studio* vol 62 1914 pp 277-292 31 illus.

Whitley, W. T. 'The National Competition of Schools of Art', *Studio* vol 65 1915 pp 247-258 29 illus.

'Arts and Crafts' a review of work executed by students in the leading art schools of Great Britain and Ireland (ed) Charles Holme. 1916 London: Studio

Twentieth century

From the tangled web of the history of later developments in education it is not possible to draw out a simple and comprehensive string of references. Consequently the next section concentrates eight threads:

1 Agitation for change and some general surveys to 1939

2 The creation and history of the Central School of Arts and Crafts

3 Postwar argument for improvement

4 The Royal College of Art

5 The widening national and international debate on the training of industrial designers

6 Situation in the 1950s

7 Ferment and change in the wake of Coldstream and 1968

8 The encouragement of design education in schools

1 Agitation and gradual change to 1939

A selection of papers to give a flavour of some of the problems and issues:

Wardle, Sir Thomas. *Address on the relationship which should exist between Art schools and technical instruction, delivered at Fenton, North Staffordshire.* 1901 Leek: Clowes 12pp

Waldstein, Sir Charles. 'The relation of industry to art', *JRSA* vol 62 August 28, September 4, September 11 1914 pp 849-859, pp 865-874, pp 881-892 (theoretical papers but dwells particularly on current educational shortcomings)

Rothenstein, William. *A plea for the wider use of artists and craftsmen, lecture to Sheffield Technical School 1916.* 1917 London: Constable 28pp

Rothenstein, William. 'Possibilities for the improvement of industrial art in England', *JRSA* vol 69 March 18 1921 pp 268-277

Richards, Charles Russell. *Art in industry. Being the report of an industrial art survey conducted under the auspices of the National Society for Vocational Education and the Department of Education of the State of New York.* 1922 New York: Macmillan 499pp (includes detailed analysis of education in Britain and Europe as a basis of comparison)

Sanderson, Harold W. 'Art schools and art in industry', *JRSA* vol 82 December 29 1933 pp 183-199

Milne, John D. 'Artist in industry', *JRSA* vol 83 January 25 1935 pp 245-253

Taylor, F. A. 'The training of art students for industry and commerce', *JRSA* vol 83 October 4 1935 pp 1014-1021, 1040-1046, 1068-1071, 1091-1096

'Art school education. Memorandum to the President of the Board of Trade submitted by the Design and Industries Association on the subject of art education with special reference to the organisation of the Royal College of Art', *Design for Today* February 1935 pp 74-76

Read, Herbert. 'Designer in industry; with plans for training and employing', *Architectural Review* vol 79 March 1936 pp 143-146

Kisby, Cyril. 'The future designer – from elementary school to college', *JRSA* vol 86 April 22 1938 pp 551-566

2 Central School of Arts and Crafts

The creation of the Central School under the terms of the Technical Education Acts 1889 and 1891 and the Local Taxation (Customs and Excise) Act 1890 set an administrative pattern for other colleges and its teaching methods were followed widely. The early history is briefly set out in:

London County Council. *The Central School of Arts and Crafts: its aim and organisation. Report by the Principal* (F. V. Burridge) 1913 LCC Central School of Arts and Crafts 19pp

and in more detail in the minutes of the LCC Technical Education Board (1893-1903) and Education Committee (1904-). There are broader surveys in:

Billington, D. 'Sixty years of design training', *Art and Industry* vol 62 April 1957 pp 131-135

Johnstone, William. 'Design training: the
Central School of Arts and Crafts',
Design vol 37 January 1952 pp 6-11

Its exhibitions and occasionally its teaching
are discussed in *Studio:*

Witley, William T. 'Central School of Arts
and Crafts', *Studio* vol 80 1920 pp 51-58

'The Central School of Arts and Crafts',
Studio vol 82 1921 pp 100-107

3 Postwar argument for improvement

Of the many critics of the existing methods
of training designers, few were as widely
read as John Gloag:

Gloag, John. *The missing technician in
industrial production.* 1944 London: Allen
and Unwin 107pp pl.16

Gloag, John. *Self training for industrial
designers.* 1947 London: Allen and
Unwin 168pp pl.16

Gloag, John. 'Preliminary studies for
industrial designers', *JRIBA* June 1947
pp 416-418

The end of the war and the creation of the
Council of Industrial Design helped bring
forward new ideas and the need for change:

Read, Herbert. 'Design review. Education of
the designer', *Architectural Review* vol 96
December 1944 pp 183-184

'Industry and education – special issue',
Architectural Review vol 99 January 1946

Moholy-Nagy, Lazlo. 'New education –
organic approach', *Art and Industry* March
1946 pp 66-77

and surveys:

Darwin, Robin. 'The training of the
industrial designer', *JRSA* vol 97 May 6
1949 pp 421-436 (author of an
unpublished report on industrial design
education for the Council of Industrial
Design)

4 Royal College of Art

It was at the Royal College of Art, under
Robin Darwin as Principal, that many of the
most striking educational changes were
introduced and design education
reinvigorated. Some of these developments
are spelled out in his paper:

Darwin, Robin. 'The Dodo and the Phoenix:
the Royal College of Art since the war',
JRSA vol 102 February 5 1954 pp 174ff

One fruit of these changes is the set of
lectures:

*The Anatomy of Design. A series of inaugural
lectures by Professors of the Royal College of
Art.* 1951 London: Royal College of Art
103pp

Further studies of the College's history are
to be found in its own publications:

Royal College of Art Yearbook 1976/77
(pp 13-17 on the history)

Royal College of Art Annual Report 1959
(pp 16-37 A Decennial review)

*Graphics RCA. 15 years work of the School of
Graphic Design.* 1963 London: Royal
College of Art

as well as smaller surveys in:

'Design progress at the Royal College',
Design 46 October 1952 pp 21-23

'Royal College of Art', special issue (ed)
Ken Baynes, *Design* 192 December 1964

'Royal College of Art and Kunstgewerbe
Schule Basel issue', *Graphis* vol 25 no 146
1970 pp 488-540

5 Education of Industrial Designers – the widening debate

In the 1950s and 1960s efforts to widen the
discussion of the needs of industrial design
education become more prominent:

*Report of a one-day conference between
industrialists and educationalists on the
training of designers for industry: furniture,
pottery, printing and textiles. 24 September.*
1957 London: Federation of British
Industry 50pp

*The training of industrial designers, engineering.
Report of a one-day conference between
industrialists and educationalists, London
1959.* 1959 London: Federation of
British Industry 61pp

*Industrial and engineering design. Report of a
working party of the Federation of British
Industries.* 1965 London: Federation of
British Industries 34pp illus.

With the rise of the International Council of
the Societies of Industrial Design (ICSID)
the debate became international:

*ICSID Report no 1 on the Education of
Industrial Designers* (Report on the first
International Seminar sponsored by
UNESCO, held in Bruges 1964)

*ICSID Report no 2 on the Education of
Industrial Designers* (Report of the second
International Seminar, Ulm 1965)

*ICSID Report no 3 on the Education of
Industrial Designers* (Report of the third
International Seminar, Syracuse, USA
1967)

One of the clearest exponents of the
problems and developments of education at
this period was Misha Black:

Black, Misha. 'The education of industrial
designers 1. The past and present, 2. The
future', *JRSA* vol 113 pp 850-862,
pp 867-882

Black, Misha. 'Education for industrial
design', *Nature* 201 March 28 1964
pp 1258-1264

Black, Misha. 'The training of industrial designers', in *Conference on the teaching of Engineering*. 1964 London: Institute of Engineering Designers pp 285-294

6 Situation in the mid 1950s

Rowntree, Diane. 'Designers in the making', *Architectural Review* vol 117 no 699, 701 March, May 1955 pp 209-212, pp 348-351

Blake, John E. 'Training product designers', *Design* 112 April 1958 pp 27-45

7 Coldstream and after

Radical changes in the awards and structure of art and design education were ushered in with the implementation of some of the recommendations of the reports submitted by the National Advisory Council on Art Education under the chairmanship of Sir William Coldstream:

National Advisory Council on Art Education. First Report. October 1960. 1960 London: HMSO

Vocational courses in colleges and schools of Art. Second report of the National Advisory Council on Art Education. June 1962. 1962 London: HMSO

Post-Diploma studies in art and design. Third report of the National Advisory Council on Art Education. April 1964. 1964 London: HMSO

Structure of art and design education in the further education sector. Report of a joint committee of the National Advisory Council on Art and Education and the National Council for Diplomas on Art and Design 1970. 1970 London: HMSO

Together with the student unrest of 1968, it is probably still too soon to arrive at a balanced historical judgement. However this period of design education and its changes has been well documented in different ways in:

Field, Dick. *Change in art education.* 1970 London: Routledge and Kegan Paul 148pp

Piper, David Warren (ed). *Readings in art and design education. 1. After Hornsey, 2. After Coldstream.* 1973 London: Davis Poynter 2 vols 150pp, 164pp illus.

Hannema, Sjoerd. *Fads, fakes and fantasies. The crisis in art schools and the crisis in art.* 1970 London: Macdonald 146pp illus. bibl.

Baynes, Ken (ed). *Attitudes in design education.* 1969 London: Lund Humphries 144pp illus.

and even later:

Baynes, Ken. *About design.* 1976 London: Design Council 159pp (substantial amount about design teaching)

Eggleston, John. *Developments in design education.* 1976 London: Open Books 144pp

8 Design education in schools

With the formation of the National Association for Design Education and the later development of the Schools Council Design and Craft Education Project, increasing attention is being drawn to the needs and problems of teaching design in schools:

Aylward, Bernard. *Design education in schools.* 1973 London: Evans 176pp illus.

Willmore, F. R. (ed). *Design education in craft and technology.* The Proceedings of the 1976 Northampton Craft Conference 1976 London: Batsford

Official bodies, professional organisations and sponsors

Royal Society of Arts

See also:

Great Exhibition 1851 *page 32*
Design at Work Exhibition 1948 *page 68*

The Society of Arts (styled Royal in 1908) is the oldest patron of the many aspects of design through exhibitions, bursaries, meetings, papers. This patronage extends from before the 1830s to the present. The most useful introduction to the history of the Society's activities is:

Hudson, Derek and Luckhurst, Kenneth William. *The Royal Society of Arts 1794-1954*. 1954 London: John Murray 411pp illus. bibl.

which is a revision of the earlier:

Wood, Sir Henry Trueman. *History of the Royal Society of Arts*. 1913 London: John Murray 558pp illus.

Later writings are noted in the typescript:

The Society's History. A bibliographical and tabular supplement. April 1954-April 1975. London: Royal Society of Arts

There are interesting earlier commentaries in:

Davenport, Samuel Taylor. *The Society of Arts, past and present*. 1869 London: W. Trouncer (reprinted from *JSA* vol 17 1869)

Wheatley, H. B. 'The Society of Arts', *Engineering* vol 51 1891 pp 83-86, 134-135, 163-164, 231-232, 361, 451-452

McMahon, Sir Henry. '180 years of pioneer work by the Royal Society of Arts', *JRSA* vol 85 November 13 1936 pp 10-21 (together with the ordinance for the conferment of distinctions on industrial designers pp 23-24)

Taylor, Basil. 'Two hundred years with industrial art', *Design* 63 March 1954 pp 21-24

Milne, Oswald P. 'The Royal Society of Arts – yesterday, today and tomorrow', *JRSA* vol 108 1959 pp 7ff

and the lectures given to commemorate their bicentenary:

Pevsner, Nikolaus. 'Arts, manufactures and commerce 1754-1954, a bicentenary lecture', *JRSA* vol 102 1954 pp 391-405

More specific historical points are covered in the *Studies in the Society's archives*, which have been a regular feature of *JRSA* since volume 106

Publications

Many pages in this bibliography bear witness to the importance of papers read to the Society. These appear in the regular publications:

Transactions of the Society vols I – LVII 1783-1851

Abstracts of Proceedings and Notes of Proceedings 1844-1851

Journal of the Society of Arts 1852-1907 becoming in 1908

Journal of the Royal Society of Arts

Role of the Society

The importance of the Society's activities on the development of many aspects of industrial design have been discussed in a number of papers:

Gloag, John. 'The contribution of the Society to industrial design', *JRSA* vol 110 April 1962 pp 311-322

Blood, Sir Hilary. 'The encouragement of arts, manufactures and commerce: a learned society looks at its role', *JRSA* vol 112 December 1963 pp 11-20

Sanderson, Harold W. 'Royal Society of Arts and art in industry', *JRSA* vol 83 February 1 1935 pp 273-277

De la Valette, John. 'Royal Society of Arts and industrial art', *JRSA* vol 85 October 15 1937 pp 1033-1039

The section on the International Exhibitions bears witness to the crucial role of the Society in many facets of its organisation and support:

Haltern, Utz. 'The Society of Arts and some of the international aspects of the Great Exhibition of 1851', *JRSA* vol 116 1968 pp 539-542, 620-622

The way in which its work paved the way for 1851 and later developments should not be overlooked – either through earlier exhibitions:

Recent British manufactures and decorative art. 1849 London: Society of Arts

or lectures:

Aikin, Arthur. *Illustrations of Arts and Manufactures, being a selection from a series of papers, read before the Society*. 1841 London: J. van Voorst 376pp

The Society has probably made its most important contribution in the educational field:

Davenport, S. T. 'A short review of the Society's past and present action in the promotion of industrial education', *JSA* vol 13 December 23 1864 pp 88-97

Dawson, R. A. 'Art training for industry and the Society's competitions', *JRSA* vol 74 May 14 1926 pp 614-641

Early manuals:

Bell, J. *Rudimentary art-instruction for artisans and others, and for schools; prepared at the request of the Society of Arts . . . Freehand outline. Part 1 – outline from outline, or from the flat. Part 2 – objects.* 1852, 1854 London

Delamotte, Philip Henry. *'Choice examples of Art-workmanship selected from the exhibition of Ancient and Medieval Art at the Society of Arts',* 1851 London: Cundall and Addey pl 60

From 1876 (as a memorial to Owen Jones) awards were made to students at schools of art. From 1924-1933 this became a more formal competition with its own detailed annual reports:

Reports on the competition of industrial designs 1924-1933 London: F. J. Parsons

Eventually this was revived to become the Industrial Art (later Design) Bursaries competition and documented in the *Journal*

For the mature designer the distinction of 'Designer (later Royal Designer) for Industry' (RDI) was introduced:

'Institution of distinction for designers for industry; with first list of names selected', *JRSA* vol 85 November 13 1936 pp 2-9, 20-21, 23-24

Russell, Gordon. 'Work of the Royal Designers for Industry', *JRSA* vol 97 October 22 1948 pp 765-770

Art Workers' Guild

See also:

Arts and Crafts Movement *page 70*
Important Designers *page 75*

A history:

Massé, Henri Louis Joseph. *The Art Workers' Guild 1884-1934.* 1935 London: Shakespeare Head Press for Art Workers' Guild. 213pp illus. (includes index of lectures and list of subjects discussed).

and commemorative exhibition:

Swell, Pat. *Art and work of the Art Workers' Guild. 'An exhibition of art, craft and design 1884-1975 presented by the National Book League and the Art Workers' Guild at the NBL, 27 February – 21 March 1975'.* London: National Book League 48pp

Addresses to the Guild often include important statements of attitude and principle:

Allsop, Bruce. *The professional artist in a changing society: an inaugural address delivered as Master to the Art Workers' Guild.* 1970 London: Oriel Press 16pp

Image, Selwyn. *An address delivered by request in the Hall of Clifford's Inn Before the Art Workers' Guild on the 25th anniversary of the Guild's foundation.* 1909 London: Chiswick Press

Journals:

The Art Workers' Quarterly 1902-1906

Artifex: journal of the crafts 5 pts in 2 vols. 1968-1971 Newcastle upon Tyne

Arts and Crafts Exhibition Society

See also:

Art Workers' Guild *page 21*
Arts and Crafts Movement *page 70*
Important Designers *page 75*

The Arts and Crafts Exhibition Society (later the Society of Designer Craftsmen) provided the main showcase for the Arts and Crafts Movement. Particularly important exhibitions were the earliest, in 1888, 1889, 1890, 1893, 1896, 1899, 1903, 1906, 1910, 1912, 1916, 1923, 1926, 1928, 1931, 1935, 1938, 1941, 1944, 1946, 1950, 1952 and 1957.

Some of the early catalogues are particularly valuable for their articles and detail:

Catalogue of the Second Exhibition. 1889 London: New Gallery, Regent Street 102pp *(Of cast iron,* by W. R. Lethaby pp 47-56; *Of dyeing as an art,* by William Morris pp 57-67; *Of book illustration and book decoration,* by Reginald T. Blomfield pp 84-93; *Of designs and working drawings,* by Lewis F. Day pp 93-102)

Catalogue of the Seventh Exhibition. 1903 London: Chiswick Press 236pp

Catalogue of the Fifth Exhibition. 1896 London: Chiswick Press 176pp (pp 11-31 a note on the work of Ford Madox Brown by Ford Madox Hueffer)

Some of the papers first published in these catalogues or presented to the society have been reprinted:

Arts and crafts essays by members of the Arts and Crafts Exhibition Society. 1893 London: Rivington, Percival & Co 1903 London: Longmans (facsimile reprint Garland Pub. 1977) 420pp

Art and life: the building and decoration of cities. 1897 London: Rivington (ABC Reprint) 262pp

*Handicrafts and reconstruction. Notes by
   members of the Arts and Crafts Exhibition
   Society.* 1919 London: John Hogg 130pp

*Four papers read by members of the Arts and
   Crafts Exhibition Society.* 1935 London:
   Longmans 70pp *(A paper on the labelling
   of exhibits,* by Edward Johnston. *Welcome!
   Machinery,* by John Farleigh. *The place of
   handwork in modern civilisation,* by J. H.
   Mason. *The crafts and education for industry,*
   by N. Rooke)

Many of the early exhibitions were very
fully documented in the *Studio* and other
journals:

'The Arts and Crafts Exhibition Society at
   the New Gallery 1893'. *Studio* vol II 1894
   pp 3-23

Wilson, Henry. 'The Arts and Crafts
   Society's Exhibition with especial
   reference to certain exhibits', *Architectural
   Review* vol VI 1899 pp 209-216

'The Arts and Crafts Society's Exhibition.
   Second notice', *Architectural Review* vol VI
   1899 pp 263-276

Vallance, Aymer. 'British decorative art in
   1899 and the Arts and Crafts Exhibition',
   Studio vol 8 1900 pp 37-57, pp 104-131,
   pp 179-194, pp 247-281

'A German view of the English Arts and
   Crafts Exhibition', *Architectural Review*
   vol VII 1900 pp 133-136

'Architecture and crafts at the Royal
   Academy 1900', *Architectural Review*
   vol VII 1900 pp 193-256

'Arts and Crafts Exhibition: a discussion',
   I Mervyn Macartney. II Conclusion – D.
   S. MacColl, *Architectural Review* vol 13
   1903 pp 141-142, pp 187-189

'Arts and Crafts Exhibition at the New
   Gallery', *Studio* vol 28 1903 pp 27-40,
   pp 117-126, pp 179-186; vol 29 1903
   pp 22-33

'Domestic architecture of the Arts and
   Crafts Exhibition', *Studio* vol 28 1903
   pp 249-260 illus.

Simpson, F. M. 'The Arts and Crafts
   Exhibition', *Architectural Review* vol 19
   January-June 1906 pp 119-120

'Arts and Crafts Exhibition at the Grafton
   Gallery', *Studio* vol 37 1906 pp 48-64,
   pp 129-144, pp 213-227

Witley, W. T. 'The Arts and Crafts
   Exhibition at the New Gallery', *Studio*
   vol 48 1910 pp 33-43, pp 105-112 illus.

'The Arts and Crafts Society: a retrospect',
   Studio vol 48 1910 pp 297-306 illus.

Witley, W. T. 'Arts and Crafts Society's
   Exhibition at the Grosvenor Gallery',
   Studio vol 57 1913 pp 290-302 illus.;
   vol 58 1913 pp 21-00 illus.

'Arts and Crafts Exhibition Society',
   Architectural Review vol 33 1914
   (June-July) pp 31-34 (illus. general
   articles on the occasion of the 10th
   exhibition)

Witley, W. T. 'Arts and Crafts at the Royal
   Academy', *Studio* vol 69 1917 pp 66-77,
   pp 120-131 46 illus.

Farleigh, John. 'The Arts and Crafts
   Exhibition Society', *Studio* vol 130 1945
   pp 137-147 illus.

National Association for the Advancement of Art and its application to industry

'The Association has been formed for the
purposes of holding an Annual Congress in
the principal manufacturing towns in the
Kingdom, in rotation, to discuss problems of
a practical nature connected with the
welfare of the Arts, Fine and Applied.'

This shortlived organisation is chiefly
important for the papers and discussions
organised by William Morris and his
contemporaries and published in:

*Transactions of the National Association for the
   Advancement of Art and its application to
   industry, Liverpool meeting.* 1888 406pp

*Transactions of the National Association for the
   Advancement of Art and its application to
   industry, Edinburgh meeting 1889.* 1890
   London 485pp

*Transactions of the National Association for the
   Advancement of Art and its application to
   industry, Birmingham meeting 1890.* 1891
   London 307pp

A selection of essays were republished:

Plan Handicrafts, being essays by artists. 1892
   London: National Association

Apart from a study of the impact of the
Liverpool meeting:

Stansky, Peter. 'Art industry and the
   aspirations of William Martin Conway',
   Victorian Studies vol 19 June 1976
   pp 465-484

little has been written in any detail.

Design and Industries Association

Founded in 1915 and the oldest voluntary
association in the field. Its history has been
recounted several times, notably through
the reminiscences of:

Carrington, Noel. *Industrial design in Britain.*
1976 London: Allen and Unwin 195pp
illus.

For more formal histories:

Design Action – DIA Yearbook 1975 The Diamond Jubilee of the Design and Industries Association

containing:

Smith, Hamilton T. *The early years.* pp 29-32 (first published in *Design for Today* May 1935)

Carrington, Noel. *The last 10 years 1925-1935.* pp 31-32. *The world, the DIA and Walter Gropius* pp 33-40 (date chart)

Pevsner, Nikolaus. *History of the DIA* pp 41-52 (first published in *DIA Yearbook* 1964-65)

Plummer, Raymond. *The history of the DIA: 1965-1974* pp 53-55

Other references are:

'1910-1935 Design and Industries Association special supplement', *Design for Today* May 1935 pp 177-205

Pevsner, Nikolaus. 'Patient progress three: the DIA', in Pevsner, Nikolaus. *Studies in Art, architecture and design. Vol 2. Victorian and After.* 1968 London: Thames and Hudson pp 226-241

50 years of the DIA. Catalogue of the Design Council exhibition. 1975 London: Design Council

Grey, John. 'The Design and Industries Association', *Art and Industry* December 1947 pp 192-194 (reprinted separately 1949)

Black, Misha. 'Fitness for what purpose?' *Design* 313 January 1975 pp 42-45

Farr, Michael. 'Old guard or avant-garde?' *DIA Yearbook* 1956 pp 33-44

Publications

Throughout its history the DIA has produced a bewilderingly wide range of papers, pamphlets and books. A detailed bibliography of publications prepared from the originals and data in the possession of Hamilton Temple Smith is to be found in:

Festival of Britain DIA Yearbook 1951 pp 37-41

and the list:

Index to the printed and manuscript material concerning the Design and Industries Association. 1972 London: Historical Manuscripts Commission

The larger-circulation publications are the best sources of information on the activities of the DIA and the period as a whole:

Journal of the Design and Industries Association March 1917 – Summer 1919

continued as:

The Monthly News-sheet of the Design and Industries Association no 1 November 1921 to no 3 February 1922

Yearbooks of the Design and Industries Association:

Design in modern industry, with an introduction by C. H. Collins Baker 1922 London: Benn illus.

Design in modern industry 1923-1924. 1924 London: Benn illus.

Design in modern life and industry 1924-1925, with an introduction by John Gloag. 1925 London: Benn illus.

Design in everyday life and things 1926-1927 (ed). John Gloag with contributions by B. J. Fletcher 'Right making'; F. Pick 'Design in cities'; W. H. Ansell 'The principles of design as applied to buildings'; C. H. Collins Baker 'Design in the home'; H. P. Shapland 'Design in furniture'. 1927 London: Benn illus.

Design in modern printing 1927-1928. 1928 London: Benn illus.

The face of the land. Yearbook 1929-1930. 1930 London: Benn illus.

DIA Quarterly. The journal of the Design and Industries Association nos 3-17 March 1928-January 1932

Design in Industry no 1 Spring 1932

Design for Today vol 1 May 1933 – vol 4 June 1936 (a monthly published by Week-end Publications Ltd)

Trend in Design of Everyday Things 1936 (two issues only)

Annual report presented to the annual general meeting 1932 and later.

DIA Cautionary guide to St Albans. 1929 Birmingham: Kynoch Press (Similar guides published to Carlisle 1930, Oxford 1930)

DIA News 1937-1939

DIA News sheet 1940-1942

DIA News, new series 1942-1944 (four issues)

DIA Yearbook and membership list 1945/1946 (later title *Design Action* added in 1970s)

Of the various leaflets and pamphlets, which are increasingly hard to trace, particularly interesting are the postwar series of booklets including:

Read, Herbert. *The future of industrial design.* 1946 DIA booklet 1 8pp

Grey, John. *Fitness – for what purpose?* 1946 DIA booklet 7pp

Bertram, Anthony. *The enemies of design.* 1946 DIA booklet 3 8pp

There have been many quite important DIA exhibitions but the documentation is noticeably slim:

'DIA exhibition at Bowmans', *Design for Today* November 1935 pp 422-424

'DIA exhibition at Dunn's of Bromley', *Design for Today* June 1936 pp 246-247

'Design round the clock', *Art and Industry* December 1942 pp 179-180

'Mass observation report', *DIA Yearbook 1953* pp 15-16 (On 'Register your choice' exhibition, followed by 7pp of illustrations)

Reilly, Paul. 'Same room: same cost. Two modern styles. Which do you prefer?', *Design* 52 April 1953 pp 8-11 (On 'Register your choice')

Forrest, D. M. 'Make or mar?' *DIA Yearbook* 1957 pp 25-28

British Institute of Industrial Art

A post First World War creation that gradually withered away after the withdrawal of the Treasury grant in 1921, but not finally expiring until the 1930s.

Its aims and early history:

Some particulars with regard to the aims and activities of the British Institute of Industrial Art. With a list of fellows. 1923 London: HMSO 15pp

Report on the work of the British Institute of Industrial Art 1919-1924. 1924 London: HMSO 82pp

The Institute is probably best remembered for its small-scale exhibitions:

'Modern crafts and manufactures.' 1920 London: 217 Knightsbridge

'Posters, colour prints and the art of the book'. 1921 London

'Present day industrial art'. 1922 London: Victoria and Albert Museum

'Industrial art of today'. 1923 London: Victoria and Albert Museum

'Exhibition 1924-1925'. Manchester: Whitworth Art Gallery

'Industrial art for the slender purse'. 1929 London: Victoria and Albert Museum

'Exhibition of British industrial art in relation to the home 1933

A number of reports were presented by different special committees:

Report to the University of London by a special committee of the British Institute of Industrial Art on the teaching of Art in relation to commerce, in connection with the commerce degree. 1921 London 16pp

The university teaching of art in relation to commerce. 1923 London 22pp

Public departments and industrial art: being a report of a special committee . . . on the influence exercised by public departments . . . on the standard of British industrial art. 1923 London 32pp

Mason, J. H. *Notes on printing, considered as an industrial art.* 1926 London 15pp

The training of the silversmith. Being a report of a joint conference of manufacturing and distributing silversmiths, principals of schools for training silversmiths. 1928 London 15pp

The art of lettering, and its uses in diverse crafts and trades. The report of a special committee. 1931 London 45pp pl. 12

In some ways as important as the actual work of the Institute were the writings and influence of its advocate, Sir Hubert Llewellyn Smith:

Smith, Sir Hubert Llewellyn. *The economic laws of art production.* 1924 Oxford University Press 246pp

Smith, Sir Hubert Llewellyn. *The place of economy in art. The inaugural lecture delivered at the LCC Central School of Arts and Crafts.* 1929 London: British Institute of Industrial Art 9pp

Society of Industrial Artists and Designers

Founded in 1930 as the Society of Industrial Artists, and reconstituted in 1945. A detailed history of the organisation has yet to be written. There are outlines in:

'SIAD The first forty years', *The Designer* October 1970 pp 4-6

1 'In the beginning' by Milner Gray

2 'The next phase' by Peter Ray

3 'The festival years' by Misha Black

4 'International relations' by F. H. K. Henrion

5 'At the crossroads' by Peter Lord

and:

Goodden, Wyndham. 'SIA 25', *Design* 82 October 1955 pp 13-18

Blake, John E. 'Growing pains of a new profession', *Design* 197 May 1965 pp 28-35

but its history is best traced through its own journal:

SIA Bulletin (to issue 13-14 September-November 1947) then *Journal of the Society of Industrial Artists* (February 1948 to May 1966) then *The Designer* (June 1966-)

Its published *Codes of Practice* and *Yearbook* could be useful archival sources

Perhaps more influential on the history of design have been the annual Milner Gray lectures (formerly the Design Oration) given since 1955:

1955 Bronowski, J. 'The shape of things'

1956 Jordan, R. Furneaux. 'Architecture as industrial design'

1957 Barman, Christian. 'Design for tomorrow's industry'

1958 Spender, Stephen. 'Thoughts on design in everyday life'

1959 Hutton, Graham. 'Graphic design in a mass culture'

1960 Hawkes, Jacquetta. 'Patterns and cultures'

1961 Read, Sir Herbert. 'Design and tradition'

1962 Burkart, A. J. 'Design as an instrument of competition'

1963 Fisher, Norman. 'Industrial design, necessity or luxury?'

1964 Llewellyn-Davies, Lord. 'Education for industrial designers'

1965 Gould, Sir Ronald. 'Design and the teacher'

1966 Penny F. D. 'Industrial design 1984'

1967 Briggs, Asa. 'Design and the historian'

1968 Darwin, Sir Robin. 'One and twenty'

1971 Wedgwood-Benn, Anthony. 'Design in the community'

1972 Sainsbury, John. 'Design comes at last'

1973 Feather, Vic. 'Design and the environment'

1974 Buchanan, Sir Colin. 'Design and urban environment'

Some of these have been republished separately:

Read, Sir Herbert. *Design and tradition.* 1962 Hemingford Grey: Vine Press

Better known is the influential review of industrial and commercial design:

Designers in Britain:

vol 1 1947 London: Wingate

vol 2 1949 London: Wingate

vol 3 1951 London: Wingate (titled 'Designers 1851-1951' and including historical essays by Nikolaus Pevsner and Milner Gray)

vol 4 1953 London: Deutsch

vol 5 1957 London: Deutsch

vol 6 1964 London: Deutsch

vol 7 1971 London: Deutsch

There have been a number of smaller manuals:

A guide to the practice of illustration. With articles by Stephen Spurrier, George W. Leech and John Farleigh. 1937 London: Lamley 21pp

Council for Art and Industry

Established in the wake of the Gorell report and under the Board of Trade, the Council prepared some of the ground for its much more powerful successor the Council of Industrial Design. Its reports provide useful evidence on the 1930s:

Design and designer in industry. 1937 London: HMSO 62pp

Education for the consumer – art in elementary and secondary school education. Report. 1935 London: HMSO 38pp illus.

Design in education being an exhibition of material for use in elementary schools, January 1937. 1937 London: HMSO 16pp

The working class home. Its furnishing and equipment. 1937 London: HMSO 66pp

Design in the jewellery, silversmithing and allied trades. Report. 1937 London: HMSO 36pp

Design in the pottery industry. Report . . . to enquire into the training of designers and craftsmen for the pottery industry. 1937 London: HMSO 27pp

and during the war:

Design and designer in the light metal trades. Report of a committee set up to consider how to give practical effect . . . to recommendations in 'Design and designer in industry'. 1944 London: HMSO 58pp

Design and the designer in the dress trade. 1945 London: HMSO 15pp

It also had a Scottish committee:

Education for the consumer. Art in general education in Scotland. 1935 Edinburgh: HMSO 52pp illus.

Printing and allied trades in Scotland. 1937 Edinburgh: HMSO 38pp

Design in the Scottish woollen industry. 1937 Edinburgh: HMSO 35pp

Exhibitions of school crafts in Scotland. 1939 Edinburgh: HMSO 28pp

The chairman of the Council, Frank Pick, was one of the most important figures in the history of design between the wars:

Pevsner, Nikolaus. 'Frank Pick'. *Architectural Review* vol 92 1942 *reprinted in* Pevsner, Nikolaus. *Studies in Art, architecture and design. Vol 2 Victorian and after* 1968 London: Thames and Hudson pp 191-209

Barman, Christian. 'Frank Pick and his influence on design in England'. *Graphis* no 21 1948 pp 70-73, 96

'Frank Pick'. *Architectural Review* vol 90 1941 p 183

Barman, Christian. 'Frank Pick'. *Architectural Review* vol 91 January 1942 pp 1-2

Pick, Frank. 'Design in industry'. Being an address to the Imperial Industries Club 1933. *Design for Today* January 1934 pp 37-39

Pick, Frank. 'The artist's place in British industry'. *Studio* vol 101 1931 p 299

Central Institute of Art and Design

Created during the war, the Institute faded away after 1948 as most of its functions were then undertaken by the Council of Industrial Design.

A history:

Report on the work of the Central Institute of Art and Design, September 1948. 1948 London: CIAD 8pp

Its own publications:

The Central Institute of Art and Design (a prospectus). 1940 London 3pp

Bulletin vol 1 no 1 – vol 1 no 12 (to June-September 1946) High Wycombe

then:

Art and Design vol 2 nos 1-3 (March 1947-January 1948) London

Primarily remembered as an organiser of exhibitions:

'Central Institute and of Art and Design. Its work for artist and art patron'. *Art and Industry* April 1942 pp 101-103

Catalogue Inn crafts exhibition 27 April – 13 May 1948. Organised for the Brewers Society by the Central Institute of Art and Design 1948 London 82pp

Council of Industrial Design

See also:

Britain Can Make It 1946 *page 68*

Festival of Britain 1951 *page 69*

The history of the Council of Industrial Design figures largely in:

MacCarthy, Fiona. *All things bright and beautiful*. 1972 London: Allen and Unwin

but apart from this there is no single history of the Council. Consequently the best sources for detail are:

Council of Industrial Design. *First annual report 1945-1946*. 1946 32pp (then published annually)

The establishment of the Council is reported in:

Parliamentary Debates (Hansard) House of Commons Official Report vol 406 no 12 Tuesday 19 December 1944 col 1612-1615

A useful survey of the period covered by the activities of the Council of Industrial Design is provided by:

Design 253 January 1970. 1970 Anniversary issue 1949-1970 pp 44-103

The early years are reviewed critically in:

'CoID: Progress report (+ Industrial Design 1951)'. *Architectural Review* vol 110 December 1951 pp 349-352 (+pp 353-359)

and defended in:

'CoID Progress report: the Director replies'. *Architectural Review* vol 111 no 662 February 1952 pp 73-75

The eventual enlargement of the Council of Industrial Design to the Design Council was heralded by the Conway report:

A National Design Council. Report of a Working Party set up by the Council of Engineering Institutions (Conway report). 1970 London: Council of Engineering Institutions 9pp

The annual reports and early Council of Industrial Design publications include a number of attempts to spell out the nature of good design and the problems involved:

Russell, Gordon. 'What is good design?' *Design* 1 January 1949 pp 2-6

Russell, Gordon. 'The problem of raising design standards in industry'. *Eighth Annual Report 1952-1953*. Council of Industrial Design. Four-page insert

CoID. *The Council of Industrial Design* (explanatory leaflet). 1946 London: Council of Industrial Design

But more interesting have been the different methods the Council employed to help improve design. The following sections indicate some of these activities and their documents in chronological lists:

1 Conferences

2 Exhibitions

3 Design Centre

4 Awards

5 Journals

6 Publications

1 Conferences

Council of Industrial Design and Federation of British Industries. *Report of the conference on Industrial Design . . . the Central Hall, Westminster on the 26 and 27 September 1946.* 1946 London: Council of Industrial Design 100pp (seven papers and discussion)

The Conference on Packaging held at 23 Knightsbridge SW1 on the 29 November 1946. 1946 London: CoID 48pp illus. pl 20

Conference on Presentation and Packaging held in the North British Hotel on Wednesday 17 September 1947. Edinburgh: CoID Scottish Committee 62pp

Council of Industrial Design. *Digest report of conferences held in connection with the Design Week at Newcastle upon Tyne . . . 8 July 1947, Industrial Design and Industry, 9 July 1947, Industrial Design and the Retail Trade.* 1947 London: CoID 36pp (eight papers)

Colour and lighting in factories and on machines. Report of a course held at RIBA November 1948. CoID and British Colour Council with the co-operation of the Building Research Station and Paint Research Station. London: CoID 96pp bibl.

Council of Industrial Design. *Design report. Ideas for industry: points from speeches made at Design Week, held at Cardiff from 12 to 17 April 1948.* Edited by Alec Davis. 1948 London: CoID 16pp

Report on the Design Conference for Retailers, 21-24 February 1949 at Westham House, Barford, Warwicks. 1949 30pp

Report on the Design Conference for Retail Staff Trainees, 9-12 May 1949 at Stoke House, Bletchley, Bucks. 1949 London: CoID 30pp

Report on the Design Course for Furniture Salesmen, February 27 to March 2 1950 at Attingham Park, Shrewsbury. London: CoID 57pp

Design Policy within Industry as a responsibility of higher level Management . . . held at the Royal College of Art September 19 and 20. 1951 London: CoID

Report on the Design Course for Furniture Salesmen, February 11 to February 15 at Attingham Park, Shrewsbury. 1951 London: CoID 51pp

Design and the Co-operative Movement. Co-operative Management Conference, Harrogate 1952 March 28-30. 1952 London: CoID 20pp

Design appreciation. Report of a conference held in Moray House Training College, Edinburgh, on November 14, 1952. 1952 Edinburgh: CoID Scottish Committee 31pp

Industrial design. Report of the series of five lectures organised by the Council of Industrial Design Scottish Committee and held at the Royal Philosophical Society, Glasgow, Winter 1952-1953. Edinburgh: CoID Scottish Committee 29pp

School Furniture Conference. Summary of papers and discussion at a one-day conference held in the North British Hotel, Edinburgh, on Tuesday 6 March 1956. 1956 Edinburgh: CoID Scottish Committee 35pp

The 1956 Design Congress. The management of design . . . held at the Victoria and Albert Museum and Royal College of Art, South Kensington, September 12 and 13, 1956. 1956 London: CoID

The management of design: report based on papers read at the second Design Congress. 1957 London: CoID 40pp

Conference on Industrial Design and the Engineering Industries, organised by the Council of Industrial Design and the Birmingham Exchange and Engineering Centre in Birmingham, 12 November 1958. 1958 London: CoID

Design policy for corporate buying. A report on the 1961 International Design Congress. 1961 London: CoID 24pp illus.

Wainwright, David. 'Design policy for corporate buying'. *Design* 156 December 1961 pp 40-53

Product planning. Papers read at a one-day seminar on product development, diversification and design, held at the Central Hotel, Glasgow on Thursday 22 March 1962 under the chairmanship of Sir Robert A. Maclean. 1962 Glasgow: CoID Scottish Committee in association with Personnel Administration Ltd. 27pp

Conference for retail management, Winchester 28 to 30 March 1965, papers given . . . 1965 London: CoID 57pp

White, J. Noel (ed). *Profit by design. Some views on design management,* published by the *Financial Times* in association with the Council of Industrial Design. 1965 London: CoID 43pp illus. bibl.

International Design Congress 1966. Profit by design. Royal Garden Hotel, Kensington, 12 and 13 October 1966. 1966 London: CoID

'Design in Industry'. (Fourth International Design Congress) *The Times* Wednesday 12 October 1966. Four-page supplement

Design for export. Management Seminars. Report June and July 1968 at The Design Centre. 1968 London: CoID

Going metric. Seminar reports (February-March) 1969 second edition London: CoID 84pp

Design in education. Report of a conference held at the National Union of Teachers Headquarters, London, 19 February 1969. 1969 London: CoID 12pp

Unity in design. Report of a conference on organisation and training in engineering design at Loughborough University of Technology, 30 September 1969. 1970 London: CoID 32pp

Design in management. Report on a conference for management consultants and industrial engineers at the Royal Society of Arts, 10 February 1970. 1970 London: CoID 32pp illus.

Farm buildings in the landscape. Report of a conference held at Agriculture House, London SW1 on 25 June 1970. 1970 London: Ministry of Housing and Local Government in association with the Ministry of Agriculture, Fisheries and Food, the Council of Industrial Design, the Countryside Commission and the Welsh Office. 22pp

2 Exhibitions

See also:

Britain Can Make It 1946 *page 68*

Design at Work 1948 *page 68*

Festival of Britain 1951 *page 69*

Many of the exhibitions staged by the Council of Industrial Design are documented only in *Design* and the daily press. There have been so many that it is not possible to list them here. The following list some of the more typical.

Design Fair: a display of ideas and things to show that good design can be good fun. 1948 London: CoID

Four ways of living, introduced by Frank Mansfield. (For sale at the Ideal Home Exhibition, Olympia 1949). 1949 London: HMSO for CoID 4pp illus.

Addition to the family. Furnishing for children and old people. (Exhibition September-October 1962) 1962 London: CoID 8pp

3 The Design Centre

Since its establishment in 1956 exhibitions at The Design Centre have been a vital aspect of the Council's work and so it may be helpful to list some of the literature concerned with its strategy:

Council of Industrial Design. *What is a Design Centre? A description and explanation of its function.* 1947 London: HMSO 16pp illus.

Design Centres. A co-operative scheme for the development of industrial design. London: CoID 1947 9pp

'Design Centre'. Special issue. *Design* 89 May 1956

Announcing The Design Centre for British Industries. 1956 London: CoID 12pp illus.

Russell, Sir Gordon. 'The Design Centre for British Industries'. *DIA Yearbook* 1956 pp 30-32

A report on The Design Centre. April 1957. London: Mass Observation Ltd 25pp typescript

The Design Centre Book. Souvenir of The Design Centre for British Industries. 1961 London: CoID 112pp illus.

The Design Centre Book 2. A record of The Design Centre for British Industries. 1962 London: CoID 78pp illus.

Johnston, Dan. 'Design Council and The Design Centre'. *Museums Journal* vol 74 December 1974 pp 118-121

Blake, John. 'Design Centre story'. *Design* 341 May 1977 pp 26-27

4 Awards and Design Index

General surveys:

Pilditch, James. 'The story so far' (on the occasion of the 20th exhibition of the Design Council's Contract Consumer Goods Awards). *Design* 340 April 1977 pp 28-34 illus.

Reilly, Paul. 'Ten years of Design Centre awards' (including illustrations of the awards). *Design* 209 May 1966 pp 58-71 (to celebrate the last year in that form)

Documents of particular awards or approved designs (and some comments):

Street lighting columns. List of approved designs 1954. 1954 London: CoID 24pp

Street lighting columns. List of approved designs. 1957 London: CoID 39pp

Designs of the Year 1958 and 1957. 1958 London: CoID 48pp

Reid, John and Sylvia. 'Far from "Outstanding"' – review of Designs of the Year 1958. *Architects Journal* 22 May 1958 pp 764-767 illus.

The Design Centre Awards 1959, 1960, 1961, 1962, 1963, 1964, 1965, 1967. London: CoID

Street furniture. List of approved designs. 1961 London: CoID 124pp illus.

Contract furniture from Design Index. 1964 London: CoID 280pp

Street furniture from Design Index. 1965 London: CoID

More recently there have been awards for design management:

Four studies in design management. The Royal Society of Arts Presidential Awards for Design Management October 1967. 1967 London: CoID 14pp typescript

Design management in five companies. The Royal Society of Arts Presidential Awards for Design Management 1969. 1969 London: CoID 24pp typescript

5 Journals

Most influential has been:

Design January 1949 – (monthly)

There was an earlier much smaller ancestor:

Design Digest 1946 (September) – 1947 (January)

6 Publications

A few other publications, principally of advice:

New home. 1946 London: CoID 32pp illus. (another edition no 2 published 1948)

Buying for your home no 1. Furnishing fabrics, by Mary Shaw. 1946 London: HMSO for CoID 30pp

Furnishing to fit the family. With drawings by Nicolas Bentley, Hugh Casson and Hilton Wright. 1947 London: HMSO 48pp (reprinted 1948, 1949)

How to buy furniture by Gordon Russell. 1947 London: HMSO 32pp illus. (new edition 1951)

Waterer, John W. *This design business.* 1947 London: CoID 4pp (proposes definitions of design)

How to buy things for the kitchen. 1948 London: CoID 64pp illus.

Design folios A-Q 1948-1951 London: CoID
A Teapots 1948
B Chairs 1949
C Boats 1949
D Radios 1949
E Woodware 1949
F Pottery 1949
G Sideboards and dressers 1949
H Glass 1949
I Easy chairs 1950
J Clocks and watches 1950
K Wall paper for the small home 1950
L Street furniture 1950
M Sports gear 1951
N Knives, spoons, forks 1951
O Home lighting 1951
P Door and drawer furniture 1951
Q Packaging 1951

Selling through display. Ideas for the smaller shop by Arthur Symes. 1948 London: CoID 32pp illus.

Ideas for your home. 1950 London: CoID 33pp

Llewellyn, Margaret. *Design and our homes.* A book on design in the home and in the shop, raising ideas for discussion and suggestions for activities in groups and classes in the Cooperative movement. 1951 Reddish: Education Dept Cooperative Union Ltd and CoID 100pp illus.

Russell, Gordon and Jarvis, Alan. *How to furnish your home.* 1953 London: Newman Neame unpaged illus.

Careers in Industrial Design. 1961 London (later editions 1961, 1968)

Stephenson, Henry and Stephenson, Lilian. *Eating, sleeping and living.* 1964 Loughborough: Education Dept of Cooperative Union and CoID 96pp illus.

'Print for Exporters'. A supplement to *Design* October 1964 84pp

Then there are the Design Centre publications
(published by Macdonald and Jane's):

Chapman, Nigel. *Heating* 1966 (revised 1971) 64pp

Prizeman, John. *Kitchens* 1966 (revised 1970) 64pp

Phillips, Derek. *Lighting* 1966

Meade, Dorothy. *Bedrooms* 1967

Rayner, Claire. *For children* 1967

Ward, Mary and Ward, Neville. *Living rooms* 1967

Salmon, Geoffrey. *Storage* 1967

Proctor, Ian. *Boats for sailing* 1967

Sharp, Peter E. M. *Sound and vision* 1967

Matthews, Peter. *Workrooms* 1969

Good, Elizabeth. *Tableware* 1969

Shepheard, Peter. *Gardens* 1969

Phillips, Derek. *Flooring* 1969

There are many other publications, often associated with Design Centre exhibitions.

The Scottish Committee of the Council of Industrial Design has also been an important publisher:

Enterprise Scotland. 1947 Edinburgh 94pp (a catalogue)

Enterprise Scotland 1947. A pictorial record of the Exhibition, (ed) Wyndham Goodden. 1947 Edinburgh 90pp

Enterprise series 1947 (Furniture, Hosiery, Printing, Shipbuilding, Tourist, Textiles, Woollens) 16pp each

Good design – good business, by John Gloag.
1947 Edinburgh 72pp illus.

The Scottish Design Congress 1954. 1954
Glasgow

*The value of good design. A report on the Scottish
Design Congress, Edinburgh, 1954,* (ed)
Alister Maynard. 1955 London: CoID
72pp 32pp of plates

Design Scotland. 1963 Glasgow 32pp illus.
(Scottish Design Centre Book)

International Council of the Societies of Industrial Design (ICSID)

History:

Black, Misha. 'The history of ICSID'. *Kogei
News* (The Journal of the Japanese
Industrial Designers Association JIDA)
vol 40 1 June 1972

*Constitution adopted at the First General
Assembly, Stockholm, Sweden* 17 September
1959 11pp

General Assemblies

After the first assembly booklets were
produced as well as minutes and other
papers:

Digest of Stile Industria no 34. October 1961
25pp (second Assembly Vienna)

*Paris Congress. 3rd Congress UNESCO
Headquarters June 1963.* 1965 Hilversum:
ICSID 38pp

*Fourth Congress WIFI Vienna September 1965.
Design and Community.* 1965 Vienna:
Österreiche Institut für Formgebung
40pp

*Canada Congress: 5th Assembly and Congress,
Ottawa-Montreal, September 1967.* 1969
Montreal: Queens Printer 104pp illus.

*6th General Assembly and Congress, London
8-12 September 1969*

Ibiza 1971 October. 1971 Barcelona:
ADIFAD 78pp

There have also been other meetings, such
as the International Seminars on Industrial
Design Education (see page   ).

Other useful publications:

Chart of Industrial Design Exhibition Centres (a
list of permanent design exhibitions
throughout the world with statistics . . .)
1973 Brussels: ICSID

*Industrial Design. An International Survey,
March 1967.* 1969 London: Newman for
ICSID on behalf of UNESCO 130pp

*Design promotion. Case histories compiled by
ICSID group VI.* ?1973

London Livery Companies

The more detailed sections of this
bibliography bear witness to the detailed
influence some of the Livery companies had
and still have on the developments in design
of their own craft. As it is not always easy to
trace the appropriate company or
documents about that company the large
bibliography in the following could be
useful:

Kahl, William F. *The development of London
Livery Companies. An essay and a
bibliography.* 1960 Boston: Baker Library,
Harvard Graduate School of Business
Administration 104pp (Kress Library of
Business and Economics no 15)

International Exhibitions

Essentially a creation of the nineteenth century, these 'tournaments of industry' have done much to influence attitudes to design in spite of strong national rivalries and even jealousies. In common with most forms of exhibition literature, documents are often very difficult to trace and there are often bewildering variants. This section concentrates on the better known international exhibitions. Equally large but national exhibitions, such as the Festival of Britain, are discussed later in the chronological studies section.

Regulation

With the proliferation of exhibitions early in the twentieth century some kind of regulation became necessary and the first attempt to establish an internationally agreed calendar was made in Berlin in 1912. After the War further attempts at agreement were made, culminating in the 'Convention regarding international exhibitions', signed in Paris in 1928. These and later draft arrangements are set out in:

Great Britain. Department of Overseas Trade. *Draft of General regulations applying to International Exhibitions*. 1934 London: HMSO 47pp

and are the basis of current conventions which are still only agreed by a fairly small number of signatories. The Bureau International des Expositions was established in Paris in 1931 to administer these convention agreements. The reluctance of the USA (until very recently) to sign these conventions is an important reason for the separate development of the American international exhibitions in the twentieth century.

General Historical Surveys

Useful introductions:

Allwood, John. *The Great Exhibitions*. 1977. London: Studio Vista 192pp illus. bibl.

Luckhurst, Kenneth W. *The story of exhibitions*. 1951 London: Studio 224pp illus. bibl.

Exhibition of exhibitions. Illustrating the origin and development of exhibitions in Great Britain and commemorating the Great Exhibition. Catalogue. 1951 London: Royal Society of Arts

A study of the architecture:

Cornell, Elias. *De stora utställingarna: arkitekturexperiment och kulturhistoria*. 1952 Stockholm: Bokforlaget Natur och Kultur 270pp illus. bibl.

The purpose of the international exhibition:

Neuberg, Hans. *Conceptions of international exhibitions*. 1969 Zurich: ABC 212pp illus.

Regnier, Noel. *Revue et examen des expositions nationales et internationales en France et à l'étranger depuis 1798 jusqu'à 1878*. 1878 Paris: Sault 483pp

RIBA Joint Committee of Foreign Relations Committee and Exhibitions Sub-Committee. 'Architecture at international exhibitions – memorandum'. *JRIBA* November 1938

Berger, H. George. *Les expositions universelles internationales. Leur passé, leur rôle actuel, leur avenir*. 1901 Paris: Arthur Rousseau 164pp (strong hostile criticism)

Studies of international exhibitions in particular countries:

France

Isay, Raymond. *Panorama des Expositions Universelles*. 1937 Paris: Gallimard 229pp illus.

Poirier, René. *Des foires, des peuples, des expositions*. 1958 Paris: Plon 258pp

Isaac, Maurice. *Les Expositions Universelles*. 1936 Paris: Librairie Larousse 406pp

Demy, Adolphe. *Essai historique sur les expositions universelles de Paris*. 1907 Paris: Picard 1096pp

Dupays, Paul. *Vie prestigieuse des expositions historiques*. 1939 Paris: H. Didier 285pp

Cinquantenaire 1885-1935. Comité français des expositions et comité national des expositions coloniales réunis par décret de Juin 1925. 1935 Paris: Comité Français des Expositions 328pp illus. bibl.

Isaac, Maurice. *Les expositions en France et dans le régime international*. 1928 Paris: Dorbon ainé 350pp (mostly post-1900 exhibitions)

Belgium

Cockx, A and Lemmens, J. *Les expositions universelles et internationals en Belgique de 1885 à 1958*. 1958 Brussels: Editorial Office 176pp

The early history of industrial exhibitions:

Jerrold, William Blanchard. *The history of industrial exhibitions from their origin to the close of the Great International Exhibition of 1862 no 1* 1862 London (no more published)

Geddes, Patrick. *Industrial exhibitions and modern progress*. 1887 Edinburgh: D. Douglas 57pp

The role of Britain and the value of these exhibitions has been discussed in a number of official reports:

Great Britain. Board of Trade. Exhibitions Branch. _Report of a committee appointed . . . to make enquiries with reference to the participation of Great Britain in great international exhibitions_. 1907 London: HMSO 2 vols in 1 Cmd 3772-3773 (Committee chaired by Sir Alfred E. Bateman)

Great Britain. Department of Overseas Trade. _Report of the committee under the chairmanship of Lord Ramsden to consider the part which exhibitions and fairs should play in the promotion of export trade in the post-war era and to advise on the policy and plans to be adapted to derive the maximum advantage from such displays_. 1946 London: HMSO 16pp Cmd 6782

Bibliographies and Lists

Only a small number of international exhibitions can be listed in the following pages, so it may be helpful to list some large sources that can help with detailed research.

A very full list of different international exhibitions up to 1907 is provided by:

'International exhibitions 1851-1907'. _JSA_ vol 55 1907 pp 1141-6

The literature is so vast that there is no one single bibliography but useful guides to different periods are provided by:

Davis, Julia Finette (comp). 'International expositions 1851-1900'. _American Association of Architectural Bibliographers. Papers_. Charlottesville vol 4 1967 pp 47-130

Exhibitions. A list of references to material in the library of the Royal Institute of British Architects. 1948 London: RIBA 32pp (cyclostyled typescript)

Plinval Salgues, Régine de. _Bibliographie des expositions industrielles et commerciales en France, depuis l'origine jusqu'à 1867_. 1960 Paris: Conservatoire National des Arts et Métiers 185pp (1020 references)

Pelletier, Monique. _L'oeuvre civilisatrice des puissances européens vue à travers les expositions coloniales et internationales de 1900 à 1931_. 1963 Paris: Mémoire INTD 63pp (255 references)

Lasnier, Albert (comp). _Références sur les expositions (1937-1964)_. 1964 Quebec: Albert Lasnier 220pp

United States. Library of Congress. Division of Bibliography. _List of references on Expositions in the United States and foreign countries 1918-1928_. 1928 Washington 16pp typescript

United States. Library of Congress. Division of Bibliography. _A selected list of references on Fairs and expositions 1928-1939_. 1938 Washington 49pp typescript

Exhibitions before 1851

Although this bibliography really starts with the Great Exhibition, it is important to realise that it marked a culmination and development of earlier ventures rather than a totally new departure:

Carpenter, Kenneth E. 'European Industrial exhibitions before 1851 and their publications'. _Technology and Culture_ vol 13 no 3 July 1972 pp 465-486

Jerrold, W. Blanchard. 'The history of industrial exhibitions'. _Illustrated London News_ May 3, May 10, May 13 1851 pp 372-3, pp 404-405, pp 433-437

The Royal Society of Arts has already been mentioned (see Royal Society of Arts) but notice should also be taken of the French Expositions des Produits de l'industrie Française:

Colmont, Achille de. _Histoire des Expositions des Produits de l'Industrie Française_. 1855 Paris: Guillaumin 566pp

Burat, Jules. _Exposition de l'Industrie Française, année 1844. Description méthodique accompagnée d'un grand nombre de planches et de vignettes_. 1844 Paris: Challamel 2 vols

Exposition des produits de l'industrie Française en 1844. Rapport du Jury Central. 1844 Paris: Fain & Thunot

'National Exposition of the Productions of Industry, Agriculture and Manufacture in France'. _Art Journal_ August, September 1849

This is all the more important as the working basis for 1851 was provided by:

Wyatt, Matthew Digby. _A report on the eleventh French exposition of the products of industry. Prepared by the direction of and submitted to, the President and council of the Society of Arts . . . September 1849_. 1849 London: Chapman and Hall 36pp

Great Exhibition of the Works of Industry of All Nations. London 1851

'It's all so wonderfully ugly' (William Morris).

'The Great Exhibition of 1851 was responsible for the greatest outpouring of printed matter of any event since the introduction of printing' (David Low [bookseller]. Catalogue no 95 1948 p 24)

Some bibliographies exist but they are not easy to trace or use:

Dilke, Sir Charles Wentworth. *Exhibition of the Works of Industry of All Nations, 1851. Catalogue of a collection of works on or having a reference to the Exhibition of 1851, in the possession of C. Wentworth Dilke.* 1855 London: W. Clowes 116pp (most of Dilke's papers have been deposited in the Victoria and Albert Museum Library)

Mitchell, Elizabeth M. *The Great Exhibition of 1851. A select bibliography.* 1950 83pp (typescript deposited in the library of the Royal Society of Arts)

Illustrations of the Great Exhibition of the Industry of all Nations: presented to the Library of the London Institution by Thomas Baring Esq MP. 1855 London: London Institution 8pp (110 items 1849-1852. Sadly the London Institution Library was dispersed before 1914)

Perhaps the most helpful introductory contemporary listing is to be found in the collection of one of its prime movers:

Kaden, Vera C. *The personal papers, manuscripts, pamphlets and other documents left by Sir Henry Cole, first director of the South Kensington Museum.* 1973 London: Victoria and Albert Museum typescript

Official Catalogues

Official descriptive and illustrated catalogue of the Great Exhibition of the Works of Industry of All Nations 1851:
1 *Raw materials and machinery*
2 *Manufactures and Fine Arts*
3 *Foreign states*
4 *Supplement – illustrations and reports*
1851 London: Clowes

The catalogue was very hastily compiled and exists in at least four editions and numerous variants. The muddle and confusion surrounding the publication of this official text was satirised in:

Dickens, Charles. 'The Catalogue's account of itself'. *Household Words* 23 August 1851

An index was compiled:

Alphabetical and classified index to the Official Catalogue of the Great Exhibition of the Works of Industry of All Nations. In two parts. Part 1. Alphabetical list of contributors and others, whose names appear in the catalogue. Part 2. Alphabetical and classified list of articles contained in the catalogue. 1851 London: Spicer printed by Clowes 99pp (or 230pp with fourth edition)

The official catalogue was also published in different sections with priced lists:

IIj Austrian section, IIk British section, IIl Russian section, IIm Saxon section, IIn Zollverein section

For a bit more information on this bibliographical nightmare:

Hasler, Charles. 'The official catalogues of the Great Exhibition of 1851. *Penrose Annual* vol 45 1951 pp 63-65

Unofficial Catalogues

Much easier to trace and use are the many catalogues and guides printed for visitors to the Exhibition and later to the Crystal Palace. Well endowed with illustrations they are particularly useful, if optimistic, sources:

The Art Journal illustrated catalogue. The Industry of All Nations 1851. 1851 London: Virtue 390pp illus. (facsimile reprint by David and Charles 1970)

which contains the valuable study:

Wornum, Ralph N. 'The exhibition as a lesson in taste'.

Tallis's history and description of the Crystal Palace and the Exhibition of the World's Industry in 1851. Illustrated by steel engravings from original drawings and daguerrotypes by Beard, Mayall. 1852-1854 London: Tallis 3 vols

The Crystal Palace and the Great Exhibition; an historical account of the building, together with a descriptive synopsis of its contents. 1851 London: H. G. Clarke 182pp

The Crystal Palace and its contents; being an illustrated cyclopaedia of the Great Exhibition of the Industry of All Nations, 1851. Embellished with upwards of 500 engravings. 1852 London: W.M. Clark 424pp (first published in weekly parts November 1851-March 1852)

The Expositor: an illustrated recorder of inventions, designs and art manufactures. 1851 London: Joseph Clayton 428pp (published in weekly instalments 2 November, 1850-25 February 1854 numbers 1-73)

Guide book to the Industrial Exhibition; with facts, figures and observations on the manufactures and products exhibited. 1851 London: Partridge and Oakley 166pp

A guide to the Great Exhibition; containing a description of every principal object of interest. With a plan, pointing out the easiest and most systematic way of examining the contents of the Crystal Palace. 1851 London: Routledge 231pp (later editions under the title *Reminiscences of the Crystal Palace*)

Hunt, Robert. *Companion to the Official Catalogue. Synopsis of the contents of the Great Exhibition of 1851.* 1851 London: Spicer and Clowes 94pp (nine different editions and a French translation)

Hunt, Robert (ed). *Hunt's handbook to the official catalogues: an explanatory guide to the natural productions and manufactures of the*

34
Fostering design

Great Exhibition of the Industry of All Nations, 1851. 1851 London: Spicer and Clowes 2 vols 948pp (guide not catalogue)

The Illustrated Exhibitor, a tribute to the World's industrial jubilee; comprising sketches, by pen and pencil, of the principal objects in the Great Exhibition of the Industry of All Nations. 1851 London: Cassell 556pp (originally published in weekly instalments 1-30, June-December 1851)

The Journal of the Exhibition of 1851. Its origin, history and progress. 1851 London: John Crockford – The Critic. 324pp illus. (first published in fortnightly instalments numbers 1-17, 9 November 1850-5 July 1851)

Stephenson, Robert. *The Great Exhibition; and its palace and principal contents. With notices of the public buildings of the metropolis, places of amusement.* 1851 London: Routledge 220pp

Timbs, John. *Yearbook of facts on the Great Exhibition: its origin and progress, constructive details of the building, the most remarkable articles and objects exhibited.* 1851 London: Bogue 348pp (Extra volume of the annual work *The Yearbook of facts in Science and Art, exhibiting the most important discoveries and improvements of the past year*)

Besides these there are many smaller guides and collections of views.

A few examples:

Jerrold, William Blanchard. *How to see the Exhibition in four visits.* 1851 London: Bradbury and Evans, 4 parts

The Great Exhibition illustrated in a series of fifty views of the most interesting and beautiful departments from original paintings by David Roberts, Louis Haghe and Joseph Nash. 1852 London: Dickinson 2 vols pp 55

Baxter's pictorial key to the Great Exhibition (forming a companion to the Official Catalogue) and visitors guide to London. In French, English, German. 1851 London: Baxter 16pp

Clarke's critical catalogue and synopsis of the Great Exhibition of the Industry of All Nations, 1851. 1951 London: H. G. Clarke 45pp

Recollections of the Great Exhibition of 1851. 1851 London: Lloyd Brothers and Simpkin Marshall 25 lithographed plates

Saunders, W. J. B. *The Palace of Industry. A comprehensive guide and popular account of the Great Exhibition building in Hyde Park.* 1851 London: Effingham Wilson 62pp

Contemporary views and comments

The Great Exhibition 1851. A collection of contemporary documents compiled by John Langdon-Davies. 1968 London: Cape (Jackdaw no 43)

Babbage, Charles. *The Exposition of 1851; or views of the industry, the science and the government of England.* 1851 London: Murray 231pp (reprint of second edition 1968 Cass)

Jones, Owen. *Gleanings from the Great Exhibition of 1851.* 1863 London: Strangeways and Walden 15pp (reprinted from *Journal of Design* June 1851)

Berlyn, Peter. *A popular narrative of the origin, history, progress and prospects of the Great Industrial Exhibition, 1851.* 1851 London: James Gilbert 186pp

Dempsey, George Drysdale. *The machinery of the nineteenth century; illustrated from original drawings, and including the best examples shewn at the Exhibition of the Works of Industry of all Nations.* 1852 London: Atchley & Son 72pp pl 30 (six parts issued but never completed)

Exhibitors Almanac for 1852, being bissextile or leap year; containing the calendar; moon's changes; and eclipses; an alphabetical list of the prizeholders of the Exhibition, giving their names and localities, a description of the articles for which prizes were awarded, and the classes in which they were exhibited; the whole forming a complete record of the Crystal Palace, together with a mass of useful information, and the ordinary contents of an almanac. 1852 London: Simpkin Marshall 166pp

Felkin, William. *The Exhibition of 1851, of the products and industry of all Nations. Its probable influence upon labour and commerce.* 1851 London: A. Hall 30pp

Fireside facts from the Great Exhibition. By the Editor of 'Pleasant Pages'. 1851 London: Houlston and Stoneman 246pp illus.

Gibbs, William. *The handbook of architectural ornament, illustrating and explaining the various styles of decoration employed in the Great Exhibition of 1851; and intended as a guide to designers and draughtsmen.* 1851 London: Ackermann 56pp

Griffiths, Thomas. *Chemistry of the Crystal Palace; a popular account of the chemical properties of the chief materials employed in its construction.* 1851 London: Parker 236pp

Humphreys, Henry Noel. *Ten centuries of art. Its progress in Europe from the 9th to 19th century. With a glance at the artistic works of classical antiquity and concluding considerations on the probable influence of the Great Exhibition, and on the state and future prospects of art in Great Britain.* 1852 London: Grant and Griffith 118pp illus.

Illustrated London News 1850-1851

Janin, Jules. *Le mois de mai à Londres et l'Exposition de 1851.* 1851 Paris: Michel Levy 172pp (eye witness account)

Knight, Charles. *Cyclopaedia of the industry of all nations.* 1851 London: C. Knight

Laborde, Leon Emmanuel Simon Joseph de, Comte. *Rapport sur l'application des arts à l'industrie, fait à la Commission Française du Jury International de l'Exposition Universelle de Londres.* 1856 Paris

Lardner, Dionysius. *The Great Exhibition and London in 1851. Reviewed by Dr Lardner.* 1852 London: Longman 630pp illus.

Semper, Gottfried. *Wissenschaft, Industrie und Kunst.* 1852 Braunschweig (Reissued 1966 Florian Kupferberg, Mainz)

The industry of nations as exemplified in the Great Exhibition of 1851. The materials of industry. 1852 London: Society for Promoting Christian Knowledge 411pp illus.

Texier, Edmond. *Lettres sur l'Angleterre. Souvenirs de l'Exposition Universelle.* 1851 Paris

The Times carried many important reports of the exhibition including 'Universal Infidelity in Principle of Design':
'The absence of any fixed principles in ornamental design is apparent in the Exhibition . . . it seems to us that the art manufacturers of the whole of Europe are thoroughly demoralized'.

Ward, James. *The Great Exhibition of 1851; or, the wealth of the world in its workshops. Comparing the relative skill of the manufacturers, designers and artisans of England with that of France, Belgium, Prussia and other continental states. By Philoponos.* 1850 London: Edward Charton 139pp

Ward, James. *The world in its workshops; a practical examination of British and foreign processes of manufacture, with a critical comparison of the fabrics, machinery and works of art contained in the Great Exhibition.* n.d. London: William S. Orr 284pp illus.

Weekes, Henry. *The prize treatise on the Fine Arts section of the Great Exhibition of 1851. Submitted to the Society of Arts in competition for their medal.* 1852 London: Vizetelly 150pp

On particular details:

Jones, Owen. *An apology for the colouring of the Greek court in the Crystal Palace (With arguments by G. H. Lewes and W. Lloyd and a fragment on the origin of Polychromy by Professor Semper)* 1854 London: Bradbury and Evans 56pp

Wyatt, Sir Matthew Digby and Waring, John Burley. *The Fine Arts courts in the Crystal Palace . . . Official handbook.* 1854 London: Crystal Palace Library. five parts:
1 *The Italian Court* 91pp
2 *The Renaissance Court* 108pp
3 *The Medieval Court* 123pp
4 *The Byzantine and Romanesque Court* 116pp
5 *A handbook to the Courts of Modern sculpture* (by Mrs Jameson) 91pp

'Ecclesiological aspect of the Great Exhibition'. *Ecclesiologist* XII 1851

Results of the exhibition:

Redgrave, Richard. *Report on Design prepared as A supplement to the Jury Reports of Class XXX of the Exhibition of 1851 at the desire of Her Majesty's Commissioners.* 1852 London: Clowes 96pp

Exhibition of the Works of Industry of All Nations, 1851. Reports by the juries on the subjects in the thirty classes into which the Exhibition was divided. 1852 London: Clowes for the Royal Commission (various editions-1 vol, 2 vols, 3 or 4 vols)

List of awards granted by the juries . . . Report of Viscount Canning on presenting the awards to the Royal Commission. HRH Prince Albert's answer. 1851 London: Clowes for the Royal Commission

A catalogue of the articles of ornamental art, selected from the Exhibition of the Works of Industry of All Nations in 1851, and purchased by the Government. Prepared at the desire of the Lords of the Committee of Privy Council for Trade. 1852 London: Chapman and Hall for Department of Practical Art 102pp

Wyatt, Matthew Digby. *The industrial arts of the nineteenth century. A series of illustrations of the choicest specimens produced by every nation at the Great Exhibition of Works of Industry, 1851.* 1851-1853 London: Day and Son 2 vols pl 158 (col)

Lectures on the results of the Great Exhibition of 1851. Delivered before the Society of Art, Manufactures and Commerce, at the suggestion of HRH Prince Albert. 1852-1853 London: David Bogue 2 vols (two series including lectures by Whewell, Wyatt, Playfair, Owen Jones)

Ruskin, John. *The opening of the Crystal Palace considered in some of its relations to the prospects of art.* 1854 London: Smith Elder 21pp

Sharp, Granville. *The Gilbart prize essay on the adaptation of recent discoveries and inventions in science and art (collected at the Great Exhibition of 1851) to the purposes of banking.* 1854 London: Groombridge 356pp (Reprinted from *Bankers Magazine* January and February 1852)

One important result of the Great Exhibition was the continuing work of the Royal Commission for the Exhibition of 1851:

An outline of its activities past and present. 1924 London: HMSO for Royal Commission

An important aspect of their work was the gathering and preservation of much of the basic materials generated and used by the Exhibition:

Collection of printed documents and forms used in carrying on the business of the Exhibition of 1851, together with some others issued without authority, but bearing upon the subject of the Exhibition. 8 vols

Exhibition of the Works of Industry of All Nations, 1851. Prospectuses of exhibitors . . . Collected under the authority of the Royal Commissioners. 16 vols

Exhibition of 1851. Catalogue of a collection of samples of raw and partly manufactured produce shown in the Exhibition of 1851: prepared by order of Her Majesty's Commissioners, for transmission to foriegn countries. 1853 London: William Clowes 34pp

Minutes of the proceedings of Her Majesty's Commissioners for the Exhibition of 1851. 11 January 1850 to 24 April 1852. 1852 London: William Clowes for HMSO

Further details of the activities of the Royal Commission are detailed in the reports of 1852 (two), 1856, 1861, 1867, 1879, 1889, 1911, 1935.

Studies of the Exhibition

Pevsner, Nikolaus. *High Victorian design: a study of the exhibits of 1851.* 1951 London: Architectural Press 162pp reprinted in Pevsner, Nikolaus. *Studies in Art, architecture and design. Vol 2 Victorian and after.* 1968 London: Thames and Hudson pp 38-95

Haltern, Utz. *Die Londoner Weltausstellung von 1851. Ein Beitrag zur Geschichte der Bürgerlich-Industriellen Gesellschaft im neunzehnten Jahrhundert.* 1971 Munster: Aschendorff 397pp bibl.

Luckhurst, K. W. 'The Great Exhibition of 1851'. *JRSA* vol 99 April 20 1951 pp 413-456

Fay, Charles Ryle. *Palace of industry 1851: a study of the Great Exhibition and its fruits.* 1951 Cambridge University Press 156pp illus.

Ffrench, Yvonne. *Great Exhibition.* 1950 London: Harvill Press 297pp

Hobhouse, Christopher. *1851 and the Crystal Palace. Being an account of the Great Exhibition and its contents; of Sir Joseph Paxton; and of the erection, the subsequent history and destruction of his masterpiece.* 1937 London: Murray 181pp illus. (another edition 1950)

Howarth, Patrick. *The year is 1851.* 1951 London: Collins 256pp (mainly social and economic background)

Richardson, John. *The real exhibitors exhibited; or, an inquiry into the condition of these industrial classes who have really represented England at the Great Exhibition.* 1851 London: Wertheim and Macintosh 122pp

Ames, Winslow. *Prince Albert and Victorian taste.* 1967 London: Chapman and Hall 238pp

Norrish, R. G. W. 'Lyon Playfair and his work for the Great Exhibition of 1851'. *JRSA* vol 99 June 1 1951 pp 537-549

Collections of photographs:

Gibbs-Smith, Charles H. *The Great Exhibition of 1851: a commemorative album.* 1950 London: HMSO 142pp

Maré, Eric de. *London 1851 The year of the Great Exhibition.* 1973 London: Folio Press/J. M. Dent 108pp

Harmsworth, Geoffrey. 'The Palace of Glass. A souvenir of 1851'. *Connoisseur* vol 127 1951 pp 98-105

Caricatures:

L'Exposition de Londres (1851). Croquis comiques par Cham (De Noé). n.d. Paris

Studies of the Crystal Palace:

Beaver, Patrick. *The Crystal Palace: 1851 to 1936.* 1970 London: Hugh Evelyn 151pp illus.

Bird, Anthony. *Paxton's Palace.* 1976 London: Cassell 179pp

Shand, P. Morton. 'The Crystal Palace as structure and precedent'. *Architectural Review* vol 81 February 1937 pp 65-72

Short, Audrey. 'Workers under glass'. *Victorian Studies* vol 10 no 2 pp 193-202

Hindley, Charles A. 'The architectural courts at the Crystal Palace'. *Architectural Review* vol 52 1922 pp 16-18

Irish National Exhibition of 1852, Cork

Maguire, John Francis. *The industrial movement in Ireland, as illustrated by the National Exhibition of 1852.* 1953 Cork: J. O'Brien 476pp

Davies, A. C. 'The first Irish National Industrial Exhibition: Cork 1852'. *Irish Economic and Social History* II 1975

Great Industrial Exhibition, Dublin 1853

Official catalogue of the Great Industrial Exhibition, 1853. 1853 Dublin

Adley, Charles C. *Synopsis of the contents of the Great Industrial Exhibition of 1853 . . . and a guide to its internal arrangements.* 1853 Dublin: Webb and Chapman 48pp

Record of the Great Industrial Exhibition 1853, being a brief and comprehensive description of the different objects of interest contained in that temple of industry. By Thomas Dillon Jones, financial officer. 1854 Dublin

Sproule, John (ed). *The Irish Industrial Exhibition of 1853: a detailed catalogue of its contents.* 1854 Dublin (Edited from his *Exhibition Expositor and Advertiser* 1853. 13 issues)

Bence-Jones, Mark. 'Ireland's Great Exhibition'. *Country Life* 153 15 March 1973 pp 666-668

Davies, A. C. 'The Society of Arts and the Dublin Exhibition of 1853'. *JRSA* vol 123 June 1975 pp 433-436

World's Fair of the Works of Industry of All Nations, New York 1853

Coleman, Earle E. 'The Exhibition in the Palace: a bibliographical essay'. *New York Public Library Bulletin* vol 64 September 1960 pp 459-477

Silliman, B. Jnr and Goodrich, C. R. (ed). *The world of Science, Art and Industry, illustrated from examples in the New York exhibition, 1853-1854.* 1854 New York: G. P. Putnam & Co 207pp 500 illus.

Greeley, Horace. *Art and Industry as represented in the exhibition at the Crystal Palace New York 1853-1854: showing the progress and state of the various useful and esthetic pursuits.* From the *New York Tribune.* 1853 New York: Redfield 386pp (University Microfilms)

Exposition Universelle, Paris 1855

Catalogues and guides:

Exposition des Produits de l'Industrie de toutes les Nations, 1855: catalogue officiel. 1855 Paris: Panis 544pp illus.

Rapports publiés sous la direction de SAI le Prince Napoléon. 1856 Paris: Imprimerie Impériale 2 vols

Recueil des pièces et documents officiels concernant l'Exposition Universelle de 1855, mis en ordre et publiés par M. E. Panis . . . éditeur des catalogues officiels de l'Exposition de 1855. 1855 Paris: Panis 264pp

Art Journal. The exhibition of art-industry in Paris 1855. 1855 London: Virtue 46pp

The official guide to the Universal Exhibition. Edited by W. Blanchard Jerrold, preceded by an historical introduction. 1855 Paris: Gervais 172pp

Paris universal exhibition 1855. Catalogue of works exhibited in the British section of the exhibition, in French and English; together with exhibitors prospectuses, prices current. 1855 London: Chapman and Hall for the Royal Commission for the Paris Exhibition 383pp illus.

Rapport sur l'Exposition Universelle de 1855 présenté à l'Empereur. 1857 Paris: Imprimerie Impériale 511pp

Reports on the Paris Universal Exhibition. 1856 London: Eyre and Spottiswoode for Royal Commission for the Paris Exhibition. 3 vols

Studies and commentaries:

Notes of some remarkable objects exhibited in the French, foreign, and British colonial departments of the Paris Universal Exhibition. Furnished to the Board of Trade by Sir William Hooker, Sir Joseph Olliffe, Professor Owen, Professor Willis, Professor W. Smyth, Charles Knight, George Wallis, H. Cole and Captain Fowke . . . and published for the information of merchants, manufacturers, workmen. 1855 London: Chapman and Hall 103pp

'By way of contrast. Some exhibits from the Paris Exhibition of 1855'. *Architectural Review* vol 69 1931 pp 81 (Collection of engravings)

Lefèbvre Laboulaye, Charles Pierre. *Essai sur l'Art industriel, comprenant l'étude des produits les plus célèbres de l'industrie à toutes les époques et des oeuvres les plus remarquées à l'Exposition Universelle de Londres en 1851, et à l'Exposition de Paris en 1855.* 1856 Paris: Bureau du Dictionnaire des arts et manufactures 256pp illus.

Barrault, Alexis and Bridel, G. *Le Palais de l'Industrie et ses annexes; description raisonné du system de construction en fer et en fonte, adopté dans ces bâtiments, avec dessins d'exécution et tableaux des poids.* 1857 Paris

Braund, John. *Illustrations of furniture, candelabra, musical instruments . . . from the Great Exhibitions of London and Paris; with examples of similar articles from royal palaces and noble mansions.* 1858 London: Braund pl 48

Visite à l'Exposition de Paris en 1855. Publié sous la direction de M Tresca. 1855 Paris: Hachette

The English and American Intelligencer no 18 June 9-no 38 October 27 1855 (Published in Paris for the English speaking visitor)

Moniteur industriel: journal de la défense du travail national. Vingt-quatrième année numbers 1979-2007. Paris

Brisse, L. Baron. *Album de l'Exposition Universelle 1855.* 1855-1859 Paris 3 vols

International Exhibition of 1862, London

Much less popular than the 1851 exhibition, the exhibition of 1862 is particularly interesting for the ways in which it reflected changes in design since 1851. Much less flamboyant in a brick rather than glass palace.

Official publications:

Official illustrated catalogue. 1862 London: HMSO 12 parts

Official catalogue of the industrial department. 1862 London: HMSO 432pp

Illustrated catalogue of the Industrial department. 1862 London: HMSO 4 vols (vols 1 & 2 British division, vol 3 Colonial and Foreign, vol 4 Foreign). Vol 1 includes an article by J. Hollinshead reviewing earlier exhibitions)

Reports by the Juries on the subjects in the 36 classes into which the exhibition was divided. 1863 London: W. Clowes for Society of Arts 1178pp including Tylor, A. 'Scientific and art education in relation to progress in manufactures. Second part of Jury Report Class XXXI'.

Popular catalogues and guides:

Art Journal Illustrated catalogue of the International Exhibition. 1862 London: Virtue 324pp illus. (Facsimile reprint 1973 E. P. Reprint)

Clark, Daniel Kinnear (ed). *The exhibited machinery of 1862: a cyclopaedia of the machinery represented at the International Exhibition.* 1864 London: Day 447pp

Hunt, Robert. *Synopsis of a complete guide to the contents of the International Exhibition of 1862.* 1862 London: Stanford 96pp

Hunt, Robert. *Handbook to the industrial department of the International Exhibition 1862 . . . published with the authority of Her Majesty's Commissioners.* 1862 London: E.' Stanford 2 vols

Macdermott, Edward. *The popular guide to the International Exhibition of 1862.* 1862 London: W. H. Smith 244pp illus.

Practical Mechanics Journal. *Scientific record of the International Exhibition of 1862; being a systematic and scientific synopsis of the chief productions shown, relating to commerce, arts and manufacture. Edited by Robert Mallet.* 1863 London: Longman 607pp illus.

The Penny guide to the International Exhibition. 1862 London: Simpkin Marshall 28pp

A plain guide to the International Exhibition. The wonders of the exhibition, showing how they may be seen at one visit. 1862 London: Sampson Low 64pp

Pardon, George Frederick. *A guide to the International Exhibition; with plans of the building, an account of its rise, progress, and completion and notices of its principal contents.* 1862 London: Routledge 205pp

Cassells Illustrated Family Paper Exhibitor, containing about 300 illustrations, with letterpress description of all the principal objects in the International Exhibition of 1862. 1862 London: Cassell, Petter and Galpin 272pp illus.

Some account of the buildings designed by Francis Fowke RE for the Exhibition. 1861 London: Chapman and Hall 36pp

Timbs, John. *The International Exhibition. The industry, science and art of the age; or the International Exhibition of 1862 popularly described from its origin to its close.* 1863 London: Bogue

Timbs, John (ed). *The Yearbook of Facts in the International Exhibition of 1862: its origin and progress; construction details of the building; the most remarkable articles and objects exhibited.* 1862 London

Serious contemporary appraisal:

Dresser, Christopher. *Development of Ornamental Art in the International Exhibition being a concise statement of the laws which govern the production and application of ornament, with references to the best examples.* 1862 London: 192pp (ABC Reprint)

Lefèbvre Laboulaye, Charles Pierre. *Etudes sur l'Exposition Universelle de Londres.* 1863

Paris 908pp (also published as *Annales du Conservatoire Impérial des Arts et Métiers* tome 3)

Fairbairn, William. *Useful information for engineers. Third series. As comprised in a series of lectures in the Applied Sciences, and other kindred subjects; together with treatises on the comparative merits of the Paris and London international exhibitions.* 1866 London: Longmans Green 330pp illus.

Hawes, William. 'On the results of the International Exhibition of 1862'. *JSA* vol 11 June 5 1863 pp 488-501

Levi, Leone. 'International Exhibition of 1862. The introductory lecture to a course on the commerce of the countries represented at the International Exhibition'. *JSA* vol 11 November 21 1862 pp 21-27

Easel, Jack *pseud* (ie C. L. Eastlake). 'The Great Ex'. *London Society* II 1862 pp 105-113

Rondot, Cyr François Natalis. *Exposition universelle de 1862.* 1863 Paris 74pp illus.

Extracts from the reports of the French jurors at the International Exhibition. 1862 London 12pp

Wallis, George. *The Art manufactures of Birmingham and the Midland Counties in the International Exhibition of 1862.* 1862 London

Burges, William. 'The International Exhibition'. *Gentleman's Magazine* July 1862 pp 3-12

A number of sumptuous collections of illustrations were prepared:

Waring, John Burley. *Masterpieces of industrial art and sculpture at the International Exhibition, 1862. Selected and described by J. B. Waring, chromolithographed by W. R. Tymms, A. Warren and G. Macculloch from photographs by Stephen Thompson.* 1863 London: Day 3 vols 301 col pl

Album des installations les plus remarquables de l'Exposition Universelle de 1862, à Londres, publié par la Commission Impériale pour servir de renseignement aux exposants des diverses nations. 1866 Paris

More detailed comments on particular items and sections of the exhibition are buried in the journals of the time:

Crace, J. G. 'On the decoration of the International Exhibition Building of 1862'. *JSA* vol 10 1862 pp 339-345

Burges, William. 'The Japanese Court'. *Gentleman's Magazine* July 1862

'The Medieval court, International Exhibition'. *Building News* 8 August 1862 pp 98-101

There have been few recent studies of the exhibition:

Bradford, Betty. 'The brick palace of 1862'. *Architectural Review* vol 132 July 1962 pp 15-21

International Exhibition of 1862. 1962 London: HMSO for Victoria and Albert Museum 36pp 28 illus. (Small picturebook no 60)

International Exhibition of Arts and Manufactures, Dublin 1865

Official catalogue of the Exhibition of Manufactures, machinery and Fine Arts. 1865 Dublin 106pp

The Official guide to the Dublin International Exhibition, 1865. 1865 Dublin

Art Journal Illustrated Catalogue of the Exhibition of Industry in Dublin. 1853 London: Virtue 64pp illus.

The illustrated record and descriptive catalogue of the Dublin International Exhibition of 1865. Compiled and edited by Henry Parkinson and Peter Lund Simmonds; aided by numerous contributions from several heads of departments and other experienced writers on special subjects. 1866 Dublin 250 illus.

Kane, Sir Robert. 'On the recent progress and present state of industry in Ireland, and the Dublin International Exhibition.' *JSA* vol 13 December 16 1864 pp 70-78

Exposition Universelle, Paris 1867

Catalogues:

Paris Universal Exhibition, 1867: the complete official catalogue, English version. 1867 London: J. M. Johnson and Sons under the authority of the Imperial Commission 1008pp illus.

Catalogue général, publié par la Commission Impériale. 1867 Paris: E. Denton 1538pp

The illustrated catalogue of the Universal exhibition, published with the Art Journal. 1868 London: Virtue 331pp

Catalogue of the British section, containing a list of the exhibitors of the United Kingdom and its colonies, and the objects which they exhibited. In French, English, German and Italian. With statistical introductions and an appendix in which many of the objects exhibited are more fully described. 1867 London: HMSO 464pp, 363pp, 322pp illus.

Paris Universal Exhibition, 1867. British section. Fine Arts division comprising objects illustrating the history of labour before 1800. 1867 London: Spottiswoode 84pp

Exposition Universelle de 1867. Illustrée publication internationale, autorisée par la

Commission Impériale. 1868 Paris:
Administration 2 vols (first issued in 60
parts)

Guides:

Black's guide to Paris and the exhibition of 1867.
Edited by David Thomas Amsted. 1867
Edinburgh: A & C Black 72pp

L'Exposition Universelle de 1867. Guide de
l'Exposant et du Visiteur avec les documents
officiels, une place et une vue de l'Exposition.
1866 Paris: Hachette 191pp illus.

Reports:

Great Britain. Imperial Commission. *Reports*
on the Paris Universal Exhibition, 1867.
Presented to both Houses of Parliament. 1868
London: HMSO 6 vols (vols 2-5 on
particular classes)

Rapport sur l'Exposition Universelle de 1867, à
Paris. Précis des opérations et listes des
collaborateurs, avec un appendice sur l'avenir
des expositions, la statistique des opérations, les
documents officiels et le plan de l'Exposition.
1869 Paris: Imprimerie Impériale
672pp plans

Rapport du Jury International publié sous la
direction de M Michel Chevalier. 1868
Paris: P. Dupont 13 vols

The views of British visitors:

Reports of artisans selected by a committee
appointed by the Council of the Society of Arts
to visit the Paris Universal Exhibition 1867.
Edited by C. Critchett. 1867 London: Royal
Society of Arts

Dexter, John Thomas (ed). *Modern*
industries; a series of reports on industry and
manufactures as represented in the Paris
Exposition in 1867 by twelve British workmen
visiting Paris under the auspices of the Paris
excursion committee of the Society of Arts.
1868 London

Hawes, William. 'On the reports of the
artisans selected to visit the Paris
Universal Exhibition of 1867'. *JSA* vol 16
January 24 1868 pp 161-180 (extensive
quotation)

Aitken, W. C. *Report presented to the council of*
the Birmingham Chamber of Commerce, on
manufactures of a similar kind to those of
Birmingham as represented in the
International Exhibition held at Paris 1867.
1967 Birmingham: M. Billing 92pp

Sala, George Augustus. *Notes and sketches of*
the Paris Exhibition. 1868 London: Tinsley
Brothers 396pp illus. (reprint of *Daily*
Telegraph articles)

Wyatt, Sir Matthew Digby. *On the arts of*
decoration at the International Exhibition at
Paris AD 1867 consisting of reports to the
British government on class XV Decoration,
class XVIII Carpets, tapestries, class XIX

Paperhangings. 1868 London: private
circulation 4 parts

Albums and collections of illustrations:

L'Exposition populaire illustrée. 1867 Paris
numbers 1-60

Grand album de l'Exposition Universelle 1867.
150 dessins par les premiers artistes de la
France et de l'étranger. 1868 Paris: Michel
Lévy frères 127pp illus.

Mesnard, Jules. *Les merveilles de l'Exposition*
Universelle de 1867. Arts-Industrie; bronzes,
meubles, orfèvrerie, porcelaines, faïences,
cristaux, bijoux, dentelles, soieries, tissus de
toutes sortes, papiers peints, tapisseries, tapis,
glaces etc. 1867 Paris: Lahure 2 vols
243pp, 239pp

Gautier, Albert Hippolyte. *Les curiosités de*
l'Exposition Universelle de 1867 suivi d'un
indicateur pratique des moyens de transport.
1867 Paris: Delagrave 190pp

A few studies:

Luchet, Auguste. *L'Art industriel à*
l'Exposition Universelle de 1867. Mobilier,
vêtement, aliments. 1868 Paris: Librairie
Internationale 475pp

Falke, Jacob. *Die Kunstindustrie der*
Gegenwart. Studien auf der Pariser
Weltausstellung im Jahr 1867. 1868
Leipzig: Quandt 269pp

Alcan, Michel. *Fabrication des étoffes: études*
sur les arts textiles à l'Exposition Universelle
de 1867. 1868 Paris: J. Baudry 2 vols

Annual International Exhibitions, London 1871-1874

An attempt to turn the taste for
international exhibitions into regular
channels, with particular classes of products
to be shown in turn in different years, the
exhibitions lost money and public interest.

Although the *Journal of the Society of Arts*
was declared the official record, other
documents are now very hard to find.

First Annual International Exhibition 1871

Catalogues and reports:

The International exhibition of 1871 (The Art
Journal Catalogue of the International
Exhibition by George Wallis). 1871 London:
Virtue 88pp

Official catalogue. Industrial department. 1871
London: HMSO 168pp

Official reports on the various sections of the
exhibition, edited by the Right Hon Lord
Houghton. Fine Arts Division Part 2. 1871
London: J. M. Johnson (Furniture and
metalwork pp 15-36)

France: Commission Supérieure. *Rapports.*
1872 Paris: J. Claye

Popular guides:

The Key: a programme and record of the London International Exhibitions. 1871 London 4 parts in 1 vol

Kelly's Post Office guide to London in 1871, visitor's handbook . . . and companion to the directory (includes brief guide to Exhibition of 1871; and the art and industrial pursuits of the Kingdom, as illustrated therein: the London annual international exhibition of fine and industrial art and scientific inventions). 1871 London: Kelly

Second Annual International Exhibition 1872

Art Journal. International Exhibition. Second division. 1872 London: Virtue 64pp illus.

Reports on the London International Exhibition of 1872. 1872 London: Society of Arts

Third Annual International Exhibition 1873

Reports on the London International Exhibition of 1873; prepared by the direction of the Council of the Society of Arts. Parts 1, 2 and 3 1873 London: Society of Arts

Fourth Annual International Exhibition 1874

Cole, H. H. 'On the London International Exhibition of 1874'. *JSA* vol 22 March 27 1874 pp 426-430 ('It is said that the idea of International Exhibitions is worn out) . . .'

Weltausstellung 1873 Wien. Vienna

Cole's quote did not apply outside Britain.

Official catalogues and reports:

Welt-Ausstellung 1873 in Wien. Offizieller General-Catalog. 1873 Vienna

Offizieller Ausstellungs-Bericht. Herausgegeben durch die General-Direktion der Weltausstellung (Edited by Carl Thomas Richter) 1873-1875 Vienna (in many parts)

The British section at the Vienna Universal Exhibition 1873 (Fine Art galleries, industrial, agricultural and machinery halls and park). Official catalogue with plans and illustrations. 1873 London: Royal Commission for the Vienna Universal Exhibition of 1873 52pp illus.

Reports on the Vienna Universal Exhibition of 1873 . . . presented to both Houses of Parliament. 1874 London: Eyre and Spottiswoode 4 vols illus. (C. 1072)

Containing a more general discussion:

Archer, T. C. 'On the influence on International Exhibitions as records of art industry'. Part 3 pp 5-12 with appendices pp 13-56

A study:

Falke, Jakob von. *Die Kunstindustrie auf der Wiener Weltausstellung 1873.* 1873 Vienna: Gerold 2 vols 431pp

Philadelphia Centennial Exhibition 1876

Catalogues and surveys:

Art Journal. Contributions to the International Exhibition at Philadelphia 1876. Illustrated with one chromolithograph, eight engravings on steel and one hundred and eighteen on wood. 1876 London: Virtue 54pp

Norton, Frank Henry. *Illustrated historical register of the Centennial Exhibition, Philadelphia 1876 and the Exposition Universelle Paris 1878.* 1879 New York: American News Company 396pp illus.

United States Centennial Commission. *International Exhibition 1876. Official catalogue.* 1876 Philadelphia 4 parts

Official catalogue of the British section. 1876 London: HMSO 2 parts

Reports on the Philadelphia International Exhibition of 1876. 1877 London: HMSO 3 vols (Cmd 1774, 1848, 1890)

Albums and examples:

McCabe, James Dabney. *The illustrated history of the Centennial Exhibition held in commemoration of the one hundredth anniversary of American independence: with a full description of the great buildings and all the objects on interest exhibited in them: embracing also a concise history of the origin and success of the exhibition and biographies of the leading members of the Centennial Commission.* 1975 Philadelphia: National Press 302pp (reprint of 1876 edition)

Magee's illustrated guide of Philadelphia and the Centennial Exhibition: a guide and description. 1975 New York: Cohen 192pp illus. (reprint of 1876 edition)

The masterpieces of the Centennial International Exhibition. 1877-1878 Philadelphia: Gebbie and Barrie 3 vols (vol 2 Industrial Art)

Ferris, George Titus. *Gems of the Centennial exhibition: consisting of illustrated descriptions of objects of an artistic character, in the exhibits of the United States, Great Britain, France.* 1877 New York: Appleton & Co 164pp illus.

Smith, Walter. *Examples of household taste (the industrial art of the International Exhibition).* 1880 New York: R. Worthington 521pp

Some visitors and reflections:

Archer, Professor. 'The Centennial Exhibition, Philadelphia 1876' *JSA* vol 25 22 December 1876 pp 84-94

Davies, A. C. 'Britain and the American Centennial Exhibition 1876'. (Studies in the Society's history and archives CXXXII) *JRSA* December 1976 pp 28-31

The Great exhibitions of the world. 1880 New York: Lovering 186pp 119 illus. ('The history of the [Philadelphia Centennial] exhibition' by Jos. M. Wilson pp 83-186)

Exposition Universelle, Paris 1878

General and official catalogues:

Art Journal. The illustrated catalogue of the Paris International Exhibition 1878. 1878 London: Virtue 212pp illus.

Catalogue officiel publié par le commissariat général. 1878 Paris: Imprimerie Nationale 5 vols

Catalogue officiel. Liste des récompenses. 1878 Paris: Imprimerie Nationale 529pp

The British section:

Official catalogue of the British section. 1878 London: Eyre and Spottiswoode for HMSO 2 vols

Paris Universal Exhibition of 1878. Statistical and descriptive notes introductory to the various classes of exhibits in the British section . . . compiled by P. L. Simmonds. 1878 London: Eyre and Spottiswoode 82pp

Official reports and observers:

Report of Her Majesty's commissioners for the Paris Universal Exhibition of 1878. 1880 London: HMSO 2 vols

Rapports du Jury International. 1880-1885 Paris: Imprimerie Nationale 9 vols (9 groups of 90 classes)

The Society of Arts artisan reports on the Paris Universal Exhibition of 1878. 1879 London: Sampson Low 664pp

Reports of artisans sent to the Paris Exhibition. 1879 Leeds: Chamber of Commerce 87pp

A guide:

Black's guide to Paris and the Exhibition of 1878. 1878 Edinburgh: A & C Black 72pp

An eye-witness:

Sala, George Augustus. *Paris herself again in 1878-1879.* 1880 London: Remington 2 vols 400 illus.

Albums:

L'art et l'industrie de tous peuples à l'Exposition universelle de 1878: description illustré des merveilles du Champs-de-Mars et du Trocadéro par les écrivains speciaux les plus autorisés. 1880 Paris: Librairie illustrée 636pp

L'Exposition universelle de 1878 illustrée. 87 belles gravures sur bois, text descriptif par S. de Vandières. 1879 Paris: Calmann Lévy 152pp 159 illus.

Gautier, Adolphe Hippolyte. *Les curiosités de l'Exposition de 1878. Guide du visiteur.* 1878 Paris: Delagrave 211pp illus.

The Illustrated Paris Universal Exhibition. 1878 London: Illustrated London News 232pp

Parville, Henri de. *Exposition universelle 1878. Ouvrage orné de 253 vignettes.* 1879 Paris: J. Rothschild 459pp

Shinn, Earl (ed). *Les chefs d'oeuvre d'art à l'Exposition universelle 1878.* 1878 Paris: L. Baschet (American edition by Gebbie and Barrie, Philadelphia) 138pp

A bibliography:

Famy, Colette. *Bibliographie analytique de l'Exposition universelle tenue à Paris en 1878.* 1962 Paris: Mémoire INTD 71pp (193 refs)

International Health Exhibition 1884 London

Perhaps more national than international, the exhibition generated a lot of material.

Official documents and reports:

Official guide. 1884 London: Clowes 45pp

Handbooks. 1884 London: Clowes 25 vols

The awards of the International juries. Confirmed and issued by the Jury Commissioners. 1884 London: Clowes 79pp

Lectures. 1884 London: Clowes 37 vols

Conferences. 1884 London: Clowes 14 vols

The Health Exhibition literature. 1884 London: Clowes 19 vols

Catalogue of decorations and designs, work of students of Schools of Art, South Kensington. 1884 London: Clowes

A popular guide:

The People's guide to the Health Exhibition . . . edited by Carter Blake. 1884 London: General Publishing Co 63pp

A study:

Hart, Ernest. 'International Health Exhibition: its influence and possible sequels'. *JSA* vol 33 November 28 1884 pp 35-58

Exposition Universelle, Paris 1889

Official catalogues and reports:

Catalogue général officiel. 1889 Lille: Imprimerie L. Danel

Bulletin officiel nos 1-157, 20 November 1886-16 November 1889. Paris

Exposition universelle internationale de 1889 à Paris. Rapport général par Alfred Picard. 1890-1892 Paris: Imprimerie Nationale 10 vols (vol 1 includes a history of international exhibitions)

Rapports du Jury International publiés sous la direction de M Alfred Picard. 1890-1892 Paris: Imprimerie Nationale 16 vols

Guide to the exhibition. 1889 London: Clowes 82pp pl 10

Special journal:

Le Courrier de l'Exposition Illustré. Edition speciale du 'Matin' no 1-45 (April 7-December 1889)

Albums:

The Paris Universal Exhibition album, 1889. 1889 London and New York: Stiassay and Rasetti 179pp illus.

L'album de l'Exposition 1889 (par) Glucq. 1889 Paris: Gaulon pl 100 (captions in English, French, Spanish)

Alphand, Adolphe. *Exposition universelle de Paris de 1889. Monographie des palais, jardins, constructions diverses et installations générales.* 1892-1895 Paris: Rothschild 3 vols

Champier, Victor. *Les industries d'art à l'Exposition universelle de 1889.* 1889-1894 Paris a series of plates

Gautier, Albert Hippolyte. *Les curiosités de l'Exposition de 1889 avec itinéraire du visiteur.* 1889 Paris: C. Delagrave 142pp

Monod, Emile. *L'Exposition universelle de 1889, grand ouvrage illustré, historique, encyclopédique, descriptif.* 1890 Paris: Denton 3 vols

Walton, William. *Chef d'oeuvre de l'Exposition universelle de Paris 1889.* 1889 Philadelphia: G. Barrie 118pp pl 75

L'art décoratif à l'Exposition universelle de 1889. Ameublement, tapisserie, bronzes, orfèvrerie, céramiques, vitraux. 1890 Paris: A. Calavas 1p pl 60

Marx, Roger. *La décoration et l'art industriel à l'Exposition universelle de 1889.* 1890 Paris: Ancienne Maison Quantin 60pp

Revue de l'Exposition universelle de 1889, F. G. Dumas directeur. 1889 Paris: L. Baschet 2 vols

An English view:

Wood, H. Trueman. 'The Paris Exhibition'. *JSA* vol 38 December 13 1889 pp 45-62

A bibliography:

Martinière, Véronique de la. *Bibliographie des documents ayant paru à l'occasion de l'Exposition universelle de 1889 à Paris.* 1959 Paris: Mémoire INTD 207pp (663 refs)

World's Columbian Exposition, Chicago 1893

Shepp, James W. and Shepp, Daniel B. *Shepp's World's Fair photographed. Being a collection of original copyrighted photographs authorized and permitted by the management of the World's Columbian Exposition.* 1893 Chicago: Globe Bible Publishing Company 528pp

Bancroft, Hubert Howe. *The book of the fair; an historical and descriptive presentation of the world's science, art and industry as viewed through the Columbian Exposition at Chicago in 1883.* 1893 Chicago: Bancroft 2 vols

Grille, M. and Falconnet, M. H. *Revue technique de l'exposition universelle de Chicago.* 1894 Paris: E. Bernard (planned as series – Part 1 only published)

Villiers, Frederick. 'An artist's view of Chicago and the World's Fair'. *JSA* vol 42 December 8 1893 pp 49-54

Exposition Universelle, Paris 1900

See also:

Art Nouveau *page 71*

Official catalogues and reports:

Catalogue général officiel. 1900 Paris: Imprimerie Lemercier 20 vols in 19

Exposition universelle internationale de 1900 à Paris. Rapport général administratif et technique par Alfred Picard . . . commissaire général. 1902-1903 Paris: Imprimerie Nationale 8 vols

Rapport du Jury International. 1902-1905 Paris: Imprimerie Nationale 46 vols

Rapport général sur les congrès de l'Exposition par M. de Chasseloup-Laubat. 1901 Paris: Imprimerie Nationale 810pp

Paris Exposition, reproduced from the official photographs taken under the supervision of the French government. 1900 New York: R. S. Peale

The British interest:

British official catalogue. 1900 London: HMSO for Royal Commission for the Paris Exhibition 1900 260pp illus.

Paris Exhibition, 1900: catalogue of the loan collection and exhibits at the British Royal Pavilion. 1900 London: HMSO 7pp

Spielmann, Sir Isadore. *The Royal Pavilion.* 1900 London: HMSO for Royal Commission for the Paris Exhibition 1900 151pp illus.

Report of Her Majesty's Commissioners for the Paris International Exhibition 1900. 1901 London: HMSO 2 vols

Some special guides:

Anglo-Saxon guide to the Paris Exhibition, 1900 with a map of Paris; map of the exhibition grounds and buildings, enlarged plans of the various sections. Edited by B. Bernard. 1900 New York: Darbyshire 232pp

International Association for the Advancement of Science, Arts and Education. *Guide to Paris; the exhibition and the assembly.* 1900 London: Paris International Assembly 228pp

Guide pratique du visiteur de Paris et de l'Exposition. 1900 Paris: Hachette 484pp illus. maps

Contemporary surveys:

Thomson, David Croal (ed). *The Paris Exposition, 1900.* 1901 London: Virtue-Art Journal Office 374pp illus.

Benn, R. Davis. 'Cabinet Maker review of the Paris Exhibition'. *Cabinet Maker* vol 21 July-February 1900-1901 pp 1-11, 29-39, 57-74, 85-93, 113-121, 141-151, 169-186, 197-214

'Round the Exhibition'. 1. The House of the 'Art Nouveau Bing' by Gabriel Mourey, 2. A Palace of Dress by Frederic Lees. *Studio* vol 20 June, July 1900 pp 164-180, 227-236

Anderson, A. 'The Paris Exhibition and some of its buildings'. *Architectural Review* vol 7 1900 pp 29-37

Grubhofer, Tony. 'Some sketches of the Paris Exhibition'. *Studio* vol 20 July 1900 p 217 – (drawings of the pavilions)

La mécanique à l'Exposition de 1900, publiée sous le patronage et la direction technique d'un comité de rédaction, composé de M Haton de la Goupillière. 1902 Paris: C. Dunod 3 vols

La décoration et l'ameublement à l'Exposition de 1900. 1900 Paris: Guérinet 6 vols 664 illus. (Vols 1-3 furniture, 4 Wall hangings, textiles, wallpaper, 5 Decorative painting, 6 Carving)

Marx, Roger. *La décoration et les industries d'art de l'Exposition Universelle de Paris 1900.* 1902 Paris: C. Delagrave 130pp illus.

Picard, Alfred. *Le bilan d'un siècle.* 1906 Paris: Imprimerie Nationale 6 vols (reflections by the Commissaire Général)

Geffroy, Gustave. *Les industries artistiques Françaises et étrangères à l'Exposition Universelle de 1900.* 1900 Paris: Librairie Centrale des Beaux Arts 62pp pl 100

Champiers, Victor. *Les industries d'art à l'Exposition Universelle de 1900.* 1902 Paris: Bureaux de la Revue des arts décoratifs 2 vols 254pp illus. (a fairly hostile view)

Journals specially published for the exhibition:

Nineteen hundred: monthly illustrated journal containing all the laws, decrees and official documents of the Paris Universal Exposition of 1900. A pictorial and literary history. 1895 Paris

1900; organe des expositions. 25 November 1898 Paris

L'Exposition de Paris (1900): publiée avec la collaboration d'écrivains speciaux et des meilleurs artistes. 1899-1900 Paris: Montgredion 3 vols (based on a weekly newspaper)

La grande revue de l'Exposition: supplément illustré de la Revue des Revues. November 1899-October 1900 nos 1-16 260pp

Albums and picture books:

Le Panorama. L'Exposition Universelle. 1900 Paris: Librairie A. Pigoreau

Campbell, James B. *Illustrated history of the Paris International exposition of 1900. A presentation of the world's achievements in literature, science, industry, art and architecture, as shown at the Paris exposition at the close of the nineteenth century.* 1900 Chicago: Chicago and Omaha Pubs 196pp illus.

Les beaux-arts et les arts décoratifs à l'Exposition Universelle de 1900. 1900 Paris: Gazette des Beaux Arts 526pp

Album de l'Exposition 1900. 120 vues et 7 plans. 1900 Paris

Detailed analytical studies:

Mandell, Richard D. *Paris 1900. The Great World's Fair.* 1967 University of Toronto Press 173pp illus. bibl. (the notes and bibliography are particularly rich and full)

Borsi, F. and Godoli, E. *Paris 1900.* 1978 London: Crosby Lockwood Staples 290pp (translation of Vockauer edition)

A growing number of exhibitions and surveys in a broader European context:

Europa 1900. Peintures – Dessins – Sculptures – Bijoux 3 juin-30 septembre 1967, Museum

voor Schone Kunsten, Ostend. Text by Emile Langui. 1967 Brussels: Editions de la Connaissance 64pp

Jullian, Philippe. *The triumph of Art Nouveau: Paris Exhibition 1900, translated by Stephen Hardman.* 1978 (new edition) Oxford: Phaidon 216pp 143 illus. (previous edition 1974)

A very great deal has been written on this exposition and so for more material:

Signat, Colette. *Bibliographie analytique des documents publiés à l'occasion de l'Exposition Universelle Internationale de 1900 à Paris.* 1959 Paris: Conservatoire national des arts et métiers 159pp (545 refs)

Wendte, Frederica. 'Reading list of magazine articles on the Paris Exposition, 1900'. *Bulletin of Bibliography* II no 3 1900 pp 42ff

Glasgow International Exhibition 1901

'The artistic side of the Glasgow International Exhibition'. *Architectural Review* vol 9 1901 pp 242-254

'Round the exhibition: German decorative art by Gabriel Mourey. Austrian decorative art by Gabriel Mourey. Scandinavian decorative art by S. Frykholm'. *Studio* vol 21 1901 pp 44-50, 113-123, 190-199

'Glasgow International Exhibition'. *Studio* vol 23 1901 pp 44-48, 165-173, 237-246

Pan-American Exposition 1901

Brush, Edward Hale. 'The artistic side of the Pan-American exposition'. *Architectural Review* vol 9, vol 10 1901 pp 99-107, 42-55

Esposizione Internazionale d'Arte Decorativa Moderna, Turin 1902

Pica, Vittorio. *L'Arte decorativa all'Esposizione di Torino del 1902.* 1903 Bergamo: Instituto Italiano d'Arti Grafiche 388pp 465 illus.

Fuchs, Georg and Newbery, F. H. *Internationale Ausstellung für dekorative Kunst in Turin, MDCCCCII.* 1903 Darmstadt: Koch 340pp illus. (Also French edition)

I mobili alla prima esposizione internazionale d'arte decorativa moderna. 1903 Turin 2 vols

'The First International Exhibition of Modern Decorative Art at Turin'. *Studio* vol 26 1902 pp 45-47, 47-52, 91-104, 204-213, 251-259

'The International Exhibition of Decorative Art at Turin'. *Studio* vol 27 1903 pp 130-134, 188-197, 273-279, 279-282

Fratini, Francesca Romana. *Torino 1902: polemiche in Italia sull'arte nuova.* 1971 Torino: Martano 303pp illus. bibl.

Franco-British Exhibition London 1908

Carden, Robert W. 'The Franco-British exhibition'. *Architectural Review* vol 24 1908 pp 32-37, 108-111

Cockburn, Sir John. 'The Franco-British exhibition'. *JRSA* vol 56 November 29 1907 pp 23-32

Horsfield, J. Nixon. 'The Franco-British exhibition of science, arts and industries London, 1908'. *JRIBA* vol 15 series 3 pp 546-556

Exposition Universelle et Internationale, Brussels 1910

Exposition universelle et internationale de Bruxelles 1910. Catalogue général officiel. 1910 Brussels 536pp

British official catalogue. 1910 London: HMSO 424pp

Reports of the British jurors at the Brussels and Turin exhibitions 1910 and 1911. 1912 London: HMSO 168pp

'The Brussels Exhibition'. *Studio* vol 50 1910 pp 308-317

Esposizione Internazionale d'Industria e de Laboro, Turin 1911

British official catalogue. Catalogo ufficiale britannico. 1911 London: HMSO 449pp

Melani, Alfredo. 'Some notes on the Turin International Exhibition'. *Studio* vol 53 1911 pp 286-293

Exposition Universelle et Industrielle, Ghent 1913

Catalogue of the British arts and crafts section. 1913 London: HMSO

Panama-Pacific Exposition, San Francisco 1915

'Panama-Pacific Exposition at San Francisco'. *Architectural Review* vol 38 1915 pp 32-35

Harada, Prof Jiro. 'Panama-Pacific International Exposition and its meaning'. *Studio* vol 65 1915 pp 186-195

The Panama-Pacific International Exposition illustrated in colour. Official publication. 1915 San Francisco: Reid 30 leaves

Macomber, Benjamin. _The Jewel City: its planning and achievement; its architecture, sculpture, symbolism and music; its gardens, palaces, and exhibitions._ 1915 San Francisco: Williams 204pp

James, Juliet Helena. _Palaces and Courts of the Exposition; a handbook of the architecture, sculpture and mural paintings with special reference to the symbolism._ 1915 San Francisco: California Book Company 151pp illus.

Nehaus, Eugen. _The art of the exposition: personal impressions of the architecture, sculpture, mural decorations, color scheme and other aesthetic aspects of the Panama-Pacific International Exposition._ 1915 San Francisco: Elder 91pp

Todd, Frank M. _The story of the Panama-Pacific International Exposition 1915._ 1921 New York 5 vols

British Empire Exhibition, Wembley 1924-1925

Official publications:

Official catalogue. 1924 London: HMSO 292pp

Official guide. 1924 London: HMSO 128pp

Official sectional catalogue of the Palace of Engineering, compiled by Mrs C. M. Glenday. 1924 London: HMSO 186pp

Commentaries and studies:

Weaver, Sir Lawrence. _Exhibitions and the arts of display._ 1925 London: Country Life 106pp (based on his experience working for the Wembley exhibition)

'Empire – special issue on the Empire exhibition'. _Architectural Review_ vol 55 June 1924 pp 205-229

'The British Empire exhibition'. _Studio_ vol 87 1924 pp 249-252, 312-317

'A Wanderer at Wembley' (general souvenir). _Illustrated London News_ May 24 1924 pp 932-974

'The British Empire Exhibition'. _Studio_ vol 88 1924 pp 27-32, 90-93

Maxwell, Donald. _Wembley in colour; being both an impression and a memento of the British Empire Exhibition of 1924 – with over one hundred sketches._ 1924 London: Longmans 112pp illus.

British Empire exhibition Wembley 1924. 50th anniversary. 1974 Wembley: Wembley Historical Society

There is also a lot of valuable material in the daily and monthly press

Exposition Internationale des Arts Décoratifs et Industriels Modernes, Paris 1925

See also:
Art Deco _page 74_
Interior Design: French _page 157_

The first great postwar international exhibition, giving its name to a much studied international design style – Art Deco

Official catalogues and reports:

Catalogue général officiel. 1925 Paris: Imprimerie de Vaugirard 847pp pl 16 plans

Encyclopédie des arts décoratifs et industriels modernes au XX siècle. 1926 Paris: Office Central d'Editions et de Librairies 12 vols pl 1152 bibl. (ABC Reprint 1977)

International exhibition of modern decorative and industrial art, Paris. British section . . . organised by the Department of Overseas Trade (a catalogue) April-October 1925. 1925 London: HMSO 242pp

Very important analyses and discussions of the significance for British design are contained in :

Reports on the present position and tendencies of the industrial arts as indicated at the International Exhibition of Modern Decorative and Decorative Industrial Arts, Paris 1925. With an introductory survey by Sir H. Llewellyn. 1926 London: HMSO 208pp illus. (15 articles by 14 hands)

The special albums prepared for the exhibition and visitors proved very influential:

Guide album de l'Exposition internationale des arts décoratifs et industriels modernes. 1925 Paris: L'Edition Moderne 112pp

Bâtiments et jardins; cent planches en héliogravures, avec une introduction et des notices par M. Roux-Spitz. 1925 Paris: Lévy 55pp

Collection des ouvrages relatifs à l'architecture, à l'ameublement et aux arts décoratifs:
tome 1 ser 1-3 Ensembles mobiliers par M. Dufrêne 3 vols
tome 2 Une ambassade française (par R. Chavance)
tome 3 L'Architecture officielle et les pavillons (par P. Patout) 1925 Paris: Moreau 6 vols

L'architecture étrangère: à l'Exposition internationale des arts décoratifs et industriels modernes. 42 planches rassemblées par Adolphe Dervaux. 1925 Paris: Moreau

Herbst, René. *Devantures, vitrines, installations de magasins à l'Exposition internationales des arts décoratifs, Paris 1925.* 1925 Paris: Moreau pl 60

Janneau, Guillaume. *Le luminaire et les moyens d'éclairages nouveaux.* 1926 Paris: Moreau

Janneau, Guillaume. *Formes nouvelles et programmes nouveaux.* 1925 Paris: Bernheim Jeune 185pp illus.

Mayor, Jacques. *Kiosques et pavillons urbains destinés à l'Exposition.* 1925 London: Moreau 8pp pl 32

Selmersheim, Pierre. *L'architecture à l'Exposition des arts décoratifs modernes de 1925. Le village moderne, les constructions régionalistes et quelques autres pavillons.* 1925 Paris: Moreau 4pp pl 48

The Modern Style. Sixty four plates in collotype and seven in colour illustrating the modern style in decorative and applied art in France. 1925 London: Benn

Memories and visitors:

Scarlett, Frank and Townley, Marjorie. *Arts Décoratifs 1925. A personal recollection of the Paris Exhibition.* 1975 London: Academy Editions 108pp illus.

Mourey, Gabriel. 'The Paris International Exhibition 1925'. *Studio* vol 90 1925 pp 16-21, 98-102, 154-157, 239-245

'Exposition Internationale des Arts Décoratifs et Industriels Modernes, Paris: MDCCCCXXV'. *Architectural Review* vol 58 no 344 pp 1-38 (special issue)

Blake, Vernon. 'Modern Decorative Art II'. *Architectural Review* vol 58 pp 181-191

A few of the special guides and special issues:

Paris, arts décoratifs; guide pratique du visiteur de Paris et de l'Exposition. 1925 Paris: Hachette 400pp illus.

Les arts décoratifs modernes 1925. 1925 Paris: Crès 188pp illus. ('Numero special de *Vient de Paraître*')

Exposition internationale des arts décoratifs et industriels modernes, Paris 1925 . . . Edité par 'L'Art Vivant'. 1925 Paris: Larousse 143pp illus.

L'Exposition internationale des arts décoratifs et industriels modernes, Paris 1925. Paris 36pp illus. (issued with *L'Illustration* Samedi 25 avril 1925)

'Le Pavillon d'Elégance – l'Exposition des Arts décoratifs et industriels modernes, Paris 1925'. *Gazette de Bon Ton* year 7 no 7 1925 (Chadwyck-Healey microform)

Two important retrospective exhibitions:

Les années '25': art déco, Bauhaus, Stijl, Esprit Nouveau. 1966 Paris Musée des Arts Décoratifs

Cinquantenaire de l'exposition de 1925. 1976 Paris Musée des Arts Décoratifs

and an introduction:

Benton, Charlotte. 'The International Exhibition of Modern Decorative and Industrial Arts, Paris 1925'. Part Four pp 62-88, in *Design 1920s.* 1975 Milton Keynes: Open University Press

Exposición Internacional de Barcelona 1929

Paris, William F. 'Barcelona exposition. A splendid but costly effort of the Catalan people'. *Architectural Forum* vol 51 November 1929 pp 481-496

Grundy, C. R. 'Barcelona today'. *Connoisseur* 85 January 1930 pp 3-7

A Century of Progress International Exposition, Chicago 1933-1934

Official guide book of the World's Fair of 1934. Chicago, A Century of Progress Exposition. 1934 Chicago 192pp (many editions)

'Century of Progress Exposition reference number, with views and plans'. *Architectural Forum* vol 59 July 1933 pp 1-69

'Chicago World's Fair'. *Studio* vol 106 1933 pp 67-70, 191-211

Haskell, D. 'Chicago Exhibition: Mixed Metaphors at Chicago'. *Architectural Review* August 1933 pp 47-49

Exposition Universelle et Internationale de Bruxelles 1935

Le livre d'or de l'Exposition universelle et internationale, Bruxelles, 1935. 1935 Brussels: Edité par le Comité exécutif de l'Exposition 635pp illus.

Universal and international exhibition. 1935 Brussels: J. E. Goossens 31pp illus.

'Brussels: the Universal and International Exhibition'. *Studio* vol 110 August 1935 pp 55-76

Gloag, John. 'Brussels exhibition'. *Architectural Review* vol 78 July 1935 pp 1-8

'The Brussels exhibition'. *Design for Today* August 1935 pp 307-312

Robertson, Howard. 'The Brussels exhibition 1935'. *Architect and Building News* vol 142 1935 pp 178-182, 209-213

Exposition Internationale des Arts et Techniques dans la vie moderne, Paris 1937

Official publications:

Le guide officiel. 1937 Paris: Editions de la Société pour le développement du tourisme 212pp illus.

Rapport général (présenté par M Edmond Labbé, rapporteur général). 1937 Paris: Imprimerie Nationale illus.

Paris 1937. 1936-1937 (official magazine published by the General Committee)

Studies and criticism:

Defries, Amelia Dorothy. *Purpose in design. A survey of the new movement seen in the studios and factories and at the Exposition Internationale des Arts et Techniques appliqués à la vie moderne, Paris 1937*. 1938 London: Methuen 238pp pl 64

Le Corbusier. *Des canons, des munitions? Merci!* 1938 Paris: L'Architecture d'Aujourd'hui illus. ('Monographie de Pavillon des Temps Nouveaux à l'Exposition Internationale . . . de Paris 1937')

Badovici, Jean. *Architecture de fêtes: arts et techniques*. 1937 Paris: Morancé 68pp illus.

Campagne, J. M. 'Les participations étrangères à l'exposition de 1937'. *Art et Décoration* 66 no 7 1937 pp 222-224

Albums:

Exposition 1937, décoration, intérieurs . . . Introduction de Jacques Greber. 1937 Paris: Editions Art et Architecture 4 vols –
  1 Pavillons Français
  2 Régionalisme
  3 Sections étrangères
  4 Décoration intérieure

Pavillon Société des artistes décorateurs, Paris. 1937 Paris: Société

L'Exposition de Paris. Introduction par Albert Laprade. 1937 Paris: Librairie des arts décoratifs pl 42

Henriot, Gabriel. *Luminaire moderne*. 1937 Paris: Moreau 8pp pl 48

La décoration française contemporaine à l'Exposition internationale de Paris 1937 (Décoration intérieure du pavillon du Comité français des expositions. Cours La Reine) 1937 Paris 111pp

Ensembles Mobiliers. 1937 – Paris: Editions Moreau

Janneau, Guillaume. *Meubles nouveaux*. 1937 Paris: Moreau 8pp pl 32

Mallet-Stevens, Robert. *Vitraux modernes*. 1937 Paris: Moreau 8pp pl 48

Special issues and contemporary views:

'The Paris Exhibition – special issue'. *Architectural Review* vol 81 September 1937 pp 85-110

'Paris International Exhibition. Things to see in the British Pavilion'. *Studio* vol 113 1937 pp 333-341

Guide souvenir de l'Exposition 'arts et techniques' 1937, par Charles de Saint-Cyr, Claude Fayard et H. de Marcley. Illustrations de Georges Dehayes. Plans de André Guérin. 1937 Paris: Editions du 'Guide de Paris' 63pp illus.

'Exposition 1937'. *Acier* no 1 1938 130pp (Published by l'Office Technique pour l'Utilisation de l'Acier)

'Exposition de Paris 1937. Arts et Techniques' *L'Illustration* 29 May 1937 supplement

British Empire Exhibition, Glasgow 1938

Guides and catalogues:

Empire exhibition, Scotland 1938. Official guide. 1938 Glasgow 232pp

Official catalogue. 1938 Glasgow 254pp illus.

Criticism:

Richards, J. M. and others. 'Glasgow Empire Exhibition 1938. A critical survey'. *Architectural Review* July 1938 pp 1-40

Holme, C. G. 'What I think of Glasgow's Empire Exhibition'. *Studio* vol 116 August 1938 pp 85-93

Westwood, B. and N. 'Empire Exhibition, Glasgow 1938'. *Architects Journal* vol 87 May 5 1938 pp 771-786

Golden Gate International Exposition, San Francisco 1939/1940

Decorative Arts. Official catalog. Department of Fine Arts. 1939 San Francisco: Exposition Division of Decorative Arts 107pp illus.

'Golden Gate exposition – special issue'. *Architectural Forum* June 1939 pp 469-500

James, Jack and Weller, Earle. *Treasure island, 'the magic city' 1939-1940; the story of the Golden Gate International Exposition*. 1941 San Francisco: Pisani 300pp illus.

Neuhaus, Eugen. *The art of Treasure island . . . first hand impressions*. 1939 Berkeley: University of California Press 185pp illus.

New York World's Fair 1939-1940

Official guide book of the New York World's Fair. 1939 New York: Exposition Publications Inc 256pp (many editions)

Guide to the Pavilion of the United Kingdom, Australia, New Zealand and the British Colonial Empire. 1939 London: Clowes 121pp

Cummings, Carlos E. *East is east and west is west; some observations on the World's Fairs of 1939 by one whose main interest is in museums.* 1940 East Aurora, New York: Ryecrofters Press 382pp

Gloag, John. 'Ever since Barnum'. *Architects Journal* vol 89 1939 pp 1034-1050

'New York World's Fair'. *Architectural Review* vol 86 August 1939 pp 54-94

Genauer, Emily. *Modern interiors today and tomorrow; a critical analysis of trends in contemporary decoration as seen at the Paris exposition of arts and techniques and reflected at the New York World's Fair.* 1939 New York: Illustrated Editions Company 255pp illus.

New York World's Fair. 1939 Paris: L'Illustration (reissue of *L'Illustration* for June 1939 with added English text)

Hall, Stanley, Easton and Robertson. 'The British Pavilion'. *Architect and Building News* 26 May 1939 p211

Exposition Universelle et Internationale de Bruxelles. Expo 58. Brussels 1958

Exposition universelle et internationale de Bruxelles 1958. Mémorial édité par le Commissariat Général du Gouvernement après l'exposition. 1959-1962 Brussels:

1 *L'organisation et le fonctionnement.* 1961

2 *Les messages et les congrès.* 1961

3 *Les participations étrangères et belges.* 1961

4 *L'architecture, les jardins et l'éclairage.* 1960 2 vols

5 *Les arts (les arts plastiques. Les manifestations culturelles).* 1960

6 *Les sciences*

7 *Message to youth*

8 *Synthèse.* 1962

Black, Misha. 'The nations displayed'. *Design* 117 September 1958 pp 23-30

Blake, John E. 'New products at Brussels'. *Design* 116 August 1958 pp 46-53

Curjel, Hans. 'Expo 58'. *Graphis* vol 14 August/September 1958 pp 288-312

Hadfield, Charles. 'The Brussels Universal and International Exhibition 1958'. *JRSA* vol 106 August 1958 pp 681-697

Read, A. B. 'Impressions of the Brussels Exhibition 1958'. *DIA Yearbook* 1958 pp 26-32

Century 21 Exposition, Seattle 1962

Morgan, Murray Cromwell. *Century 21: the story of the Seattle World's Fair.* 1963 Seattle: Acme Press 159pp illus.

Universal and International Exhibition, Montreal. Expo 67. 1967

Expo 67: official guide. 1967 Toronto: Maclean-Hunter 350pp illus.

Expo 67: survey of building materials, systems and techniques used at the Universal and International Exhibition of 1967 Montreal Canada, prepared by I. Kalin. 1969 Ottawa: Queen's Printer 307pp illus.

'Expo 67 special issue'. *Architectural Review* vol 142 August 1967

'Expo 67 issue'. *Graphis* vol 23 no 132 1967 pp 322-392

Crosby, Theo. 'Design and purpose in World Exhibitions'. *JRSA* vol 116 February 1968 pp 239-257

Ferrabee, Lydia. 'The shape of Expo 67'. *Design* 217 January 1967 pp 24-29

Taylor, Nicholas. 'Crowd scenery at Expo'. *Design* 224 August 1967 pp 22-37

Japan World Exposition. Expo 70. Osaka 1970

Expo 70 official guide. 1970 Osaka: Suita for the Japan Association for the 1970 World Exposition 352pp

Expo 70, Osaka, Japan. 1969 Tokyo: Shinjudo Co 133pp illus.

'Expo 70, special issue'. *Architectural Review* vol 148 August 1970

'Expo 70. Market place and Festival'. *Design* 259 July 1970 pp 22-73

'Expo 70'. *Graphis* vol 26 no 150 1970 pp 296-388

Esposizione Triennale Internazionale delle Arti Decorative e Industriali Moderne e dell'Architettura Moderna

This recurrent international exhibition (named the Biennale when at Monza, the Triennale after its move to Milan) has excited considerable British interest and involvement since its inauguration after the First World War.

A useful summary and bibliography of its history is:

Pica, Agnoldomenico. *Storia della Triennale di Milano 1918-1957.* 1957 Milano: Edizione del Milione 126pp pl 109 bibl pp 95-127

Accounts of particular exhibitions are provided by:

Carra, Carlo. *L'Arte decorativa contemporanea alla prima Biennale Internazionale di Monza.* 1923 Milan: Edizioni Alpes 153pp illus.

'International Exhibition at Monza'. *Studio* vol 98 1929 p 459

Giangeff, F. A. 'The significance of Monza: a new Italian Renaissance. *Studio* vol 100 1930 pp 25-26

'A triumph of British decorative art. Monza exhibition of industrial and decorative art'. *Studio* vol 100 1930 pp 7-18

Holme, C. G. 'Designing for modern needs: the Monza School'. *Studio* vol 101 1931 pp 359-366

Catalogo ufficiale (5th 1933). 1933 Milan: Ceschina 884pp illus.

Muzio, G. and others. 'Triennial exhibition of industrial art'. *Architectural Review* September 1933 p 108, pp 111-114

'Modern design in Italy. The fifth international exhibition at Milan of modern decorative and industrial art and architecture'. *Studio* vol 106 1933 pp 141-144

'La Quinta Triennale di Milano – special issue'. *Rivista* August 1933 197pp

Guida della Sesta Triennale. A cura di Agnoldomenico Pica. 1936 Milan 192pp

Catalogo. 1951 Milano 482pp (9th 1951)

Decima triennale di Milano. Catalogo. 1954 Milan 581pp

Farr, Michael. 'Impressions from the "Triennale".' *Design* 72 December 1954 pp 14-19

Undicesima Triennale. 1957 Milan: Messagerie Italiane (Text in Italian with shorter English guide) 216pp illus.

12 Triennale di Milano, Palazzo dell'arte (Catalogo a cura di Pier Carlo Santini). 1960 Milan: Artigrafiche Crespi 126pp

Farr, Michael. 'Triennale – Crisis in Italian design'. *Design* 143 144 November, December 1960 pp 68-75, pp 56-59

Tredicesima Triennale di Milano. Tempo libero. 1964 Milan 201pp illus.

Blake, John E. 'Triennale. Fourteen nations discuss leisure'. *Design* 189 September 1964 pp 28-39

Quattordicesima Triennale di Milano. 1968 Milano: Artigrafiche Crespi e Occhipinti 186pp illus.

British Industries Fair

Although by no means an international exhibition, the British Industries Fair has been a very important design showcase for over 60 years. Individual exhibitions (eg Festival of Britain) are considered separately in the Chronological Studies and Documents and recurrent more specialised exhibitions (eg Ideal Home in Interior Design) are considered in the more particular sections, but this Fair has been very general in application and interest.

A summary of its early history is contained in:

Great Britain. Board of Trade. *Report of the sub-committee of the exhibitions advisory committee to review the present arrangements for the British Industries Fair.* 1953 London: HMSO Cmd 9013 11pp

Held annually since 1915 (with the exception of 1925 and 1940-1946) in London and Birmingham, many of the early catalogues are large and detailed (eg 440 pages in 1929). Reported fitfully in many of the main design journals, the best source of detailed criticism is often the daily press and special supplements eg postwar *The Times Survey of the British Industries Fair*).

Museums and collections

The connection between international exhibitions and museums is clear, but has rarely been discussed in much detail:

Ferguson, Eugene S. 'Technical museums and international exhibitions'.*Technology and Culture* Winter vol 6 no 1 1965 pp 30-46

Reekie, Gordon. 'Expositions, exhibits and today's museums'. *Natural History* vol 73 no 6 1964 pp 20-29

Many museums were created with the ostensible purpose of promoting good design by example and many papers and books throughout the period suggest how this could be achieved:

Webster, Thomas. 'On museums for technical instruction in the industrial arts and manufactures of the United Kingdom and the surplus of the inventor's fee fund'. *JSA* vol 22 January 14 1874 pp 136-145

Ablett, William H. 'Museums of trade patterns and industrial examples'. *JSA* vol 34 January 15 pp 144-155

Vauchon, Marius. *Rapport sur les musées et les écoles d'art industriel en Angleterre, 1889.* 1890 Paris: Ministre de l'Instruction Publique et des Beaux Arts ('L'Angleterre veut reconquérir à tout prix la suprématie industrielle et commerciale qu'on lui dispute')

Brown, Gerard Baldwin. *Industrial . museums in their relation to art.* 1901 Edinburgh: Museums Association 14pp

Bach, Richard F. *Museums and the industrial world.* 1926 New York: Metropolitan Museum of Art 8pp (address before the American Federation of Arts 19 May 1920)

Richards, Charles Russell. *The industrial museum.* 1925 New York: Macmillan 117pp

Richards, Charles R. *Industrial art and the museum.* 1927 New York: Macmillan (Includes historical survey of British developments) 102pp

Kaufmann, Edgar Jnr. 'Museums and industrial design'. *JRSA* vol 97 August 12 1949 (based on his experience at the Museum of Modern Art, New York) pp 714-728

Harrison, Molly. 'The museum and visual education'. *Eidos* no 1 May/June 1950 pp 42-45

Zetterberg, Hans Lennart. *Museums and adult education.* 1968 London: Evelyn Adams and Mackay for International Council of Museums 89pp illus. bibl.

A useful anthology of actual responses is:

Hudson, Kenneth. *A social history of museums: what the visitors thought.* 1975 London: Macmillan 210pp

The Victoria and Albert Museum and the Science Museum have been particularly important:

Ashton, Sir Leigh. '100 years of the Victoria and Albert Museum'. *JRSA* vol 101 December 26 1952 pp 79-90

The history of the Victoria and Albert Museum. 1976 (second edition) London: HMSO 32pp illus. (Small picture book no 31)

Conway, Moncure Daniel. *Travels in South Kensington with notes on decorative art and architecture in England.* 1882 London: Trubner 234pp (includes large section on the genesis and development of the South Kensington Museums)

The Science Museum. The First hundred years. 1957 London: HMSO 85pp illus.

The influence of the collections and particularly the catalogues on individual designers is a very rich area:

South Kensington. Catalogues of reproductions of objects of art in metal, plaster, and fictile ivory, chromolithography, etching and photography. Selected from the . . . Museum . . . For the use of Schools of Art, for prizes and for general purposes of public instruction. 1870 London: HMSO 7 vols in 1

Catalogue of the articles of ornamental art, selected from the Exhibition of the Works of Industry of all Nations in 1851, and purchased by the government. 1852 London: HMSO (5 editions by May 1853)

Apart from the main museum collections that are listed in directories such as:

Hudson, Kenneth and Nicholls, Anne. *The Directory of Museums.* 1975 London: Macmillan 846pp

Museums of the World. 1975 (second edition) London: Bowker 808pp

Museums Yearbook. (annual) London: Museums Association

there are many other potential sources for the design historian. Some help can be obtained from:

TIP Handbook 77/78. Transport and Industrial Preservation. A Guide to what, where and when. Derek Burns (ed). 1977 Crawley: DB Publication 140pp

Smith, Norman A. F. *Victorian technology and its preservation in modern Britain.* 1970 Leicester University Press 74pp (a report submitted to the Leverhulme Trust)

Design and designers

Theories of design and craftsmanship – evolution of design methods

Industrial design began to develop its own distinctive literature after the First World War. Earlier theories of design are very much involved with individual designers and their practice, and so are best studied in terms of their own work and statements.

Historical developments

Nineteenth century

The whole field of nineteenth-century design theory is extremely complex and confusing. There is a short elderly introduction in:

Bøe, Alf. *From Gothic Revival to Functional Form. A study in Victorian theories of design.* 1957 Oxford: Blackwell 183pp illus. bibl.

and the older and philosophical roots of 'Functionalism' are discussed in:

De Zurko, Edward Robert. *Origins of Functionalist theory.* 1957 New York: Columbia University Press 265pp illus. bibl.

However, there is no short cut to a detailed study of the works of Morris, Ruskin, Semper, Jones, Day and others presented separately in the section on Important Designers *page 75*.

Twentieth century

The contribution of bodies such as the DIA and the British Institute of Industrial Art is discussed elsewhere in the section on Official bodies, professional organisations and sponsors *page 20*

It was not until the 1930s that a serious body of theory and explanation was developed with:

Read, Herbert. *Art and industry. The principles of industrial design.* 1934 London: Faber 143pp illus. (later editions with different illustrations and altered text in 1944, 1953, 1956, 1966)

and:

Gloag, John. *Industrial art explained.* 1934 London: Allen and Unwin 192pp (later larger edition 1946)

Discussion of principles and the role of the designer became important at many different levels:

Gossop, R. P. 'The place of the designer in commerce', *Architectural Association Journal* February 1931 pp 247-265

Higgins, W. 'Design and mass production', *Studio* 107 February 1934 pp 68-72

White, L. W. Thornton. 'Design and Industry: the next step', *Architectural Review* November 1935 p 188

Nobbs, Percy Erskine. *Design: discovery of form.* 1937 London: Oxford University Press. 412pp

Richards, J. M. 'Black and white: an introductory study of a national design idiom', *Architectural Review* November 1937 pp165-176

Fawcett, John R. *Designing for mass production.* 1939 London: Pitman 141pp

The efforts of the Council for Art and Industry noted earlier were also very important in this direction.

With the war and, later, the evolution of the Council of Industrial Design, theoretical writing began to proliferate in two main directions.

1. The search for good taste and valid criteria for good design:

Pevsner, Nikolaus. *Visual pleasures from everyday things. An attempt to establish criteria by which the aesthetic qualities of design can be judged.* 1946 London: Batsford (Council for Visual Education Booklet 4) 19pp

Harrison, Tom. 'Public taste and public design' (address to DIA), *Art and Industry* September 1943 pp 83-85

Russell, Gordon. 'What we mean by Good Design', *Architects Journal* 15 July 1948 pp 66-67 (a paper repeated elsewhere in different forms)

Clark, K. W. 'What is good design (in industrial manufacture)', *Art and Industry* January 1948 pp 2-7

Wilkes, Edward. 'The fundamentals of good design', *Art and Industry* May 1948 pp 184-189

Bulley, Margaret H. *Art and Everyman: a basis for appreciation, forming a general* introduction to the study of art of all types, ages and countries. 1951 London: Batsford 2 vols.

Mundt, Ernest. *Art Form and Civilisation.* 1952 Berkeley: University of California Press. 246 pp illus.

Black, Misha. 'Taste, Style and the Industrial Designer', *Motif* 4 March 1960 pp 61-67

There are many others, notably in the papers of the Council of Industrial Design, DIA, SIAD.

2. Discussion of the place of design and the designer:

Conference on industrial design 26 and 27 September 1946: full account and papers in:

Report of the Conference on industrial design. 1946 London: Council of Industrial Design. 99pp

some papers republished in:

'Conference on industrial design', *JRSA* 25 October 1946 pp 690-703

Further references are:

Goodale, E. W. 'Design and the manufacturer', *JRSA* vol 89 April 4 1941 pp 282-294 with discussion

Gloag, John. 'Planning research for industrial design', *JRSA* 17 January 1947 pp 118-133 with discussion

Gloag, John. 'The architect's responsibility for industrial design', *JRIBA* January 1948 pp 95-103

Gloag, John. 'British Industrial Design and World Markets', *JRSA* vol 97 May 20 1949 pp 445-461 with discussion

Edwards, R. S. 'Social and economic aspects of industrial design, *JRSA* 3 December 1948 pp 25-38

Gray, Milner. 'The Industrial designer and consumer goods', *JRSA* vol 97 9 April 1949 pp 339-355 with discussion

Russell, Gordon. 'The Industrial designer's responsibility', *JRSA* vol 97 22 April 1949 pp 379-392 with discussion

Thomas, M. Hartland. 'Industrial Design and the engineering industries', *JRSA* vol 97 January 1949 pp 155-173 with discussion

Gloag, John. 'Identity and development of Industrial design', *Eidos* no 2 September/October 1950 pp 34-43, no 3 November/December 1950 pp 34-40

The 1940s also witnessed the increasing impact of American theory and practice, particularly from:

Loewy, Raymond. 'Selling through design', *JRSA* vol 90 January 1942 pp 91-103 with discussion

In the 1950s and later the discussions of design theory and practice become more international:

The Aspen Papers: twenty years of design theory from the International Design Conference in Aspen edited with a commentary by Reyner Banham. 1974 London: Pall Mall Press 224pp

and wide ranging. A few of the most important works are:

Conway, H. G. *Industrial Design and its relation to Machine Design.* 1951 London: Institute of Mechanical Engineers. 8pp

Braun-Feldweg, Wilhelm. *Normen und Formen industrieller Produktion.* 1954 Ravensburg: Otto Maler. 159pp illus.

Anderson, Donald Meyers. *Elements of Design.* 1961 New York: Holt Reinholt and Winston. 218pp

Estetica industriale. Sele arte Sept-Oct 1954. 'Il Rapporto Generale del Congresso Internazionale di Estetica Industriale, Parigi, Settembre 1953'.

Reilly, Paul. 'Influence of national character on design', *JRSA* vol 104 26 October pp 919-939 with discussion

Jordan, R. Furneaux. 'Design and creative process', *Architects Yearbook* no 8 1957 pp 169-177 (reprinted from SIA *Journal* February 1957)

Kipping, Sir Norman. *Design applied to industry.* 1959 London: Association of Technical Institutions. 8pp

Redmayne, Paul Brewis. *The changing shape of things.* 1960 London: John Murray 56pp illus. (previous edition 1945)

Grillo, Paul Jacques. *What is design?* 1960 London: Tiranti. 238pp illus.

Dorfles, Gillo. *Il disegno industriale e la sua estetica.* 1963 Bologna: Cappelli 103pp (with bibliography pp 89-92)

Gerstner, Karl. *Designing programmes: four essays and an introduction.* English version by D. Q. Stephenson 1964 London: Tiranti 95pp illus.

Gasson, Peter. *Theory of Design.* 1973 London: Batsford 230pp bibl.

Then there are the many papers prepared for ICSID and the Council of Industrial Design detailed elsewhere. The range of documents is truly bewildering, especially as many of these are very closely related to an individual designer's experience and preferences, as in the case of:

Glegg, Gordon L. *The Design of Design.* 1969 Cambridge University Press 94pp (general laws and basic advice)

Glegg, Gordon L. _The Selection of Design._
1972 Cambridge University Press. 84pp
(inventing, problems, principles,
practice)

Glegg, Gordon L. _The Science of Design._
1973 Cambridge University Press 94pp
(research for engineering design and
design data)

Perhaps the clearest to emerge is still:

Pye, David. _The Nature of Design._ 1964
London: Studio Vista 96pp illus.

It is still difficult to discern clear trends in
thought although there is a useful 'state of
the art' survey of current thinking in:

Cornford, Christopher. 'Cold rice pudding
and revisionism', _Design_ 231 April 1968
pp 46-48

The last decade or so of the period has
witnessed a growth in the literature
stressing the visual/perceptual aspects of
design, often to radically different
purposes:

Collier, Graham. _Form, space and vision:
discovering design through drawing._ 1963
London, Englewood Cliffs: Prentice
Hall 256pp illus.

Rowland, Kurt. _Looking and seeing series: 1.
Pattern and Shape._ 1964 London: Ginn
128pp illus. _2. The Development of Shape._
1964 London: Ginn 128pp illus.

De Sausmarez, Maurice. _Basic design: the
dynamics of visual form._ 1964 London:
Studio Vista 96pp

Sneum, Gunnar. _Teaching Design & Form._
1965 London: Batsford 125pp

Kepes, Gyorgy (ed). _Education of Vision._
1965 London: Studio Vista 233pp illus.

Kepes, Gyorgy (ed). _The Manmade object._
1966 London: Studio Vista 230pp illus.

Kepes, Gyorgy. _Structure in art and science._
1965 London: Studio Vista 189pp illus.

Kranz, Stewart and Fisher, Robert. _The
Design Continuum. An approach to
understanding visual forms._ 1976 New
York: Van Nostrand Reinhold 152pp
illus. (first published 1966)

Reichardt, Jascia. 'Design as an attitude'.
Studio International 1967 pp 166-167

Thomas, Richard K. _Three dimensional
design: a cellular approach._ 1969 New
York: Reinhold 96pp illus.

Rowland, Kurt. _Visual Education and beyond._
1976 London: Looking and Seeing
148pp illus.

The plea for design to adopt a much
broader role is a comparatively recent
evelopment and finds its most powerful
xpression in:

Papanek, Victor. _Design for the real world.
Making to Measure._ 1972 London:
Thames and Hudson 339pp illus. bibl.

So far only the general works on design
theory and practice have been introduced,
but one of the most noticeable post-war
developments has been the growth of more
specialised literature relating to design
methods, management, engineering design
and ergonomics.

Design Methods

The first popular handbook was:

Ashford, Frederick C. _Designing for industry –
some aspects of the product designer's work._
1955 London: Pitman 222pp illus.

even though techniques had been discussed
much earlier:

Gloag, John. 'Planning research for
industrial design', _JRSA_ vol 95 January 17
1947 pp 118-133

and in the technical press.

Perhaps the most helpful introduction to
the evolution of thinking about design
method is contained in Part 1 of:

Jones, J. Christopher. _Design methods: seeds of
human futures._ 1970 Wiley-Interscience
408pp illus.

Discussions of methods and techniques raise
extremely complex issues and so it is not
possible to discuss the literature helpfully in
general terms. However the following have
acquired wide currency:

Jones, J. Christopher. 'Automation and
Design' '1. Automation and Design'
'2. Input/output devices' '3. The Products'
'4. Work and Leisure' '5. Social and
Aesthetic effects', _Design_ July 1957
pp 27-30, August 1957 pp 15-19, October
1957 pp 44-51, December 1957 pp 50-53,
February 1958 pp 42-47

Jones, J. Christopher and Thorley, D. G.
(eds). _Papers presented at the conference on
Systematic and Intuitive methods in
engineering, industrial design, architecture._
. . . 1963 Oxford: Pergamon 222pp
illus.

Starr, Martin Kenneth. _Product Design and
Decision Theory._ 1963 Englewood Cliffs,
New Jersey: Prentice Hall

Archer, L. Bruce. _Systematic methods for
designers._ 1965 London: Council of
Industrial Design 40pp illus.

Pilditch, James and Scott, Douglas. _The
business of product design._ 1965 London:
Business Publications 166pp

Dixon, John R. *Design Engineering. Inventiveness, Analysis and Decision Making.* 1966 New York: McGraw Hill 354 pp illus.

Jones, J. Christopher. 'Design methods compared – 1. Strategies, 2. Tactics', *Design* 212 August 1966 pp 32-35, 213 September 1966 pp 46-52

Gregory, Sydney A. (ed). *The Design Method.* 1966 Butterworth on behalf of the Design and Innovation Group, University of Aston 354pp bibl.

Mayall, William Henry. *Machines and perception in industrial design.* 1968 London: Studio Vista 96pp illus.

Ellinger, J. H. *Design Synthesis.* 1968 London and New York: J. Wiley 2 vols (text, drawings)

Rodenacker, W. *Systematic Design Method (Methodisches Konstruieren)* 1970 Berlin: Springer 233 pp illus.

Batty, Michael. 'An approach to rational design', *Architectural Design* July 1971 pp 436-437

Bonya, J. P. 'Design method or Beaux Arts?' *Architectural Association Quarterly* 10 1970 pp 4-12

Cross, Nigel (ed). *Design Participation.* 1972 Wiley 124pp illus.

Archer, L. Bruce. *Technological innovation – a methodology.* 1971 Frimley: Inforlink 66pp illus.

and an important technique:

Knoblaugh, Ralph R. *Modelmaking for industrial design.* 1958 New York: McGraw Hill 276pp

Quite apart from the convoluted discussions of method, the standard handbook of practice has proved to be:

Goslett, Dorothy. *The Professional Practice of Design.* 1971 London: Batsford. 272pp (first published 1960)

Special Case Design

In the past 25 years a vast range of technical reports and articles have been produced on specialised research, from the Royal College of Art research on the hospital bed to much smaller projects. The range of literature concerned with designing for the disabled is enormous. Perhaps the most accessible documents to give a general sense of the issues are:

Bayes, Kenneth and Francklin, Sandra (eds). *Designing for the Handicapped.* 1971 London: Godwin 96pp

Goldsmith, Selwyn. *Designing for the disabled.* 1976 (third edition) London: RIBA 525pp illus.

Ergonomics

Although only coined as a word in 1949, this aspect of human engineering has long been a very important factor in design, even though it was not widely recognised until the planning of military equipment in the Second World War. There were three early reports by the Industrial Fatigue Research Board of the Medical Research Council, which may have had wide but difficult to calculate consequences:

Report no 36. The Design of Machinery in Relation to the Operator. 1926 London: HMSO

Report no 44. Physique of Women in Industry. 1927 London: HMSO

Report no 71. Physique of Men in Industry. 1935 London: HMSO

Subsequent developments can often only be traced by a close search of the relevant specialised literature eg:

Hugh-Jones, P. 'The effect of seat position on the efficiency of bicycle pedalling'. *Journal of Physiology* 106(2) 1947 pp186-193

and the report of the Karolinska Institute, Stockholm, that started much research on chairs:

Akerblom, Bengt. *Standing and sitting posture.* 1948 Stockholm: Nordiska Aktiebolaget 187pp

Although discussed in a general way earlier:

Thomas, Mark Hartland. 'Human aspects of engineering design', *Art and Industry* January 1950 pp 2-11, 28-37

interest quickens in the mid-1950s with the publication of:

Ergonomics 1957- (monthly) London: Taylor and Francis

and the appearance of guides and handbooks:

Woodson, Wesley E. *Human Engineering guide for equipment designers.* 1954 Berkeley: University of California Press

McCollom, I. N. and Chapanis, Alphonse. *Human Engineering Bibliography.* 1956 San Diego State College, California 128pp

McCormick, E. J. *Human Factors Engineering.* 1957 McGraw Hill 467pp

Jones, J. Christopher. 'Ergonomics, human data for design', *Design* 66 June 1954 pp 13-17

In the next decade support in the form of conferences and specially commissioned documents by the Department of Scientific and Industrial Research and the Ministry of Technology makes for a very great number of reports and technical documentation in all fields to be served by:

Ergonomics Abstracts 1968- (quarterly)
London: Taylor and Francis and
Ergonomics Information Analysis Centre,
Department of Engineering Production,
University of Birmingham

and:

Applied Ergonomics 1969- (quarterly)
London: Iliffe

as well as the continuing stream of
handbooks and general advice:

Morgan, C. T. and others. *Human
Engineering Guide to Equipment Design.*
1963 McGraw Hill

Kellerman, Frans Thomas and others
(eds). *Vademecum: Ergonomics in Industry.*
1964 London: Cleaver-Hume Press 92pp

Perin, Constance. *With Man in Mind: an
interdisciplinary prospectus for Environmental
Design* 1970 Cambridge, Mass: M.I.T.
Press 168pp

Croney, John. *Anthropometrics for Designers.*
1971 London: Batsford 176pp

A very important influence has also been
the interest and writing of Henry Dreyfuss
and his organisation:

Dreyfuss, Henry. *The Measure of Man.* 1967
(revised edition) New York: Whitney
Library of Design

Computer-aided Design

A very important development of the 1960s
has been the increasing application of
computers to solve complex design
problems, culminating in the establishment
of the Computer-Aided Design Centre in
Cambridge in 1969. It is probably still too
early for a history of this aspect of design
but the growing literature reflects important
shifts in attitudes and techniques:

Fetter, William A. *Computer Graphics in
Communication.* 1965 McGraw Hill
110pp illus.

Prince, David. *Interactive graphics for
computer-aided design.* 1971 New York:
Addison-Wesley (includes 'History and
heritage of CAD' after 10 years)

Copp, H. 'Computers and Design',
Engineering Designer March 1966

Ministry of Technology. *Computer Aided
Design NEL Report no 242.* 1966 London:
HMSO

Mischke, Charles R. *Introduction to Computer
Aided Design.* 1968 Prentice Hall 207pp

Furmann, T. T. *The use of Computers in
Engineering Design.* 1970 London: English
University Press 296pp

Tree, Michael. 'Software and hardware –
changing attitudes to design', *JRSA*
vol 119 December 1970 pp 18-27 with
discussion

*The scope for computer aids to design in
the engineering industry.* 1970 (June)
London: Urwick Technology
Management
for Department of Trade and Industry

Computer-aided design for industry. 1972
Cambridge: Computer-Aided Design
Centre

Fleck, Glen (ed). *A Computer Perspective
by the office of Charles and Ray Eames.*
1973 Cambridge, Mass: Harvard
University Press 174pp illus.

Hyman, Anthony. *The Computer in design.*
1973 London: Studio Vista 112pp bibl.
illus.

Two useful journals:
Bulletin of Computer Aided Design 1970 –

Computer Aided Design 1968 – (quarterly)
London: IPC

See also: Computer Graphics *page 115*

Management

With the evolution of the power of the
Council of Industrial Design has come
an increasing emphasis on the importance
of design as an aspect of management
and the importance of the effective
management of design services:

Houghton, Arthur A. *Design policy within
industry as a responsibility of high-level
management* (paper delivered at the
international congress of the Council of
Industrial Design . . . 1951) 44pp

Farr, Michael. *Design management.* 1966
London: Hodder and Stoughton 162pp

Archer, L. Bruce. 'A place for design
in management education', *Design* 220
April 1967 pp 38-43

'Design Management. A Symposium by
Owen Green, J. T. Reynolds, Lord
Maclay, John Sainsbury', *JRSA* vol 116
December 1967 pp 11-32

Evans-Vaughan, George Frederick. *Design
in industry.* 1970 Henley: Administrative
Staff College 19pp

*Design in management: report on a conference
for management consultants and industrial
designers at the Royal Society of Arts* 1970
London: Council of Industrial Design
32pp illus.

Black, Misha. 'The Function of Design
in Long Range Planning', *Journal of the
Long Range Planning Society* vol 5 no 2
1972

Farr, Michael. *Control systems for industrial
design.* 1972 London: Gower Press
160pp illus.

White, James Noel. *The Management of
Design Services.* 1973 London: Allen and
Unwin 180pp illus.

and the efficient development of product design:

Brichta, A. M. and Sharp, Peter E. M. *From project to production.* 1970 Oxford: Pergamon 296pp illus.

Buck, Christopher Hearn. *Problems of product design and development.* 1963 Oxford: Pergamon 172pp

Design has often made a point of including articles on particularly outstanding design management, eg:

Hughes-Stanton, Corin. 'Design Management. Pioneering Policies' (London Transport), *Design* 197 May 1965 pp 36-47

Engineering Design

The extension of the Council of Industrial Design to the Design Council to include Engineering Design (in 1972) gave concrete recognition to the growing identification and importance of engineering design through the previous quarter century. Although there is no history of engineering design yet written, there is a useful introduction to many of the most important documents in :

Rodwell, Christopher. 'Current Reading on Design for Management' pp 83-91 in Barty, Euan. *Management and engineering design.* 1972 London: Design Council 108pp illus.

and many of the most important developments can be traced through the pages of *The Engineering Designer* (1950-)

Not surprisingly there is quite a literature on the role of the engineering designer and its relation to industrial design:

Wallis, Barnes N. 'Artist or engineer?', *JRSA* vol 111 1963 pp 724-735

Mayall, W. H. 'Let's not build barriers with words'. *Design* 214 October pp 26-31

Ashford, Frederick Clark. *The aesthetics of engineering and design.* 1969 London: Business Books 128pp illus.

Black, Misha. 'Engineering and industrial design', *Transactions of the Institute of Mechanical Engineers* vol 186 74/75 1972

Engineering Design. Report of a committee appointed by the Council of Scientific and Industrial Research to consider the present standing of mechanical engineering design. 1963 London: HMSO (often referred to as the 'Feilden report' after its chairman)

Design Departments. A survey of the role, organisation and functioning of design departments and drawing offices in European engineering firms. 1967 Paris: OECD

as well as formal concern with technique:

Beresford-Evans, John. *Form in Engineering Design. The Study of appearance during design and development.* 1954 Oxford: Clarendon Press 96pp

Booker, Peter J. *Principles and Precepts in Engineering Design.* 1962 London: Institute of Engineering Designers

Asimow, Morris. *Introduction to Design.* 1962 Englewood Cliffs, New Jersey: Prentice Hall 135pp

Matousek, R. *Engineering Design: a systematic approach.* 1963 Glasgow: Blackie 264pp

'Design in Engineering' (special issue), *Design* 202 October 1965

Krick, Edward V. *An Introduction to Engineering and Engineering Design.* 1965 London: Wiley 220pp illus.

Roylance, T. F. (ed). *Engineering Design: papers given at the University of Nottingham September 1964.* 1966 Oxford: Pergamon 345pp

Redford, G. D. *Mechanical Engineering Design.* 1966 London: Macmillan 446pp

Dixon, John R. *Design engineering – inventiveness, analysis and decision making.* 1966 New York: McGraw Hill 354pp

Mayall, W. H. *Industrial Design for Engineers.* 1967 London: Iliffe 142pp

French, M. J. *Engineering Design: the conceptual stage.* 1971 London: Heinemann Educational Books 238pp illus.

Garner, R. H. *Mechanical design for electronic engineers.* 1956 London: Newnes 223pp

Pitts, G. *Techniques in Engineering Design.* 1973 London: Newnes 160pp

Some case studies:

Great Britain. Ministry of Technology. *Good design – Good business. Case studies in engineering design.* 1965 London: HMSO 26pp illus. (10 examples)

W. H. Mayall (ed). *More value by design.* 1971 London: Council of Industrial Design 52pp (to accompany Design Centre exhibition)

Design Consultants

One very clear development of post-war British design has been the increase in importance and numbers of industrial design consultants. A clear early statement of their role is:

Mercer, Frank A. 'The Industrial Design Consultant', *JRSA* vol 93 June 8 1945 pp 342-353 with discussion

later published in a different form as:

The Industrial Consultant. Who he is and what he does. 1947 London: Studio 144pp

Gradually histories of some of these groups are emerging and no doubt will soon be able to fill a substantial separate bibliography. Some of the most accessible are:

Henrion, F. H. K. 'Design Consultants: a new profession', *DIA Yearbook* 1959 pp 26-32 illus.

Hughes-Stanton, Corin. 'How consultant designers work' (David Carter, John Barnes, Alan Bednall), *Design* 214 October 1966 pp 36-43

Bendixson, Terence. 'Professional Practice. Does the versatile designer make sense?', *Design* 177 September 1963 pp 29-38

Kinsayder, John. 'How designers design: Procter, Ingles & Palmer', *DIA Yearbook* 1967-1968 pp 25-28

Burns, Jim. *Arthropods. New Design Futures.* 1971 168pp illus. (achievements of over 30 international groups)

Thomas, Doina. 'How Designers Design: Allied International Designers', *DIA Yearbook 1969-1970* pp 45-49 illus.

Pentagram Design Partnership. *Pentagram.* 1972 London: Lund Humphries 192pp illus.

Pentagram Design Partnership. *Living by Design.* 1977 London: Lund Humphries 280pp 800 illus.

Hughes-Stanton, Corin. 'Designers on the payroll', *Design* 215 November 1966 pp 52-63

Design Research Unit

Perhaps the best known and one of the oldest and best documented consultancies:

Blake, John and Avril. *The Practical Idealists. Twenty Five Years of Designing for Industry.* 1969 London: Lund Humphries 147pp

Goldsmith, Maurice. 'Design Research Unit. An English Design Cooperative', *Graphis* vol 4 no 23 1948 pp 262-267

Blake, John E. 'Design Research Unit. Twenty five years of design for industry', *Graphis* vol 26 no 147 pp 72-77

Craftsmanship

Methods of handcrafts and machine production are very closely related to design even though craftsmanship has mistakenly often been regarded as an opposite to industrial design rather than an aspect of it.

In this section there are a number of books that try to indicate the nature of craftsmanship as well as sensitive descriptive writing, such as:

Sturt, George. *The Wheelwright's shop.* 1923 Cambridge University Press 236pp illus.

There are useful discussions in material as diverse as:

Gloag, John. *Artifex or the future of craftsmanship.* 1926 London: Kegan Paul 96pp

Williams-Thomas, H. S. 'Craftsmanship in industry', *Journal of the Society of Glass Technology* August 1938 pp 153-164

Farleigh, John. *The creative craftsman.* 1950 London: Bell 268pp

Robertson, Seonaid. *Craft and contemporary culture.* 1961 London: Harrap-Unesco 158pp illus.

Perhaps the clearest discussion is contained in:

Pye, David. *The nature and art of workmanship.* 1968 Cambridge University Press 102pp illus.

Perhaps craftsmanship is best studied in the light of the particular craft or trade but there are some useful general historical surveys to supplement information available from *Crafts* and the many crafts organisations that now exist:

Wymer, Norman. *English town crafts: a survey of their development from earliest times to the present day.* 1975 East Ardsley: EP (first published 1949 Batsford) 208pp illus.

Wymer, Norman. *English country crafts.* 1946 London: Batsford 116pp illus.

Jenkins, J. Geraint. *Traditional Country Craftsmen.* 1965 London: Routledge and Kegan Paul 236pp illus.

Jenkins, J. Geraint. *The Craft Industries.* 1972 London: Longman 128pp illus. bibl.

Williams, William Morgan. *The Country craftsman: a study of some rural crafts and the Rural Industries Organisation in England.* 1958 London: Routledge 214pp

Turner, Walter James (ed). *British craftsmanship.* 1948 London: Collins 322pp illus.

There are of course many studies of individuals or groups, such as:

Lucie-Smith, Edward. *World of the makers: today's master craftsmen and craftswomen.* 1975 London: Paddington Press 224pp

but a lot of useful historical fact can be obtained from:

Agricultural Economic Research Institute. *The Rural Industries of England and Wales.* Four reports. 1926-1927 London: Oxford University Press

and the 'Craftsmanship' series of articles/papers presented to the Royal Society of Arts in 1948:

JRSA vol 96 1948 pp 28-37, 356-372, 224-236, 245-260, 372-381, 460-477, 520-536, 628-640, 665-674, 675-685

General chronological studies, periods and tendencies

General Surveys

Studies ranging over the whole period are still very patchy as so much research is needed to create a firm basis for an authoritative study. Of the surveys that have been written a useful introduction is provided by:

MacCarthy, Fiona. *All things bright and beautiful: design in Britain 1830 to today.* 1972 London: Allen and Unwin 327pp illus. bibl. (revised edition 1979 *A History of British Design 1830-Today*)

A number of earlier more universal studies exist, but their discussion of design in Great Britain is much more superficial:

Ferebee, Ann. *A history of design from Victorian era to the present: a survey.* 1970 New York: Van Nostrand Reinhold 120pp 100 illus.

Schaeffer, Herwin. 'Design: an international survey 1851-1956', pp 393-430 in Maccurdy, Charles (ed). *Modern Art, a pictorial anthology.* 1958 New York: Macmillan

Rosenthal, Rudolf and Ratzka, Helen. *The story of modern applied art.* 1948 New York: Harper 296pp illus.

There is a more incisive critical discussion in French:

Noblet, Jocelyn de. *Design: introduction à l'histoire de l'évolution des formes industrielles de 1820 à aujourd'hui (avec la collaboration de C. Bressy).* 1974 Paris: Stock 381pp illus. bibl.

Prolonged study of some of the longer-established journals is still the best general introduction to the general history of the period. Not surprisingly a number of the liveliest general discussions are contained therein:

Pevsner, Nikolaus. 'Design in relation to industry through the ages', *JRSA* December 1948 pp 90-101

Lindinger, Herbert. 'Design Geschichte/Die 19 Jahrhundert Materialen/Zur Europäischen Produktgestaltung vor der Französischen Revolution/Betrachtungen zur Antike-Produktformen von 1850 bis 1965'. *Form* nos 26, 27, 28, 30, June, September, December, 1964, June 1965, pp 18-26, 26-32, 37-43, 36-44

Betjeman, John. 'There and back: AD 1851 to AD 1933; a history of the revival of good craftsmanship; with a symposium by craftsmen', *Architectural Review* 74 July 1933 pp 4-8

McGrath, R. 'Progress and period charts of English design', *Architectural Review* 74 July 1933 pp 8a-8b

Design 1860-1960. Sixth annual conference at the Royal College of Art 1968. 1970 London: Victorian Society 28pp illus.

The centenary of 1851 was the cause of a number of surveys:

Reilly, Paul. 'A century of British design', *JRSA* 1 June 1951 pp 519-536

reprinted with five other addresses in:

A Century of British Progress 1851-1951. 1951 London: Royal Society of Arts

Carrington, Noel and Harris, Muriel. 'The British contribution to industrial art', *Design* 29-30 May-June, 31 July 1951 pp 2-6, 2-7

Mechanisation and the functional tradition are tackled in a spirited but idiosyncratic fashion in:

Giedion, Siegfried. *Mechanisation takes command: a contribution to anonymous history.* 1948 New York, reprinted 1970: Oxford University Press 743pp illus. bibl.

Schaefer, Herwin. *The roots of modern design: functional tradition in the 19th century.* 1970 London: Studio Vista 211pp illus. bibl.

Banham, Reyner. 'Machine aesthetic', *Architectural Review* vol 117 April 1955 pp 225-228 illus.

The patriotic element is explored in:

Gloag, John. *English tradition in design.* 1947 Harmsworth: Penguin 89pp illus. (later editions 1959, 1960)

Histories of architecture and design are more numerous and accessible but also very selective in their choice of design:

Pevsner, Nikolaus. *Pioneers of modern design from William Morris to Walter Gropius.* 1970 (revised edition) Harmondsworth: Penguin 256pp illus. bibl. (first published as *Pioneers of the Modern Movement* 1936 Faber)

Pevsner, Nikolaus. *The sources of modern architecture and design.* 1968 London: Thames and Hudson 216pp illus. bibl.

Pevsner, Nikolaus. *Studies in Art, Architecture and Design vol 2 Victorian and after.* 1968 London: Thames and Hudson 288pp illus. bibl.

Banham, Reyner. *Theory and design in the first machine age.* 1960 London: Architectural Press 338pp illus.

Giedion, Siegfried. *Space, time and architecture: the growth of a new tradition.* 1967 (fifth edition) New York: Harvard University Press 897pp 531 illus.

Muthesius, Stefan. *Das Englische Vorbild. Eine Studie zu den deutschen Reformbewegungen in Architektur, Wohnbau und Kunstgewerbe im späteren 19 Jahrhundert.* 1974 Munich: Prestel Verlag 258pp illus. bibl.

Rowland, Kurt. *A history of the Modern Movement: art, architecture and design.* 1976 (revised edition) London: Looking and Seeing 240pp illus. bibl. (first published 1973 Van Nostrand Reinhold)

The central interest in the evolution of the Modern Movement and its main exponents is clear. Unfortunately this tends towards literature and exhibitions seeking out heroes and classics rather than deeper surveys of the complexities of the period:

Classics of Modern Design (Catalogue by Bernard Gay) 1977 London: Camden Arts Centre 40pp illus. bibl.

Dictionaries and Encyclopaedias

The growing numbers of dictionaries and companions do contain a range of useful historical information, even though they reveal a heavy and very uneven bias in favour of the decorative arts and earlier periods:

Fleming, John and Honour, Hugh. *The Penguin dictionary of Decorative Arts.* 1977 Harmondsworth: Allen Lane-Penguin 896pp illus. bibl. notes

Osborne, Harold (ed). *The Oxford companion to the Decorative Arts.* 1976 Oxford University Press 880pp 600 illus. (over 1000 entries)

Limited help with terminology is provided by:

Walker, John A. *Glossary of art, architecture and design since 1945: terms and labels describing movements, styles and groups derived from the vocabulary of artists and critics.* 1973 London: Bingley 240pp bibl. (second edition 1977)

The need for an encyclopaedic work/dictionary to cover most forms of industrial design has yet to be satisfied.

Writing for the collector (particularly of the nineteenth century) is fairly well established and so could be a useful source of detail:

The Collector's encyclopaedia. Victoriana to Art Deco. 1974 London: Collins 303pp illus. bibl. (1851-1939)

Mackay, James. *An encyclopaedia of small antiques.* 1975 London: Ward Lock 320pp illus. bibl.

Pearsall, Ronald. *Collecting Mechanical antiques.* 1973 Newton Abbot: David and Charles 192pp illus.

Information on many aspects of design can be culled from the texts forming the Open University course History of Architecture and Design 1890-1939 and its accompanying anthology:

Benton, Charlotte and Benton, Tim with Sharp, Dennis. *Form and function. A sourcebook for the History of Architecture and Design 1890-1939.* 1975 London: Crosby Lockwood Staples/Open University Press 252pp illus.

Particular Periods

Nineteenth Century

Given the complexity and variety of this period it is not surprising that the general surveys that exist tend to be very selective:

Gloag, John. *Victorian comfort: a social history of design from 1830-1900.* 1973 (second edition) Newton Abbot: David and Charles 252pp (first edition 1961 Black)

Gloag, John. *Victorian taste: some social aspects of architecture and industrial design from 1820-1900.* 1972 Newton Abbot: David and Charles 175pp illus. (first published 1962)

Kaufmann, Edgar Jnr. 'Nineteenth century design', *Perspecta* 1960 no 6 pp 56-57

For a bit more detail there are a number of encyclopaedias:

Bridgeman, Harriet and Drury, Elizabeth (eds). *The Encyclopaedia of Victoriana.* 1975 Feltham: Country Life 368pp (a collection of 16 chapters by different specialists)

Sutherland, Gilbert D. *An encyclopaedia of the arts, manufactures and commerce of the United Kingdom. The Victorian era 1837-1897.* 1897 London: Love and Wyman 488pp

Some of the most incisive analysis is to be found in the works concerned primarily with architecture:

Ferriday, Peter (ed). *Victorian architecture.* 1963 London: Cape 305pp illus.

Hitchcock, Henry Russell. *Early Victorian architecture in Britain.* 1954 London: Architectural Press 2 vols

Most of the other exhibitions and studies have concentrated very heavily on the decorative arts and the richest introduction to this area is provided by:

Victorian and Edwardian decorative arts. 1952 London: HMSO for Victoria and Albert Museum 150pp (catalogue of a pioneering exhibition)

and the smaller:

Victorian and Edwardian decorative arts. 1952 London: HMSO for Victoria and Albert Museum 40pp (small picture book no 34)

followed by the later exhibition:

Victorian and Edwardian decorative art. The Handley-Read collection. (Catalogue of an exhibition held at the Royal Academy 4 March-30 April 1972). 1972 London: Royal Academy 139pp illus. bibl.

Jervis, Simon. 'Victorian decorative art at the Royal Academy. Charles Handley-Read's collecting achievements', *Connoisseur* vol 179 no 720 pp 89-98

There are a number of more general surveys:

Day, Lewis F. 'Victorian progress in applied design', *Art Journal* Royal Jubilee Number June 1887 pp 185-202

Wallis, George. *British art, pictorial, decorative and industrial. A fifty years retrospect 1832 to 1882. A paper read before the Arts Society at the Museum, Nottingham Castle on Tuesday October 31 1882.* 1882 London: Chapman and Hall 27pp

Floud, Peter. 'The decorative arts under Queen Victoria', *The Listener* September 11 1952

Madsen, Stephan Tschudi. 'Victoriansk Dekorativ Kunst 1837-1901', pp 9-92 in *Nordenfjelske Kunstindustrimuseum Arbok* 1952 Trondheim (Norwegian text)

Norbury, James. *The world of Victoriana: illustrating the progress of furniture and the decorative arts in Britain and America from 1837 to 1901.* 1972 Feltham: Hamlyn 128pp illus.

Lichten, Frances. *Decorative art of Victoria's era.* 1950 New York: Scribner 274pp illus.

There are very many other shorter articles relating Victorian discoveries/inventions with present-day practice, eg:

Schwab, Frances Troy. 'Victorian prototypes of the present', *Architectural Record* September 1945 pp 70-75 (kitchen units to tubular chairs)

Even so there are very large areas left to explore and the best general introduction to further research is:

Madden, Lionel. *How to find out about the Victorian period.* 1970 Oxford: Pergamon 188pp

Useful starting points could well be more localised exhibitions:

1850-1875 art and industry in Sheffield. 1976 Sheffield City Art Galleries 36pp

or collections, eg:

Reed, H. S. T. 'Decorative arts – the Valentine Museum. The eclectic taste of nineteenth-century Richmond', *Antiques* vol 103 pp 167-174

Design to about 1860

The section on the 1851 Great Exhibition has already detailed some of the important early studies it produced. The most useful for a general introduction to the design of that period are:

Redgrave, Richard. *Report on Design prepared as a supplement to Jury report of Class XXX of the Exhibition of 1851.* 1852 London: Clowes 96pp

and:

Wyatt, Matthew Digby. *The industrial arts of the nineteenth century.* 1851-1853 London: Day and Son 2 vols

There are more general later surveys in:

Edwards, Ralph and Ramsey, L. G. G. (eds). *The early Victorian period 1830-1860.* 1958 London: Connoisseur 180pp illus.

Steegman, John. *Victorian taste: a study of the arts and architecture from 1830 to 1870; with a foreword by Sir Nikolaus Pevsner.* 1970 London: Nelson 202pp illus. (first published 1950 as *Consort of Taste* by Sidgwick and Jackson)

but some of the most interesting material is yet to be exploited in contemporary documents and papers, eg:

Dodd, George. *Curiosities of industry and the applied sciences.* 1854 London: Routledge

Wallis, George. 'Recent progress in design, as applied to manufactures', *JSA* vol 4 no 173 1856 pp 291-301

and his manuscript notebook:

Records of art and industry, the commonplace book of George Wallis (deposited in the National Art Library)

The vital importance of Sir Henry Cole and his friends has long been recognised even though little has been published recently:

Cole, Sir Henry. *Fifty years of public work.* 1884 London: Bell 2 vols

Bury, Shirley. 'Felix Summerly's art manufactures', *Apollo* January 1967 pp 28-33

Journal of Design 1849-1853 London: Chapman and Hall

Denvir, Bernard. 'A nineteenth century patron' (Sir Henry Cole), *Design* 32 August 1951 pp 22-25

Gray, Nicolette. 'Prophets of the Modern Movement', *Architectural Review* vol 81 February 1937 pp 49-50 (Redgrave, Wyatt and Jones in the early 1850s)

The interest of the Prince Consort is an area for further study:

Fulford, Roger. 'The Prince Consort – Victorian philosopher 1851: his vision of industry and art', *Architectural Review* vol 109 May pp 275-277

High Victorian Design

Concise introductions to a very complicated subject are provided by:

Handley-Read, Charles. 'High Victorian Design: an illustrated commentary', pp 23-27 in *Design 1860-1960, Sixth Conference Report of the Victorian Society.* 1968 London: Victorian Society

Jervis, Simon. *High Victorian Design. A travelling exhibition organized by the Victoria and Albert Museum for the National Programme of the National Gallery of Canada, Ottawa 1974-1975.* 1974 Ottawa: National Gallery of Canada 300pp illus. bibl. (identifies a number of main strands – Creative antiquary, Rococo revival, Victorian neo-classicism, Naturalism, Reformed Gothic style, Renaissance revival, Exotic, Geometric style)

Other selections:

High Victorian design. 1974-1975 London: Whitechapel Art Gallery

Burty, Philippe. *Chefs d'Oeuvre of the Industrial Arts . . . céramique, verrerie et vitraux, émaux, métaux, orfevrerie et bijouterie, tapisserie, edited by W. Chaffers.* 1869 London: Chapman and Hall 391pp 200 engravings

Maskell, William. *Industrial arts: historical sketches with numerous illustrations.* 1876 London: Chapman and Hall for the Committee of the Council on Education 276pp (South Kensington. Science Handbooks)

Davis, Owen W. *Art and work. As shown in the several artistic industries employed in the use of marble, stone, and terra cotta; metal, wood and textile fabrics; as well as in various details associated with decorative art – the whole exemplified by 85 lithographic drawings.* 1885 London: author 36pp illus.

Aesthetic Movement

A number of important changes in design and craftsmanship have been lumped together by Walter Hamilton as the 'Aesthetic Movement':

Hamilton, Walter. *The aesthetic movement in England.* 1882 London: Reeves and Turner 127pp (particularly stressing 'a Renaissance of Medieval art and culture')

Exhibitions:

The Aesthetic Movement 1869-1890. Catalogue of an exhibition at the Camden Arts Centre London 15 August-7 October 1973 edited by Charles Spencer. 1973 London: Academy editions 94pp 96 illus. bibl.

The Aesthetic Movement and the Cult of Japan; exhibition held on 3-27 October 1972; designed by Stuart Durant and Hannah Oothuys. 1972 London: Fine Art Society 56pp illus. bibl.

General studies:

Aslin, Elizabeth. *The Aesthetic Movement: prelude to Art Nouveau.* 1969 London: Elek 192pp 136 illus.

Spencer, Robin. *The Aesthetic Movement: theory and practice.* 1972 London: Studio Vista 160pp 120 illus.

Farmer, Albert John. *Le Mouvement Esthétique et Décadent en Angleterre (1873-1900).* 1931 Paris: H. Champion 413pp

Crane, Lucy. *Art and the formation of taste; six lectures.* 1882 London: Macmillan 292pp illus. (ABC Reprint)

Some of its sources have been traced in the activities of the Pre-Raphaelites:

Watkinson, Raymond. *Pre-Raphaelite Art and Design.* 1970 London: Studio Vista 208pp illus.

Fredeman, William Evan. *Pre-Raphaelitism: a bibliocritical study.* 1965 Cambridge, Mass.: Harvard University Press 327pp illus.

Hunt, William Holman. *Pre-Raphaelitism and the Pre-Raphaelite brotherhood.* 1905-1906 London: Macmillan 2 vols (later editions)

End of the Century

See also:

Important Designers *page 75*

Arts and Crafts Movement *page 70*

Art Nouveau *page 71*

Useful introductions are provided by:

Les sources du XXe siècle. Les Arts en Europe de 1884 à 1914. 1960-1961 Paris: Musée National d'Art Moderne for

Council of Europe 410pp illus. (Architecture et les Arts Décoratifs pp 259-410 with a short essay by Nikolaus Pevsner pp 259-262)

Bury, Shirley. 'British decorative arts, of the late 19th century in the Nordenfjeldske Kunstindustrimuseum', *Nordenfjeldske Kunstindustrimuseum Arbok* 1961-1962 Trondheim pp 37-106

and the contemporary:

Bode, Wilhelm. *Kunst und Kunstgewerbe am Ende des neunzehnten Jahrhunderts.* 1901 Berlin 168pp

Ward, Henry Snowden (ed). *Useful arts and handicrafts, planned by Charles Godfrey Leland.* 1900-1901 London: Dawbarn and Ward 4 vols

Some aspects of popular taste and preference are indicated in the exhibitions of the Home Arts and Industries Association:

Wood, Esther. 'The Home Arts and Industries exhibition', *Studio* vol 17 1899 pp 99-109 illus.

Wood, Esther. 'Home Arts and Industries exhibition at the Albert Hall', *Studio* vol 20 1900 pp 78-88

Wood, Esther. 'Home Arts and Industries exhibition', *Studio* vol 23 1901 pp 106-110

Wood, Esther. 'The Home Arts and Industries Association', *Studio* vol 26 1902 pp 129-134

Revivals

The nineteenth century is notable for the depth of research into the styles and detail of earlier periods. The associated revivals of different sorts have long been recognised, even though many of these revival styles have been discussed primarily with reference to architecture.

GREEK REVIVAL:

Crook, J. Mordaunt. *The Greek Revival: neo-classical attitudes in British architecture 1760-1870.* 1972 London: John Murray 204pp pl 250

GOTHIC REVIVAL:

Clark, Sir Kenneth. *The Gothic Revival. An essay in the history of taste.* 1974 London: J. Murray 248pp illus. (first published 1928 with many later editions. Basically to 1860)

Eastlake, Charles Lock. *A history of the Gothic Revival, an attempt to show how the taste for mediaeval architecture which lingered in England during the last two centuries has since been encouraged and developed.* (reprint of second revised edition edited and

introduced by J. Mordaunt Crook). 1970 Leicester University Press (first published 1872)

Ferriday, Peter. 'The Revival: (Gothic) stories ancient and modern', *Architectural Review* vol 121 March 1957 pp 155-157

Hitchcock, Henry-Russell. 'High Victorian Gothic', *Victorian Studies* vol 1 no 1 September 1957 pp 47-71

Hersey, George L. *High Victorian Gothic: a study in associationism.* 1972 Baltimore: Johns Hopkin University Press 234pp illus. bibl.

Frankl, Paul. *The Gothic. Literary sources and interpretations through eight centuries.* 1960 New Jersey: Princeton University Press 916pp pl 57 bibl. notes

Germann, Georg. *Gothic Revival in Europe and Britain: sources, influences and ideas, translated by Gerald Owen.* 1972 London: Lund Humphries with the Architectural Association 263pp illus. bibl. notes

Gwynn, Denis. *Lord Shrewsbury, Pugin and the Gothic Revival.* 1946 London: Hollis and Carter 155pp

'Gothic number', *Architectural Review* vol 98 December 1945 pp 149-180

Lang, S. 'The principles of the Gothic Revival in England', *Journal of the Society of Architectural Historians* vol 25 no 4 1966 pp 240-267

Paley, Frederick Apthorp. *A manual of Gothic mouldings, with full directions for copying them and for determining their dates.* 1845 London: J. Van Voorst 72pp pl 16 (many later editions 1847, 1865, 1877, 1891, 1902)

QUEEN ANNE:

Girouard, Mark. *Sweetness and light: the 'Queen Anne' movement 1860-1900.* 1977 Oxford: Clarendon Press 250pp pl 8 illus. bibl. refs

Harbron, Dudley. 'Queen Anne taste and aestheticism', *Architectural Review* vol 94 July 1943 pp 15-18

Saint, Andrew. *Richard Norman Shaw.* 1976 New Haven: Yale University Press 487pp 291 illus.

Antiques

With the increasing interest in all types of Victoriana, quite a range of surveys of antiques written primarily for the collector can yield useful detail on Victorian design:

Woodhouse, Charles Platten. *The Victoriana Collector's handbook.* 1970 London: Bell 240pp pl 78

Wood, Violet. *Victoriana: a collector's guide.* 1960 London: Bell 175pp

Howe, Bea. *Antiques from the Victorian home.*
1973 London: Batsford 240pp illus.

Hughes, George Bernard and Hughes,
Therle. *After the Regency. A guide to late
Georgian and early Victorian collecting
1820-1860.* 1952 London: Lutterworth
Press 231pp pl 48

The literature is quite large and can be very
useful if well endowed with illustrations:

Lambton, Lucinda. *Vanishing Victoriana.*
1976 Oxford: Elsevier-Phaidon 142pp
128 illus.

Twentieth Century

Compared with the previous century there
is a distinct poverty of good general surveys
apart from those detailed at the beginning
of this section. Certainly there are a number
of brief journal surveys:

'The first third of the Twentieth Century',
Architectural Review vol 75 May 1934
pp 153-196

'The first half century. The Architectural
Review records the Revolution in two acts
and distinguishes the main plot',
Architectural Review vol 101 January 1947
pp 27-36

Briggs, Asa. 'A cavalcade of tastes',
Architectural Review vol 161 April 1977
pp 227-234

and selections based on a leading collection:

Drexler, Arthur and Daniel, Greta.
*Introduction to twentieth century from the
collection of the Museum of Modern Art, New
York.* 1959 New York: Museum of
Modern Art 94pp illus.

Drexler, Arthur. *The Design collection: selected
objects.* 1971 New York: Museum of
Modern Art 112pp 55 illus.

For more information it is necessary to go
back to Banham, MacCarthy and the
general books or on to more specific studies
and documents.

To 1914

Apart from the lavish documentation of the
Studio and the *Architectural Review* a useful
introduction is provided by a catalogue of
an exhibition held in 1914:

Great Britain. Board of Trade. Exhibitions
Branch. *Arts décoratifs de Grande Bretagne
et d'Irlande, exposition organisée par le
gouvernement Britannique. Palais du Louvre,
Pavillon de Marsan 1914.* 1914
Letchworth: Arden Press for HMSO
168pp (mainly Arts and Crafts with essays
by Crane, Cockerell).

There are a number of general surveys
written with the collector in mind but they
are decidedly thin:

Garner, Philippe. *The world of Edwardiana.*
1974 Feltham: Hamlyn 128pp

Hughes, Therle and Kelly, Alison.
Edwardiana for collectors. 1977 London:
Bell 128pp

As other parts of this bibliography show,
there is no shortage of material but it is to
be found in more specific areas.

1914-1918

See also:

Design and Industries Association *page 22*

Perhaps the most noticeable design event
was the jolt provoked by the Board of
Trade exhibition of German and Austrian
design:

Great Britain. Board of Trade. *Exhibition of
German and Austrian articles typifying
successful design (an explanatory pamphlet).*
1915 London: HMSO 6pp

Great Britain. Board of Trade. *Exhibition of
British design for surface decoration.* 1915
London: HMSO 47pp (part of the
British Industries Fair and a direct
follow up of the German and Austrian
exhibition)

The problem of design also figured in the
plans for reconstruction:

Great Britain. Ministry of Reconstruction.
*Reconstruction Problems 17. Art and
Industry.* 1919 London: HMSO 20pp ('we
have got to believe that art is
indispensible in life')

1920s

See also:

British Institute of Industrial Art *page 24*

Most published surveys of the 1920s tend
to concentrate on European, and
particularly French, design:

Battersby, Martin. *The decorative twenties.*
1969 London: Studio Vista 216pp 201
illus.

Brunhammer, Yvonne. *The nineteen twenties
style.* 1969 Feltham: Hamlyn 159pp
(translation of *Lo Stile 1925*)

Veronesi, Giulia. *Into the twenties. Style and
design 1909-1929, translated by Diana
Barron.* 1968 London: Thames and
Hudson 367pp illus (translation of *Style
1925*)

*Les années 25. Art Deco-Bauhaus
de-Stijl-Esprit Nouveau.* Catalogue by
Yvonne Brunhammer. 1966 Paris:
Musée des Arts Décoratifs. Vol 1. Art
Déco, Bauhaus, L'Esprit Nouveau vol 2
Collection of the Museum

Harcourt-Smith, Cecil. 'The modern note in industrial art'. *JRSA* vol 74 November 27 1925 pp 32-47 (especially on the impact of the Paris exhibition)

From the early 1920s the *Architectural Review's Craftsman's Portfolio* of well designed products in different techniques becomes a useful visual index of industrial and craft design. Other documents are widely scattered, often in some unusual combinations:

Daily Mail Ideal Labour-saving home. The three prize designs in the Daily Mail competition with other designs. Including a report of the Household appliances committee of the Design and Industries Association. 1920 London: Associated Newspapers 69pp illus.

1930s

Any study of industrial design in Britain in the 1930s must start with its most thoroughly researched study:

Pevsner, Nikolaus. *An enquiry into industrial art in England.* 1937 Cambridge University Press 234pp illus.

based on the series of articles in the *Architectural Review:*

Read, Herbert. 'The designer in industry', *Architectural Review* vol 79 March 1936 pp 143-146

and

Pevsner, Nikolaus. 'The designer in industry 1. Carpets, 2. Furnishing fabrics, 3. Gas and electric fittings Part 1 fires, Gas and electric fittings Part 2 lighting fittings, 4. Architectural metalwork, 5. New materials and new processes, 6. The role of the architect', *Architectural Review* vol 79 April, June, vol 80 July, August, September, October, November 1936 pp 185-190, pp 291-296, pp 45-48, pp 87-90, pp 127-129, pp 179-182, pp 227-230

A few more general studies:

Battersby, Martin. *The decorative thirties.* 1971 London: Studio Vista 208pp 145 illus.

Sembach, Klaus-Jurgen. *Into the thirties: style and design 1927-1934, translated from the German by Judith Filson.* 1971 London: Thames and Hudson 175pp illus. (6000 word essay and 120 pictures)

Campbell, Louise. 'History of taste 5. The good new days', *Architectural Review* vol 162 September 1977 pp 177-183

Naylor, Gillian. 'History of taste 4. Modernism threadbare or heroic?', *Architectural Review* vol 162 August 1977 pp 107-111

Hampstead in the thirties – a committed decade. 1974 London: Camden Arts Centre 66pp 33 illus bibl.

Perhaps more valuable are the other surveys written during the decade:

De la Valette, John (ed). *The conquest of ugliness: a collection of contemporary views on the place of art in industry.* 1935 London: Methuen 207pp pl 16 (19 essays in five parts: Aspects of art applied to industry/Role of producer, distributor, consumer, educator/Various industries/Display and presentation/Summing up)

'Industrial design special issue', *Architectural Review* vol 78 December 1935 (includes essay by J. M. Richards 'Towards a rational aesthetic. An examination of the characteristics of modern design with particular reference to the influence of the machine' and an illustrated 'catalogue of what well designed objects of everyday use are available on the market today')

Dowling, Henry G. *A survey of British industrial arts.* 1935 Benfleet: F. Lewis 55pp pl 100

Design in modern life. April 1933 London: BBC 17pp 31 illus. bibl. (to accompany a series of broadcast talks)

Gloag, John and others. 'Towards a style: symposium'. *Architectural Review* vol 74 July 1933 pp 27-42

Hoffmann, Josef. 'Rebirth of design in craftsmanship', *Studio* April 1933 pp 240-245

Gloag, John (ed). *Design in modern life.* 1934 London: Allen and Unwin 138pp illus. (based on the 1933 broadcast talks)

Holme, Geoffrey. *Industrial design and the future.* 1934 London: Studio 160pp (subtitled *A challenge to the producer*)

reviewed and discussed in:

Holme, G. 'Forgotten landmarks 1. 1934 – Industrial Design and the Future', *Art and Industry* February 1948 pp 57-65

Johnson, Philip. *Machine Art.* 1934 New York: Museum of Modern Art 112pp illus. (Arno Reprint 1970)

Gaunt, William. 'How to improve the design of British goods', *JRSA* vol 82 April 20 1934 pp 603-620

Carrington, Noel. *Design and a changing civilisation.* 1935 London: John Lane 140pp

'The trend of design in pottery, furnishing, fabrics', *Studio* vol 110 pp 267-275

Circle: international survey of constructive art, edited by J. L. Martin, Ben Nicholson, Naum Gabo. 1971 London: Faber 292pp illus. (facsimile of 1937 edition)

Bertram, Anthony and others. 'Design in everyday things series', *Listener* 1937

(Includes – 'What does the public
want?' October 6: pp 701-711, 'What is a
house?' October 13: pp 780-782, 'Living
rooms and kitchens' October 20:
pp 840-842, Bedrooms and bathrooms'
October 27: pp 910-912, 'Heat light and
sound in the home', November 3:
pp 971-972, 'Housing the workers',
November 10: pp 1007-1009, 'Our streets',
November 4: pp 1125-1127, 'Public
buildings', December 1: pp 1188-1190,
'Places of work', December 8:
pp 1261-1263, 'Places of pleasure',
December 15: pp 1324-1326, 'From
aeroplanes to nutcrackers', December 22
p 1385)

Bertram, Anthony. *Design in daily life*. 1938
London: Methuen 98pp

Martin, John Leslie and Speight, Sadie
(eds). *The flat book*. 1939 London:
Heinemann 200pp illus. (slightly
misleading title – very good anthology of
well designed objects)

Carrington, Noel. *The shape of things. An
introduction to design in everyday life*. 1939
London: Nicholson and Watson 209pp
illus.

'Design and character in British goods'.
Studio vol 108 1934 pp 234-245

The important works by Herbert Read,
John Gloag and others developing theories
and explanations of the nature of industrial
design are set out in the first section in this
chapter Theories of design and
craftsmanship *page 52*.

The 1930s witnessed a quickening of official
interest in design from the Gorell report
onwards:

Great Britain. Board of Trade. *Report of the
committee appointed by the Board of Trade
under the chairmanship of Lord Gorell on the
production and exhibition of articles of good
design and everyday use*. 1932 London:
HMSO illus.

See also:

Council for Art and Industry *page 25*

With the improvement in economic
conditions it became possible to stage
exhibitions:

DORLAND HALL EXHIBITION 1933

'British industrial art – special issue',
Architectural Review vol 74 July 1933

Thorpe, W. A. 'Exhibition of British
industrial art at Dorland Hall', *Apollo* 18
July 1933 pp 46-48

'Exhibition of British industrial art', *Studio*
vol 106 1933 p 108

DORLAND HALL EXHIBITION 1934

Frost, A. E. '(Dorland Hall) exhibition of
contemporary industrial design in the
home', *Architects Journal* November 1
1934 pp 642-648

Bertram, Anthony. 'Contemporary
industrial design. The Dorland Hall
exhibition', *Design for Today* December
1934 pp 451-460

EXHIBITION OF BRITISH ART IN
INDUSTRY, BURLINGTON HOUSE
1935

See also:

Royal Society of Arts *page 20*

A guide:

British Art in Industry. Illustrated souvenir.
1935 London: Royal Academy 107pp
illus.

Accounts of its genesis and objectives by its
creators and supporters:

De la Valette, John and, Lewis J. 'Royal
Academy exhibition of British art in
industry', *JRIBA* vol 42 series 3 March 23
1935 pp 573-592

De la Valette, John. 'Collaboration between
manufacturers and artists', *JRSA* vol 82
March 23 1934 pp 511-534

Milne, John A. 'Arts and commerce
promoted', *JRSA* vol 83 November 16
1934 pp 2-11

Milne, John A. 'Art in industry', *JRSA* vol 83
January 25 1935 pp 245-253

Symonds, R. W. 'Exhibition of British
industrial art at Burlington House', *JRSA*
vol 83 February 1935 pp 347-349

'Art in industry; conference at the Royal
Society of Arts', *JRSA* vol 83 March 29
1935 pp 445-456

Milne, John A. 'The 1935 exhibition – and
after', *JRSA* vol 86 May 6 pp 614-633

Some of its reviewers and critics:

'Forgotten landmarks 2. The Royal
Academy exhibition of British art in
industry', *Art and Industry* March 1948
pp 82-89

'Art in industry', *Architectural Review* vol 77
January 1935 pp 3-10

Read, Herbert. 'Novelism at the Royal
Academy', *Architectural Review* vol 77
February 1935 pp 45-50

Chamot, Mary. 'British art in industry at
Burlington House', *Apollo* January 1935
pp 26-30

Furst, Herbert. 'Exhibition of British art in
industry at Burlington House', *Apollo*
February 1935 pp 85-89

Lamb, W. R. M. 'Art in industry at the Royal Academy', *Listener* January 9 1935 pp 47-51

'The Royal Academy exhibition of British Art in Industry', *Studio* vol 109 February 1935 pp 52-71

Holme, C. G. 'My ideal exhibition of industrial art', *Studio* vol 109 March 1935 pp 115-117

Smith, A. Llewellyn. 'British industrial art at the Royal Academy', *JRIBA* January 12 1935 pp 313-316

Barman, Christian. 'Industrial art at the Academy', *Design for Today* January 1935 pp 5-11

Quigley, Hugh. 'The Royal Academy of British Art in Industry', *Design for Today* February 1935 pp 48-52 (critical)

DESIGN IN EVERYDAY THINGS 1936

Design in everyday things. Exhibition catalogue. 1936 London: Royal Institute of British Architects 67pp

'Design in Everyday Things by a man in the street', *Design for Today* April 1936 pp 144-153

World War Two and after

A very general introduction:

Hillier, Bevis. *Austerity binge: the decorative arts of the Forties and Fifties.* 1975 London: Studio Vista 208pp 460 illus. bibl.

WARTIME

In spite of the deprivations of war, it is interesting to notice how interest in design is sustained in journals, reviews and even exhibitions:

Capey, Reco. 'Design in daily life', *JRSA* vol 88 February 23 1940 pp 342-363

Prentis, Betty. 'British designers change the face of fashion', *Studio* vol 120 1940 pp 110-115

Pevsner, Nikolaus. 'Design parade', *Studio* vol 119, vol 120 1940 pp 137-140, pp 180-183, pp 221-223, pp 29-31

McAndrew, John. 'New standards for industrial design', *Museum of Modern Art Bulletin* January 1940

'British design for Spring export. Reviewed by Grace Lovat Fraser', *Studio* vol 121 1941 pp 108-123

Lewis, Frank. *British designers, their work. With an introduction by Ernest W. Goodale.* 1942 Leigh on Sea: F. Lewis

Exhibition of modern British crafts. Organised by the British Council, London. 1942 New York: Metropolitan Museum 79pp 12 illus.

'Design in Everyday Life – review of exhibition by British Institute of Adult Education', *Art and Industry* September 1942 pp 76-78

Cursiter, Stanley. *Art in industry. With special reference to conditions in Scotland.* 1943 Edinburgh: Oliver and Boyd for Saltire Society 32pp illus. (Saltaire Pamphlets no 4)

Bossom, A. C. 'Pre-Fabrication and good design', *JRSA* vol 93 December 4 1944 pp 22-31

UTILITY

An interesting development was the evolution of a series of standards and specifications to make the most of wartime and post-war shortages. A useful introduction is provided by the catalogue:

Utility furniture and fashion 1941-1951. 1974 London: Geffrye Museum 48pp

Brutton, Mark. 'Utility: strengths and weaknesses of government controlled crisis design', *Design* 39 September 1974 pp 66-69

'Utility or austerity', *Architectural Review* vol 93 1942 pp 3-4, 28

Board of Trade Utility schedules were evolved for many industries and exist in printed or (more usually) cyclostyled form. The most accessible relate to furniture and are detailed separately.

See also:

Furniture: Utility *page 176*

POST-WAR SURVEYS

As well as the work initiated by the Council of Industrial Design and the search for better design and education, detailed separately, the immediate post-war period is notable for a number of reports touching on many aspects of industrial design:

The Visual Arts. A report sponsored by the Dartington Hall Trustees. 1946 London: Oxford University Press for PEP 182pp (very critical of most current aspects of industrial design)

Great Britain. Board of Trade. *Working party reports.* 1946-1948 London: HMSO:

Boots and shoes. 1946 190pp

Cotton. 1946 278pp

Furniture. 1946 209pp

Hosiery. 1946 224pp

Jewellery and silverware. 1946 105pp

Pottery. 1946 51pp

Heavy clothing. 1947 208pp

Lace. 1947 163pp

Linoleum and felt base. 1947 48pp

Wool. 1947 231pp

Wool. 1947 231pp

Cutlery. 1947 29pp

Light clothing. 1947 52pp

Rubber proofed clothing. 1947 52pp

Carpets. 1947 117pp

Handblown domestic glassware. 1947 143pp

Jute. 1948 121pp

China clay. 1948 67p

Heath, Sir H. Frank and Hetherington, A. L. _Industrial research and development in the United Kingdom: a survey._ 1946 London: Faber 375pp illus.

and even the practice of design:

Read, Herbert (ed). _The practice of design by Alastair Morton and others. Edited with an introduction by Herbert Read._ 1946 London: Lund Humphries 227pp illus.

Another important event was the Council of Industrial Design's first major exhibition:

BRITAIN CAN MAKE IT 1946

Britain can make it. Exhibition. Organised by the Council of Industrial Design at the Victoria and Albert Museum opening September 24th 1946. Catalogue. 1946 London: HMSO 242pp

Design '46. Survey of British industrial design as displayed at the 'Britain can make it' exhibition, edited by W. H. Newman. 1946 London: Council of Industrial Design 143pp

'Industrial design – special issue', _Architectural Review_ vol 100 no 598 October 1946 pp 91-117 (special supplement issued as a reprint for the Council of Industrial Design)

'Britain can make it. The exhibition of British postwar products', _Board of Trade Journal_ 28 September 1946 supplement 24pp illus

Austen, Peter. 'Britain can make it: the Council of Industrial Design', _Graphis_ vol 2 no 14 March-April 1946 pp 258-261 illus.

'Britain can make it exhibition, Victoria and Albert Museum September 24-October 31', _Form_ (Sweden) 9 1946 pp 183-199

and two years later:

DESIGN AT WORK 1948

Design at work: an introduction to the industrial designer with a study of his methods of working and the position he holds in British industry today: exhibition handbook. 1948 London: Royal Society of Arts and Council of Industrial Design 40pp

Logan, Malcolm. 'Design at work (Royal Designers for Industry exhibition)', _Art and Industry_ December 1948 pp 203-208

'R(oyal) D(esigners for) I(ndustry) exhibition at Burlington House', _Architects Journal_ October 21 1948 pp 375-376

A few more general surveys and comments from later in the 1940s:

Carrington, Noel. 'State and industrial design', _Graphis_ vol 3 no 18 pp 108-117

'Industrial design' series in _Britain Today_ 1948 ('Pottery' June pp 24-28, 'Exhibition display' July pp 34-38, 'Domestic equipment', August pp 37-41, 'Table glass', September pp 34-36, 'Radio', October pp 14-18, 'Motor cars', November pp 25-30, 'Books', December pp 25-29)

Carrington, Noel. 'Decoration in contemporary industrial design', _Design_ 5 May 1949 pp 2-7

Fejer, George. 'Contrary to popular belief (Cooperation between designer and manufacturer)', _Art and Industry_ April 1948 pp 140-145

From July 1947 _Art and Industry_ included a regular survey of new industrial designs under the heading 'New Designs from the factories'.

Mid-Century and after

The situation in 1950 or a little later:

Farr, Michael. _Design in British industry: a mid-century survey; with a foreword and postscript by Nikolaus Pevsner._ 1955 Cambridge University Press 333pp pl 88

Bill, Max. _Form. A balance sheet of mid-twentieth-century trends in design. English version by P. Morton Shand._ 1952 Basel: Karl Werner AG 168pp illus. (a picture book laying no claim to completeness or balance)

and a few shorter papers:

Reilly, Paul. 'The maturing taste of the mid-century', _Penrose Annual_ 1954 pp 24-27

Reilly, Paul. 'The changing face of modern design and what it may mean commercially (1938-1951)', _Design_ 44 August 1952 pp 15-21

Thorough histories of the remaining 20 years are yet to come but there are useful summaries in:

'Anniversary issue 1949-1970. A visual record of twenty one years', _Design_ 253 January 1970

'Quarter-century review-preview, in praise of pacemakers. Twenty five years of British influential products', _Design_ 342 June 1977

'Living in Britain 1952-1977, special issue', _Architectural Review_ vol 162 no 969 November 1977

Gloag, John. 'The remaining third', *Architectural Review* September 1967

Possibly the most important and debated event was the
FESTIVAL OF BRITAIN 1951
Perhaps the best introductions are provided by its prime mover:

Barry, Sir Gerald. 'The influence of the Festival of Britain on design today', *JRSA* vol 109 June 1961 pp 503-515 illus.

Barry, Sir Gerald. 'The Festival of Britain. Three Cantor lectures', *JRSA* August 22 1952 pp 667-704

and the material assembled for the 1976 commemorative exhibition:

Banham, Mary and Hillier, Bevis (eds). *A Tonic to the Nation: Festival of Britain 1951.* 1976 London: Thames and Hudson 200pp 196 illus. bibl.

The range of exhibitions, documents and reviews are many and various and I have already detailed some in:

Coulson, Anthony J. (comp). *The Festival of Britain and Design History. A preliminary bibliography.* 1976 Milton Keynes: author 9pp

Most important are the official publications:
Catalogue of exhibits, South Bank exhibition. 1951 London: HMSO

The South Exhibition: a guide to the story it tells by I. Cox. 1951 London: HMSO

The Festival Exhibition 1951: Land travelling exhibition. Catalogue and guide. 1951 London: HMSO

Exhibition of Science, South Kensington: a guide to the story it tells. 1951 London: HMSO

Exhibition of Industrial Power, Kelvin Hall, Glasgow (Catalogue and guide). 1951 London: HMSO

The event captured the attention of the press of all sorts and there are many supplements and special issues to choose, eg:

'The Festival Story 1943-1951', *The Times* 1951.

'Festival Supplement Festival of Britain 1951: preview and guide', *Daily Mail* 1951.

'Special issue on the South Bank Exhibition', *Architectural Review* vol 110 no 656 August 1951

'FOB exhibitions review', *Architectural Review* vol 110 September 1951 pp 191-202

and then there are numerous details in *Design.*

Particularly interesting from a design point of view are:

Design in the Festival, illustrating a selection of well designed British goods in production in the Festival year 1951, with an introduction by Gordon Russell, and articles by eleven contributors. 1951 London: HMSO for Council of Industrial Design 131pp illus.

Reilly, Paul. 'The printed publicity of the Festival of Britain', *Penrose Annual* vol 46 1952 pp 23-27

Thomas, Mark Hartland. 'Festival Pattern group', *Design* 29-30 May-June 1951 pp 12-24 (also issued separately)

Association of Consulting Engineers, London. *Selected designs, Festival of Britain: some examples of Britain's contribution to engineering.* 1951 London: Princes Press 321 89pp illus.

Some later criticism:

Frayn, Michael. 'The Festival of Britain' in Sissons, Michael and French, Philip (eds). *The Age of Austerity.* 1963 London: Allen and Unwin

'FOB + 10', *Design* 149 May 1961 pp 40-51

Pevsner, Nikolaus. 'Ten years after the Festival', *DIA Yearbook* 1961-1962 pp 14-21 illus.

Some later material on the 1950s:

Banham, Reyner. 'Design by choice 1951-1961: an alphabetical chronicle of landmarks and influences', *Architectural Review* vol 130 no 773 July 1961 pp 43-48 illus.

Industriell Formgivning, Storbritannien. Industrial design in Great Britain . . .with a complete catalogue of the British exhibition at H55. 1955 London: Council of Industrial Design on the occasion of Halsingborg H55 35pp illus.

'Focus on British design' (review of the decade's achievements), *Design* 121 January 1959

Elvin, Rene. 'A festival of British industrial design in Zurich', *Art and Industry* October 1952 pp 110-117

Binney, H. A. R. 'The contemporary role of industrial standards', *JRSA* vol 101 September 4 1953 pp 744-758

Idea 53: International design annual edited by Gerd Hatje. 1952 Stuttgart: Verlag Hatje 129pp illus. (similar volumes for 1953-1955 of 'best works in the sphere of industrial design')

Gloag, John. 'Contemporary design', *DIA Yearbook* 1957 pp 18-24

Designs of the year 1959. Selected from The Design Centre and including the Duke of Edinburgh's prize for elegant design. 1959 London: Council of Industrial Design 24pp

Russell, Sir Gordon. 'Modern trends in industrial design', *JRSA* vol 108 July 1960 pp 565-567, 578-595

and the 1960s:

Baynes, Ken. *Industrial design and the community.* 1967 London: Lund Humphries 96pp illus. bibl.

Arts and Crafts Movement

See also:

Art Workers' Guild *page 21*

Arts and Crafts Exhibition Society *page 21*

Important Designers *page 75*

Areas of Design Activity, especially Furniture, Metals *pages 173, 226*

A tendency rather than a single movement, much of the detail is best studied through the work and writings of leading individuals such as Ashbee, Morris, Crane etc. However there are useful general introductions in:

Naylor, Gillian. *The arts and crafts movement: a study of its sources, ideals and influence on design theory.* 1971 London: Studio Vista 208pp illus. bibl.

Triggs, Oscar Lovell. *Chapters in the history of the arts and crafts movement.* 1902 Chicago: The Bohemia Guild of the Industrial League. 198pp plates (facsimile reprint Arno 1976. University Microfilms Books in Demand reprint)

'Fifty years of arts and crafts', review by Nikolaus Pevsner and commentary by Bernard Shaw, *Studio* vol 116 1938 pp 225-230 illus. (reproduces Bernard Shaw's article from *The World* October 3 1888 'In the Picture Galleries' – review of the first Arts and Crafts Exhibition pp 229-230)

Callen, Anthea. *Angel in the studio: the women of the arts and crafts movement 1870-1914.* 1978 London: Astragal 208pp illus.

Neve, C. 'Complex crusade for a plain utopia, the arts and crafts movement', *Country Life* vol 154 October 11 1973 pp 1048-1049

The exhibition:

Arts and crafts movement. Artists, craftsmen and designers 1890-1930. 1973 London: Fine Art Society in association with Haslam and Whiteway Ltd illus. bibl. (four-page introduction by Lionel Lambourne with representative selection of printing, sculpture, metalwork, furniture, ceramics)

'Artists, craftsmen and designers 1890-1930. The Fine Art Society, London exhibition', *Connoisseur* October 1973 no 184 pp 148

Interesting parallel developments in America:

The arts and crafts movement in America 1876-1916. Edited by Robert Judson Clark. 1972 New Jersey: Princeton University Press

A vital journal documenting some of the most important years:

The Century Guild Hobby Horse edited by A. H. Mackmurdo, 1884-1892, then *The Hobby Horse* 1893-1894

One of the leading theorists of the movement:

Cobden-Sanderson, Thomas James. *The arts and crafts movement.* 1905 Hammersmith Publishing Society 39pp (also ABC Reprint)

Cobden-Sanderson, Thomas James. *Ecce Mundus, industrial ideals, the book beautiful.* 1902 London: Hammersmith Publishing Society 36pp (ABC Reprint)

Cobden-Sanderson, Thomas James. *The journals of Thomas James Cobden-Sanderson 1879-1922.* 1926 London: R. Cobden-Sanderson 2 vols

Cobden-Sanderson, Thomas James. *Of art and life.* 1897 London 70pp (facsimile reprint Bloomfield Books 1975. Originally published in *Art and life and the building and decoration of cities* 1897 London: Art Workers' Guild)

As well as the studies of major designers presented separately there is a growing number of writings on lesser figures:

Service, Alastair. 'Arts and crafts extremist: Charles Harrison Townsend (1851-1928)', *Architectural Association Quarterly* vol 6 no 2 1974 pp 4-12 illus.

Browning, Julian. 'Arts and crafts loyalist', *Country Life* vol 156 1974 pp 700-702 (on Henry Wilson)

Grillet, C. 'Edward Prior, born 1852', *Architectural Review* vol CXII 1952 pp 302-308.

Rothenstein, William. *Men and memories.* 1931-1939 London: Faber 3 vols

and on the smaller guilds and groups:

Morrison, Barbara June. *The saga of the renowned Guild of Decorative Arts.* Birmingham: A. J. Morrison 56pp illus. (Bromsgrove Guild of Decorative Arts)

Birmingham Guild Ltd. *The Birmingham Guild Ltd architectural and decorative metalworkers.* 1935 Birmingham 128pp

Wood, Esther. 'The School of Arts and Crafts', *Architectural Review* vol II 1897 pp 240-244 pt 1, pp 285-292 pt 2

Local organisations and exhibitions were also important:

Arts and Crafts Exhibition. 1904 Leeds: City Art Gallery

Manchester. Northern Art Workers Guild. *Catalogue of works exhibited by members of the Guild, 1898.* 1898 Manchester 72pp

Wood, Esther. 'Manchester Arts and Crafts Exhibition', *Studio* vol 15 1899 pp 121-127 illus. (first exhibition of the Northern Art Workers Guild)

Art Nouveau

See also:

Important Designers, especially Mackintosh *page 75*

Exposition Universelle 1900 *page 43*

Areas of Design Activity, especially Jewellery, Glass, Metalwork *pages 234, 219, 226*

Europe *page 88*

Predominantly a series of short-lived European developments. A particular study of Art Nouveau in Britain:

Art Nouveau in Britain. February 6-July 17 1965. (Text by Nikolaus Pevsner) 1965 Glasgow Art Gallery and Museum 24pp

Much more has been written and exhibited on this subject than almost any other area of design. What follows is a very brief selection.

General

Madsen, Stephen Tschudi. *Sources of Art Nouveau.* 1956 Oslo and New York: H. Aschehoug 490pp 264 illus. (Da Capo reprint 1976. University Microfilms very detailed bibliography pp 455-470)

Pevsner, Nikolaus. 'Beautiful and if need be useful', *Architectural Review* vol 122 no 730 November 1957 pp 297-299 (criticism of Art Nouveau as a term and of Madsen's book)

Madsen, Stephen Tschudi. *Art Nouveau.* 1967 London: Weidenfeld and Nicolson 256pp 84 illus.

Richards J. M. and Pevsner, Nikolaus, (eds). *The Anti-rationalists.* 1973 London: Architectural Press 210pp illus.

Schmutzler, Robert. *Art Nouveau, translated by E. Roditi.* 1964 London: Thames and Hudson 322pp illus.

Selz, Peter and Constantine, Mildred. *Art Nouveau: art and design at the turn of the century.* 1975 revised edition London: Secker and Warburg 196pp 193 illus. (previous edition to accompany the 1960 Museum of Modern Art exhibition)

Casteels, Maurice. *The new style in architecture and decorative design.* 1931 London: Batsford 54pp 144 pl (first published 1901 London. Translation of *L'Art moderne primitif*)

Seling, Helmut (ed). *Jugendstil. Der Weg ins 20 Jahrhundert.* 1959 Heidelburg: Keyser 459pp illus. bibl.

Abbate, Francesco (ed). *Art Nouveau: the style of the 1890s.* 1972 London: Octopus 158pp

Bott, Gerhard. *Kunsthandwerk um 1900: Jugendstil, art nouveau, modern style, nieuwe Kunst.* 1965 Darmstadt: Roether 411pp illus. (Kataloge des Hessischen Landesmuseums no 1)

Barilli, Renato. *Art Nouveau.* 1969 Feltham: Hamlyn 157pp (first published in Italian 1966)

Battersby, Martin. *Art Nouveau.* 1969 Feltham: Hamlyn 90pp illus.

Benton, Tim and Millikin, Sandra. *Art Nouveau 1890-1902.* 1975 Milton Keynes: Open University Press 64pp pl 132 illus. bibl. (History of Architecture and Design 1890-1939 Units 3-4)

Bini, Vittoria and Trabuchelli, Angioletta. *L'Art Nouveau.* 1957 Milan: G. de Silvestri 123pp illus. bibl.

Bode, Wilhelm. *Kunst und Kunstgewerbe am Ende des neunzehnten Jahrhunderts* 1901 Berlin: E. Cassirer 168pp

Bossaglia, Rossana. *Art nouveau: revolution in interior design.* 1973 London: Orbis 64pp 109 illus. (translation of *Il Mobile Liberty.* 1971 Istituto geografico De Agostini 1971)

Cremona, Italo. *Il Tempo dell'Art Nouveau: Modern Style, Sezession, Jugendstil, Arts and Crafts, Floreale, Liberty.* 1964 Firenze: Valuchi 230pp

Lahor, Jean. *L'Art Nouveau: son histoire, l'Art Nouveau étranger à l'Exposition, l'Art Nouveau au point de vue social.* 1901 Paris: Lemerre 104pp

Lenning, Henry F. *The Art Nouveau.* 1951 The Hague: Nijhoff 142pp illus. bibl. pp 132-135

Thiis, Jens Peter. *Arbog 1898-1901.* Nordenfjeldske Kunstindustrimuseum Trondheim: Trykt l Aktierykkeriet 205pp

A natural subject for pictorial anthologies:

Rheims, Maurice. *The age of Art Nouveau. European and American Arts in 1900.* 1966

London: Thames and Hudson 450pp 598 illus.

Amaya, Mario. *Art Nouveau.* 1966 London: Studio Vista 168pp illus.

Day, Joanne Christine. *Art Nouveau: cut and use stencils: 66 full-size stencils printed on durable stencil paper.* 1977 London: Constable 32 leaves

Garner, Philippe. *Art nouveau for collectors.* 1974 Feltham: Hamlyn 127pp illus. (all colour)

Gillon, Edward Vincent. *Art Nouveau: an anthology of design and illustration from the 'Studio'.* 1969 New York: Dover 89pp

Klamkin, Marion. *The collector's book of Art Nouveau.* 1971 Newton Abbot: David and Charles 112pp illus.

Warren, Geoffrey. *Art Nouveau.* 1972 London: Octopus Books 72pp 100 illus.

Reade, Brian. *Art Nouveau and Alphonse Mucha.* 1963 London: HMSO 66pp illus. (V & A large picturebook no 18)

Art Nouveau in Particular Countries

In Belgium:

Brussels 1900: capital of Art Nouveau. 1972 Brussels: Archives de l'Architecture Moderne

Bruxelles 1900: capitale de l'Art Nouveau. 1971 Brussels: École Nationale Superieure d'Architecture et des Arts Visuels 106pp illus. (Chadwyck Healey microfiche)

Borsi, Franco and Portoghesi, Paolo. *Victor Horta.* 1970 Brussels: Eds Vockauer 1969 Rome: Edizioni del Tritone 192pp illus.

Madsen, Stephen Tschudi. 'Horta', *Architectural Review* vol 118 no 708 December 1955 pp 388-392

In France:

Witt, Cleo. *French Art Nouveau for English collectors (catalogue of an exhibition at the) City of Bristol Museum and Art Gallery.* 1977 City of Bristol Museum and Art Gallery

'Paris Art Nouveau', *Architectural Review* vol 155 March 1974 pp 173-178

Graham, F. Lanier. *Hector Guimard.* 1971 New York: Museum of Modern Art 36pp illus.

The activities of Samuel Bing are central to an understanding of the growth in popularity of Art Nouveau:

Weisberg, Gabriel P. 'Samuel Bing: patron of Art Nouveau'. '1 The appreciation of Japanese art'. '2 Bing's sales of Art Nouveau'. '3 The House of Art Nouveau Bing'. *Connoisseur* vol 172 no 692

October 1969 pp 119-125; vol 172 no 694 December 1969 pp 294-299; vol 173 no 695 January 1970 pp 61-68

Weisberg, Gabriel P. 'Samuel Bing: international dealer of Art Nouveau'. 4 parts. *Connoisseur* vol 176 no 709 March 1971 pp 200-207; vol 176 no 710 April 1971 pp 275-283; vol 177 no 711 May 1971 pp 49-57; vol 177 no 713 July 1971 pp 211-219

Salon de l'Art Nouveau. 1896 Paris: Hotel Bing (Chadwyck Healey microfiche)

In Germany:

Bott, Gerhard. *Jugendstil; vom Beitrag Darmstadts zur internationalen Kunstbewegung um 1900, zusammengestellt und erlautert von Gerhard Bott.* 1965 Darmstadt: E. Roether 30pp

Citroën, K. A. *Jugendstil.* 1962 Darmstadt: Hessisches Landesmuseum 181pp

Ein Dokument Deutscher Kunst 1901. 1976. 1977 Darmstadt: Roether for Hessisches Landesmuseum 5 vols:

    1 Ein Dokument Deutscher Kunst 1901-1976

    2 Kunst und Dekoration 1851-1914

    3 Akademie-Sezession-Avantgarde um 1900

    4 Die Kunstler der Mathildenhohe

    5 Künstlerkolonie Mathildenhohe 1899-1914

Kruft, Hanno Walter. 'Ein Dokument Deutscher Kunst 1901-1976' (review of exhibition, Darmstadt 1976-1977), *Burlington Magazine* January 1977

Fred, W. 'The Darmstadt Artists' Colony', *Studio* vol 24 1902 pp 22-30; pp 91-100; pp 268-276

Schuckmann, Angelika von. 'Jugendstil in Munich', *Apollo* November 1971 pp 366-377 illus.

Der Jugendstil in Hamburg. 1965 Hamburg: Museum für Kunst und Gewerbe (picture book no VII)

Dingelstedt, Kurt. *Jugendstil in der angewandten Kunst. (Le Modern Style dans les arts appliqués).* 1959 Braunschweig/Paris 46pp

Goldschmiedekunst des Jugendstils; Schmuck und Gerät um 1900. 1963 Pforzheim Schmuckmuseum

Herman, Jost. *Jugendstil. Ein Forschungsbericht 1918-1964.* 1965 Stuttgart: J. B. Metzlersche Verlagsbuchhandlung

Hoffman, Julius. *Auswahl von Motiven aus dem Modernen Stil.* 1906? Stuttgart: Julius Hoffman pl 36

In Austria:

Levetus, A. S. 'The Exhibition of the Vienna Secession', *Studio* vol 25 1902 pp 267-275 illus. (thirteenth exhibition)

Levetus, A. S. 'The twenty-third exhibition of the Vienna Secession', *Studio* vol 34 1905 pp 53-63 illus.

Schmalenbach, Fritz. *Jugendstil. Ein Beitrag zu Theorie und Geschichte der Flächenkunst.* 1935 Wurzburg: K. Triltsch 160pp illus.

Vienna Secession. Art Nouveau to 1970. 1971 London: Royal Academy of Arts (Chadwyck Healey microfiche)

Waissenberger, Robert. *Die Wiener Sezession. Eine Dokumentation.* 1971 Vienna: Jugend und Volk 295pp

Wien um 1900. 1964 Vienna: Oesterreichisches Museum für angewandte Kunst

Kossatz, Horst-Herbert. 'The Vienna Secession and its early relations with Great Britain', *Studio International* January 1971 pp 9-23

In Italy:

Brosio, V. *Lo stile liberty in Italia.* 1967 Milan: Antonio Vallardi Editore 168pp

Amaya, Mario. 'Liberty and the Modern Style', *Apollo* February 1963 pp 109-115 illus.

Bossaglia, Rossana. *L'Italia Liberty. Arti Decorative. Art Nouveau Italy. Decorative Arts.* 1975 Milan: Görlich 368pp illus.

In England:

'Pillory: l'Art Nouveau at South Kensington', *Architectural Review* vol X 1901 pp 104-107

Schmutzler, Robert. 'The English origins of Art Nouveau', *Architectural Review* vol CXVII no 698 February 1955. pp 108-116

British sources of Art Nouveau. 1969 Manchester: Whitworth Art Gallery 64pp

Art Nouveau in England und Schottland. 1968 Hagen: Karl Ernst Osthaus Museum 36 illus. (Chadwyck Healey microfiche)

Art Nouveau in Britain. 1965 London: Arts Council (exhibition in Goldsmith's Hall)

Malton, John. 'Art Nouveau in Essex' pp 159-169 in Richards, J. M. and Pevsner, Nikolaus (eds). *The Anti-Rationalists.* 1973 London: Architectural Press 211pp illus. bibl. notes

Rotzler, W. 'Der Englische Jugendstil und die Schule von Glasgow', *Du Atlantis* (Zurich) September vol 25 1965 pp 684-699

Wordsall, Francis. 'Art Nouveau and Talwin Morris', *Apollo* January 1967 pp 64-65 illus.

There have been very many exhibitions. Some of the most important are:

Europa 1900. 1967 Ostend: Kursaal, Museé des Beaux Arts 3 vols

Kunstgewerbe Museum, Zurich. *Um 1900. Art Nouveau und Jugendstil, Kunst und Kunstgewerbe aus Europa und Amerika.* 1952 Zurich: Prokop & Co for Kunstgewerbe Museum 48pp 24pp of pl (Chadwyck Healey microfiche)

Art Nouveau: art and design at the turn of the century, edited by Peter Selz and Mildred Constantine. 1959 New York: Museum of Modern Art 192pp

Werke um 1900. Kunstgewerbe Museum Berlin von Wolfgang Scheffler. 1966 Berlin: Kunstgewerbe Museum 217pp illus.

Jugendstil. Sammlung K. A. Citroën, Amsterdam. 1962 Darmstadt: Hessisches Landesmuseum 217pp

'Art Nouveau in Zurich' (Um 1900, Art Nouveau und Jugendstil), *Architectural Review* vol 113 no 674 February 1953 pp 128-130 illus.

Le Bijou 1900. 1965 Brussels

Art Nouveau. 1965-1966 London: Grosvenor Gallery

Art Nouveau: Belgium/France. 1976 Chicago: Art Institute

Art Nouveau, Jugendstil, Niewe Kunst. 1972 Amsterdam: Bulletin van het Rijksmuseum

A few influences:

Grady, James. 'Nature and the Art Nouveau', *Art Bulletin* vol XXXVII no 3 1955 pp 187-192

Lancaster, Clay. 'Oriental contributions to Art Nouveau', *Art Bulletin* vol XXXIV December 1952 pp 297-310

Schmutzler, Robert. 'Blake and Art Nouveau', *Architectural Review* vol 118 no 704 August 1955 pp 90-97 illus.

Periodicals

Die Jugend 1896-1933 Munich

Nebehay, Christian (ed). *Ver Sacrum 1898-1903.* 1978 London: Thames and Hudson illus.

Pan nos 1-21, vols 1-5. 1895-1900 Berlin (Chadwyck Healey microfiche)

Bibliographies

Grady, James. 'A bibliography of the Art Nouveau', *Journal of the Society of Architectural Historians* vol XIV no 2 1955 pp 18-27

Kempton, Richard. *Art Nouveau – an annotated bibliography. Vol 1: Austria, Belgium and France.* 1977 Los Angeles: Hennessy and Ingalls 328pp

Art Deco

See also:

Exposition Internationale des Arts Décoratifs et Industriels Modernes, Paris 1925 *page 46*

Chronological Studies *page 59*

Areas of Design Activity *page 114*

A very fashionable movement closely related to the 1925 Paris Exhibition.

General studies:

Hillier, Bevis. *Art Deco of the Twenties and Thirties.* 1968 London: Studio Vista 168pp illus.

Minneapolis Institute of Arts. *The world of Art Deco: catalogue of an exhibition organised by the Minneapolis Institute of Arts July-September 1971.* Text by Bevis Hillier. 1971 London: Studio Vista 224pp illus. bibl.

L'évolution artistique. Revue destinée à la diffusion des idées d'art moderne dans l'industrie et contenant des réproductions d'oeuvres d'artistes des groupes 'La Stèle' et 'Evolution'. Textes par Yvanhoe Rambossom. 1926 Paris: Goldscheider

An ideal subject for picturebooks:

Klein, Dan. *All colour book of Art Deco.* 1974 London: Octopus 72pp

Lesieutre, Alain. *The spirit and splendour of Art Deco.* 1974 London: Paddington Press 304pp illus. bibl.

Loeb, Marcia. *Art deco designs and motifs.* 1972 New York: Dover 75pp

Rowe, William. *Original art deco designs.* 1973 New York: Dover 80pp (Dover pictorial archive series)

Maenz, Paul. *Art Deco. Formen zwischen Zwei Kriegen.* 1974 Verlag DuMont Schauberg 243pp illus. bibl.

Menten, Theodore. *The Art Deco Style in household objects, architecture, sculpture, graphics, jewellery.* 468 authentic examples. 1972 New York: Dover 183pp

Walters, Thomas. *Art Deco* 1973 London: Academy Editions 88pp illus.

and for collectors:

McClinton, Katharine Morrison. *Art Deco: a guide for collectors.* 1972 New York: Crown 278pp illus. bibl.

Johnson, S. J. 'The new antiques: art deco and modernism', *Antiques* vol CI no 1 pp 230-236 illus.

Some exhibitions:

Art Deco: French decorative arts in the Twenties. 1975 London: Victoria and Albert Museum 15pp illus.

Art Deco 1920-1930. 1967 Milan: Galleria Milano

More detailed studies:

Hunter, Penelope. 'Art Deco and the Metropolitan Museum of Art', *Connoisseur* vol 179 no 722 pp 273-281

Julian, P. 'Les années '20 revues dans les années '70 chez Yves Saint Laurent', *Connaissance des Arts* no 262 December 1973 pp 102-109

'Biba: an art deco pleasure palace in London', *Interiors* vol 133 March 1974 pp 14ff

Kitsch

Kitsch is not by any stretch of the imagination a movement, but there has been recent study of the nature of Kitsch or deliberate commercial bad taste:

Dorfles, Gillo. *Kitsch.* 1974 London: Thames and Hudson 316pp

Sternberg, Jacques. *Kitsch.* 1972 London: Academy Editions 96pp illus.

Important designers

Ashbee, Charles Robert

1863-1942

See also:

Metals: Cast Iron *page 228*

Metals: Silver *page 231*

Ashbee, Charles Robert. *Craftmanship in competitive industry, being a record of the workshops of the Guild of Handicraft and some deductions from their twenty one years experience.* 1898 London: Grant 297pp 37 illus. (1908 edition: Essex House Press) ABC Reprint

Ashbee, Charles Robert. *Decorative art from a workshop point of view. A paper read at the Edinburgh Art Congress, November 1889.* 1889 Edinburgh 11pp

Ashbee, Charles Robert. *A description of the work of the Guild of Handicraft.* 1902 London: Guild and School of Handicraft 13pp

Ashbee, Charles Robert. *An endeavour towards the teaching of J. Ruskin and W. Morris.* 1901 London: Edward Arnold Essex House Press. ABC Reprint 52pp

Ashbee, Charles Robert. *A few chapters in workshop reconstruction and citizenship.* 1894 London: Guild and School of Handicraft 166pp ABC Reprint

Ashbee, Charles Robert. *From Whitechapel to Camelot. Illustrated by M-or-N.* 1982 London: Guild of Handicraft 80pp

Ashbee, Charles Robert. *The Guild of Handicraft.* 1909 Essex House Press

Ashbee, Charles Robert. *The ideals of the craftsman.* 1889 London 12pp (address to the Guild and School of Handicraft)

Ashbee, Charles Robert (ed). *Manual of the Guild of Handicraft. Being a guide to County Councils and technical teachers.* 1892 London: Cassell 124pp ABC Reprint

Ashbee, Charles Robert. 'The "Norman Chapel" buildings at Broad Campden, in Gloucestershire', *Studio* vol 41 1908 pp 289-296 illus.

Ashbee, Charles Robert. 'Province of the arts and handicrafts in a mechanical society', *Hibbert Journal* April 1915 pp 95-104

Ashbee, Charles Robert. *Should we stop teaching art?* 1911 London: Batsford 122p ABC Reprint. (attempt to relate Art and Craft movement to problems of machines and twentieth century)

Ashbee, Charles Robert. 'A short history of the Guild and School of Handicraft', *Transactions of the Guild and School of Handicraft* vol 1 1890 pp 19-31

Ashbee, Charles Robert. *Socialism and politics.* 1906 Essex House Press

Ashbee, Charles Robert. *Where the great city stands. A study in new civics.* 1917 London: Batsford and Essex House Press 164pp illus.

Burrough, B. G. 'C. R. Ashbee, his Guild and School of Handicraft', *Antique Dealer and Collector's Guide* January 1974 pp 67-69

Burrough, B. G. 'Three disciples of William Morris. 2 Charles Robert Ashbee'. Part 1 *Connoisseur* vol CLXXII no 692 October 1969 pp 85-90 illus. Part 2 *Connoisseur* vol CLXXII no 694 December 1969 pp 262-266

Crawford, Alan. 'Ten letters from Frank Lloyd Wright to Charles Robert Ashbee', *Journal of the Society of Architectural Historians* 1970 vol 13 pp 64-76 (includes a list of Ashbee's works)

'The Guild of Handicraft. A visit to "Essex House"', *Studio* vol 12 1898 pp 27-36 illus.

Proofs on hand-made Japanese vellum of the illustrations of the Transactions of the Guild and School of Handicraft volume 1 1890. Touched up by the artists. 1890 London: Guild and School of Handicraft 16 pl

A set of illustrations of the works of the Guild of Handicraft. 1900 London: Guild and School of Handicraft

Transactions of the Guild and School of Handicraft. Edited by C. R. Ashbee. 1890- London: Guild and School of Handicraft

Rowley, Charles. *A Workshop Paradise and other papers.* 1905 London: Sherratt and Hughes 280pp illus.

'C. R. Ashbee obituary note', *Architectural Review* vol 92 pp xxxiii-xxxiv

Ashbee, Charles Robert. *Memoirs* typescript 1938-1940. (unpublished MSS in the Victoria and Albert Museum)

Baillie Scott, Mackay Hugh

1865-1945

See also:

Interior Design *page 147*

Fireplaces *page 161*

Textiles: Needlework *page 195*

Baillie Scott, Mackay Hugh. 'House building: past and present', *JRSA*

vol 63 October 29 1915 pp 989-996;
November 5 1915 pp 1004-1013;
November 12 1915 pp 1019-1030

Baillie Scott, Mackay Hugh. *Houses and
gardens*. 1906 London: George Newnes
247pp 17 col pl illus.

Kornwolf, James David. *M. H. Baillie Scott
and the arts and crafts movement: pioneers of
modern design*. 1972 Baltimore: Johns
Hopkins Press 588pp

Wilson, Michael. 'The piano designs of
Baillie Scott (1865-1945)', *Country Life*
January 22 1976 pp 198-199

Benson, William Arthur Smith

1854-1924

Benson, William Arthur Smith. *Drawing – its
history and uses with a memoir by the Hon. W.
N. Bruce*. 1925 Oxford University Press
109pp

Benson, William Arthur Smith. *Elements of
handicraft and design*. 1893 London:
Macmillan 151pp illus.

Benson, William Arthur Smith. *Rudiments of
handicraft*. 1919 London: Murray 151pp
illus.

Bury, Shirley. 'A craftsman who used the
machine' (W. A. S. Benson), *Country Life*
CXXXVII 1965 pp 624, 627

Bury, Shirley. 'The metalwork of W. A. S.
Benson', *Country Life* March 18 1965

Brangwyn, Frank

1867-1956

Furst, Herbert Ernest Augustus. *Decorative
art of Frank Brangwyn. A study of the
problems of decoration*. 1924 London: John
Lane 231pp

Holme, C. G. 'Frank Brangwyn designs for
British industry', *Studio* vol 100 1930
pp 440-445 illus.

'A bedroom decorated by Frank Brangwyn',
Studio vol 19 1900 pp 175-180 illus.

Finch, Arthur. 'Recent decorative work of
Frank Brangwyn A. R. A.' '1 Mural
paintings on the Panama-Pacific Export'
(9 illus.) '2 Mosaic designs for St Aiden's
Church, Leeds' (6 illus.) *Studio* vol 72
pp 3-14, 142-147

Burges, William

1827-1881

See also:

Church Plate *page 237*

Burges, William. *The architectural designs of
W. Burges ARA. Details of stonework. Edited
by Richard Popplewell Pullan*. 1887
London: Batsford 8pp pl 39

Burges, William. *Architectural drawings*.
1870 London: Clewes 29pp pl 75

Burges, William. *Art applied to industry.
A series of lectures 1865*. 1865 Oxford:
Parker 120pp

Burges, William. 'The Loan Museum
1862', *Gentleman's Magazine* 1862

Handley-Read, Charles. 'William Burges'.
pp 185-220 in Ferriday, Peter (ed.)
Victorian architecture. 1963 London: Cape

Burges, William. *The designs of William
Burges ARA edited by R. P. Pullan*. 1885
London: Batsford 9pp pl 23

Pullan, Richard Popplewell. *The house of
William Burges*. 1886 London: Batsford
14pp pl 40

Briggs, R. A. 'The art of William Burges:
an appreciation (of the decoration and
furniture of his own house)', *JRIBA*
19 February 1916 pp 131-139 8 figs.

Pullan, Richard Popplewell. 'The works
of the late William Burges, ARA Fellow',
RIBA Transactions 1881-1882 pp 183-195

Taylor, Nicholas and Symondson,
Anthony. 'Burges and Morris at Bingley:
a discovery', *Architectural Review* vol 144
no 857 July 1968 pp 34-38 illus.

Burne-Jones, Edward

1833-1898

See also:

Stained Glass *page 223*

Tapestries *page 196*

Bell, Malcolm. *Edward Burne-Jones*. 1902
London: G. Bell & Sons 151pp pl
(first published 1892)

Burne-Jones, Georgiana Lady. *Memorials of
Edward Burne-Jones*. 1904 London:
Macmillan 2 vols illus. New York: B.
Blom reprint 704pp illus.

'Burne-Jones issue', *Apollo* November 1975

Christian, John. 'Burne-Jones studies',
Burlington Magazine 115 1973 pp 93-109
illus.

*Drawings and designs by Sir Edward Coley
Burne-Jones*. Fitzwilliam Museum,
Cambridge 1971 Catalogue

Fitzgerald, Penelope. *Edward Burne-Jones:
a biography*. 1975 London: Michael
Joseph 320pp

Harrison, Martin and Waters, Bill.
Burne-Jones. 1973 London: Barrie and
Jenkins 209pp 330 illus.

Slater, John Atwood. 'An ethical retrospect
of the traditions and aims of Edward
Burne-Jones', *Architectural Review* VI
1900 pp 70-

Vallance, Aymer. *The decorative art of Sir E. Burne-Jones.* 1900 Art Journal Easter Art Annual 32pp

Wilson, H. 'The work of Sir Edward Burne-Jones: more especially in decoration and design', *Architectural Review* 1 1897, pp 171-181 (part 1), pp 225-234 (part 2), pp 273-281 (part 3)

Coates, Wells Wintemute
1895-1958

Cantacuzino, Sherban. *Wells Coates.* 1978 London: Gordon Fraser 112pp 200 illus.

Boumphrey, Geoffrey. 'The designers. Wells Coates', *Architectural Review* vol 79 January 1936 pp 45-46

Crane, Walter
1845-1915

See also:

Wallpaper *page 207*

Book Illustration *page 127*

Interior Design: Decoration *page 147*

Catalogue of a collection of designs by Walter Crane. 1891 London: Fine Art Society 28pp

Catalogue of a collection of designs by Walter Crane with prefatory and explanatory notes by the artist, at the Nicholson Institute, Leek. 1892 Leek: Nicholson Institute 24pp

Crane, Walter. *An artist's reminiscences . . . with one hundred and three illustrations by the author.* 1907 London: Methuen 520pp

Crane, Walter. *The bases of design.* 1898 London: G. Bell & Sons 365pp ABC Reprint

Crane, Walter. *Cartoons for the cause: designs and verses for the socialist and labour movement 1886-1896.* (A souvenir of the International Socialist Workers and Trade Union Congress 1896). 1976 London: Journeyman Press 40pp illus. (first published 1896)

Crane, Walter. *The claims of decorative art.* 1892 London: Lawrence and Bullen 191pp

Crane, Walter. *Ideals in Art: papers, theoretical, practical, critical.* 1905 London: G. Bell & Sons 301pp ABC Reprint

Crane, Walter. *Illustration et décoration du livre.* 1914 Paris: British Arts and Crafts Exhibition

Crane, Walter. *Line and form.* 1900 London: G. Bell & Sons 282pp

Crane, Walter. *Moot points. Friendly disputes on art and industry between Walter Crane and*

Lewis F. Day. Caricatures by Walter Crane. 1903 London: Batsford 94pp

Crane, Walter. *The relation of art to education and social life. Being an address.* 1892 Leek: Leek Press 25pp

Crane, Walter. *William Morris to Whistler. Papers and addresses on art and craft and the commonweal.* 1911 London: G. Bell & Sons 276pp illus.

Konody, Paul George. *Art of Walter Crane.* 1902 London: George Bell & Sons 147pp illus.

Spencer, Isobel. *Walter Crane.* 1975 London: Studio Vista 208pp 92 illus.

The work of Walter Crane. With notes by the artist. 1898 London: J. S. Virtue Easter Art Annual 1898 32pp

Day, Lewis Foreman
1845-1910

See also:

Ornament *page 103*

Embroidery *page 195*

Enamelling *page 236*

Day, Lewis Foreman. *Everyday art: short essays on the arts not-fine.* 1882 London: Batsford 283pp ABC Reprint (325pp 35 pl)

Day, Lewis Foreman. *Instances of accessory art: original designs and suggestive examples of ornament, with practical and critical notes.* 1880 London: Batsford 120pp 29 pl ABC Reprint

Dresser, Christopher
1834-1904

See also:

Ornament *page 102*

1862 International Exhibition *page 38*

Dresser, Christopher. ' "Art Industries", "Art Museums", "Art Schools" 3 lectures delivered in Philadelphia', *Penn Monthly* January, February, March 1877

Dresser, Christopher. 'On Eastern art, and its influence on European manufacturers and taste', *JSA* vol 22 February 6 1874 pp 211-221

Dresser, Christopher. 'Art manufactures of Japan, from personal observation', *JSA* vol 26 February 1 1878 pp 169-178

Dresser, Christopher. *Japan, its architecture, art and art manufactures.* 1882 London: Longmans 467pp ABC Reprint

Dresser, Christopher. *Principles of art . . . adopted by the Art Furnishers Alliance.* 1881 London 28pp

Dresser, Christopher. *Principles of decorative design.* 1873 London: Cassell 167pp

Dresser, Christopher. 'Articles on "Principles in Design"' in *The Technical Educator* 2 vols 1870

Dresser, Christopher. *Rudiments of botany, structural and physiological: being an introduction to the study of the vegetable kingdom, and comprising the advantages of a full glossary of technical terms.* 1859 London: Virtue 433pp illus.

Dresser, Christopher. *Studies in design for house decorators, designers and manufacturers.* 1876 London: Cassell, Peter and Galpin 40pp

Dresser, Christopher. *Unity in variety, as deduced from the vegetable kingdom: being an attempt at developing that oneness which is discoverable in the habits, mode of growth and principle of construction of all plants.* 1859 London: J. S. Virtue 162pp ABC Reprint 1977

Christopher Dresser 1834-1904: pottery, glass, metalwork. Catalogue by J. Jesse and R. Dennis. 1972 London: Fine Arts Society 38pp

Garner, P. 'Aesthete of the machine age' (Christopher Dresser), *Art and Antiques Weekly* 14 May 1977 pp 20-22

Pevsner, Nikolaus. 'Minor masters of the nineteenth century; Christopher Dresser, industrial designer', *Architectural Review* 81 April 1937 pp 183-186

'The work of Christopher Dresser', *Studio* vol 15 1899 pp 104-114 illus.

Gimson, Ernest

1864-1919

See also:

Furniture *page 173*

Burrough, B. G. 'Ernest Gimson and the "Cotswold School" ', *House and Garden* February 1971 pp 100

Burrough, B. G. 'Three disciples of William Morris. 1 Gimson'. Part 1 *Connoisseur* August 1969 vol CLXXI no 690 pp 228-232. Part 2 *Connoisseur* September 1969 vol CLXXII no 691 pp 8-14

Ernest Gimson. 1969 Leicester Museum 46pp illus.

Lambourne, Lionel. 'The art and craft of Ernest Gimson', *Country Life* August 7 1969 pp 338

Lethaby, W. R. and others. *Ernest Gimson, his life and work.* 1924 London: Shakespeare Head Press 180pp pl 60 (ABC Reprint called 'Life and Work')

Jewson, Norman. *By chance I did rove.* 1973 Kineton, Warwick: Roundwood Press 145pp (Gimson's last pupil)

Godwin, Edward William

1833-1886

'The greatest aesthete of them all' (O. Wilde)

See also:

Furniture *page 173*

Harbron, Dudley. *The conscious stone: the life of Edward William Godwin.* 1949 London: Latimer House 190pp

Harbron, Dudley. 'Edward Godwin', *Architectural Review* vol 98 August 1945 pp 48-52

Aslin, Elizabeth. 'E. W. Godwin and the Japanese taste', *Apollo* December 1962 pp 779-784

Godwin, Edward William. *Dress and its relation to health and climate.* 1884 London: International Health Exhibition 80pp

Service, A. 'James MacLaren and the Godwin legacy', *Architectural Review* vol 154 August 1973 pp 111-118 bibl.

Lethaby, William Richard

1857-1931

See also:

Education *page 14*

Design and Industries Association *page 22*

Lead *page 230*

Studies

Rubens, Godfrey. *William Lethaby: his life and work 1857-1931.* 1976 London: Architectural Press 256pp illus.

Roberts, A. R. N. (ed). *William Richard Lethaby 1857-1931. A volume in honour of the School's first principal prepared by A. R. N. Roberts at the suggestion of William Johnstone OBE.* 1957 LCC Central School of Arts and Crafts 88pp

Troup, F. W. W. R. 'Lethaby' (obituary), *JRIBA* vol XXXVIII 8 August 1931 pp 696-698

Blomfield, Sir Reginald. 'W. R. Lethaby, an impression and tribute', *JRIBA* Series III vol 39 no 8 February 1932 pp 293-302

Thomas, B. and others. 'W. R. Lethaby: a symposium in honour of his centenary', *JRIBA* series III vol LXIV 1957 pp 218-225

Roberts, A. R. N. 'The life and work of W. R. Lethaby', *JRSA* vol 105 29 March 1957 pp 355-371

Bayley, Stephen. 'W. R. Lethaby and the cell of tradition', *JRIBA* April 1975 pp 29-31

Burrough, B. G. 'Three disciples of William Morris. III W. R. Lethaby', *Connoisseur* vol CLXXIII no 695 January 1971 pp 33-37

Faulkner, Thomas. 'W. R. Lethaby: tradition and innovation', pp 4-25 in *Design 1900-1960: design and popular culture of the 20th century*, edited by T. Faulkner. 1976 Newcastle Polytechnic

Rooke, Noel. 'The work of Lethaby, Webb and Morris', *JRIBA* March 1950 pp 167-175

Rubens, G. 'Lethaby and the revival of printing', *Penrose Annual* 1976 pp 219-232

Ward, Basil. 'Lethaby – architect, designer and teacher', *Design* no 103 July 1957 pp 44-46

Weir, Robert W. S. *William Richard Lethaby (paper read before the Art Workers' Guild on 22 April 1932)*. 1938 Central School of Arts and Crafts 22pp (reprinted from *Architectural Association Journal*)

Lethaby's Writings

Lethaby, William Richard. *About beauty*. 1928 Birmingham School of Printing 9pp (reprinted from *Architecture*)

Lethaby, William Richard. *Architecture. An introduction to the history and theory of the art of building*. 1912 Williams & Norgate 256pp (other editions 1929, 1939)

Lethaby, William Richard. *Architecture, mysticism and myth, with introduction by Godfrey Rubens*. 1975 London: Architectural Press reprint 280pp (first edition 1892 Percival & Co, rewritten in parts in *The Builder* 1928, then republished as *Architecture, nature and magic*. 1956 Duckworth)

Lethaby, William Richard. *Art and workmanship*. 1915 London: Design and Industries Association 11pp

The artistic crafts. Series of technical handbooks edited by W. R. Lethaby. 1901 London: John Hogg

Lethaby, William Richard. 'Education for industry' in *Handicrafts and reconstruction*. 1919 Arts and Crafts Exhibition Society. pp 75

Lethaby, William Richard. *Form in civilization: collected papers on art and labour, with an introduction by Lewis Mumford*. 1957 London: Oxford University Press 242pp (previous edition 1922)

Lethaby, William Richard. *Home and country arts*. Reprinted from *Home and Country*. 1924 second edition London: Home & Country 119pp illus. (third edition 1930 143pp with additional chapter)

Lethaby, William Richard. *Londinium. Architecture and the crafts*. 1923 London: Duckworth 248pp 176 figs (illus. facsimile reprint 1976, New York: Arno Press)

Lethaby, William Richard. *The study and practice of artistic crafts: an address*. 1901 Birmingham: College of Art and Crafts 21pp

William Richard Lethaby . . .A bibliography of his literary works. Compiled by the Royal Institute of British Architects library staff in collaboration with the Design and Industries Association 1950 41pp typescript (includes index)

Mackintosh, Charles Rennie
1868-1928

See also:

Furniture *page 173*

Metals *page 226*

Art Nouveau *page 71*

Fullest introduction is:

Howarth, Thomas. *Charles Rennie Mackintosh and the Modern Movement*. 1952 (revised edition 1977) London: Routledge and Kegan Paul 521pp illus. bibl.

There are shorter studies in:

Macleod, R. *Charles Rennie Mackintosh*. 1968 London: Country Life

Pevsner, Nikolaus. *C. R. Mackintosh*. 1950 Milan: Il Balcone 152pp illus. bibl. (in Italian) reprinted in a revised translation by Adeline Hartcup in *Studies in Art, Architecture and Design vol 2 Victoria and After*. 1968 London: Thames and Hudson pp 152-175

Taylor, E. A. 'A Neglected Genius – Charles Rennie Mackintosh', *Studio* vol 105 1933 pp 345-352 illus.

Two papers in Richards, J. M. and Pevsner, Nikolaus (eds). *The Anti-Rationalists*. 1973 London: Architectural Press:

Walker, David. 'The Early Works of Mackintosh', pp 116-135

Sekler, Eduard F. 'Mackintosh and Vienna', pp 136-142 (both published earlier in *Architectural Review* November and December 1968)

'C. R. Mackintosh', *Casabella* no 376 1973 pp 17-26

Alison, Filippo. 'Critical survey of Mackintosh's works', *Casabella* no 380-381 1973 pp 33-42

Bedford, June and Davies, Ivor. 'Remembering Charles Rennie Mackintosh, a recorded interview with

Mary Newberry Sturrock', *Connoisseur*
vol 183 no 738 August 1973 pp 280-288

Blackie, W. 'Memories of Charles Rennie
Mackintosh', *Scottish Arts Review* vol XI
no 4 1968

Taylor, J. 'Modern Decorative Art at
Glasgow. Some Notes on Miss Cranston's
Argyle Street Tea-House', *Studio* vol 39
1907 pp 31-36

Brown, Timothy. 'Charles Rennie
Mackintosh', *Antique Dealer and Collector's
Guide* August 1974 pp 84-89

Garner, Philippe. 'Charles Rennie
Mackintosh and the Glasgow style', *Art
and Antiques Weekly* 19 March 1977
pp 24-26

Other very valuable sources of information
are the exhibition catalogues:

*Charles Rennie Mackintosh. Margaret
MacDonald Mackintosh. Memorial Exhibition.*
1933 Glasgow: McLellan Galleries

*Exhibition of work by Charles Rennie Mackintosh
(organised by) Saltaire Society and the Arts
Council of Great Britain.* Catalogue and text
by Thomas Howarth. 1953 Edinburgh:
Saltaire Society

*Mackintosh and the modern interior (organised
by) the British Council.* 1961 Glasgow:
School of Art

*Charles Rennie Mackintosh (1868-1928)
Architecture, Design and Painting.*
Exhibition at the Royal Scottish Museum.
Catalogue prepared with an introduction
by Andrew MacLaren Young. 1968
Edinburgh: Scottish Arts Council 74pp

Charles Rennie Mackintosh 1868-1928. 1969
Darmstadt: Hessisches Landesmuseum
139pp

Charles Rennie Mackintosh. 1969 Vienna:
Museum des 20 Jahrhunderts 52pp

Charles Rennie Mackintosh. 1974 New York:
Museum of Modern Art

Mackmurdo, Arthur Heygate

1851-1942

See also:

Arts and Crafts *page 70*

Art Nouveau *page 71*

Much of his own work is still unpublished
(manuscript *Memoirs* and *History of the Arts
and Crafts Movement* in the William Morris
Gallery, Walthamstow) but a useful
introduction is provided by:

*A. H. Mackmurdo and the Century Guild
Collection Catalogue.* 1967 Walthamstow:
William Morris Gallery 35pp

Useful short studies are:

Pevsner, Nikolaus. 'Arthur H. Mackmurdo.
A Pioneer Designer', *Architectural Review*
vol 83 1938 pp 141-143 (republished in
Pevsner, Nikolaus. *Studies in Art,
Architecture and Design vol 2 Victorian and
after.* 1968 London: Thames and
Hudson pp 132-139

Pond, Edward. 'Mackmurdo Gleanings',
Architectural Review vol 128 no 766
pp 429-431 (republished in Richards, J.
M. and Pevsner, Nikolaus (eds). *The
Anti-Rationalists.* 1973 London:
Architectural Press pp 111-115)

Haslam, Malcolm. 'Pioneer of Art Nouveau,
Arthur Heygate Mackmurdo
(1851-1942)', *Country Life* February 27
1975 pp 504-506

Horne, H. P. 'The Century Guild', *Art
Journal* September 1887 New Series VII
pp 295-298

Vallance, Aymer. 'A. H. Mackmurdo and
the Century Guild', *Studio* vol 17 1899
pp 183-192

Then there are his published works:

Mackmurdo, Arthur Heygate. *A People's
Charter or the Terms of Prosperity and
Freedom within a Community.* 1933
London: Williams and Norgate 269pp

Mackmurdo, Arthur Heygate (ed). *Plain
Handicrafts: being essays by artists setting forth
the principles of designs and established
methods of workmanship: a guide to
Elementary Practice.* 1892 London:
Percival & Co 63pp

Mackmurdo, Arthur Heygate (ed). *Letters
of Selwyn Image.* 1932 London: ABC
Reprint 220pp

and the journal he edited:

The Century Guild Hobby Horse 1884-

Morris, William

1834-1896

See also:

Wallpaper *page 207*

Book Design *page 117*

Furniture *page 173*

Interior Design *page 147*

Tapestry *page 196*

Carpets *page 199*

Writings

Morris, William. *The collected works of William
Morris. With an introduction by his daughter
May Morris.* 1910-1915 London:
Longmans, Green & Co 24 vols

Morris, William. *Lectures.* 1898-1901
London: Longmans 5 vols
1 *Address delivered . . . at the distribution of
prizes to students of the Birmingham*

Municipal School of Art, February 21 1894. 1898 25pp

2 Art and the beauty of the earth. 1898 31pp

3 Some hints on pattern designing. 1899 45pp

4 Architecture and history at Westminster Abbey. 1900 50pp

5 & 6 Art and its producers and the Arts and Crafts Today; two lectures delivered before the National Association for the Advancement of Art. 1901 47pp

Lemire, Eugene D. compiler. The unpublished lectures of William Morris. 1969 Detroit: Wayne State University 331pp bibl. (includes checklist of Morris's speeches and lectures pp 291-322)

Morris, William. The letters of William Morris to his family and friends. Edited with an introduction and notes by Philip Henderson. 1950 London: Longmans 406pp illus.

Morris, William. The aims of art. 1887 London: Office of 'The Commonweal' 39pp

Morris, William. Architecture, industry and wealth. Collected papers by William Morris. 1902 London: Longmans Green & Co 163pp

Morris, William. The decorative arts, their relation to modern life and progress. An address delivered before the Trades Guild of Learning. 1878 London: Ellis and White 32pp (later published as 'The Lesser Arts' in Hopes and fears for Art)

Morris, William. Hopes and fears for Art. Five lectures. 1882 London: Ellis & White 217pp

Morris, William. Signs of change. Seven lectures. 1888 London: Reeves and Turner 262pp

Morris, William. 'The revival of handicraft', Fortnightly Review November 1888

Selections

Selected writings and designs (of) William Morris edited with an introduction by Asa Briggs; with a supplement by Graeme Shankland on William Morris, designer. 1977 Harmondsworth: Penguin 312pp illus. pl 24 (first edition 1962)

William Morris: selected writings edited by G. D. H. Cole. 1948 London: Nonesuch Press 696pp

Exhibitions

Catalogue of a collection of examples illustrating the works of William Morris, introduction by S. Cockerell. 1908 Manchester College of Art.

Catalogue of an exhibition in celebration of the centenary of William Morris, February 9th-April 8th 1934. 1934 London: Victoria and Albert Museum 42pp pl 11

William Morris Society. The work of William Morris. Catalogue of an exhibition at The Times Bookshop 1962

William Morris Gallery. Catalogue of the Morris Collection. 1969 second edition Walthamstow: William Morris Gallery 76pp (previous edition 1958)

William Morris and Company

Morris and Company 1861-1940. A commemorative centenary exhibition. 1961 London: Arts Council (held at the Victoria and Albert Museum)

A brief sketch of the Morris movement and of the firm founded by William Morris to carry out his designs and of the industries revived or started by him. Written to commemorate the firm's fiftieth anniversary in June 1911. 1911 London: privately printed by Charles Whittingham & Co 63pp illus.

'William Morris issue', Du vol 25 September 1965 (article by Barbara Morris 'Morris and Company' pp 658-670)

Morris, Barbara. 'William Morris and Company', Discovering Antiques Part 73 1971 pp 1734-1739 illus. bibl.

Morris and Co. (Exhibition March-May 1975). 1975 California: Stanford University Art Museum 75pp (Stanford Art Book 15)

The printed sales catalogues of the company are also very useful sources of information and illustration

Wilson, Arnold. 'More from Morris and Company', Apollo July 1964 pp 57-59 illus.

Studies

Watkinson, Raymond. William Morris as designer. 1967 London: Studio Vista 68pp pl 90 bibl.

Mackail, J. W. The life of William Morris. 2 vols 1899 London: Longmans Green & Co 750pp (reissued in Oxford University Press World's Classics Series 1950 and as an Arno Reprint 1976, 2 vols in 1) the standard life

Lindsay, Jack. William Morris. His life and work. 1975 London: Constable 432pp illus. (includes very thorough 10 page bibliography of books and articles)

Vallance, Aymer. William Morris, his art, writings and public life. A record. 1897 revised 1909 London: Bell 462pp illus.

Vallance, Aymer. The art of William Morris . . . With reproductions from designs and fabrics printed in colours of the originals . . . also a classified bibliography by Temple Scott. 1897 London: Bell & Sons 167pp

Bloomfield, Paul. 'The life and work of William Morris', *JRSA* vol 82 September 21 1934 pp 1103-1116 and September 28 1934 pp 1119-1132

Day, Lewis F. 'William Morris and his art 1899', London: Virtue *(Art Journal, Easter Art Annual)* 32pp

Crow, Gerald H. 'William Morris Designer'. Special Winter number of *The Studio* 1934 120pp illus. bibl.

Journal of the William Morris Society 1961- Walthamstow

Transactions of the William Morris Society 1960- Walthamstow

Lethaby, William Richard. *Morris as Work-Master. A lecture.* 1902 London: John Hogg 23pp

Thompson, Paul. *The work of William Morris.* 1977 London: Quartet Books 325pp pl 16 bibl. (first published 1967 Heinemann)

Arnot, Robert Page. *William Morris, the man and the myth. Including letters of William Morris to J. L. Mahon and Dr. John Glass.* 1964 London: Lawrence and Wishart 131pp

Arnot, Robert Page. *William Morris, a vindication.* 1934 London: Martin Lawrence 31pp

Atkins, William. *William Morris, artist, printer and man of business.* 1918 London: St. Bride's Foundation Printing School 16pp

Bradley, Ian. *William Morris and his world.* 1978 London: Thames and Hudson

Cary, Elisabeth L. *William Morris, poet, craftsman and socialist.* (Bibliography prepared by S. C. Cockerell) 1902 London: Putnams 296pp illus.

Clutton-Brock, Arthur. *William Morris: his work and influence.* 1914 London: Williams and Norgate 256pp (Home University Library of Modern Knowledge)

Colebrook, Frank. *William Morris, master printer.* 1897 Tonbridge Wells: Hepworth & Co 39pp

Compton-Rickett, Arthur. *William Morris: a study in personality.* 1913 London: Herbert Jenkins 325pp

Cuffe, Lionel. 'William Morris', *Architectural Review* vol LXIX 1931 p 151 illus.

Ellis, F. S. 'The life work of William Morris', *JSA* vol 46 May 27 1898 pp 618-630

Faulkner, Peter. *William Morris and Eric Gill.* 1975 Walthamstow: William Morris Society

Floud, Peter. 'Dating Morris patterns', *Architectural Review* July 1959 pp 14-20

Floud, Peter. 'The inconsistencies of William Morris', *The Listener* October 14 1954

Floud, Peter. 'William Morris as an artist: a new view', *The Listener* October 7 1954

Forman, Harry Buxton. *The books of William Morris described with some account of his doings in literature and in the allied arts.* 1897 London: F. Hollings 224pp

Fryberger, Betsy and others. *The William Morris work and essay book.* 1975 California: Stanford University Art Museum 135pp illus.

Grey, Lloyd Eric. *William Morris; prophet of England's new order.* 1949 London: Cassell 386pp

Henderson, Philip (ed). *William Morris: his life, work and friends.* 1967 London: Thames and Hudson 388pp illus.

Jackson, Holbrook. *William Morris, craftsman and socialist.* 1926 London: Cape 160pp (first edition 1908. University Microfilms Books in Demand 1970)

Jackson, Holbrook. *William Morris and the Arts and Crafts.* 1934 Berkeley, New Jersey: Oriole Press 17pp

Jordan, Robert Furneaux. *The Medieval vision of William Morris; a lecture, number 14, 1957 at the Victoria and Albert Museum.* 1960 London: William Morris Society 30pp

Lahor, Jean *pseud* (ie Henry Cazalis). *William Morris et le mouvement de l'art décoratif.* 1897 Geneva: Eggiman 73pp illus.

Mackail, J. W. 'William Morris', *JRIBA* series 3 vol 41 April 14 1934 pp 557-565

Macleod, Robert Duncan. *Morris without Mackail – as seen by his contemporaries.* 1954 Glasgow: W. & R. Holmes 23pp

Morris, May. *Introductions to the collected works of William Morris edited by J. R. Dunlop.* 1977 New York: Oriole Editions 2 vols 762pp illus.

Morris, May. *William Morris artist, writer, socialist.* 1936 Oxford: Blackwell 2 vols (includes a memoir by G. B. Shaw)

Mumford, Lewis. 'Polytechnic creativity', *JRIBA* October 1973 pp 481-486 illus.

Prouting, Norman. 'Morris and the Victorian revival', *Apollo* 7 1951 pp 17-21, 51-56 illus.

Roebuck, George Edmund (ed). *William Morris 1834 to 1934: some appreciations.* 1934 Walthamstow Antiquarian Society 36pp

Tames, Richard. *An illustrated life of William Morris 1834-1896.* 1972 Tring: Shire 47pp

Thiis, J. 'Engelsk stil og William Morris', *Nordenfjeldske Kunstindustrimuseums Arbog*, Trondheim 1900 pp 179-208

Thompson, Edward Palmer. *William Morris from Romantic to Revolutionary*. 1977 (revised edition) London: Merlin Press 850pp (first edition 1955)

Vidalenc, Georges. *William Morris*. 1920 Paris: F. Alcan 166pp illus.

Rigby, J. Scarrat. 'Remarks on Morris's work and its influence on British decorative arts of today', *Art Workers Quarterly* vol 1 1902 pp 3ff

William Morris. *Illustrated booklet of designs*. 1958 London: HMSO for Victoria and Albert Museum (small picture book no 43)

Bibliographies

So much has been and is being published on Morris that the best way to keep up to date is to study the publications of the William Morris Society and the collection at the William Morris Gallery, Walthamstow. Apart from the bibliographies in the larger studies already cited useful guides are:

William Morris Society. *A handlist of the public addresses of William Morris to be found in generally accessible publications (compiled by R. C. H. Briggs)*. 1961 London: Dolmen Press 16pp

Scott, Temple. *Bibliography of the works of William Morris*. 1897 London: Bell 120pp

Nash, Paul
1889-1946

See also:

Interior Design *page 147*

Textiles *page 184*

Nash, Paul. *Complete graphic work, edited by Alexander Postan*. 1973 London: Secker and Warburg 87pp 98 illus.

Paul Nash as designer. An exhibition catalogue by Susan Lambert. 1975 London: Victoria and Albert Museum

Nash, Paul. *Outline, an autobiography and other writings*. 1949 London: Faber 271pp

Paul Nash. An exhibition of applied design 1908-1942. 1943 London: Council for the Encouragement of Music and the Arts

Bertram, A. 'Paul Nash', *Architectural Review* vol 72 October 1932 pp 144-145

Bertram, Cyril Anthony George. *Paul Nash. The portrait of an artist*. 1955 London: Faber 336pp pl 32

Gaunt, William. 'Paul Nash, the man and his work', *Studio* vol 104 1932 pp 350-352 illus.

Omega Workshops and Fry, Roger Eliot
1866-1934

Exhibition of furniture, textiles and pottery made at the Omega Workshops 1913-1918 4-25 May 1946. Catalogue 1946 London: Victoria and Albert Museum, published by the Arts Council

Lipke, William C. 'The Omega Workshops and Vorticism', *Apollo* March 1970 pp 224-231 illus.

Pevsner, Nikolaus. 'Omega', (Roger Fry's Omega Workshops, industrial art enterprise 1913-1919), *Architectural Review* vol 90 August 1941 pp 45-48 illus.

Fry, Roger Eliot. *Vision and design*. 1957 (first edition 1920) London: Chatto and Windus 302pp illus.

Vision and design: the life, work and influence of Roger Fry, 1866-1934. Arranged by the Arts Council and the University of Nottingham. 1966 Nottingham: University of Nottingham

Ironside, J. 'Roger Fry: a summing up', *Architectural Review* vol 88 1940 pp 99-100

Bell, Quentin. *Roger Fry*. 1964 Leeds: University Press 20pp

Woolf, Virginia. *Roger Fry. A biography*. 1940 London: Hogarth Press 307pp illus.

Furniture, textiles and pottery made at the Omega Workshops 1913-1918 Lewes: Miller's Art Centre

Pugin, Augustus Welby Northmore
1812-1852

See also:

Furniture *page 173*

Interior Design: Churches *page 162*

Ornament *page 99*

Writings

Pugin, Augustus Welby Northmore. *An apology for the revival of Christian architecture in England*. 1843 London: J. Weale 51pp pl 9 (reprinted 1969 Oxford: St Barnabas Press)

Pugin, Augustus Welby Northmore. *Contrasts: a parallel between the Noble Edifices of the fourteenth and fifteenth centuries and similar buildings of the present day, shewing the present decay of taste*. 1836 London: the Author 50pp (reissued 1969 Leicester University Press)

Pugin, Augustus Welby Northmore.
*Floreated ornament: a series of thirty nine
designs.* 1849 London: Bohn 4pp pl
col 31

Studies

Ferrey, Benjamin. *Recollections of Pugin.
Introduction and index by Clive and Jane
Wainwright.* 1977 London: Scolar Press
552pp (first published 1861)

Stanton, Phoebe B. *Pugin.* 1971 London:
Thames and Hudson 216pp 169 illus.

Pevsner, Nikolaus (comp). 'A short Pugin
florilegium', *Architectural Review* vol 94
August 1943 pp 31-34 illus.

Bury, Shirley. 'Pugin and the Tractarians',
Connoisseur January 1972 pp 15-20

Clark, Alexander Gordon. 'A. W. N. Pugin',
pp 137-152 in Ferriday, Peter (ed).
Victorian architecture. 1963 London: Cape

Cornforth, J. 'Pugin revival at Westminster',
Country Life vol 160 November 11 1976
pp 1367-1371

Stanton, A. P. 'Some comments on the life
and work of Augustus Welby Northmore
Pugin', *JRIBA* vol LX December 1952
pp 47-54

Trappes-Lomax, Michael. *Pugin, a medieval
Victorian.* 1932 London: Sheed and
Ward 358pp illus.

Waterhouse, Paul. 'The life and work of
Welby Pugin', *Architectural Review* vol III
1898 pp 167-177 part 1, pp 211-221 part
2, pp 264-272 part 3. *Architectural Review*
vol IV 1898 pp 23-27 part 4, pp 67-72
part 5, pp 115-118 part 6, pp 159-165
part 7

Ruskin, John

1819-1900

Writings

Ruskin, John. *The complete works of John
Ruskin. Edited by E. T. Cook and A.
Wedderburn.* 1903-1912 London:
Longmans (reprinted in Microcards
Edition) 39 vols

Ruskin, John. *The diaries of John Ruskin
1848-1873. Edited by Joan Evans and John
Howard Whitehouse.* 1956 London: Oxford
University Press 3 vols

Ruskin, John. *Education in art, an address to
the National Association for the Promotion of
Social Science.* 1858 Oxford: J. W. Parker
(reprint from *Transactions of the National
Association for the Promotion of Social Science*
pp 311-316)

Ruskin, John. *The elements of drawing.* 1973
revised edition New York: Dover 228pp
51 illus. (first edition 1857)

Ruskin, John. *Elements of perspective, arranged
for the use of schools and intended to be read in
conexion with the first three books of Euclid.*
1859 London: Smith Elder 144pp

Ruskin, John. *Fors clavigera. Letters to the
workmen and labourers of Great Britain.*
1871-1887 Orpington 9 vols (other
editions 1883, 1896)

Ruskin, John. *General statement explaining the
nature and purposes of St George's Guild.*
1882 Orpington: George Allen 32pp

Ruskin, John. *The Guild of St George. Master's
report.* 1885 London: Guild of St George
8pp

Ruskin, John. *The nature of Gothic: a chapter
from 'The Stones of Venice', edited by William
Morris.* 1892 Kelmscott Press 80pp (ABC
Reprint 1977). (*Stones of Venice* first
published 1853)

Ruskin, John. *Seven lamps of architecture.*
1849 London: Smith Elder & Co 205pp

Ruskin, John. *Stones of Venice.* 1851-1853
London: Smith Elder & Co 3 vols (many
later editions)

Ruskin, John. *Ruskin today. Chosen and
annotated by Kenneth Clark.* 1964 London:
John Murray 362pp pl bibl.

Ruskin, John. *Two paths: being lectures on art
and its application to decoration and
manufacture, delivered in 1858-1859.* 1859
London: Smith Elder 271pp (contains
Modern Manufacture and Design. Many later
editions)

Studies

Bell, Quentin. *Ruskin.* 1978 (revised
edition) London: Chatto and Windus
144pp

Collingwood, William Gershon. *The art
teaching of John Ruskin.* 1891 London:
Percival 376pp

Cook, Edward. *Studies on Ruskin. Some aspects
of the work and teaching of John Ruskin.*
1972 Kennikat Press 334pp illus.

Cook, Sir Edward Tyas. *The life of John
Ruskin.* 1911 London: George Allen &
Co
2 vols

Earland, Ada. *Ruskin and his circle.* 1910
London: Hutchinson 340pp (reprinted
1972 AMS Press)

Harrison, Frederic. *John Ruskin.* 1902
London: Macmillan 216pp

Hewison, Robert. *John Ruskin: the argument
of the eye.* 1976 London: Thames and
Hudson 228pp illus.

Jolly, William. *Ruskin on education. Some
needed but neglected elements restated and
reviewed by W. Jolly.* 1894 London: G.
Allen 167pp

Ladd, Henry Andrews. *The Victorian morality of art. An analysis of Ruskin's ethics.* 1932 New York: Long and Smith Inc 418pp (analysis of Ruskin's aesthetics)

Landow, George P. *The aesthetic and critical theories of John Ruskin.* 1971 New Jersey: Princeton University Press 468pp

Leon, Derrick. *Ruskin, the great Victorian.* 1949 London: Routledge 595pp illus.

Mather, J. Marshall. *John Ruskin: his life and teaching.* 1897 London: Frederick Warne & Co 184pp (first edition 1883)

Penny, N. 'Ruskin's ideas on growth in architecture and ornament', *British Journal of Aesthetics* vol 13 no 3 Summer 1973 pp 276-286 bibl.

Pevsner, Nikolaus. *Ruskin and Viollet-Le-Duc.* 1970 London: Thames and Hudson 48pp illus. (Walter Neurath Memorial Lecture)

Rosenberg, John. *The darkening glass. A portrait of Ruskin's genius.* 1963 London: Routledge & Kegan Paul 287pp illus.

Sizeranne, Robert de la. *Ruskin et la Religion de Beauté.* 1901 Paris: Hachette 360pp

Spence, Margaret E. 'The Guild of St George: Ruskin's attempt to translate his ideas into practice', *Bulletin of the John Rylands Library* vol XL September 1957 pp 147-201

Wilenski, Reginald Howard. *John Ruskin. An introduction to the further study of his life and work.* 1933 London: Faber 406pp

Russell, Sydney Gordon
1892-

See also:

Council of Industrial Design *page 26*

Furniture *page 173*

Russell, Gordon. *Designer's trade. Autobiography of Gordon Russell.* 1968 London: Allen & Unwin 328pp illus.

Russell, Gordon. 'Taste in design', *Art and Industry* August 1944 pp 49-53

Hughes-Stanton, Corin. 'Gordon Russell today', *Design* 233 June 1968 pp 62-63

Pevsner, Nikolaus. 'Patient Progress Two: Gordon Russell', *Architectural Review* vol CXXXII 1962, republished in *Studies in art, architecture and design vol 2 Victorian and after.* 1968 London: Thames and Hudson pp 210-225

Pevsner, Nikolaus. 'Roots and branches. (Russell's development of industrial design)', *Design* 132 December 1959 pp 28-35

Boumphrey, Geoffrey. 'The designers. 2 Gordon Russell', *Architectural Review* vol 78 August 1935 pp 77-78

Sedding, John Dando
1838-1891

Sedding, John Dando. *Art and handicraft.* 1893 London: Kegan Paul, Trench, Trubner & Co 179pp (ABC Reprint)

Sedding, John Dando. *A memorial of the late J. D. Sedding, being illustrations from some of his work, compiled by the Architectural Association . . . with a short sketch of his life by H. Wilson.* 1892 London: Batsford 16pp

Cooper, J. P. 'The work of John Sedding, architect', *Architectural Review* vol III 1898 pp 35-41 part 1; pp 69-77 part 2; pp 125-133 part 3; pp 188-194 part 4; pp235-242 part 5; vol IV 1898 pp 33-36 part 6

Semper, Gottfried
1803-1879

Semper, Gottfried. *Der Stil in den technischen und tektonischen Künsten oder Praktische Asthetik. Ein Handbuch für Techniker, Künstler und Kunstfreunde von Gottfried Semper.* 1863 München (second edition) 2 vols (third volume never printed. Title translates as 'Style in the technical and tectonic arts, or a practical aesthetic')

Semper, Gottfried. *On the study of polychromy and its revival.* Museum of Classical Antiquities no III London July 1851

Semper, Gottfried. *Kleine Schriften (ed Manfred Hans Semper).* 1884 Berlin and Stuttgart: Spemann 516pp

Semper, Gottfried. *Wissenschaft, Industrie und Kunst. Vorschlage zur Anregung nationalen Kunstgefühles. Bei dem Schlüsse der Londoner Industrie-Austellung.* 1852 Braunschweig: F. Vieweg und Sohn 76pp

Ettlinger, L. D. 'On science, industry and art. Some theories of Gottfried Semper', *Architectural Review* vol CXXXVI 1964 pp 57-60

Fröhlich, Martin. *Gottfried Semper. Zeichnerischer Nachlass an der ETH Zürich Kritischer Katalog von Martin Fröhlich.* 1974 Basel und Stuttgart: Birkhauser Verlag 310pp illus. bibl.

Harvey, Lawrence. 'Semper's theory of evolution in architectural ornament', *Transactions RIBA* no 1 1885 pp 29

Gottfried Semper und die Mitte des 19 Jahrhunderts Symposium vom 2 bis 6 Dezember 1974 veranstaltet durch das Institut für Geschichte und Theorie der Architektur an der Erdgenössischen Technischen Hochschule Zürich. 1976 Basel und Stuttgart: Birkhauser Verlag 387pp (collection of papers, some in English. Includes Rykwert, Joseph. Semper and the conception of style pp 67-82)

Semper, H. *Gottfried Semper, ein Bild seines Lebens und Wirkens.* 1880 Berlin: Calvary 35pp

Stockmeyer, Ernst. *Gottfried Sempers Kunsttheorie.* 1939 Zürich und Leipzig: Glarus 91pp

Silver Studio

Darracott, Joseph. 'The Silver Studio collection and the history of design', *Connoisseur* vol 170 no 684 February 1969 pp 84-86

'A studio of design. An interview with Mr A. Silver', *Studio* vol iii 1898 pp 117-122

'End of the Silver Studio', *Country Life* vol CXL 1966 pp 1595-1596 illus.

Turner, Mark. 'The Silver Studio's contribution to British wallpaper design 1890-1930' pp 73-78, in Bishop T. (ed). *Design History: Fad or Function?* 1978 London: Design Council 102pp illus.

Stevens, Alfred

1817-1875

Beattie, Susan. *Alfred Stevens 1817-1875.* 1975 London: HMSO V & A exhibition catalogue

Armstrong, Walter. *Alfred Stevens. A biographical study.* 1881 London: Remington 47pp

MacColl, D. S. 'Alfred Stevens, sculptor, painter, architect', *JRSA* vol 78 February 28 1930 pp 428-436 illus.

Morris, Edward. 'Alfred Stevens and the School of Design', *Connoisseur* vol 190 no 763 September 1975 pp 3-11 illus.

Stannus, Hugh. *Alfred Stevens and his work: being a collection of 57 autotypes with a brief memoir and an account of his principal productions.* 1891 London: Autotype 39pp

Towndrow, Kenneth Romney. *Alfred Stevens, architectural sculptor, painter and designer. A biography with new material.* 1939 London: Constable 294pp pl 42

Voysey, Charles Francis Annesley

1857-1941

See also:

Wallpaper *page 207*

Interior Design *page 147*

'An interview with C. F. A. Voysey, architect and designer', *Studio* vol 1 1897 pp 231 ff

Voysey, Charles Francis Annesley. *Individuality.* (essays) 1915 London: Chapman and Hall 142pp

'Some recent designs by Mr C. F. A. Voysey', *Studio* vol 7 1896 pp 209-218 14 illus.

Voysey, Charles Francis Annesley. *Reason as a basis of art.* 1906 London: Elkin Mathews 29pp

Betjeman, John. 'C. F. Annesley Voysey, 1874 and after', *Architectural Review* vol LXX 1931 pp 91-96

Brandon-Jones, John. *C. F. A. Voysey: architect and designer, 1857-1941.* 1978 London: Lund Humphries

Brandon-Jones, John. 'C. F. A. Voysey', pp 267-288 in Ferriday, Peter (ed). *Victorian architecture.* 1963 London: Cape

Pevsner, Nikolaus. 'C. F. A. Voysey, translated by Caroline Doggart and revised by the author', in *Studies in art, architecture and design. Vol 2 Victorian and after.* 1968 London: Thames and Hudson pp 140-151 (first published *Elseviers Maandschrift* May 1940)

Pevsner, Nikolaus. 'Charles F. Annesley Voysey 1857-1941', *Architectural Review* vol 89 1941 pp 112-113 illus.

Gebhard, David. *Charles F. A. Voysey, architect.* 1975 Los Angeles: Hennessey and Ingalls 184pp illus. bibl.

Gebhard, David. *Charles F. A. Voysey.* 1970 Santa Barbara 75pp

Walton, George

1867-1933

Pevsner, Nikolaus. 'George Walton', *JRIBA* third series vol XLVI 1939, republished in *Studies in art, architecture and design vol 2 Victorian and after* 1968 London: Thames and Hudson pp 177-188

Webb, Philip Speakman

1831-1915

Lethaby, William Richard. *Philip Webb and his work.* 1935 London: Oxford University Press 234pp

Riley, Noel. 'Philip Webb and Standen'. *Antique Dealer and Collector's Guide* 1977 pp 76-79 illus.

Wyatt, Sir Matthew Digby
1820-1877

See also:

Great Exhibition 1851 *page 32*

Pottery *page 209*

Metalwork *page 226*

Illustration *page 127*

Exposition Universelle 1867 *page 39*

Textiles *page 184*

Wyatt, Sir Matthew Digby. *Fine art: a sketch of its history, theory, practice and application to industry; being a course of lectures delivered at Cambridge in 1870.* 1870 London: Macmillan 375pp

Wyatt, Sir Matthew Digby. *An attempt to define the principles which should determine form in the decorative arts. Read to the Society of Arts April 21 1852.* 1852 (lecture on the results of the Great Exhibition)

Pevsner, Nikolaus. *Matthew Digby Wyatt.* 1950 Cambridge University Press. Reprinted in *Studies in art, architecture and design vol 2 Victorian and after.* 1968 London: Thames and Hudson pp 96-107

Wyatt, Matthew. *Memoirs of T. H. Wyatt and Sir M. D. Wyatt, architects.* 1888 Basingstoke: private printing 32pp

Europe and elsewhere

The purpose of this section is to pick out
a few themes and areas of design activity
outside Britain that have excited interest
but cannot be effectively presented in
relation to more detailed studies
elsewhere. It is not intented as a
mini-encyclopaedia of world design
developments, but is deliberately very
selective since a lot of information relating
to things such as International Exhibitions
and French Interior Design is presented
elsewhere. Most periodicals are to be
found in the Journals section.

Austria

(particularly in the early twentieth century)

Holme, Charles (ed). *The Art Revival in
Austria*. 1906 London: Studio special
issue 56pp illus.

Powell, Nicholas. *The Sacred Spring: the arts
in Vienna 1898-1918*. 1974 London:
Studio Vista 224pp illus.

Eisler, Georg. 'Achievements of the Vienna
Secession', *Apollo* January 1971 pp 44-51

Art and Design in Vienna 1900-1930. 1972
Paris: La Boetie in association with Robert
K. Brown

Levetus, A. S. 'Arts and Crafts at the
Austrian Museum for Art and Industry,
Vienna', *Studio* vol 55 1912 pp 28-38

Levetus, A. S. 'A Viennese exhibition of
Arts and Crafts', *Studio* vol 57 1913
pp 217-226

The Wiener Werkstätte:

*Die Wiener Werkstätte, modernes
Kunsthandwerk von 1903-1932. Ausstellung
des Bundesministeriums für Unterricht 22
Mai bis 20 August 1967*. 1967 Vienna:
Oesterreichisches Museum fur
Angewandte Kunst 100pp illus.

Flögl, Mathilde (ed) *Die Wiener Werkstätte
1903-1928. Modernes Kunstgewerbe.*
1929 Vienna: Krystall illus.

Levetus, A. S. 'The "Wiener Werkstätte",
Vienna', *Studio* vol 52 1911 pp 187-196

A few individuals:

Levetus, A. S. 'An Austrian decorative artist:
Koloman Moser', *Studio* vol 33 1905
pp 111-117

Designs of Josef Hoffmann. 1977 London:
Fischer Fine Art

Khnopff, Fernand. 'Josef Hoffmann.
Architect and decorator', *Studio* vol 22
1901 pp 261-266

*Josef Hoffmann mit einer Einleitung von Leopold
Kleiner*. 1927 Berlin: F. E. Hubsch 90pp
illus.

Hoffmann, Josef. 'Rebirth of design in
craftmanship', *Studio* vol 105 1933
pp 240-245

Shand, P. Morton. 'Josef Hoffmann', *DIA
Quarterly* 14 January 1931 pp 9-11

*Joseph Maria Olbrich. Die Zeichnungen in der
Kunstbibliothek Berlin. Kritischer Katalog . . .
Karl Heinz Schreyl*. 1972 Berlin: Gebruder
Mann 360pp illus.

*Joseph M. Olbrich 1867-1908; das Werk des
Architekten (Exhibition catalogue)*. 1967
Darmstadt: Hessischen Landesmuseum
353pp illus.

Loos, Adolf. *Die Schriften von Adolf Loos –
vol 1: Ins Leere gesprochen 1897-1900, vol 2:
Trotzdem 1900-1930*. 1931-1932
Innsbruck: Brenner Verlag 222pp,
257pp

Münz, Ludwig and Künstler, Gustav. *Der
Architekt Adolf Loos*. 1964 Vienna: Verlag
Anton Schroll 200pp illus. bibl.
(Translation by Harold Meck published
1966 by Praeger)

Worbs, D. 'Adolf Loos in Vienna; aesthetics
as a function of retail trade
establishments', *Architects Yearbook* 14
1974 pp 181-196

Levetus, A. S. 'Otto Prutscher: a young
Viennese designer of interiors', *Studio*
vol 37 1906 pp 33-41

Henry van de Velde

Schrijver, Elke. 'Henry van de Velde
1863-1957', *Apollo* February 1965
pp 110-115

*Henry van de Velde 1863-1957. Persönlichkeit
und Werk*. 1958 Zurich:
Kunstgewerbemuseum illus.
(Chadwyck-Healey Microfilm)

*Henry van de Velde zum 100 Geburtstag.
Ausstellung 19 Oktober bis 24 November
1963*. 1963 Stuttgart: Württembergischer
Kunstverein 53pp illus.

Henry van de Velde. Extracts from his
memoirs 1891-1901, introduced and
translated by P. Morton Shand',
Architectural Review vol 112 September
1952 pp 143-155

Van de Velde, Henry. *Essays*. 1910 Leipzig:

Hammacher, Abraham Marie. *Die Welt
Henry van de Velde*. 1967 Köln: Dumont
Schauberg 354pp illus. bibl.

Hüter, Karl-Heinz. *Henry van de Velde*.
1967 Berlin: Akademie Verlag

Staber, Margit. '100 Jahre Henry van de
Velde', *Form* 21 March 1963 pp 2-7

Baudin, Fernand. 'Henry van de Velde and book design', *Penrose Annual* vol 65 1972 pp 117-132

see also Art Nouveau

Germany

Late nineteenth century:

Hansen, Hans Jurgen (ed). *Late nineteenth century art; the art, architecture and applied art of the 'Pompous age', translated by Marcus Bullock.* 1972 New York: McGraw Hill 264pp illus. bibl. (first published 1961 *Das Pompöse Zeitalter*)

Deutscher Werkbund

Eckstein, Hans (ed). *50 Jahre Deutscher Werkbund.* 1958 Frankfurt/Main Metzner 57pp pl 64 (includes contributions by Theodor Heuss, Henry van de Velde, Richard Riemerschmid, Hermann Muthesius)

Posener, Julius. *Anfänge des Funktionalismus. Von Arts and Crafts zum Deutschen Werkbund.* 1964 Berlin: Ullstein 231pp 49 illus.

Benton, Tim and others. 'Part 6 Industry, the Werkbund and German design from the machine', in *Europe 1900-1914. The reaction to historicism and Art Nouveau.* 1975 Milton Keynes: Open University Press (History of Architecture and Design 1890-1939 units 5-6)

Jahrbuch des Deutschen Werkbundes:

1912 Die Durchgeistigung der Deutschen Arbeit

1913 Die Kunst in Industrie und Handel

1914 Verkehr

1915 Deutsche Form in Kriegsjahr. Die Ausstellung Köln 1914 Munich: Bruckmann

Interwar period;

Die Form: Monatsschrift für gestaltende Arbeit vol 1-10 no 7 October 1925-January 1935 Berlin: Reckendorf

Schwarz, Felix and Gloor, Frank (comps). *Die Form. Stimme des Deutschen Werkbundes 1925-1934.* 1969 Gütersloh: Bertelsmann Fachverlag 357pp illus.

Pfleiderer, Wolfgang. *Die Form ohne Ornament: Werkbundausstellung 1924.* 1924 Stuttgart: Deutsche Verlagsanstalt 89pp pl 172

Kropp, Ernst. *Wandlungen der Form in XX Jahrhundert, dem Deutscher Werkbund gewidmet.* 1926 Berlin: Reckendorf 48pp pl 80

Kollman, Franz. *Schönheit der Technik.* 1928 Munich: Langen 251pp illus. bibl.

Section allemande, exposition de la société des artistes décorateurs, Grand Palais 14 mai-13 juillet (by H. Bayer). 1930 Berlin: Reckendorf

Weissenhofsiedlung exhibition 1927

Joedicke, Jurgen and Plath, Christian. *Die Weissenhofsiedlung.* 1968 Stuttgart: Karl Kramer 60pp illus. bibl.

Bau und Wohnung: die Bauten der Weissenhofsiedlung in Stuttgart errichtet 1927 nach Vorschlagen des Deutschen Werkbundes im Auftrag der Stadt Stuttgart und im Rahmen der Werkbundausstellung 'Die Wohnung' herausgegeben vom Deutschen Werkbund. 1927 Stuttgart: Wedekind 152pp illus. plans

Innenraume: Raume und Inneneinrichtungsgegenstände aus der Werkbundausstellung 'Die Wohnung', insbesondere aus dem Bauten der Städtischen Weissenhofsiedlung in Stuttgart. Herausgegeben im Auftrage des Deutschen Werkbundes von Werner Gräff. 1928 Stuttgart: Wedekind 168pp illus. (Text by Le Corbusier and others)

Special issues devoted to Weissenhofsiedlung:

L'Architecture Vivante 1928 (Spring and Summer issues)

Cahiers d'Art vol 2 no 7-8 pp 287-292

Bassett Lowke, W. J. 'A wonderful experiment at Stuttgart', *DIA Quarterly* no 2 December 1927 pp 8-10

Hilberseimer, Ludwig (ed). *Internationale neue Baukunst. Im Auftrag des Deutschen Werkbundes.* 1928 Stuttgart: Julius Hoffman

Lotz, Wilhelm. *Licht und Beleuchtung: lichttechnische Fragen unter berücksichtigung der Bedurfnisse der Architektur.* 1928 Berlin: Reckendorf 60pp pl 79

Deutsche Werkstätten

60 Jahre Deutsche Werkstätten. Deutsche Werkstatten 1898-1958 (text by Herbert Hoffmann). 1958 Munich: Deutsche Werkstatten 24pp 32 illus.

Koch, Alexander. *Das neue Kunsthandwerk in Deutschland und Oesterreich,* 1923 Darmstadt: Koch 263pp 384 illus.

European Arts and Crafts Exhibition, Leipzig 1927

Europäisches Kunstgewerbe; Berichte über die Ausstellung Europäisches Kunstgewerbe 1927 von M. R. J. Brinkgren. 1928 Leipzig: E. A. Seemann 85pp pl 112

Peach, H. H. 'The European arts and crafts exhibition at Leipzig', *Architectural Review* vol 61 May 1927 pp 200-202

Bauhaus

One of the most fully documented areas of design history still yielding many research possibilities. A few introductory works:

Wingler, Hans Maria. _The Bauhaus – Weimar, Dessau, Berlin, Chicago, translated from the German by W. Jabs and B. Gilbert._ 1969 Cambridge, Mass: MIT Press 653pp illus. bibl. (the fullest and certainly the largest single volume)

Naylor, Gillian. _The Bauhaus._ 1968 London: Studio Vista 160pp illus.

Benton, Tim. 'Background to the Bauhaus', pp 26-41 in Faulkner, T. (ed). _Design 1900-1960._ 1976 Newcastle Polytechnic

Hirschfeld-Mack, Ludwig. _The Bauhaus. An introductory survey._ 1963 London: Longmans 54pp

Adams, George. '1919 + 50 = 1969', _Decorative Art in Modern Interiors_ vol 59 1969 pp 7-10

Gaunt, William. 'The remarkable story of the Bauhaus', _Connoisseur_ vol 169 November 1968 pp 157-161

Richards, J. M. 'The Bauhaus in retrospect', _Design_ 237 September 1968 pp 44-47

Wingler, Hans M. (ed). _Graphic work from the Bauhaus, translated from the German by Gerald Onn._ 1969 London: Lund Humphries 168pp illus. (first published as _Die Mappenwerke Neue Europäische Graphik_)

Weimar phase:

Franciscono, Marcel. _Walter Gropius and the creation of the Bauhaus in Wiemar: the ideals and artistic theories of its founding years._ 1971 Urbana: University of Illinois Press 320pp illus.

Scheidig, Walther. _Crafts of the Weimar Bauhaus 1919-1924: an early experiment in industrial design. Photos by Klaus G. Beyer._ 1967 London: Studio Vista 150pp illus. bibl. (translation of _Bauhaus Weimar 1919-1924_)

Benton, Tim. 'The Weimar Bauhaus Part 4', pp 53-65 in Benton, Tim _The New Objectivity._ 1975 Milton Keynes: Open University Press (History of Architecture and Design 1890-1939 Units 11-12)

Von Erffa, Helmut. 'Bauhaus: first phase', _Architectural Review_ vol 122 August 1957 pp 103-105

Necker, W. F. 'Bauhaus '23-'24', _Architectural Review_ vol 134 September 1963 pp 157-159

Dessau:

The Bauhaus Journal – Bauhaus: Zeitschrift für Gestaltung nos 1-15 1926-1931 (facsimile reprint 1976 Art Book Company. List of contents and index in Wingler, H. M. _Bauhaus_ pp 628-631)

Benton, Tim. 'German design and the Bauhaus 1925-1932', pp 7-49 in Benton, Tim and Charlotte. _Design 1920s._ 1975 Milton Keynes: Open University Press (History of Architecture and Design 1890-1939 Units 15-16)

Suschitsky, Edith. 'University of commercial art', _Commercial Art_ March 1931 pp 113-114

Besides these there are the Bauhausbücher and many other publications detailed in Wingler's book and shown in exhibitions since:

50 years Bauhaus. Catalogue of an exhibition mounted by the Württembergischer Kunstverein Stuttgart and shown at the Royal Academy London. 1968 London: Royal Academy 363pp illus.

Bauhaus 1919-1928, edited by Herbert Bayer, Walter Gropius, Ise Gropius. 1976 London: Secker and Warburg 224pp 550 illus. (first published 1938 by Museum of Modern Art, New York to accompany exhibition)

Concepts of the Bauhaus: the Busch-Reisinger Museum collection. 1971 Cambridge, Mass: Busch-Reisinger Museum 136pp

Bauhaus-Archiv: Arbeiten aus der Graphischen Drückerei des Staatlichen Bauhaus in Weimar 1919-1925. 1963 Darmstadt: Mathildenhöhe 35pp

Memories:

Neumann, Eckhard (ed). _Bauhaus and Bauhaus people. Personal opinions and recollections of former Bauhaus members and their contemporaries._ 1970 New York: Van Nostrand Reinhold 256pp illus.

Adams, George. 'Memories of a Bauhaus student', _Architectural Review_ vol 144 September 1968 pp 192-194

Post-war developments

Werk und Zeit: Monatszeitung des Deutschen Werkbundes vol 1 no 1. 1952 Berlin

König, Heinrich. 'Industrielle Formentwicklung in Deutschland' pp 100-122 in Thiele, E. _Die situation der bildenden Kunst in Deutschland._ 1954 Stuttgart-Koln illus. bibl.

Made in Germany. Produktform. Industrial Design. Forme Industrielle. 1966 Munich: Peter Winkler Verlag 274pp illus. (text in English, German, French 'a brief survey of industrial production in Germany during the seventh decade of the twentieth century')

Some important individual designers

BAYER

Bayer, Herbert. *Printer, designer, architect.* 1967 London: Studio Vista 211pp illus. bibl.

BEHRENS

Peter Behrens (1868-1940). Gedenkschrift mit Katalog aus Anlass der Ausstellung. 1966-1967 Kaiserlautern: Pfalzgalerie 107pp illus. bibl.

'Numero dedicato a Peter Behrens', *Casabella* no 240 Giugno 1960 pp 3-55 (includes bibliography)

Cremers, Paul Joseph. *Peter Behrens: sein Werk von 1909 bis zur Gegenwart.* 1928 Essen: G. D. Baedeker 168pp illus.

BREUER

Breuer, Marcel. *Marcel Breuer: new buildings and projects 1960-1970 and work in retrospect 1921-1960 by Tician Papachristou.* 1970 London: Thames and Hudson 240pp

Breuer, Marcel. *Buildings and projects 1921-1961.* 1962 London: Thames and Hudson 262pp

Breuer, Marcel. *Marcel Breuer: sun and shadow. The philosophy of an architect. Editing and notes by Peter Blake.* 1956 New York: Longmans Green 205pp

Breuer, Marcel. 'Where do we stand', *Architectural Review* vol 77 1937 pp 133 ff

Blake, Peter. *M. Breuer architect and designer.* 1949 New York: Museum of Modern Art 128pp

Argan, Guilio Carlo. *Marcel Breuer, disegno industriale ed architettura.* 1957 Milan: Goerlich 123pp illus. bibl. (text in Italian and English)

GROPIUS

Giedion, Siegfried. *Walter Gropius: work and teamwork, translated by Jacqueline Tyrwhitt.* 1954 London: Architectural Press 249pp illus.

Gropius, Walter. 'Education toward creative design', *American Architect* May 1937 pp 26-30

Gropius, Walter. *New architecture and the Bauhaus, translated by P. Morton Shand.* 1935 London: Faber 80pp illus.

Gropius, Walter. 'Bauhaus', *JRIBA* May 19 1934

Herbert, Gilbert. *The synthetic vision of Walter Gropius.* 1959 Johannesburg: Witwatersrand University Press 57pp (University Microfilms)

Pritchard, Jack. 'Gropius, the Bauhaus and the future', *JRSA* vol 117 January 1969 pp 75-94

ITTEN

Itten, Johannes. *Design and form: the basic course at the Bauhaus.* 1975 (revised edition) London: Thames and Hudson 136pp illus.

KLEE

Klee, Paul. *Pedagogical sketchbook.* 1968 London: Faber 64pp 90 illus.

MEYER

Schnaidt, Claude. *Hannes Mayer.* 1965 London: Academy Editions 124pp 98 illus.

MIES VAN DER ROHE

Blaser, Werner. *Mies van der Rohe: the art of structure (English version by D. Q. Stephenson).* 1965 London: Thames and Hudson 226pp illus.

Drexler, Arthur. *Mies van der Rohe.* 1960 London: Mayflower 127pp illus. bibl.

Hilbersheimer, Ludwig. *Mies van der Rohe.* 1956 Chicago: Paul Theobald 200pp illus.

Johnson, Philip C. *Mies van der Rohe.* 1953 (second edition) New York: Museum of Modern Art 215pp illus. bibl. (first edition 1947)

MOHOLY-NAGY

Kostelanetz, Richard. *Laszlo Moholy-Nagy.* 1970 London: Allen Lane 238pp illus.

Moholy-Nagy, Laszlo. *Painting, photography, film, translated by Janet Seligman.* 1969 London: Lund Humphries 152pp illus.

Moholy-Nagy, Sibyl. *Moholy-Nagy: experiment in totality.* 1971 (second edition) Cambridge, Mass: MIT Press 288pp illus. (first edition 1950)

Moholy-Nagy, Laszlo. *The new vision and abstract of an artist.* 1967 New York: Wittenborn 92pp illus. (based on fourth revised edition of 1947)

SCHAROUN

Jones, Peter Blundell. *Hans Scharoun.* 1978 London: Gordon Fraser 128pp 260 illus.

SCHLEMMER

Oskar Schlemmer und die abstrakte Bühne. 1961 Zürich: Kunstgewerbemuseum 53 illus. (Chadwyck-Healey microfiche)

WAGENFELD

Du Bauhaus à l'industrie: Wilhelm Wagenfeld, objets quotidiens. 1973 Köln: Kunstgewerbemuseum

Wilhelm Wagenfeld: 50 Jahre Mitarbeit in Fabriken. 1973 Köln: Kunstgewerbemuseum

Brunhammer, Yvonne. 'Wilhelm Wagenfeld du Bauhaus à l'industrie', *L'Oeil* 238 May 1975 pp 62-67

*Wilhelm Wagenfeld: 30 Jahre künstlerische
Mitarbeit in der Industrie.* 1961 Munich:
Neue Sammlung illus.

Italy

Ambasz, Emilio (ed). *Italy: the new domestic
landscape; achievements and problems of
Italian design.* 1972 New York: Museum
of Modern Art distributed by New York
Graphic Society 430pp illus. bibl.

Bo, Lina and Pagani, Carlo (ed). *Quaderni
de Domus.* 1945- Milan: Domus

Pica, Agnoldomenico and others. *Forme
Nuova in Italia.* 1957 Rome: Bestetti
218pp illus. (text and captions in
English)

*Modern Italian design (presented by) Compagnia
Nazionale Artigiana.* 1956 Manchester City
Art Gallery

Ottagono. Rivista trimestrale di architettura
arredamento e industrial design no 1
April 1966- Milan: Co.P.In.A.
(Chadwyck-Healey microfiche 1974 issues
include four articles by Gregotti, Vittorio.
'For a history of Italian design')

See also:
Journals *page 284*

Japan

Nineteenth-century interest:

Moser, David H. *Japanese ornamentation: for
the use of sign painters, decorators, silversmiths
etc.* 1880 New York: Honey pl 11

Audsley, George Ashdown. *The ornamental
arts of Japan.* 1882-1885 London:
Sampson Low, Searle and Rivington
2 vols

Morse, Edward Sylvester. *Japanese houses and
their surroundings.* 1885 London:
Trübner 372pp illus.

Liberty, Sir Arthur Lazenby. *The industrial
arts and manufactures of Japan.* 1891
London 13pp (reprinted from *Artistic
Japan*)

Hart, Ernest. 'Japanese art industries', *JSA*
vol 43 September 13 1895 pp 869-876,
881-885

See also:
Dresser *page 77*

Later:

*Official report of the Japan British exhibition
1910 at the Great White City, Shepherd's
Bush, London.* 1911 London: Unwin
Brothers 551pp illus.

Yamamoto, Hisaci. 'Japan industrial design
renaissance', *Design* 130 October 1959
pp 52-56 (post-war developments)

Gerrit Rietveld

Brown, Theodore M. *The work of G. Rietveld
architect.* 1958 Utrecht: Bruna and Zoon
198pp illus.

G. Rietveld, architect. 1972 London: Arts
Council illus.

Wilson, Colin St. John. 'Gerrit Rietveld
1888-1964', *Architectural Review* vol 136
December 1964 pp 399-402

De Stijl

De Stijl vol 1 1917-1920, vol 2 1921-1932.
1968 Amsterdam: Atheneum (complete
reprint of magazine)

Jaffé, Hans Ludwig C. *De Stijl 1917-1931:
the Dutch contribution to modern art.* 1956
London: Tiranti 293pp pl 48 (later
paperback editions)

De Stijl. 1951 Amsterdam: Stedelijk
Museum

Mondrian, De Stijl and their impact. 1964 New
York: Marlborough-Gerson Gallery
54 illus. (Chadwyck Healey microfiche)

De Stijl. 1968 London: Camden Arts Centre

Housden, Brian. 'De Stijl: the other face of
tradition', *Design* 231 March 1968
pp 26-31

Overy, Paul. *De Stijl.* 1969 London: Studio
Vista 168pp illus.

Van Doesburg, Theo. *Principles of neoplastic
art, translated from the German by J.
Seligman.* 1969 London: Lund
Humphries 84pp illus. (translation with
texts by H. M. Wingler and H. L. C. Jaffé
of *Grundbegriffe der Neuen gestaltenden
Kunst. Bauhausbuch 6,* 1925)

Benton, Tim. 'Part 1 Dutch architecture and
De Stijl', 'Part 3 De Stijl after 1921 and
Elementarism', pp 8-31, 42-52 in Benton,
Tim *The New Objectivity.* 1975 Milton
Keynes: Open University Press (History
of Architecture and Design 1890-1939
Units 11-12)

Scandinavia

A few general works:

Scandinavian design. 1974 Jerusalem: Israel
Museum 52pp (includes brief history of
industrial design in Scandinavia)

Zahle, Erik (ed). *Scandinavian domestic
design.* 1963 London: Methuen 300pp
illus.

*Design from Scandinavia: Scandinavian
production in furniture, textiles, illumination,
arts and crafts and industrial design.* 1966 –
Copenhagen: World Pictures A-S illus.
(text in English/French/German)

Design in Scandinavia, Finland, Norway and Sweden. 1954 Oslo: Kirstes Boktr. 125pp illus.

Denmark

Two centuries of Danish design. 1968 London: Victoria and Albert Museum

Danish domestic design. 1946/1947 London: Arts Council

Rasmussen, S. E. 'Modern Danish design', *JRSA* vol 96 January 30 1948 pp 138-145

'Denmark – special issue', *Architectural Review* vol 109 November 1948

Contemporary Danish design: exhibition arranged by the permanent exhibition of Danish arts and crafts, the Danish Society of Arts and Crafts and Industrial Design (and) the Danish Institute. 1960 London: Arts Council

Norway

Vreim, Halvar. *Norwegian decorative art today.* 1937 Oslo: Fabritius and Sonner 91pp illus.

See also:
Journals *page 284*

Finland

'Finland reaches her fifty', *Design* 226 October 1967 pp 35-44 (series of articles)

Sjöman, Bror (ed). *Designed in Finland.* 1961 Helsinki: Finnish Foreign Trade Association 52pp illus. (later editions)

Finlandia: modern Finnish design (organised by the Finnish Society of Crafts and Design). 1961-1962 London: Victoria and Albert Museum

The Ornamo book of Finnish design. 1963 Helsinki: Finnish Society of Crafts and Design/Tiranti (includes a historical survey)

Reilly, Paul. 'Report from Finland', *Design* 38 February 1952 pp 4-9

Hård af Segerstad, Ulf. *Modern Finnish design.* 1969 London: Weidenfeld and Nicolson 62pp pl 64

ALVAR AALTO

Fleig, Karl (ed). *Alvar Aalto.* 1963 London: Pall Mall Press

Fleig, Karl (ed). *Alvar Aalto vol 2 1963-1970.* 1971 London: Pall Mall Press 248pp illus.

Giedion, Sigfried. 'Alvar Aalto', *Architectural Review* vol 107 February 1950 pp 77-84

Labo, Giorgio. *Alvar Aalto.* 1948 Milan: Balcone 157pp illus.

Gutheim, Frederick Albert. *Alvar Aalto.* 1968 London: Mayflower 128pp illus.

Möbel aus Holz und Stahl: Alvar Aalto, Mies van der Rohe. 1957 Basel: Kunstgewerbemuseum (exhibition catalogue)

EERO SAARINEN

Spade, Rupert. *Eero Saarinen.* 1971 London: Thames and Hudson 130pp

Saarinen, Eero. *Eero Saarinen on his work*, edited by A. B. Saarinen. 1968 (second edition) New Haven: Yale University Press 117pp

Sweden

Useful general introductions:

Lindkvist, Lennart (ed). *Design in Sweden.* 1972 Stockholm: Svenska Institutet 144pp illus. (current trends with brief history since 1917)

Paulsson, Gregor. 'During 100 years' *Form* no 1 1945 pp 3-7 (Swedish industrial art and Stockholm exhibitions)

Wettergren, Erik. *The modern decorative arts of Sweden.* 1927 London: Country Life 207pp illus.

Surveys of more particular periods:

Bröchner, Georg. 'The exhibition of Swedish applied art at Stockholm', *Studio* vol 47 1909 pp 202-216

Wettergren, Erik. 'Applied art in Sweden', *Studio Yearbook* 1921 pp 107-122

Paulsson, Gregor. *Swedish contemporary decorative arts.* 1927 New York: Gilliss Press for Metropolitan Museum of Art 8pp

Wollin, Nils Gustaf Axelsson. *Modern Swedish decorative art.* 1931 London: Architectural Press 30pp pl 207

Swedish industrial art. 1931 London: Dorland Hall

'Swedish exhibition of industrial arts and crafts, London 1931', *Studio* vol 101 1931 pp 290-291

Biggs, E. J. 'Art and mass production in Sweden', *Studio* vol 106 1933 pp 305-308

Stavenow, Ake (ed). *Swedish modern – Swedish arts and crafts – a movement towards sanity in design.* 1939 New York: Royal Swedish Commission, New York World's Fair

Yerbury, F. R. 'Design in everyday things in Sweden', *Art and Industry* March 1944 pp 80-84

Plath, Iona. *The decorative arts of Sweden.* 1948 London: Scribners 246pp illus.

Hald, Arthur and Skawonius, Sven Erik. *Contemporary Swedish design. A survey in pictures.* 1951 Stockholm: Nordisk Rotogravyr 179pp illus.

Svensk Form – God Form. Exhibition at the Design Centre. 1961 Stockholm: Svensk Form 64pp illus.

Perhaps the event to excite most interest was the Stockholm Exhibition of 1930:

'Living shipshape – the lesson of the Stockholm Exhibition', *Studio* vol 100 1930 pp 164-181

'Special Sweden number', *DIA Quarterly* July 1930

Shand, P. Morton. 'Stockholm 1930', *Architectural Review* August 1930 pp 67-72

Paulsson, Gregor. 'White industry' (with pictorial supplement), *Architectural Review* vol 69 1931 pp 78-100

Paulsson, Gregor. *Design and mass production* 11pp supplement to *DIA Quarterly* September 1931

Shand, P. Morton. 'E. Gunnar Asplund. A tribute to the famous Swedish architect . . . with special reference to his work at the Stockholm Exhibition, 1930', *Architectural Review* vol 90 1941 pp 99-102

Paulsson, G. 'The exhibition 1930, its jubilee', *Form* no 5 1940 pp 89-100

'H55 (Hälsingborg)', *Architectural Review* vol 118 October 1955 pp 222-236 (celebration of developments since 1930 in a special exhibition held in Hälsingborg)

See also:
Journals *page 284*

United States of America

The history of design in the USA is touched on in a general way in many of the works cited in the Chronological Studies section. Curiously there is no effective summary to act as a sequel to:

Dunlap, William. *History of the rise and progress of the arts of design in the United States. Notes and additions by Frank W. Bayley and Chalres D. Goodspeed.* 1964 New York: B. Blom 3 vols 1325pp (mid 18th century to 1834)

There is a rather elderly study in:

Cheney, Sheldon and Cheney, Martha Candler. *Art and the machine. An account of industrial design in 20th century America.* 1936 New York: McGraw Hill 307pp illus.

Many of the most accessible studies relate to smaller time spans:

Bing, Samuel. *La culture artistique en Amérique.* 1896 Paris: 121pp (University Microfilms)

Frankl, Paul Theodore. *Machine made leisure.* 1932 New York: Harper 192pp illus.

Kahn, Ely Jacques. *Design in art and industry.* 1935 New York: Scribner 204pp illus. (international interest)

'Portfolio of industrial design', *Architectural Record* 77 April 1935 pp 235-242

Bush, Donald, J. *The streamlined decade.* 1975 New York: Braziller 214pp illus. bibl. (1927 to World War Two)

'Design decade', *Architectural Forum* October 1940 (special issue)

Conference on industrial design, a new profession. Museum of Modern Art, New York 1946 Minutes. 1947 New York: Society of Industrial Designers 77pp

'Design review. A design exhibition' (Design for use at the Museum of Modern Art), *Architectural Review* vol 104 May 1948 pp 88-92 (especially streamlining)

'Design review. Borax, or the chromium-plated calf by Edgar Kaufmann', *Architectural Review* vol 104 May 1948 pp 88-92 (especially streamlining)

'Design review. Counter-Borax', *Architectural Review* vol 104 December 1948 pp 300-401

Industrial design in the United States. Project no 278. 1959 Paris: Organization for European Economic Cooperation 140pp illus. (reports of 26 experts after 6 weeks visit in 1955)

Christensen, Erwin Ottomar. *The index of American design.* 1959 New York: Macmillan-Smithsonian 229pp (first edition 1951)

'America – special issue', Design 193 March 1964 (includes Caplan, Ralph. 'Background to the ID idea' pp 21-31)

Wurman, Richard Saul and Chermayeff, Ivan. *The design necessity: a casebook of federally initiated projects in visual communications, interiors and industrial design, architecture, landscaped environment.* 1963 Cambridge, Mass: MIT Press 80pp (for first Federal Design Assembly)

There is a great deal of other more detailed material, some of which is presented in Karpel's bibliography, but there is scope for a much more detailed listing, particularly of exhibitions that provide a concise introduction, eg:

19th century America: furniture and other decorative arts: an exhibition in celebration of the hundredth anniversary of the Metropolitan Museum. 1970 New York: Metropolitan Museum 260pp illus. bibl.

Machine art. March 6 to April 30 1934. 1934 New York: Museum of Modern Art (Arno Reprint 1969)

An American Museum of Decorative Art and Design: designs from the Cooper-Hewitt collection, New York. Exhibition June-August 1973 at the Victoria and Albert Museum. 1973 London: Arts Council

Studies of individual designers often provide the most convenient points of approach to this exceptionally rich and complex subject.

DESKEY

Deskey, Donald. 'The rise of American architecture and design', *Studio* vol 105 1933 pp 266-273

DREYFUSS

Dreyfuss, Henry. *Designing for people.* 1955 New York: Simon and Schuster 240pp illus. (autobiography)

Dreyfuss, Henry. *Industrial design.* 1939-1957 New York: Dreyfuss 4 parts: *vol 1. 10 years of industrial design; Henry Dreyfuss 1929-1939 vol 2. A record of industrial designs 1929 through 1947 vol 3. Industrial design, a progress report 1929-1952 vol 4. Industrial design, a pictorial accounting 1929-1957*

Dreyfuss, Henry. 'The industrial designer as consultant', *Art and Industry* September 1944 pp 75-79

EAMES

Drexler, Arthur. *Charles Eames; furniture from the Design collection, the Museum of Modern Art.* 1973 New York: Museum of Modern Art 56pp illus.

FULLER

Meller, James (ed). *The Buckminster Fuller reader.* 1969 London: Cape 383pp illus.

Marks, Robert W. *The Dymaxion world of Buckminster Fuller.* 1960 New York: Reinhold 232pp illus.

Dymaxion index: bibliography and published items regarding Dymaxion and Richard Buckminster Fuller 1927-1953. 1953 Forest Hills, New York: Fuller Research Foundation 64pp

McHale, John. 'Buckminster Fuller', *Architectural Review* vol 120 July 1956 pp 12-20

Fuller, Richard Buckminster. *4D Time Lock.* 1970 New York: Lama Foundation

GEDDES

Geddes, Norman Bel. *Horizons (on design in machines and objects of common use. With illustrations from designs by the author and others).* 1934 London: John Lane 293pp illus. (1977 Constable reprint)

Benton, Tim. 'Design case study: Norman Bel Geddes' pp 21-27 in *Introduction.* 1975 Milton Keynes: Open University

Press (History of Architecture and Design 1890-1939 Units 1-2)

LOEWY

Loewy, Raymond. *Never leave well enough alone (the personal record of an industrial designer).* 1951 New York: Simon and Schuster 377pp illus.

Loewy, Raymond. 'Selling through design', *JRSA* vol 90 January 1942 pp 92-103

Loewy, Raymond. 'Selling through design', *Art and Industry* February 1942 pp 32-40

Designs of Raymond Loewy. 1975 Washington: Smithsonian

Loewy, Raymond. *The locomotive: its esthetics.* 1937 London: Studio 108pp illus.

Bouverie, David Pleydell and Davis, Alec. 'Popular art organized: the manner and methods of Raymond Loewy Associated', *Architectural Review* vol 110 November 1951 pp 319-326

Clarke, C. F. O. 'Raymond Loewy Associated; modern industrial designing', *Graphis* vol 1 no 13 January-February 1946 pp 94-97

NEUTRA

Neutra, Richard. *Survival through design.* 1970 New York: Oxford University Press 400pp illus. (first edition 1954)

TEAGUE

Teague, Walter Dorwin. *Design this day, the technique of order in the machine age.* 1940 New York: Harcourt Brace 237pp pl 128 (later edition 1947 London: Studio)

Teague, Walter Dorwin. 'Growth and scope of industrial design in the United States' (Trueman Wood lecture), *JRSA* vol 107 1959 pp 640 ff

Teague, Walter Dorwin. 'A quarter century of industrial design in the United States', *Art and Industry* November 1951 pp 154-161, 182

Details of more specific design activities will be found spread through the more detailed sections of this bibliography.

USSR

A difficult area to research as the documentation is incomplete, scattered and very difficult to obtain. A few introductory works:

Art in Revolution: Soviet Art and Design since 1917. 1971 London: Arts Council

Art in the USSR. 1935 London: Studio 140pp (includes sections on handicrafts, pottery, cartoon art and architecture)

Gibian, G. and Tjalsma, H. W. (eds).
*Russian modernism – Culture and the
Avant-Garde 1900-1930*. 1976 Ithaca:
Cornell University Press 256pp illus.

Height, Frank. 'Design in the Soviet Union',
Design 228 December 1967 pp 28-32

Colour, ornament and pattern

The history of design is strewn with arguments about the formal elements of design as a means to improve current weakness. These range from:

Clegg, Samuel. *Architecture of machinery. An essay on propriety of form and proportion, with a view to assist and improve design.* 1842 London: Architectural Library 64pp pl 8

to:

Ashford, Fred. 'Visual organisation', *Design* 213 September 1966 pp 58-65 (on the importance of visual perception in product design)

Most of these discussions are more clearly understood in terms of a specific design activity or a particular historical period, and that is where they can be found in this bibliography. More general theories and statements have been included in the section on Theories of Design and Craftmanship *page 52*.

However, two general aspects that have built up their own distinctive literature are colour and ornament and pattern and so they are treated separately.

Colour

See also:

Interior Design: Colour *page 158*
Textiles: Dyed fabrics *page 193*
Colour printing *page 131*

Theories

The Royal College of Art has built up a very large collection of works on colour. A detailed annotated catalogue has been prepared and, if this can be published, it should provide a fine introduction to the large literature of this subject.

A short introduction to the whole area is provided by:

Birren, Faber. *Principles of color: a review of past traditions and modern theories of color harmony.* 1969 New York: Van Nostrand Reinhold 96pp illus.

Short historical studies:

Birren, Faber, *The story of color, from ancient mysticism to modern science.* 1941 Connecticut: Crimson Press 338pp illus.

Bossert, Helmuth Theodor. *Encyclopaedia of colour decoration from the earliest times to the middle of the 19th century.* 1928 London: Gollancz 34pp pl 120

but there is no reliable way of shortcutting original theoretical writings of some of the main theorists and their exponents:

GOETHE

Goethe, Johann Wolfgang von. *Theory of colours, translated from the German by Charles L. Eastlake.* 1967 London: Cass 428pp illus. (first published 1810 *Zur Farbenlehre*, first edition 1840. Another recent edition 1970 MIT Press)

CHEVREUL

Chevreul, Michel Eugene. *The principles of harmony and contrast of colours, and their application to the arts, translated by C. Martel.* 1916 London: Bell 465pp (first published 1854 with many later editions)

MUNSELL

Munsell, Albert H. *A grammar of color. A basic treatise on the color system of Albert H. Munsell edited with an introduction by Faber Birren.* 1969 New York: Van Nostrand Reinhold 96pp illus.

Judd, Deane B. and Wyszecki, Gunter W. *Color in business, science and industry.* 1975 (revised edition) New York: Wiley 570pp illus. First edition 1952)

OSTWALD

Ostwald, Wilhelm. *The color primer: a basic treatise on the color system of Wilhelm Ostwald edited by F. Birren.* 1969 New York: Van Nostrand Reinhold 96pp illus.

Jacobson, Egbert. *Basic color: an interpretation of the Ostwald color system.* 1948 Chicago: Paul Theobald 207pp illus. bibl.

Sargant-Florence, M. *Colour co-ordination.* 1940 London: John Lane 352pp illus.

Sloane, Patricia. *Colour: basic principles, new directions.* 1969 London: Studio Vista 96pp illus.

ITTEN

Itten, Johannes. *The art of color. The subjective experience and objective rationale of color, translated by Ernst van Haagen.* 1961 New York: Reinhold 155pp illus.

Itten, Johannes. *The elements of color. A treatise on the color system of Johannes Itten based on his book The art of color, edited with evaluation by Faber Birren, translated by Ernst van Haagen.* 1970 New York: Van Nostrand Reinhold 96pp (title of Itten's original work: *Kunst der Farbe. Studien Ausgabe*)

ALBERS

Albers, Josef. *Interaction of color.* 1975 (revised edition) New Haven: Yale University Press 74pp illus. (first published 1963 in 2 vols)

RENNER

Renner, Paul. *Color: order and harmony. A color theory for artists and craftsmen, translated from the German by Alexander Nesbitt.* 1965 London: Studio Vista 80pp illus. (first published *Ordnung und Harmonie der Farben*)

BIRREN

Birren, Faber. *Light, color and environment: a thorough presentation of facts on the biological and psychological effects of color – plus historical data and detailed recommendations for the . . . use of color in modern human environments.* 1969 New York: Van Nostrand Reinhold 131pp illus. bibl.

Birren, Faber. *New horizons in color.* 1955 New York: Reinhold 200pp illus. bibl.

GERRITSEN

Gerritsen, Frans. *Theory and practice of colour: a colour theory based on laws of perception.* 1975 London: Studio Vista 180pp illus.

Application

Works on the particular application of colour to textiles, interior decoration are presented elsewhere.

Some of the earlier more theoretical writings of the nineteenth century are valuable for the light they cast on current practice:

Hay, David Ramsay. *A nomenclature of colours, hues, tints and shades applicable to the arts and natural sciences, to manufactures and other purposes of general utility.* 1845 Edinburgh 72pp (revised edition 1846)

Field, George. *Chromatography: or, a treatise on colours and pigments and of their power in painting.* 1835 London (many later editions)

This set the chromatic equivalents followed by Owen Jones and others:

Jones, Owen. *An attempt to define the principles which should regulate the employment of colour in the decorative arts, with a few words on the present necessity of an architectural education on the part of the public. Read before the Society of Arts April 28, 1852.* 1852 London: G. Barclay 59pp illus.

Redgrave, Richard. *An elementary manual of colour, with a catechism to be used with the diagram illustrating the harmonious relations of colour.* 1853 London: Chapman and Hall 36pp bibl. (the official manual for the schools of design)

Moore, G. B. *The principles of colour applied to decorative art.* 1851 London: Taylor, Walton and Moberly

Audsley, William James and Audsley, George Ashdown. *Polychromatic decoration as applied to buildings in the Medieval styles.* 1882 London: H. Sotheran & Co 32pp pl 36 (in colours and gold)

Goodwin, Thomas G. *A short account of the art of Polychrome, historical and practical.* 1860 London

Crace, J. D. 'The decorative use of colour', *JSA* vol 36 May 11 1888 pp 696-704

Crace, J. D. 'On colour', *Builder* November 30, December 7 1867

In the present century the British Colour Council and the evolution of a whole range of British Standards have led to much more scientific measurement of colour:

The British Colour Council dictionary of colour standards. 1934 London: British Colour Council 2 parts (second edition 1951)

Wilson, Robert F. 'Colour and colour nomenclature', *JRSA* vol 83 February 15 1935 pp 307-323

Physical Society Colour Group. *Report of colour terminology.* 1948 London: Physcial Society 56pp

Wright, William david. *The measurement of colour.* 1944 London: Adam Hilger 223pp

Wright, Lance. 'Standardized colour (BS 2660: 1955)', *Architectural Review* vol 119 May 1956 pp 283-284

Textbooks provide quite a useful guide to current practice:

Ward, James. *Colour harmony and contrast for the use of art-students, designers and decorators.* 1903 London: Chapman and Hall 140pp

Irwin, Beatrice. *The new science of colour.* 1916 London: W. Rider 127pp

Carpenter, Henry Barrett. *Colour: a manual of its theory and practice.* 1933 London: Batsford 86pp

Evans, Ralph Merrill. *An introduction to colour.* 1948 London: Chapman and Hall 340pp pl 15 bibl.

Taylor, Francis Arthur. *Colour technology for artists, craftsmen and industrial designers.* 1962 Oxford University Press 140pp pl 9

Verity, Enid. *Colour.* 1967 London: Frewin 164pp illus. bibl.

A general discussion:

'Colour in modern life'(Cantor lectures) '1 One man's colour' by Hulme Chadwick, '2 Scientific aspects' by T. Vickerstaff, '3 Colour in the community' by Hulme Chadwick, *JRSA* vol 112 1964 pp 145-173

More specific applications:

Chambers, Bernice Gertrude. *Color and Design. Fashions in man's and woman's clothing and home furnishings*. 1953 New York: Prentice Hall 603pp

Wilson, Robert F. 'Colour as a factor in industrial design', *JRSA* vol 93 May 11 1945 pp 304-312

Later there developed much greater attention to colour co-ordination in industrial design:

Gloag, Bill and Keyte, Michael. '1 Colour co-ordination for manufacturer and user', '2 Co-ordinating a range', *Design* 123 March 1959 pp 34-40, 129 September 1959 pp 33-37

Forsyth, Susan and Blake, John E. 'A co-ordinated approach to colour', *Design* 227 November 1967 pp 36-38

Gloag, H. L. 'Colour co-ordination applied to material', *Design* 227 November 1967 pp 39-42

Colour co-ordination of factory made products. A statement to the Council of Industrial Design by its advisory committee on colour and industrial design. 1967 London: Council of Industrial Design 8pp

An individual designer's viewpoint:

Klein, Bernat. *Eye for colour*. 1965 Galashiels: Bernat Klein with Collins 136pp illus.

The psychology of colour has been studied in great detail. Some useful introductions are:

Ladd-Franklin, C. *Colour and colour theories*. 1929 London: Kegan Paul 305pp

Katz, David. *World of colour*. 1935 London: Kegan Paul Trench, Trubner 300pp illus. (translation of *Der aufbau der farbwelt* by R. B. Macleod and C. W. Fox)

Sharpe, Deborah T. *The psychology of color and design*. 1975 Totowa, New Jersey: Littlefield Adams & Co

Perhaps the most obvious application of colour is paint:

Betjeman, John and Casson, Hugh. *A handbook on paint*. 1939 London: Silicate Paint Company

'Paint as protection and decoration. A review by William Tatton Brown', *Architectural Review* vol 85 1939 pp 153-158

150 years of paint and varnishing manufacturing. 1952 London: Thomas Parsons & Sons 63pp illus.

The first half century: a history of the Paint Research Association 1926-1976. 1976 Teddington: Paint Research Association 30pp illus.

Ornament and pattern

See also:

Important Designers: Day, Dresser, Morris *pages 75-*

Surveys

Useful introductions to this bewildering large, diverse and often contradictory field are:

Justema, William. *Pattern. A historical panorama*. 1976 London: Elek 202pp illus. bibl.

Evans, Joan. *Pattern: a study of ornament in Western Europe from 1180 to 1900*. 1975 New York: Hacker Art Books 2 vols 380pp 687 illus. (reprint of 1931 edition Clarendon Press)

Perhaps the clearest way to approach the subject as a whole is through individual speculation and selection:

Justema, William. *The Pleasures of pattern*. 1968 New York: Van Nostrand Reinhold 233pp illus. bibl.

Evans, Joan. *Style in ornament*. 1950 Oxford University Press 64pp

Durant, Stuart. 'Ornament in an industrial civilisation', *Architectural Review* vol 160 no 955 September 1976 pp 139-143 illus. (large bibl.)

For terminology:

Stafford, Maureen and Ware, Dora. *An illustrated dictionary of ornament*. 1974 London: Allen and Unwin 246pp illus.

Victorian Ornament

'Ornamental art is rather abstractive and reproductive than imitative' (William Dyce)

In view of the wealth of surviving evidence it is surprising that more has not been published recently on this extremely complex subject, even though the problems of identification and documentation are enormous. A concise introduction is provided by:

Bøe, Alf. 'Victorian theory of ornament', *British Journal of Aesthetics* vol 3 no 4 pp 317-329

and a visual anthology by:

Durant, Stuart. *Victorian ornamental design*. 1972 London: Academy Editions 103pp 97 illus.

Some of the main figures are introduced in:

Haité, George C. 'Design and designers of the Victorian reign', *Architectural Review* 2 1897 pp 81-89, 141-146

Any serious study of this subject must start with one of its most influential theorists:

Wornum, Ralph. *Analysis of ornament – the characteristics of styles, an introduction to the study of the history of ornamental art.* 1856 London: Chapman and Hall 215pp (many editions – 10th 1896)

and the many rich collections of plates that began to be studied and published in the 1830s:

Shaw, Henry. *The encyclopaedia of ornament.* 1974 London: Academy Editions 96pp illus. (facsimile of 1842 Pickering edition)

Zahn, Wilhelm. *Ornamente aller classischen Kunstepoken nach den Originalen (Ornaments of all classical epochs of art after the originals)* 1843-1848 Berlin 2 vols (first issued 1831)

Julienne, Eugène. *L'Ornemaniste des Arts Industriels. Recueil complet de tous les styles d'ornements employés et ajustés dans la décoration, avec les notes descriptives de chaque style. Les sujets par F. Reignier.* 1844 Paris: Letouze 5 vols pl 198

Examples of ornament, selected chiefly from the works of art in the British Museum, the Museum of Economic Geology, the Museum of Ornamental Art at Marlborough House, and the Crystal Palace. Drawn from original sources by Francis Bedford, Thomas Scott, Thomas Macquoid and Henry O'Neill, and edited by Joseph Cundall. 1855 London 5pp pl 24

Robinson, John Charles. *The Treasury of Ornamental Art: illustrations of objects of art and vertu. Photographed from the originals and drawn on stone by F. Bedford.* 1857 London: Day 145pp pl 70

Griesbach, C. B. *Historic ornament: pictorial archive: 900 fine examples from ancient Egypt to 1800 suitable for reproduction.* 1975 New York: Dover 280pp 900 illus. (originally published late nineteenth century as *Muster-Ornamente aus allen Stilen in historischer Anordnung*)

Dolmetsch, H. *The historic styles of ornament, containing 1500 examples from all countries and periods.* 1898 London: Batsford 3pp pl 100 (further edition 1912)

There are many others. As their use was central to many aspects of the teaching of the schools of design and their successors, many of the early folios are helpfully listed in:

Books of plates of ornament available at the Central School, Marlborough House. Appendix to Third report of the Council of the School of Design reprinted in British Parliamentary papers. Industrial design. Design 3

1840-1849. 1971 Shannon: Irish Universities Press pp 148-151

The textbooks and manuals produced throughout the period are also useful guides to current practice and preference:

Dyce, William. *The drawing book of the Government School of Design, published in the years 1842-1843 under the direction of William Dyce Esq RA.* 1854 London

The Ornamentist; or artisan's manual in the various branches of ornamental art: being a series of designs selected from the works of Dietterlin, Berain, Blondell, Meisonier, LePautre, Zahn, Boetticher, and the best French and German ornamentalists. With an introductory essay on ornamental art by W. B. Scott. 1845 London: A. Fullarton 21pp illus.

Leith, Samuel (ed). *The tradesman's book of ornamental designs. Essay on ornamental art as applicable to trade and manufactures by J. Ballantine.* 1847 London: Virtue 36pp pl 40

Richardson, Charles James. *Studies in ornamental design.* 1848 London: J. Weale pl 8

Dyce, William. 'Lecture on ornament delivered to the students of the London School of Design', *Journal of Design* 1849 pp 26-29, 64-67, 91-94

Martel, Charles. *The principles of form in ornamental art.* 1856 London

Wilson, George. *The relation of ornamental to industrial art. A lecture December 1856.* 1857 Edinburgh

Burn, Richard Scott. *Ornamental drawing and architectural design, with notes historical and practical. With upwards of 200 illustrations.* 1857 London: Ward Lock and Tylor 124pp

Marshall, Julian. *Handbook of engravers of ornament, produced for the use of schools of art, and generally, for public instruction.* 1869 London: Eyre 39pp illus.

Gibbs, William. *Designers' and draughtsmen's handbook of ornament, illustrating the various styles of decoration.* 1851 London

Gibbs, John. *Studies for art designers and manufacturers.* 1869 Oxford: John Gibbs 4pp pl 32

Lyon, J. T. *Creative and imitative art; decoration and ornamentation.* 1873 Brussels: M. Weissenbruch 138pp illus.

Bourgoin, Jules. *Theorie de l'ornement.* 1873 Paris: A. Lévy 366pp 330 motifs (later edition 1883)

The Designer. All kinds of ornament for lithographers, architects . . . edited by Klimsch and Co. Part 1-16. 1877 London: Asher & Co pl 96

Hay, J. Marley. *Ornament and ornamentalists.* 1886 Aberdeen: author 22pp

Jackson, Frank G. *Lessons on decorative design.* 1888 London: Chapman and Hall 173pp pl 34

Jackson, Frank G. *Theory and practice of design . . . being a sequel to the author's 'Lessons on Decorative Design'.* 1894 London: Chapman and Hall 216pp 700 illus.

Burn, Richard Scott. *Ornamental draughtsman and designer. By several practical draughtsmen and designers.* 1892 London: Ward Lock 142pp pl 37

Schauermann, François Louis. *Theory and analysis of ornament applied to the work of elementary and technical schools.* 1892 London: Sampson Low 208pp

Leland, Charles G. *Drawing and designing: in a series of lessons.* 1888 London: Whittaker 79pp

White, Gleeson (ed). *Practical designing, a handbook on the preparation of working drawings.* 1893 London: Bell 328pp illus.

Meyer, Franz Sales. *A handbook of ornament systematically arranged for the use of architects, decorators, handicraftsmen and all other classes of art students, translated from the fourth revised German edition and revised by Hugh Stannus.* 1893 London: Batsford 580pp illus. (available as a Dover reprint)
also available as:

Meyer, Franz Sales. *A handbook of ornament, edited by Tony Birks.* 1974 London: Duckworth 300 illus.

Stannus, Hugh. 'Some principles of form design in applied art', *JSA* October 14, 21, 28, November 4 1898 pp 885-889, 897-903, 909-916, 922-931

Blount, Godfrey. *Arbor Vitae. A book on the nature and development of imaginative design for the use of teachers, handicraftsmen and others.* 1899 London: Dent 240pp illus. (reflects the fervour of the arts and crafts movement at its height)

Hatton, Richard George. *Design; an exposition of the principles and practices of making patterns.* 1902 London: Chapman and Hall 182pp illus. (later editions 1914, 1925)

Dawson, Charles Frederick. *Elementary design. A systematic course of lessons for students.* 1903 London: Chapman and Hall 96pp

Rhead, George Wooliscroft. *The principles of design. A textbook for teachers, students and craftsmen.* 1905 London: Batsford 186pp illus. (another edition 1913)

Harrison, T. E. and Townsend, W. G. P. *Terms commonly used in ornamental design.* 1906 London: Batsford 111pp

Moody, Francis W. *Lectures on decorative art: being an introduction to a practical and comprehensive scheme.* 1908 London: Bell 176pp pl 24

Meurer, M. *Vergleichende Formenlehre des Ornamentes und der Pflanze, mit besonderer Berücksichtigung der Entwicklungsgeschichte der architektonischen Kunstformen.* 1909 Dresden: Gerhard Kühtmann 596pp

Most of the most influential work in ornament and design is based on very detailed research of the past and so it may be helpful to list some of the most influential histories:

Shaw, Henry. *The decorative arts, ecclesiastical and civil, of the Middle Ages.* 1851 London: W. Pickering 90pp pl 41

Collingwood, William Gerson. *The Philosophy of ornament: eight lectures on the history of decorative art.* 1883 Orpington: George Allen 220pp

Guillaume, Edmond. *L'Histoire de l'art et de l'ornement.* 1886 Paris: Musée Pedagogique 133pp

Glazier, Richard. *Historical and descriptive notes of ornament, with illustrative sketches.* 1887 Manchester: J. Heywood 43pp

Glazier, Richard. *A manual of historic ornament. Treating upon the evolution, tradition and development of architecture and the other applied arts.* 1899 London: Batsford 136pp 470 illus. (sixth edition 1948)

Balfour, Henry. *The evolution of decorative art. An essay upon its origins and development as illustrated by the art of modern races of mankind.* 1893 London: Rivington, Percival & Co 131pp

Balfour, Henry. 'The evolution of decorative art', *JSA* vol 42 April 27 1894 pp 455-471

Brown, William Norman. *A history of decorative art.* 1900 London: Scott Greenwood 98pp

Christie, Archibald H. *Pattern design: an introduction to the study of formal ornament.* 1969 New York: Dover 313pp 359 figs (facsimile reprint of *Traditional methods of pattern designing; an introduction to the study of decorative art.* 1929 Clarendon Press first edition 1910)

Speltz, Alexander. *The styles of ornament from prehistoric times to the middle of the nineteenth century.* 1910 London: Batsford 864pp

Hamlin, Alfred Dwight Foster. *A history of ornament, ancient and medieval.* 1916 London: Batsford 406pp 400 illus.

Hamlin, Alfred Dwight Foster. *A history of ornament Renaissance and Modern.* 1923 London: Batsford 521pp 464 illus.

Bossert, Helmuth Theodor. *Encyclopaedia of ornament: collection of applied decorative forms from all nations and all ages.* 1937 London: Simpkin Marshall 48pp pl 120

and much later:

Humbert, Claude. *Ornamental design: Europe, Africa, Asia, the Americas, Oceania: a source book with 1000 illustrations.* 1970 London: Thames and Hudson 236pp

Some important individual designers and their statements:

OWEN JONES

Jones, Owen. *The Grammar of ornament.* 1856 London: Day 104pp 100 col pl (1856 best edition. Facsimile of 1865 edition published 1972 by Van Nostrand Reinhold)

Jones, Owen. *On the leading principles in the composition of ornament of every period, from the Grammar of Ornament. Read before the RIBA December 15 1856.* 1856 London

Jones, Owen. *On the true and the false in the decorative arts. Lectures at Marlborough House June 1852.* 1863 London: private pub 112pp

Jones, Owen. *Designs for mosaic and tesselated pavements; with an essay on their material and structure by F. O. Ward.* 1842 London: J. Weale 17pp pl 11

Jones, Owen. *The Alhambra Court of the Crystal Palace. Erected and described by O. J.* 1854 London: Crystal Palace Library and Bradley & Evans 119pp illus.

Jones, Owen. *Examples of Chinese ornament selected from objects in the South Kensington Museum and other collections.* 1867 London: Day pl 50

Jones, Owen. *One thousand and one initial letters. Designed and illuminated by Owen Jones.* 1864 London: Day 1pp col pl 27

Jones, Owen. *702 monograms.* 1864 London: De La Rue

Bibliographical catalogue of the work of the late Owen Jones. 1874 London (produced for Annual International Exhibition 1874)

LEWIS (LUDWIG) GRUNER

Grüner, Lewis. *Specimens of ornamental art, selected from the best models of the classical epochs . . . text by Emil Braun.* 1850 London: Thomas Mclean pl 80

Grüner, Ludwig. *Die dekorative Kunst. Beitrage zur Ornamentik für Architektur und Kunstgewerbe aus dem Schatzen des Königs. Sammlung für Handzeichnungen und Kupferstich.* 1879-1882 Dresden: G. Gilbers 2pp pl 100

A. W. N. PUGIN

Pugin. A. W. N. *Floreated ornament.* 1849 London: H. G. Bohn pl 31

D. R. HAY

Hay, David Ramsay. *Essay on ornamental design, with an attempt to develop its principles, and to point out an easy method of acquiring facility in its practice.* 1884 London: D. Bogue 43pp

Hay, David Ramsay. *The natural principles and analogy of the harmony of form.* 1842 London: W. Blackwood 50pp

Hay, David Ramsay. *Original geometrical diaper designs, accompanied by an attempt to develop and elucidate the true principles of ornamental design, as applied to the decorative arts.* 1844 London: D. Bogue 43pp pl 57

Hay, David Ramsay. *First principles of symetrical beauty.* 1864 Edinburgh: W. Blackwood 88pp pl 100

Hay, David Ramsay. *A catalogue raisonné of the works of D. R. Hay; with critical remarks by various authors.* 1849 Edinburgh: W. Blackwood 32pp

RICHARD REDGRAVE

Redgrave, Richard. *Manual of design, compiled from the writings and addresses of R. Redgrave by Gilbert R. Redgrave.* 1876 London: Chapman and Hall 173pp illus.

Redgrave, Richard. *Richard Redgrave CBRA. A memoir compiled from his diary by F. M. Redgrave.* 1891 London: Cassell 399pp

JOHN LEIGHTON

Limmer, Luke *pseud* (ie John Leighton). *Suggestions in design, being a comprehensive series of original sketches in various styles of ornament arranged for application in the decorative and constructive arts.* 1880 London: Blackie pl 101 (earlier edition 1853)

CHRISTOPHER DRESSER

See also:

Important Designers *page 75*

Dresser, Christopher. *The art of decorative designs.* 1862 London: Day 280pp (ABC Reprint 1977)

Dresser, Christopher. *Modern ornamentation, being a series of original designs for the patterns of textile fabrics, for the ornamentation of manufacturers in wood, metal.* 1886 London: Batsford 106pp pl 50 (ABC Reprint)

Dresser, Christopher. *Principles of decorative design.* 1973 London: Academy Editions 182pp 188 illus. (facsimile of 1873 Cassell, Petter and Galpin)

Dresser, Christopher. 'The art of decorative design', *The Builder* March 15 1862 pp 182-185

Dresser, Christopher. 'On decorative art', *Planet* January 1862 no 1 14pp

AUDSLEY and AUDSLEY

Audsley, George Ashdown and Audsley, Berthold. *The art of polychromatic and decorative turning.* 1911 London: Allen 109pp pl 21

Audsley, George Ashdown and Audsley, Maurice Ashdown. *The practical decorator and ornamentist, for the use of architects, practical painters, decorators and designers.* 1892 Glasgow: Blackie 36pp pl 100

Audsley, William and Audsley, George Ashdown. *Designs and patterns from historic ornament.* 1968 New York: Dover 93pp illus. (facsimile of 1881 Sampson Low edition)

Audsley, William James and Audsley, George Ashdown. *Guide to the art of illuminating and missal painting.* 1862 London: G. Rowney 72pp pl 8

Audsley, William James and Audsley, George Ashdown. *Outlines of ornament in the leading styles. A book of reference for the architect, sculptor, decorative artist, and practical painter.* 1881 London: Sampson, Low, Marston, Searle and Rivington 14pp pl 60

JAMES WARD

Ward, James. *Historic ornament: treatise on decorative art and architectural ornament.* 1897 London: Chapman and Hall 2 vols

Ward, James. *Elementary principles of ornament.* 1890 London: Chapman and Hall 91pp

Ward, James. *The principles of ornament, edited by G. Aitchison.* 1892 London: Chapman and Hall 139pp (later editions)

Ward, James. *Progressive design for students.* 1902 London: Chapman and Hall 49pp 42 illus.

LEWIS F. DAY

Day, Lewis F. *Textbooks of ornamental design* series:

The anatomy of pattern. 1887 53pp pl 35

The planning of ornament. 1887 49pp pl 38

The application of ornament. 1888 73pp pl 42

Some principles of everyday art. 1890 148pp

Nature in ornament. 1892 246pp pl 123

Alphabets old and new. 1898 39pp

Art in needlework. A book about embroidery. 1900 262pp London: Batsford (second edition 1889-1901 in 6 parts)

Day, Lewis F. *Pattern design. A book for students, treating in a practical way of the anatomy, planning and evolution of repeated ornament.* 1933 (second edition) London: Batsford 306pp illus. (additional chapter by Amor Fenn on 'Development of pattern design')

Day, Lewis F. 'Principles and practice of ornamental design', *JSA* vol 35 December 24, December 31 1886, January 7, January 14 1887 pp 91-100, 105-115, 118-128, 132-144

Day, Lewis F. 'Some masters of ornament', *JSA* vol 41 July 14, July 21, July 28, August 11 1893 pp 793-803, 805-815, 817-826, 830-840

GEOMETRIC ORNAMENTATION

Billings, Robert William. *The infinity of geometric design exemplified.* 1849 London: Blackwood 19pp pl 39

Billings, Robert William. *The power of form applied to geometric tracery. One hundred designs and their foundations resulting from one diagram.* 1851 Edinburgh: Blackwood 26pp illus.

Lorch, Adolf. *Modern geometric design.* 1971 London: Oaktree Press 79pp

Hornung, Clarence Pearson. *Handbook of designs and devices. Geometric elements. With 1836 examples drawn by the author.* 1932 New York: Harper 204pp illus.

Wedd, J. A. D. 'Beans and boomerangs (use of geometrical form in modern design)', *Art and Industry* February 1954 pp 46-51

EXOTIC DESIGN

Cutler, Thomas William. *A grammar of Japanese ornament and design with introductory, descriptive and analytical text.* 1880 London: Batsford 31pp pl 58

ORNAMENT DEVELOPED FROM PLANT FORMS

Dresser, Christopher. 'Botany as adapted to the Arts and Art manufacture', *Art Journal* 1857-1858 11 articles

Butterfield, Lindsay P. *Floral forms in historic design mainly from objects in the Victoria and Albert Museum.* 1922 London: Batsford pl 18

Colling, James Kellaway. *Art foliage, for sculpture and decoration; with an analysis of geometric form, and studies from nature, of buds, leaves, flowers and fruit.* 1865 London: author 136pp pl 72 (second edition 1878)

Colling, James Kellaway. *Examples of English mediaeval foliage and coloured decoration, taken from buildings of the twelfth and fifteenth century.* 1874 London: author and B. T. Batsford 72pp pl 76

Cole, Herbert. *Heraldry and floral forms as used in design.* 1922 London: Dent 248pp illus.

Grasset, Eugene. *Plants and their application to ornament.* 1897 London: Chapman and Hall pl 77

Haité, George Charles. *Plant studies for artists, designers and art students.* 1886 London: B. Quaritch 71pp

Hulme, Frederick Edward. *Art studies from nature as applied to design: for the use of architects, designers and manufacturers.* 1872 London: Virtue

Hulme, F. E. *The birth and development of ornament.* 1893 London: Swann Sonnenschein 340pp

Hulme, F. E. *Plants, their natural growth and ornamental treatment.* 1874 London: Marcus Ward

Hulme, F. E. *Principles of ornamental art.* 1875 London: Petter and Galpin (University Microfilms Books in demand)

Hulme, F. E. *A series of sketches from nature of plant form.* 1868 London: Day

Hulme, F. E. *Suggestions on floral design.* 1878-1879 London: Cassell, Petter and Galpin

Lilley, A. E. V. and Midgley, W. *A book of studies in plant form with some suggestions for their application to design.* 1902 (sixth edition) London: Chapman and Hall 183pp illus. (many editions)

Lindley, John. *The symetry of vegetation. An outline of the principles to be observed in the delineation of plants: being the substance of three lectures delivered to students of practical art at Marlborough House in November 1852.* 1854 London: Chapman and Hall 51pp

Redgrave, Richard. 'Importance of the study of botany to the ornamentist', *Journal of Design* 1849 pp 147-151, 178-185

Stannus, Hugh. 'The decorative treatment of natural foliage', *JSA* vol 39 October 9, October 16, October 30, November 6 1891 pp 859-866, 874-884, 905-913, 917-932

Strange, E. F. *Flowers and plants for designers and schools.* 1907 London: Hodder and Stoughton 95pp

Townsend, W. G. Paulson. *Plant and floral studies for designers, art students and craftsmen.* 1901 London: Truslove, Hanson and Combe 137pp

Wadsworth, J. W. *Designing from plant forms.* 1910 London: Chapman and Hall 122pp

Whitaker, Henry. *Materials for a new style of ornamentation consisting of botanical subjects and compositions drawn from nature.* 1849 London: John Weale

OPPOSITION TO ORNAMENT

Banham, Reyner. 'Ornament and crime', *Architectural Review* vol 121 no 721 February 1957 pp 85-88

a shortened translation of:

Loos, Adolf. *Ornament und verbrechen.* 1908 Munchen reprinted in *Trotzdem.* 1931 Innsbruck: Brenner Verlag 257pp

A bibliography:

Great Britain. Science and Art Department. *A list of works on ornament in the National Art Library.* 1882 London: Eyre and Spottiswode for HMSO 101pp

Decoration

Kahn, Ely Jacques. 'The province of decoration in modern design', *Studio* vol 98 1929 pp 885-889

Fenn, Amor. *Abstract design. A practical manual on the making of patterns for the use of students, teachers, designers and craftsmen.* 1930 London: Batsford 204pp illus.

Cannon, N. I. *Pattern and design.* 1948 London: Lund Humphries 160pp pl 12

Megaw, Helen. 'The investigation of crystal structure', *Architectural Review* vol 109 April 1951 pp 236-240

Wedd, John Anthony Dunkin. *Sources of design: pattern and texture.* 1956 London: Studio 96pp

Kadleigh, Sergei. 'A new grammar of ornament', *JRSA* vol 105 11 October 1957 pp 896-908

White, Gwen. *A world of pattern.* 1957 London: Murray 76pp

Farleigh, John. *Design for applied decoration in the crafts.* 1959 London: Bell 128pp illus.

Alexander, Mary Jean. *Handbook of decorative design and ornament.* 1965 New York: Tudor Pub 128pp illus.

Inchbald, Jacqueline. *Decoration and design.* 1971 London: Cassell 184pp

Critchlow, Keith. *Order in space: a design source book.* 1969 London: Thames and Hudson 120pp illus.

Particular motifs:

Rice, Brian and Evans, Tony. *The English sunrise.* 1972 London: Matthews Miller Dunbar 79pp all illustrations

Technical, social and economic factors

This section introduces some books that can provide avenues into many of the background issues necessary to an understanding of design change. Four main groups have been selected:

1 Technical developments
2 Inventions and patents
3 Social history
4 Economic and business history

1 Technical Developments

The most accessible general introduction to the whole area is provided by the enormous *A history of technology* series:

Singer, Charles and others (eds). *A history of technology vol V. The late nineteenth century c 1850-1900.* 1958 Oxford: Clarendon Press

Williams, Trevor (ed). *A history of technology vols VI and VII. The twentieth century c 1900-c 1950 Parts 1 and 2.* 1978 Oxford: Clarendon Press (in preparation)

General histories of technology

There is a growing range of large-span studies:

Kranzberg, Melvin and Pursell, Carroll W. Jnr. (eds). *Technology in Western civilization.* 1967 Oxford University Press 2 vols illus. bibl. *vol 1 Emergence of modern industrial society to 1900* 802pp *vol 2 Technology in the twentieth century* 722pp

Landes, David S. *The unbound Prometheus: technological change and industrial development in Western Europe from 1750 to the present.* 1969 Cambridge University Press 566pp illus.

Thring, Meredith Wooldridge. *Man, machines and tomorrow.* 1973 London: Routledge and Kegan Paul 127pp illus.

Fyrth, Hubert Jim. *Science, history and technology.* 1969 London: Cassell
Book 2 part 1: The age of confidence: the 1840s to the 1880s
Book 2 part 2: The age of uncertainty: the 1880s to the 1940s
Book 2 part 3: The age of choice: the 1940s to 1960s

Chaloner, William Henry and Musson, Albert Edward. *Industry and technology: a visual history of Britain.* 1963 London: Vista Books 202pp illus.

Buchanan, Robert Angus. *Technology and social progress.* 1965 Oxford: Pergamon 172pp illus.

Francastel, Pierre. *Art et techniques aux XIX et XXe siècles.* 1956 Paris: Editions de Minuit 307pp illus. bibl.

Derry, Thomas Kingston and Williams, Trevor. *A short history of technology from the earliest times to AD 1900.* 1970 Oxford University Press 784pp illus.

Dunsheath, Percy (ed). *A century of technology 1851-1951.* 1951 London: Hutchinson 346pp illus.

Bernal, John Desmond. *Science in history.* 1969 Harmondsworth: Penguin 4 vols

Pyke, Magnus. *The science century.* 1967 London: Murray 183pp illus.

NINETEENTH CENTURY

Bernal, John Desmond. *Science and industry in the nineteenth century.* 1953 London: Routledge and Kegan Paul 230pp illus. (Indiana University Press reprint 1970)

Habakkuk, Hrottger John. *American and British technology in the nineteenth century. The search for labour saving inventions.* 1962 Cambridge University Press 222pp

Smith, Norman Alfred Fisher. *Victorian technology and its preservation in modern Britain: a report submitted to the Leverhulme Trust.* 1970 Leicester University Press 74pp (not a general history but 'this report embodies the findings of the Victorian Technology Survey which was carried out by the Department of Science and Technology at Imperial College, London')

TWENTIETH CENTURY

Lovell, Maurice. *The expanding world: changes in twentieth century life caused by applied science.* 1970 London: Methuen Educational for British Society for International Understanding 120pp illus. bibl.

Humphreys, Mary Eleanor B. and Humphreys, D. W. *The scientific and industrial revolution of our time.* 1964 London: Allen and Unwin 47pp illus.

and a popular exhibition:

Taylor, Gordon Rattray. *A salute to British genius.* 1977 London: Secker and Warburg 160pp illus.

Histories of Engineering

A few general studies:

Armytage, Walter Harry Green. *Social history of engineering.* 1976 (fourth edition) London: Faber 381pp illus. (first edition 1961)

Pannell, J. P. M. *Man the builder. An illustrated history of engineering.* 1977 (revised edition) London: Thames and Hudson 252pp illus.

Fleming, Sir Arthur Percy Morris and Brocklehurst, Harold John Stanley. *A history of engineering.* 1925 London: Black 312pp

Perhaps the richest sources are journals:

The Engineer: the weekly for engineering management. 1856- London: Morgan-Grampian (in particular its 100-year cumulative index and the centenary number January 1956)

Engineers Digest 1940- (monthly) London

MECHANICAL ENGINEERING

Burstall, Aubrey F. *History of mechanical engineering.* 1963 London: Faber 465pp illus.

Institution of Mechanical Engineers. *Engineering heritage: highlights from the history of mechanical engineering.* 1963, 1966 London: Heinemann 2 vols illus. bibl.

Cressy, Edward. *One hundred years of mechanical engineering.* 1937 London: Duckworth 340pp pl 114

English Mechanic, London. A weekly magazine. 1865-1926 124 vols (a new series started 1926 changed to *Mechanics* 1 May 1942)

Machine Design 1929- (28 per year) Cleveland (University Microfilms)

The steam engine is particularly important:

Dickinson, Henry W. *A short history of the steam engine.* 1939 Cambridge University Press 255pp pl 10 (Frank Cass reprint 1963)

Watkins, George. *The stationary steam engine.* 1968 Newton Abbot: David and Charles 128pp illus. (51 illustrated examples)

Buchanan, Robert Angus and Watkins, George. *The industrial archaeology of the stationary steam engine.* 1976 London: Allen Lane 199pp illus.

ELECTRONICS AND ELECTRICAL ENGINEERING

Dunsheath, Percy. *History of electrical engineering.* 1962 London: Faber 368pp illus.

Handel, Samuel. *The electronic revolution.* 1967 Harmondsworth: Penguin 252pp illus. bibl.

Zeluff, V. and Markus, J. '100 years of electricity and electronics', *Scientific American* 173 July 1945 pp 7-12

Braun, Ernest and Macdonald, Stuart. *Revolution in miniature. The history and impact of semi-conductor electronics.* 1978 Cambridge University Press 240pp illus.

and a bibliography:

Shiers, George and Shiers, Mary (eds). *History of electronics; a bibliography.* 1972 Metuchen, New Jersey: Scarecrow Press 323pp

and some pioneers:

Weiher, Sigfrid von. 'The Siemens brothers, pioneers of the electrical age in Europe', *Transactions of the Newcomen Society* vol 45 pp 1-13

Scott, John Dick. *Siemens brothers 1858-1958. An essay in the history of industry.* 1958 London: Weidenfeld and Nicolson 279pp illus.

Ridding, Arthur. *S. Z. Ferranti – pioneer of electrical power.* 1964 London: HMSO for Science Museum 32pp illus.

Sources of energy

Vowles, William Hugh Pembroke and Vowles, Margaret Winifred. *The quest for power from prehistoric times to the present day.* 1931 London: Chapman and Hall 354pp illus.

Chandler, Dean and Lacey, A. Douglas. *The rise of the gas industry in Britain.* 1949 London: British Gas Council 156pp

Benjamin, Park. *A history of electricity.* 1975 New York: Arno 611pp illus. bibl. (reprint of 1898 edition)

Organisation and manufacture

A complex and specialised area with a growing literature in its own right. The following raise a number of the basic issues:

Schwarz, A. 'The evolution of mills and factories', *CIBA Review* no 1 1968 pp 2-39 (concentrates on textile developments to 1900)

Strassmann, Wolfgang Paul. *Risk and technological innovations. American manufacturing methods during the nineteenth century.* 1959 Ithaca: Cornell University Press 249pp

Amber, George H. and Amber, Paul S. *The anatomy of automation.* 1963 Englewood Cliffs, New Jersey: Prentice Hall 245pp illus.

and in a more specialised direction:

Taylor, F. Sherwood. *A history of industrial chemistry.* 1956 London: Heinemann 467pp

Technology and Design

Discussions of the relationship are often broad enough to invite any amount of speculation. More practical argument is to be found in:

Quimby, Ian M. G. and Earl, Polly Anne (eds). *Technological innovation and the Decorative Arts*. 1974 University of Virginia Press 373pp (Winterthur Conference report 1973)

Cornford, Christopher. *The kinship of art and technology*. 1966 London: Association of art and technology 15pp

Richardson, E. G. *Physical science in art and industry*. 1946 London: English Universities Press 299pp (first edition 1940)

and the writings of Lewis Mumford:

Mumford, Lewis. *The myth of the machine; technics and human development*. 1967 London: Secker and Warburg 342pp pl 32 bibl.

Mumford, Lewis. *Art and technics*. 1960 New York: Columbia University Press 162pp (first edition 1952)

Mumford, Lewis. *Technics and civilisation*. 1934 London: Routledge 495pp illus. bibl.

Engineering Design

Engineering design has already been touched on in the section on Theories of Design. A large but very specialised field with many crucial local problems, it needs a bibliography in its own right. The issues can be seen in a general way through some of the journals:

Engineering 1866- (now monthly) London: Design Council

Design and Components in Engineering 1961- London: Engineering Chemical and Marine Press

which is now combined with

Engineering Materials and Design 1958-(monthly) London: IPC Industrial Press

Design Engineering: the ideas journal for design engineers. 1964- (monthly) London: Morgan Grampian

Engineering Designer 1955- (monthly) Potters Bar: Kennett

Encyclopaedias and Biographical Dictionaries

Many early technical encyclopaedias are invaluable sources of information on techniques, processes and even products:

Useful arts and manufactures of Great Britain. 1845 London: Society for Promoting Christian Knowledge (second edition 1850)

Tomlinson, Charles (ed). *Cyclopaedia of useful arts, Mechanical and chemical, manufactures, mining and engineering*.

1854 London: Virtue 2 vols (further 3 vol edition 1861-1866)

Ure, Andrew. *A dictionary of arts, manufactures, and mines*. 1853 London 2 vols (many later editions, seventh 1875)

Encyclopaedia of the industrial arts, manufactures, and raw commercial products. 1882 London: E. & F. N. Spon

More recently part-works (issued in instalments) and pictorial encyclopaedias are also valuable for their carefully researched visual material:

How things work. The universal encyclopedia of machines. 1967 1971 London: Paladin 2 vols 590pp each vol

There is no shortage of biographical material on the early engineers:

Bell, Samuel Peter (comp). *A biographical index of British engineers in the 19th century*. 1975 London: Garland 246pp (lists obituaries of 3,500 British engineers 1837-1900)

Smiles, Samuel. *Industrial biography: iron workers and tool makers*. 1967 Newton Abbot: David and Charles 342pp pl 16 (reprint of 1863 edition with added plates and introduction by L. T. C. Rolt)

Smiles, Samuel. *Lives of the Engineers, with an account of their principal works; comprising also a history of inland communication in Britain*. 1968 Newton Abbot: David and Charles 3 vols (facsimile of 1862 edition with added notes and introduction by L. T. C. Rolt)

or even the union:

Jefferys, James Bavington. *The story of the engineers 1800-1945*. 1946 London: Amalgamated Engineering Union 301pp

Journals

Particularly valuable for the history of engineering and technology are:

Technology and Culture; devoted to the study of the development of technology and its relations with society and culture 1959-(quarterly) University of Chicago Press

Transactions of the Newcomen Society vol 1 1920-1921 (annual) General index to Transactions vol 1-32 (1920-1960 bound with vol 32 1959-1960

Many of the longer established general scientific journals also frequently contain valuable historical material:

Nature 1869- (weekly) London

Scientific American 1845- (monthly) New York

Annals of Science 1936- (quarterly) London

Bibliographies

Rider, Kenneth John. *The history of science and technology.* 1970 (second edition) London: Library Association 75pp (first edition 1967. LA Special Subject List no 48)

Ferguson, Eugene Shallcross. *Bibliography of the history of technology.* 1968 Cambridge, Mass: MIT Press 347pp (based on an earlier series of articles in *Technology and Culture* Winter 1962-Winter 1965)

and the annual:

'Current bibliography in the history of technology', in *Technology and Culture* 1964-

More general studies of the history of science can also be most useful:

ISIS cumulative bibliography: a bibliography of the history of science formed from the ISIS critical bibliographies 1913-1965, edited by Magda Whitrow. 1971 London: Mansell 2 vols

2 Inventions and Patents
General studies of inventions

Baker, R. *New and improved. Inventors and inventions that have changed the modern world.* 1976 London: British Museum Publications for British Library 168pp illus. bibl.

Jewkes, John. *Sources of invention.* 1969 (revised edition) London: Macmillan 372pp illus. (first edition 1958)

Clark, Ronald William. *The scientific breakthrough: the impact of modern invention.* 1974 London: Nelson 208pp illus. (concentrates on six main areas: photography, air, man made materials, nuclear energy, genetics, inspection)

Schmookler, Jacob. *Invention and economic growth.* 1967 Cambridge, Mass: Harvard University Press 350pp illus.

Schmookler, Jacob. *Patents, invention and economic change: data and selected essays edited by Zvi Griliches and Leonid Hurwicz.* 1973 Cambridge, Mass: Harvard University Press 310pp

Duckworth, J. C. 'Progress and innovation', (Peter Le Neve lecture), *JRSA* vol 111 March 1963 pp 259-271

and many lighter more popular surveys:

De Bono, Edward (ed). *Eureka! An illustrated history of inventions from the wheel to the computer.* 1974 London: Thames and Hudson 248pp illus.

Larsen, Egon. *A history of invention.* 1969 (revised edition) London: Dent 382pp pl 33 (previous edition 1961 Phoenix House)

Larsen, Egon. *Ideas and invention.* 1960 London: Spring Books 383pp

Odle, Francis. *The picture history of British inventions.* 1966 London: World Distributors 157pp illus.

Hornsby, Jeremy. *The story of inventions.* 1977 London: Weidenfeld and Nicolson 142pp illus.

Timbs, John. *Wonderful inventions: from the Mariner's compass to the electric telegraph cable . . . with engravings.* 1882 (new edition) London: Routledge 423pp (first edition 1868)

Local studies:

Prosser, Richard Bissell. *Birmingham inventors and inventions: being a contribution to the industrial history of Birmingham.* 1970 East Ardsley: EP 264pp (facsimile reprint of 1881 edition)

Lists:

Carter, Ernest Frank (ed). *Dictionary of inventions and discoveries.* 1969 (revised edition) London: Muller 204pp illus.

Robertson, Frank. *Shell book of firsts.* 1974 London: Michael Joseph 256pp illus.

NINETEENTH CENTURY

Routledge, Robert. *Discoveries and inventions of the nineteenth century.* 1876 London: Routledge (twelfth edition 1900 820pp 456 illus.)

De Vries, Leonard. *Victorian inventions, compiled in collaboration with Ilonka van Amstel.* 1973 London: John Murray 192pp illus. (first edition 1971. Based on illustrations from *Scientific American, La Nature* and *De Natuur*)

TWENTIETH CENTURY '

Crowther, James Gerald. *Discoveries and inventions of the twentieth century.* 1966 London: Routledge and Kegan Paul 400pp illus.

Cressy, Edward. *Discoveries and inventions of the twentieth century.* 1914 London: Routledge 398pp illus. (second edition 1923, third 1929, fourth 1955)

Rickards, Maurice. *New inventions: a comprehensive survey of scientific and technical progress in the arts, sciences and manufactures as published during the reign of Her Majesty.* 1969 London: Hugh Evelyn 72pp

Particular types of inventions:

Usher, Abbot Payson. *A history of mechanical inventions.* 1929 New York: McGraw Hill 401pp illus. (second edition 1954 Harvard University Press. Reprinted 1970)

Dummer, Geoffrey William Arnold. *Electronic inventions 1745-1976.* 1976 Oxford: Pergamon 164pp illus.

Patents

As Baker's book suggests, the key to detailed appreciation of many inventions is provided by patent literature.

Two works to give an idea of the changes in procedure and documentation, particularly during the period of this bibliography:

Harding, Herbert. *Patent Office centenary; a story of 100 years in the life and work of the Patent Office.* 1953 London: HMSO 48pp illus.

Gomme, A. A. *Patents of Invention. Origin and growth of the Patent system in Britain.* 1948 London: Longmans Green

Patent literature is complex and so introductions can be valuable:

Great Britain. Patent Office. *Searching British Patent Literature.* 1970 London: HMSO

Houghton, Bernard. *Technical information sources. A guide to Patents literature and technical reports literature.* 1972 London: Bingley

Newby, Frank. *How to find out about Patents.* 1967 Oxford: Pergamon 192pp

Capsey, Sydney Ross. *Patents: an introduction for engineers and scientists.* 1973 London: Butterworth 96pp

For those wishing to trace the minutiae of legal changes:

Patent Law of the United Kingdom. Text, commentary and notes on practice by the Chartered Institute of Patent Agents. Being a revised edition of The Patent Acts 1949-1961. (second edition 1968 with annual supplements to 1974). 1975 London: Sweet and Maxwell

White, T. A. Blanco. *Patents for inventions and the protection of Industrial Designs.* 1974 (fourth edition) London: Stevens

White, T. A. Blanco and Jacob, Robin. *Patents, trade marks, copyright and industrial design.* 1970 London: Sweet and Maxwell 189pp

Parsons, Charles Sidney. *Patents, designs and trade marks; a practical exposition of the nature, use and value in business of patents, designs and trade marks.* 1938 London: 183pp (supplement 1951)

The central documents are the Patent Specifications and the fine range of retrieval tools published by the Patent Office:

Patents for Inventions. Abridgements of Specifications. 1617-
(1617-1876 an unillustrated chronological listing in 100 subject classes
1855-1908 illustrated listing in 146 classes with 9 vols each class
1909-1930 illustrated listing in 271 classes with 4 vols each class
1931-1963 illustrated listing in 46 classes with volumes covering successive ranges of 20,000 consecutively published specifications)

Classification key

The reference index to the Classification key. (Alphabetic list of catchwords, details of structure and subjects)

Forward concordance to the Classification key (to link pre and post 1963 classifications)

Backward concordance to the Classification key (to link pre and post 1963 classifications)

The index to names of applicants in connection with published specifications complete (each volume covers 20,000 specifications, 25,000 after British Patent 1,000,000)

The divisional allotment index to Abridgements of Specifications (indicates in which division of the Classification Key an abridgement has been published)

Fifty years subject index, 1861-1910

Official Journal (Patents) 1884-(weekly) London: Patent Office (lists forthcoming specifications and specifications accepted)

To supplement these there are a number of 'unofficial' publications:

Fleet Street Patent Law Reports 1963- London

British Patent Abstracts 1951-(weekly) London: Derwent Publications

Woodcroft, Bennet. *Alphabetical index of Patentees of Inventions 1617-1852.* 1969 London: Evelyn Adams and Mackay 655pp

Industrial Designs

Registered industrial designs (as defined by the Registered Designs Acts 1949-1961, Copyright Act 1956 and Design Copyright Act 1968) differ legally from Patents both in protection and documentation.

Perhaps the best introduction to their nature is provided by the report:

Great Britain. Board of Trade. *Departmental Committee on Industrial Designs. Report.* 1962 London: HMSO 143pp

and the general guide:

Johnston, Dan. *Design protection. A guide to the law on plagiarism for manufacturers and designers.* 1978 London: Design Council 127pp

For legal details:

Russell-Clarke, Alan Daubeney. *Copyright in Industrial Designs.* 1974 (fifth edition) London: Sweet and Maxwell 360pp

Copinger, Walter Arthur and James, Francis Edmund Skone. *Copyright.* 1971 (eleventh edition) London: Sweet and Maxwell 920pp

Standardisation Literature

There are now many types of standards published: dimensional standards, standards of performance or quality, standards of testing, standardised terminology, and codes of practice. For British standards the central body is the British Standards Institution (founded 1901 as the Engineering Standards Committee of the Institute of Civil Engineers, obtaining a Royal Charter 1929 and adopting the title British Standards Institution in 1931) although it must be realised that the standards evolved by its Divisional Councils and over 4,000 technical committees have no mandatory implications, but are simply the basis for voluntary application. The main publications are:

British Standards Yearbook (a numerical listing of the various series of standards, brief descriptions and international recommendations)

Sectional Lists of Standards (for broad subjects such as plastics)

British Standard Handbooks

and the individual *Standards* themselves.

3 Social History

General Surveys

Marsh, David Charles. *The changing structure of England and Wales 1871-1951*. 1958 London: Routledge and Kegan Paul 266pp

Ryder, Judith and Silver, Harold. *Modern English society: history and structure 1850-1970*. 1970 London: Methuen 352pp illus.

Armytage, Walter Harry Green. *The rise of the technocrats: a social history*. 1965 London: Routledge and Kegan Paul 448pp

Williams, Raymond. *Culture and Society 1780-1950*. 1958 London: Chatto and Windus 348pp bibl. (Penguin edition 1961)

These touch on general issues, for detail:

Quennell, Charles Henry Bourne and Quennell, Marjorie. *A history of everyday things in England vol 4: 1851-1914*. 1958 (sixth edition) London: Batsford 228pp (many other editions) illus.

Ellacott, S. E. *A history of everyday things in England vol 5: 1914-1968* London: Batsford 224pp illus.

and then there are many more general histories that help to put social developments in a wider perspective, eg:

Webb, Robert Kiefer. *Modern England from 18th century to the present*. 1969 London: Allen and Unwin 652pp bibl.

Studies of working people can be very useful indicators of some of the social factors attendant on design changes:

Burnett, John (ed). *Useful toil: autobiographies of working people from the 1820s to the 1920s*. 1974 London: Allen Lane 368pp illus.

Fussell, George Edwin. *The English rural labourer. His home, furniture, clothing and food from Tudor to Victorian times*. 1949 London: Batchworth Press 160pp (Greenwood Press Reprint 1976)

The revolution in domestic service is particularly important:

McBride, Theresa M. *The domestic revolution: the modernisation of household service in England and France 1820-1920*. 1976 London: Croom Helm 160pp bibl.

Dawes, Frank. *Not in front of the servants: domestic service in England 1850-1939*. 1973 London: Wayland 160pp

PICTORIAL PRESS

The longest lived illustrated magazines are very useful and accessible sources of social and design detail:

Art Journal 1849-1912 London (previously *The Art Union* 1839-1848)

The Graphic. An illustrated weekly newspaper. 1869-1932 London

Illustrated London News 1842- (weekly) London (University Microfilms)

A number of anthologies and selections have been made, eg:

Bishop, James. *The Illustrated London News social history of Edwardian Britain*. 1977 London: Angus and Robertson 160pp illus. bibl.

L'Illustration 1843-1944 Paris

Picture Post 1935-1957 London

Punch 1841- (weekly)

Some selections:

Adburgham, Alison. *A Punch history of manners and modes 1841-1940*. 1961 London: Hutchinson 367pp illus.

'Punch as referee of a hundred years of household taste, introduction by James Laver, commentary by William Gaunt', *Architectural Review* vol 107 May 1950 pp 309-323

Nineteenth century

Taste and manners:

Dutton, Ralph S. *Victorian home. Some aspects of nineteenth century taste and manners*. 1954 London: Batsford 206pp illus.

Laver, James. *The Age of Optimism. Manners and morals 1848-1914.* 1966 London: Weidenfeld and Nicolson 272pp illus. bibl.

Morley, John. *Death, heaven and the Victorians.* 1971 London: Studio Vista 208pp illus. bibl.

Illustrations:

Evans, Hilary and Evans, Mary. *The Victorians: at home and at work as illustrated by themselves.* 1973 Newton Abbot: David and Charles 112pp

Bentley, Nicolas. *The Victorian scene 1837-1901.* 1968 London: Weidenfeld and Nicolson 296pp (later edition 1971 Hamlyn)

and many, many others.

London:

De Maré, Eric. *The London Doré saw: a Victorian evocation.* 1973 London: Allen Lane 230pp

Metcalf, Priscilla. *Victorian London.* 1972 London: Cassell 190pp illus. bibl.

Increasing literacy and responses to industrialisation:

Altick, Richard D. *The English common reader: a social history of the mass reading public 1800-1900.* 1957 University of Chicago Press 430pp

Sussman, H. L. *Victorians and the machine: literary response to technology.* 1968 Cambridge, Mass: Harvard University Press 274pp illus.

Harvie, Christopher and others. *Industrialisation and culture 1830-1914.* 1970 London: Macmillan 460pp illus.

Life and labour:

Tobias, Richard C. 'Popular studies of Victorian life', *Victorian Studies* vol 17 December 1973 pp 209-215 (introductory review)

Fay, Charles Ryle. *Life and labour in the nineteenth century: being the substance of lectures delivered at Cambridge.* 1920 Cambridge University Press 319pp (fourth edition 1947)

Chancellor, Valerie Edith (ed). *Master and artisan in Victorian England. The diary of William Andrews and the autobiography of Joseph Gutteridge.* 1969 London: Evelyn Adams and Mackay 238pp

Wright, Thomas. *Some habits and customs of the working classes, by a journeyman engineer.* 1867 London 276pp illus.

Booth, Charles. *Life and labour of the people of London.* 1889 London: Williams and Norgate 2 vols (many later editions and selections)

Early and middle part of the reign:

Houghton, Walter E. *The Victorian frame of mind 1830-1870.* 1957 New Haven: Yale University Press 467pp bibl.

Clark, George Kitson. *The making of Victorian England.* 1962 London: Methuen 328pp

Best, Geoffrey. *Mid Victorian Britain 1851-1875.* 1971 London: Weidenfeld and Nicolson 316pp illus. bibl.

Young, George Malcolm (ed). *Early Victorian England 1830-1865.* 1934 London: Oxford University Press 2 vols

Young, George Malcolm. *Victorian England; portrait of an age.* 1936 Oxford University Press 213pp

Burton, Elizabeth. *The early Victorians at home 1837-1861.* 1972 London: Longman 336pp illus.

De Vries, Leonard (ed). *Panorama 1842-1865.* 1967 London: John Murray 160pp

Later:

Bott, Alan John (ed). *Our fathers 1870-1900: manners and customs of the ancient Victorians: a survey in pictures and text of their history, morals, wars, sports, inventions and politics.* 1931 London: Heinemann 249pp illus.

Bott, Alan John (ed). *Our mothers: a cavalcade in pictures, quotation and description of late Victorian women 1870-1900.* 1932 London: Gollancz 219pp illus.

Wiseman, E. J. *Victorian do-it-yourself: handicraft and pastimes of the 1880s.* 1976 Newton Abbot: David and Charles 168pp illus. (a selection from *Amateur Work*)

Pike, Edgar Royston (ed). *Human documents of the Victorian Golden Age.* 1967 London: Allen and Unwin 378pp

The 1890s:

Jackson, Holbrook. *The eighteen nineties: review of art and ideas at the close of the nineteenth century.* 1976 (fourth revised edition) Hassocks: Harvester Press 296pp (first edition 1913. History in terms of personalities)

Twentieth century

Halsey, Alfred H. (ed). *Trends in British society since 1900: a guide to the changing social structure of Britain.* 1972 London: Macmillan 578pp

Early:

Pike, Edgar Royston (ed). *Human documents of the age of the Forsytes.* 1969 London: Allen and Unwin 320pp illus.

Pike, Edgar Royston (ed). *Human documents of the Lloyd George era*. 1972 London: Allen and Unwin 272pp

Laver, James. *Edwardian promenade*. 1958 London: Hulton 236pp illus.

Clephane, Irene. *Ourselves (1900-1930)*. 1933 London: John Lane 240pp illus. (sequel to Bott's two studies)

After 1914:

Taylor, Alan John Percival. *English history 1914-1945*. 1965 Oxford University Press 709pp bibl.

Thomson, David. *England in the twentieth century 1914-1963*. 1965 Harmondsworth: Penguin 304pp bibl. (first edition 1964 Cape)

Marwick, Arthur. *The explosion of British society 1914-1970*. 1971 London: Macmillan 202pp bibl.

Between the wars:

Glynn, Sean and Oxborrow, John. *Interwar Britain: a social and economic history*. 1977 London: Allen and Unwin 276pp

Blythe, Ronald George. *The age of illusion: England in the twenties and thirties, 1919-1940*. 1963 London: Hamish Hamilton 293pp (Penguin edition 1964)

1920s:

Jenkins, Alan. *The twenties*. 1974 London: Heinemann 224pp illus.

Montgomery, John M. *The twenties. An informal social history*. 1957 London: Allen and Unwin 235pp pl 15

1930s:

Cole, G. D. H. and Cole, Margaret. *The condition of Britain*. 1937 London: Gollancz 471pp

Jenkins, Alan. *The thirties*. 1976 London: Heinemann 224pp illus.

Branson, Noreen and Heinemann, Margot. *Britain in the 1930s*. 1971 London: Weidenfeld and Nicolson 368pp

Garland, Madge. *The indecisive decade. The world of fashion and entertainment in the thirties*. 1968 London: Macdonald 254pp illus.

Graves, Robert and Hodge, Alan. *The Long weekend: a social history of Great Britain 1928-1939*. 1940 London: Faber 472pp

Muggeridge, Malcolm. *The thirties 1930-1940 in Great Britain*. 1940 London: Hamish Hamilton 326pp

Symons, Julian. *The thirties*. 1975 London: Faber 160pp illus.

Symons, Julian. *The angry thirties*. 1976 London: Eyre Methuen 128pp illus. (Picturefile series)

War:

Longmate, Norman. *How we lived then, a history of everyday life during the Second World War*. 1973 London: Hutchinson 586pp pl 16

1940s:

Sissons, Michael and French, Philip (eds). *The age of austerity 1945-1951*. 1963 London: Hodder and Stoughton 349pp illus.

1950s:

Montgomery. John M. *The fifties*. 1965 London: Allen and Unwin 368pp

Thompson, Alan. *The day before yesterday. An illustrated history of Britain from Attlee to Macmillan*. 1971 London: Sidgwick and Jackson 223pp illus.

1960s:

Levin, Bernard. *The pendulum years: Britain and the sixties*. 1977 London: Pan 447pp (first edition 1970 Cape)

Economic and business history

General studies:

Hobsbawn, Eric John. *Industry and empire: an economic history of Britain since 1750*. 1968 London: Weidenfeld and Nicolson 336pp illus.

Breach, R. W. and Hartwell, R. M. *British economy and society 1870-1970*. 1972 London: Oxford University Press 406pp

Feinstein, C. H. *National income, expenditure and output of the United Kingdom 1855-1965*. 1972 Cambridge University Press 244pp

Sayers, R. S. *A history of economic change in England 1880-1939*. 1969 Oxford University Press

More particular studies:

Milward, Alan Steele. *The economic effects of the world wars on Britain; prepared for the Economic History Society*. 1970 London: Macmillan 64pp bibl.

Tames, Richard. *Economy and society in nineteenth century Britain*. 1972 London: Allen and Unwin 156pp

Harrison, George Major and Mitchell, Frank C. *The home market. A handbook of statistics*. 1936 London: Allen and Unwin 149pp (later editions 1939, 1950 edited and enlarged by M. A. Abrams)

Dunning, John Harry. *American investment in British manufacturing industry*. 1958 London: Allen and Unwin 365pp

Jefferys, James Bavington. *Retail trading in Britain 1850-1950*. 1954 Cambridge University Press 497pp pl 13

Industrial history:

Henderson, W. O. *Britain and industrial Europe 1750-1870. Studies in British influence on the industrial revolution in Western Europe.* 1972 (third edition) Leicester University Press 268pp

Checkland, Sydney George. *The rise of industrial society in England 1815-1885.* 1964 London: Longman 471pp

Hammond, John Lawrence LeBreton and Hammond, Lucy Barbara. *The rise of modern industry.* 1925 London: Methuen 280pp (many later editions)

Fay, Charles Ryle. *Round about Industrial Britain 1830-1860.* 1952 University of Toronto Press 227pp

Chamberlin, E. R. *The awakening giant. Britain in the Industrial Revolution.* 1976 London: Batsford 168pp illus.

Dunning, John Harry and Thomas, Clifford J. *British industry. Change and development in the twentieth century.* 1961 London: Hutchinson 232pp

Erickson, Charlotte. *British industrialists: steel and hosiery 1850-1950.* 1959 Cambridge University Press 276pp

Buxton, Neil K. and Aldcroft, Derek (eds). *British industry between the wars.* 1977 London: Scolar Press 330pp (10 case studies: cotton and wool textiles, coalmining, shipbuilding, iron and steel, mechanical engineering, chemicals, motorcars, aircraft, electrical engineering, rayon)

Allen, George Cyril. *The industrial development of Birmingham and the Black Country 1860-1927.* 1929 London: Allen and Unwin 479pp illus. (Frank Cass reprint 1966)

Timmins, Samuel (ed). *Resources, products and industrial history of Birmingham and the Midland hardware district: a series of reports collected by the local industries association committee of the British Association at Birmingham in 1865.* 1866 London

Business history:

Barker, T. C. and others. *Business history.* 1971 London: Historical Association 39pp

Business History 1959- (two per year) London: Frank Cass

Areas of design activity

Graphic and print design

This section will pass swiftly from a few introductory pages on histories of graphic art and design in general to the more specific areas of book design, typography, illustration and associated activities.

General Survey and studies

Writing the history of the whole span of visual communication is a daunting task, but there is a history of graphic design in its broadest sense in:

Müller-Brockmann, Josef. *A history of visual communication. From the dawn of barter in the Ancient world to the visualized conception of today, translated from the German by D. Q. Stephen.* 1971 London: Academy Editions 336pp 570 illus.

Much smaller areas are covered by:

Cleaver, James. *A history of graphic art.* 1977 Wakefield: EP 282pp pl 64 bibl. (first published 1963 Peter Owen)

and:

Stubbe, Wolf. *History of modern graphic art.* 1963 London: Thames and Hudson 317pp illus.

PARTICULAR PERIODS

Beyond these there are a number of studies, particularly of graphic art of smaller periods.

Nineteenth century:

Roger-Marx, Claude. *Graphic art of the 19th century, translated by E. M. Gwyer.* 1962 London: Thames and Hudson 254pp illus. (first published as *La Gravure originale au XIX siècle*)

Jussim, Estelle. *Visual communication and the graphic arts: photographic technologies in the nineteenth century.* 1974 New York: Xerox 364pp illus.

Southward, John. *Progress in printing and the Graphic Arts during the Victorian era.* 1897 London: Simpkin Marshall 96pp illus.

Hamerton, P. G. *The Graphic arts.* 1882 London: Seeley, Jackson and Halliday 384pp illus.

Art Nouveau:

Menten, Theodore (ed). *Art Nouveau and early Art Deco.* 1973 New York: Dover 87pp illus.

Walters, Thomas. *Art Nouveau graphics.* 1972 London: Academy Editions 104pp illus.

Twentieth century

The graphic arts of Great Britain: drawing, line-engraving, etching, mezzotint, aquatint, lithography, wood engraving, colour printing. Text by Malcolm C. Salaman. Edited by Charles Holme. 1971 London: Studio 156pp illus.

Neumann, Eckhard. *Functional graphic design in the 20s.* 1967 New York: Reinhold 96pp 100 illus. (relation of fine art and commercial art, particularly in Germany)

Jones, James. *Graphic art of World War II.* 1975 London: Leo Cooper 272pp

Rosner, Charles. 'Graphic and advertising art in Britain', *Graphis* vol 16 no 92 November/December 1969 pp 466-489

Gerstner, Karl and Kutter, Markens. *Die neue Graphik – the new Graphic Art. English version by D. Q. Stephenson.* 1959 London: Tiranti 247pp illus.

Hamilton, Edward A. *Graphic design for the computer age: visual communication for all media.* 1970 New York: Van Nostrand Reinhold 192pp illus. bibl.

Lambert, Frederick W. *Graphic design Britain.* 1967 London: Owen 206pp

Lambert, Frederick W. (ed). *Graphic Design Britain 70.* 1970 London: Studio Vista 176pp illus.

Keen, Graham and La Rue, Michel (eds). *Underground graphics.* 1970 London: Academy Editions 92pp 80 illus.

Murgatroyd, Keith. *Modern graphics.* 1969 London: Studio Vista 160pp illus.

Then there are many more detailed surveys of specific areas arising from conference reports, eg:

Recent developments in graphic arts research: proceedings of the Tenth International Conference of Printing Research Institutes held in Krems, Austria, 1969, edited by W. H. Banks. 1971 Oxford: Pergamon 373pp illus.

JOURNALS

Perhaps the best sources of historical information on this extremely diverse area are the journals:

Arts et Métiers Graphiques September 15 no 1 1927-(Chadwyck-Healey 1927-1939. Index 1927-1939 published 1940)

Graphis. Internationale Monatsschrift für freie Graphik, Gebrauchs-graphik und Dekoration. September 1944- (German and English. Cumulative Index 1944-1953)

Die Graphischen Künste. 1879-1938 Vienna

Motif. A journal of the visual arts. November 1958-1967 London

Penrose Annual: review of the graphic arts 1895- (1895-1915 known as *Process Yearbook*)

There is a useful anthology in:

Printing in the 20th century. A Penrose anthology edited by James Moran. 1974 London: Northwood Publications 332pp (1895-1973)

and an index in:

Taylor, John. 'A checklist of Penrose articles 1895-1968', *Penrose Annual* vol 62 1969 pp 257-292

For more detail there are the indexes:

Graphic Arts Literature Abstracts 1954- (monthly) Rochester, New York Rochester Institute of Technology (previously *Graphic Arts Progress*)

Graphic Arts Abstracts: a digest of scientific technical and educational information for the Graphic Communication Industries 1947-(monthly) Pittsburg: Graphic Arts Technical Foundation

Graphic Arts Index: a classified list of the leading articles on printing trade journals and other periodicals on file at the United Typothetae of America Research Library 1923-1934 Washington (later published in *Typothetae Bulletin* and then the *UTA Service Bulletin*).

NATURE OF GRAPHIC DESIGN

There are a number of general discussions of the nature of graphic design and its applications which will provide a useful introduction to the varied aspects of graphic design. As time passes they become useful indexes to current thinking at the time of writing:

Rand, Paul. *Thoughts on design . . . introduction by E. McKnight Kauffer; illustrations from the author's work.* 1947 New York: Wittenborn 159pp illus. (many later editions)

Ivins, William M. Jnr. *Prints and visual communication.* 1953 London: Routledge and Kegan Paul 190pp illus.

Lewis, John and Brinkley, John. *Graphic design, with special reference to lettering,* *typography and illustration.* 1954 London: Routledge and Kegan Paul 198pp illus.

Anderson, Donald Meyers. *Elements of design.* 1961 New York: Holt Rinehart and Winston 222pp illus.

Bradshaw, Christopher. *Design.* 1964 London: Vista Books 127pp illus.

Fletcher, Alan and others. *Graphic design: visual comparisons.* 1964 London: Studio Vista 96pp illus.

Muller-Brockmann, Josef. *The graphic artist and his design problems.* 1971 London: Academy Editions 186pp (earlier editions published by Niggli, Teufen)

Levens, Al S. *Graphics: analysis and conceptual design.* 1968 (second edition) New York: Wiley 786pp illus.

Davis, Alec. *Graphics: design into production.* 1973 London: Faber 154pp 124 illus.

Glaser, Milton. *Graphic Design.* 1973 London: Secker and Warburg 242pp illus.

Turnbull, T. and Baird, Russel N. *The graphics of communication.* 1975 (third edition) New York: Holt Rinehart and Winston 462pp illus. bibl.

Craig, James. *Production for the graphic designer.*1975 London: Pitman 263pp illus. bibl.

Computer graphics have caused radical changes in design:

Siders, R. A. *Computer graphics; a revolution in design.* 1966 New York: American Management Association 160pp illus.

International Computer Graphics Symposium, Brunel University, 1968. Computer graphics: techniques and applications, edited by R. D. Parslow, R. W. Prowse and R. Elliot Green. 1969 London: Plenum 247pp illus. bibl.

Franke, Herbert W. 'Computer graphics', *Graphis* vol 28 no 161 pp 206-221

Green, Richard Elliot and Parslow, Robert Douglas (eds). *Computer graphics in management: case studies of industrial applications.* 1970 London: Gower Press 226pp illus.

For information on individual designers:

Commander, John (ed). *17 graphic designers.* 1963 London: Balding and Maunsell (chiefly illustrations)

Friend, Leon and Hefter, Joseph. *Graphic design. A library of old and new masters in the graphic arts.* 1936 New York: McGraw Hill 407pp illus.

Who's who in graphic art. An illustrated book of reference to the world's leading graphic designers, illustrators, typographers and

cartoonists, edited by Walter Amstutz. 1962
Zurich: Amstutz and Herdeg/Graphis
586pp illus. bibl.

*Graphic designers in Europe, edited by Henri
Hillebrand vol 1, vol 2* 1971, 1972 London:
Thames and Hudson –
*vol 1: Jan Lenica, Jean-Michel Folon, Joseph
Müller-Brockman, Dick Effers
vol 2: Edward Bawden, Hans Hillman,
Herbert Leupin, Giovanni Pintori.*

International organisations and their papers
and congresses are notable developments in
the 1960s.

IARIGAI (International Association of
Research Institutions for the Graphic Arts
Industry):

Hoare, Kenneth N. 'IARIGAI – ten years',
Penrose Annual vol 68 1975 pp 89-93

ICOGRADA (International Council of
Graphic Design Associations):

Icograda News Bulletin 1963 –

Icographic 1971 –

Print Design

The richest sources of general material are
some of the histories of printing:

Lewis, John. *Anatomy of printing: the
influences of art and history on its design.*
1970 London: Faber 228pp illus. (an
attempt to draw up the full historical
context of printing)

Twyman, Michael. *Printing 1770-1970: an
illustrated history of its development and uses
in England.* 1970 London: Eyre and
Spottiswode 283pp illus.

Berry, William Turner and Poole, Herbert
Edmund. *Annals of printing. A chronological
encyclopaedia from the earliest times to 1960.*
1966 London: Blandford 336pp

Clair, Colin. *A chronology of printing.* 1969
London: Cassell 228pp

Clair, Colin. *A history of European printing.*
1976 London: Academic Press 526pp
illus. bibl.

Clair, Colin. *A history of printing in Britain.*
1965 London: Cassell 314pp illus.

Handover, Phyllis M. *Printing in London from
1476 to modern times.* 1960 Cambridge,
Mass: Harvard University Press 224pp
illus.

Steinberg, Sigfrid Heinrich. *Five hundred
years of printing.* 1962 Harmondsworth:
Penguin 400pp (first published 1955)

Rosner, Charles. *Printer's progress: a
comparative survey of the craft of printing
1851-1951 dedicated to 100 years of British
printing by Balding and Mansell printers and
produced by them at their works at Wisbech,*

Cambridgeshire. 1951 London: Sylvan
Press 170pp illus.

Smaller periods:

McLean, Ruari. 'Printing', pp 167-173 in
Edwards, Ralph and Ramsey, L. G.
(eds). *The Early Victorian period
1830-1860.* 1958 London: Connoisseur

*Art for commerce: illustrations and designs in
stock at E. S. and A. Robinson, Printers,
Bristol in the 1880s, introduction by Michael
Turner and David Vaisey.* 1973 London:
Scolar Press 384pp (facsimile of stock
book)

Morison, Stanley. *Modern fine printing. An
exhibition of printing issued in England, the
United States of America . . . during the
twentieth century and with few exceptions
since the outbreak of the war.* 1925
London: Benn 64pp 328 illus.

See also:

Design and Industries Association *page 22*

Tarr, John Charles. *Printing today.* 1945
Oxford University Press 184pp pl 24

Some important journals:

British Printer: the leading technical journal
of the printing industry 1888-
(monthly) London: Maclean-Hunter
(numerous supplements with examples
of printers work)

Printing World 1878-(weekly) London:
Benn

Print Design and Production 1965- London:
Cox and Sharland

Print in Britain May 1953-December 1968

For scholarly reviews and historical
articles:

Library 1889-(quarterly) London:
Bibliographical Society (cumulative index
1877-1932)

Imprint 1913- London

Signature 1935-1940 (nos 1-15), 1946-1954
(nos 1-18)

Journal of the Printing Historical Society
1965- (annual) London

and shorter notices in:

Printing Historical Society Newsletter
1974-(quarterly)

See also journals detailed in the other
sections of Graphic Design.

A useful point of entry to the great mass
of commercial and technical information
that may now be historically useful is
provided by:

Printing Abstracts 1950-(monthly).
Leatherhead: Printing Industries
Research Association (formerly *PATRA
Journal* 1946-1950)

Machinery and practical techniques can make a useful introduction to some of the detailed considerations of the history of design:

Moran, James, *Printing presses: history and development from the fifteenth century to modern times*. 1973 London: Faber 263pp pl 64

Carter, John Waynflete and Muir, Percival Horace. *Printing and the mind of man: a descriptive catalogue illustrating the impact of print on the evolution of western civilisation during five centuries*. 1967 London: Cassell 280pp (expanded version of the catalogue of printed materials on display at the International Printing Machinery and allied trades exhibition, London 1963)

Handbooks and manuals are also invaluable:

Brinkley, John. *Design for print: a handbook of design and reproduction processes*. 1949 London: Sylvan Press 175pp

Thorp, Joseph. *Printing for business: a manual of printing practice in non-technical idiom*. 1919 London: John Hogg 180pp illus.

Warford, H. S. *Design for print production: the interaction between design, planning and production of print.* 1971 London: Focal Press 176pp pl 33

Gibson, Peter. *Modern trends in letter-press printing*. 1966 London: Studio Vista 110pp. illus.

Apart from these suggestions there are many more in the large bibliographies:

Bigmore, E. C. and Wyman, C. W. H. (eds). *A bibliography of printing. 1880-1884*. London: Quaritch 3 vols (reprinted in 1 volume by Holland Press 1969 996p)

Dictionary catalog of the history of printing from the John M. Wing Foundation, the Newberry Library, Chicago. 1962 Boston: G. K. Hall 6 vols and first supplement 1970 3 vols

Ulrich, Carolyn F. and Kup, Karl. *Books and printing. A selected list of periodicals 1800-1942*. 1943 Woodstock, Vermont: William E. Rudge for New York Public Library 244pp

Book Design
General introductions:

McLean, Ruari. *Modern book design from William Morris to the present day*. 1958 London: Faber 115pp pl 16 bibl.

McLean, Ruari. *Modern book design*. 1951 London: Longman for British Council 48pp pl 16

A bibliography to introduce some of the many aspects:

Myers, Robin. *The British book trade, from Caxton to the present day. A bibliographical guide to the libraries of the National Book League and St Bride's Institute*. 1973 London: Andre Deutsch/Grafton. 405pp

Then there are many much more general studies:

Escarpit, Robert Charles Etienne Georges. *The book revolution*. 1966 London: Harrap 160pp

Aldis, Harray Gidney. *The printed book . . . revised and brought up to date by John Carter and Brooke Crutchley*. 1951 (third revised edition) Cambridge University Press 141pp

Studies and documents of particular periods:

McLean, Ruari. *Victorian book design and colour printing*. 1972 (revised edition) London: Faber 253pp illus. (first edition 1963)

Lewis, John. *The twentieth century book, its illustration and design*. 1967 London: Studio Vista 272pp illus.

Smaller time-spans:

Hillier, Bevis. 'Books of 1874', *Connoisseur* January 1974 66-69pp

Krishnamurti, Gutala. *The eighteen-nineties (catalogue of) a literary exhibition (held at the National Book League 4-21) September 1973*. 1973 London: National Book League 204pp pl 8

British Bookmaker: devoted to the interests of the book printer, the book illustrator, the book cover designer, the bookbinder, librarians and lovers of books generally. 1887-1894 London (from 1887-1890 known as *Bookbinder* and later absorbed by *British Printer*)

Taylor, John Russell. *The art nouveau book in Britain*. 1966 London: Methuen 176pp illus.

Garvey, Eleanor M. *The turn of a century, 1885-1910; Art Nouveau – Jugendstil books. Catalogue by Eleanor M. Garvey, Anne B. Smith and Peter A. Wick*. 1970 Cambridge, Mass: Harvard University Dept of Printing and Graphic Arts 124pp illus. bibl. (exhibition at Houghton Library)

Eidelberg, Martin. 'Edward Colonna's, "Essay on Broom-Corn": a forgotten book of early art nouveau', *Connoisseur* vol 176 February 1971 pp 123-130

Die Insel. Monatsschrift mit Buchschmuck und Illustrationen, later Aesthetisch-belletristische Monatsschrift mit Bilderbeilagen. 1899-1901 Leipzig (Chadwyck Healey)

Holme, Charles (ed). *The art of the book. A review of some recent European and American work in typography, page decoration and binding.* 1914 London: *Studio* special number 276 illus.

Catalogue of the British section of the International Exhibition of the book industry and graphic arts. 1914 London: HMSO 309pp (Board of Trade catalogue for Leipzig exhibition)

Modern book production. 1928 London: *Studio* special number 186pp illus.

Miles, Hamish. 'The art of the book: recent work of some English presses', *Studio* vol 97 1929 pp 308-313

Symons, A. J. A. 'The art of the book in Great Britain', *Studio* vol 107 1934 pp 227-240

Symons, A. J. A. 'Book design this year, Illustration – Typography – Binding', *Studio* vol 110 1935 pp 319-325

Newdigate, Berhard H. *The art of the book.* 1938 London: *Studio* special Autumn number 104pp illus.

Ede, Charles (ed). *The art of the book. Some record of work carried out in Europe and the USA 1939-1950.* 1951 London: Studio 214pp illus.

Meynell, Francis. *English printed books.* 1946 London: Collins 46pp illus. (a general survey but reflecting its time)

Le livre et ses amis. Revue mensuelle de l'art du livre nos 1-18, November 1945-April 1947 Paris (Chadwyck Healey microfiche)

Exhibition of books arranged by the National Book League at the Victoria and Albert Museum (Catalogue compiled by John Hadfield). 1951 London: Cambridge University Press for National Book League 224pp (exhibition for the Festival of Britain)

Books for our time 1951. Edited and designed by Marshall Lee (a catalogue). 1951 New York: Oxford University Press 128pp

British book design (exhibition) 1945- London: National Book League (sizeable catalogues published 1945, 1951, 1952, 1956, 1957, 1974)

British book production (exhibition). 1960- London: National Book League (substantial catalogues 1960, 1964, 1965, 1966, 1970)

Taylor, Kim. 'The modern paperback', *Graphis* vol 15 no 83 May/June 1959 pp 238-243

Book Design and Production vol 1 no 1 Spring 1958-vol 7 no 4 Winter 1964 London

Textbook design exhibition 1966. Catalogue of an exhibition of books published between May 1962 and May 1965. 1966 London: National Book League 72pp illus.

and two bibliographies:

Myers, Robin. *A handlist of books and periodicals on British book design since the war to accompany the Galley Club exhibition of book design 45-66 selected by Will Carter.* 1967 London: Galley Club 12pp

Folio 21: a bibliography of the Folio Society 1947-1967 with an appraisal by Sir Francis Meynell. 1968 London: Folio Society 207pp illus.

Texts and manuals on the practice of design can provide a useful introduction to historical changes:

Williamson, Hugh Albert Fordyce. *Methods of book design: the practice of an industrial craft.* 1966 (second edition) London: Oxford University Press 433pp (first edition 1956)

Diringer, David. *The hand produced book.* 1953 London: Hutchinson 603pp illus.

Jennett, Sean. *The making of books.* 1973 (fifth edition) London: Faber 554pp 209 illus.

Hurlburt, Allen. *Publication design: a guide to page layout, typography, format and style.* 1976 New York: Van Nostrand Reinhold 138pp

Wilson, Adrian. *The design of books.* 1967 London: Studio Vista 160pp illus.

CHILDREN'S BOOK DESIGN

The main issues are best approached through the more general surveys of childrens books:

Muir, Percival Horace. *English children's books 1600-1900.* 1954 London: Batsford 255pp illus.

Hurlimann, Bettina. *Three centuries of children's books in Europe, translated and edited by Brian W. Alderson.* 1967 London: Oxford University Press 346pp illus.

Darton, Frederick Joseph Harvey. *Children's books in England; five centuries of social life.* 1958 (second edition) Cambridge University Press 367pp illus. (first edition 1932)

Field, Louise Frances. *The child and his book. Some account of the history and progress of children's literature in England.* 1891 London: Wells Gardner 356pp illus.

Two exhibitions:

Victorian children's books selected from the library of the Victoria and Albert Museum. 1973 London: National Book League 107pp illus.

Children's books of yesterday; a catalogue of an exhibition held . . . during May 1946. 1946 London: Cambridge University Press for the National Book League 192pp bibl.

Some surveys:

James, Philip. *Children's books of yesterday, edited by Geoffrey Holme.* 1933 London: *Studio* special Autumn number 128pp illus. bibl.

Holme, Charles Geoffrey. *The children's art book.* 1937 London: Studio 96pp illus.

There are many other studies that cannot be included here, including those aimed at the collector, eg:

Quayle, Eric. *The collector's book of children's books.* 1971 London: Studio Vista 144pp 166 illus.

DETAILS OF BOOK DESIGN

Title pages:

Simon, Oliver. 'The title page', *Fleuron* no 1 1923 pp 93-109

Stephen, George Arthur. *Modern decorative title pages . . . reprinted from Penrose's Pictorial Annual.* 1915 London: Penrose 32pp

Bookjackets:

Rosner, Charles. *The growth of the bookjacket.* 1954 London: Sylvan Press 74pp

Curl, Peter. *Designing a bookjacket.* 1956 London: Studio 96pp illus.

Rosner, Charles. *The art of the book jacket.* 1949 London: HMSO for Victoria and Albert Museum 12pp

Pearsall, Ronald. *Victorian sheet music covers.* 1972 Newton Abbot: David and Charles 112pp illus.

Stephen, George A. 'Publishers' book jackets', *Penrose Annual* vol 26 1924 pp 57-66

Grimsditch, Herbert B. 'British book wrappers', *Studio* vol 92 1926 pp 17-21

Symons, A. J. A. 'How the jacket sells the book', *Art and Industry* vol 22 June 1937 pp 213-227

Floud, Peter and Rosner, Charles. 'The book jacket comes of age', *Graphis* no 29 1950

Weidemann, Kurt. *Book jackets and record sleeves.* 1969 London: Thames and Hudson 149pp (originally published as *Buchumschlage und Schallplattenhüllen* 1969)

Carr, Richard. 'Hardbacks sell soft', *Design* 255 March 1970 pp 34-39

Tanselle, G. Thomas. *Book jackets, blurbs and bibliographers.* 1971 London: Bibliographical Society (reprinted from 'Transactions of the Bibliographical Society', *The Library* June 1971 pp 91-134)

Illustrated endpapers:

Matthews, Maleen. 'The forecourts of pleasure', *Art and Antiques Weekly* July 23 1977 pp 16-19 (100 years)

PRIVATE PRESSES

Some of the most vital influences on developments in book design in general have been the experiments and revival of craft techniques in the private press.

Two general introductions:

Franklin, Colin. *The Private Presses.* 1969 London: Studio Vista 239pp illus. bibl. (pp 183-232)

Cave, Roderick. *The Private Press.* 1971 London: Faber 376pp illus

and a bibliography:

Modern British and American Private Presses (1850-1965). Catalogue of the holdings of the British Library compiled by P. A. H. Brown. 1976 London: British Museum Publications for the British Library 211pp

A few studies of some of the more important presses:

Chiswick Press:

Keynes, Geoffrey. *William Pickering, publisher.* 1969 (revised edition) London: Galahad Press 126pp illus. (employer of Chiswick Press)

Curwen Press:

Harley, Basil H. *The Curwen Press, a short history.* 1971 London: Curwen Press 40pp illus.

Simon, Herbert. *Song and words: history of the Curwen Press.* 1973 London: Allen and Unwin 261pp illus.

Gilmour, Pat. *Artists at Curwen: a celebration of the gifts of artists' prints from the Curwen Studio.* 1977 London: Tate Gallery 167pp illus. (pp 9-95 on the Curwen Press)

Curwen Press News Letter 1932- (irregular)

Essex House Press:

Ashbee, Charles Robert. *The private press: a study in idealism. To which is added a bibliography of the Essex House Press.* 1909 Chipping Campden: Privately printed

Golden Cockerell Press:

Gibbings, Robert. 'Art of the book: the Golden Cockerell Press', *Studio* vol 97 1929 pp 98-101

Gregynog Press:

Child, Harold. 'The complete book-builder. A survey of the Gregynog Press', *Studio* vol 99 1930 pp 277-282

Hutchins, Michael (ed). *Printing at Gregynog. Exhibition catalogue.* 1976 Cardiff: Welsh Arts Council 32p illus

Kelmscott Press and William Morris:

Sparling, Henry Halliday. *The Kelmscott Press and William Morris, master-craftsman.* 1975 London: Dawsons 177pp illus. (first published 1924 Macmillan)

Morris, William. *A note by William Morris on his aims in founding the Kelmscott Press. Together with a short description of the press by S. C. Cockerell and an annotated list of books printed thereat.* 1969 Shannon: Irish Universities Press 70pp (facsimile of 1898 Kelmscott Press edition)

Morris, William. *The ideal Book, a paper read . . . before the Bibliographical Society London. June 19, 1893.* 1907 London: L.C.C. Central School of Arts and Crafts 13pp

Dreyfus, John. 'New light on the design of types for the Kelmscott and Doves presses', *Library* fifth series 29 1974 pp 26-41

Franklin, Colin. *Emery Walker; some light on his theories of printing and on his relations with William Morris and Cobden-Sanderson.* 1973 Cambridge: Privately printed 35pp illus.

In fine print: William Morris as book designer. Catalogue of an exhibition 18 December-19 March 1977. 1977 London: William Morris Gallery 77pp illus. bibl.

William Morris and the art of the book. 1976 New York: Pierpont Morgan Library 140pp illus. (includes studies of Morris as book collector, calligrapher, typographer)

See also Important designers: William Morris *page 80*

NEWSPAPER DESIGN

Two compact introductions:

Hutt, Allen. *The changing newspaper: typographic trends in Britain and America 1622-1972.* 1973 Bedford: Gordon Fraser Gallery 224pp illus. bibl.

Morison, Stanley. *The English newspaper. Some account of the physical development of journals printed in London between 1622 and the present day.* 1932 Cambridge University Press 335pp

There is scope for a lot more research along the lines of:

Howe, Ellis. 'Newspaper printing in the 19th century', *Alphabet and Image* 4 1947 pp 5-31

Studies of current practice make a useful starting point for historical enquiry:

Evans, Harold. *Editing and design.* 1972-1974 London: Heinemann 5 vols – especially *Book 5: Newspaper Design.* 1974 214pp bibl.

Hutt, Allen. *Newspaper design.* 1967 (revised edition) Oxford University Press 326pp illus. (first edition 1960)

A few details and surveys:

Hutt, Allen. 'A new face for newspaper text', *Penrose Annual* vol 49 1955 pp 56-57

Hutt, Allen. 'Newspaper format: broadsheet to tabloid', *Penrose Annual* vol 54 1960 pp 70-72

Evans, Harold, 'Newspaper graphics', *Penrose Annual* vol 63 1970 pp 77-88

Meynell, Francis. *Typography of newspaper advertisements . . . With a display of typefaces . . . and a gallery of contemporary advertisements.* 1929 London: Benn 240pp

The Times has been particularly well documented:

Printing 'The Times' since 1785. Some account of the means of production and changes of dress of the newspaper. Illustrated with . . . facsimiles of pages . . . and line engravings. 1953 London: The Times 195pp pl 52

Printing 'The Times'. A record of the changes introduced in the issue for October 3, 1932. 1932 London: The Times 36pp

Morrison, Stanley. *The history of 'The Times'.* 1935-1952 London: The Times 4 vols

Magazine Design

The only work attempting to survey the whole field is:

McLean, Ruari. *Magazine design.* 1969 Oxford University Press 354pp illus.

There is a general history of periodicals in:

Dudek, Louis. *Literature and the press.* 1960 Toronto: Ryerson Press 238pp

and for particular types of magazines:

The Art Press. An exhibition of two centuries of art magazines at the Victoria and Albert Museum, London 1976. 1976 London: Art Book Company (there is also a complete photographic record of the exhibition on microfiche)

White, Cynthia L. *Women's magazines 1693-1968.* 1970 London: Joseph 348pp

Individual journals:

Spielmann, M. H. *The history of 'Punch'.* 1895 London: Cassell 592pp illus.

Wynn-Jones, Michael. '*Nova*. A magazine for the modern woman'. *Graphis* vol 24 no 137 1968 pp 250-257

Blake, John E. and Garland, Kenneth. 'Design analysis 21: *Radio Times*', *Design* 150 June 1961 pp 68-77

Typography

General histories of typography:

Blumenthal, Joseph. *Art of the printed book 1455-1955. A history of typography from the invention of printing to the present day.* 1973 New York: Pierpont Morgan Library 192pp illus.

Updike, Daniel Berkeley. *Printing types: their history, forms and use: a study in survivals.* 1962 Cambridge, Mass: Harvard University Press 2 vols (previous edition 1937)

Morison, Stanley. *The typographic book 1450-1935.* 1963 London: Benn 98pp pl 377 ('A study of fine typography through five centuries exhibited in upwards of 350 title and text pages drawn from the presses working in the European tradition. With introductory essay by Stanley Morison and supplementary material by Kenneth Day')

Johnson, Alfred Forbes. *Type designs: their history and development.* 1966 (third revised edition) London: Deutsch 183pp bibl. (previous edition 1960)

Dowding, Geoffrey. *An introduction to the history of printing types: an illustrated summary of the main stages in the development of type design from 1440 up to the present day; an aid to type identification.* 1961 London: Wace 278pp

Reiner, Imre. *Modern and historical typography. An illustrated guide.* 1948 (third edition) St Gallen: Zollikofer (translation of *Typo-grafik, Studien und Verstudien*)

Caslon, H. D. 'Developments in typefounding since 1720', *JRSA* vol 82 March 16 1934 489-505

Day, Kenneth (ed). *Book typography 1815-1965 in Europe and the United States of America.* 1966 London: Benn 432pp, especially Handover, P. M. 'British book typography', pp 137-174

Studies of shorter periods and some contemporary thoughts:

Johnson, A.F. '19th century typefounders and mechanical inventions', *Alphabet and Image* 3 December 1946 pp 37-47

Gray, Nicolette. *Nineteenth century ornamental typefaces.* 1976 (new edition) London: Faber 238pp illus. (first edition 1938)

Johnson, J. R. 'On certain improvements in the manufacture of printing types', *JSA* vol 21 March 1873 pp 330-338

Reed, Talbot Baines. 'Old and new fashions in typography', *JSA* vol 38 April 18 1890 pp 527-538

Twentieth century:

Lewis, John Noel Claude. *Typography: basic principles, influences and trends since the 19th century.* 1967 London: Studio Vista 96pp illus (first edition 1964)

Spencer, Herbert. *Pioneers of modern typography.* 1969 London: Lund Humphries 160pp illus. (stresses links with modern art and architecture)

Simon, Oliver and Rodenberg, Julius. *Printing of today. An illustrated survey of post-war typography in Europe and the United States. Introduction by Aldous Huxley.* 1928 London: Curwen Press 83pp

Typographical design and layout. 1930 London: Linotype and Machinery Ltd 93pp illus.

McMurtrie, Douglas C. *The fundamentals of modernism in typography.* 1930 Chicago: Eyncourt Press 17pp

McMurtrie, Douglas C. *Fitness to purpose vs. beauty in book typography.* 1933 New York: private printing 8pp

Ehrlich, Frederic. *The new typography and modern layouts.* 1934 London: Chapman and Hall 120pp pl 70

Curwen, Harold, Farleigh, John and Evans, Bertram. 'Modern typography', *JRSA* vol 86 October 14, October 21, October 28 1938 pp 1130-1140, 1150-1162, 1166-1179

Davis, Alec. 'Type comes into its own', *Art and Industry* December 1946 pp 172-179

Hutchings, R. S. 'The use and abuse of decorated printing types', *Art and Industry* December 1947 pp 198-205

Cheetham, Dennis and Grimbly, Brian. 'Design analysis. Typeface', *Design* 186 June 1964 pp 61-71

Many of the most recent changes and shifts in opinion are to be found in texts of current practice:

Lewis, John. *Typography design and practice.* 1978 London: Barrie and Jenkins 192pp

Bastien, Alfred James. *Practical typography explained for students.* 1955 (second revised edition) West Drayton: Bastien 118pp (first edition 1942)

Biggs, John Reginald. *Basic typography.* 1969 London: Faber 176pp

Dair, Carl. *Design with type*. 1967 London: Benn 164pp illus. (first edition 1952)

Klingspor, Karl. *Uber Schönheit von Schrift und Druck. Erfahrungen aus fünfzig Jahre Arbeit.* 1949 Frankfurt: Schauer 155pp (pioneer of *Fraktur*. Important section on nineteenth century attempts to reshape type)

Roberts, Raymond. *Typographic design.* 1966 London: Benn 224pp illus.

Ruder, Emil. *Typography design manual.* 1971 London: Academy Editions 274pp 500 illus. (text in German, English, French. Earlier edition 1967)

Simon, Oliver. *Introduction to typography, edited by David Bland.* 1963 London: Faber 164pp illus. (first edition 1945)

Swann, Cal. *Techniques of typography.* 1969 London: Lund Humphries 96pp illus.

Tarr, John Charles. *Design in typography. An introduction.* 1951 London: Phoenix 31pp

Warde, Beatrice Lamberton. *The Crystal Goblet: sixteen essays in typography. Selected and edited by Henry Jacob.* 1956 London: Sylvan Press 221pp

Miller, Anthony Mackay. *Type for books: a designer's manual.* 1976 (third edition) London: Bodley Head.

Other useful sources are encyclopedias, atlases and collections of type-faces:

Berry, W. Turner, Jaspert, W. Pincus and Johnson, A. F. *Encyclopaedia of type faces.* 1970 (fourth edition) London: Blandford 420pp illus.

Sutton, J. and Bartram, A. *An atlas of type forms.* 1968 London: Lund Humphries 116pp illus.

Hutchings, Reginald Salis. *The western heritage of type design: a treasury of currently available typefaces.* 1963 London: Cory, Adams and Mackay 127pp

Cowell, W. S. *A handbook of printing types with notes on the style of composition and graphic processes used by Cowells.* 1948 Ipswich: W. S. Cowell 115pp (first edition 1947)

Hutchings, Reginald Salis. *A manual of script typefaces; a definitive guide to series in current use, selected and arranged with an introduction, commentaries and appendices.* 1965 London: Cory Adams and Mackay 92pp bibl.

Hutchings, Reginald Salis. *A manual of decorated typefaces. A definitive guide to series in current use.* 1965 London: Cory Adams and Mackay 96pp

Rosen, Ben. *Type and typography: the designer's type book.* 1976 (revised edition) New York: Van Nostrand Reinhold 406pp illus.

and the more specialised:

Bastien, Alfred James (ed). *Encyclopaedia typographica. Part 1. Decor and classification of type. Part 2.* 1953, 1961 West Drayton: Encyclopaedia Typographica Pub. Co 332pp 267pp

Bastien, Alfred James (ed). *Printing types of a new world: monograph on a major British typographic alphabetics documentation compromising reproductions of alphabets from 'Typographica' (Bastien 1933) and recent sources illustrating the effect of world events in the early and mid-twentieth century on international type design.* 1963 West Drayton: Encyclopaedia Typographica 34pp

The printed word; first linotype and books . . . pages from books of leading publishers. 1938 London: Linotype and Machinery Ltd (type specimens)

Leaves out of books. Brought together as examples of 20 classic 'Monotype' faces at work. 1938 London: Monotype Corporation 6pp (11 leaves from 80 current books)

Balston, Thomas. *The Cambridge University Press collection of private press types: Kelmscott, Ashendene, Eragny, Cranach.* 1951 Cambridge University Press 45pp

Art Nouveau and early Art Deco: type and design from the Roman Scherer catalogue, edited by T. Menten. 1972 New York: Dover 87pp

A small introduction:

MacRobert, T. M. *Printed books. A short introduction to fine typography.* 1957 London: HMSO 6pp pl 46

Some journals rich in historical material:

Alphabet and Image nos 1-8 1946-1948 London: Shenval Press (quarterly resumption of *Typography*. After issue 5 called *Art and Technics*. Art Book Company Reprint)

Ars Typographica vols 1-3 1918-1934 New York (Art Book Company Reprint)

Bastien Typographica 1935 – (irregular) West Drayton

Fleuron. A journal of Typography 1923-1930 London 7 vols (edited by Stanley Morison and Oliver Simon. Art Book Company Reprint)

Image nos 1-3 1949-1952 London (Art Book Company Reprint)

Journal of Typographic Research 1967-1970 London (1971- titled *Visible Language*)

Monotype Recorder. A journal for users and prospective users of 'Monotype' machines 1901- (later absorbed by *Monotype Newsletter*)

Signature: a quadrimestrial of typography and graphic arts. Original series nos 1-15

November 1935-December 1940, New series nos 1-18 July 1946-1954 London (edited by Oliver Simon. Chadwyck Healey microfiche)

Typographica: contemporary typography and graphic art. 1949-1958, new series 1960-1967

Typography 1937-1939 London (edited by James Shand and Robert Harling)

A bibliography:

Williamson, Hugh Albert Fordyce. *Book typography: a handlist for book designers.* 1955 London: Cambridge University Press for National Book League 15pp

LETTERFORMS

Surveys and papers now of historical interest:

Day, Lewis F. 'Design in lettering', *JSA* vol 45 September 24, October 1 1897 pp 1103-1112, 1115-1125

Gray, Nicolette. 'Expressionism in lettering', *Architectural Review* vol 125 April 1959 pp 273-276

British Institute of Industrial Art. *The art of lettering and its uses in divers crafts and trades.* 1930 London: Oxford University Press 50pp

Gray, Nicolette. 'Lettering: the modern movement', *Architectural Review* vol 125 May 1959 pp 336-340

Oliver, M. C. 'The revival of lettering', *JRSA* vol 98 September 22 1950 pp 907-918 (particularly Smith and Johnston)

Holme, C. Geoffrey (ed). *Lettering of today.* 1937 London: *Studio* special autumn number 146pp

Laker, Russell. 'This lettering business', *Art and Industry* November 1946 pp 142-149

Reiner, Imre. *Lettering in book art, translated by C. C. Palmer.* 1948 St Gallen: Zollikofer 95pp illus.

Nesbitt, Alexander. *Lettering: the history and technique of lettering as design.* 1950 New York: Prentice Hall 300pp

Brinkley, John (ed). *Lettering today, a survey and a reference book.* 1964 London: Studio Vista 146pp (University Microfilms Books in demand)

More general and current texts are important, raising issues that have been historically interesting:

Greer, Alan and Greer, Rita. *Introduction to lettering.* 1972 London: Pitman 128pp 105 illus.

Ballinger, Raymond Aldwyn. *Lettering art in modern use.* 1966 London: Studio Vista 96pp illus. (previous edition 1952)

Biggs, John R. *Letterforms and lettering.* 1977 London: Blandford Press 128pp

Harvey, Michael. *Lettering design: form and skill in the design and use of letters.* 1975 London: Bodley Head 160pp

Gray, Milner and Armstrong, Ronald. *Lettering for architects and designers.* 1962 London: Batsford 160pp illus.

Carter, Harry G. 'Letter design and typecutting', (Percy Smith memorial lecture), *JRSA* vol 102 1954 pp 878 ff

Hewitt, William Graily. *Lettering students and craftsmen.* 1930 London: Seeley Service 336pp illus.

Hornung, Clarence Pearson. *Lettering from A to Z.* 1946 New York: Ziff-Davis Publishing Co 153pp

Thompson, Tommy. *The script letter: its form, construction and application.* 1966 London: Constable 128pp (revision of first edition 1939)

Leach, Mortimer. *Letter design in the graphic arts.* 1960 New York: Reinhold 192pp illus.

ALPHABETS

Some general studies:

Staples alphabet exhibition. The alphabet through the ages and in many lands. 1953 London: Staples

Diringer, David. *The Alphabet.* 1968 London: Hutchinson 2 vols 473pp 452pp illus.

Scarfe, Laurence. *Alphabets.* 1954 London: Batsford 191pp illus.

Day, Lewis F. *Alphabets old and new.* 1910 (third edition) London: Batsford 256pp (first edition 1898)

Gray, Nicolette. 'Alphabet', *Architectural Review* vol 120 August 1956 pp 109-114

Nineteenth century:

Delamotte, F. G. *Examples of modern alphabets, plain and ornamental.* 1859 London: Spon 48pp (many later editions)

Delamotte, F. G. *The book of ornamental alphabets, ancient and medieval, from 9th century to the 19th century.* 1858 London: Spon 50pp (many later editions – eighth 1874)

Victorian display alphabets: 100 complete fonts selected and arranged by Dan X. Solo from the 'Solotype Typographers Catalog'. 1976 New York: Dover 112pp

Strange, Edward Fairbrother. *Alphabets: a manual of lettering for the use of students with historical and practical descriptions.* 1898 (third edition) London: Bell 298pp

Art Nouveau:

Baurmann, Roswitha. 'Art Nouveau script', *Architectural Review* vol 123 June 1958 pp 369-372

Art Nouveau display alphabets: 100 complete fonts selected and arranged by Dan X. Solo. 1976 New York: Dover 100pp

Art Deco:

Loeb, Marcia. *New Art Deco alphabets.* 1975 New York: Dover 75pp

Later twentieth-century developments:

Smith, Percy John Delf. *Lettering: a handbook of modern alphabets.* 1936 London: Black 100pp

Bastien, Alfred James (ed). *Lettering alphabets for draughtsmen, advertisement designers, architects and artists.* 1942 West Drayton: Bastien (many later editions)

Reiner, Imre and Reiner, Hedwig, *Alphabets.* 1947 St Gallen: Zollikofer

Spencer, Herbert and Forbes, Colin. *New alphabets A to Z.* 1973 London: Lund Humphries 96pp

Particular letters:

Handover, Phyllis Margaret. *Grotesque letters: a history of unseriffed type faces from 1816 to the present day.* 1964 Redhill: Monotype Corporation 8pp illus. (reprinted from *Monotype Newsletter* no 69)

Megaw, Denis. '20th century san serif types', *Typography* 7 1938 pp 27-35

Lettering and its application:

Smith, Percy. 'Lettering and its uses today', *JRSA* vol 84 September 18, September 25, October 2 1936 pl 1111-1125, 1129-1141, 1145-1158

Bartram, Alan. *Lettering in the British Isles: street name lettering, fascia lettering, tombstone lettering.* 1978 London: Lund Humphries 3 vols 96pp each

Public lettering:

Barman, Christian. 'Public lettering', (Percy Smith memorial lecture) *JRSA* vol 103 March 18 1955 pp 281-293

Mansell, George. 'The planning and lettering of public notices and signs', *JRSA* vol 80 November 20 1931 pp 23-45

On buildings:

Bartram, Alan. *Lettering on architecture.* 1975 London: Lund Humphries 176pp

Gray, Nicolette. *Lettering on buildings.* 1960 London: Architectural Press 191pp illus.

Gray, Nicolette. 'Lettering on buildings', *Motif* 13 1967 pp 17-47

Tracy, Walter. 'Typography in buildings', *Motif* 4 1960 pp 82-87

Display:

Bain, Eric K. *Display typography (a comprehensive guide with practical exercises to the technique of display typography).* 1970 London: Focal Press 182pp illus. bibl.

Sharp, John. 'Design review. Fascia lettering', *Architectural Review* vol 122 October 1957 pp 281-286

Advertising:

Davis, Alec. *Type in advertising.* 1951 Leicester: Raithby Lawrence & Co 80pp

Day, Kenneth. *The typography of press advertisements.* 1956 London: Benn 320pp illus.

Tregurtha, C. Maxwell. *Types and type faces: an introduction to the study of type display and advertisement layouts.* 1927 London: Pitman 47pp (reprinted from *Modern Advertising)*

Reiner, Imre. 'Typography in advertising', *Art and Industry* vol 23 December 1937 pp 205-216

Schmoller, Heinrich. 'Modern typography in advertising', *Graphis* vol 9 no 48 1953 pp 290-301

Street lettering:

Gray, Nicolette. 'Street lettering', *Architectural Review* vol 121 April 1957 pp 225-229

Railway lettering:

Strevens, Peter. 'Railway lettering', (for GWR), *Architectural Review* vol 126 July 1959 pp 53-56

Wardle, B. L. 'Standardization of type by the LNER', *Commercial Art* vol 16 June 1934 pp 213-216

Business printing:

Spencer, Herbert. *Design in business printing.* 1952 London: Sylvan Press 104pp

Pickard, Peter. 'A designer's approach to commercial printing', *Art and Industry* February 1957 p 54

Government printing:

Carter, Harry. 'The typographical design of government printing', *Alphabet and Image* 5 September 1947 pp 3-15

McLean, Ruari. 'Design policy. Printing for the Crown', *Design* 179 November 1963 pp 37-43

CALLIGRAPHY

Child, Heather. *Calligraphy today.* 1976 London: Studio Vista 112pp illus. (c. 1850-1974. Previous edition 1962)

Some Important Individual Designers

ERIC GILL

Gill, Eric. *Autobiography.* 1940 London: Cape 283pp

Gill, Eric. *An essay in typography.* 1936 (second edition) London: Sheed and Ward 133pp (first edition 1931)

Gill, Eric. *The letter forms and type designs of Eric Gill, notes by Robert Harling.* 1976 Westerham: Eva Svensson 64pp (first published in *Alphabet and Image* 6 January 1948)

An exhibition of the work of Eric Gill, master of lettering, held at Monotype House, London, October 14th 1958. 1958 London: Monotype Corporation 6pp Illus.

Gill, Eric. 'What is lettering?', *Architectural Review* vol 73 1933 pp 26-28

Memoirs and studies:

Brewer, Roy. *Eric Gill the man who loved letters.* 1973 London: Muller 86pp

Speaight, Robert. *The life of Eric Gill.* 1966 London: Methuen 323pp illus.

Brady, Elizabeth. *Eric Gill: twentieth century book designer.* 1975 New York: Scarecrow Press 150pp illus.

Chesterton, G. K. 'Eric Gill and no nonesense', *Studio* vol 99 1930 pp 231-234

Gill, Cecil, Warde, Beatrice and Kindersley, David. *The Life and works of Eric Gill. Papers read at a Clark Library Symposium 22 April 1967.* 1968 Los Angeles: California University Press 67pp illus.

A tribute to Eric Gill. 1976 Oxford: Studio One

Warde, B. L. 'This month's personality: Eric Gill', *Commercial Art* vol 14 June 1933 pp 213-216

A bibliography:

Gill, Evan R. *Bibliography of Eric Gill.* 1953 London: Cassell 223pp illus.

EDWARD JOHNSTON

Johnston, Edward. *Writing and illuminating and lettering.* 1977 London: Pitman (first published 1906 J. Hogg)

Edward Johnston. *The House of David, his inheritance: a book of sample scripts 1914 AD.* 1966 London: HMSO for Victoria and Albert Museum 32pp

Johnston, Priscilla. *Edward Johnston.* 1969 London: Faber 316pp illus.

Cockerell, Sir Sydney Carlyle. *Edward Johnston. A tribute. One of six short papers read at a memorial meeting convened by the Society of Scribes and Illuminators.* 1947 Maidstone: Maidstone School of Art and Crafts 7pp

Hawkes, Violet. 'Edward Johnston at the Royal College of Art 1920-1935', *Alphabet and Image* 1 Spring 1946 pp 52-58

JOHN MASON

J. H. Mason RDI: leaves from my father's notebooks, a selection from the notebooks of a scholar-printer made by his son John Mason, illustrated by Rigby Graham. 1961 Leicester: Twelve by Eight Press 44pp

Mason, J. H. *Notes on printing considered as an industrial art.* 1926 London: British Institute of Industrial Art 24pp

John Henry Mason. Royal Designer for Industry. 1955 London: Central School of Arts and Crafts 31pp illus.

Owens, L. T. *J. H. Mason.* 1976 London: Muller 208pp illus.

FRANCIS MEYNELL

Meynell, Francis. *My lives.* 1971 London: Bodley Head 336pp illus.

Meynell, Sir Francis. *The typography of advertising: annual livery lecture of the Stationers' and Newspaper Makers' Company.* 1960 London: Institute of Practitioners in Advertising 24pp illus.

STANLEY MORISON

Morison, Stanley. *The art of the printer, 250 title and text pages selected from books composed in the Roman letter printed from 1500 to 1900.* 1925 London: Benn

Morison, Stanley. *First principles of typography.* 1936 Cambridge University Press 29pp (first published in *Fleuron* no 7 1920. Many later editions)

Morison, Stanley. *Four centuries of fine printing: one hundred and ninety two facsimiles of pages from books printed at presses established between 1465 and 1924.* 1960 (fourth edition) London: Benn 254pp (earlier editions 1924, 1949, 1957)

Morison, Stanley. *On type designs, past and present: a brief introduction.* 1962 London: Benn 80pp illus (first published 1923 as *On type faces*)

Morison, Stanley. *Politics and script: aspects of authority and freedom in the development of Graeco-Latin script from the Sixth Century B.C. to the twentieth century A.D. Edited and completed by Nicholas Barker.* 1972 London: Oxford University Press 368pp illus.

Morison, Stanley. *A review of recent typography in England, the United States, France and Germany.* 1927 London: Fleuron 62pp illus.

Morison, Stanley. *A tally of types, edited by Brooke Crutchley.* 1973 Cambridge University Press 138pp

Morison, Stanley. *The typographic arts (past present and future).* 1949 London: Sylvan Press 106pp pl 32

Studies:

Moran, James. *Stanley Morison: his typographical achievement.* 1971 London: Lund Humphries 184pp illus.

Jones, Herbert. *Stanley Morison displayed. An examination of his early typographic work.* 1976 London: Muller 128pp illus.

Barker, Nicholas. *Stanley Morison.* 1972 London: Macmillan 566pp illus.

Dreyfus, John. 'The impact of Stanley Morison', *Penrose Annual* vol 62 1969 pp 94-111

Moran, James. 'A tribute to Stanley Morison, RDI', *JRSA* vol 118 July 1969 pp 535-545

Warde, Beatrice. 'Stanley Morison: innovator', *Architectural Review* vol 129 May 1961 pp 341-343

Stanley Morison – a portrait (catalogue of an exhibition held in the King's Library, British Museum, 8th July-3rd October 1971). 1971 London: British Museum 64pp illus. bibl.

Bibliographies:

Appleton, Tony. *The writings of Stanley Morison: a handlist.* 1976 Brighton: Appleton 144pp

Carter, John Waynflete. *A handlist of the writings of Stanley Morison compiled by J. Carter with some notes by Mr Morison and indexes by Graham Pollard.* 1950 Cambridge University Press 45pp

Handover, Phyllis Margaret. *Stanley Morison: a second handlist, 1950-1959.* 1960 London: Shenval Press 57pp (reprinted from *Motif* 3)

HERBERT SPENCER

Smith, Bryan H. 'Penrose portrait: Herbert Spencer', *Penrose Annual* vol 68 1975 pp 193-208

WALTER TRACY

Hutt, Allen. 'Walter Tracy, type designer', *Penrose Annual* vol 66 1973 pp 101-115

JAN TSCHICHOLD

Tschichold Jan. *Asymetric typography, translated by Ruari McLean.* 1967 London: Faber 94pp (first published as *Typographische Gestaltung.* 1935 Basel)

Tschichold, Jan. *Designing books: planning a book, a typographer's composition rules, fifty eight examples . . . translated by Joyce Wittenborn.* 1951 New York: Wittenborn 21pp (first published as *Im Dienste des Buches.* 1951 St Gallen)

Tschichold, Jan. *An illustrated history of lettering and writing.* 1946 London: Zwemmer 18pp pl 70 (*Geschichte der Schrift in Bildern*)

Tschichold, Jan. 'New paths in poster work', *Commercial Art* June 1931 pp 242-247

Tschichold, Jan. 'The new typography', in Martin, J. L. and others. *Circle.* 1971 London: Faber

Tschichold, Jan. 'On mass-producing the classics, *Signature* 3 March 1947

Tschichold, Jan. 'Origin and development of contemporary typography', *Isomorph translation* 3 (1946)

Tschichold, Jan. *These are the fundamental ideas of my typography – typographical work of Jan Schichold.* 1935 London: Lund Humphries 8pp

Tschichold, Jan. *Treasury of alphabets and lettering: a source book of the best letter forms of past and present.* 1966 New York: Reinhold 236pp illus. (translation of *Meisterbuch der Schrift*)

Tschichold, Jan. 'Type mixtures', *Typography* no 3 1937 pp 2-7

Two exhibitions:

Jan Tschichold: an exhibition . . . 9 April-30 May 1975 (Catalogue complied by James Mosley). 1975 London: St Bride's Institute 23pp

Jan Tschichold, Typograph und Schriftenwerfer 1902-1974 das Lebenswerk. 1976 Zurich: Kunstgewerbemuseum 78pp illus. (very full bibliography. pp 64-77 by Rudolf Hostettler).

Tributes/studies:

Rand, Paul. 'Tschichold', *Print* vol 23 1969 pp 45-59 (part of a special issue titled 'Great Graphic Designers of the 20th Century')

McLean, Ruari. *Jan Tschichold: typographer.* 1975 London: Lund Humphries 160pp illus. (particularly on the influence of *Die neue typographie* 1928)

McLean, Ruari. 'Jan Tschichold', *Penrose Annual* vol 63 1970 pp 88-104

McLean, Ruari. 'Book design's debt to Tschichold', *Penrose Annual* vol 68 1975 pp 181-185

Layout

Some of the earlier annuals and theories are guides to changes:

Bartels, Samuel. *The art of spacing; a treatise on the proper distribution of white space in typography.* 1926 Chicago: Inland Printer 110pp illus.

Knights, Charles Cromwell and Swann, Edward. *Layout and commercial art.* 1932 London: Butterworth 388pp pl 192

Tolmer, André. *Mise en page: the theory and practice of layout.* 1931 London: Studio (text also in French. Examples and text)

'Forgotten landmarks 3. 1931 Mise en Page by A. Tolmer' (the effect of Tolmer's study of theory and practice on book lay-out and design) *Art and Industry* May 1948 pp 174-183

Wade, Cecil. *Layout; its theory and practice in modern commercial art.* 1934 London: Pitman 92pp illus.

Steer, Vincent. *Printing design and layout: the manual for printers, typographers and all designers and users of printing and advertising.* 1934 London: Virtue 400pp (many later editions – fourth 1951)

Dowding, Geoffrey. *Finer points in the spacing and arrangement of type.* 1954 London: Wace 60pp (another edition 1966)

Ballinger, Ramond Aldwyn. *Layout and graphic design.* 1970 London: Studio Vista 96pp illus.

Setting and Composition

Moran, James. *The composition of reading matter.* 1966 London: Wace 80pp (surveys history of type composition)

Huss, Richard E. *The development of printers' mechanical typesetting methods 1822-1925.* 1972 Charlottesville: University Press of Virginia 307pp illus.

Southward, John. *Type-composing machines of the past, the present and the future.* 1890 London: Truslove and Shirley 51pp

Barnett, Michael P. *Computer type-setting: experiments and prospects.* 1966 Cambridge, Mass: MIT Press 272pp illus.

Brewer, Roy. 'Typesetting by computer – a new challenge to graphic designers', *Design* 212 August 1966 pp 40-43

Legibility

Towards the end of the period studies of legibility became more formalised and detailed:

Spencer, Herbert. *The visible word.* 1969 (second edition) London: Lund Humphries for Royal College of Art 107pp illus. bibl. pp 85-107 (previous edition 1968)

Zachrisson, Bror. *Studies in the legibility of printed text.* 1965 Stockholm: Almqvist and Wiksell 225 pp bibl. (Stockholm studies in educational psychology 11)

Legibility Research Abstracts 1970- London: Lund Humphries (Research later dropped from title)

Book Illustration

Some general period studies:

Hofer, Philip and Garvey, Eleanor. *The artist and the book 1860-1960.* 1967 London: John Lewis

Bland, David. *A history of book illustration: the illuminated manuscript and the printed book.*

1969 (second edition) London: Faber 459pp illus. (first edition 1958)

Bland, David. *The illustration of books. Part 1. History of Illustration Part 2. Processes and their application.* 1951 London: Faber 200pp illus. bibl.

Slythe, R. Margaret. *The art of illustration 1750-1900.* 1970 London: Library Association 144pp illus.

Surveys of nineteenth-century illustration:

Wakeman, Geoffrey. *Victorian book illustration. The technical revolution.* 1973 Newton Abbot: David and Charles 182pp illus. bibl.

Wakeman, Geoffrey. *XIX century illustration: some methods used in English books.* 1970 Loughborough: Plough Press (15 prints and pamphlet)

Muir, Percy. *Victorian illustrated books.* 1971 London: Batsford 287pp illus. bibl.

Ruemann, Arthur. *Das illustrierte Buch des XIX Jahrhunderts in England, Frankreich und Deutschland 1790-1860.* 1930 Leipzig: Insel Verlag 380pp illus. bibl.

James, Philip. *English book illustration 1800-1900.* 1947 London: Penguin 72pp illus. bibl.

Balston, Thomas. 'English book illustrations 1800-1900' chapter in Carter, John Waynflete (ed). *New paths in book collecting. Essays by various hands.* 1934 London: Constable 294pp

Harvey, John. *Victorian novelists and their illustrators.* 1970 London: Sidgwick and Jackson 240pp illus.

Kitton, Frederic George. *Dickens and his illustrators.* 1899 London: Redway 256pp

Maré, Eric de. 'The boxwood illustrators,' *Penrose Annual* vol 63 1970 pp 49-68.

Shorter periods:

Reid, Forrest. *Illustrators of the sixties: an illustrated survey of the work of 58 British artists.* 1928 London: Faber and Gwyer 295pp illus. (1975 Dover reprint)

White, Gleeson. *English illustration. 'The sixties' 1855-1870.* 1897 London: Constable 496pp (1970 Bath: Kingsmead reprint)

Pennell, Joseph. 'English book illustrations 1860-1870', *JSA* vol 44 April 3 1896 pp 455-456

Thorpe, James. *English illustration in the Nineties.* 1935 London: Faber 268pp pl 123 (Blom reprint)

More technical papers and advice:

Carr, J. Comyns. 'Book illustration, old and new', *JSA* vol 30 October 13, October 20, October 27 1882 pp 1035-1040, 1045-1053, 1055-1062

Hudson, James Shirley. *An historical and practical guide to art illustration.* 1884 London: Sampson 224pp illus.

Blackburn, Henry. 'The art of book and newspaper illustration', *JSA* vol 42 December 29 1893, January 5, January 12 1894 pp 93-99, 105-112, 121-127

Blackburn, Henry. *The art of illustration.* 1894 London: Allen 251pp (third edition 1904)

Hinton, Horsley. *A handbook of illustration.* 1894 London: Dawbarn and Ward 120pp illus.

Harper, C. G. *Practical handbook of drawing for modern methods of reproduction.* 1894 London: Chapman and Hall 161pp illus.

Layard, George Somes. *Tennyson and his Pre-Raphaelite illustrators. A book about a book.* 1894 London: Elliott Stock 68pp

White, Gleeson (ed). *Practical designing.* 1893 London: Bell 327pp illus. (Drawing for reproduction pp 181-223)

White, Gleeson. 'Drawing for process reproduction', *JSA* vol 43 February 15 1895

Twentieth-century illustration:

Sketchley, R. E. D. *English book illustration of today.* 1903 London: Kegan Paul 175pp illus.

Holme, Charles and Halton, Ernest G. (eds). *Modern book illustrators and their work.* Text by M. C. Salaman. 1914 London: Studio 12pp text 179pp illus.

Bradshaw, Percy Venner. *The art of the illustrator.* 1918 London: Press Art School 20 parts (each part consists of plates and commentary)

Salaman, Malcolm C. *British book illustration, yesterday and today.* 1923/1924 London: *Studio* special Winter number 176pp illus.

Darton, F. J. Harvey. *Modern book illustration in Great Britain and America.* 1931 London: *Studio* special Winter number 144pp

Sullivan, Edmund J. *The art of illustration.* 1921 London: Chapman and Hall 257pp illus.

Child, Harold. 'Modern illustrated books: artist and typographer set a standard for the connoisseur', *Studio* vol 100 1930 pp 33-41

Farleigh, John. 'The designer and his problem 6. Illustrating a book', *Design for Today* October 1933 pp 227-230

Gossop, Robert Percy. *Book illustration: a review of the art as it is today.* 1937 London: Dent 45pp illus.

Biggs, John Reginald. *Illustration and reproduction.* 1950 London: Blandford Press 240pp

Boswell, James. 'English book illustration today', *Graphis* vol 7 no 34 1951 pp 42-57

Ross, Robert. *Illustration today.* 1963 Scranton: International Textbook Co. 292pp illus. bibl.

These are a mere handful of references to introduce an easily documented subject. There are very many shorter reviews in the more popular design journals, eg:

Miles, Hamish. 'Some recent illustrated books', *Studio* vol 99 1930 pp 20-25

CHILDREN'S BOOK ILLUSTRATION

Feaver, William. *When we were young. Two centuries of children's book illustration.* 1977 London: Thames and Hudson 96pp illus.

Mahony, Bertha E. Latimer, Louise Payson and Folmbee, Beulah. *Illustrators of children's books, 1744-1945.* 1947 Boston: Horn Books 527pp illus. bibl. (with *Supplement 1946-1956,* compiled by Ruth Hill Viguers, Marcia Dalphin and Bertha Mahony Miller. 1957 299pp. *Supplement 1957-1966* compiled by Lee Kingman, Joanna Foster and Ruth Giles Lontoft. 1968 295pp)

Morris, Charles. *The illustration of children's books.* 1957 London: Library Association 18pp (Pamphlet no 16)

White, Gleeson. *Children's books and their illustrators.* 1897/1898 London: *Studio* special Winter number 68pp illus.

Gottlieb, Gerald. *Early children's books and their illustrations.* 1975 Oxford University Press 263pp illus.

Smith, Janet Adam. *Children's illustrated books.* 1948 London: Collins 49pp illus.

Taylor, Judy and Ryder, John. 'Children's book illustration in England', *Graphis* vol 23 no 131 1967 pp 232-241 (early 1960s)

Particularly Kate Greenaway:

Engen, Rodney. *Kate Greenaway.* 1978 London: Macdonald and Jane's 320pp illus.

Holme, Bryan (comp). *The Kate Greenaway book.* 1976 London: Warne 114pp illus.

Spielmann, M. H. and Layard, G. S. *Kate Greenaway.* 1905 London 321pp illus. (Blom reprint)

SPECIALISED FORMS

Scientific illustration:

'The artist in the service of science', *Graphis* 29 no 165 1973/74 pp 6-95 (series of short historical surveys)

Ridgway, John Livesey. *Scientific illustration.* 1938 California: Standford University Press 208pp (University Microfilms)

Blunt, Wilfrid Jasper Walter. *The art of botanical illustration.* 1950 London: Collins 304pp

Knight, David. *Zoological illustration.* 1977 Folkestone: Dawsons 192pp illus.

Hill, Thomas George. *The essentials of illustration. A practical guide to the reproduction of drawings and photographs for the use of scientists and others.* 1915 London: Wesley 91pp

Engineering drawing:

Booker, Peter Jeffrey. *A history of engineering drawing.* 1963 London: Chatto and Windus 239pp illus.

Science fiction and fantasy:

Frewin, Anthony. *One hundred years of science fiction illustration.* 1974 London: Jupiter Books 128pp illus.

Peppin, Brigid. *Fantasy: book illustration 1860-1920.* 1975 London: Studio Vista 192pp illus.

Diagrams:

Lockwood, Arthur. *Diagrams: a visual survey of graphs, maps, charts and diagrams for the graphic designer.* 1969 London: Studio Vista 144pp illus.

Fashion:

Bradshaw, Percy Venner. *Fashion drawing and designing.* 1936 London: Press Art School 6 parts

See also Costume and fashion *page 238*

Illustrated press:

Jackson, Mason. *Pictorial press.* 1885 London: Hurst and Blackett 363pp illus.

Blackburn, Henry. 'The art of popular illustration', *JSA* vol 23 March 12 1875 pp 367-375 (particularly newspaper illustration)

Townsend, Horace. 'Modern development of illustrated journalism', *JSA* vol 42 February 16 1894 pp 233-246

Waterhouse, R. 'News that's fit to draw: *The Sunday Times* and *The Observer*', *Design* no 307 July 1974 pp 52-57

See also *Illustrated London News* and other journals in Technical, social and economic factors: Social history *page 110*

Surveys of a few developments elsewhere in Europe:

Lang, Lothar. *Expressionist book illustration in Germany 1907-1927.* 1976 London: Thames and Hudson 246pp illus.

Pichon, Leon. *The new book illustration in France, translated by Herbert M. Grimsditch.* 1924 London: *Studio* special number 168pp

The exhibitions of book illustrations often provide one of the simplest introductions to the subject whether they concern themselves with broad periods:

The decorated page: eight hundred years of illuminated manuscripts and books. 1971 London: Victoria and Albert Museum

English book illustration since 1800. 1943-1944 London: Society for the Encouragement of Music and the Arts

The artist and the book, 1860-1960 in Western Europe and the United States (Exhibition held at the Museum of Fine Arts, Boston May 4-July 16, 1961) Introduction by Philip Hofer. Catalogue by Eleanor M. Garvey. 1961 Cambridge, Mass: Harvard College Library, Dept of Printing and Graphic Arts 232pp illus. bibl.

or shorter spans:

Book illustration of the Sixties (A reissue of the catalogue of the 1923 exhibition at the National Gallery). 1924 London: Whitechapel Art Gallery

British book illustration, 1935-1945, with introduction by Philip James. 1946 London: National Book League

Book illustration in England 1949-1954. 1954 London: Arts Council 12pp

or individuals:

Eric Ravilious 1903-1942: an exhibition of watercolours, wood engravings, illustrations, designs. 1958 Sheffield: Graves Art Gallery

The literature on book illustration is very large. While most of the larger studies include detailed lists, convenient introductions are provided by:

Bland, David. 'A bibliography of book illustration', *The Book* no 4 1955 16pp (published by the National Book League)

and the large bibliography in:

Ray, Gordon N. (ed). *The illustration and the book in England from 1790 to 1914.* 1976 New York: Oxford University Press 370pp 296 illus.

SOME INDIVIDUAL ILLUSTRATORS

Book illustrators 1860-1900. 1977 Birmingham: Birmingham Bookshops 200pp (a bibliography of over 100 British book illustrators published during this period)

EDWARD BAWDEN

Harling, Robert. *Edward Bawden.* 1950 London: Art and Technics 104pp

AUBREY BEARDSLEY

Reade, Brian. *Beardsley*. 1967 London: Studio Vista 338pp

Gallatin, Albert Eugene. *Aubrey Beardsley. Catalogue of drawings and bibliography*. 1945 New York: Grolier Club 141pp

WALTER CRANE

Engen, Rodney K. *Walter Crane as book illustrator*. 1975 London: Academy Editions 105pp illus.

Crane, Walter. *Of the decorative illustration of books old and new*. 1896 London: Bell 337pp illus. (later editions 1901, 1922 – reissued 1972. Facsimile reprint 1977)

Crane, Walter. 'The decoration and illustration of books', *JSA* October 18, October 25 1889 pp 863-873, 875-881, 887-898

Massé, Gertrude C. E. *A bibliography of the first editions of books illustrated by Walter Crane*. 1923 London: Chelsea Publishing Co 59pp (facsimile reprint 1977 Carl Slienger)

GEORGE CRUIKSHANK

McLean, Ruari. *George Cruikshank: his life and work as a book illustrator*. 1948 London: Art and Technics 100pp illus.

Jones, Michael Wynn. *George Cruikshank. His life and London*. 1978 London: Macmillan 224pp illus.

Cohn, Albert M. 'George Cruikshank: a catalogue raisonné 1806-1877', *Bookmans Journal* 1924

RICHARD DOYLE

Hambourg, Daria. *Richard Doyle*. 1948 London: Art and Technics 96pp illus.

EDMUND DULAC

White, Colin. *Edmund Dulac*. 1976 London: Studio Vista 208pp illus.

ERIC FRASER

Davis, Alec. *The graphic work of Eric Fraser*. 1975 London: Uffculme Press 80pp illus.

GILES

Melville, Robert. 'Giles', *Architectural Review* vol 121 March 1957 pp 177-182

GEORGE HIM

Rosner, Charles. 'George Him', *Graphis* vol 18 no 94 1961 pp 146-155

LYNTON LAMB

Lamb, Lynton. 'The true illustrator. Lynton Lamb . . . writes on what makes artists into true book illustrators', *Motif* 2 February 1959 pp 70-77

Lamb, Lynton. *Drawing for illustration*. 1962 Oxford University Press 211pp pl 23

EDWARD LEAR

Lehmann, John. *Edward Lear and his world*. 1977 London: Thames and Hudson 128pp illus. bibl.

GEORGE DU MAURIER

Whiteley, Derek Pepys. *George du Maurier, his life and work*. 1948 London: Art and Technics 112pp illus.

PHIL MAY

Fletcher, Geoffrey. 'The incisive eye of Phil May', *Apollo* December 1962 pp 799-800

Thorpe, James. *Phil May*. 1932 London: Harrap 211pp illus.

Thorpe, James. *Phil May*. 1948 London: Art and Technics 96pp

JOSEPH PENNELL

Pennell, Joseph. *Modern illustration*. 1895 London: Bell 146pp illus.

Pennell, Joseph. *The illustration of books*. 1896 London: T. Fisher Unwin 166pp illus.

Pennell, Joseph. *Adventures of an illustrator*. 1925 London: T. Fisher Unwin 372pp illus.

ARTHUR RACKHAM

Gettings, Fred. *Arthur Rackham*. 1975 London: Studio Vista 176pp illus.

Hudson, Derek. *Arthur Rackham: his life and work*. 1973 London: Heinemann 181pp illus.

ERIC RAVILIOUS

Harling, Robert. *Notes on the wood-engravings of Eric Ravilious*. 1947 London: Faber for Shenval Press 72pp illus.

CHARLES ROBINSON

Salaman, Malcolm C. 'Charles Robinson', *Studio* vol 66 1916 pp 176-185

WILLIAM HEATH ROBINSON

Lewis, John. *Heath Robinson: artist and comic genius*. 1973 London: Constable 223pp

Baldry, A. L. 'The art of Mr W. Heath Robinson', *Studio* vol 89 1925 pp 243-249

REYNOLDS STONE

Piper, Myfanwy. *Reynolds Stone*. 1951 London: Art and Technics 96pp

EDMUND J. SULLIVAN

Salaman, Malcolm C. 'Edmund J. Sullivan: a master book-illustrator', *Studio* vol 88 1924 pp 303-309

SIR JOHN TENNIEL

Sarzano, Francis. *Sir John Tenniel.* 1948 London: Art and Technics 96pp

REX WHISTLER

Whistler, Laurence. *Rex Whistler 1905-1944: his life and drawings.* 1948 London: Art and Technics 103pp

Processes of Illustration

A few general works:

Brunner, Felix. *Handbook of graphic reproduction processes.* 1962 London: Tiranti

Lilien, Otto M. *History of industrial gravure printing up to 1920.* 1972 London: Lund Humphries 155pp (first edition 1957)

Eichenberg, Fritz. *The art of the print.* 1976 London: Thames and Hudson (includes some historical material)

Sotriffer, Kristian. *Printmaking: History and technique.* 1968 London: Thames and Hudson

Lewis, Charles Thomas Courtney. *The story of picture printing in England during the nineteenth century; or forty years of wood and stone.* 1928 London: Sampson Low 405pp pl 61

Lewis, John and Smith, Edwin. *The graphic reproduction and photography of works of art.* 1969 London: Faber 144pp illus.

Some earlier manuals and surveys:

Davenport, S. T. 'On prints and their production', *JSA* vol 18 December 10 1869 pp 62-71 (covers all methods available at time)

Burton, William Kinninmond. *Practical guide to photographic and photo-mechanical printing.* 1887 London: Marion & Co 355pp

Jacobi, Charles T. 'The printing of modern illustrated or decorated books, *JSA* vol 50 June 6 1902 pp 617-632

Poortenaar, Jan. *The technique of prints and art reproduction processes. A study of technical processes.* 1933 London: Bodley Head 174pp illus.

Curwen, Harold. *Processes of graphic reproduction.* 1934 London: Faber 143pp illus. (later edition 1946)

The technical aspects of book illustration are extremely complex and the number of historical surveys are comparatively few. A very fruitful approach to the subject is through the biographies of active practitioners, eg:

Dalziel, George and Dalziel, Edward. *The brothers Dalziel, a record of fifty years work, in conjunction with many of the most distinguished artists of the period, 1840-1890.* 1901 London: Methuen 359pp illus.

Evans, Edmund. *The reminiscences of Edmund Evans, edited by Ruari McLean.* 1967 Oxford: Clarendon Press 92pp illus.

Farleigh, John. *Graven image.* 1940 London: Macmillan 388pp illus.

COLOUR PRINTING

A general work:

Yule, John Arthur Carslake. *Principles of color reproduction applied to photomechanical reproduction, color photography and the ink, paper and related industries.* 1967 New York: Wiley 428pp illus.

An early history and surveys:

Burch, R. M. *Colour printing and colour printers.* 1910 (second edition) London: Pitman 279pp illus.

Peddie, R. A. 'The history of colour printing', *JRSA* vol 62 February 13 1914 pp 262-270

Dalziel, Harvey. 'Three colour printing', *JSA* vol 51 February 20 1903 pp 292-299

Nineteenth century studies:

Wakeman, Geoffrey and Bridson, Gavin D. R. *A guide to Nineteenth century colour printers.* 1975 Loughborough: Plough Press 127pp illus.

Wakeman, Geoffrey. *The production of nineteenth century colour illustration.* 1976 Loughborough: Plough Press

Tooley, Ronald Vere. *English books with coloured plates, 1790 to 1860; a bibliographical account of the most important books illustrated by English artists in colour aquatint and colour lithography.* 1954 London: Batsford 424pp illus. (reprint 1973 Dawsons)

Hardie, Martin. *English coloured books.* 1906 London: Methuen 340pp illus. (Kingsmead facsimile 1973)

Chromolithography:

Audsley, George Ashdown. *The art of chromolithography popularly explained and illustrated by forty four plates.* 1883 London: Sampson Low

Chromolithograph. A Journal of Art, decoration and the accomplishments . . . November 1867-September 1869 (an attempt to popularise colour printing. Includes series of articles by Christopher Dresser on the 1867 Paris Exhibition)

ENGRAVING

A general history:

Hind, Arthur Mayger. *A history of engraving and etching from the 15th century to the year 1914.* 1923 London: Constable 487pp illus. bibl. (Dover reprint 1963. Earlier editions 1908, 1911)

Wood engraving:

Garrett, Albert. *A history of British wood engraving*. 1978 Tunbridge Wells: Midas 416pp

Bliss, Douglas Percy. *A history of wood engraving*. 1928 London: Dent 263pp

Lindley, Kenneth. *The woodblock engravers*. 1970 Newton Abbot: David and Charles 128pp illus.

Hind, Arthur M. *An introduction to a history of the woodcut*. 1963 New York 2 vols (first edition 1935)

The nineteenth century:

Jackson, John and Chatto, W. A. *A treatise on wood engraving*. 1861 (second edition) London: Chatto and Windus 664pp illus. (first edition 1839)

Gilks, Thomas. *The art of wood engraving*. 1866 London: Winsor and Newton 58pp illus.

Linton, William James. *The masters of wood engraving*. 1889 London: B. F. Stevens (lavish folio of reproductions)

Linton, William James. *Wood engraving: a manual of instruction*. 1884 London: Bell 127pp illus.

Linton, W. J. 'Engraving in wood, old and new. Concerning the use of lines in engraving', *JSA* vol 38 April 4 1890 pp 487-494

Morris, William. 'The woodcuts of Gothic books', *JSA* vol 40 February 12 1892 pp 246-260

Holmes, C. J. 'Original wood engraving', *Architectural Review* vol 6 1900 pp 106-116

The twentieth century:

Holme, Geoffrey (ed). *Modern woodcuts and lithographs by British and French artists with commentary by Malcolm C. Salaman*. 1919 London: *Studio* special issue 204pp

Beedham, R. John. *Wood-engraving; with introduction and appendix by Eric Gill*. 1921 London: Faber (many later editions – sixth 1946)

Holme, Geoffrey (ed). *The woodcut at home and abroad. Commentary by Malcolm C. Salaman*. 1927 London: *Studio* special number 182pp

Furst, Herbert. *The modern woodcut; a study of the evolution of the craft*. 1924 London: John Lane 271pp illus.

Woodcut: an annual 1927-1930 London

Vox, Maximilian. 'British wood engraving of the present day', *Studio* vol 99 1930 pp 155-172

Salaman, Malcolm C. *The new woodcut*. 1930 London: *Studio* Spring special number 176pp

Leighton, Clare. *Wood engraving of the 1930s*. 1936 London: *Studio* special Winter number 192pp

Wood engraving in modern English books. The catalogue of an exhibition arranged by Thomas Balston . . . October-November 1949. 1949 London: Cambridge University Press for National Book League 48pp illus.

Balston, Thomas. *English wood engraving 1900-1950*. 1951 London: Art and Technics 84pp

Wright, John Buckland. *Engraving and etching: techniques and the modern trend*. 1973 New York: Dover 240pp 156 illus. (first edition 1952)

Bibliographies:

Hassall, John. *Wood engravings: a reader's guide*. 1949 London: Cambridge University Press for National Book League 16pp

Levis, H. C. (ed). *A descriptive bibliography of the most important books in the English language relating to the art and history of engraving and the collecting of prints*. 1912 (13th edition) London: Ellis 736pp (Dawson Reprint 1974)

ETCHING

General histories and surveys:

Guichard, Kenneth M. *British etchers 1850-1940*. 1977 London: Robin Garton 87pp pl 81 bibl.

Laver, James. *A history of British and American etching*. 1929 London: Benn 195pp

Bell, Frederick. *Etching in England*. 1895 London: Bell 184pp illus.

Sparrow, Walter Shaw. *Book of British etching from Francis Barlow to Francis Seymour Haden*. 1926 London: Lane 227pp illus. (much very early material)

Particularly nineteenth century:

Wedmore, Frederick. *Etching in England*. 1895 London: Bell 185pp illus.

English Etchings 1881-1891

The Etcher 1879-1883

Hamerton, Philip George. *Etching and etchers*. 1868 London: Macmillan 354pp illus.

Lalanne, Maxime. *A treatise on etching, translated by Koehler*. 1880 London: Sampson Low (original French edition 1866) 79pp illus.

Short, Frank. *On the making of etchings*. 1889 (third edition) London: Robert Dunthorne 43pp illus.

Paton, Hugh. *Etching drypoint, mezzotint. The whole art of the painter-etcher. A practical treatise*. 1895 London: Raithby 182pp

Twentieth century:

Holme, Charles (ed). *Modern etching and engraving*. 1902 London: *Studio* special Summer number 67pp

Holme, Charles (ed). *Modern etchings, mezzotints and drypoints*. 1912-1913 London: Studio special winter number 279pp

Holme, C. Geoffrey (ed). *Etchings of today. Introduction by W. Gaunt*. 1929 London: *Studio* special Spring number 24pp pl 1200

Buckland-Wright, John. *Etching and engraving*. 1953 London: Studio 240pp illus.

Gross, Anthony. *Etching, engraving and intaglio printing*. 1970 Oxford University Press 172pp illus.

LITHOGRAPHY

General:

Weber, Wilhelm. *History of lithography*. 1966 London: Thames and Hudson 259pp illus. (translation of *Saxa loquuntur*. 1964 Munich)

Floud, Peter. '150 years of lithography', *The Modern Lithographer and Offset Printer* October 1948

Simpson, William. 'Lithography; a finished chapter in the history of illustrative art', *JSA* vol 39 February 1891 pp 189-201

Man, Felix H. *150 years of artist's lithographs*. 1953 London: Heinemann 62pp illus. bibl.

Nineteenth century:

Wakeman, Geoffrey. *Aspects of Victorian lithography, anastatic printing and photozincography*. 1970 Melton Mowbray: Brewhouse Press 63pp

Pennell, Joseph and Pennell, Elizabeth Robins. *Lithography and lithographers; some chapters in the history of art*. 1898 London: T. Fisher Unwin 279pp illus.

British Lithographer 1891-1895 Leicester (merged with *British Printer*)

Richmond, W. D. *The grammar of lithography. A practical guide for the artist and printer*. 1912 (12th edition) London: Myers 254pp (first edition 1878)

McCulloch, George. 'Lithography as a mode of artistic expression', *JSA* vol 45 February 26 1897 pp 272-278

Twentieth century:

Cumming, David. *Handbook of lithography; a practical treatise for all who are interested in the process. Third edition thoroughly revised and with additional chapters dealing with offset printing, photo-lithography and other modern processes by C. Parkinson*. 1932 London: Black 368pp illus. (first edition 1904)

Pennell, Joseph. 'Artistic lithography', *JRSA* vol 62 July 3, July 10, July 17 1914 pp 701-724, 729-747, 753-760

Lithographie. Journal des Artistes et Imprimeurs 1936- Paris

Lawson, Leslie Edward. *Offset lithography*. 1963 London: Vista 184pp illus.

Faux, Ian. *Modern lithography*. 1973 London: Macdonald and Evans 336pp 187 illus.

Bookbinding

A small but well documented craft and industry.

General histories:

Nixon, Howard M. *Five centuries of English bookbinding*. 1978 London: Scholar Press 216pp pl 102 (based on 25 years of 'English bookbindings' series in *The Book Collector*)

Sadleir, Michael T. H. *The evolution of publishers binding styles 1770-1900*. 1930 London: Constable 95pp pl 12

Carter, John Waynflete. *Binding variants in English publishing 1820-1900*. 1932 London: Constable 172pp pl 14 (Bibliographia no 6)

Carter, John Waynflete. *More binding variants . . . with contributions by Michael Sadleir*. 1938 London: Constable 52pp

Wheatley, Henry B. 'The history and art of bookbinding', *JSA* vol 28 April 16 1880 pp 449-468

Harthan, John Plant. *Bookbindings*. 1961 (second revised edition) London: Victoria and Albert Museum 33pp (illustrated booklet no 2)

Howe, Ellie and Child, John. *The Society of London Bookbinders 1780-1951*. 1952 London: Sylvan Press 288pp

Studies of particular periods:

Nineteenth century:

Carter, John Waynflete. *Publisher's cloth: an outline history of publisher's binding in England 1820-1900*. 1970 Aberystwyth: CLW-University Microfilms 48pp (first edition 1935 Constable)

McLean, Ruari. *Victorian publishers' book bindings*. 1974 Bedford: Gordon Fraser 160pp 200 illus.

Price, Bernard. 'Some Victorian book-bindings', *Antique Dealer and Collectors Guide* November 1970 pp 78-82

Nixon, Howard M. 'Bookbinding' pp 163-166 in Edwards, Ralph and Ramsey, L. G. G. (eds). *The early*

Victorian period 1830-1860. 1958
London: Connoisseur

Modern bookbindings and their designers.
1899-1900 London: *Studio* special
Winter number 82pp illus.

Twentieth century:

Prideaux, Sarah T. *Modern bookbindings
their design and decoration.* 1906 London:
Constable 131pp

Leighton, Douglas. *Modern bookbinding. A
survey and a prospect.* 1935 London:
Dent 63pp illus.

Mansfield, Edgar. 'New directions in
modern bookbinding', *Graphis* vol 15
no 84 July-August 1959 pp 350-357

Robinson, Ivor and Middleton, Bernard
(ed). *Modern British bookbindings.
Illustrated catalogue of works by members
of the Designer Bookbinders.* 1971 London:
Designer Bookbinders 32pp illus.

Smith, Philip. *New directions in bookbinding.*
1975 London: Studio Vista 208pp illus.

Technical aspects of bookbinding:

Zaehnsdorf, Joseph William. *The art of
book binding.* 1890 (second edition)
London: Bell 190pp illus. (first edition
1880)

Wheatley, Henry Benjamin. *Bookbinding
considered as a fine art, mechanical art
and manufacture.* 1882 London: E. Stock
27pp

Wheatley, Henry B. 'Principles of design
applied to book binding', *JSA* vol 36
February 17 1888 pp 359-377

Vaughan, Alexander James. *Modern
bookbinding: a treatise covering both
letterpress and stationery branches of the
trade, with a section on finishing and design.*
1960 London: Skilton 218pp (first
published 1929 Raithby Lawrence)

Chivers, Cedric. 'Bookbinding', *JRSA*
vol 73 November 1925 pp 1077-1096

Darley, Lionel S. *Introduction to bookbinding.*
1965 London: Faber 118pp illus.

Hasluck, Paul N. *Bookbinding.* 1920
London: Cassell 160pp illus. (earlier
editions 1902, 1906, 1912)

Machine bookbinding:

Comparato, Frank E. *Books for the millions:
a history of the men whose methods and
machines packaged the printed word.* 1971
New York: Stackpole 374pp illus. bibl.
(eighteenth century to the present)

Stephen, George A. 'Modern machine
bookbinding', *JRSA* vol 59 February 17
1911 pp 339-360

Stephen, George A. *Commercial bookbinding.*
1910 London: Stonehill 59pp

Stephen, George A. *Machine book-sewing, with
remarks on publishers' binding.* 1908
Aberdeen: University Press 26pp

Darley, Lionel Seabrook. *Bookbinding then
and now: a survey of the first 178 years of
James Burn and Co.* 1959 London: Faber
127pp

Aspects of craft binding:

Middleton, Bernard Chester. *A history of
English craft bookbinding technique.* 1963
London: Hafner Publishing 307pp pl 11

Mason, John. *Edition case binding.* 1946
London: Pitman 69pp illus.

Mason, John. *Letterpress bookbinding.* 1946
London: Pitman 88pp illus.

Mason, John. *Stationery bookbinding.* 1946
London: Pitman 70pp illus.

Town, Lawrence. *Bookbinding by hand for
students and craftsmen.* 1951 London:
Faber 281pp illus.

Horne, Herbert Percy. *The binding of books.*
1915 (second edition) London: Kegan
Paul 232pp illus. (includes 'An essay on
the history of gold tooling' first edition
1895)

Designer Bookbinders Review 1973 – includes
some historical coverage, and other
collectors journals, such as *Book Collector*,
very often have articles on the more
specialised aspects of book binding. A
useful bibliography:

Hobson, Anthony Robert Alwyn. *The
literature of bookbinding.* 1955 London:
Cambridge University Press for the
National Book League 15pp

Some important individuals:

ROSSETTI

Grieve, Alastair. 'Rossetti's applied art
designs 2 Bookbindings', *Burlington
Magazine* February 1973 pp 79-84

COBDEN-SANDERSON

*Bookbindings by T. J. Cobden-Sanderson; an
exhibition at the Pierpont Morgan Library
September 3-November 3 1968. Catalogue
compiled by Frederick B. Adams Jnr.* 1968
New York: Pierpont Morgan Library
32pp pl 36

'The art of bookbinding, interview with Mr
Cobden-Sanderson', *Studio* vol 2 1898
pp 53 ff

'Cobden-Sanderson binding', *British Museum
Quarterly* July 1933 pp 37-38

DOUGLAS COCKERELL

Cockerell, Douglas. 'The binding of books',
JRSA vol 87 May 19 1939 pp 686-701

Cockerell, Douglas. *Bookbinding and the care
of books, revised by Sidney Cockerell.* 1978

London: Pitman 364pp illus. (first edition 1901)

Cockerell, Douglas. *Some notes on bookbinding.* 1929 Oxford University Press 105pp illus.

EDGAR MANSFIELD

Mansfield, Edgar. *Modern design in bookbinding. The work of Edgar Mansfield.* 1966 London: Owen 119pp pl 76

Exhibitions are a major source of information. A few of the most important:

Modern British bookbinders: an exhibition of modern British bookbinding by members of Designer Bookbinders. 1972 New York: Pierpont Morgan Library 64pp illus. (additional 18pp supplement printed to accompany transfer of exhibition to the Victoria and Albert Museum)

The history of bookbinding 1525-1950 AD 1957-1958 Baltimore Museum of Art

Bindings by members of the Guild London: Foyle Art Gallery for Guild of Contemporary Bookbinders (exhibitions 1955, 1956, 1960, 1962 held in Bournemouth-Southampton 1963, 1965, 1967, 1968, 1970 last two held at Hatchards Bookshop)

Publicity and Advertising

See also:

Posters *page 138*

Package design *page 144*

GENERAL HISTORIES

Elliott, Blanche Beatrice. *A history of English advertising.* 1962 London: Business Publications in association with Batsford 231pp pl 20

Turner, Ernest Sackville. *The shocking history of advertising.* 1965 London: Penguin 303pp (first edition 1952 M. Joseph)

Schuwer, Philippe. *History of advertising.* 1967 London: Leisure Arts 112pp (first published as *Histoire de la publicité*)

Sampson, Henry. *A history of advertising from earliest times, illustrated by anecdotes, curious specimens and bibliographical notes.* 1875 London: Chatto and Windus 616pp illus.

Sparrow, Walter Shaw. *Advertising and British art. An introduction to a vast subject.* 1924 London: John Lane 189pp pl 107

Preston, Gillian. *Advertising.* 1971 London: Batsford 96pp 65 illus. (*Past into Present* series)

PARTICULAR PERIODS

Nineteenth century:

Lauterbach, Edward S. 'Victorian advertising and magazine stripping',

Victorian Studies vol 10 no 4 June 1967 pp 431-444

De Vries, Leonard. *Victorian advertisements. Compiled in collaboration with Ilonka van Amstel.* 1968 London: John Murray 136pp illus.

Hindley, Diana and Hindley, Geoffrey. *Advertising in Victorian England 1837-1901.* 1972 London: Wayland 207pp illus.

Day, Lewis F. 'Art in advertising', *Art Journal* 1897 pp 49-53

Anthology of early material:

Hornung, Clarence Pearson. *Handbook of early advertising art vol 1 Pictorial, vol 2 Typographical.* 1956 (third edition) New York: Dover 242pp, 312pp

Twentieth century:

World graphic design: fifty years of advertising art, selected by Felix Gluck. 1968 London: Studio Vista 178pp illus.

Early years:

Field, Eric. *Advertising. The forgotten years.* 1959 London: Benn 158pp illus. (first 25 years of twentieth century)

Fairchild, E. C. 'Press advertising 1900-1926', *Commercial Art* vol 2 January 1927 pp 31-36

Official catalogue of the International Advertisers Exhibition, Crystal Palace, May 1900 70pp (issued with *The Poster* vol 5 no 29)

Haste, Cate. *Keep the home fires burning: propaganda in the First World War.* 1977 London: Allen Lane 230pp illus. bibl.

Postwar:

Jones, Sidney R. *Art and publicity. Fine printing and design. Edited by Geoffrey Holme.* 1925 London: *Studio* special Autumn number 172pp (includes letterheadings, booklets, boxpapers and labels, showcards, press adverts)

Bradshaw, Percy Venner. *Art in advertising. A study of British and American pictorial publicity.* 1925 London: Press Art School 496pp illus.

Menten, Theodore. *Advertising art in the Art Deco style.* 1975 New York: Dover 169pp illus.

Russell, Gilbert. *Nuntius. Advertising and its future.* 1926 London: Kegan Paul 96pp

Harrison, G. P. 'Humour in advertising', *DIA Quarterly* no 5 1928

Young, Frank H. *Modern advertising art.* 1928 London: Library Press 199pp

Harrison, John. 'New lamps for old', *Studio* vol 98 1929 pp 786-791

Sell to Britain through the 'Daily Mail'. 1930 London: Associated Newspapers 270pp illus. (comprehensive analysis of British Isles as a market)

'Press advertisements reviewed', *Commercial Art* vol 15 August 1933 pp 76-79

'Advertising and marketing at Olympia', *Commercial Art* vol 15 September 1933 pp 81-103

Levetus, A. S. 'What is wrong with present day advertising? interview with J. Klinger', *Commercial Art* vol 15 November 1933 pp 192-195

Butler, W. E. 'Selling power of the trade press', *Commercial Art* vol 17 October 1934 pp 125-137

'Modern art gets down to business; Herbert Bayer uses new method in design of brochure to announce the Miracle of Life exhibition, Berlin', *Commercial Art* vol 18 April 1935 pp 156-161

'Modern lay-out of booklets', *Commercial Art* vol 18 April 1935 pp 221-227

Pearce, K. 'Publicity through display', *JRSA* vol 83 July 26 1935 pp 862-874

'Survey of catalogues, brochures, press ads, and packaging for sports goods', *Commercial Art* vol 18 June 1935 pp 220-225

'Illustrated review of the trade press', *Commercial Art* vol 20 February 1936 pp 37-51

'Cross section of British press advertising', *Art and Industry* vol 22 January 1937 pp 1-16

Tolmer, André. 'Notes on the trend of art in publicity', *Art and Industry* vol 22 March 1927 pp 84-98

'British press advertising, 1937 vintage', *Art and Industry* vol 24 pp 78-88

Kauffer, E. McKnight. 'Advertising art; the designer and the public', *JRSA* vol 87 November 25 1938 pp 52-70

Gruber, L. F. 'Humoristische englische Werbung', (British humourous advertising)', *Gebrauchsgraphik* 15 January 1938 pp 2-17 (English and German texts)

Brumwell, J. R. M. 'Modern art in advertising', *Penrose annual* 1938-1939 pp 17-21

Wartime:

Rhodes, Anthony. *Propaganda. The art of persuasion World War II.* 1976 London: Angus and Robertson 320pp illus.

Mercer, Frank A. and Fraser, Grace Lovat. *Modern publicity in war.* 1941 London: Studio

Whitehouse, Roger. 'Rationed advertising (Small advertisements: an analysis of a

contemporary trend)', *Art and Industry* July 1940 pp 2-7

'Publicity in wartime – special issue', *Art and Industry* December 1940

Hobson, John. 'The influence and techniques of modern advertising 1. The social and economic context, 2. The techniques, 3. The influence of advertising on mass media and communications', *JRSA* vol 92 1944 pp 565-596

Since 1945:

Kaldor, Nicholas and Silverman, Rodney. *A statistical analysis of advertising and the revenue of the press.* 1948 Cambridge University Press 199pp (National Institute of Economic and Social Research. Economic and Social Studies no 8)

Reiner, Imre. *Grafika: modern design for advertising and printing.* 1947 St Gallen: Zollikofer 120pp

Art in British advertising: a selection from an exhibition organised by the Advertising Creative Circle and sponsored by 'The Times'. 1956 London: Arts Council

Gloag, John. *Advertising in modern life.* 1959 London: Heinemann 183pp pl 16

Design and Art Direction 1963- London: Designers and Art Directors Association (annual exhibition. First annual published 1964 Studio Vista)

Journals and annuals are prime historical sources:

AD: the international survey of advertisements, edited by Kurt Weidemann. 1966- New York: Praeger

Advertisers Weekly

The Advertising Review Summer 1954-November-December 1958

Annual of advertising and editorial art and design. 1922- (Art Director's Club of New York. Later editions published in UK by Pitman)

Commercial Art and Industry vol 1-5 no 6 October 1922-June 1926, new series vols 1-20 July 1926-1936 (continued as *Art and Industry)*

Display International: journal of commercial presentation. 1970- (previously *Display* 1919-1970)

Gebrauchsgrafik. International advertising art 1924-1943, 1950-1971 (continued as *Novum Gebrauchsgraphik* 1972-. Chadwyck Healey microfiche)

Graphis annual. International yearbook of advertising art. 1952-1953

Modern Publicity 1930- (previously *Posters and their designers* 1924, *Art and Publicity* 1925, special autumn numbers of *Studio*

1924-1926, *Posters and Publicity*
1926-1929)

Publicité 1936- Paris

Publicité et Arts Graphiques. Revue de la
publicité et des arts graphiques
1946-1947 Geneva (later *Packaging and
Window Dislay*)

WIDER ISSUES

Packard, Vance Oakley. *The hidden
persuaders*. 1957 London: Longman
275pp

Peach, Harry H. 'The advertiser and the
disfigurement of the countryside', *JRSA*
vol 78 December 20 1929 pp 144-162

SOME INDIVIDUALS

Havinden, Ashley. *Advertising and the artist*.
1956 London: Studio 48pp illus.

Havinden, Ashley. 'Advertising and
commercial design', *JRSA* vol 96 January
30 1948 pp 145-157

Gowing, Mary. 'The creative art in
advertising: influence of Ashley
Havinden', *Art and Industry* January 1957
pp 11-15

Henrion, F. H. K. 'Design's debt to Ashley',
Penrose Annual vol 67 1974 pp 33-46

James, R. H. 'Eric Fraser, creator of Mr
Therm', *Art and Industry* vol 22 May 1937
pp 183-192

Some early works on technique:

Gossop, Robert Percy. *Advertisement design*.
1927 London: Chapman and Hall 254pp

Freshwater, G. J. and Bastien, Alfred.
*Pitman's dictionary of advertising and
printing*. 1930 London: Pitman 447pp

Danvers, Verney L. *Training in commercial
art; the principles and technique of the subject*.
1926 London: Pitman 177pp illus.

Russell, Gilbert. *Planning advertisements*.
1935 London: Allen and Unwin 159pp
illus.

Layout:

Cox, R. H. W. *The layout of advertisements*.
1931 London: Pitman 196pp

Knights, Charles Cromwell. *Layout and
commercial art*. 1932 London:
Butterworth 388pp pl 192

Young, Frank H. *Technique of advertising
layout*. 1947 (revised edition) London:
Partridge Publications 185pp (first
edition 1936)

Sharpe, Leonard. *Advertisement layout in
practice. A guide for designers, illustrators and
advertisers*. 1937 London: Black 44pp

Ballinger, Raymond A. *Layout*. 1956 New
York: Reinhold 244pp illus. bibl. (later
edition 1970)

Baker, Stephen. *Advertising layout and art
direction*. 1959 New York: McGraw Hill
326pp illus. bibl.

Illustration:

Aymar, Gordon Christian. *An introduction to
advertising illustration*. 1929 New York:
Harper 236pp illus.

Fry, Roger. *Art and commerce*. 1926 London:
Woolf 22pp

Poulton, T. L. 'Scraper board, its nature,
uses and advertising value', *Art and
Industry* vol 21 July 1936 pp 4-17

Twining, Ernest W. and Holdich, Dorothy
E. M. *Art in advertising; a treatise on artists'
works in connection with all branches of
publicity*. 1931 London: Pitman 190pp

COLOUR

Knights, Charles Cromwell. *Colour in
advertising and merchandise display*. 1926
London: Crosby Lockwood 122pp illus.

Binder, Joseph. *Colour in advertising*. 1934
London: Studio 29pp pl 24

Biggs, Ernest. *Colour in advertising*. 1956
London: Studio 160pp illus.

Copy writing:

Russell, Gilbert. *Advertisement writing*. 1927
London: Benn 248pp

Press advertising:

Turner, John R. *What the press artist should
know*. 1936 London: Pitman 153pp illus.

Farmer, Courtney Douglas. *Advertisement
production for newspapers and periodicals: a
guide to the writing and designing of
advertisements*. 1950 London: Pitman
146pp

Outdoor advertising:

See also:

Posters *page 138*

Houck, John William (ed). *Outdoor
advertising: history and regulation*. 1969
University of Notre Dame 250pp illus.

Nelson, Richard and Sykes, Anthony
Edmund. *Outdoor advertising. Its function in
modern advertising and marketing*. 1953
London: Allen and Unwin 116pp

DETAILED STUDIES

There are a number of detailed studies of
advertising that has been evolved to serve
particular companies:

A history of Bovril advertising, compiled by Peter
Hadley. 1970 London: Bovril Ltd. 111pp

Williams, Iolo Aneurin. *The firm of Cadbury
1831-1931*. 1931 London: Constable
295pp illus.

'Design in relation to the problem: Cadbury
bros', *Commercial Art* vol 13 December
1913 pp 257-264

'Design in relation to the problem: the Gramophone Co Ltd', *Commercial Art* vol 13 November 1932 pp 210-220

Wilson, Roger Burdett. *Go Great Western: a history of GWR publicity.* 1970 Newton Abbott: David and Charles 198pp illus.

The first 25 years. History as mirrored in advertising of Shell-Mex and BP Ltd 1932-1957. 1957 London: Shell-Mex and BP Ltd 73pp

Connolly, Cyril. 'The new Medici (Shell-Mex and BP exhibition of pictures in advertising)', *Architectural Review* vol 76 July 1934 pp 2-4

Righyni, S. L. 'Simpson advertising, a campaign of ideas', *Art and Industry* vol 22 June 1937 pp 245-252

'Style and the product: Yardley's; interview with E. C. Morgan', *Commercial Art* March 1932 pp 107-111

Car advertising has attracted considerable interest:

Frostick, Michael. *Advertising and the motor-car, with a prologue by Ashley Havinden.* 1970 London: Lund Humphries 159pp illus.

Roberts, Peter. *Any colour as long as it's black: the first fifty years of automobile advertising.* 1976 Newton Abbott: David and Charles 144pp illus.

Wells, S. A. 'Evolution of motor advertising', *Commercial Art* vol 11 November 1931 pp 182-195

'Launching a new car; methods adopted by the British Ford Motor Co', *Art and Industry* vol 22 February 1937 pp 50-61

The role of the advertising agency and its methods has only been patchily studied. An introduction:

Treasure, John. *The history of British advertising agencies 1875-1939.* 1977 edinburgh: Scottish Academic Press 20pp

There is a great amount of other evidence concerned with particular campaigns and advertisements awaiting the researcher. Finally, a bibliography to introduce contemporary practice and its literature:

Thompson, J. Walter Company. *Advertising: an annotated bibliography.* 1972 London: National Book League 35pp

Posters

A popular subject for exhibitions and many picture books.

GENERAL HISTORICAL STUDIES

Barnict, John. *A concise history of posters: 1870-1970.* 1972 London: Thames and Hudson 288pp illus.

Hillier, Bevis. *Posters.* 1969 London: Weidenfeld and Nicolson 287pp illus. (covers period 1871-1968)

Hutchinson, Harold Frederick. *The poster. An illustrated history from 1860.* 1968 London: Studio Vista 216pp illus.

Müller-Brockmann, Josef. *History of the poster.* 1971 London: Academy Editions 244pp 291 illus.

Rickards, Maurice. *The rise and fall of the poster.* 1971 New Abbot: David and Charles 111pp illus.

Gallo, Max. *The poster in history, translated from the French by L. Emmet.* 1973 Feltham: Hamlyn 232pp illus.

Word and Image. Posters from the collection of the Museum of Modern Art. Selected and edited by Mildred Constantine. Text by Alan M. Fern. 1968 New York: New York Graphic Society 160pp illus. bibl.

Earlier studies:

Kauffer, Edward McKnight (ed). *The art of the poster. Its origin, evolution, purpose.* 1924 London: Cecil Parker 190pp illus. bibl.

Sheldon, Cyril. *A history of poster advertising, together with a record of legislation and attempted legislation affecting outdoor advertising.* 1937 London: Chapman and Hall 316pp

Hiatt, Charles. *Picture posters: a short history of the illustrated placard.* 1895 London: Bell 317pp

SPECIFIC PERIODS

Nineteenth century:

Wood, Robert William. *Victorian delight.* 1967 London: Evans 159pp illus. (reproductions of playbills, posters and printed notices by John Procter c.1830-1880 of Hartlepool)

Cirker, Hayward and Harward, Blanche. *The golden age of the poster.* 1971 London: 80pp illus. (last years of the century)

L'Affiche anglaise: les années 90. 1972 Paris: Musée des Arts Décoratifs

Posters 1890-1920. 1962-1963 London: Lord's Gallery

Rhead, Louis John. *Catalogue of an exhibition of sixty original designs for posters.* 1897 London: Hare 11pp

Gleeson, Gleeson. 'The poster and its artistic possibilities', *JSA* vol 44 January 17 1896 168-179pp

Spielmann, M. H. 'Posters and poster-designing in England', *Scribners Magazine* vol 18 July 1895 pp 34-47

Art Nouveau:

Sainton, Roger (comp). *Art nouveau posters and graphics.* 1977 London: Academy Editions 95pp illus.

Melvin, Andrew. *Art nouveau: posters and designs.* 1971 London: Academy Editions 105pp illus.

Rickards, Maurice. *Posters at the turn of the century.* 1968 London: Evelyn Adams and Mackay 72pp 32 illus.

Wember, Paul. *Die Jugend der Plakate 1887-1917.* 1961 Krefeld: Scherpe Verlag 342pp illus. bibl.

Twentieth century:

Rogers, W. S. *A book of the poster . . . illustrated with examples of the work of the principal poster artists of the world.* 1901 London: Greening 146pp illus.

Price, Charles M. *Posters.* 1913 New York: G. W. Bricka 380pp

Rogers, W. S. 'The poster: its essentials and significance', *JRSA* vol 62 January 23 1914 pp 186-194

Yockney, Alfred. 'Some recent London posters', *Studio* vol 63 1915 pp 281-292

Price, Charles M. *Posters: a critical study of the development of poster design in continental Europe, England and America.* 1918 New York: G. W. Bricka 386pp illus.

Darracott, Joseph and Loftus, Belinda (eds). *First World War posters.* 1972 London: Imperial War Museum 72pp illus.

Rickards, Maurice. *Posters of the First World War.* 1971 London: Evelyn Adams and Mackay 32pp 242 illus.

Pennell, Joseph. *Joseph Pennell's liberty loan poster: a text-book for artists and amateurs, governments and teachers and painters, with notes, an introduction and essay on the poster by the artist.* 1918 London: J. B. Lippincott

Hardie, Martin and Sabin, Arthur K. *War posters issued by belligerent and neutral nations 1914-1919.* 1920 London: Black 159pp illus. (University Microfilms)

Catalogue of war literature issued by HM Government 1914-1919 including recruiting, war savings and other pictorial posters. 1921 London: HMSO

Between the wars:

Rickards, Maurice. *Posters of the nineteen-twenties.* 1968 London: Evelyn Adams and Mackay 72pp 32 illus.

Taylor, Horace. 'The poster revival 1. Mr E. McKnight Kauffer, 2. Mr F. Gregory Brown', *Studio* vol 79, 80 1920 pp 140-147, pp 147-150

Jones, Sydney Robert. *Posters and their designers, edited by Geoffrey Holme.* 1924 London: *Studio* special Autumn number 11pp + 150pp illus.

'Forgotten landmarks III 1924 "Posters and their designers"', *Art and Industry* March 1948 pp 130-137

International posters exhibition. 1924 London: Whitechapel Art Gallery (further exhibition 1925)

Jones, Sydney R. *Posters and publicity. Fine printing and design.* 1926 London: *Studio* special Autumn number 165pp

Jones, Sydney R. *Posters and their designers.* 1927 London: *Studio* special Autumn number 150pp

Raffé, W. G. *Poster design.* 1929 London: Chapman and Hall 223pp illus.

Cassandre, A. M. (*pseud*) (ie Mouron, Adolph Edouard). *Posters (Plakate).* 1948 St Gallen: Zollikofer 188pp (study of various posters 1923-37)

Cooper, Austin. *Making a poster.* 1945 London: Studio 96pp (first edition 1938)

Mercer, Frank Alfred and Gaunt, William (eds). *Poster progress.* 1939 London: Studio 128pp illus.

Second World War:

Judd, Dennis (ed). *Second World War posters.* 1972 London: Imperial War Museum 72pp

Rotter, V. 'The war in posters. A review', *Art and Industry* September 1945 pp 66-79

'The other war: propaganda problems', *Art and Industry* July 1940 pp 14-15

Newton, Eric. 'The poster in war time Britain', *Art and Industry* July 1943 pp 2-16

Postwar:

Eckersley, Tom. 'British hoardings under fire', *Art and Industry* October 1949 pp 130-135 (criticism of postwar developments)

Souvenir catalogue International Poster Exhibition London 1951. 1951 London: Council of Industrial Design for Society of Industrial Artists (includes essay 'The changing background of the poster' by C. Rosner)

Allner, Walter Heinz (ed). *Posters: fifty artists and designers analyze their methods, and their solution to poster design and poster advertising.* 1952 New York: Reinhold 119pp illus.

Games, Abram. 'A future for British posters?', *Design* 123 March 1959 pp 23-27

'British posters', *The Times* 30 October 1961
(four-page supplement to mark the
centenary of the British Poster
Advertising Association)

Adams, James W. R. *Posters look to the future.*
1965 London: Poster Advertising
Planning Committee 48pp illus.

Posters and the planner in the 70s. 1969
London: Council of Industrial Design
28pp illus.

INDIVIDUAL CAMPAIGNS

*Original posters designed for the Empire
Marketing Board.* 1926 London: Royal
Academy of Arts

'Great advances in posters: Shell-Mex and
BP Ltd', *Commercial Art* vol 15 July 1933
pp 11-15

Holme, C. G. 'Thought behind a poster
campaign; the British Industries Fair',
Commercial Art vol 17 November 1934
pp 187-190

Lancaster, Osbert. 'Posters for British films
(Ealing Studios)', *Architectural Review* vol
105 February 1949 pp 88-89

Carr, Richard. 'The "For God's sake"
campaign', *Design* 236 August 1968
pp 32-36 (Salvation Army campaign)

*Posters for the Victoria and Albert Museum
designed by Peter Bradfield.* 1971 London:
Architectural Association

NOTABLE INDIVIDUALS

TOM ECKERSLEY

Eckersley, Tom. *Poster design.* 1954
London: Studio 96pp illus.

Elvin, René. 'Tom Eckersley and the art of
the poster', *Penrose Annual* 1976 vol 69
pp 33-45

Elvin, René. 'Tom Eckersley', *Graphis* vol
10 no 56 1954 pp 468-473

ABRAM GAMES

Games, Abram. *Over my shoulder.* 1960
London: Studio 84pp

Games, Abram. 'The poster in modern
advertising', *JRSA* vol 110 April 1962
pp 323-332

Games, Abram. 'Poster appeal to the army',
Art and Industry September 1942 pp 62-64

Games, Abram and Henrion, F. H. K. 'The
poster designer and his problems', *Art and
Industry* July 1943 pp 17-26

Tritton, Ronald. 'Abram Games', *Graphis* no
44 1953 pp 194-205

Levy, Mervyn. 'Abram Games and the
poster', *Studio* February 1963 pp 72-77

'War office posters by Abram Games', *Art
and Industry* January 1942 pp 9-11

E. McKNIGHT KAUFFER

Haworth-Booth, Mark. 'E. McKnight
Kauffer', *Penrose Annual* vol 64 1971
pp 83-96

Grigson, G. 'E. McKnight Kauffer:
evolution of a master designer',
Commercial Art vol 18 May 1935
pp 202-206

Rosner, Charles. 'In memoriam E.
McKnight Kauffer', *Graphis* vol 11 no 57
1955 pp 10-19

Symon, David. 'Simplicity and symbolism.
Some reflections on the work of E.
McKnight Kauffer', *Design for Today* May
1935 pp 163-167

Kauffer, Edward McKnight. *The art of the
poster, its evolution and purpose arranged
and edited by E. McKnight Kauffer.* 1924
London: Palmer 190pp illus. bibl.

*Posters by E. McKnight Kauffer . . . foreword
by Aldous Huxley.* 1937 New York:
Museum of Modern Art 24pp illus.

The work of E. McKnight Kauffer. 1935
London: Lund Humphries (exhibition)

*Memorial exhibition of the work of E.
McKnight Kauffer . . . Presented by the
Society of Industrial Artists with the support
of the Royal Society of Arts.* 1955 London:
Victoria and Albert Museum

E. McKnight Kauffer: poster art 1915-1940.
1973 London: Whitechapel Art Gallery

COLLECTIONS

It is becoming increasingly popular to
republish batches of particular types of
posters:

Rennert, Jack (ed). *100 years of bicycle
posters.* 1973 London: Hart Davis 112pp

Terry, Walter and Rennert, Jack (eds).
100 years of dance posters. 1975 London:
M. Dempsey 112pp

Rennert, Jack (ed). *100 years of circus
posters.* 1974 London: Studio Vista
112pp

Rickards, Maurice. *Banned posters; presented
and reviewed by Maurice Rickards.* 1969
London: Evelyn Adams and Mackay
72pp

Rickards, Maurice. *The public notice: an
illustrated history.* 1973 Newton Abbot:
David and Charles 128pp 265 illus.

Hillier, Bevis. *Travel posters.* 1976 London:
Phaidon 104pp 96 illus.

Shackleton, J. T. (comp). *The golden age of
the railway poster.* 1976 London: New
English Library 128pp

London Transport posters are especially popular:

Levey, Michael (comp). *London Transport posters.* 1976 London: Phaidon 96pp

Hutchinson, Harold F. *London Transport posters.* 1963 London Transport Board 124 colour illus.

Art for all: an exhibition of posters and their originals produced by London Transport, 1908-1949. 1949 London: Victoria and Albert Museum

Guyatt, Richard. 'London Transport. The posters of a public service', *Graphis* vol 15 no 83 May/June 1959 pp 194-201

A few useful journals and annuals with historical material on posters:

L'Estampe móderne nos 1-24 1897-1899 (Chadwyck Healey microfiche)

International Poster Annual '50. 1950 London: Pitman (many later editions published by Arthur Niggli, Teufen, Switzerland)

Les Maîtres de l'Affiche contenant la reproduction des plus belles affiches illustrées des grands artistes, francais et étrangers 1896-1900 Paris (Chadwyck Healey microfiche)

The Poster, an illustrated monthly becoming *The Poster and Art Collector* 1898-1901 (Chadwyck Healey microfiche)

The Poster collector's circular 1899 continued as *The Poster and Post card collector* 1903

Posters and Publicity. Commercial Art Annual 1927-(*Modern Publicity* 1930-1940, *Modern Publicity in War* 1941 then *Modern Publicity*)

There are many other studies of posters elsewhere in Europe, eg:

Abdy, Jane. *The French poster: Cheret to Cappiello.* 1969 London: Studio Vista 176pp illus.

Zucker, Irving (comp). *A source book of French advertising art . . . with over 5000 illustrations from the turn of the century.* 1964 London: Faber 256pp illus.

Lyakov, V. *The Soviet advertising posters 1917-1922.* 1973 Moscow: Soviet Arts 126pp illus.

These will have to wait for a much larger listing.

Stamps

Many books have been written specifically for the philatelist, but comparatively recently the general principles and practice of stamp design have received more attention.

Finlay, William. *Illustrated history of stamp design.* 1974 London: P. Lowe. 187pp illus.

Lewy, Edgar. 'Stamp design – a neglected tradition', *Design* 94 October 1956 pp 37-41

Rose, Stuart. 'Stamp on it. Some aspects of postage stamp design', *Icographic* 1974 no 8 pp 8-11

Gentleman, David. *Design in miniature.* 1972 London: Studio Vista. 104pp illus. (includes matchbox design)

Gentleman, David. 'The design and production of postage stamps', *Philatelic Journal of Great Britain* vol 84 no 2 June 1974 pp 30-37

Gentleman, David. 'The design and production of postage stamps', *JRSA* vol 122 1974 pp 431-439 illus.

Easton, John. *British postage stamp design.* 1946 (fourth edition) London: Faber 384pp

Harrison, Guy. 'The postage stamp', *JRSA* vol 88 May 31 1940 pp 650-662 (problems of making up and printing stamps)

Some of the histories of stamps can provide a lot of interesting detail on design changes:

Todd, T. *A history of British postage stamps.* 1941 London: Duckworth. 274pp pl 40

Easton, John. *The De La Rue history of British and foreign postage stamps 1855 to 1901.* 1958 London: Faber for the Royal Philatelic Society

Lowe, Robson. *The British postage stamp: being the history of the nineteenth century postage stamps based on the collection presented to the nation by Reginald M. Phillips of Brighton.* 1968 London: National Postal Museum 280pp illus.

Potter, David C. D. *British Elizabethan stamps. The story of the postage stamps of the United Kingdom, Guernsey, Jersey and the Isle of Man, from 1952 to 1970.* 1971 London: Batsford. 190pp illus.

Gibbons, Cecil W. 'British postage stamp designs and the Elizabethan stamps', *Connoisseur* vol 131 March 1953 pp 76-79 illus.

Postage stamps of Great Britain. 1934- London: Royal Philatelic Society

For more information there are the Stanley Gibbons catalogues and:

G. B. Journal 1956- (bi-monthly) Leigh on Sea: Great Britain Philatelic Society

Postal History International 1972- (monthly) London: Proud Bailey Co

Stamp Collecting 1913- (weekly) London: Stamp Collecting Ltd

A bibliography:

Strange, Arnold M. *A list of books on the postal history, postmarks and adhesive postage and revenue stamps of Great Britain.* 1971 (second edition) Brighton: Great Britain Philatelic Society 48pp

Ephemera

See also:

Package design *page 144*

Publicity and Advertising *page 135*

Recently considerable attention has been paid to the collection and study of minor types of printing and ephemera of all sorts. This has led to the formation of an Ephemera Society and the publication of a number of special studies. The whole subject is introduced concisely by:

Lewis, John Noel Claude. *Printed ephemera: the changing use of type and letter forms in English and American printing.* 1969 London: Faber 128pp (first edition 1962 Cowells)

Lewis, John. *Collecting printed ephemera.* 1976 London: Studio Vista 176pp 166 illus.

CHRISTMAS CARDS

Buday, György. *The history of the Christmas card.* 1954 London: Rockliff 304pp illus.

Carrington, Noel. '. . . but once a year. Thirty years progress in Christmas card design', *Design* 36 December 1951 pp 4-7

COMICS

Gifford, Dennis. *British comic catalogue 1874-1974.* 1975 London: Mansell 272pp illus.

Gifford, Denis. *Victorian comics.* 1976 London: Allen and Unwin 144pp illus.

LETTERHEADS

Lehner, Ernst. *The letterhead: history and progress.* 1955 New York: Museum Books Inc (unpaged) (a brief history, especially US and France)

Pickard, Peter. 'The history of the letterhead: a study of its development and its design today', *Printing Review* no 75 Autumn 1957

PLAYING CARDS

Beal, George. *Playing cards and their story.* 1975 Newton Abbot: David and Charles 120pp illus. bibl. pp 115-116

Hoffmann, Detleff. *The playing card: an illustrated history, translated by C. S. V. Salt.* 1973 London: George Prior Publishers.

Denning, Trevor. 'The hidden design of playing cards', *Design* 229 January 1968 pp 40-43

Tilley, Roger. *A history of playing cards.* 1973 London: Studio Vista 192pp illus.

Konstam, K. W. 'Modern playing card designs', *Graphis* vol 14 no 77 May/June 1958 pp 262-268

Denning, Trevor. *Translucent playing cards.* 1976 Birmingham: The Author 51pp

Clark, Freida (comp). *Playing card collectors' handbook: description and checklist. English royalty and cards issued by . . . (the) Company of Makers of Playing Cards.* 1954 London: Worshipful Company of Makers of Playing Cards 64pp

POSTCARDS

Carline, Richard. *Pictures in the post: the story of the picture postcard and its place in the history of popular art.* 1971 Bedford: Gordon Fraser 128pp illus. bibl. (first edition 1959)

Duval, William. *Collecting postcards in colour 1894-1914.* 1977 London: Blandford 160pp (64pp of illus.)

Weill, Alain. *Art Nouveau postcards.* 1978 London: Thames and Hudson

Holt, Tonie and Holt, Valmai. *Picture postcards of the Golden Age.* 1971 London: MacGibbon and Kee 214pp 32 illus.

Klamkin, Marion. *Picture postcards.* 1974 Newton Abbot: David and Charles 192pp illus.

Staff, Frank. *The picture postcard and its origins.* 1966 London: Lutterworth Press 96pp illus. bibl.

The picture postcard 1870-1920. 1971 London: Victoria and Albert Museum

VALENTINES

Staff, Frank. *The valentine and its origins.* 1969 London: Luterworth 144pp

Lee, Ruth Webb. *A history of valentines.* 1953 London: Batsford 239pp illus.

ENVELOPES

Girouard, Mark. 'Stamped addressed and illustrated: Irish decorated envelopes of the Victorian era', *Country Life* 148 1970 pp 290-291

TICKETS

Journal of the Transport Ticket Society 1964- (monthly) Luton: Transport Ticket Society (previously *Ticket and Fare Collection Society Newsletter* 1946-1963)

SOUVENIRS

Henderson, Ian T. *Pictorial souvenirs of Britain.* 1974 Newton Abbott: David and Charles 160pp illus. (particularly 1880-1914)

Rodgers, David. *Coronation souvenirs and commemoratives.* 1975 London: Latimer New Dimensions 152pp 140 illus.

Medwin, A. Gardner. 'Designing Coronation souvenirs', *Design* 54 June 1953 pp 16-19

Hasler, Charles. 'Arms, stamps and money', *Architectural Review* vol 113 no 673 January 1953 pp 27-37 (designs for Coronation)

Almost anything is collected and so this list could be virtually limitless . . .

Signs, Symbols and Trademarks

Although the science of semiology is beyond the scope of this work, it may be helpful to look at some of the collections of signs, symbols and identifying marks that exist and some of the studies.

General collections and discussions of signs and symbols:

Dreyfuss, Henry. *Symbol source book: an authoritative guide to international graphic symbols.* 1972 New York: McGraw Hill 320pp illus.

Handbook of pictorial symbols: 3,250 examples from international sources (compiled by) Rudolf Modley. 1976 New York: Dover 143pp bibl. (Dover Pictorial Archive series)

Kepes, Gyorgy (ed). *Sign, image and symbol.* 1966 London: Studio Vista 282pp illus. bibl.

Shepherd, Walter. *Glossary of graphic signs and symbols.* 1972 London: Dent 598pp illus.

For more information on particular systems:

Whittick, Arnold. *Symbols for designers. A handbook on the application of symbols and symbolism to design.* 1935 London: Crosby Lockwood 168pp 56 illus.

Whittick, Arnold. *Symbols, signs and their meanings.* 1960 London: L. Hill 408pp

Crosby, Theo and others. *A sign systems manual.* 1970 London: Studio Vista 80pp illus.

Signs

DIRECTION SIGNS

Sutton, James. *Signs in action.* 1965 London: Studio Vista 96pp (a general visual introduction)

Carr, Stephen. *City signs and lights.* 1973 Cambridge, Mass: MIT Press 272pp bibl.

Smith, Percy Delf. 'Beauty in signs and civic lettering', *JRSA* vol 93 March 30 1945 pp 214-222

Carrington, Noel. 'Legibility of "architectural appropriateness", South Bank lettering', *Design* 32 August 1951 pp 27-29

Carrington, Noel. 'In all directions', *Design* 76 April 1955 pp 23-27 (criticism of road signs)

Cullen, Gordon. 'Alphabet or image', *Architectural Review* vol 120 no 717 October 1956 pp 240-247 (visual codes for traffic)

ILLUMINATED SIGNS

Browne, Kenneth. 'Illuminated signs', *Architectural Review* vol 143 no 856 June 1968 pp 427-432

Davis, Alec. 'Letters of fire. The topography and typography of neon signs', *Design* 111 March 1958 pp 49-54

INN SIGNS

Bell, M. C. Farrar. 'Inn signs', *Art and Industry* November 1947 pp 166-171

Benham, Sir Gurney. *Inn signs – their history and meaning.* 1939 London: Brewers Society 16 leaves

Delderfield, Eric R. *British inn signs and their stories.* 1965 Newton Abbot: David and Charles 160pp illus.

Larwood, Jacob and Holton, John Camden. *English inn signs, revised and modernised edition of History of signboards.* 1951 London: Chatto and Windus 336pp pl 64 (original work published in 1886. Revision includes additional chapter 'Some notes on the modern inn sign' by Gerald Miller and a bibliography)

Swift, Charles Robert. *Inns and inn signs: sacred and secular.* 1947 St Albans: author 47pp

Tomlin, G. A. *Pubs; a collection of hotel, inn and tavern signs in Great Britain and Ireland, to which are added a few foreign cafe signs, classified by G. A. Tomlin.* 1922 London: Spottiswode 120pp illus.

Other advertising signs:

Baglee, Christopher and Morley, Andrew. *Street jewellery: an illustrated history of enamel advertising signs.* 1978 London: New Cavendish Books

Makers names and monographs

Macdonald-Taylor, Margaret S. (comp). *A dictionary of marks: metalwork, furniture, ceramics.* 1976 London: National Magazine Co (earlier editions 1962, 1973)

Haslam, Malcolm. *Marks and monograms of the Modern Movement 1875-1930. A guide to the marks of artists, designers, retailers and manufacturers from the period of the Aesthetic movement to Art Deco and Style Moderne.* 1977 London: Lutterworth Press

Turbayne, A. A. *Monograms and cyphers.* 1905 London: Caxton 160pp (Dover reprint 1969)

Davis, Alec. 'Signatures of industry', *Design* 163 July 1962 pp 40-45

Trademarks

Historical studies of trademarks:

Caplan, David and Stewart, Gregory. *British trademarks and symbols: a short history and a contemporary selection.* 1966 London: Owen 128pp 134 illus. (previous edition 1956)

Great Britain. Department of Trade. *A century of trade marks 1876-1976: commentary on the work and history of the Trade Marks Registry.* 1976 London: HMSO 60pp illus.

Johnson, Christopher G. A. Yate. *Trade marks and industrial designs, their history, development and protection.* 1950 Edinburgh: Johnsons 30pp (Presidential address to the Royal Scottish Society of Arts)

The problems of designing trade marks:

Jacobson, Egbert (ed). *Seven designers look at trade mark designs: Herbert Bayer and others.* 1955 New York: Paul Theobald 171pp

Werkman, C. J. *Trade marks: their creation, psychology and perception.* 1974 London: Longmans 496pp

Anthologies of marks:

Kamekura, Yusaku. *Trade marks and symbols of the world. Preface by Paul Rand.* 1956 New York: Wittenborn 164pp illus. bibl.

Kuwayama, Y. *Trade marks and symbols 2 vols. vol 1 Alphabetical designs, vol 2 Symbolic designs.* 1973 New York: Van Nostrand 193pp, 186pp

Trade marks and symbols, edited by Amstutz and Walter Herdeg. 1948 Zurich: Graphis Press

Ricci, Franco Maria and Ferrari, Corinna (eds). *Top symbols and trade marks of the world.* 1973 Milan/New York: Marquis Who's Who Inc. 7 vols (3,000 pages of illustrations)

A bibliography and directory:

Rimmer, Brenda M. *Trade marks. A guide to the literature and directory of lists of trade marks.* 1976 London: British Library Science Reference Library 63pp

For more details:

Trade Marks Journal vol 1 1876- London: HMSO

Package Design

The history of packaging has enormous possibilities given the range of evidence, but up to the present the whole area has only been partly explored.

General Surveys

Davis, Alec. *Package and print. The development of container and label design.* 1967 London: Faber 112pp 208 illus. bibl. (mainly developments to 1914)

Gray, Milner. 'The history and development of packaging', *JRSA* vol 87 no 4511 May 5 1939 pp 633-658 illus.

Dutton, Norbert. 'The progress of packaging', *Design* 79 July 1955 pp 17-23 (developments 1930s-1960s)

Bitting, Arvill Wayne. *Appetizing, or the art of canning: its history and development.* 1937 San Francisco: Trade Pressroom 852pp

'An outline of packaging history', *Shelf Appeal* July, September 1938

Exhibitions:

The Pack Age – a century of wrapping it up. The history of package design and promotional material from 1800 to the present day. Exhibition catalogue. 1975 London: Victoria and Albert Museum

The Package. 1959 New York: Museum of Modern Art (details in *Museum of Modern Art Bulletin* vol 27 no 1 Fall 1959 pp 1-39)

Seasons greetings: British biscuit tins 1868-1939. 1974 London: Whitechapel Art Gallery (earlier Victoria and Albert circulating exhibition)

Company histories include useful information on changes in design and technique:

Reader, W. J. *Metal Box: a history.* 1976 London: Heinemann 272pp illus.

Forty years 1921-1961: commemorating the 40th anniversary of Boxfoldia. 1961 Birmingham: Boxfoldia 16pp

House, Jack. *A century of boxmaking: a history of Andrew Ritchie and Son Ltd from 1850 to 1950.* 1950 Glasgow: Maclehose

Smaller surveys

Much smaller surveys reflecting developments at particular points of time:

Simon, A. P. 'The Manchester exhibition of containers', *DIA Quarterly* no 8 July 1929 pp 11-12

Gray, Milner. 'Shape, design and colour of the package', *Commercial Art* vol 17 October 1934 pp 147-157

'Package? no package? or any old package?', *Commercial Art* vol 18 June 1935 pp 242-251

'Packaging: recent efforts surveyed by Jopa', *Commercial Art* vol 20 April 1936 pp 147-149

'Designs for packages', *Gebrauchsgrafik* vol 14 April 1937 pp 58-60

Gray, Milner. 'This packaging', *Penrose Annual* vol 42 1940

Rosner, Charles. 'New art forms in packaging', *Penrose Annual* vol 42 1940

Packaging: a design folio. 1951 London: Council of Industrial Design 7pp pl 12

Rosner, Charles. 'Wrapping papers: a new conception', *Penrose Annual* vol 46 1952 pp 68-70

Herdeg, Walter. *Packaging: an international survey of package design* Zurich: Amstutz and Herdeg – vol 1 1959 322pp, vol 2 1970 356pp

Gray, Milner. 'Packaging progress', *JRSA* vol 107 August 1959 pp 621-639

Crouwel, Wim and Weidemann, Kurt (eds). *Packaging: an international survey.* 1968 London: Thames and Hudson 188pp illus.

Neubauer, Robert G. *Packaging the contemporary media.* 1973 New York: Van Nostrand 208pp 287 illus. (Chapter 9: Package histories)

'A package tour', *Designer* December 1973 pp 3-11

Scott, Gerald. 'Packaging the throwaway society', *JRSA* vol 122 March 1974 pp 188-202

Graphis record covers: the evolution of graphics reflected in record packaging, edited by Walter Herdeg. 1974 Zurich: Graphis Press 192pp illus.

The techniques involved in packaging are crucial and so further sources of information are earlier manuals, advice and technical surveys:

Harrison, V. G. W. 'Technical advances in packaging', *JRSA* vol 109 October 1961 pp 821-839 illus.

Jones, Harry. *Planned packaging.* 1950 London: Allen and Unwin 216pp illus. (includes historical examples)

Franken, Richard Benjamin and Larrabee, Carroll B. *Packages that sell.* 1928 New York: Harper 302pp illus.

Powell, Leona. 'Merchandising through packaging', *Penrose Annual* vol 35 1933 pp 87-89

Larrabee, Carroll Burton. *How to package for profit. A manual.* 1935 New York: Harper 211pp

Charlton, Demetrius E. A. The art of packaging. 1937 London: Studio 127pp

Richardson, Edward. 'What is packaging?', *Art and Industry* November 1945 pp 130-136 (design problems)

Packaging and Display encyclopaedia. 1948 London: Newnes (many later editions – fifth edition 1959)

Verstone, Philip Eason. *The manufacture of paper containers. A textbook on paper box and bag making.* 1949 London: Verstone 293pp (earlier editions 1922, 1932)

Sutnar, Ladislav. *Package design: the force of visual selling.* 1953 New York: Arts Inc

Gray, Milner. *Package design.* 1955 London: Studio 128pp (*How to do it* series no 59)

Labels

Humbert, Claude. *Label design, evolution, design and function of labels from earliest times to the present day.* 1973 London: Thames and Hudson 252pp 1000 illus. (mainly examples with short history)

Davis, Alec. 'Towards a history of tin-printing', *Journal of the Printing Historical Society* no 8 1972 pp 53-64

Corley, T. A. B. 'Towards a history of tin-printing. Some further signposts', *Journal of the Printing Historical Society* no 9 1973-1974 pp 1-5

Davis, Alec. 'The picture on the pack', *Penrose Annual* vol 50 1956 pp 60-62

Journals

Some long-lived journals that may be useful for more detail:

Canning Industry and Packaging Trades Gazette. January 1931-September 1939 (then merged with *The Tin Printer and Box Maker*)

Graphics in Packaging 1958- New York: American Institute of Graphic Arts

Modern Packaging. 1927- (monthly) New York

Packaging and the Packing Record 1930- London: Tudor Press (from 1930-1933 titled *The Packing Record*)

Packaging Abstracts 1944- (monthly) Leatherhead: Printing Industries Research Association

Packaging Review 1897- (monthly) London: IPC Industrial Press (originally titled *The Box Makers Journal*)

Tin Printer and Box Maker 1924- (monthly) London: Canning Publication (from 1939-1953 titled *The Tin Printer and Box Maker and Canning Industry*)

Packaging Technology and Management 1948-(quarterly) London: Institute of Packaging

For further information on all types of packaging:

Jones, G. (comp). *Packaging: a guide to information sources.* 1967 Detroit: Gale Publishing 285pp

As the collection of old packaging has become part of the antique trade a range of specialised guides have grown up. These often contain useful notes on specialised changes in design and method, eg:

Hunt, Chris. *Collecting cream pots.* 1977 Bradford: John England 50pp (1866-c. 1920)

For packaging in specific materials see also the Designing in particular materials sections

Corporate Identity and Design Co-ordination

In the past twenty years much more attention has been directed towards corporate design programmes and other attempts to co-ordinate the image of a company.

There has not yet been much historical writing but the manuals and guides provide a lot of information which could be useful:

Blake, John E. (ed). *A management guide to Corporate Identity.* 1971 London: Council of Industrial Design 100pp illus. (based on three earlier conferences with some case histories)

Henrion, F. H. K. and Parkin, Alan. *Design co-ordination and corporate image.* 1967 London: Studio Vista 208pp illus.

Henrion, F. H. K. and Parkin, Alan. 'Systematic methods in design co-ordination', *DIA Yearbook* 1967-1968 pp 33-42 illus.

Pilditch, James. *Communication by design, a study in corporate identity.* 1970 London and New York: McGraw Hill 208pp

Rosen, Ben. *The corporate search for visual identity.* 1970 New York: Van Nostrand 259pp illus. (Based on programmes of US and Canadian companies)

Eksell, Olle. *Corporate design programs, translated from the Swedish by Charles Harrison-Wallace.* 1967 London: Studio Vista 96pp illus.

There are a number of case histories:

Schmittel, Wolfgang. *Design concept realisation.* 1976 London: Academy Editions 228pp 1000 illus. (profiles of Braun, Citroën, Herman Miller, Olivetti, Sony, Swissair)

Reynolds, Jim. 'Total design, or, design for the people by the people', *Design Action DIA Yearbook* 1976 p 5 (British Thornton Ltd)

Scholberg, Philip. 'Cape Graphic', *DIA Yearbook* 1964-1965 pp 94-101

Masson, Georgina. 'Olivetti. The creation of a house style', *Architectural Review* vol 121 no 725 June 1957 pp 431-439

A different sort of corporate identity:

Leeson, R. A. *United we stand: an illustrated account of trade union emblems.* 1971 Bath: Adams and Dart 72pp illus.

Studies in the development of corporate design or house style policies are a popular feature in *Design* magazine:

'House Style – special issue by Alec Davis', *Design* 95 November 1956 (includes useful bibliography)

Reilly, Paul. 'Appearance design in the AEI Companies', *Design* 41 May 1952 pp 3-7

Reilly, Paul. 'Design policy in industry. The Radiation group of companies', *Design* 47 November 1952 pp 23-28

White, J. Noel. 'A company's livery (Pest Control Ltd)', *Design* 84 December 1955 pp 32-35

Davis, Alec. 'House-style: the face of the firm', *Design* 124 April 1959 pp 32-37 (on the DIA exhibition at the Ceylon Tea centre)

McNab, Archie. 'Shop shape (James Galt & Co Ltd – toys)', *Design* 163 July 1962 pp 28-31

Naylor, Gillian. 'The designer v Jack with the paint brush', *Design* 210 June 1966 pp 40-51

Baynes, Ken and Baynes, Kate. 'Her Majesty's house style', *Design* 238 October 1968 pp 64-67

Miller, Russell. 'A century of Sainsbury's', *Design* 243 March 1969 pp 64-69

Interior design

This section is divided into five main areas:

1 Domestic interiors and decoration
2 Public interiors – offices, churches, shops, pubs, ships and others
3 Services – lighting, plumbing
4 Retail and point of sale design
5 Exhibition design

Many detailed and specific factors are involved in the planning of 2-5 and for these reasons the coverage is much more selective.

1 Domestic Interiors and Decoration

General surveys

General histories of interior design provide only very sketchy coverage of most aspects of this period:

Praz, Mario. *An illustrated history of interior decoration: from Pompeii to art nouveau,* translated *by William Weaver.* 1964 London: Thames and Hudson 396pp 400 illus. bibl. (first published as *La filosofia dell' arredamento*)

Bauer, Franz. *European interiors.* 1961 London: Macdonald 204pp illus. (translation by Mervyn Savill of *Das schöne Zuhause*)

Potter, Margaret and Potter, Alexander. *Interiors: a record of some of the changes in interior design and furniture from mediaeval times to the present day.* 1957 London: John Murray 48pp illus.

More specifically British:

Barley, M. W. *The house and home. A review of 900 years of house planning and furnishing in Britain.* 1971 London: Studio Vista 208pp illus. (first published 1963)

Yarwood, Doreen. *The English home: a thousand years of furnishing and decoration.* 1956 London: Batsford 393pp illus. bibl.

Dutton, Ralph. *The English interior (1500-1900).* 1948 London: Batsford 192pp pl 171

Keogh, Brian and Gill, M. *British domestic design through the ages.* 1970 London: Arthur Barker 126pp illus.

Harrison, M. *People and furniture: a social background to the English home.* 1971 London: E. Benn 160pp illus. bibl.

There are some useful wide-ranging discussions of the principles of interior design:

Denby, Elaine. *Interior design, history, principles and practice.* 1963 London: Country Life 206pp illus.

Allsopp, Bruce. *Decoration and furniture.* 1952-1953 London: Pitman 2 vols: *vol 1 The English tradition.* 1952 233pp illus. *vol 2 Principles of modern design.* 1953 205pp illus.

Denby, Elaine. *What's in a room? Some aspects of interior design.* 1971 London: BBC 41pp illus.

Kaufmann, Edgar. *What is modern interior design?* 1953 New York: Museum of Modern Art (reprinted introduction from *Modern rooms of the last fifty years* 1947 Museum of Modern Art)

Some brief introductions in journals:

Betjeman, John. '1830-1930 – still going strong. A guide to the recent history of interior decoration', *Architectural Review* vol 67 May 1930 pp 231-240 followed by illustrated supplement pp 241-272

Fraser, Grace Lovat. 'Design in interior design', *JRSA* vol 93 August 3 1945 pp 464-472

Trethowan, Harry. 'Decorative art 1893-1943', *Studio* 125 1943 pp 144-148

General long-established journals probably provide the most detailed introduction:

Architektur und Wohnform 1946- (formerly *Innendekoration.* Die gesamte Wohnungskunst in Bild und Wirt 1900-1943/1944, previously *Illustrierte kunstgewerbliche Zeitschrift für Innen-Dekoration* 1890-1899)

Casabella: rivista di urbanistica, architettura e disegno industriale 1928- (monthly) Milan

Decorative art in modern interiors 1961/1962- (previously *Decorative Art:* the Studio yearbook of international furnishing and decoration 1926-1960/1961, previously *The Studio yearbook of decorative art* 1906-1925

Domus; architettura arredamento arte 1928- (monthly) Milan (There is a useful anthology: *Domus: 45 ans d'architecture, design, art 1928-1973.* 1973 Milan: Editorale Domus)

Furnishing 1945- London: National Trade Press (previously *Furnishing Trades Organiser* 1920-1944)

Furnishing World 1931- (two per month) London: Trade Chronicles (later absorbed into *Cabinet Maker and Retail Furnisher* but available on University Microfilms)

Good Housekeeping 1929- (monthly) London: National Magazine Co

Home Furnishing 1971- (superseded *Furnishing Review*)

Homes and Gardens 1919- (monthly) London: IPC

House and Garden 1934- (10 per year) London: Condé Nast

House and Home 1952- (monthly) New York: McGraw Hill

Ideal Home 1920- (monthly) London: IPC

Interior design 1957- (monthly) Mordern: Westbourne (1957-1959 titled *Contract Furnishing. Incorporating Furnishing International and British Institute of Interior Design. Annual yearbook of interior design and contract furnishing*)

Interior design 1932- (monthly) New York: Whitney (available University Microfilms)

Interiors 1940 (vol 100 no 5) – New York: Whitney (previously *Interior Decorator* 1935-November 1940, *Upholsterer and Interior Decorator* 1888-1935) (available on University Microfilms)

Many of the architectural journals, eg *Architectural Review, Architects Journal, Builder, Architectural Design,* are very rich sources of contemporary information on interior design. Then there are the more general journals such as *Studio* and *Country Life.*

Interior design is quite a long-established profession:

Weller, John. 'British Institute of Interior Design', *Design Action DIA Yearbook* 1976 p 25

Incorporated Institute of British Decorators and Interior Designers. 75th anniversary: special commemorative publication. 1974 London: Sterling 108pp illus.

Adams-Acton, M. 'Conference of the Institute of British Decorators; the position of the decorative designer', *Apollo* 16 September 1932 pp 113-115

Garrett, Stephen. 'Interior design, an enquiry into current training, prospects and practices', *Design* 128 August 1959 pp 28-35

Bonellie, Helen-Janet. *The status merchants: the trade of interior decoration.* 1972 New York: Barnes/Yoseloff 109pp 80 illus.

Campbell, Kenneth. *Campbell Smith and Company 1873-1973. A centenary of decorative craftmanship. The story of a successful venture in architectural interior decoration. An outline history of church architecture, colour and decoration. Reference lists and illustrations of decorative works.* 1973 London: Campbell, Smith & Co 78pp illus.

A bibliography:

Lackschewitz, Gertrud. *Interior design and decoration. Bibliography compiled for the American Institute of Decorators.* 1961 New York Public Library 86pp

Studies and Documents of particular periods

NINETEENTH CENTURY

A useful introductory review of books on Victorian interior design:

Ames, Winslow. 'Inside Victorian walls', *Victorian Studies* vol 5 no 2 December 1961 pp 151-162 illus.

Some general studies:

Dutton, Ralph. *The Victorian home: some aspects of nineteenth century taste and manners.* 1954 London: Batsford 206pp illus.

Goodhart-Rendel, H. S. 'The Victorian home', pp 71-84 in Ferriday, Peter (ed). *Victorian architecture.* 1963 London: Cape

Rubinstein, David. *Victorian homes.* 1975 Newton Abbot: David and Charles 287pp (200 extracts from contemporary documents reflecting changes)

Lochhead, Marion Cleland. *The Victorian household.* 1964 London: J. Murray 226pp illus.

Harling, Robert. *Home: a Victorian vignette.* 1938 London: Constable 166pp illus.

Girouard, Mark. *The Victorian country house.* 1971 Oxford University Press 218pp illus. bibl.

Geffrye Museum. *Nineteenth century English homes.* 1974 London: Inner London Education Authority 16pp illus. bibl.

For more architectural detail:

Physick, John and Darby, Michael. '*Marble Halls' drawings and models for Victorian secular buildings exhibition.* 1973 London: HMSO for Victoria and Albert Museum 220pp 150 illus.

(There is a wealth of further detail in the more general studies listed in the Chronological Studies section *page 59*)

The period to about 1860:

Hinton, Denys. 'Architecture and interior decoration', pp 17-32 in Edwards, Ralph and Ramsey, L. G. G. (eds). *The early Victorian period 1830-1860.* 1958 London: Connoisseur 180pp

Cornforth, J. 'Some early Victorians at home', *Country Life* December 4 1975 pp 1530-1534

Some very important early works:

Arrowsmith, H. W. and Arrowsmith, A. *The house decorator and painter's guide; continuing a series of designs for decorating apartments, suited to the various styles of architecture.* 1840 London: T. Kelly 120pp pl 61 (second edition 1861. Pattern book by decorators to Queen Victoria)

Loudon, John Claudius. *An encyclopaedia of cottage, farm and villa architecture and furniture; containing numerous designs for dwellings from the cottage to the villa, including farm houses, farmeries and other agricultural buildings; several designs for country inns, public houses and parochial schools; with the requisite fittings-up, fixtures and furniture; and appropriate offices, gardens and garden scenery; each design accompanied by analytical and critical remarks, illustrative of the principles of architectural science and tqste on which it is composed.* 1833 London: Longman 3 vols 1138pp illus. (republished 1835, 1836, 1839, 1842, 1846, 1847, 1850, 1853, 1857, 1863, 1867)

1870s and 1880s:

Loftie, William John (ed). *Art at home series.* 1876-1878 London: Macmillan 7 vols (ABC Reprint in 2 vols) consisting of:

Garrett, Rhoda and Garrett, Agnes. *Suggestions for house decoration in painting, woodwork and furniture.* 1879 90pp illus.

Loftie, William John. *A plea for art in the house with special reference to the economy of collecting works of art and the importance of taste and education and morals.* 1877 100pp illus.

Loftie, Martha Jane. *The dining room.* 1878 128pp illus.

Orrinsmith, Lucie. *The drawing room: its decorations and furniture.* 1878 145pp illus.

Barker, Lady (Mary Anne Stewart Barker). *The bedroom and the boudoir.* 1878 116pp illus.

Oliphant, Margaret. *Dress.* 1878 103pp illus.

Hullah, John Pyke. *Music in the house.* 1877 79pp illus.

See also:

William Burges: *page 00*

Colquhoun, Ian. 'Montagu Norman designer', *Design* 71 November 1954 pp 36-38

CHARLES LOCK EASTLAKE

Eastlake, Charles Lock. *Hints on household taste in furniture, upholstery and other details,* new introduction by John Gloag. 1969 New York: Dover 304pp (facsimile reprint of fourth edition 1878 Longmans. Also Blom Reprint of 1872 edition)

Madigan, Mary Jean Smith. *Eastlake-influenced American furniture 1870-1890. Catalogue of an exhibition November 18, 1873- January 6 1974).* 1974 New York: Hudson River Museum 66pp illus. bibl.

Gould, Cecil. 'The Eastlakes', *Apollo* May 1975 pp 350-353

ROBERT WILLIAM EDIS

Edis, Robert William. *Decoration and furniture of the town house. A series of Cantor lectures delivered before the Society of Arts 1880 amplified and enlarged.* 1972 East Ardsley: EP 292pp (facsimile of second edition. First edition 1881)

Edis, Robert William. 'The building of town houses. Their arrangement, aspect, design and general planning, *JSA* vol 32 September 19, September 26, October 3 1884 pp 1023-1033, 1039-1049, 1057-1067

Edis, Robert William. *Healthy furniture and decoration.* 1884 London: W. Clowes for Executive Council of the International Health Exhibition and the Council of the Royal Society of Arts 75pp illus.

MRS HAWEIS

Haweis, Mary Eliza. *The art of beauty.* 1878 London: Chatto and Windus 298pp illus.

Haweis, Mary Eliza. *The art of decoration.* 1881 London: Chatto and Windus 431pp (ABC Reprint)

Haweis, Mary Eliza. *Beautiful houses; being a description of certain well-known artistic houses.* 1882 London: Sampson Low 115pp illus.

WILLIAM MORRIS

Lethaby, W. R. 'Kelmscott manor and William Morris', *Architectural Review* vol 45 1919 pp 67-69

Mitchell, William. 'William Morris at St James's Palace', *Architectural Review* vol 101 January 1947 pp 37-39

Morris, Barbara. 'The Harbourne room', *Victoria and Albert Museum Bulletin* vol IV no 3 July 1968 pp 82-95

Grylls, R. Glynn. 'Wightwick manor – a William Morris period-piece', *Connoisseur* January 1962 pp 2-11

Some other important contemporary
writings:

Yapp, George Wagstaffe. *Art industry.
Furniture, upholstery and house decoration.
Illustration of the arts of the carpenter, joiner
cabinet maker, painter, decorator and
upholsterer.* 1880 London: Virtue (Gregg
reprint 1972. Yapp's catalogue first
appeared in 1851 and represents many
aspects of approved mid-Victorian taste)

Crane, Lucy. *Art and the formation of taste; six
lecture: . . . with illustrations by Thomas and
Walter Crane.* 1882 London: Macmillan
292pp

Facey, James William. *Elementary decoration.
A guide to the simpler forms of everyday art as
applied to the interior and exterior decoration
of dwelling houses.* 1882 London: Crosby
Lockwood 120pp illus. (number 229 of
Weale's Rudimentary series)

Smith, John Moyr. *Ornamental interiors,
ancient and modern.* 1887 London: Crosby
Lockwood 236pp (useful on public
buildings)

Sylvia's Home Help Series. *Artistic homes, or
how to furnish with taste.* 1881 London:
Ward Lock 130pp (ABC Reprint)

Armitage, George Faulkner. *Decoration and
furnishing.* 1885 Manchester: Manchester
and Salford Sanitary Association (Health
Lectures series 8 no 6)

Late nineteenth-century interiors:

Lemere, H. Bedford. *The opulent eye: late
Victorian and Edwardian taste in interior
decoration. Text by Nicholas Cooper.
Photographs from the Bedford Lemere archive.*
1976 London: Architectural Press
200pp 200 illus.

Holme, Charles (ed). *Modern British domestic
architecture and decoration.* 1901 London:
Studio special Summer number 212pp
illus.

Lancaster, Osbert. 'A room of the nineties',
Country Life January 22 1943 pp 168

Morhange, Angela. 'Late Victorian
interiors', *Antique Collector* March 1975

Peel, Dorothy Constance. *The new home:
treating of the arrangement and furnishing
decoration of a house of medium size and a
moderate income.* 1903 (second edition)
London: Constable 287pp (first edition
1898)

Gardiner, Florence Mary. *Furnishing and
fittings for every home.* 1894 London:
Record Press 130pp

Crouch, Joseph and Butler, Edmund. *The
apartments of the house. Their arrangement,
furnishing and decoration.* 1900 London:
Unicorn Press 197pp illus.

Panton, Jane Ellen. *A gentlewomen's home: the
whole art of building furnishing and
beautifying the home.* 1896 London: The
Gentlewoman 443pp

Heaton, John Aldam. *Beauty and art.* 1897
London: Heinemann 208pp (includes a
survey of furniture pattern books)

Wharton, Edith and Codman, Ogden. *The
decoration of houses.* 1897 New York:
Scribners 204pp pl 56 bibl. (London
edition 1898)

Watson, Rosamund Marriott. *The art of the
house.* 1897 London: Bell 185pp illus.
(*Connoisseur* series edited by Gleeson
White)

O'Brien, Kevin H. F. '"The house beautiful",
A reconstruction of Oscar Wilde's
American lecture', *Victorian Studies* vol 17
June 1974 pp 395-418

Bodenhausen, E. von. 'Englische Kunst im
Haus', *Pan* 2 Jahrgang Heft 4 pp 329-336

There are many more general magazines
and popular books that cannot be included,
but a short introduction is:

Lasdun, Susan. 'Keeping one's house in
order: Victorian magazines and
furnishing taste', *Country Life* September 9
1976

EARLY TWENTIETH CENTURY

See also:

M. H. Baillie Scott, C. F. A. Voysey *pages 75,
86*

Weaver, Lawrence (ed). *The house and its
equipment.* 1911 London: Country Life
212pp illus.

Sparrow, Walter Shaw. *The British house of
today. A book of modern domestic architecture
and applied art.* 1904 London: Hodder
and Stoughton illus. (includes articles by
Norman Shaw, Brangwyn)

Studio Yearbook of Decorative Art 1906 276pp
(first)

Jennings, H. J. *Our homes and how to beautify
them.* 1902 London: Harrison & Sons
254pp illus.

Muthesius, Hermann. *Das moderne Landhaus,
und seine innere Ausstattung. 320
Abbildungen moderner Landhäuser aus
Deutschland, Oesterreich, England, und
Finnland, mit Grundrisse und Innenraumen.*
1905 Munich: F. Bruckmann 216pp
illus

Dyson, H. Kempton. 'Cheap cottages
exhibition at Letchworth', *Architectural
Review* 18 1905 pp 108-115, 154-169

Binstead, Herbert E. *Useful details
(concerning furniture and interior decoration)
in several styles.* 1906 London: A. H.
Botwright 152pp illus.

Elder-Duncan, John Hudson. *The house beautiful and useful. Being practical suggestions on furnishing and decoration.* 1907 London: Cassell 224pp illus.

Watson, Rosamund Marriott. *The art of the home.* 1907 London: Bell 185pp illus.

Sparrow, Walter Shaw. *Hints on home furnishing.* 1909 London: Eveleigh Nash 307pp pl 59 (section on furniture by Baillie Scott)

Sparrow, Walter Shaw. *Our homes and how to make the best of them.* 1909 London: Hodder and Stoughton 280pp illus.

Shapland, Henry Percival. *Style schemes in antique furnishing. Interiors and their treatment. Written by H. P. Shapland, the schemes being designed by H. Pringner Benn.* 1909 London: Simplin Marshall 71pp pl 2

Muthesius, Hermann. *Das Englische haus.* 1904-1908 Berlin: Wasmuth 3 vols illus.

Muthesius, Hermann. *Die Englische baukunst der gegenwart.* 1909 Leipzig: Cosmos 174pp pl 110

The perfect home and how to furnish it. 1913 London: Daily Mirror 256pp

Mendl, Elsie. *The house in good taste.* 1914 London: Pitman 322pp illus.

Parsons, Frank Alvah. *Interior decoration: its principles and practice.* 1915 Garden City, New York: Doubleday 284pp pl 57 (distinctive US viewpoint)

and on the Tudor revival:

Simpson, Duncan. 'History of taste 3. Beautiful Tudor'. *Architectural Review* vol 162 no 965 July 1977 pp 29-36 (approx 1890-1915)

Notable individuals:

Voysey, C. F. A. 'Remarks on domestic entrance halls', *Studio* vol 21 1901 pp 242-246 8 illus.

Voysey, C. F. A. 'The orchard, Chorleywood, Hertfordshire', *Architectural Review* vol 10 1901 pp 32-38

Baillie Scott, M. H. 'Decoration and furniture for the New Palace, Darmstadt', *Studio* vol 17 1899 pp 107-115 10 illus.

Baille Scott, M. H. 'A country house', *Studio* vol 19 1900 pp 30-38 8 illus.

Taylor, Nicholas. 'Baillie Scott's Waldbuhl', *Architectural Review* vol 138 no 826 1966 pp 456-458 illus.

See also Important designers *page 75*

Manuals of domestic economy were an important development of the nineteenth century. Their successive editions yield useful information on many aspects of domestic design:

Beeton, Isabella Mary. *The book of household management.* 1861 London: S. O. Beeton. 1112pp illus. (first of many editions)

Webster, Thomas and Parkes, Mrs William. *An encyclopeadia of domestic economy comprising such subjects as are most immediately connected with housekeeping.* 1844 London

Walsh, J. H. *A manual of domestic economy suited to families spending from £100 to £1000 a year including directions for the management of the nursery and sickroom and preparation and administration of domestic remedies.* 1857 (second edition) London: Routledge 736pp (many other editions to 1890)

Cassell's household guide: being a complete encyclopaedia of domestic and social economy and forming a guide to every department of practical life. 1869-1871 London: Cassell 4 vols (many later editions)

Marks, Montague. *Cyclopaedia of home arts with nearly 600 illustrations and designs.* 1899 London: C. A. Pearson 438pp

Gregory, Edward W. *The art and craft of home-making.* 1913 London: T. Murby 190pp illus. (second edition 1928 Batsford)

Davidson, Hugh Coleman (ed). *The book of the home.* 1905 London: Gresham 8 vols 1500pp ('all matters relating to the house and household management')

Frederick, Christine. *Scientific management in the home: household engineering.* 1920 London: Routledge and Kegan Paul 527pp (first edition 1915 New York. Many later editions)

The Ideal Home exhibition was first held at Olympia in 1910 and provides an index of many aspects of twentieth-century British domestic design:

The Ideal Home exhibition organized by the Daily Mail. Catalogue. April 8th to 23rd 1910 at Olympia, London. 1910 London: Associated Newspapers 127pp

Other large catalogues exist for 1923, 1937, 1939, 1950-2, 1954, 1958.
Daily Mail Ideal Home series. 1955-London: Associated Newspapers.
Daily Mail Ideal Home book. 1950/1-1955. London: Associated Newspapers.

The later publications of the Good Housekeeping Institute perform the same function:

Good Housekeeping Institute. *The happy home; a universal guide to household management; compiled and edited for the Gas Council.* 1955 London: Grosvenor Press 374pp

INTER-WAR PERIOD

This period witnessed a notable expansion in writing on interior design for all types of homes. Much of this appeared in the major architectural journals and monographs of the time.

General surveys:

Ward, N. *Home in the 20s and 30s.* 1977 Shepperton: Allan 128pp illus.

Kauffman, Edgar Jnr. *Modern rooms of the last fifty years.* 1947 New York: Museum of Modern Art (reprinted from *Interiors* 106 February 1947 pp 68-82)

Garland, Madge. 'The fahionable interior', *Country Life* 137 4th February 1965 pp 224-226 illus.

Gould, J. *Modern houses in Britain 1919-1939.* 1977 London: Society of Architectural Historians of Great Britain (Architectural History Monograph 1) 86pp pl 53 24 plans (mostly architectural but good gazetteer and bibliographical references)

Aloi, Roberto. *L'arredamento moderno; trecentosessanta artisti, venti nazioni, settecentodieci illustrazioni.* 1934 Milan: U. Hoepli 18pp 204pp illus. (first of a series of pictorial anthologies, sixth series 1955)

Studies of chronological interest:

'Conference on house furnishings', *JRSA* 5 March 1920 pp 248-258

Wainwright, Shirley B. 'On the decoration and furnishing of small rooms', *Studio Yearbook* 1920 pp 1-26

Wright, Richardson Little. *House and Gardens book of interiors, containing over three hundred illustrations.* 1920 New York: Condé Nast 126pp (a second book of interiors was published in 1926)

Townsend, W. G. Paulson. *Modern decorative art in England, its development and characteristics.* 1922 London: Batsford

'Interiors, British, continental, American', *Studio Yearbook of Decorative Art* 1923 pp 39-73

James, Charles Holloway and Yerbury, F. R. (eds). *Modern English houses and interiors.* 1925 London: Benn 6pp pl 99

Hayward, Charles Harold. *English rooms and their decoration at a glance.* 1925 London: Architectural Press 2 vols

'Ultra modern interiors', *Architect* 14 January 1927 pp 102-105

Phillips, R. Randal. *The modern English interior.* 1928 London: Country Life 192pp illus.

Robertson, Howard. 'Modern art in decoration and furnishing. The exhibition at the galleries of Waring and Gillow', *Architect and Building News* vol 120 1928 pp 693-697

Rogers, John C. 'Modern decoration at Warings', *DIA Quarterly* no 6 December 1928 pp 4-6

Todd, Dorothy and Mortimer, Raymond. *The new interior decoration. An introduction to its principles, and an international survey of its methods.* 1929 London: Batsford 42pp (illustrations by McKnight Kauffer)

Frankl, Paul Theodore. *Form and reform. A practical handbook of modern interiors.* 1930 New York: Harper 203pp pl 109 bibl. (facsimile reprint Hacker Art Books 1972)

Nash, Paul. 'Modern English furnishing', *Architectural Review* vol 67 1930 pp 43-46

'Modern English interior decoration', *Architectural Review* vol 67 May 1930 pp 241-272

Decorative Art. Studio Yearbook 1929 (includes Wainwright, Shirley B. 'The new movement. Rational design in the home', pp 6-58, Todd, Dorothy. 'The modern interior' pp 59-102 and 'Furniture and decoration of today', pp 103-150)

Hoffmann, Herbert. *Modern interiors in Europe and America.* 1930 London: Studio 7pp pl 208 (English version of *Farbige Raumkunst* 1929)

Wainwright, Shirley B. 'The Modern home and its decoration', *Decoration Art Studio Yearbook* 1930 pp 59-84

Lutyens, Robert. 'The art of furnishing: a survey of modern styles', *Studio* vol 101 1931 pp 383-399 22 illus.

Nash, Paul. *Room and book.* 1932 London: Soncino Press 98pp illus.

Platz, Gustav Adolf. *Wohnraume der Gegenwart.* 1933 Berlin: Propylaen 516pp illus. (very comprehensive and worldwide coverage)

Anderson, M. L. 'The living room of to-day', *Design for Today* vol 1 May 1933 pp 4-14 (includes historical survey)

Yorke, F. R. S. *The modern house.* 1934 London: Architectural Press 192pp illus. (many later editions but none as important as the first)

'The art of home planning – series', *Studio* 110 1935 pp 153-173, pp 190-211, pp 250-275, pp 339-353

'The trend of design in home decoration', *Studio* 110 1935 pp 169-173

'The interior of the house of today', *Decorative Art. Studio Yearbook* 1935 pp 31-40

Smithells, Roger and Woods, S. John. *The modern home. Its decoration, finishing and equipment.* 1936 Benfleet: F. Lewis 180pp illus.

'Interior design and decoration', *Studio* vol 112 September 1936 pp 148-155

'Interior house equipment bulletin of standard designs', *Architectural Review* 79 March 1936 pp 144-145

Yorke, F. R. S. *The modern house in England.* 1937 London: Architectural Press 144pp illus (later editions 1944; 1948)

Great Britain. Council of Art and Industry. *The working class home; its furnishing and equipment.* 1937 London: HMSO 63pp

'Interior design – special issue', *Architectural Review* vol 82 December 1937 pp 223-298

Storey, Walter Rendall. *Period influences in interior decoration.* 1937 New York: Harper 211pp illus bibl.

Abercrombie, Patrick. *The book of the modern house; a panoramic survey of contemporary domestic design.* 1939 London: Hodder and Stoughton 378pp illus.

Lancaster, Osbert. *Homes sweet homes.* 1939 London: John Murray 78pp illus.

Fraser, Grace Lovat. 'Interior decoration and furnishing in 1939', *Decorative Art. Studio Yearbook.* 1940 pp 40-48

Fraser, Grace Lovat. 'New design and decoration in Great Britain', *Studio* 120 1940 pp 118-135

This was also an important period for advice and handbooks:

Phillips, R. Randal and Wollrich, Ellen. *Furnishing the house.* 1921 London: Country Life 152pp illus.

Gloag, John and Gloag, Helen. *Simple furnishing and arrangement.* 1921 London: Duckworth 165pp illus.

Holloway, Edward Stratton. *The practical book of furnishing the small house and apartment.* 1922 London: J. B. Lippincott 296pp pl 153

House and Garden (English edition) 1920-1924 (previously *Our Homes and Gardens* 1919-1923, later merged with *Vogue*)

Jennings, Arthur Seymour. *The decoration and renovation of the home. A practical handbook for house owners, tenants, architects, decorators and others . . . With a chapter on 'Period furniture and appropirate mural decoration' by Herbert E. Binstead.* 1923 London: W. R. Howell 220pp illus. bibl.

Gloag, John and Mansfield, Leslie. *The house we ought to live in.* 1923 London: Duckworth 160pp illus.

Rothery, Guy Cadogan. *Furnishing a small house or flat.* 1923 London: Collins 265p illus.

Northend, Mary Harrod. *The small house, its possibilities.* 1924 London: Williams and Norgate 243pp illus.

Seal, Ethel Davis. *Furnishing the little house.* 1924 london: Century Co 200pp illus.

Bateman, Robert Allen. *How to own and equip a house.* 1926 London: R. A. Bateman 355pp

Minter, David (ed). *The book of the home. A practical guide to the modern household.* 1925 London: Gresham 4 vols

Gloag, John. *Modern home furnishing.* 1929 Eyre and Spottiswode 127pp

Phillips, R. Randal. *The house improved.* 1931 London: Country Life 144pp illus.

Carrington, Noel. *Design in the home.* 1933 London: Country Life 191pp (later editions as *Design and decoration in the home* 1938, revised 1952 Batsford)

Decoration of the English Home July 1934-December 1936 (replacing *Decoration, Beauty and the Home* 1930-1934 as a radical alternative to *Studio* and *Homes and Gardens*)

Bertram, Anthony. *The house; a machine for living in: summary of the art and science of homemaking considered functionally.* 1935 London: Black 116pp illus. (later edition 1945)

Rutt, Anna Houg. *Home Furnishing.* 1935 London: Chapman and Hall 408pp illus. bibl.

Briggs, Martin Shaw. *How to plan your house.* 1937 London: English Universities Press. 210pp pl 16

Merivale, Margaret. *Furnishing the small home volume 1.* 1938 London: Studio 112pp illus (reprinted 1944, 1946)

Aronson, Joseph. *The book of furniture and decoration: period and modern.* 1938 London: Pitman 347pp illus.

Tomrley, Cycill Geraldine. *Furnishing your home; a practical guide to inexpensive furnishing and decorating.* 1940 London: Allen and Unwin 244pp illus. bibl.

The interior planning of flats becomes a subject of attention:

Yorke, F. R. S. *The modern flat.* 1934 London: Architectural Press 199pp illus (later editions 1948, 1958)

Flats. Municipal and private enterprise. 1938 London: Ascot Gas Company 285pp illus.

Joel, Betty. 'Space saving in the small flat', *Studio* 112 1936 pp 89-98

Gibberd, F. 'Furnishing the small apartment. Suggestions for the rational design and arrangement of furniture in homes where space is limited', *Studio* 114 1937 pp 169-172

and humorously:

Robinson, William Heath and Browne, Kenneth Robert Gordon. *How to live in a flat*. 1936 London: Hutchinson 128pp.

A few individual designers:

Adams, Maurice S. R. *Modern decorative art. A series of two hundred examples of interior decoration, furniture, lighting fittings and other ornamental features*. 1930 London: Batsford 249pp illus. (based on 25 years of Maurice Adams Ltd)

Patmore, Derek 'British decorators of today 1. Rodney Thomas', *Studio* 103 1932 p 294

Patmore, Derek. 'British interior architects of today II Duncan Miller, III Ronald Dickens, IV John Hill, V Jack Killick, VI Betty Joel, VII Allan Walton, VII Ronald Fleming, IX Syrie Maugham, X Serge Chermayeff, XI Derek Patmore', *Studio* vols 103 1932, 104 1932, 105 1933 pp 358-359; pp 50-51, pp 92-93, pp 174-175, pp 276-277, pp 338-339, pp 40-41, pp 312-313, pp 112-113, pp 392-393

Patmore, Derek. 'British interior decorators. Herman Schrijver', *Studio* vol 106 1933 pp 100-101

Boumphrey, Geoffrey. 'The designers 3. Arundell Clarke, 4. J. Duncan Miller 5. Betty Joel', *Architectural Review* vol 78, September October November 1935 pp 115-116, pp 159-160, pp 205-206

Holme, C. G. 'Designs for modern needs. Atelier 1,' *Studio* 101 May 1931 pp 358-365

Bernard, Oliver Percy. *Cock sparrow. A true chronicle*. 1936 London: Cape 384pp

Trevor, John. 'Interior decorators of today. John and Shelagh Butler', *Studio* 116 1938 pp 100-103

A few interiors:

'Decoration: two town house interiors designed by Oliver Hill', *Architectural Review* vol 55 1924 pp 58-63

Frost, A. C. 'Finella. A house for Mansfield D. Forbes', *Architectural Review* 66 December 1929 pp 264-272

Garland, Madge. 'The 1930 look in British decoration. A room decorated by Vanessa Bell and Duncan Grant', *Studio* vol 100 1930 pp 142-143

'The designer and her problem. Furnishing for £200. A "Design for Today" house at Welwyn', *Design for Today* September 1933 pp 175-184

Chermayeff, Serge. 'Remodelling a flat', *Studio* 109 1935 pp 269-271

'A space saving flat. The London home of Miss Jeanne de Casalis', *Studio* 110 1935 pp 165-167

Breuer, Marcel. 'A house in Bristol' (Crofton E. Gane's), *Design for Today* December 1935 pp 459-462

WARTIME AND RECONSTRUCTION

The Postwar home, a series of lectures on its interior and equipment. 1942 London: Studio for Royal Society of Arts 120pp (13 papers reprinted from *JRSA* vol 90 1942)

A similar series of articles in *Art and Industry* from 1945 was republished in book form:

Robertson, Howard. *Reconstruction and the home*. 1947 London: Studio 87pp illus.

Daily Mail book of postwar houses based on the ideas and opinions of the women of Britain and specially compiled for the Daily Mail by Mrs M. Pleydell-Bouverie. 1944 London: Daily Mail 175pp illus.

Design in the home. Arranged by the Victoria and Albert Museum '(an exhibition). 1943 London: Council for the Encouragement of Music and the Arts

Designs at home (an exhibition) 1945 London: Council for the Encouragement of Music and the Arts

POSTWAR

Surveys:

Casson, Hugh (ed). *Inscape, the design of interiors*. 1968 London: Architectural Press 208pp illus.

Aloi, Roberto. *L'arredamento moderno; terza serie*. 1945 Milan: Hoepli 347pp (mostly illustrations)

Yerbury, F. R. (ed). *Modern homes illustrated*. 1947 London: Odhams 320pp

Aloi, Roberto. *Esempi di arredamento di tutto il mundo*. 1950- Milan: Hoepli (series with captions in English, French and German. Titles of later series vary)

Survey of the British furnishing industry. A guide for buyers, traders and importers; prepared by 'Furnishings for Britain'. 1950 London: National Trade Press 244pp (other editions 1952 and later)

Gilliatt, Mary. *English style in interior decoration*. 1967 London: Bodley Head 144pp illus. (concentrates on post-Festival examples)

Garland, Madge. 'The eclectic interior 1950-1965', *Country Life* October 14 1965 pp 958-960

Whiton, Sherrill. *Elements of interior design and decoration.* 1951 Chicago: Lippincott. 829pp illus. (first edition 1937. Revised to include subsequent historical developments)

Penraat, Sherrill. *Elements of interior 1950-1965', Country Life* October 14 1965 pp 958-960

Carney, Clive Carney. *International interiors and designs: outstanding achievements by leading architects, interior designers and decorators of the world.* 1959 Sydney: Angus and Robertson 194pp

House and Garden. *Small houses.* 1961 New York: Condé Nast 208pp illus.

House and Garden. *Book of interiors.* (ed). Robert Harling 1962 London: Condé Nast 216pp illus.

Buzas, Stefan. 'Modern trends in interior decoration', *JRSA* vol 111 September 1963 pp 802-813

House and Garden. *The modern interior.* (ed). Robert Harling. 1964 London: Condé Nast 304pp illus.

ID & D: interior design and decoration compiled and designed by Design Yearbook Ltd. 1965- London: M. Joseph 319pp illus.

Daily Mail book of furnishing, decorating and kitchen plans annual review. 1968- London: Associated Newspapers

Skurka, Norma and Gili, Oberto. *Underground interiors: decorating for alternate life styles.* 1972 London: Macdonald 122pp illus. (period 1965-1971)

Hicks, David. 'Design in interior decoration', *JRSA* March 1976 pp 181-192

Guides and some advice:

New home. 1946 London: Council of Industrial Design 36pp bibl.

Council of Industrial Design. *Furnishing to fit the family.* 1947 London: HMSO for Council of Industrial Design (10 designed rooms for different types of family)

Llewellyn, Margaret. *Design and our homes.* (1951?) London: Council of Industrial Design and Education Department, Cooperative Union. 100pp

Hennessey, William J. *Modern furnishings for the home.* 1952, 1956 New York: Reinhold 2 vols

Merivale, Margaret. *Furnishing the small home vol 2.* 1953 London: Studio 96pp

Russell, Gordon and Jarvis, Alan. *How to furnish your home . . . With a shopping guide by Veronica Nisbet.* 1953 London: Newman Neame

Young, Dennis. *Home furnishing on a small income.* 1955 London: Hutchinson 128pp illus.

Stephenson, Henry and Stephenson, Lilian. *Interior design.* 1960 London: Studio 96pp

Ball, Victoria Kloss. *The art of interior design: a text in the aesthetics of interior design.* 1960 New York: Macmillan 352pp illus. bibl.

Living in one room. Three different solutions to the problem of living in one room (exhibition catalogue) n.d. London: Council of Industrial Design 8pp plans

Stephenson, Henry. *Design and decoration in the home.* 1962 London: Blandford 80pp

Hatje, Gerd and Hatje, Ursula. *Design for modern living; a practical guide to home furnishing and interior decoration.* 1962 New York: Abrams 318pp 550 illus. (translation of *Knaurs Wohnbuch*)

Peluzzi, Giulio and Revista Dell' Arredamento. *Living the modern way; form and colour in modern interiors.* 1964 London: Studio Vista 210pp

Rowntree, Diana. *Interior design. Drawings by Ian Lacey.* 1965 Harmondsworth: Penguin 215pp

Ward, Mary and Ward, Neville. *Living rooms.* 1967 London: Macdonald in association with the Council of Industrial Design 64pp illus.

Bonellie, Helen-Janet. *Introduction to interior design.* 1968 New York: Yoseloff 80pp

Black, Maggie (ed). *Design for living.* 1970 London: Ward Lock 256pp illus. plans

Friedmann, Arnold and others. *Interior design: an introduction to architectural interiors.* 1976 Oxford: Elsevier 425pp illus. bibl. (previous edition 1970)

Demachy, Alain. *Interior architecture and decoration. English translation by J. A. Underwood.* 1974 London: Studio Vista 163pp illus. (translation of *Architecture d'interieur et décoration*)

A few encyclopaedias:

Harling, Robert (ed). *House and Garden dictionary of design and decoration.* 1973 London: Collins 544pp illus. (from *House and Garden* 1962-1971)

Sheridan, Michael (ed). *The furnisher's encyclopaedia.* 1953 London: National Trade Press 541pp (later edition 1955)

Pegler, Martin. *The dictionary of interior design.* 1967 London: Barker 500pp

Ergonomics:

Panero, Julius. *Anatomy for interior designers, illustrated by Nino Repetto.* 1966 (third edition) New York: Whitney Publications 146pp illus. (first published 1962)

Design of Particular Rooms

BATHROOMS

See also:

Interior Design: Plumbing *page 169*

A convenient introduction to the whole subject is provided by:

Giedion, Siegfried. *Mechanization takes command: a contribution to anonymous history.* 1948 reprinted 1970 Oxford Univeristy Press. *Part VII The mechanization of the bath* pp 628-711

a condensed version of which appeared as:

Giedion, Siegfried. 'The mechanisation of the bath', *Architectural Review* vol 102 October 1947 pp 119-126

More popular histories are:

Wright, Lawrence. *Clean and decent: the fascinating history of the bathroom and water closet, and of sundry habits, fashions and accessories of the toilet principally in Great Britain, France and America.* 1960 London: Routledge and Kegan Paul 280pp illus. bibl.

Ashe, Geoffrey. *The tale of the tub. A survey of bathing through the ages.* 1950 London: Newman Neame for the County Chemical Company 63pp

Scott, George Ryley. *The story of baths and bathing.* 1939 London: Werner Laurie 290pp illus.

Pudney, John. *The smallest room. Decorations by David Knight.* 1954 London: Joseph 150pp (a history of lavatories)

An exhibition:

A pageant of baths (held at the Bath Festival). 1964 London: Allied Ironfounders Ltd

The bathroom at a more specific point of history:

Yorke, F. R. S. 'Modern bathroom', *Architectural Review* vol 72 October 1932 pp 147-156 illus.

'Famous dancer's bathroom designed by Paul Nash', *Architectural Review* vol 73 June 1933 pp 254a-b

'Fine craftmanship. The bathroom and its design', *Studio* vol 107 1934 pp 150-154 illus.

Braddel, Dorothy. 'The bathroom', *Design for Today.* February 1934 pp 57-63

Dunnett, H. McG. 'Design review. Bathroom equipment', *Architectural Review* vol 112 September 1952 pp 172-178 (mostly illustrations)

Report to the Council of Industrial Design . . . on bathrooms. 1966 London: Council of Industrial Design 24pp

Goulden, Gontran. *Bathrooms: a guide to bathroom design.* 1966 London: Macdonald in association with the Council of Industrial Design 64pp illus.

Kira, Alexander. *The bathroom: criteria for design.* 1966 Ithaca: Cornell University Center for Housing and Environmental Studies (revised edition 1976 Viking Press Based on a very extensive research programme)

a lot of this book has been republished in:

Kira, Alexander. *The bathroom book.* 1976 Harmondsworth: Penguin 288pp illus.

For much earlier material there is:

'A bibliography on baths and bathing', *American Architect* vol 87 1905 pp 14-15

KITCHENS

See also:

Domestic Equipment *page 253*

An introduction:

Harrison, Molly. *The kitchen in history.* 1972 London: Osprey 142pp 122 illus.

The evolution of the kitchen:

Ravetz, Alison. 'The Victorian coal kitchen and its reformers', *Victorian Studies* June 1968 pp 435-460 illus.

The model kitchen and reception room in Empire woods arranged by the Design and Industries Association for the Empire Marketing Board. 1929 London: Empire Marketing Board 12pp illus.

'The Modern kitchen', *Design and Industries Association Journal* no 2 1932

Denby, E. 'In the kitchen', *Architectural Review* vol 74 November 1935 pp 199-200

Denby, Elizabeth. 'Women and kitchens', *Design for Today* July 1933 pp 113-115

Denby, Elizabeth. 'Designs in the kitchen', pp 59-70 in Gloag, John (ed). *Design in Modern Life.* 1934 London: Allen and Unwin

Veasey, Christine. 'Design and colour in the kitchen', *Studio* 108 1934 pp 85-88

Merivale, Margaret. 'Problems for the designer: kitchens. The kitchen workshop of the house', *Art and Industry* October 1943 pp 113-116

Ballantyne, Adie. *Choose your kitchen. A book for the housewife.* 1944 London: Faber 84pp

Ward, Mary. 'Design review. Kitchen fittings', *Architectural Review* vol 114 no 680 August 1953 pp 125-127 illus.

'Science in kitchen planning: two papers read to the Royal Society of Arts. Principles of planning by Mrs Mildred Wheatcroft. The kitchen of today and tomorrow by Miss Joan E. Walley', *JRSA* February 1957 pp 187-206

Walley, Joan E. *The kitchen in catering: a handbook on food service planning and organisation.* 1960 London: Constable (third edition 1970. A basic textbook)

'Modern kitchens', *Ideal Home* April 1966 supplement 63pp

Prizeman, John. *Kitchens.* 1966 London: Macdonald & Co in association with the Council of Industrial Design 64pp

DINING ROOMS:

Speyer, Marion. 'Dining rooms 1834-1934', *Design for Today* September 1934 pp 350-353

The dining room. Some simple suggestions for its treatment. 1910 London: Decorative Art Journals Company Ltd 28pp illus.

Iles, J. Bird. 'The problem of the small dining room', *Studio* 113 1937 pp 39-41

French Interior Design

See also:

Furniture: French *page 178*
International Exhibitions *page 31*

In many ways and at different times French interior design has influenced ideas of interior design both in Britain and elsewhere.

NINETEENTH CENTURY

Daly, César. *L'Architecture privée au XIX siècle. Troisième série. Décorations intérieures: salons, salles à manger, boudoirs etc.* 1974-1976 2 vols

Blake, Vernon. 'Morris, Munich and Cezanne. The origin of the modern French decorators', *Architectural Review* vol 65 1929 pp 207-208

Blanc, Charles. *Grammaire des arts décoratifs, décoration intérieure de la maison.* 1886 (new edition) Paris: Renouard 495pp illus. (first edition 1882)

Mourey, Gabriel. 'Decorative art in Paris: the exhibition of the "Six",' *Studio* vol 13 1898 pp 83-91

TWENTIETH CENTURY

Two basic documents:

The modern style. Le style moderne. Contribution de la France. With a foreword in English by John Gloag and in French by Henry van de Velde. 1925 London: E. Benn 15pp pl 64

Le Corbusier *pseud* (ie Charles Edouard Jeanneret). *L'Art décoratif d'aujourd'hui.* 1925 Paris: G. Cres 218pp illus.

An exhibition:

Le décor de la vie, de 1900 à 1925. 1937 Paris: Musée des Arts Décoratifs

Mourey, Gabriel. 'French decorative art', *Studio* vol 78 1919 pp 13-20, 53-57

Les arts de la maison. 1923 Paris: Albert Morance

Verne, Henri et Chavancé, René. *Pour comprendre l'art décoratif moderne en France.* 1925 Paris: Hachette 515 illus.

Deshairs, Leon. *Modern French decorative art. A collection of examples of modern French decorative art with an introduction by Leon Deshairs.* 1926 London: Architectural Press pl 188 (selected from *Art et Décoration*)

'The Modern Movement in Continental decoration', *Architectural Review* vol 59-62 1926-1927 pp 248-251, pp 302-305; pp 40-42, pp 120-123, pp 164-167; pp 34-36, pp 112-115; pp 86-87, pp 156-158 (nine articles on different parts of the house)

Deshairs, Leon. *Modern French decorative art. Second series.* 1930 London: Architectural Press 168pp

Kahle, Katherine Morrison. *Modern French decoration.* 1930 London: Putnam 219pp

Dufrène, Maurice. 'Interior decoration in Europe and America', *Decorative Art. Studio Yearbook* 1931 pp 35-66

Trevor, John. 'Paris trends in modern interior decoration. Did the 1937 exhibition set an improved standard?', *Studio* 115 1938 pp 267-273

Eudes, Georges. *Modern French interiors, translated by M. I. Martin.* 1959 London: Thames and Hudson 136pp

Particularly important groups:

Société des Artistes-Décorateurs (founded 1901, annual exhibitions 1907-)

Regularly reported in the *Studio*

Société du Salon d'Automne (founded 1903, annual exhibitions)

Catalogues 1904-1913. Chadwyck Healey Microfiche

Also regular reports in the *Studio*

Union des Artistes Modernes

Annual exhibitions 1930 – with detailed published catalogues (1950- titled *Formes Utiles*)

A few individuals:

Vago, Picrre. 'An interview with Jacques Adnet', *Studio* 118 1939 pp 73-75

Thornton, Lynne. 'Jean Dunand and his friends', *Apollo* October 1973 pp 294-299

Valotaire, Marcel. 'Interior design today: a talk with Maurice Jallot', *Studio* 101 1931 pp 181-186

Janneau, Guillaume. *Technique du décor intérieur moderne.* 1928 Paris: A. Morancé 213pp illus.

Janneau, Guillaume. *Le style directoire. Mobilier et décoration.* 1937 Paris: G. Moreau 62pp pl 48

Jourdain, Francis. *Intérieurs.* 1929 Paris: Moreau 4pp pl 48

Moussinac, Leon. 'Francis Jourdain', *Studio* vol 103 1932 pp 228-231

Garner, Philippe. 'Pierre Legrain – décorateur', *Connoisseur* 189 June 1975 pp 130-137

Mallet-Stevens, Robert. *Dix années de réalisations en architecture et décoration.* 1930 Paris: Massin pl 72

Mourey, Gabriel. 'A great French furnisher – J. E. Ruhlmann', *Studio* vol 92 1926 pp 244-250

Elements of Interior Design

COLOUR

See also:

Colour *page 97*

Surveys:

Birren, Faber. *Color for interiors. Historical and modern. An essential reference work covering the major period styles of history and including modern palettes from the authentic decoration of houses, institutional and commercial interiors.* 1963 New York: Whitney Library of Design 210pp

The British Colour Council Dictionary of colours for interior decoration. 1949 London: British Colour Council 3 vols (vols 1 and 2 samples)

Porter, Tom and Mikellides, Byron. *Colour for architecture.* 1975 London: Studio Vista 176pp 104 illus.

Library bibliography 232 Colour in buildings. 1969 Garston: Building Research Station. Design Division. Colour Section (1870 to present)

Domestic applications:

Hay, David Ramsay. *The laws of harmonious colouring, adapted to house painting and other interior decorations . . . to which is added An attempt to define aesthetic taste.* 1847 (sixth edition) Edinburgh (first edition 1828)

Duveen, Edward J. *Colour in the home, with notes on architecture, sculpture, printing and upon decoration and good taste.* 1912 London: Allen and Unwin 167pp pl 44 (20 in colour)

Grace, John Dibblee. *Art of colour decoration. Being an explanation of the purposes to be kept in view and the means of attaining them.* 1913 London: Batsford 89pp pl 20 (primarily historical examples but with a final section on his own and his father's work)

Ward, James. *Colour decoration of architecture, treating on colour and decoration of the interiors of buildings.* 1913 London: Chapman and Hall 135pp

Barker, Roland G. 'Colour schemes in domestic decoration', *Journal Society of Architects* July 1915 pp 326-329 (paper to the Incorporated Institute of British Decorators)

Thorpe, Hall. 'On colour in the cottage', *Studio Yearbook* 1919 pp 65-74

Gloag, John. *Colour and comfort in decoration . . . with illustrations and original designs by Palmer-Jones.* 1924 London: Duckworth 186pp illus.

Ionides, Basil. *Colour and interior decoration.* 1926 London: Country Life 81pp illus. (deals with the effects of individual colours)

Holmes, John M. *Colour in interior decoration.* 1931 London: Architectural Press 91pp col pl bibl.

Patmore, *Colour schemes for the modern home.* 1933 London: Studio 29pp col pl bibl. 29pp (revised edition 1936)

Shand, P. Morton. 'An adventure in colour. Ideal Home exhibition', *Design for Today* May 1934 pp 172-175

Ionides, Basil. *Colour in everyday rooms, with remarks on sundry aspects of decoration.* 1934 London: Country Life 115pp illus.

Colour designs for modern interiors. 1935 London: Architectural Press pl 80

Miller, Duncan. *More colour schemes for the modern home.* 1938 London: Studio 24pp illus.

Patmore, Derek. *Colour schemes and modern furnishing.* 1945 London: Studio 35pp pl 73

Holmes, John M. *Colour in the home.* 1950 London: Pitman 51pp illus.

Carrington, Noel. *Colour and pattern in the home.* 1954 London: Batsford 160pp illus.

Smithells, Roger. *Colour in interior decoration.* 1966 London: Batsford 128pp illus.

Halse, Albert O. *The use of colors in interiors.* 1968 New York: McGraw Hill 134pp

Factories:

Nelson, J. H. 'The colour factor in working conditions', *Art and Industry* July 1946 pp 19-25

Colour as applied to the decoration of factories and offices. 1949 Hounslow: Deeds

Wilson, Robert Francis. *Colour and light at work*. 1953 London: Seven Oaks Press 148pp pl 12 (by art director of British Colour Council)

Wilson, Robert Francis. *Colour in industry today. A practical book on the functional use of colour*. 1960: Allen and Unwin 90pp illus. bibl.

Gloag, Herbert Lawrence. *Colouring in industry today. A practical book on the functional use of colour*. 1960: Allen and Unwin 90pp illus. bibl.

Gloag, Herbert Lawrence. *Colouring in factories*. 1961 London: HMSO 19pp (Factory Building Studies 8. Code 47-212-8)

There are a number of more technical studies published by the British Colour Council, such as the different editions of *Colour and Lighting in factories*.

Public buildings:

Horsley, Gerald C. 'Structural colour decoration of the interior of public buildings', *JSA* vol 50 April 1902 pp 429-440

DECORATION

This section concentrates on surface and applied decoration rather than the more general interior design aspects already presented.

General surveys:

Savage, George. *A concise history of interior decoration*. 1966 London: Thames and Hudson 285pp illus. bibl.

Jeans, Herbert. *The periods in interior decoration. A practical guide. (with a chapter on the progress of paperhanging in England by Metford Warner)*. 1921 London: Trade Papers Publishing Co 118pp (Chapter IX The Regency – the Victorian period – the Morris influence)

and for exterior decoration:

Barnard, Julian. *The decorative tradition*. 1973 London: Architectural Press 144pp illus.

Studies and writings of chronological interest:

The Decorator's Assistant 1847 London 5 vols

The Universal Decorator illustrated by W. Gibbs. 1858 (3 vols), 1860 (second series), 1861-3 (third series)

The Decorator: an illustrated practical magazine for the furnishing trades. 1864/5 2 vols

Gibbs, John. *Domestic architecture and ornament in detail: being a series of designs for windows, doorways, doors, capitals, cornices, iron railings, furniture etc., after the manner of the Romanesque, English, and foreign, the Gothic and other styles*. 1868 Oxford: author 8pp pl 21

Pitman, William. 'On surface decoration', *JSA* vol 18 March 18 1870 pp 378-386

Davidson, Ellis A. *A practical manual of house-painting, graining, marbling etc.* 1875 London: Crosby Lockwood (ninth edition 1904)

The House decorator and school of design numbers 1-28, (18 June-24 December 1880)

Journal of Decorative Art. An illustrated technical journal for the house painter, decorator and the art workman. 1881- Manchester

Decoration 1880-1888

James, M. E. *How to decorate our ceilings, walls and floors*. 1883 London: Bell 86pp

Miller, Fred. *Interior decoration. A practical on surface decoration*. 1885 London: Wyman 145pp illus. (includes chapters on Japanese decoration)

Facey, James William. *Practical house decoration. A guide to the art of ornamental painting, the arrangements of colours in apartments and the purposes of decorative design . . . with some remarks upon the nature . . . of pigments*. 1886 London: Crosby Lockwood 184pp

Pearce, Walter John. *Painting and decorating*. 1898 London: C. Griffin 312pp pl 34

Crane, Walter. *Of the decoration of public building, edited by A. Baker*. 1975 Doncaster: Bloomfield Books. 58pp (second lecture given at Arts and Crafts Exhibition Society's exhibition 1896)

Brown, William Norman. *House decorating and painting*. 1900 London: Scott Greenwood 156pp illus.

Dowling, Henry George. *Painters' and decorators' work*. 1916 London: Routledge 151pp illus. bibl.

Giles, Godfrey. 'Legitimate use of imitations in decoration (read before the Incorporated Institute of British Decorators)', *Building News* 15 March 1916 pp 254-257

Gloag, John. *Simple schemes for decoration, illustrated by E. J. Warner*. 1922 London: Duckworth 151pp

Vince, M. *Decoration and care of the home. Some practical advice.* 1923 London: Collins 255pp illus.

Jennings, Arthur Seymour and Rothery, Guy Cadogan. *The modern painter and decorator. A practical treatise on house, church, theatre and public buildings painting and decorating.* 1924 London: Caxton Publishing 3 vols *(vol 1. Painting and materials, vol 2. wallpapering, Vol 3. design style and decoration)*

McClelland, Nancy. *The practical book of decorative wall-treatments.* 1926 Philadelphia: J. B. Lippincott 273pp illus. (includes historical survey)

'Allan Walton, a modern decorator', *Studio* vol 93 1927 pp 250-255

Tree, Viola. 'Old and new in interior decoration. The work of Curtis Moffat', *Studio* vol 98 1929 pp 792-799

Ionides, Basil. 'Modern interior decoration', *Studio* vol 97 1929 pp 341-345

Block, Robert.'Reflections on modern decoration', *Studio* vol 98 1929 pp 535-540

Davis, A. J. 'Some aspects of contemporary decoration', *JRSA* vol 79 March 27 1931 pp 453-463

Johnson, C. S. *Interior decoration; a textbook for handymen and housewives who are interested in their homes.* 1931 London: Pitman 122pp illus.

'Decoration portfolio', *Architectural Review* vol 77 1935 pp 33-36, pp 73-76, pp 121-124

Patmore, Derek. 'Interior decoration', *JRSA* vol 83 January 18 1935 pp 209-221

Patmore, Derek. *Modern furnishing and decoration.* 1936 (revised edition) London: Studio 40pp pl 48 (first published 1934)

Patmore, Derek. *I decorate my home.* 1936 London: Harper 176pp illus.

Miller, Duncan. *Interior decorating.* 1937 London: Studio 79pp illus. (reprinted 1944)

Eberlein, Harold Donaldson. *The practical book of interior decoration.* 1937 London: Lippincott 477pp pl 191

Patmore, Derek. *Decoration for the small home.* 1938 London: Purnam 202pp illus.

Marshall, Herbert George Hayes. *Interior decoration today.* 1938 Leigh on Sea: F. Lewis 287pp pl 231pp

Schrijver, Hermann. *Decoration for the home.*1939 Leigh on Sea: F. Lewis 96pp illus.

Gillies, Mary Davis. *All about modern decorating.* 1942 London: Harper 225pp pl 40 bibl.

The practical painter and decorator . . . A comprehensive and authoritative introduction to the most modern methods of painting and decorating for learners and more experienced craftsmen. 1945 London: Odhams 284pp

Marshall, Herbert George Hayes. *Within four walls: a book about interior decoration, colour schemes and furnishing the home.* 1948 Leigh on Sea: F. Lewis 171pp

Llewellyn, Margaret. *Colour and pattern in your home. A book on design, with 'do it yourself' ideas, colour schemes, house decoration and practical hints.* 1951 Loughborough: Cooperative Union Education Department and Council of Industrial Design 34pp illus.

Tubb, L. F. J. *Painting and decorating (advanced).* 1951 London: Newnes 160pp illus.

Holmes, John M. *The art of interior design and decoration.* 1951 London: Longmans 195pp illus bibl.

Patmore, Derek. *A decorator's notebook.* 1952 London: Falcon Press 88pp

Gatz, Konrad (ed). *Decorative designs for contemporary interiors* 1960 London: Peter Owen 240pp 506 ills. (first published 1956 New York)

Connaissance Des Arts. *The art of interior decoration, edited by Souren Melikian.* 1962 Paris: Hachette 2 vols illus.

Hicks, David. *On decoration.* 1967 New York: Macmillan 152pp illus.

House and Garden. *Guide to interior decoration. Editor Robert Harling.* 1967 London: Condé Nast 304pp illus.

Gundrey, Elizabeth (ed). *The book of home decoration . . . produced in collaboration with the Wall Paper Manufacturers Ltd.* 1968 London: Spectator Publications 64pp illus.

Some journals:

The Decorator: official organ of the London association of master decorators 1902-1967 (monthly) London: Trade Publications (absorbed *Paint and Wallpaper* July 1928. Continued as *Decorating Contractor* 1967-)

Painting and Decorating Journal 1969-(monthly) Southport: Sutherland Pub. Co. (previously *Journal of Decorative Art and British* Decorator 1881-1954, *Painting and Decorating* 1954-1968)

PLASTERWORK

Most surveys of plasterwork concentrate on much earlier periods.

Useful general studies for our period are:

Weaver, Sir Lawrence. *Tradition and modernity in plasterwork.* 1928 London: G. Jackson & Son 63pp

Millar, William. *Plastering plain and decorative. A practical treatise on the art and craft of plastering and modelling.* 1897 London: Batsford 604pp over 500 illus.

Articles occasionally appear in architectural journals, eg:

'Modern British plasterwork', *Architectural Review* vol 23, vol 24, 1908 pp 221-233, pp 276-284, pp 329-338, pp 25-31

'Plaster technique. A review by E. H. Ellis', *Architectural Review* vol 85 1939 pp 207-214

An individual:

Bankart, George P. 'The craft of the plasterer', *Architectural Review* vol 59 1926 pp 160-165

Bankart, George P. and Bankart, G. Edward. *Modern plasterwork design.* 1928 London: Architectural Press pl 100

Radford, Ernest. 'Modern English plastering: Mr G. P. Bankart's work', *Studio* vol 27 1903 pp 267-273

Vallance, Aymer. 'Of some recent plaster work by Mr G. P. Bankart', *Studio* vol 39 1907 pp 144-150

FLOORS

See also:

Textiles: Carpets *page 199*

History and manufacture of floor coverings. 1899 New York: Review Publishing Company 98pp illus.

Williams, Llewellyn E. 'Modern floor coverings', *Architects Journal* vol 74 1931 pp 605-609

Chermayeff, Serge. 'A grammar of groundwork', *Architectural Review* vol 74 September 1933 pp 147-154

Dugdale, Michael. 'Modern domestic floors', *Design for Today* March 1934 pp 98-101

Holme, C. G. 'Take the floor', *Decorative Art. Studio Yearbook* 1942 pp 43-46

Dunnett, H. McG. 'Design review. Top dressing. A review of flooring materials', *Architectural Review* vol 113 no 674 February 1953 pp 115-121

HANDLES AND DOOR FURNITURE

Tomrley, C. G. 'Problems of handles', *Design* 39 March 1952 pp 8-13

Door and drawer furniture: a design folio. 1951 London: Council of Industrial Design 6pp pl 12

Dunnett, H. McG. 'Design review. Door and window furniture', *Architectural Review* vol 112 August 1952 pp 116-121

Austin, Frank. 'Design review. Cabinet ironmongery', *Architectural Review* vol 116 no 692 August 1954 pp 127-129

Whitworth, Peter. 'Survey. Door furniture', *Design* 179 November 1963 pp 48-55

Whitworth, Peter. 'At last – British door furniture gets co-ordinated', *Design* 208 April 1966 pp 33-37

Parkin, Alan. 'Waiting for the air curtain: an ergonomic survey of doors, handles and locks', *Design* 241 January 1969 pp 50-53

Jones, J. Christopher. 'Handles. The ergonomic approach', *Design* 72 December 1954 pp 34-38

STAIRCASES

Marwick, T. P. *The history and construction of staircases.* 1888 Edinburgh: Gray 138pp pl 14

Rothery, Guy Codogan. *Staircases and garden steps.* 1912 London: Werner Laurie 250pp illus. bibl.

Tomlinson, Harold. 'The staircase', *Architectural Review* vol 73 1933 pp 215-222

FIREPLACES

See also:

Domestic Appliances: Solid Fuel *page 255*

Kelly, Alison. *The book of English fireplaces.* 1968 Feltham: Country Life 96pp illus.

West, Trudy. *The fireplace in the home.* 1976 Newton Abbot: David and Charles 160pp illus.

Rothery, Guy Cadogan. *Chimneypieces and inglenooks. Their design and ornamentation.* 1912 London: Werner Laurie 239pp illus. bibl.

Edwards, Frederick. *Our domestic fireplaces: a treatise on the economic use of fuel.* 1865 London: Hardwicke (another edition 1870)

Baillie Scott. M. H. 'The fireplace of the suburban house', *Studio* vol 6 1896 pp 101-108 and 'The modern fireplace', *Studio* vol 106 July 1933 pp53-54

Royere, Jean. 'Designing a modern fireplace', *Studio* vol 114 1937 pp 29-32

'Progress in fireplace design', *Design* 37 January 1952 pp 20-21, 34

Trade catalogues of major or long-lived companies are another prime source.

2 Public Interiors

Public interiors have only recently been studied in general and historical terms. Consequently a lot of raw material for further research is buried in more specific or technical areas which are not widely accessible. What follows is a brief selection of some historically interesting material.

Two general but recent surveys:

Black, Misha. *Public interiors. An international survey.* 1960 London: Batsford 192pp (a selection of post-1945 work)

'Inscape – special issue', *Architectural Review* vol 139 no 831 May 1966

Offices

A general survey:

Cowan, Peter with Joint Unit for Planning Research. *The office: a facet of urban growth.* 1969 London: Heinemann Educational Books 280pp illus. bibl.

Some historical studies:

Wallen, James. *Things that live forever, being the story of office equipment from the dawn of thought to the age of metal.* 1921 Jamestown New York: Ryecrofters for the Art Metal Construction Company 71pp

'Modern interior decoration: Guaranty Trust Company of New York, 50 Pall Mall East, SW1', *Architectural Review* November 1920 pp 112-118

Stark, Gordon. 'Furnishing and decoration of the modern office', *Architectural Review* vol 68 July 1930 pp 35-37

Gloag, John. 'Modern office; with craftsman's portfolio', *Architectural Review* vol 75 April 1934 pp 139-148

Thomas, Mark Hartland. 'The interior design of factories and offices', *Design* 34 October 1951 pp 4-11

McCallum, Ian. Prestige and utility (Time Life's London offices) *Architectural Review* vol 113 no 675 March 1953 pp 157-172

'Time Life building special issue', *Design* 51 March 1953

'Office equipment', *Design* 63, 65, 67, 69, 71 March, May July, September, November 1954 pp 10-17, pp 30-33, pp 31-34, pp 38-42, pp 31-35

Goodden, Wyndham. 'Conversion to a modern office', *Design* 65 May 1954 pp 24-28

Rosenauer, Michael. *Modern office buildings.* 1955 London: Batsford 163pp illus.

'Modern offices – special issue', *Architectural Design* July 1958

Better Offices 1. 1961 London: Institute of Directors

Better Offices 2. 1964 London: Instutute of Directors 216pp

Pilkington Research Unit. *Office design: a study of environment, edited by Peter Manning.* May 1965 University of Liverpool Department. of Building Science 160pp illus.

'Interior design – office interiors', *Architectural Review* vol 143 no 855 May 1968 pp 372-380

'Inside the office', *Design* 263 November 1970 pp 29-43

Kaleidoscope: diversity by design. An exhibition of furnishings by the Supplies Division, *Department of the Environment.* 1971 London: Council of Industrial Design (Design Centre exhibition)

Broadcasting House

Broadcasting house. 1932 London: BBC 116pp illus.

Coates, Wells, Goodesmith, Walter and Yorke, F. R. S. 'Broadcasting house', *Architectural Review* vol 72 January 1932 pp 42-78 (lavishly illustrated)

Factories

See also:

Interior design: colour *page 158*

Mills, Edward. *Modern Factory.* 1959 London: Architectural Press 215pp

Better factories. 1963 London: Institute of Directors 279pp illus. bibl.

Public auditoria

'Royal Festival Hall special issue', *Architectural Review* vol 109 June 1951

Sharp, Dennis. *The picture palace and other buildings for the movies.* 1969 London: Hugh Evelyn 228pp illus.

First night. Exhibition of Odeon cinemas 1931-1939. 21 February-8 March 1973. Wolverhampton Polytechnic Faculty of Art and Design 24pp illus.

Worthington, Clifford. *The influence of the cinema on contemporary auditoria design.* 1952 London: Pitman 123pp

Churches

See also:

Metals: Church plate *page 237*

This is an area meriting a bibliography in its own right. I hope the following will provide a brief introduction to some important features.

A general survey:

Anson, Peter Frederick. *Fashions in church furnishings 1840-1940.* 1965 (second edition) London: Faith Press 383pp illus.

Other general introductions:

Addleshaw, G. W. O. and Etchells, Frederick. *The architectural setting of Anglican worship. An inquiry into the arrangements for public worship in the Church of England from the Reformation to the present day.* 1948 London: Faber 288pp illus. bibl.

Little, Bryan D. G. *Catholic churches since 1623: a study of Roman Catholic churches in England and Wales from penal times to the present decade.* 1966 London: Hale 256pp pl 48

Briggs, Martin S. *Puritan architecture and its future.* 1946 London: Lutterworth 90pp pl 22

A useful starting point for research of individual churches:

Betjeman, John (ed). *Pocket guide to English parish churches vol 1. The South, vol 2. The North.* 1968 London: Collins

A long-established company:

Campbell, Kenneth. *Church decoration – Campbell Smith and Company 1873-1973. A century of decorative craftsmanship.* 1973 London: Campbell Smith and Co. 78pp illus.

A valuable bibliographical introduction:

The conservation of churches and their treasures. A bibliography. 1970 London: Council for the Care of Churches

Victorian churches

A concise introduction:

Victorian church art: catalogue of an exhibition November 1971-January 1972. 1971 London: Victoria and Albert Museum 184pp illus. bibl.

Exhibition of Victorian and Edwardian church art. 1967 London: Victorian Society.

Architectural studies:

Hitchcock, Henry Russell. *Early Victorian architecture in Britain.* 1973 London: Trewin Copplestone (first edition Yale University Press 1954)

Clarke, Basil F. L. *Churchbuilders of the nineteenth century. A study of the Gothic Revival in England.* 1969 Newton Abbot: David and Charles 296pp illus. (first edition SPCK 1939)

Howell, Peter. *Victorian churches.* 1968 London: RIBA 64pp illus. bibl. (RIBA Drawings series)

Muthesius, Hermann. *Die neuere kirchliche Baukunst in England.* 1901 Berlin: W. Ernst & Sohn 1761 pl 32

Leatherbarrow, Joseph Stanley. *Victorian period piece. Studies occasioned by a Lancashire church.* 1954 London: SPCK 260pp illus. (full and serious study of Swinton church)

Ferriday, Peter. 'The church restorers', *Architectural Review* vol 136 no 810 August 1964 pp 87-95

Howe, Bea. 'Dressing the Victorian church', *Country Life* vol 152 1972 pp 162, 164

'Internal decoration and arrangement of churches', *Quarterly Review* 1857 39pp

A strong influence was provided by the Ecclesiological Society (1837-1868):

Ecclesiologist 1841-1868

Instrumenta Ecclesiastica. 1847 London: Ecclesiological Society (another edition 1856 'a variety of working drawings of details and fittings, appertaining to churches . . .')

White, William. 'Modern design', *Ecclesiologist* 1853

Burges, William. 'Why we have so little art in our churches', *Ecclesiologist* 1867

The Camden Society:

White, James Floyd. *The Cambridge Movement. The Ecclesiologists and the Gothic Revival.* 1962 Cambridge University Press 272pp pl 8

A few designers:

Ricardo, Halsey. 'John Francis Bentley. '1 Church buildings', *Architectural Review* vol 11 1901 vol 12 1902 pp 155-164, pp 18-30

Warren, Edward. 'George Frederick Bodley', *Architectural Review* vol 11 1901 pp 131-138

Warren, Edward. 'The life and work of George Frederick Bodley', *JRIBA* vol 17 3rd series 1909-1910 pp 305-336

Thompson, Paul. *William Butterfield.* 1971 London: Routledge and Kegan Paul 526pp illus. bibl.

PUGIN

Pugin, A. N. W. *The true principles of pointed or Christian architecture set forth in two lectures delivered at St Marie's, Oscott.* 1841 London: J. Weale 67 + 40pp pl 9 (reprinted 1969 St Barnabas Press, Oxford, 1973 Academy Editions, London)

Pugin, A. W. N. *Glossary of ecclesiastical ornament and costume, compiled and illustrated from ancient authorities and examples. Faithfully translated by the Rev. Bernard Smith.* 1844 London: Henry G. Bohn 245pp pl 73 (other editions 1848, 1868. Important chromolithographs)

Pugin, A. W. N. *The present state of ecclesiastical architecture in England.* 1843 London: C. Dohman 153pp illus.

Pugin, A. W. N. *A treatise on chancel screens and rood lofts, their antiquity, use and symbolic signification.* 1851 London: C. Dolman 124pp pl 14

GEORGE GILBERT SCOTT

Scott, George Gilbert. *Personal and professional recollections, edited by his son G. G. Scott.* 1879 London: Sampson Low 436pp

Sir George Gilbert Scott. (1811-1878). A list of his buildings and writings and a bibliography. Compiled by the RIBA Library. 1956/1957 typescript

Scott, Sir George Gilbert. *A plea for the faithful restoration of our ancient churches.* 1850 London: Parker 155pp

Briggs, Martin Shaw. 'Sir Gilbert Scott I', *Architectural Review* vol 24 1908 pp 92-99, pp 147-152, pp 180-185, pp 290-294

Cole, D. 'George Gilbert Scott', in Ferriday, Peter (ed). *Victorian architecture.* 1963 London: Cape

Millard, Walter. 'Notes on some works of the late George Gilbert Scott MA FSA – Gilbert Scott the Younger', *Architectural Review* vol 5 1898 pp 59-67, pp 124-132

GEORGE EDMUND STREET

Street, Arthur Edmund. *Memoir of George Edmund Street RA 1824-1881.* 1881 London: J. Murray 441pp

ART'NOUVEAU

Malton, John. 'Art Nouveau in Essex', (St Mary the Virgin, Great Warley) *Architectural Review* vol 126 no 751 1959 pp 100-103

Beazley, Elizabeth. 'Watts chapel', *Architectural Review* vol 130 no 775 September 191 pp 166-177 both reprinted in Richards, J. M. and Pevsner, Nikolaus (eds). *The Anti-Rationalists.* 1973 London: Architectural Press

TWENTIETH CENTURY

Unwin, Frederick Sydney. *The decorative arts in the service of the church.* 1912 London: Mowbray 198pp

Sutherland, W. G. *Church decoration.* 1912 Manchester: Decorative Art Journal Company 44pp

Durst, Alan L. 'Ecclesiastical ornament', *Architectural Review* vol 59 1926 pp 194-199

'Old standards and modern problems in decoration. The work of the Diocesan committees', *Architectural Review* vol 62 1927 pp 27-41

Gill, Eric. 'Church furniture', *Architectural Review* vol 62 1927 pp 52-53

Maufe, Edward. 'Furnishing of churches; with craftsman's portfolio', *Architectural Review* vol 76 October 1934 pp 144-150

Short, Ernest (ed). *Post-war church building.* 1947 London: Hollis and Carter 202pp illus.

Mellor, Richard. *Modern church design.* 1948 London: Skeffington and Son 136pp

Hammond, Peter. *Liturgy and architecture.* 1960 London: Barrie and Rockliff 191pp illus. bibl.

Hammond, Peter (ed). *Towards a church architecture.* 1962 London: Architectural Press 262pp illus.

Ireland, Marion P. *Textile art in the church: vestments, paramats and hangings in contemporary worship, art and architecture.* 1971 Nashville: Abingdon Press 285pp (University Microfilms)

Hotels

Borer, Mary Cathcart. *The British hotel through the ages.* 1972 London: Lutterworth Press 264pp illus.

'Hotels – special issue', *Design* 109 January 1958

'Hotels – a special issue', *Architectural Review* vol 128 no 764 October 1960

Margetson, Stella. 'The era of the railway hotel', *Country Life* 152 1972 pp 798-800

Margetson, Stella. 'The rise of the luxury hotel', *Country Life* 146 13 November 1969 pp 1265, 1269

Jackson, Stanley. *The Savoy. The romance of a great hotel.* 1964 London: Muller 316pp illus.

Fry, Maxwell. 'Cumberland hotel', *Architectural Review* vol 75 January 1933 pp 13-17

Blake, John E. 'Leofric shatters a myth', (Leofric hotel, Coventry), *Design* 82 October 1955 pp 22-26

Council of Industrial Design:

Report to the Council of Industrial Design by its advisory committee on hotels and restaurants on tableware. 1963 London 19pp

Report to the Council of Industrial Design by its advisory committee on hotels and restaurants on carpets. 1965 6pp

Report to the Council of Industrial Design . . . on bedroom furniture, banqueting tables and chairs, restaurant and dining room tables. 1966 revised edition 22pp (first edition 1962)

Report to the Council of Industrial Design . . . on design requirements for food storage equipment. 1969 London 22pp

Restaurants

Curtis-Bennett, Sir Francis Noel. *The food of the people, being the history of industrial feeding.* 1949 London: Faber 320pp

Koch, Alexander. *Restaurants, cafés, bars.* 1939 Stuttgart: Koch 407pp illus.

Fengler, Max. *Restaurant architecture and design.* 1971 London: L. Hill 202pp illus. (first published 1969 as *Hotelbauen*)

Lehrian, Paul. *The restaurant . . . illustrated by Kenneth Prowen.* 1953 London: Practical Press 149pp

'Bars on land and sea. Decoration and craftsmanship supplement', *Architectural Review* vol 73 1933 pp 35-44

'Restaurants', *Architectural Review* vol 74
December 1933 pp 235-244

Hotels – Cafés – Restaurants. 1938 Boulogne:
L'Architecture d'Aujourd'hui (collection
of articles by Pierre Vago and others)

Newton, Eric. 'Meals and murals',
Architectural Review vol 94 August 1943
pp 41-48 (on British restaurants in
wartime)

Wyatt, Harold. 'The evolution of the railway
refreshment room', *Architectural Review*
vol 104 September 1948 pp 133-138

Ward, Mary. 'Design review. Canteen
equipment', *Architectural Review* vol 116
no 694 October 1954 pp 268-273

Laski, Marghanita and Gardiner, Stephen.
'Espresso/Coffee bars', *Architectural
Review* vol 118 no 705 September 1955
pp 165-174

Atkin, William Wilson and Adler, John.
Interiors book of restaurants. 1961 London:
Tiranti 215pp illus. (especially US
developments)

Stewart, John. 'Cafeterias and food halls',
Architectural Review vol 143 no 856 June
1968 pp 457-458

Dahinden, Justus and Kuhne, Gunther.
Neue restaurants: an international survey.
1973 Stuttgart: Hatje 156pp

Public Houses

Monckton, H. A. *A history of the English public
house.* 1969 London: Bodley Head 175pp

Girouard, Mark. *Victorian pubs.* 1975
London: Studio Vista 224pp illus. bibl.
(pp 127-170 on fittings)

Spiller, Brian. *Victorian public houses.* 1972
Newton Abbot: David and Charles 112pp
illus.

Taylor, Nicholas. 'The Black Friar',
pp 181-186 in Richards, J. M. and
Pevsner, Nikolaus (eds). *The
Anti-Rationalists.* 1973 London:
Architectural Press

Williams, E. E. *The new public house.* 1924
London: Chapman and Hall 204pp

Oliver, Basil. *The modern public house.* 1934
London: Westminster Press 46pp illus.

Oliver, Basil. *The renaissance of the English
public house.* 1947 London: Faber 181pp
illus.

Yorke, F. R. S. *The planning and equipment of
public houses.* 1949 London: Architectural
Press 210pp illus.

Gorham, Maurice and Dunnett, H. McG.
Inside the pub. 1950 London:
Architectural Press 138pp 136 illus.

'The pub tradition recaptured', (results of
Architectural Review's competition),
Architectural Review vol 107 May 1950
pp 383-396

Spiller, Brian. 'Brewers house styles',
Architectural Review vol 118 no 708
December 1955 pp 372-381

Crawford, Alan and Thorne, Robert.
Birmingham pubs 1890-1939. 1976
Birmingham: Centre for Urban and
Regional Studies, Birmingham University
in association with the Victorian Society
Birmingham Group 52pp illus.

Shops

See also:

Retail and Point of Sale Design *page 170*

Some general surveys:

Adburgham, Alison. *Shops and shopping
1800-1914: where and in what manner the
well dressed Englishwoman bought her clothes.*
1964 London: Allen and Unwin 304pp
illus.

Artley, Alexandra (ed). *The golden age of
shop design. European shop interiors
1880-1939.* 1975 London: Architectural
Press 128pp illus.

Adburgham, Alison. 'History of taste 2.
Edwardian taste in interior decoration as
interpreted in the shops', *Architectural
Review* vol 161 no 963 May 1977
pp 295-301

Edwards, Arthur Trystan. *The architecture of
shops.* 1933 London: Chapman and Hall
75pp pl 84

Westwood, Bryan and Westwood, Norman.
Smaller retail shops. 1937 London:
Architectural Press 120pp illus.

Westwood, Bryan and Westwood, Norman.
The modern shop. 1952 London:
Architectural Press 183pp 191pp
(revised edition 1955)

Eldridge, Mary. 'The plate glass shop front',
Architectural Review vol 123 no 734 March
1958 pp 193-195 (a history of its
adoption in the nineteenth century)

Turner, Michael L. and Vaisey, David.
*Oxford shops and shopping. A pictorial survey
from Victorian and Edwardian times.* 1972
Oxford: Illustrated Press 64pp 140 illus.

Some developments through the period:

Ince, Harold. 'The design of London
shopfronts', *Architectural Review* vol 14
1903 pp 75-87

Lanchester, H. V. 'The design and
architectural treatment of the shop', *JRSA*
vol 61 April 25 1913 pp 577-592

Chatterton, Frederick. *Shop front. A selection
of English, American and continental*

examples. 1927 London: Architectural Press 104pp illus.

Robertson, Howard. 'The new shop-front', *DIA Quarterly* no 6 December 1928 pp 6-9 illus.

Tayler, Herbert. 'Shops', *Architectural Review* vol 121 no 721 February 1927 pp 98-111 (includes a survey history from 1851)

Hammond, Albert Edward. *Shop fittings and display.* 1927 London: Pitman 131pp illus.

Emberton, Joseph. 'Shopfittings and shop-fronts', *DIA Quarterly* no 11 April 1930 pp 8-10 illus.

Yorke, F. R. S. 'Shop fronts and fittings', *Architectural Review* vol 70 1931 pp 173-177

Hammond, A. Edward. 'Shop fronts', *Design for Today* June 1934 pp 210-213

Schumacher, Adolf. *Ladenbau.* 1934 Stuttgart: Hoffman 165pp 478 illus.

Hammond, Albert Edward. *Store interior planning and display.* 1939 London: Blandford 247pp illus.

Levy, Hermann Joachim. *The shops of Britain. A study in retail distribution.* 1948 London: Kegan Paul, Trubner 246pp

Ketchum, Morris. *Shops and stores.* 1949 London: Chapman and Hall 308pp (American but very influential)

Parnes, Louis. *Planning stores that pay: organic design and layout for efficient merchandising.* 1948 New York: F. W. Dodge Corporation 313pp illus.

Atkinson, F. 'Towards an architecture: post war shop fronts in London', *Architectural Review.* vol 109 February 1951 pp 99-106

Pasdermadjian, Hrant. *The department store: its origins, evolution and economics.* 1954 London: Newman Books 217pp illus. bibl.

Somake, Ellis E. and Hellberg, Rolf. *Shops and stores today, their design, planning and organisation.* 1956 London: Batsford 232pp illus.

Koch, Alexander and Gutmann, Robert. *Ladengestaltung; shop design.* 1956 Stuttgart: A. Koch 195pp illus.

Daykin, Leonard E. (ed). *Outstanding new supermarkets.* 1969 New York: Progressive Grocer 230pp illus.

'Shops: a special issue', *Design* 167 November 1962

Beazley, Elizabeth. 'Supermarkets', *Architectural Review* vol 140 no 837 November 1966 pp 329-334

Shopfitting International 1969- (monthly) London: Batsford (previously *Shop and Shopfitting Review* 1955-1968)

Schools

A little on a very big area:

Seaborne, Malcolm. *The English school: its architecture and organisation 1370-1870.* 1971 London: Routledge and Kegan Paul 317pp illus. bibl.

Seaborne, Malcolm and Lowe, Roy. *The English school: its architecture and organisation vol II: 1870-1970.* 1977 London: Routledge and Kegan Paul 320pp illus. bibl.

Seaborne, Malcolm. *Primary school design.* 1971 London: Routledge and Kegan Paul 92pp illus. (covers 120 years)

Hospitals

Thompson, John D. and Goldin, Grace. *The hospital: a social and architectural history.* 1975 New Haven: Yale University Press 320pp illus. bibl.

Ship interiors

See also:

Transport: Water *page 280*

General studies:

Anderson, Sir Colin. 'Interior design of passenger ships', (Thomas Gray memorial lecture), *JRSA* vol 114 March 1966 pp 477-493

Greenhill, Basil and Giffard, Ann. *Travelling by sea in the nineteenth century: interior design in Victorian passenger ships.* 1972 London: Adam and Charles Black 168pp pl 78

De La Valette, John. 'Fitment and decoration of ships from the Great Eastern to the Queen Mary', *JRSA* vol 84 May 22 1936 pp 705-726

'Architecture of the liner', *Architectural Review* vol 35 1914 pp 87-110

'The architecture of the liner', *Architectural Review* vol 70 1931 pp 61-65

Traveller. 'Shipshape design', *DIA Quarterly* 15 May 1931 pp 9-12

Some of the most illuminating studies concentrate on individual liners:

'Empress of Britain: the decoration of a liner', *Studio* vol 102, 1931 pp 21-43

Anderson, Sir Colin. 'Ship interiors: when the breakthrough came', *Architectural Review* vol 141 no 844 June 1967 pp 449-452 (reviews changes that came with the Orion in 1935)

Grigson, Geoffrey. 'Design of the temporary home. SS Orion', *Studio* vol 110 1935 pp 190-201

'Design in ships. RMS Orion. SS Normandie', *Design for Today* October 1935 pp 381-386, 387-390

Brown, William Tatton. 'Architecture afloat. The Orion sets a new course', *Architectural Review* vol 78

'Designing for ocean travel – the Caronia', *Art and Industry* August 1949 pp 60-71

Maynard, Alister. 'Ships cabins: a complex design problem', *Design* 39 March 1952 pp 22-23

Blake, John E. 'Fifth in line' (Orsova of Orient Line), *Design* 65 May 1954 pp 9-11

Farr, Michael. 'Towards a modern liner', (SS Southern Cross), *Design* 78 June 1955 pp 26-30

McCallum, Ian. 'Ship interiors', *Architectural Review* vol 119 no 710 February 1956 pp 133-140

'ID. The passenger ship: backward or forward?' *Architectural Review* vol 128 no 765 November 1960 pp 362-367

Scholberg, Philip. 'Design for the voyager', *DIA Yearbook* 1961-1962 pp 22-30

'Interior design: SS Canberra, SS Oriana', *Architectural Review* vol 130 September 1961 pp 181-193

Salmon, Geoffrey. 'Canberra', *Design* 153 September 1961 pp 63-69

'Interior design: SS Canberra', *Architectural Review* vol 130 no 776 October 1961 pp 261-266

Casson, Hugh. 'A ship is an island', *Architectural Review* vol 145 1969 pp 399-409

'Queen Elizabeth 2', *Design* 244 April 1969 pp 36-77

'Queen Elizabeth 2 a special issue edited by Sherban Cantacuzino', *Architectural Review* vol 145 no 868 1969 (interiors pp 422-462)

'QE2: design for future trends in world travel', *Architects Journal* 149 1969 pp 985-996

Aircraft interiors

See also:

Transport: Air *page 277*

Woolcombe, Joan. 'Inside an air liner', *Design for Today* August 1933 pp 126-133

Chadwick, Hulme. 'Modern air transport interior design', *Art and Industry* September 1946 pp 73-79

Holmes, Kenneth. 'Design for air travel', *Art and Industry* May 1947 pp 130-152

Gaunt, William. 'Interior design in the air', *Design* 50 February 1953 pp 8-13 (the comet)

Burrey, Suzanne. 'Aircraft interiors. British and American designs compared', *Design* 87 March 1956 pp 18-23

Spark, Robert. 'Survey. Aircraft interiors', *Design* 201 September 1965 pp 38-53

Nason, Gerald. 'Inside-up. Interior design and the air liner', *Architectural Review* vol 140 no 838 December 1966 pp 413-422

Carr, Richard. 'Designing interiors for the SRN4', *Design* 227 November 1967 pp 48-53

Cooper, Ian. 'A little bit of help on the flight deck', *DIA Yearbook* 1967/8 pp 21-24 (reorganisation of head-up display)

Public conveniences

Crawford, David and Williams, Alma. 'Public conveniences', *Design* 213 September 1966 pp 32-44

3 Services

See also:

Domestic Equipment *page 253*

Introductions to the whole area.

Banham, Reyner. *The architecture of the well-tempered environment.* 1973 (new edition) London: Architectural Press 292pp illus. bibl. (first edition 1969)

Banham, Reyner. *Mechanical services.* 1975 Milton Keynes: Open University Press (especially pp 6-28)

This section concentrates on three elements: Lighting, Plumbing and Air conditioning. Heating and other services dependent on appliances are dealt with in the section on Domestic Appliances.

Lighting

General studies:

O'Dea, William T. *A short history of lighting.* 1958 London: Science Museum 39pp illus. (first published as *Darkness into Daylight* 1948)

O'Dea, William T. *The social history of lighting.* 1959 London: Routledge and Kegan Paul 253pp illus. bibl.

Robins, Frederick William. *The story of the lamp (and the candle).* 1970 Bath: Kingsmead Reprints 155pp illus. (first edition 1939 Oxford University Press)

Thwing, Leroy. *Flickering flames. A history of domestic lighting through the ages.* 1958 Rutland, Vermont: Tuttle 138pp illus.

Let there by light. 1964 Hartford, Connecticut: Wadsworth Atheneum 54pp illus.

Henriot, Gabriel. *Encyclopédie du luminaire. Appareils de toutes les époques et de tous les styles. Choix d'objets de formes et de décors apparentes depuis l'antiquité jusqu'à 1870.*

1933 Paris: Les Editions Guerinet 6 vols (especially Tome VI *XIX siècle*. Well illustrated but poorly dated)

Wechssler-Kümmel, Sigrid. *Schöne Lampen Leuchter und Lanternen*. 1962 Heidelberg: Keysersche Verlagsbuchhandlung 440pp illus. bibl. (pp 115-137 Nineteenth century, pp 138- Twentieth century)

Wells, Stanley. *Period lighting*. 1975 London: Pelham 166pp illus. bibl.

Defries, D. N. 'On artificial illumination', *JSA* vol 15 February 15 1867 pp 193-197

Gaster, Leon. 'Modern methods of artificial illumination', *JSA* vol 57 August 6, August 13, August 20, August 27, September 3, September 10 1909 pp 757-772, pp 775-788, pp 795-810, pp 815-837, pp 843-861, pp 867-890

GAS LIGHTING

Chandler, Dean. *Outline of history of lighting by gas*. 1936 London: Chancery Lane Printing Works 279pp illus.

Audouin, Paul and Berard, Paul. *On the different varieties of burners used for gas lighting. Etude sur les divers becs employés pour l'éclairage au gaz et recherches des conditions les meilleurs pour sa combustion*. 1862 Paris: Mallet-Bachelieur 75pp

Haddan, St George Lane Fox. 'Automatic gas-lighting', *JSA* vol 26 March 8 1878 pp 321-326

Harcourt, A. Vernon. 'Improvements in gas illumination', *JSA* vol 30 March 10 1882 pp 438-447

Lewes, Vivian B. 'The use of gas for domestic lighting', *JSA* vol 45 December 25 1896, January 1 January 8 1897 pp 89-98, pp 101-111, pp 113-123

Lewes, Vivian B. 'The incandescent gas mantle and its uses', *JSA* vol 48 October 19 1900 pp 841-847, pp 853-859, pp 865-873

'Gas lighting; twenty years of progress', *Illuminating Engineer* 21 January 1928 pp 38-41

Hodgson, R. B. 'Romance of the gasholder', *Gas Journal* (London) 180 November 23 1927 pp 547-554

Journal of the Institution of Gas Engineers. 1960- (monthly) London (previously *Transactions of the Institution of Gas Engineers* 1863-1959)

ELECTRIC LIGHTING

O'Dea, William T. *Electric illumination. An account of the principles, applications and development of electric lighting*. 1936 London: HMSO 40pp (revised edition 1937)

Bright, Arthur Aaron. *The electric lamp industry; technological change and economic development from 1800 to 1947*. 1972 New York: Arno 526pp (reprint of 1949 edition)

Preece, William Henry. 'Electric lighting at the Paris electrical exhibition', *JSA* vol 30 December 16 1881 pp 98-107

Dredge, James (ed). *Electric illumination*. 1882-1885 London: Engineering 2 vols

Hibben, S. G. 'Forty years of lighting progress', *Illuminating Engineering Society Transactions* 28 September 1933 pp 640-642

Pope, Franklin Leonard. *Evolution of the electric incandescent lamp*. 1889 Elizabeth, New Jersey: Henry Cook 91pp illus.

Gaster, Leon 'Progress in electric lighting', *JSA* vol 54 February 9 1906 pp 321-340

Janneau, Guillaume. *Le luminaire et les moyens d'éclairages nouveaux*. 1925 Paris: Berheim Jeune (a series)

Jolley, Leonard B. W., Waldram, J. M. and Wilson, G. H. *The theory and design of illuminating engineering equipment*. 1930 London: Chapman and Hall 709pp illus.

Henriot, Gabriel. *Exposition internationale de 1937. Luminaire moderne*. 1937 Paris 8pp pl 48

Jenkins, H. G. 'Fluorescent lighting', *JSA* vol 90 April 3 1942 pp 282-298

Hammond, A. Edward. 'Fluorescent lighting. An impartial review of its development, scope, advantages and limitations', *Art and Industry* August 1946 pp 34-40

Ward, Neville. 'Design review. Fluorescent light fittings', *Architectural Review* vol 115 no 687 March 1954 pp 207-211

Technical and commercial design developments are probably best traced through the pages of:

Light and Lighting and environmental design. Journal of the Illuminating Engineering Society vol 29 no 1 January 1936- (bi-monthly) London (previously *The Illuminating Engineer* 1908-1935 University Microfilms)

International Lighting Review 1950- (quarterly) Netherlands

A few surveys and company histories:

Stevens, Richard. 'Surveys of industry no 3. Lighting', *Design* 149 May 1961 pp 54-65

Durrant, D. W. (ed). *Interior lighting industry*. 1973 (fourth edition) London: Lighting Industry Federation 130pp

Stern, Bernard. 'Never leave well enough alone', *Design* 210 June 1966 (Rotaflex light fittings)

Gray, John. 'Modern lighting in mass production', *Design* 74 February 1955 pp 18-22 (G.E.C.)

Casimir, H. B. G. and Gradstein, S. (eds). *An anthology of Philips research.* 1966 Eindhoven: NV Philips Gloeilampenfabrieken 469pp (first 144pp more general background)

Benoy, J. M. 'Design policy in industry', Joseph Lucas Ltd. *Design* 49 1953 pp 6-11

Dunnett, H. McG. 'Light fittings from a family firm', *Design* 57 September 1953 pp 26-32 (Merchant Adventurers Ltd)

There are a large number of standards and other technical advice:

Department of Scientific and Industrial Research. Building Research Board. Lighting Committee. *The Lighting of buildings.* 1944 London: HMSO 163pp (Postwar building studies no 12)

More specific detail on domestic illumination:

Brewer, Robert W. A. 'Country house lighting', *Architectural Review* vol 34 1913 pp 21-22, pp 41-42, pp 85-86, pp 107-108 (includes petrol and acetylene)

Thorpe, F. W. 'Development and design of lighting fixtures in relation to architecture, interior decoration and illumination', *Illuminating Engineer* March 1915 pp 102-144

'A craftsman's portfolio. Hall lights', *Architectural Review* vol 59 1926 pp 252-256

Rathbone, M. 'Modern electric light fittings', *Studio* vol 98 1929 pp 495-498

Carroll, Leon. 'The new art of light', *Studio* vol 99 1930 pp 173-183

'Aladdin at Cambridge or the magic lamp', *Studio* vol 99 1930 pp 184-185 (McGrath's light effects at Finella)

'Craftsman's portfolio. Indirect lighting', *Architectural Review* vol 67 1930 pp 49-50

'Lighting effects' edited by R. W. Maitland. *Architectural Review* vol 67 161-162

McGrath, Raymond. 'Quantity and quality in architectural illumination', *DIA Quarterly* 14 January 1931 pp 4-7

Taut, Bruno. 'Lighting and heating', *Decorative Art. Studio Yearbook* 1931 pp 97-122

Bernard, Oliver P. 'Modern lighting', *Studio* vol 102 1931 pp 183-187

Smithells, Roger. 'Light in the home', *Design for Today* October 1933 pp 208-217

Rena, Maurice. 'Lighting – decorative and efficient. Basic principles discussed', *Studio* vol 114 1937 pp 224-232

Pleydell-Bouverie, David. 'Modern lighting', *Architectural Review* vol 81 1937 pp 109-118

Read, A. B. *Lighting the home.* 1938 London: Country Life 71pp illus.

Haslett, Caroline. 'Electricity in the home', *JRSA* vol 95 August 15 1947 pp 639-654

'Light fittings from postwar Europe, review of the Scottish Design Council exhibition', *Design* 15 March 1950 pp 2-7

Home lighting: a design folio. 1961 London: Council of Industrial Design 8pp

Mills, D. Dewar. 'Design review. light fittings', *Architectural Review* vol 112 November 1952 pp 315-321

Hiscock, R. C. 'Light fitting design problems', *Design* 48 December 1952 pp 25-27

Brookes, Malcolm J. 'Design analysis 18. Pendant light fittings', *Design* 137 May 1960 pp 44-48

Phillips, Derek. *Lighting: The principles and planning of home lighting.* 1966 London: Council of Industrial Design 64pp

Hopkinson, R. G. and Collins, J. B. *The ergonomics of lighting.* 1970 London: Macdonald 272pp illus

Nuckolls, James Lawton. *Interior lighting for environmental designers.* 1976 Chichester: Wiley 384pp illus.

Plumbing

Appliances:

Reyburn, Wallace. *Flushed with pride: the story of Thomas Crapper.* 1969 London: Macdonald 95pp illus. (sanitary appliances 1872-1910)

More general plumbing:

Eassie, William. *Sanitary arrangements for dwellings, intended for the use of officers of health, architects, builders and householders.* 1874 London: Smith Elder 188pp illus.

Hellyer, Samuel Stevens. *The plumber and sanitary houses. A practical treatise on the principles of internal plumbing work, or the better means of excluding noxious gases from our houses.* 1900 (sixth edition) London: Batsford 489pp (first edition 1877)

Hellyer, Samuel Stevens. *The principles and practice of plumbing.* 1893 (second edition) London: Bell 294pp

Plumbers work: past and present. A brief commentary and a descriptive account of the museum and workshops established by the Worshipful Company of Plumbers at King's College London for the extension of the technical training of student plumbers. 1896 London: Charles Call and Sons 35pp

Davies, Philip John. *Standard practical
plumbing.* 1905 (fifth edition) London:
Spon 3 vols (first published 1885)

Moore, Edward C. S. and Silcock, E. J.
*Sanitary engineering: a practical treatise on
the collection, removal and final disposal of
sewage.* 1901 (second edition) London:
Batsford 791pp (first edition 1898)

Palmer, Roy. *The water closet. A new history.*
1973 Newton Abbot: David and Charles
141pp illus bibl.

Robins, Frederick William. *The story of water
supply.* 1946 London: Oxford University
Press 207pp pl 26

Lamb, H. A. J. 'Sanitation: an historical
survey', *Architects Journal* March 4th 1937

Air conditioning

Faber, Oscar and Kell, John Robert. *Heating
and air conditioning of buildings.* 1943
(second edition) London: Architectural
Press 580pp pl 31 (first edition 1936)

'Ventilating and air conditioning of the
interior', *Architectural Review* vol 84 1938
pp 80-88

Retail and Point of Sale Design

Aspects of shop interior design have already
been discussed in the Public Interiors
section *page 165.* This section is concerned
with retail display and individual shop
design.

GENERAL SYSTEMS DESIGN

Gosling, David and Maitland, Barry. *Design
and planning of retail systems.* 1975
London: Architectural Press 250pp
illus. bibl. (includes history of the
development of retailing systems)

Davis, Dorothy. *A history of shopping.* 1966
London: Routeledge and Kegan Paul
322pp illus.

'Shopping issue', *DIA Yearbook* 1960/1

Sutnar, Ladislav. *Design for point of sale.*
1952 New York: Pellegrini and Cundahy
illus.

Trethowan, Harry. 'Design and the retailer',
JRSA vol 88 April 19 1940 pp 507-519

DISPLAY

Capey, Reco. 'Display and relevant factors',
Art and Industry September 1948 pp 88-93

Nelson, George (ed). *Display.* 1953 New
York: Whitney Publications 190pp illus.
(includes section on Festival of Britain)

Heath, Alec. 'Surveys of industry 9. Display
fittings', *Design* 161 May 1962 pp 50-57

Useful journals:

Display International 1970- (monthly)
London (previously *Display 1919-1970*)

Shelf Appeal 1933-1946 (later *Sales Appeal*
1947 then *Freight and Sales Appeal*
1947-1949, then *Sales Appeal* 1949-1959
then *Sales Appeal and Packaging technology*
1959-1964 then *Merchandising and Sales
Appeal* 1964 and then incorporated with
Packaging News)

Window display:

Trethowan, Harray and others. *Selling
through the window.* 1935 London: Studio
96pp illus.

Picken, James Hamilton. *Principles of window
display.* 1927 Chicago: A. W. Shaw
436pp illus.

Down, H. Ashford. *The art of window display.
A complete guide to modern methods of shop
publicity, shop lighting, interior display and the
work of the display man.* 1931 London:
Pitman 213pp illus.

Black, Misha. 'The designer and his
problem VII. Shop window display',
Design for Today December 1933
pp 313-316

Beeching, C. (ed). *Modern grocery display. A
practical work on window display and interior
display.* 1933 London: Caxton 376pp

Hammond, Albert Edward (ed). *Modern
footwear display. A practical work on window
showmanship and interior planning and
equipment.* 1937 London: Caxton 339pp
illus. (first edition 1935)

Grieve, E. W. 'Display sense', *JRSA* vol 89
May 30 1941 pp 414-426 (by display
director of Harrods)

Downing, George Henry. *Art applied to
window display.* 1932 (second edition)
London: Blandford 96pp (first edition
1929)

Pick, Berverley. 'Display and the product',
Art and Industry. September 1947
pp 80-87

Oeri, Georgine. 'The display window as a
sign of the times', *Graphis* 4 number 24
1948 pp 378-385

Oeri, Georgine. 'Exhibition design and
window display', *Graphis* 5 number 28
1949 pp 332-337

*Display illustrated: up to the minute displays for
the large and small shop.* 1949 London:
Blandford 136pp illus.

*International Window Display edited by Walter
Herdeg.* 1951- Zurich: Herdeg.

Erhardt, Hans. 'An international survey of
the art of window display', *Graphis* vol 18
no 94 1953 pp 122-139

Herdeg, Walter (ed). *Window display, an
international survey of the art of window
display.* 1962 London: Sylvan Press
282pp illus.

Kaspar, Karl (ed). *International window
display. Etalages internationaux. Schaufenster
international.* 1966 London: Thames and
Hudson.

Shopping catalogues

Shopping catalogues are also a useful index
of current design. Some recent facsimiles
are:

*Victorian shopping: Harrod's 1895 Catalogue,
edited with an introduction by Alison
Adburgham.* 1972 Newton Abbot: David
and Charles 1560pp

*Edwardian shopping. A selection from the Army
and Navy Stores catalogues 1893-1913,
compiled by R. H. Langbridge.* 1975 Newton
Abbot: David and Charles 270pp

Exchange and Mart 1868-1948. Selected issues.
1972 Newton Abbot: David and Charles.

*Gamages Christmas Bazaar 1913 being a
facsimile reprint of the 1913 Christmas
catalogue of A. W. Gamage Ltd of Holborn,
London, with some pages from the 1911
General Catalogue. Introduced by Alison
Adburgham.* 1974 Newton Abbot: David
and Charles 528pp illus.

Hornung, Clarence P. (comp). *A sourcebook
of antiques and jewelry designs.* 1978
London: Hale 244pp illus. (engravings
from Nineteenth Century mail order
catalogues)

*Yesterday's shopping. The Army and Navy Stores
catalogue 1907. A facsimile of the Army and
Navy Cooperative Society's 1907 issue of Rules
of the Society and price list of articles sold at
the stores. Introduced by Alison Adburgham.*
1969 Newton Abbot: David and Charles
1282pp

More recently:

'A selection from the 100 good catalogues
exhibition', *Design* 70 October 1954
pp 34-42

Individual shops

Their distinctive retail style:

Newton, Douglas. 'Dunn and Dunn's.
Designer and retailer', *Design* 58 October
1953 pp 22-26

Rees, G. *St Michael. A history of Marks and
Spencer.* 1969 London: Weidenfeld and
Nicolson 284pp

JS 100. The story of Sainsbury's. 1969
London: J. Sainsbury 96pp

Johnson, P. 'A hundred years of Boots', *Art
and Antiques Weekly* 21st May 1977
pp 26-30

Carrington, Noel. 'Artists and industry at
Harrods', *Design for Today* December 1934
pp 461-464

Exton, E. Nelson. 'Design for selling',
(Joseph Emberton and Simpsons)
Designs for Today June 1936 pp 225-228

Two shops have been perhaps studied more
than most:

LIBERTY'S

Adburgham, Alison. *Liberty's: biography of a
shop.* 1975 London: Allen and Unwin
160pp illus.

*Liberty's 1875-1975: an exhibition to mark the
firm's centenary July-October 1975. Catalogue
edited by Shirley Bury.* 1975 London:
Victoria and Albert Museum 128pp
illus. bibl.

HEAL'S

Hughes-Stanton, Corin. 'Design
management. A shop with high
standards', *Design* 199 July 1965 pp 42-47

Benton, Tim. 'History of taste 6. Up and
down at Heal's 1929-35', *Architectural
Review* vol 153 no 972 February 1978
pp 109-116

Wainwright, Shirley B. 'Heal and Son',
Studio vol 101 November 1927 pp 334-338

Weaver, Sir Lawrence. 'Tradition and
modernity in craftsmanship II:
Furnishing and shopkeeping', *Architectural
Review* vol 63 1928 pp 247-249

Tomrley, C. 'Exhibition at Heal's. Interiors
and furniture by seven architects', *Design
for Today* June 1936 pp 229-233

See also:

Corporate Identity *page 146*

5 Exhibition Design

The major international exhibitions have
been presented in the section on Fostering
design, *page 31.* However there have been a
number of notable and interesting
developments in exhibition techniques of all
sorts throughout the period. A small but
distinctive literature has emerged.

General studies:

Black, Misha. *Exhibition design.* 1950
London: Architectural Press 195pp

Rattenbury, Arnold. *Exhibition design: theory
and practice.* 1971 London: Studio Vista
96pp illus.

Clasen, Wolfgang. *Exhibitions, exhibits and
trade fairs.* 1968 London: Architectural
Press 208pp

Franck, Klaus. *Ausstellungen. Exhibitions.*
1961 Teufen: Niggli 251pp illus.
(English and German text)

Askwith, Lord. 'Exhibitions', *JRSA* vol 72
November 23 1923 pp 2-13

Some practical advice:

Auger, Hugh Ambrose. *Trade fairs and exhibitions. Guide to cost, design and presentation.* 1967 London: Business Publications 215pp illus. ('The exhibition past and present' pp 1-27)

Wright, Alan. *INDEX: industrial exhibitions: the theory, techniques and practice of exhibiting.* 1970 London: Lintex 55pp

Carmel, James H. *Exhibition techniques, travelling and temporary.* 1962 New York: Reinhold 216pp illus.

Much of the literature provides a very detailed reflection of prevailing taste and particular problems:

'The exhibition stand: an architectural treatment', (London Gas companies' stand at the Women's Exhibition, Olympia. Designed by H. Austen Hall), *Architects Journal* 26 July 1922 pp 127-128

Yorke, F. R. S. 'An architect visits the Ideal Home Exhibition', *Architectural Review* vol 71 May 1932 pp 216-

'Exhibitions. Decoration and craftmanship supplement', *Architectural Review* vol 74 September 1933 pp 107-116 (includes an article by John Gloag 'Advertising in three dimensions')

Jeffcott, Ian. 'The designer and his problem III: Designing an exhibition (Ideal Home)', *Design for Today* July 1933 pp 88-90

Pearce, K. 'Power of exhibition display', *Commercial Art* vol 16 June 1934 pp 213-222

Black, Misha. 'Exhibition planning', *Architectural Review* vol 76 September 1934 pp 101-108

Jeffcott, I. 'Exhibition architect explains why planning pulls; Ideal Home exhibition', *Commercial Art* vol 18 June 1935 pp 236-238

Black, Misha. 'The designer and his problems. The exhibition architect', *Design for Today* October 1935 pp 399-402

Kallman, G. S. 'The wartime exhibition. Analysis of technique amd scope of exhibitions', *Architectural Review* vol 94 October 1943 pp 95-106

Pick, Beverley. 'Displaying the Ideal Home', *Art and industry* July 1948 pp 2-9

Black, Misha. 'Dissecting the problem 4. Exhibition design', *Art and Industry* September 1948 pp 82-87

Gardner, James. 'Exhibition display', *JRSA* vol 96 January 30 1948 pp 158-166

Belle, J. Cleveland. 'The first Design Centre. Exhibitions in Manchester keep the cotton industry informed of design developments in many centres and in a variety of industries', *Design* 9 September 1949 pp 7-11

Gray, Milner. 'Exhibitions: in or out', *Art and Industry* October 1952 pp 110-119 (criticism of current post-Festival trends)

Lohse, Richard P. *Neue Ausstellungsgestaltung. New design in exhibitions. 75 examples of the new form of exhibitions.* 1953 Erienbach, Zurich: Verlag für Architektur 260pp illus. (text in English, German and French)

Osborn, Elodie. *Manual of travelling exhibitions.* 1953 Paris: UNESCO 111pp

Gutmann, Robert and Koch, Alexander. *Exhibition stands (Ausstellungstade)* vol 1, vol 2. 1954, 1962 Stuttgart: A. Koch (titles and text in German, English, French)

'Interiors. The Design Centre, London SW1', *Architectural Review* vol 120 no 714 July 1956 pp 55-59

See also:

Council of Industrial Design *page 26*

Gardner, James and Heller, Caroline. *Exhibition and display.* 1960 London: Batsford 191pp illus.

Furniture design

World surveys of furniture tend to pass over work of the past hundred years very swiftly in favour of earlier periods. However some of these larger span works are useful in providing context:

Gloag, John. *A social history of furniture design from BC 1300 to AD 1960.* 1966 London: Cassell 202pp illus. bibl. (pp 171-192 The nineteenth century and after)

Aronson, Joseph. *The encyclopedia of furniture.* 1966 (third edition) London: Batsford 484pp illus. (earlier editions 1939, 1952)

Boger, Louise Ada. *The complete guide to furniture styles.* 1961 London: Allen and Unwin 438pp illus.

Reeves, David. *Furniture: an explanatory history.* 1959 London: Faber 199pp (reissued 1965. First edition 1957)

Gloag, John. *A short dictionary of furniture, containing 1707 terms used in Britain and America.* 1969 (revised edition) London: Allen and Unwin 814pp illus.

Singleton, Esther. *French and English furniture. Distinctive styles and periods.* 1904 London: Hodder and Stoughton 394pp pl 68

Binstead, Herbert E. *The furniture styles.* 1929 London: Pitman 193pp illus. (first edition 1904. Chapter 11 L'Art Nouveau, 12 British New Style, 13 Modern Style).

There are a number of wide-ranging discussions of style and design. Particularly appropriate to this period are:

Pritchard, J. C. 'The changing character of furniture', *JRSA* vol 100 February 22 1952 pp 237-255

Symonds, R. W. 'Principles of design in furniture', *Connoisseur* 94 September 1934 pp 167-173

'Furniture history issue', *Burlington Magazine* vol 111 no 800 November 1969

There are many more general surveys of English furniture:

Tomlin, Maurice. *English furniture: an illustrated handbook.* 1972 London: Faber 180pp 225 illus. bibl.

Gloag, John. *English furniture.* 1973 London: Black (first edition 1934)

Jones, Barbara. *English furniture at a glance.* 1971 London: Architectural Press 100pp 120 illus (first edition 1954)

Wills, Geoffrey. *English furniture 1760-1900.* 1971 Enfield: Guiness Superlatives 268pp illus.

Macdonald-Taylor, Margaret. *English furniture: from the Middle Ages to modern times.* 1965 London: Evans 290pp illus. bibl.

Bird, Anthony. *English furniture for the private collector.* 1961 London: Batsford 216pp illus.

Brackett, Oliver. *Furniture illustrated. A pictorial review of English furniture from Chaucer to Queen Victoria, revised by H. Clifford Smith.* 1950 London: Benn 300pp pl 240 (Chapter 5 Victorian Furniture)

Gloag, John. *British furniture makers.* 1945 London: Collins 48pp illus. ('brief essay in a great tradition')

Joy, Edward T. *The Country Life book of English furniture.* 1964 London: Country Life. 104pp illus.

Litchfield, Frederick. *Illustrated history of furniture from the earliest to the present time.* 1892 London: Truslove and Shirley 280pp (pp 229-250 1851 to the present. 7 editions to 1922)

A short history of English furniture. 1966 London: HMSO for Victoria and Albert Museum 32pp pl 100 (Large picture book no 20)

Traditional furnituremaking is a very popular subject for exhibitions and studies:

Roe, Frederick. *English cottage furniture.* 1961 (revised edition) London: Phoenix 240pp (first published 1949)

Filbee, Marjorie. *Dictionary of country furniture.* 1977 London: Connoisseur 200pp illus. bibl.

An exhibition of town and country furniture, illustrating the vernacular tradition. 1972 Leeds: Temple Newsam Museum 64pp illus. (includes material to 1920)

Twiston-Davies, L. and Lloyd-Jones, H. J. *Welsh furniture: an introduction.* 1950 Cardiff: University of Wales Press 53pp illus.

Apart from local studies the furniture industry has not been studied as a whole until comparatively recently. Useful introductions to the history of the whole industry are provided by:

Oliver, J. L. *The development and structure of the furniture industry.* 1966 Oxford: Pergamon. 187pp illus. bibl. footnotes

Julius, Leslie. 'The furniture industry', *JRSA* vol 115 May 1967 pp 430-447

One of the best short guides to the mechanical production of furniture in all materials is:

Logie, Gordon. *Furniture from machines.*
1948 London: Allen and Unwin 150pp
159 illus.

Studies of Particular Periods

There is no adequate history of the
complete period covered by this
bibliography. However there are brief
surveys in:

Joel, David. *Furniture design set free: the
British furniture revolution from 1851 to the
present day.* 1969 London: Dent 108pp
pl 128 (first published as *The Adventure of
British furniture* 1953)

'Furniture and furnishings 1880-1955'
Cabinet Maker July 1955 128pp illus.
(special issue to celebrate 75 years of the
journal with a number of essays)

Nineteenth Century

See also:

Important designers *page 75*

Helpful surveys of the century as a whole
are provided by:

Aslin, Elizabeth. *Nineteenth century English
furniture.* 1962 London: Faber 93pp illus.
bibl.

*Pictorial dictionary of British 19th century
furniture design, introduction by Edward Joy.*
1977 Woodbridge: Antique Collectors
Club 585pp illus bibl. (a very rich
anthology of reproduced furniture
designs from Sheraton 1802 to Norman
and Stacey 1910)

Jervis, Simon. *Victorian furniture.* 1968
London: Ward Lock 96pp pl 97

Symonds, Robert Wemyss and Whineray,
Bruce Blundell. *Victorian furniture.* 1962
London: Country Life 232pp illus.

Roe, Frederick Gordon. *Victorian furniture.*
1952 London: Phoenix house 160pp
illus.

Grant, Ian. 'The Machine Age: the
nineteenth century', in *The History of
Furniture.* 1976 London: Orbis

Handley-Read, Charles. 'England
1830-1901', in Hayward, Helena (ed).
World Furniture. 1965 Feltham: Hamlyn

Edwards, Ralph. 'Victorian furniture',
Connoisseur 152 1963 pp 103-105

Symonds, R. W. 'An assessment of Victorian
furniture', *Antique Collector* December
1957 pp 219-224

Victorian furniture. 1962 London: HMSO
for Victoria and Albert Museum 5pp
pl 27 (Small picture book no 59)

Andrews, John. *Price guide to Victorian
furniture.* 1973 Woodbridge: Antique
Collectors Club 350pp 341 illus.

Printed source materials, original pattern
books, studies and theories are numerous
but until recently only patchily recorded.
Some of the problems and documents are
set out in:

Cooper, Jeremy. 'Victorian furniture, an
introduction to the sources', *Apollo* vol
95 no 120 February 1972 pp 115-122

Cooper, Jeremy. 'A guide to Victorian
furniture from contemporary sources',
Antique Dealer and Collector's Guide August
1971 pp 76-79

BEFORE 1851

The period after 1851 was very greatly
influenced by earlier developments.
Convenient surveys of this earlier period
are provided by:

Joy, Edward. *English furniture 1800-1851.*
1977 London: Ward Lock/Sotheby
Parke Bernet Publications 320pp illus
(particularly useful on the evolution of
techniques and design)

Heal, Ambrose. *London furniture makers
from the Restoration to the Victorian era
1660-1840. A record of 2500 cabinetmakers,
upholsterers, carvers and gilders . . . With a
chapter on the problem of identification of
the furniture they produced.* 1953 London:
Batsford 276 (Dover reprint 1973)

Some very important designers:

Loudon, John Claudius. *Loudon furniture
designs from the Encyclopaedia of cottage,
farmhouse and villa architecture and
furniture 1839, with an introduction by
Christopher Gilbert.* 1970 East Ardsley: SR
135pp illus.

Gloag, John. *Mr Loudon's England. The life
and work of John Claudius Loudon, and his
influence on architecture and furniture
design.* 1970 London: Oriel Press
224pp illus.

Pugin, Augustus Welby Northmore. *Gothic
furniture in the style of the Fifteenth century
designed and etched by A. W. N. Pugin*
24 pl (many later editions. Republished
with other Pugin works by Gregg
International 1972)

1851-1914

Some chronological studies:

Floud, Peter. 'Furniture', pp 33-50 in
Edwards, Ralph and Ramsey, L. G. G.
(eds). *The Early Victorian period
1830-1860.* 1958 London: Connoisseur

Bird, Anthony. *Early Victorian furniture.*
1964 London: Hamish Hamilton 63pp
illus.

Pevsner, Nikolaus. 'Art furniture of the
Eighteen Seventies', *Architectural Review*
vol 111 no 661 January 1952 pp 43-50

Cooper, H. J. *The art of furniture on Rational and Aesthetic principles.* 1876 London: H. S. King 116pp (another edition 1879)

Agius, Pauline. *British furniture 1880-1915.* 1978 Woodbridge: Antique Collectors Club 200pp 200 illus.

Bennett, Ian. 'The rebirth of design: arts and crafts and Art Nouveau'. in *The History of Furniture.* 1976 London: Orbis

Hughes, Therle. 'Edwardian furniture: from the traditional to the avant-garde', *Antique Dealer and Collector's Guide* August 1975 pp 68-73

Gilbert, Christopher. 'A windfall of Edwardian furniture catalogues', *Antique Finder* vol 14 no 7 July 1975

Foley, Edwin. *The books of decorative furniture: its form, colour and history.* 1910-1911 London: T. C. and E. C. Jack 2 vols 1,000 text illus. 100 col pl. bibl.

Influences:

Joy, Edward. 'The influence of Victorian exhibitions on furniture', *Antique Finder* vol 15 no 4 April 1976

Wyatt, Mathew Digby. *Paris Universal Exhibition. Report on furniture and decoration.* 1856 London

Pollen, J. Hungerford. *Report on furniture and metalwork, London International Exhibition 1871* 1871 London

Joy, E. T. 'The overseas trade in the nineteenth century', *Furniture History* vol 6 1970

Jervis, Simon. 'Ruskin and furniture', *Furniture History* vol 9 1973 pp 97-

Eastlake, C. L. 'The fashion of furniture', *The Cornhill Magazine* vol 9 March 1864 pp 337-349

Pollen, John Hungerford. *Ancient and modern furniture and woodwork in the South Kensington Museum. Published for the Science and Art Department of the Committee of the Council of Education.* 1974 London: Chapman and Hall 415pp (later editions)

Particular styles:

Joy, E. T. 'Victorian revivals of eighteenth century furniture', *Antique Finder* October 1975 pp 12-15

Archer, Michael. 'PreRaphaelite painted furniture', *Country Life* April 1 1965 pp 720-722

Gothic:

Gloag, John. 'Nineteenth century Gothic furniture in England', *Antiques* vol 101 no 6 pp 1047-1051

Luff, R. W. T. 'An introduction to Gothic furniture', *Antique Collector* 32 1961 pp 233-238

Seymour, Sarah. 'Gothic revival furniture', *Antique Collector* August 1976 pp 10-14

Gibbs, John. *Designs for Gothic ornaments and furniture, after the ancient manner, for ecclesiastical and domestic purposes vol 1.* 1854 London: Bell 14pp pl 48

Statz, Vincenz and Ungewitter, Georg Gottlob. *The Gothic model-book. The architecture of the Middle Ages and its associated arts, translated by Monicke.* 1858 London: Trubner (very correct Gothic styles)

Gothic album for cabinet-makers; comprising a collection of designs for Gothic furniture. 1868 London: H. C. Baird 2pp pl 23

Spofford, Harriet Prescott. *Art decoration applied to furniture.* 1878 New York: Harper 237pp illus.

Talbert, Bruce J. *Examples of ancient and modern furniture, metalwork, tapestries, decoration.* 1876 London: Batsford (1971 Gregg Reprint)

Talbert, Bruce J. *Gothic forms applied to furniture, metalwork and decoration for decorative purposes.* 1868 London: S. Birkbeck (1971 Gregg Reprint)

See also:

Chronological studies *page 59*

Interior Design *page 147*
(particularly for C. L. Eastlake)

Some collections of designs:

English furniture designs 1800-1914: a bibliography of 120 pattern books and trade catalogues in the library of the Victoria and Albert Museum. Compiled by J. Bunston. 1971 London: Victoria and Albert Museum 28pp

The Cabinet Maker's Assistant. A series of original designs for modern furniture with descriptions and details of construction. Preceded by practical observations on the materials and manufacture of cabinet work and instructions in drawing adapted to trade. 1853 London: Blackie 417 designs (1970 Dover reprint with introduction by John Gloag)

Thomson, P. *The cabinet-maker's sketchbook. A series of original details for modern furniture.* c 1860 Glasgow: Mackenzie

Schwenke, Friedrich. *Designs for decorative furniture and modern chamber arrangement; including a practical guide to upholstery, illustrated by seventy two elaborate engravings, exhibiting the latest improvements in this branch of industrial art; accompanied by minute working plans.* 1882 London: H. Sotheran

Hasluck, Paul Nooncree (ed) *Cabinet work and joinery, comprising designs and details of construction with 2,021 working drawings and 12 coloured plates.* 1907 London: Cassell 568pp (later editions)

Bowers, R. S. and others. *Furniture making. Designs, working drawings and complete details of 170 pieces of furniture, with practical information on their construction.* 1915 London: Cassell 407pp illus.

There are many others, often closely associated with the more sumptuously produced trade catalogues.

INTERWAR PERIODS

See also:

Important designers *page 75*

Radio *page 261*

There is no effective single volume covering the history of this period. What follows is a selection of references drawn from the time or later that may help build up a picture of some of the developments.

1920s:

'On cottage furniture, with illustrations of examples designed by Percy A. Wells', *Studio Yearbook* 1919 pp 75-86

Wells, Percy A. *Furniture for small houses. A book of designs for inexpensive furniture with new methods of construction and decoration.* 1920 London: Batsford 35pp pl 57

Adams, Maurice S. R. *My book of furniture.* 1926 London: Adams 108pp

Rogers, John C. 'Modern craftsmanship: furniture', *Architectural Review* vol 59 1926 pp 176-181

Rogers, John C. 'English furniture 1 & 2 Cabinets with glazed doors, 3 Modern writing and book tables, 4 Tables for dining with fixed frames, 5 Chairs, 6 & 7 Sideboards, 8 Chests of drawers, 9 Standing cupboards and shelves, 10 Beds, 11 Bedroom furniture, *Architectural Review* vol 59 1926 pp 246-247, pp 297-299; vol 60 1926 pp 38-39, pp 82-84, pp 206-208, pp 254-257; vol 61 1927 pp 75-76, pp 161-163, pp 239-241; vol 62 1927 pp 121-123, pp 194-196, pp 246-249

Shapland, Henry Percival. *The practical decoration of furniture.* 1926-1927 London: Benn 3 vols

'Modern furniture and glass, *Studio* vol 93 1927 pp 319-321 (exhibition at Messrs James Powell & Sons)

Wainwright, Shirley B. 'Shoolbred's exhibition', *Studio* vol 95 1928 pp 318-325 ('The exhibition of modern furniture and decorative art')

Rogers, John C. 'Modern furniture at Shoolbred's. The enterprise of a furnishing trades organiser', *Architectural Review* vol 63 1928 pp 116-118

Maufe, Prudence. 'Modern painted and decorated furniture', *Architectural Review* vol 63 1928 pp 32-35

Stark, R. Gordon. 'New Furniture and new prices', *Architectural Review* vol 63 1928 pp 201-204

Wainwright, Shirley B. 'Modern furniture: the Waring Exhibition', *Studio* vol 97 1929 pp 131-135

1930s:

Arman, F. Marcus. 'The shape of austerity (furniture of the 30s)', *Art and Antiques Weekly* September 3 1977 pp 34-36

McGrath, Raymond. 'New Materials – new methods', *Architectural Review* vol 67 1930 pp 273-280

Rogers, John C. *Modern English furniture.* 1930 London: Country Life 208pp illus. (later edition 1935. Photographs of the work of 42 contemporary designers)

Moffat, Curtis. 'Furniture and hangings', *Decorative Art Studio Yearbook* 1931 pp 67-96

Rogers, John C. *Furniture and furnishing.* 1932 Oxford University Press 110pp illus. ('Little craft book')

Coates, Wells. 'Furniture today, furniture tomorrow', *Architecterual Review* vol 72 July 1932 pp 29-38

Wells, Percy A. *Design in woodwork.* 1934 London: Batsford 60pp

Dennison, Baird. 'From angles to body curves', *Architectural Review* vol 74 August 1933 pp 69-72

Shapland, H. P. 'Furniture design: fashions and essentials', *JRSA* vol 83 November 30 1934 pp 53-67

Jourdain, Margaret. 'Furniture at the Burlington House exhibition', *Apollo* February 1934 pp 90-94

Yakobson, L. N. 'Standard furniture', *Design for Today* September 1935 pp 336-342

Rena, Maurice. 'Design of furniture in Britain', *Studio* vol 113 1937 pp 266-275

Russell, Gordon. 'The trend of design in modern furniture', *Studio* vol 117 1939 pp 6-11

WARTIME AND UTILITY

See also:

Chronological Surveys: Utility *page 67*

The Board of Trade advisory committee on utility furniture and the recommended ranges of designs are probably the most noticed and reported facets of a whole wartime and postwar policy:

'Utility', (interviews with Sir Gordon Russell, O dwin Clinch, and Christopher Heal). *Design* 309 September 1974 pp 62-71

Neve, C. 'Virtue born of utility: new furniture in wartime', *Country Life* 156 September 26 1974 pp 828-829

'Utility furniture' (exhibition at the Building Centre reviewed) *Art and Industry* January 1943 pp 25-27

Russell, Gordon. 'Design review. National furniture production', *Architectural Review* vol 100 December 1946 pp 183-185

Publications of the committee and its schedules are prime historical sources:

Utility furniture. 1943 London: HMSO 16pp illus.

Utility furniture. Catalogue 1947 London: HMSO 48pp

Domestic furniture. Designs and specifications for licensed manufacturers. 1947 London: HMSO 20pp illus.

POSTWAR

One view:

Radford, Penny. 'Innovation: furniture to the present day', in *The History of Furniture*. 1976 London: Orbis

A very concise survey of the furniture industry and trade at the end of the war and under austerity is provided by:

Great Britain. Board of Trade. *Working party report on the furniture trade*. 1946 London: HMSO 209pp (includes a section on design)

Surveys, books of advice and conferences give some idea of postwar developments:

Russell, Gordon. *How to buy furniture*. 1947 London: HMSO for Council of Industrial Design 30pp (another edition 1951)

Hooper, John and Hooper, Rodney. *Modern furniture and fittings: a treatise dealing with the design and construction of modern furniture for houses and public buildings . . . with specialised sections*. 1948 London: Batsford 326pp pl 70 (further edition 1955)

'Modern furniture, its nature, its sources and its probable future', *Interiors* 108 July 1949 pp 76-117

Furniture design. Report of a conference held at the Royal Institute of British Architects, London W1 from Monday 18 July to Friday 22 July. 1949 London: Council of Industrial Design 195pp bibl.

British furniture 1950. A pre-view of the British Trades Exhibition. 1950 London: Cabinetmaker 208pp

Bradman, William Albert George. *Modern furniture projects*. 1950 London: Jenkins 182pp illus.

Russell, Richard D. 'Tuppence plain: penny coloured', in *The Anatomy of Design*. 1951 London: Royal College of Art

Dunnett, H. McG. 'Furniture since the war', *Architectural Review* vol 109 March 1951 pp 151-166

Pye, David W. 'Developments in the design and construction of furniture. Paper to a meeting of the RIBA Architectural Science Board December 1950', *JRIBA* vol 58 no 3 January 1951 pp 94-99 illus.

Goldfinger, Ernö. *British furniture today*. 1951 London: Tiranti 20pp pl 32

Dunnett, H. McG. 'Packaged furniture', *Architectural Review* vol 111 April 1952 pp 241-250 (traces developments since introduction of the Trivia range in 1947)

Ward, Neville and Austin, Frank. 'Design review. UK Furniture 1953', *Architectural Review* vol 114 no 684 December 1953 pp 405-406

Russell, Sir Gordon. *Furniture (Things we see)*. 1953 London: Penguin 64pp illus. (previous edition 1949)

Ward, Neville and Austin, Frank. 'Design review. UK Furniture 1954-1955', *Architectural Review* vol 117 no 699 March 1955 pp 205-209

Hatje, Gerd (ed). *Neue möbel, new furniture*. 1954-. 1954 Stuttgart: Hatje

Dal Fabbro, Mario. *Furniture for modern interiors: a progressive architecture book*. 1954 New York: Reinhold 206pp illus.

'A new approach to furniture design. Symposium. 1. Research in the furniture industry by M. J. Merrick, 2. Application of research to furniture construction by T. Kotas, 3. Effect of the research on the character of cabinets by Robin Day', *JRSA* vol 104 March 30 1956 pp 368-386

Dal Fabbro, Mario. *Modern furniture: its design and construction*. 1958 (revised edition) New York: Reinhold 210pp (first edition 1950)

Heppenstall, Brian Weston. *Contemporary furniture designs*. 1960 London: Murray 80pp

Crowther, John. 'Surveys of industry 8. Furniture', *Design* 159 March 1962 pp 49-61

Young, Dennis and Young, Barbara. *Furniture in Britain today*. 1964 London: Tiranti 310 illus.

Russell, Sir Gordon. *Looking at furniture*. 1964 (revised edition) London: Lund Humphries 64pp illus.

Moody, Ella. *Modern furniture.* 1966 London: Studio Vista 160pp illus. bibl.

Simpson, Thomas. *Fantasy furniture: design and decoration.* 1968 New York: Reinhold 96pp illus.

Duckett, Margaret. 'New furniture: the domestic market . . . the competition', *Design* no 242 February 1969 pp 44-59

About buying furniture. 1970 London: Consumer Council 24pp illus.

European developments

France

The importance of French interior design, particularly between the wars, has already been noted. Unfortunately there is no space for much on French furniture design here, but happily there is a very good bibliography to help:

Viaux, Jacqueline. *Bibliographie du meuble. Mobilier civil français.* 1966 Paris: Société des Amis de la Bibliothèque Forney 587pp

and the following may help to introduce the interwar period:

Benton, Charlotte. 'Furniture as an architectural element in the avant-garde interior', Part Five pp 69-73 of Benton, Tim and others. *Design 1920s.* 1975 Milton Keynes: Open University Press

Dufrène, Maurice. *Meubles du temps présent.* 1930 Paris: Moreau pl 40

Germany

Two general introductions amongst many:

Kreisel, Heinrich. *Die Kunst des Deutschen Möbels. Dritter Band: Klassizismus/Historismus/Jugendstil, von Georg Himmelheber.* 1973 Munich: Verlag C. H. Beck 417pp (enormous bibliography pp 288-324)

Schneck, Adolf G. *Neue Möbel vom Jugendstil bis heute.* 1962 Munich: Bruckmann 159pp

THONET

This company and its bentwood techniques have had an enormous impact on European furniture design:

Portoghesi, P. and Massobrio, G. *La seggiola di Vienna. Thonet and the history of bentwood techniques.* 1975 Turin: Martano 324pp illus. (text in English and Italian)

Bentwood furniture: the work of Michael Thonet. Exhibition catalogue by K. Mang. 1968 London: Victoria and Albert Museum-Bethnall Green Museum 12pp

'Thonet furniture', *Architectural Review* vol 146 no 860 October 1968 pp 281-286

Bugholzmöbel: das Werk Michael Thonet. 1965 Vienna: Osterreichisches Bauzentrum (exhibition catalogue)

Form from process – the Thonet chair. Historic bentwood furniture from the collection of John Sailer, Vienna. (Catalogue by Hans Buchwald). 1967 Cambridge: Harvard University Carpenter Center for the Visual Arts

Russell, Gordon. 'Design policy for new techniques', *Design* 60 December 1933 pp 7-10

'Bent-construction furniture', *Architectural Review* vol 74 August 1933 pp 69-72, pp 77-78

Scandinavian

Hard af Segerstad, Ulf. *Modern Scandinavian furniture, translated by Nancy and Edward Maze.* 1963 London: Studio 131pp

Christiansen, Gertrud Købke. 'The Danish tradition in furniture making', *Connoisseur* vol 149 February 1962 pp 104-107

Malmsten, Carl. *Swedish furniture. Schwedische Möbel.* 1954 Basel: Wepf 139pp illus.

Individual Designers and Manufacturers

See also:

Important designers *page 75*

Some of the very famous are included in:

Honour, Hugh. *Cabinet makers and furniture designers.* 1969 London: Weidenfeld and Nicholson 320pp illus. (later edition 1972 Spring Books)

BAILLIE SCOTT

Furniture made at the Pyghtle works, Bedford by John P. White. Designed by M. H. Baillie Scott. 1901 Bedford 39pp illus. (82 items)

Baillie Scott, M. H. 'Some furniture for the New Palace, Darmstadt', *Studio* vol 14 1898 pp 91-97 illus.

BARNSLEYS

Burrough, B. G. 'Edward Barnsley', *Connoisseur* vol 184 no 742 December 1973 pp 250-255

Good citizen's furniture: the work of Ernest and Sidney Barnsley: catalogue of an exhibition . . . 5 November 1976-15 January 1977. 1977 Cheltenham Art Gallery and Museum 49pp

Edwards, Tudor. 'Genesis of the Cotswold movement. The Barnsley brothers and Ernest Gimson', *Country Life* 160 December 9 1976 pp 1770

BRANGWYN

Seddon, Jill. 'Furniture designed by Frank Brangwyn', *Furniture History* vol 10 1973 pp 100-101

BURGES

The designs of William Burges, edited by R. P. Pullan. 1886 London: Batsford 9pp pl 23

Handley-Read, Charles. 'Notes on William Burges's painted furniture', *Burlington Magazine* 1963 pp 496-509

DAY

Day, Robin. 'Designing for Hille', *DIA Yearbook* 1964-1965 pp 88-91

ERCOL

Ercolani, L. R. *A furniture maker: his life, his work and his observations: an autobiography.* 1975 London: Benn 182pp illus.

GILLOW

Burkett, Mary E. Tyson, Edith and How, Davidson. *The furniture of Gillow of Lancaster.* 1970 Lancaster Museum 8pp

GIMSON

'Ernest Gimson, artist in furniture design', *Architectural Review* October 1919 pp 100

GODWIN

Furniture by Godwin and Breuer. 1976 Bristol City Art Gallery

Aslin, Elizabeth. *The furniture designs of E. W. Godwin.* 1967 London: Victoria and Albert Museum Bulletin reprint 13

Watt, William. *Art furniture from designs by E. W. Godwin and others, with hints and suggestions on domestic furniture and decoration by William Watt.* 1877 London: Batsford 8pp pl 24 (ABC Reprint. Illustrated catalogue of William Watt's Art Furniture Warehouse)

HEAL

A booklet to commemorate the centenary exhibition of the life of Sir Ambrose Heal (Foreword by John Gloag). 1972 London: Heal and Son 24pp illus.

Boumphrey, Geoffrey. 'The designers 1. Sir Ambrose Heal', *Architectural Review* vol 78 August 1935 pp 39-40

The firm Heal's played an important role in many aspects of furniture design:

Benton, Tim. 'History of taste 6. Up and down at Heal's: 1929-1935', *Architectural Review* no 972 February 1978 pp 109-116

The catalogues are an invaluable source of information. A selection has been reprinted in:

Heal's catalogues 1853-1934. 1972 Newton Abbot: David and Charles

Particularly important catalogues are:

Heal's Plain Oak Furniture 1898

Dining room and living furniture 1935. 52pp illus. (171st catalogue)

White, Gleeson. *A note on simplicity of design in furniture for bedrooms with special reference to some recently produced by Messrs Heal and Son.* 1898 London: Heal 32pp

HOLLAND

Jervis, Simon. 'Holland and Sons, and the furnishing of the Atheneum', *Furniture History* vol 6 1970 pp 43-61

HOPKINSON

Hopkinson, James. *Victorian cabinetmaker: the memoirs of James Hopkinson 1819-1894, edited by Jocelyne Baty Goodman.* 1968 London: Routledge and Kegan Paul 138pp

ISOKON

Isokon. Exhibition catalogue by Alastair Grieve. 1975 Norwich: University of East Anglia

KEITH

Reilly, Paul. 'Twenty years contribution to modern furniture', *Design* 70 October 1954 pp 14-17 (Howard Keith and armchairs 1935-)

MACKINTOSH

Alison, Filippo. *Charles Rennie Mackintosh as a designer of chairs.* 1973 London: Warehouse Publications 108pp 156 illus.

Some examples of furniture by Charles Rennie Mackintosh in the Glasgow School of Art collection; selected and described by Jefferson Barnes. 1969 Glasgow School of Art 70pp illus.

Howarth, Thomas. 'Some Mackintosh furniture preserved', *Architectural Review* vol 100 August 1946 pp 32-34 (78 Southpark Avenue, Hillhead)

MARSH AND JONES

Boynton, L. O. J. 'High Victorian furniture: the example of Marsh and Jones of Leeds', *Furniture History* vol 3 1967 pp 54-92

MORRIS

Cromey-Hawke, N. 'William Morris and Victorian painted furniture', *Connoisseur* vol 191 no 767 January 1976 pp 32-43

Kaufman, Edgar. 'Furniture (Morris chair)', *Architectural Review* vol 108 August 1950 pp 127-129

The various catalogues of Morris and Company (eg. Dining Room Furniture, Drawing Room Furniture) are very useful.

PRATTS

*Victorian and Edwardian furniture by Pratts of Bradford. Catalogue by Christopher Gilbert.*1970 Bradford City Art Gallery and Museums 25pp pl 6

Joy, E. T. 'Victorian and Edwardian furniture by Pratts of Bradford', *Connoisseur* vol 180 no 725 July 1972 pp 198-200

RACE

Naylor, Gillian. 'Ernest Race', *Design* 184 April 1964 pp 54-55

Race furniture. 1951 London: Ernest Race 22 leaves illus.

'Design review. Trends in factory made furniture by Ernest Race', *Architectural Review* vol 103 May 1948 pp 218-220

Skjalm, H. 'Ernest Race', *Dansk Kunsthandverk* (Copenhagen) 6 1965 pp 198-199

RUSSELL

'Furniture by Russell and Sons', *Studio* vol 93 1927 pp 319

Furniture designed by Gordon Russell and made by the Russell Workshops Ltd. 1928 London: Arlington Gallery

Gloag, John. 'Gordon Russell and Cotswold craftsmanship', *Architects Journal* August 15 1928 pp 219-226

SEDDON

Heal, Sir Ambrose. 'The firm of Seddon, cabinet makers 1756-1868, *Country Life* 1934 pp 72-73

VINCENT

Tucker, M. T. *Vincent and Son Ltd cabinet makers, Brick Lane, London: a short history of the firm's history, work and equipment.* 1977 London: Greater London Industrial Archaeology Society 8pp illus.

WAALS

Alexander, Russell. *The furniture and joinery of Peter Waals. A series of plates.* 1930 Chipping Campden: Alcuin Press 7pp

WOOD AND SELLERS

Partnership in style: Edgar Wood and J. Henry Sellers. 1975 Manchester City Art Gallery 96pp

Seddon, Jill. 'The furniture designs of Edgar Wood (1860-1935)', *Burlington Magazine* December 1975 pp 859-867

Furniture of particular areas

Joy, Edward.'The Royal Victorian furniture makers, 1837-1887', *Burlington Magazine* vol 111 no 800 November 1969 pp 677-686

Furniture made in Yorkshire 1750-1900. Catalogue by Christopher Hutchinson. 1974 Leeds: Temple Newsam Museum 36pp bibl.

Hutchinson, Christopher. 'Victorian furniture-makers of Leeds', *Country Life* vol 141 no 3900 pp 550-551

*Furniture from Broughton Hall made by provincial firms 1788-1909.*1971 Leeds: Temple Newsam Museum 11p

Weaver, Sir Lawrence. 'High Wycombe furniture', 1929 London: Fanfare Press 84pp illus. (History to 1920s)

Weaver, Sir Lawrence. 'Tradition and modernity in craftsmanship. IV Furniture at High Wycombe', *Architectural Review* vol 65 1929 pp 45-47

Types of Furniture

For children

Children's furniture 1600-1900. 1977 Burnley: Towneley Hall 40pp illus. bibl.

Beds

Wright, Lawrence. *Warm and snug: the history of the bed.* 1962 London: Routledge 368pp illus.

Reynolds, Reginald. *Beds: with many noteworthy instances of lying in, under or about them.*1952 London: Deutsch 239pp

Koch, Alexander. *Bett und Couch.* 1937 Stuttgart: Koch (mainly illustrations. German examples)

Myers first century 1876-1976. 1976 London: Horatio Myer & Co Ltd 52pp illus.

Luff, R. W. P. 'Three centuries of cradles', *Country Life* December 21 1961 pp 1576-1577

Chairs

Frey, Gilbert. *The modern chair.* 1970 London: Tiranti 187pp illus. bibl. (English/German/French text)

Agius, Pauline. *101 chairs and stools collected, with the assistance of the Furniture History Society . . . to show the historical evolution of chair design in Great Britain* (Exhibition catalogue). 1968 Oxford: Divinity School 56pp illus.

Gloag, John. *The Englishman's chair: origins, designs and social history of seat furniture in England.* 1964 London: Allen and Unwin 485pp

Boumphrey, G. M. 'Nationality in easy chairs', *Design for Today* May 1933 pp 25-28

English chairs. 1970 (third edition) London: HMSO for Victoria and Albert Museum 129 illus. (Large picturebook no 10)

A history of the English chair by Ralph Edwards, revised by Desmond Fitzgerald. 1970 London: HMSO 28pp 127 illus (issued by the Victoria and Albert Museum)

Traditional chairs and variants:

Roe, Frederick Gordon. *Windsor chairs.* 1953 London: Phoenix 96pp pl 33

Sparkes, Ivan G. *The English country chair: an illustrated history of chairs and chairmaking.* 1973 Bourne End: Spurbooks 160pp illus.

Sparkes, Ivan G. *The Windsor chair: an illustrated history of a classic English chair.* 1975 Bourne End: Spurbooks 143pp

Gloag, John. 'Smoker out of Windsor', *Connoisseur* 190 1975 pp 166-169

Gloag, John, 'The nomenclature of mid-Victorian chairs', *Connoisseur* vol 168 no 678 August 1968 pp 233-236

Twentieth century:

Modern chairs 1918-1970; an international exhibition. 1970 London: Whitechapel Art Gallery 26pp + 120pp designs (Published by Lund Humphries. Includes essays by Reyner Banham, Sherban Cantacuzino, Dennis Young and Joseph Rykwert)

Meadmore, Clement. *The modern chair: classics in production.* 1974 London: Studio Vista 190pp illus.

Hogben, Carol. 'Sitting pretty/50 years of chair design', *Observer Colour Supplement* 19 July 1970 pp 24-31

Darty, Peter. *Chairs, a guide to choosing, buying and collecting.* 1972 London: Barrie and Jenkins 118pp illus. bibl.

Wilson, Richard. 'Chair design in the 20th century', pp 42-55 in *Design 1900-1960. Studies in Design and Popular Culture of the 20th Century, edited by T. Faulkner.* 1976 Newcastle Polytechnic

Pevsner, Nikolaus. 'The evolution of the easy chair', *Architectural Review* vol 91 March 1942 pp 59-62

Mayes, L. J. *The history of chairmaking in High Wycombe.* 1960 London: Routledge 174pp illus.

Cabinets

Cooper, Jeremy. 'Some eminent Victorian cabinet makers', *Antique Dealer and Collector's Guide* September 1972 pp 69-73

Hooper, John and Wells, Percy. *Modern cabinetwork and fitments.* 1952 (sixth revised edition) London: Batsford (earlier editions 1909, 1918, 1922, 1925, 1928, 1938) 378pp illus.

Bonnett, Denise (ed). *Contemporary cabinet design and construction.* 1956 London: Batsford 238pp illus.

Built-in furniture

Gibberd, Frederick. *Built-in furniture in Great Britain.* 1948 London: Tiranti 43pp illus.

Brown, William Albert George. *Built-in furniture.* 1953 London: Muller 84pp

Thomas, Mark Hartland. 'Unit furniture built-in furniture and modular coordination', *Design* 68 August 1954 pp 28-35

'Decoration as storage', *Architectural Review* vol 87, vol 88, 1940 pp 219-224, pp 31-34, pp 61-64, pp 93-96, pp 126-128, pp 155-158, pp 187-190

'Design review. Household storage', *Architectural Review* vol 121 no721 pp 137-140

Stanley book of designs for home storage, written and edited by Eric Winter. 1970 London: Spectator 92pp

Furniture in materials other than wood

Metal

Aslin, Elizabeth. 'The iron age of furniture', *Country Life* 134 October 17 1963 pp 936-937 (nineteenth century)

Groneman, Chris Harold. *Bent tubular furniture.* 1949 Milwaukee: Bruce Publishing Co 128pp illus.

Sharp, Dennis, Benton, Tim and Cole, Barbie Campbell. *Pel and tubular steel furniture of the thirties.* 1977 London: Architectural Association 64pp illus.

'Pel and tubular steel furniture of the thirties', *Architectural Association Quarterly* vol 8 no 3 1976 pp 3-32 (series of short articles)

Archer, L. Bruce. 'Steel furniture for new markets', *Design* 85 January 1956 pp 35-38

Pfannschmidt, Ernest Erik. *Metallmöbel. Metal furniture.* 1962 Stuttgart: Hoffmann 160pp 406 photos (mostly contemporary but some historical material)

Perriand, Charlotte. 'Wood or metal?' *Studio* vol 97 1929 pp 278-279

Plastics

Buttrey, D. N. (ed). *Plastics in the furniture industry.* 1964 London: Macdonald 183pp illus. (later edition 1976 Applied Science)

Carr, Richard. 'Design analysis. Polypropylene chair', *Design* 194 February 1965 pp 32-37 (Day's chair for Hille)

Young, Dennis. 'New forms for seating. Material and processes', *Design* 118 October 1958 pp 28-33 (includes glass fibre, moulded plastic)

Manser, José. 'Freeform furniture', (Plastic furniture in Britain and Europe). *Design* 240 December 1968 pp 28-33

Rubber and upholstery

'The use of rubber in furniture', *Bulletin of the Rubber Growers Association* September 1937 (available as offprint 23pp)

Young, Dennis. *Sitting in comfort.* 1952 London: British Rubber Development Board

Latex foam in furniture. Report of the Conference held in London May 27 1954. 1954 London: British Rubber Development Board 47pp

Young, Dennis. *Upholstering with latex foam.* 1957 (revised edition) London: National Rubber Development Board (first edition 1952)

Johnston, Dan. 'Upholstery: a survey', *Design* 127 July 1959 pp 32-41

Plywood

Pevsner, Nikolaus. 'The early years history of plywood', *Architectural Review* vol 86 1939 pp 129-130 (to 1914)

Pevsner, Nikolaus. 'The first plywood furniture', *Architectural Review* vol 84 1938 pp 75-76

Wainwright, Shirley B. *Modern plywood.* 1927 London: Benn 66pp pl 32 (includes use in furniture)

Weaver, Sir Lawrence. 'Tradition and modernity in craftsmanship VI A study in laminated board', *Architectural Review* vol 66 1929 pp 253-254

Weaver, Sir Lawrence. *Laminated board and its uses . . . A study of modern furniture and decoration. Edited by Christopher Hussey.* 1930 London: Fanfare Press 82pp

'Plywood. A review by Bryan Westwood', *Architectural Review* vol 86 1939 pp 133-142

Wood, Andrew D. and Linn, T. G. *Plywoods of the world, their development manufacture and application.* 1963 Edinburgh: Johnston and Bacon 489pp illus.

Design Factors

Patents for inventions:

Patents for inventions. Abridgments of specifications relating to furniture and upholstery AD 1620-1866. 1869 London: Eyre and Spottiswode 575pp

Abridgments to specifications relating to furniture class 52. Furniture and upholstery 1855-1908. London: Patent Office 9 vols

Patents for inventions. Abridgments of specifications Class 52 i-v Furniture and upholstery 1909-1915, 1916-1920, 1921-1925, 1926-1930 HMSO

Furniture was an early subject for ergonomic studies:

Akerblom, Bengt. *Standing and sitting posture.* 1948 Stockholm: A. B. Nordiska Bokhandeln

Akerblom, Bengt. *The principles of restful sitting and their significance in the construction of comfortable seats.* Paper to the Ergonomics Research Society, Birmingham April 1951

O'Donovan, Brigid. 'Sitting in comfort', *Design* 67 July 1954 pp 17-21

Furniture Development Council. Research and Information Committee. *A design manual for cabinet furniture: basic scientific principles concerning its construction.* 1958 Oxford: Pergamon 49pp

Darcus, Merrick and Barkla. *Anthropometric data for chair designers.* 1960 London: Furniture Development Council

Measurements for comfortable sitting. A short guide for chair designers. 1960 London: Furniture Development Council 8pp

Berglund, Erik. *Skåp redovisning av praktiska krav på bostadens forvaringsmöbler (cupboards – a practical study of space requirements for storage furniture).* 1960 Stockholm: Svenska Slojdsforeningen 140pp illus. bibl.

O'Donovan, Brigid. 'Seating dimensions: theory and practice', *Design* 145 January 1961 pp 31-33 (comparison of British Standards and Furniture Development data)

Rykwert, Joseph. 'The sitting posture', *Arena* June 1967

Grandjean, E. (ed). *Proceedings of the symposium on sitting posture.* 1969 London: Taylor and Francis 253pp

Tools and Machines

See also:

Tools *page 250*

Salaman, R. A. *Dictionary of tools used in the woodworking and allied trades c 1700-1970.* 1975 London: Allen and Unwin 545pp illus. bibl.

Blackburn, Graham. *The illustrated encyclopedia of woodworking handtools, instruments and devices.* 1974 London: John Murray 232pp

Goodman, W. L. *British plane makers from 1700.* 1968 London: Bell 136pp (Chapter 4 'The plane-making industry 1800-1960')

Goodman, W. L. *The history of woodworking tools.* 1964 London: Bell 208pp

Goodman, W. L. *Woodwork.* 1962 Oxford: Blackwell 72pp 38 illus. (supplement to his history)

Sellens, Alvin. *The Stanley Plane: a history and descriptive inventory.* 1975 South Burlington, Vermont: Early American Industries Association 216pp illus. bibl. (traces history from its introduction in 1869)

A brief history of the woodworker's plane. 1961 Sheffield: Stanley 12pp

Jones, P. d'A. and Simons, E. N. *Story of the saw. Spear and Jackson Limited 1760-1960. Published to mark the second centenary of the world's oldest sawmakers.* 1960 80pp illus.

Richards, John. *On the arrangement, care and operation of woodworking factories and machinery: forming a complete operator's handbook.* 1885 (revised edition) London: Spon 150pp (first edition 1873)

Richards, John. *A treatise on the construction and operation of woodworking machines: including a history of the origina and progress of the manufacture of wood-working machinery . . . showing the modern practice of prominent engineers in England, France and America.* 1872 London: Spon 283pp engravings (University Microfilms)

Periodicals

The main historical journal is:

Furniture History: the journal of the Furniture History Society vol 1 1965 (annual)

A lot of useful historical material may be found in the issues of:

Cabinet Maker and Retail Furnisher 1880- (weekly) London: Benn

Furniture Record (which absorbed *Furniture Gazette* 1872-1893, *Furniture and Decoration* 1890-1899 and is now part of *Cabinet Maker*)

Furniture Forum 1951- New York: Reinhold

Furniture Manufacturer: the international journal for the manufacturer 1935- (monthly) Oxted (formerly called *Furniture and Bedding Production*)

Mobilia 1955- (8 per year) Snekkersten, Denmark

Mobilier et Décoration. Revue mensuelle des arts décoratifs appliqués et de l'architecture moderne 1920-

Woodworker 1901- (monthly)

For more technical information:

FIRA Bulletin 1962- (quarterly) Stevenage: Furniture Industry Research Association

Bibliographies

The most useful listing for the design historian is the annual bibliography published in *Furniture History.*

Other useful listings are:

Furniture Index 1970- (quarterly) North Carolina State University

Furniture Literature, compiled by Patricia Bristow. 1975 + Supplements Stevenage: Furniture Industry Research Association (earlier edition 1968. Excludes trade literature but includes very wide span of more technical material and some historical works incidentally)

Furniture and allied trades. Catalogue of the books in the special collection of Shoreditch Public Libraries. 1950 Shoreditch Public Library 53pp

Symonds, Robert Wemyss. *Readers guide: English furniture.* 1951 London: Cambridge University Press for National Book League 19pp

List of books in the National Art Library illustrating furniture. 1885 (second edition) London: South Kensington Museum 64pp

Sparkes, Ivan. 'A checklist of books and articles on rural chairs, the windsor chair and chairmaking', *Furniture History* vol 12 1976

and for further addresses of all kinds:

Information sources in the furniture and joinery industry. 1977 Vienna: United Nations Industrial Development Organisation (Guides to information sources no 4)

Designing in particular materials

Some materials produce very special types of design problems, so distinctive and often very full literatures have grown up to serve these fields of design.

Reasons of space have made it necessary to exclude architecture from this bibliography, so it is not possible to include much on the properties of structural materials. However, useful general introductions to this area are provided by:

Gordon, J. E. *The new science of strong materials: or why you don't fall through the floor.* 1968 Harmondsworth: Penguin 272pp

Timoshenko, Stephen P. *History of the strength of materials with a brief account of theory of elasticity and theory of structures.* 1953 New York: McGraw Hill 452pp illus.

Textiles

See also:

Costume and Fashion *page 238*

Interior Design *page 147*

In view of the diversity of textile design, this section is divided into five main parts:

1 General surveys, collections and discussions

2 Fabrics made from particular fibres –cotton, linen, silk, velvet, wool, artificial fibres

3 Textiles made by particular processes or techniques –printed, dyed, woven, felts, rope, needlework, tapestry, knitting, hosiery, lace

4 Particular applications –furnishing, dress

5 Carpets

General Surveys

The designer has long been regarded as a vital part of the textile manufacturing process –so much so that even historical designs and patterns are often fiercely guarded and can only be studied with difficulty. Consequently a detailed study will often start with a collection accessible to the general public. These are helpfully detailed in:

Lubell, Cecil (ed). *Textile collections of the world.* 1977 London: Studio Vista *vol 1; United States and Canada* 320pp 400 illus. *vol 2; United Kingdom and Ireland* 224pp 505 illus.

The second volume is particularly valuable for the concise essay:

Rothstein, Nathalie. 'A history of British textile design' pp 53-64

Developments can be traced more closely through some of the large general encyclopaedias of textiles:

American Fabrics Magazine. *Encyclopedia of textiles.* 1972 (second edition) Englewood Cliffs: Prentice Hall 636pp illus. (first published 1960)

or the smaller:

Flemming, Ernst. *Encyclopedia of textiles, completely revised with an introduction by Renate Jacques.* 1958 London: Zwemmer 288pp. pl 16 (first edition 1928 but only covering history to early nineteenth century)

Weibel, Adele Conlon. *2000 years of textiles.* 1975 New York: Hacker Art Books 169pp illus. (first published 1952 Pantheon, New York)

As textile design is very closely related to the problems posed by different fabrics, a study of the different editions of some of the standard general technical works could be a useful introduction:

Wingate, Isabel B. *Textile fabrics and their selection.* 1976 (seventh edition) Englewood Cliffs: Prentice Hall 620pp (first published 1935)

Hall, A. John. *Standard handbook of textiles.* 1975 (eighth edition) London: Iliffe 450pp 139 illus. (first published 1946)

Matthews, Joseph Merritt. *Matthews Fibers edited by H. R. Mauersberger.* 1954 (sixth edition) London: John Wiley 1283pp illus. bibl. (first published 1904)

or the earlier vast:

Miles, L. J. (ed). *The textile educator. A comprehensive, practical and authoritative guide for all engaged in the textile industries.* 1927 London: Pitman 3 vols illus.

Murphy, William S. *The textile industries. A practical guide to fibres, yarns and fabrics in every branch of textile manufacture.* 1910 London: Gresham Publishing Company 8 vols illus.

For help with the terminology the most useful guides are:

Farnfield, Carolyn A. and Alvey, P. J. (eds). *Textile Terms and Definitions.* 1975 (seventh edition) Manchester: The Textile Institute 228pp illus. (first edition 1954)

A very wide range of concise surveys of more particular areas of textile design and manufacture are contained in:

CIBA Review 1937-1970, *CIBA-Geigy Review* 1971-1975/1

As the textile industry is so varied it is helpful to have some idea of its industrial base:

Briscoe, Lyndon. *The textile and clothing industries of the United Kingdom.* 1971 Manchester University Press 211pp

Walton, Perry. *The story of textiles: a birds-eye view of the history of the beginning and growth of the industry by which mankind is clothed.* 1936 London: Tudor Press 274pp

Then there are many valuable regional studies:

Miles, Caroline. *Lancashire textiles: a case study of industrial change.* 1968 Cambridge University Press 124pp (National Institute of Economic and Social Research Occasional Papers 23)

Ponting, Kenneth G. *A history of the West of England cloth industry.* 1957 London: Macdonald 168pp

or of distinctive local industries, such as the West Riding shoddy and mungo trade:

Burrows, Hermann. *A history of the rag trade.* 1956 London: MacLaren and Sons 93pp

Historical Surveys

A compact visual introduction to the period covered by this bibliography is provided by:

A century of British fabrics 1850-1950. Carpets by J. H. Mellor. Printed and woven fabrics by Frank Lewis. Wallpapers by E. A. Entwisle. 1955 Leigh on Sea: F. Lewis 33pp pl 32

Although a new comprehensive work is promised:

Geijer, Agnes. *The history of textile art.* (to be published with the support of the Pasold Institute)

Many of the general surveys of historical textile design are rather old and reflect the interests of their time:

Townsend, W. G. Paulson. *Modern decorative art in England; its development and characteristics.* 1922 London: Batsford *vol 1: Woven and printed fabrics, wallpapers, lace and embroidery* (the only volume ever published in this series)

Glazier, Richard. *Historic textile fabrics. A short history of the tradition and development of pattern in woven and printed stuffs.* 1923 London: Batsford 119pp colour pl bibl.

Thurstan, Violetta. *A short history of decorative textiles and tapestries.* 1934 London: Pepler and Sewell 112pp

Schulze, Paul. 'History and development of pattern designing in textiles', *JSA* vol 41 April 21 1893 pp 533-564

Institutional histories and exhibitions can also be useful sources of general information:

The Clothworkers Company, past and present. An exhibition held during the Leeds Triennial Music Festival. 1970 Leeds: Temple Newsam House

Girtin, Tom. *Triple Crowns: a narrative history of the Draper's Company, 1364-1964.* 1964 London: Hutchinson 400pp

Turner, A. J. 'The early history of the Textile Institute', *Journal of the Textile Institute* vol 55 July 1965 pp 59-72 (covers the period to about the end of World War One)

Then there is no shortage of books and articles surveying textile design at particular points of time. Some useful ones are:

Morris, Barbara. 'Textiles', pp 113-128 in Edwards, Ralph and Ramsey, L. G. G. (eds). *The Early Victorian Period 1830-1860.* 1958 London: Connoisseur 180pp

Hoffmann, Julius. *Der Moderne Stil. Eine internationale Rundschau über die besten Leistungen der auf gewerblichen Gebiete tätigen Künstler unserer Zeit, mit besonderer Berücksichtigung des Auslandes.* 1899 Stuttgart: Hoffmann pl 120 (includes a range of English material)

Hunter, George Leland. *Decorative textiles.* 1918 London: J. B. Lippincott 457pp 580 illus. bibl.

Ionides, Basil. 'Textiles', *Architectural Review* vol 59 1926 pp 182-187

Dane, M. 'English textiles of modern design', *Studio* vol 98 1929 pp 489-494

Migeon, Gaston. *Les arts du tissu.* 1929 Paris: H. Laurens 468pp illus. (important bibliographies at the ends of chapters)

'Craftsman's portfolio XLVIII Accessories to decoration', *Architectural Review* vol 67 1930 pp 287-300

Bonney, Louise. 'Modern fabrics. Leading designs and materials at the International Exhibition of the American Federation of Arts', *Studio* vol 101 1931 pp 256-261

'New design in British fabrics', *Studio* vol 104 1932 pp 172-173

'Select fabrics. The work of seven leading British manufacturers', *Studio* vol 103 1932 pp 354-358

Jackson, Holbrook. 'Modern textile design', *Design for Today* July 1933 pp 98-102

Conran, L. 'Recent textile design; with craftsman's portfolio', *Architectural Review* vol 76 November 1934 pp 177-184

'A choice of fabrics', *Studio* 110 1935 pp 154-162

Rena, Maurice. 'How textiles are made', *Studio* 113 1937 pp 88-102 (47 illus.)

Iles, J. B. 'The beauty of modern fabrics. A review of recent design', *Studio* 116 1938 pp 182-188

Marshall, Herbert George Hayes. *British textile designers today, with introduction and chapters on the designer and design, notes on colour, definitions and descriptions, methods of manufacture, yarns.* 1939 Leigh on Sea: F. Lewis 326pp illus.

'Design in fabrics', *Studio* 118 1939 pp 164-167

Simpson, R. D. *Scottish Enterprise. Textiles.* 1947 Glasgow: Council of Industrial Design Scottish Committee 16pp

Constantine, Mildred. *Beyond craft – the art fabric.* 1973 New York: Van Nostrand Reinhold 304pp 330 illus. (survey of textiles c. 1930-1972)

Fraser, Grace Lovat. *Textiles by Britain.* 1948 London: Allen and Unwin 181pp pl 48

Whiston, P. 'Design and colour in textiles', *Textile Institute Journal* 39 June 1948 pp 193-199

Lewis, Frank. *British textiles.* 1951 Leigh on Sea: F. Lewis 21pp pl 91 (part of 'A survey of world textiles' series)

Koch, Alexander. *Dekorationsstoffe; Tapeten, Teppiche.* 1953 Stuttgart: A. Koch 150pp mostly illus. (German/French/English text)

Lewis, Frank. *Best design versus best seller in relation to textiles and wallpaper.* 1965 Leigh on Sea: F. Lewis 13pp pl 42 (92 illus.)

In such a competitive field design outside Britain cannot be ignored:

Schwartz, P. R. and Micheaux, R. de. *A century of French fabrics 1850-1950.* 1964 Leigh on Sea: F. Lewis 16pp 102 illus. (part of quite a large and useful series of introductions to important national textile designs throughout the world)

Troupp, Lotte. *Modern Finnish textiles.* 1962 Helsinki: Ottava 63pp illus.

Published Collections of Designs

Although manufacturers tend to guard their pattern books very carefully, many do find their way into public collections, even though a lot are still deliberately destroyed. To trace a few could be a life's work and there must be millions still in existence. All this bibliography can do in these circumstances is to suggest types of books and journals that might help open a few doors into this area.

Albums and Catalogues

Some published collections for textbook use can provide a useful point of approach to more detailed work:

Ashenhurst, Thomas R. *An album of textile designs containing upwards of 7,000 patterns, suitable for fabrics of every description, and an explanation of their arrangements and combinations.* 1881 Huddersfield: J. Broadbent & Co 220pp

Audsley, W. and Audsley, G. *Designs and patterns from historic ornament.* 1968 London: Dover 92pp (1882 edition reprint)

See also:

Ornament and Pattern *page 99*

Old catalogues of public collections can also help in this way but perhaps the richest (and often most difficult to trace) sources are the catalogues and reports of exhibitions, ranging from the international (eg *Second International Textile Exhibition 1955 Brussels*) to individuals (eg *Brown/Craven/Dodd: 3 textile designers.* 1965 Manchester: Whitworth Art Gallery).

Reports in the technical press can be a useful starting point for detailed consideration of attitudes and influences, eg:

'British Industries Fair 1933 Textiles Section White City'. 'A. Technical survey of the exhibits by W. Wilkinson' 'B. Design and colour survey by a manufacturer' 'C. The retailer's point of view by A. Trevor Handley' *Journal of the Textile Institute Proceedings* March 1933 vol 24 pp 37-40

Studies of Individual Designers

General histories and studies tend to be very general and repeat the familiar:

Clarke, Leslie J. *Craftsmen in textiles.* 1968 London: Bell 160pp illus. bibl.

and so the richest source of visual and other evidence tends to be buried in journals, eg:

Braddell, Darcy. 'Textile designs of Paul Nash', *Architectural Review* vol 60 1928 pp 161-165

Reilly, C. H. 'Design for textiles. The work of Jacqueline Groag', *Art and Industry* October 1942 pp 45-49

or in memoirs, eg:

Farleigh, John. *It never dies: a collection of notes and essays, 1940-1946.* 1946 London: Sylvan Press 97pp illus. (contains: Backcloth. Action and inaction. The future of furnishing fabrics. Art education and the future. The future of wood engraving. Painting and the unknown quantity. The designer and the textile trade. On exhibitions. Artist and client. Fine crafts. Design and book production. Conclusion)

Company histories

A very rich source of information, even if the best researched independent studies have concerned themselves with economic rather than design history:

Wells, Frederick Arthur. *Hollins and Viyella. A study in business history.* 1968 Newton Abbot: David and Charles 264pp

Coleman, D. C. *Courtaulds: an economic and social history vol 1: The nineteenth century, silk and crêpe vol 2: Rayon.* 1969 Oxford University Press

Plummer, Alfred and Early, Richard E. *The blanket makers 1669-1969: a history of Charles Early and Marriot (Witney) Ltd.* 1969 London: Routledge and Kegan Paul 205pp illus.

Company celebrations (centenaries, exhibitions, new releases) are generally richer sources of visual information:

Gray, Patience. 'Centenary fabrics and wallpapers (Arthur Sanderson & Sons Ltd)', *Design* 136 April 1960 pp 39-45

Berisfords the ribbon people. The story of 100 years 1858-1958. 1958 York: William Sessions 81pp

A century of Warner fabrics 1870 to 1970. 1970 London: Victoria and Albert Museum

The Mortons. Three generations of textile creation. 1973 London: Victoria and Albert Museum

Morton, Jocelyn. *Three generations in a family textile firm.* 1971 Routledge and Kegan Paul 481pp (Morton Sundour Fabrics Ltd)

A history of 250 years of clothworking in London. 1962 London: Perrotts Organisation 46pp

There are many other shorter studies and articles. Those in the more accessible journals, such as *Design,* could be particularly helpful:

Benoy, J. M. 'Design policy in industry. Morton Sundour Fabrics Limited', *Design* 52 April 1953 pp 12-19

Frostick, Michael. 'New moquette for old markets', (John Holdsworth & Co) *Design* 64 April 1954 pp 18-21

'New Sanderson patterns', *Design* 61 January 1954 pp 7-10 (postwar development of the company)

Manuals of textile design

A useful approach to a detailed historical problem might be to consult some of the more general technical manuals to clarify the area of enquiry:

Watson, William. *Textile design and colour, revised by E. G. Taylor and J. Buchanan.* 1975 (seventh edition) London: Newnes Butterworth 416pp (first published 1912)

Watson, William. *Advanced textile design.* 1947 (third edition) London: Longmans 519pp (first published 1913 now rewritten as Grosicki, Z. J. *Watson's Advanced textile design.* 1977 London: Newnes Butterworth 435pp)

Older textbooks and statements of principles could also be a useful introduction to current practice of the period studied:

Wyatt, Matthew Digby. 'On the principles of design applicable to textile art', pp 71-82 in Waring, John Burley. *Examples of weaving and embroidery.* 1858 London

Ashenhurst, Thomas R. *Design in textile fabrics.* 1885 London: Cassell 248pp illus. (Manuals of Technology)

Barker, Alfred Farrer. *The analysis and reproduction of textile fabrics.* 1894 Manchester: Marsden 230pp

Posselt, E. A. *Technology of textile design: a practical treatise on the construction and application of weaves for all textile fabrics and the analysis of cloth, containing also an appendix describing all the latest methods and improvements in designing and manufacturing.* 1896 (second edition) London: Sampson Low 292pp (first edition 1889)

Barker, Alfred Farrer. *An introduction to the study of textile design.* 1903 London: Methuen 211pp pl 16 (traces the product from yarn structure to the finished product)

Woodhouse, Thomas and Milne, Thomas. *Textile design, pure and applied.* 1912 London: Macmillan 515pp illus.

Wood, F. G. 'Textile designs and motives', *JRSA* vol 79 Feb 27 1931 pp 355-366

Read, John H. *Elementary textile design and fabric structure.* 1956 Manchester: Textile Institute 111pp 64 illus. (first published 1931)

Woods, H. J. 'The geometrical basis of pattern design:

Part 1. Point and line symmetry in simple figures and borders

Part 2. Nots and sateens

Part 3. Geometrical symmetry in plane patterns

Part 4. Counterchange symmetry in plane patterns',

Journal of the Textile Institute 1935 vol 26 T197-T210, T293-T308, 1936 vol 37 T341-T357, T305-T320

Hunt, Antony. *Textile design*. 1937 London: Studio 80pp pl 34 (another edition 1951)

Martin, Kenneth. 'The fundamentals of textile design', *Artist* 1939 vol 18 pp 29-30, 61-62, 88-89, 124-126, 153-155, 181-183 illus.

Strong, John Henry. *Foundations of fabric structure*. 1946 London: National Trade Press 254pp (later edition 1953)

Wright, Robin Harcourt. *Modern textile design and production*. 1949 London: National Trade Press 168pp 96 illus.

Shorter, S. A. 'An enumeration problem in textile design', *Journal of the Textile Institute* vol 40 1949 T189-199, T735-T748, vol 41 1950 T333-T348

Birrell, Verla Leone. *The textile arts, a handbook of fabric structure and design processes: and ancient and modern weaving, braiding, printing and other textile techniques*. 1959 New York: Harper 514pp

Harrison, P. W. (ed). *Studies in modern fabrics. Conference Proceedings*. 1970 Manchester: Textile Institute 218pp

Discussion of the role of the designer

As well as official enquiries and papers, eg:

The Textile designer in industry. Report by the county advisory committee for the textile industries. May 1964 Leeds: Council for Further Education (pamphlet no 82)

more general papers can be a useful guide to current attitudes and practice at more specific periods:

Wilcock, Arthur. 'Decorative textile industries and the designer's relation thereto', (Cantor lectures) *JRSA* vol 63 19 Feb, 26 Feb, 5 March 1915 pp 271-284, 320-321, 346-348

Brookes, A. E. G. 'Design in relation to fabrics', *Journal of the Textile Institute* March 1917 vol III no 1 pp 36-43

Morton, W. E. 'The designing of fabrics to meet consumers requirements', *Journal of the Textile Institute Proceedings* vol 39 June 1948 P187-P192

Russell, Gordon. 'Changing standards of design and the effect on textiles', *Journal of the Textile Institute Proceedings* vol 35 1954 P345-P349

Nicholson, Roger. 'The designer', *Journal of the Textile Institute Proceedings* vol 51 pp 499-506

Journals

The main historical journal in this field is primarily concerned with economic and business history:

Textile History 1968- (annual) Newton Abbot: David and Charles

Consequently the design historian will need to consult the longer runs of some of the more technical journals:

International Textiles 1933- (monthly) Amsterdam: International Textiles Ltd (University Microfilms)

Journal of the Textile Institute 1910- (monthly) Manchester: Textile Institute

Textile Manufacturer 1875- (monthly) Manchester (University Microfilms)

Textile Month 1968- (monthly) Manchester: Textile Business Press (incorporating *Skinner's Record of Manmade Fibres Industry and Man Made Textiles* and *Textile Recorder*)

Textile Recorder 1883-1915, 1918-1967 (monthly) Manchester

Bibliographies, Indexes and sources of Further Information

The most convenient single volume is:

A guide to sources of information in the textile industry, edited by Carolyn A. Farnfield. 1974 Manchester: Textile Institute 130pp

For historical studies there is now increasing coverage of the nineteenth century in the bibliography of:

Centre International d'Etude des Textiles Anciens. Bulletin de Liaison 1955- (semi-annual) Lyons

Textile History is a useful bibliographical source, eg:

Harte, N. and Ponting, K. G. 'A review of periodical literature on textile history published in 1973', *Textile History* vol 6 1975 pp 165-169

Current practice and technical innovations can be traced through:

Review of Textile Progress; a survey of world literature vol 1 1949- (annual) Manchester: Textile Institute

World Textile Abstracts 1969- (twice a month) Manchester: Shirley Institute (continuation of *Journal of the Textile Institute: Abstracts Section* 1918-1966/7, *Textile Abstracts* 1967/8-1968/9 and the *Shirley Institute Summary of Current Literature* 1921-1968)

a selection of which now appears as:

Digest of English Language Textile Literature 1973- (monthly) Manchester

There are a number of useful much older bibliographies:

Flemming, Ernst. *Textil Künste; Weberei, Stickerei, Spitze, Geschichte, Technik, Stilenwickelung.* 1923 Berlin: Verlag für Kunstwissenschaft 384pp (basically a literature guide)

Patent Office, London. *Subject lists of works on the textile industries and wearing apparel including the culture and chemical technology of the textile fibres in the library of the Patent Office.* 1919 London: HMSO 329pp

Victoria and Albert Museum. *A list of books and pamphlets in the Library. Part 1 illustrating textile fabrics. Part 2 lace and needlework.* 1888 London: Eyre and Spottiswode 86pp

Textile Foundation. *Textile design: a bibliography and directory.* 1932 Washington: Textile Foundation

2 Fabrics from particular fibres

A useful introduction to this section is provided by:

Cook, James Gordon. *Handbook of textile fibres. Vol 1 Natural fibres. Vol 2 Manmade fibres.* 1968 (fourth edition) Newcastle: Merrow (first edition 1959)

There is also a helpful earlier set of Cantor lectures:

'1. The manufacture of modern textile fibres by Claude Diamond' '2. The chemical and physical properties of modern textile fibres by J. K. Berry'. '3. The Application of modern textile fibres by R. S. Greenwood', *JRSA* vol 94 May 24 1946 pp 382-403, 403-417, 418-426

Cotton

A very general survey:

'Cotton', *CIBA Review* no 95. 1952

Techniques and materials:

Hough, Walter. *Encyclopaedia of cotton fabrics.* 1948 (sixth edition) Manchester: Sherratt 91pp (first edition 1920)

Marsden, Richard. *Cotton weaving, its development, principles and practice.* 1895 London: G. Bell 533pp illus.

Taylor, John T. *Cotton weaving and designing.* 1924 London: Longmans Green 352pp

Up to the present most historical study has concentrated on the great growth period of the cotton industry terminating early in our period:

Mann, James A. *The cotton trade of Great Britain: its rise, progress and present extent.* 1968 London: Cass 134pp (reprint of 1860 edition)

Boyson, Rhodes. *Ashworth cotton enterprise: the rise and fall of a family firm, 1818-1880.* 1970 Oxford University Press 269pp

In the design field however this period is important for an early report:

Great Britain. Board of Education. *Design and the cotton industry; being a report by HM Inspectors on existing conditions in the industry and schools, together with recommendations of the joint standing committee (industry and education) of the British cotton industry research association.* 1929 London: HMSO 59pp (Educational pamphlets no 75. Industry series no 8)

The activities (particularly in the 1940s) of the Cotton Board and its exhibitions:

Fraser, Grace Lovat. 'British cotton and rayon textiles', *Art and Industry* February 1941 pp 30-41

Although concerned primarily with technical matters there may be useful design history material now in the publications of the Shirley Institute (Cotton and Manmade Fibres Research Association)

Shirley Institute Memoirs 1922-
Shirley Institute Bulletin 1928-
Shirley Institute Yearbook 1951-

For further information about the cotton industry in general:

Yates, Bryan. *How to find out about the United Kingdom cotton industry.* 1967 Oxford: Pergamon 188pp

Linen

A small but long-established textile industry with strong local roots:

Crawford, R. H. 'Design and the linen industry', *Journal of the Textile Institute Proceedings* vol 53 1962 P371-P377

Moore, Alfred S. *Linen from raw material to the finished product.* 1914 London: Pitman 132pp (Common commodities and industries series)

Warden, Alex J. *The linen trade, ancient and modern.* 1967 London: Gass 745pp illus. (originally published 1864)

Crawford, Sir William. 'Irish linen and some features of its production', *JSA* vol 58 1910

Campbell, Etta. *Linen embroideries.* 1935 London: Pitman 41pp

Silk

A useful introduction to this very small but well documented industry is:

The Silk Book. 1951 London: Silk and Rayon Users Association 107pp

A larger general history:

Algoud, Henri. *La soie, art et histoire*. 1928 Paris: Payot 255pp illus.

For more technical information:

Goodale, E. W. 'The history and activities of the Silk Association', *Journal of the Textile Institute Proceedings* vol 30 1939 P79-P90

Howitt, Frederick Oliver. *Bibliography of the technical literature on silk*. 1946 London: Hutchinson 248pp (15 critical essays and a detailed bibliography)

Some historical surveys:

Winkworth, Thomas. 'The British silk manufacture considered in its commercial aspects', *JSA* vol 4 1856 pp 460-467

Godden, Geoffrey A. *Stevengraphs and other Victorian silk pictures*. 1971 London: Barrie and Jenkins 492pp illus.

Wardle, Thomas. *Report on the English silk industry*. 1885 London: Eyre and Spottiswode for HMSO 106pp (submission to the Royal Commission on Technical Education)

Clarke, Purdon. 'English brocades and figured silks', *JSA* vol 40 April 22 1892 pp 576-588

Wardle, Thomas. 'Improvements in the designing, colouring and manufacture of British silk since the Egerton exhibition of 1890', *JSA* vol 43 May 31 1895 pp 666-685

Sericulture: or ancient and modern silk fabrics. And the British silk renaissance. 1891 London: Liberty & Co 43pp

Cole, Alan S. *Ornament in European silks*. 1899 London: Debenham and Freebody 226pp illus.

Warner, Frank. 'The British silk industry', *JSA* vol 52 January 1 1904 pp 123-139

Warner, Frank. 'The British silk industry: its development since 1903', *JRSA* vol 60 February 23 1912 pp 392-415

Warner, Sir Frank. *The silk industry of the United Kingdom*. 1921 London: Drane 664pp

Woodman, H. 'Decorative silks – the development of design', *Journal of the Textile Institute Proceedings* vol 17 1926 P220-P223

Slomann, Vilhelm. *Bizarre designs on silk: trade and traditions translated by Eve M. Wendt*. 1953 Copenhagen: Munksgaard for Ny Carlsberg Foundation 270pp illus. bibl.

Velvet

'Velvet', *CIBA Review* no 96 1953

Wool

A general introduction:

Jenkins, J. Geraint (ed). *Wool textile industry in Great Britain*. 1972 London: Routledge and Kegan Paul 309pp illus. bibl. (Section A: Historical Studies, Section B: Technical Studies, Section C: Regional Studies)

There are a number of very full industrial histories, but a distinct lack of historical studies of wool textile design:

Lipson, Ephraim. *The history of the woollen and worsted industries*. 1965 London: Cass (reprint of 1921 edition) 273pp

Ponting, Kenneth G. *Wool trade. Past and present*. 1961 Buxton: Columbine Press 196pp

Some of the earlier histories are particularly useful for details of conditions:

Baines, Edward. *Baines's account of the woollen manufacture of England, with a new introduction by K. G. Ponting*. 1970 Newton Abbot: David and Charles 199pp

Burnley, James. *The history of wool and wool combing*. 1969 New York: Augustus M. Kelley 487pp (first published 1889 by Sampson Low)

Some publications of the International Wool Secretariat and the Wool Education Society do have a relevance to design:

Cavanagh, John. *Designing in wool*. 1955 London: Wool Education Society 20pp illus.

Cunnington, C. W. *Wool in the pageant of English fashion*. 1952 London: Wool Education Society

Goodden, Wyndham Swayne. *Trends in the design of modern wool textiles*. 1955 London: Wool Education Society 16pp

The worsted industry:

Dumville, Joseph and Kershaw, Samuel. *Worsted industry*. 1954 (revised edition) London: Pitman 157pp (first published 1924)

Sigsworth, Eric Milton. *Black Dyke Mills. A history . . . with introductory chapters on the development of the worsted industry in the nineteenth century*. 1958 Liverpool University Press 385pp

James, John. *History of worsted manufacture in England from the earliest times*. 1968 London: Cass (facsimile of 1857 edition) 640pp

There are a growing number of regional and local design studies. Perhaps the most accessible are those relating to Scottish woollens:

Stillie, T. A. 'The evolution of pattern design in the Scottish woollen textile industry in the nineteenth century', *Textile History* vol 1 no 3 1970 pp 309-331

Johnston, E. Y. 'Design and Scottish woollens', *Journal of the Textile Institute Proceedings* vol 51 1960 P74-P77

Scottish Woollens. 1956 Edinburgh: National Association of Scottish Woollen Manufacturers 245pp illus. (based on an earlier leaflet series)

Tweeds and checks have been particularly well documented:

Gulvin, Clifford. *Tweedmakers: a history of the Scottish fancy woollen industry 1600-1914.* 1973 Newton Abbot: David and Charles 240pp illus. bibl.

Christie, D. R. *Scottish tweeds. Four hundred years of fashion.* 1958 London: Wool Education Society

Sinclair, W. P. H. 'Fifty years of design in Scottish tweeds', *Design* 33 September 1951 pp 5-8

Thompson, Francis. *Harris tweed: the story of a Hebridean industry.* 1969 Newton Abbot: David and Charles 191pp illus.

Johnston, Robert. *Tweed designers handbook.* 1888 Galashiels: John M'Queen 56pp pl 18

Welsh, Thomas. 'Designing and colouring of Scottish tweeds', *Journal of the Textile Institute* November 1912 vol III no 2 pp 261-275

Harrison, Edward Stroud. *Our Scottish district checks.* 1968 Edinburgh: National Association of Scottish Woollen Manufacturers 166pp

More specific design detail for wool in general has to be tracked down through the general journals:

Wool Knowledge 1948- (quarterly) London: International Wool Secretariat

Wool Record and Textile World 1909- (fortnightly) Manchester: Textile Business Press (University Microfilms)

or the technical press and specialised bodies conveniently listed in:

Lemon, Hugo. *How to find out about the wool textile industry.* 1968 Oxford: Pergamon Press 217pp

Mixture Fabrics

(pre-synthetic fibres)

'Mixture fabrics', *CIBA Review* no 141 December 1960 (includes a brief guide to mixture fabrics of the nineteenth century pp 27-28)

Goodale, Ernest W. 'The blending and mixture of textile fibres and yarns', *JRSA* vol 100 16 November 1951 pp 4-14

Artificial Fibres

The evolution and use of manmade fibres is probably one of the most important developments of this period. A very complex area perhaps best approached through some of the encyclopaedic works:

Moncrieff, Robert Wighton. *Manmade fibres.* 1975 (sixth edition) London: Newnes-Butterworth 1086pp illus. (first published as *Artificial Fibres* 1950)

Press, Jack Joshua (ed). *Man-made textile encyclopaedia.* 1959 New York: Textile Book Publishers 913pp

Roff, William John. *Fibres, plastics and rubber. A handbook of common polymers.* 1956 London: Butterworths 400pp illus.

There are a number of convenient historical surveys:

Potter, H. V. 'Synthetic fibres, historical survey', *Chemistry and Industry* December 17 1949 pp 879-885

Ridge, B. P. 'The new textiles: their impact on manufacturers and users', *Journal of the Textile Institute Proceedings* vol 42 1951 P885-P893

Urquhart, R., Hegan, A. J. and Loasby, G. *The development of some manmade fibres.* 1951 Manchester: Textile Institute 79pp

Loasby, G. 'The development of the synthetic fibre', *Journal of the Textile Institute Proceedings* vol 42 1951 pp 411-441 (307 bibl. refs)

Hague, Douglas Chalmers. *The economics of man-made fibres.* 1957 London: Duckworth 315pp illus. (Industrial Innovation series)

The back issues of:

Manmade Textiles and Skinners Record 1924-1967 Manchester (University Microfilms)

could be a useful source of information.

The histories of particular types of synthetic fibre:

Artificial silk

'Artificial silk', *CIBA Review* 1967 issue 2

Brough, Thomas. 'Artificial silk', *JRSA* vol 75 December 10 1926 pp 97-115

Cash, Joseph. 'Artificial silk', *JSA* vol 48 December 8 1899 pp 61-67

Rayon

Beer, Edwin J. *The beginning of rayon.* 1962 Paignton: Beer 210pp

Harrop, J. 'The international rayon industry between the wars', *Textile History* vol 1 no 2 1969 pp 170-183

Robinson, A. T. C. *Rayon fabric construction.* 1951 Manchester: Skinner 180pp

'Rayon supplement', *Design* 43 July 1952 pp 15-31

'Rayon company histories', *Textile World* 86 September 1936 pp 1820-1827

Nylon

Du Pont de Nemours, E. I. and Company. *Nylon, the first 25 years.* 1963 Wilmington, Delaware: E. I. Du Pont de Nemours & Co 32pp illus.

Viscose

Hegan, H. J. 'The historical development of and outlook for viscose fibres', *Journal of the Textile Institute* vol 42 1951 pp 395-410

Jackson, Cyril Henry Ward. *A history of Courtaulds. An account of the origin and rise of Courtaulds Limited and its associate the American Viscose Corporation.* 1941 London: Curwen Press 177pp illus.

3 Textiles made by particular process or technique

Printed textiles

General introductions:

Robinson, Stuart. *A history of printed textiles: block, roller, screen, design, dyes, fibres, discharge, resist, further sources for research.* 1969 London: Studio Vista 152pp

Turnbull, Geoffrey. *A history of the calico printing industry of Great Britain.* 1951 Altrincham: Sherratt 501pp pl 43

Design by the yard; textile printing from 800 to 1956. 1956 New York: Cooper Union Museum for the Arts of Decoration 24pp illus. bibl.

A concise survey:

Floud, Peter. 'A calendar of English printed textiles 1775-1905', *Architectural Review* August 1956 pp 126-133

A few designers:

Dauriac, J. P. 'Raoul Dufy: his famous Art Deco textile designs', *Graphis* 30 no 176 1974-1975 pp 530-533

Holtom, Gerald. 'The printed fabric designs by Jacqueline Groag', *Art and Industry* June 1947 pp 174-179

Newton, Douglas. 'Printed textiles: the work of the Younger English Designers', *Architectural Review* vol 111 no 663 March 1952 pp 190-195

Discussions of technique and practice:

Burch, Joseph. 'On the printing of fabrics, with special reference to shawls and carpets', *JSA* vol 4 no 180 1856 pp 401-408

MacMahon, Percy A. 'The design of repeating patterns for decorative work', *JRSA* vol 70 June 30 1922 pp 567-582

Hubbard, H. 'Colour block prints: history, colour block print of the present and future, practice of the craft', *JRSA* vol 82 January 1926 pp 266-281, pp 287-302

Wainwright, Shirley B. 'Modern printed textiles', *Studio* vol 92, 1926 pp 394-400

Knecht, Edmund and Fothergill, James Best. *The principles and practices of textile printing.* 1952 (fourth edition) London: Griffin 1084pp (first edition 1912)

Fletcher, S. Bernice. *Pattern design for printed dress fabrics, a practical guide for the industrial artist.* 1937 London: Pitman 88pp illus.

'Design Review. Designs for printed textiles', *Architectural Review* vol 98 August 1945 pp 52-56 (review of Cotton Board's Colour, Design and Style Centre)

King, Donald. 'Textile printing in London and the Home Counties', *Journal of the Society of Dyers and Colourists* LXXI July 1955

Conran, Terence. *Printed textile design.* 1957 London: Studio 95pp illus. (How to do it series no. 74)

Clarke, William. *Introduction to textile printing.* 1974 (fourth edition) London: Newnes-Butterworth 276pp illus. (first edition 1964)

Storey, Joyce. *The Thames and Hudson manual of textile printing.* 1974 London: Thames and Hudson 188pp 188 illus.

A useful bibliography (to form the basis of a much larger work eventually):

Clark, C. O. 'List of books and important articles on the technology of textile printing', *Textile History* 6 1975 pp 89-118

Some mechanical developments:

Dalton, John. 'Improvements in machinery for printing calico and other fabrics by which ten or more different colours may be worked simultaneously and with accurate register', *JSA* July 8 1853 pp 405-409

Fishenden, R. B. 'The lithographic printing of textile fabrics', *Journal of the Society of Dyers and Colourists* June 1915

Wilcock, Arthur. 'Surface printing by rollers in the cotton industry', *JRSA* vol 70 February 24 1922 pp 260-268

Textile ornamentation:

'Textile Ornament', *CIBA Review* no 37 1941

Cole, Alan S. 'Textile ornamentation', *JRSA* vol 58 July 15 1910 pp 779-796, pp 799-812, pp 819-830

Barker, Alfred Farrer. *Ornamentation and textile design.* 1930 London: Methuen 30pp pl 94

Chintz

English chintz, two centuries of changing taste (catalogue of) an exhibition assembled by the Victoria and Albert Museum at the Cotton Board, Colour, Design and Style Centre, Manchester. 1955 London: HMSO 58pp illus. bibl.

Bunt, Cyril and Rose, Ernest Arthur. *Two centuries of English chintz exemplified by the productions of Stead, McAlpin & Co.* 1957 Leigh on Sea: F. Lewis 85pp

Lewis, Frank. *English chintz from earliest times to the present day.* 1935 Benfleet: F. Lewis 36pp pl 152 (revised edition 1942)

'English printed textiles', *CIBA Review* 1961 issue 1 (includes sections on development of design in English printed textiles, influence of William Morris)

Dyed textiles

See also:

Colour *page 97*

General historical introductions:

Robinson, Stuart. *A history of dyed textiles: dyes, fibres, painted bark, batik, starch resist, discharge, tie-dye, further sources for research.* 1969 London: Studio Vista 112pp

Hannay, J. R. 'An historical survey of dyeing and calico-printing', *Journal of the Society of Dyers and Colourists* XL, 10,317 1924

Morton, James. 'History of the development of fast dyeing and dyes', *JSA* vol 77 April 12 1929 pp 544-574

Two very important technical journals:

The Dyer 1881- (changed to *International Dyer*. 1963-) London (includes annual lists of books on textiles and dyeing)

Journal of the Society of Dyers and Colourists 1884- Bradford (includes monthly abstracts and reviews)

The historical articles in the 1934 Jubilee issue of the latter are particularly useful.

Historical developments of dyes:

Forrester, Stanley D. 'The history of the development of the light fastness testing of dyed fabrics up to 1902', *Textile History* 6 1975 pp 52-87

Mellor, C. M. and Cardwell, D. S. L. 'Dyes and dyeing 1775-1860', *British Journal for the History of Science* 1 no 3 June 1963 Part III no 3 pp 265-275

Abrahart, E. H. 'Discovery, invention and colour', *Manchester Literary and Philosophical Society, Memoirs and Proceedings* 117 (1974-1975) pp 5-11 (on the development of synthetic dyes in Britain)

Calvert, Grace. 'Dyes and dyestuffs other than aniline', *JSA* vol 19 October 6, October 13, October 20 1871 pp 803-807, pp 815-819, pp 825-831, pp 841-846

Hummel, J. J. 'Fast and fugitive dyes', *JSA* vol 39 May 15 1891 pp 535-551

Perkin and after:

Perkin, W. H. 'Cantor lectures. On the aniline or coal tar colours', *JSA* vol 17 January 1, January 8, January 15 1869 pp 99-105, pp 109-114, pp 121-126

'Sir William Henry Perkin', *CIBA Review* no 115 1956

Perkin centenary, London. 100 years of synthetic dyestuffs. 1958 Oxford: Pergamon 136pp

Gardner, Walter M. (ed.) *The British coal-tar industry. Its origins, development and decline.* 1915 London: Williams and Norgate 436pp (useful papers on Perkin and dyes)

Technique:

Whittaker, Croyden Meredith and Wilcock, C. C. *Dyeing with coal tar dyestuffs.* 1949 (fifth edition) London: Bailliere, Tindall and Cox 375pp illus. (first edition 1918)

Dye colours:

Colour Index. 1957-1964 Bradford: Society of Dyers and Colourists 5 vols with annual supplements (details trade names, chemical constituents and methods of use)

'Scarlet', *CIBA Review* no 7 March 1938

'Purple', *CIBA Review* no 4 1937

'Madder and Turkey Red', *CIBA Review* no 39 May 1941

'Indigo', *CIBA Review* no 85 1951

Some more specialised technical aspects of dyeing and its design:

Crookes, William. *A practical handbook of dyeing and calico printing.* 1874 London: Longmans Green 730pp illus.

Hummel, John James. *The dyeing of textile fabrics.* 1885 London: Cassell 534pp illus. (many later editions)

Mercurization. A practical and historical manual, by the editors of 'The Dyer and Calico Printer'. With plates and illustrations in the

text and specimens of dyed fabrics and yarns. 1903 London: Heywood 2 vols

Jackson, Holbrook. 'Colour determination in the fashion trades', *JRSA* vol 78 March 14 1930 pp 492-513

Whiston, P. 'Design and colour in textiles', *Journal of the Textile Institute Proceedings* vol 39 1948 pp 193-199

Bird, C. L. *The theory and practice of wool dyeing.* 1972 (fourth edition) Bradford: Society of Dyers and Colourists 249pp illus. (first edition 1948)

Morton, Alastair. 'The designer's approach to colour', *Journal of the Textile Institute Proceedings* vol 35 1954 pp 497-503

Hall, Archibald John. *Handbook of textile dyeing and printing.* 1955 London: National Trade Press 216pp illus.

Blackshaw, H. and Brightman, R. *Dictionary of dyeing and textile printing.* 1961 London: Newnes 221pp illus.

Storey, Joyce. *The Thames and Hudson manual of dyes and fabrics.* 1978 London: Thames and Hudson

A full bibliography to serve both this and the previous section:

Lawrie, Leslie Gordon. *A bibliography of dyeing and textile printing. Comprising a list of books from the sixteenth century to . . . 1946.* 1949 London: Chapman and Hall 143pp

Woven textiles

General introductions:

Lewis, Ethel. *The romance of textiles; the story of design in weaving.* 1937 New York: Macmillan 377pp pl 40 bibl.

Nisbet, Harry. *Grammar of textile design.* 1906 London: Scott, Greenwood 276pp 490 illus. ('a treatise upon the fundamental principles of structural design in woven fabrics'. Later edition 1927 Benn)

Some historical technical works and surveys:

Watson, John. *The theory and practice of the art of weaving by hand and power with calculations and tables for the use of those connected with the trade.* 1863 Glasgow: G. Watson 380pp (another edition 1888)

Ashenhurst, Thomas Rutherford. *A practical treatise on weaving and designing of textile fabrics: principles of construction of the loom, calculations and colour.* 1879 Bradford: T. Brear 246 illus. (fifth edition 1893)

Barlow, Alfred. *The history and principles of weaving by hand and by power.* 1879 London: Sampson Low 443pp

Bell, T. F. *Jacquard weaving and designing.* 1895 London: Longmans Green 303pp illus.

Stephenson, Charles and Suddards, F. *A textbook dealing with ornamental design for woven fabrics.* 1897 London: Methuen 273pp (later edition 1924)

Beaumont, Robert. *Colour in woven design being a treatise on the science and technology of textile colouring (woollen, worsted, cotton and silk materials).* 1912 (second edition) London: Whittaker 372pp illus. (first edition 1890)

Oelsner, Gustaf Hermann. *A handbook of weaves. Translated and revised by Samuel S. Dale including a supplement on the analysis of weaves and fabrics.* 1961 New York: Dover 402pp (reprint of 1915 edition)

Mairet, Ethel. *Handweaving today. Traditions and changes.* 1939 London: Faber 144pp

Sutherland, O. S. 'Design review. Woven furnishing textiles', *Architectural Review* vol 114 no 682 October 1953 pp 265-268

Hindson, Alice. *Designer's drawloom: an introduction to drawloom weaving and repeat pattern planning.* 1958 London: Faber 236pp bibl.

Albers, Anni. *On designing.* 1962 Middletown (Connecticut): Wesleyan University Press 80pp illus.

Robinson, A. T. C. and Marks, R. *Woven cloth construction.* 1967 London: Butterworth 180pp illus.

Regensteiner, Else. *The art of weaving.* 1970 London: Studio Vista 184pp illus.

Willcox, Donald J. *New design in weaving.* 1970 New York: Van Nostrand Reinhold 128pp illus.

Histories of companies and professional groups can provide useful incidental information:

Goodale, Sir Ernest. *Weaving and the Warners 1870-1970.* 1971 Leigh on Sea: F. Lewis 150 illus.

Adamczewski, F. 'Point about weaving (achievements of Archie Brennan and the Edinburgh tapestry company)', *Design* no 307 July 1974 pp 58-61

Plummer, Alfred. *The London Weavers Company 1600-1970.* 1972 London: Routledge and Kegan Paul 476pp illus.

The machinery involved in weaving should not be overlooked:

'The loom', *CIBA Review* no 16 1938

'The mechanical loom', *CIBA Review* 1966/2

Beaumont, Roberts. 'Recent inventions in weaving machinery', *JSA* vol 50 February 28 1902 pp 301-315

Duxbury, V. and Wray, G. R. (ed). *Modern developments in weaving machinery.* 1962 London: Columbine Press 184pp

Felts and Nonwoven Textiles

'Felt', *CIBA Review* no 129 November 1958

'Nonwovens', *CIBA Review* 1965/1

Hawkins, James Harford. *History of the Worshipful Company of Feltmakers of London.* 1917 London: Crowther and Goodman 172pp

Rope and Jute

Dickinson, H. W. 'A condensed history of rope-making', *Transactions of the Newcomen Society* XXIII 1942/3 pp 71-92

'Ropemaking then and now', *CIBA Review* 1971/1

Tyson, William. Rope. *A history of the hard fibre cordage industry in the United Kingdom.* 1962 London: Wheatlands Journal 160pp illus.

Woodhouse, Thomas and Briand, A. *A century of progress in jute manufacture.* 1934 Dundee: Winter and Son 196pp illus.

Needlework

General introductions:

Kendrick, Albert Frank. *English needlework, revised by Patricia Wardle.* 1967 (second edition) London: Black 212pp pl 31 bibl.

Symonds, M. and Preece, L. *Needlework through the ages. A short survey of its development in decorative art, with particular regard to its inspirational relationship with other methods of craftmanship.* 1928 London: Hodder and Stoughton 412pp illus. bibl.

Clabburn, Pamela. *The needleworkers dictionary.* 1976 London: Macmillan 296pp illus.

Quite a large number of historical studies exist with particular emphasis on the nineteenth century and with the collector in mind:

Hughes, Therle. *English domestic needlework 1660-1860.* 1961 London: Lutterworth 255pp pl 48

Warren, Geoffrey. *A stitch in time: Victorian and Edwardian needlecraft.* 1976 Newton Abbot: David and Charles 144pp 90 illus.

Caulfield, Sophia F. A. and Saward, Blanche C. *Encyclopaedia of Victorian needlework.* 1972 (new edition) New York: Dover 697pp (2 vols)

Cust, Marianne Margaret (Viscountess Alford). *Needlework as art.* 1886

London: Sampson Low 422pp pl 85 (ABC Reprint in preparation)

A few later surveys and collections:

Christie, Grace I. *Samplers and stitches.* 1950 (fifth edition) London: Batsford 152pp illus. (first edition 1921)

Needlework classics: nostalgic designs from the Butterick archives for decorating clothing and accessories, edited by Becky Stevens Cordello. 1976 New York: Butterick, distributed by Vogue Pattern Service 128pp illus.

Worthington, Arthur Pearson. *Survey of literature on stitches and seams for garments 1950-1974.* 1975 Manchester: Cotton Silk and Manmade Fibres Research Association, Shirley Institute 75pp

Needlework has been more intensively studied historically in its two main decorative branches, embroidery and tapestry.

Embroidery

General introductions:

Jones, Mary Eirwen. *A history of western embroidery.* 1969 London: Studio Vista 159pp 85 illus.

Snook, Barbara. *English embroidery.* 1974 (revised edition) London: Mills and Boon 136pp illus. (previous edition Batsford 1960)

Wardle, Patricia. *Guide to English embroidery.* 1971 London: HMSO for Victoria and Albert Museum 40pp pl 57 bibl.

Schuette, Marie and Müller-Christensen, Sigfrid. *The art of embroidery (text translated by Donald King).* 1964 London: Thames and Hudson 336pp illus.

Victorian embroidery:

Markrich, Lilo and Kiewe, Heinz Edgar. *Victorian fancywork: nineteenth century needlepoint patterns and designs.* 1975 London: Pitman 283pp illus.

Morris, Barbara J. *Victorian embroidery.* 1962 London: Jenkins 238pp illus. (Victorian collector series)

Lockwood, Mary Smith and Glaister, Elizabeth. *Art embroidery. A treatise on the revived practice of decorative needlework.* 1878 London: Marcus Ward 105pp pl 19 (ABC Reprint)

Delamotte, Freeman Gage. *The embroider's book of design, containing initials, emblems, cyphers, monograms, ornamental borders, ecclesiastical devices, mediaeval and modern alphabets and national emblems, colected and engraved by F. Delamotte.* 1860 London: Spon pl 19

Levey, Santina. *Discovering embroidery of the 19th century.* 1971 Tring: Shire 71pp illus.

Art Nouveau embroidery:

Day, Lewis F. and Buckle, M. *Art Nouveau embroidery*. 1975 London: Oak Tree Press 94pp

and a reprint of the work from which it is derived:

Day, Lewis F. and Buckle, M. *Art in needlework: a book about embroidery*. 1900 London: Batsford 294pp pl 94 (ABC Reprint)

Some later ideas and surveys:

Baillie-Scott, M. H. 'Some experiments in embroidery', *Studio* vol 28 1903 pp 279-284 7 illus.

Cole, Alan S. 'Some aspects of ancient and modern embroidery', *JRSA* vol 53 August 11, August 18 1905 pp 956-960, pp 973-985

Taylor, J. 'The Glasgow school of embroidery', *Studio* vol 50 1911 pp 124-145 21 illus.

Rayner, E. Ruth. 'The Embroiderers Guild exhibition', *Studio* vol 87 1924 pp 17-21 7 illus. (its first really important exhibition)

Drew, Joan H. *Embroidery and design. A handbook of the principles of decorative art as applied to embroidery*. 1915 London: Pitman 103pp illus.

Hogarth, Mary. *Modern embroidery*. 1933 London: *Studio* special Spring number 128pp illus.

Booker, Molly. *Embroidery design*. 1933 London: Studio 79pp illus. (How to do it series no 9)

Crompton, Rebecca. *Modern design in embroidery. Edited by Davide C. Minter*. 1936 London: Batsford 72pp pl 51 (reissued by HMSO 1950)

Mann, Kathleen. *Embroidery design and stitches*. 1937 London: A & C Black 48pp line drawings

Catalogue of embroideries given to the museum by the Needlework Development scheme. 1965 Edinburgh: Royal Scottish Museum 72pp pl 24

'Needlework Development scheme', *Design* 33 September 1951 pp 9-12

Whyte, Kathleen. *Design in embroidery*. 1969 London: Batsford 240pp illus.

Embroidery for church decoration:

Beese, Pat. *Embroidery for church*. 1975 London: Studio Vista 104pp illus. bibl.

Dolby, Anastasia. *Church embroidery, ancient and modern, practically illustrated*. 1867 London: Chapman and Hall 176pp pl 20

Antrobus, Mary and Preece, Louisa. *Needlework in religion*. 1924 London: Pitman 229p pl 35

Hall, Maud R. *English church needlework. A handbook for workers and designers*. 1901 London: Grant Richards 139pp (later edition 1913)

Dean, Beryl. *Ecclesiastical embroidery*. 1958 London: Batsford 258pp illus.

Dean, Beryl. *Church needlework*. 1961 London: Batsford 136pp illus.

Dean, Beryl. *Ideas for church embroidery*. 1968 London: Batsford 192pp illus.

Journals:

The Embroideress 1922 London: James Pearsall

Embroidery 1932- (quarterly) London: Embroiderers Guild

Particular embroidery techniques:

Edwards, Joan. *Crewel embroidery in England*. 1975 London: Batsford 248pp illus.

Giltsoff, Natalie. *Fashion bead embroidery*. 1971 London: Batsford 88pp illus.

Leach, Agnes Mary Minto. *Drawn fabric embroidery*. 1959 London: Hulton 118pp

Dawson, Barbara. *Metal thread embroidery*. 1976 (second edition) London: Batsford 216pp illus. (first edition 1968)

Mann, Kathleen. *Appliqué design and method*. 1937 London: A & C Black 48pp illus.

Colby, Averil. *Samplers, yesterday and today*. 1964 London: Batsford 266pp

Machine embroidery:

Risley, Christine. *Machine embroidery. A complete guide*. 1973 London: Studio Vista 212pp illus. bibl. (contains 'Machine embroidery – historical survey' by Patricia Wardle pp 7-26)

Gray, Jennifer. *Machine embroidery: technique and design*. 1973 London: Batsford 256pp illus.

Needlework tools

Groves, Sylvia. *A history of needlework tools and accessories*. 1973 Newton Abbot: David and Charles 136pp illus. (first edition 1966 Country Life)

Bond, S. 'History of sewing tools', *Embroidery* vols 13 and 14 1945, 1946

Tapestry

Very general introductions:

Thomson, William George. *A history of tapestry from the earliest times until the present day*. 1973 East Ardlsey: EP Publishing 620pp illus. (facsimile reprint of 1930 edition)

Hunter, George Leland. *Tapestries, their origins, history and renaissance*. 1912 New York: John Lane 438pp illus.

The revival of production by Morris and Burne-Jones:

Marillier, Henry Currie. *History of the Merton Abbey tapestry works founded by William Morris*. 1927 London: Constable 37pp pl 28

Vallance, Aymer. 'The revival of tapestry weaving. An inverview with William Morris', *Studio* vol 3 1894

Vallance, Aymer. 'Some examples of tapestry designed by Sir E. Burne-Jones and J. H. Dearle', *Studio* vol 45 1909 pp 13-24 10 illus.

Parry, Linda L. A. 'The tapestries of Edward Burne-Jones', *Apollo* 102 November 1975 pp 324-328 illus.

Some later work:

Lurçat, Jean. *Designing tapestry, translated by B. Crocker*. 1950 London: Rockliff 61pp 53 examples (first published 1947 as *Tapisserie Francaise*)

Beaumont-Nesbitt, Brian. 'The tapestries of Archie Brennan', *Connoisseur* vol 186 no 749 pp 196-199

Knitting

General studies:

Kiewe, Heinz. *History of knitting. First exhibition*. 1977 London: Foyles Art Gallery

Kiewe, Heinz Edgar. *The sacred history of knitting*. 1967 Oxford: Art Needlework Industries 222pp pl 87

Norbury, James. *The knitter's craft*. 1950 London: Paton and Baldwins in association with Brockhampton Press 116pp

Norbury, James. 'The knitter's craft', *JRSA* vol 99 January 26 1951 pp 216-228 (historical study by chief designer, Paton & Baldwins)

A distinctive local craft and design:

Don, Sarah. *Fair Isle knitting*. 1978 London: Studio Vista 96pp

Hosiery

Historical development:

Wells, F. A. *British hosiery and knitwear industry: its history and organisation*. 1972 (second edition) Newton Abbot: David and Charles 256pp (first edition 1935)

Grass, Milton N. *A history of hosiery, from the piloi of ancient Greece to the nylons of modern America*. 1955 New York: Fairchild Publications 283pp illus. bibl.

Felkin, W. *Felkin's history of the machine-wrought hosiery and lace manufacturers. With a new introduction of*

S. D. Chapman. 1967 Newton Abbot: David and Charles 595pp (reprint of 1867 edition)

Chandler, T. J. 'The development of the British wool hosiery industry Part 11 (1840-1900), Part III (1900-1955)', *Wool Knowledge* vol 3 no 11, no 12 1956 pp 16-19, pp 11-13

Holmes, Kenneth. 'Cooperation between manufacturers and art schools with special reference to the hosiery and knitted fabric industry', *JRSA* vol 85 May 21 1937 pp 628-645

A bibliography of material to the beginning of the twentieth century:

Ginsburg, Madeleine. 'Hosiery: a bibliography', *Costume* no 2 1968 pp 39-45

Some company histories:

Jopp, Keith. *Corah of Leicester 1815-1965*. 1965 Leicester: Newman Neame (Northern) 58pp illus.

The Pick knitwear story 1856-1956. 1956 Leicester: J. Pick and sons.

Journals are now a rich source of historical information:

British Knitwear Fashion 1969- London (previously *British Hosiery and Knitwear* 1949-1969)

Hosiery Times. The monthly journal for hosiery and knitwear manufacturers 1929-1970 (continued as *British Knitting Industry* October 1970-)

Knitting International 1894- (monthly) Leicester: Ferry Pickering (formerly called *Hosiery Trade Journal*)

For more technical detail there are the publications of the Hosiery and Allied Trades Research Association, particularly:

Hosiery Abstracts 1949- (monthly) Nottingham: HATRA.

Handframe knitting:

Rapley, Jane. 'Handframe knitting: the development of patterning and shaping', *Textile History* 6 1975 pp 18-52

Framework knitting:

Quilter, J. H. and Chamberlain, J. *Framework knitting and hosiery manufacture*. 1911-1914 Leicester: Hosiery Trade Journal 3 vols

Wheatley, B. 'Historical survey of warp knitting'. *Knitting Times* vol 43 no 17 25 April 1974 pp 104-108, 243 (1775 to present)

Stockings:

Eley, A. W. *Stockings, silk cotton, rayon, nylon.*
1953 Leicester: Hosiery Trade Journal
226pp illus. bibl.

'The stocking', *CIBA Review* no 106 October
1954

Love, D. M. 'The silken ladder', *DIA
Yearbook* 1968/1969 pp 39-42

Lace

General histories and surveys:

Bath, Virginia Charlotte. *Lace.* 1974
London: Studio Vista 320pp illus.

'Lace', *CIBA Review* no 73 April 1949

Jones, Mary Eirwen. *The romance of lace.*
1951 London: Staples 172pp illus. bibl.

Moore, N. *The lace book.* 1905 London:
Chapman and Hall 206pp illus.

Cole, Alan S. 'The art of lacemaking', *JSA*
September 9-30 1881 pp 769-776,
pp 779-789, pp 799-809

Jackson, Emily Nevill. *A history of handmade
lace with supplementary information by
E. Jesurum.* 1900 London: Gill 254pp
illus.

Palliser, Mrs. Bury. *History of lace, entirely
revised, rewritten and enlarged under the
editorship of M. Jourdain and Alice Dryden.*
1976 Wakefield: EP 536pp pl 150
(facsimile of 1903 Sampson Low
edition)

Wright, Thomas. *The romance of the
lace-pillow: being the history of lace-making.*
1977 London: Minet 272pp illus.
(facsimile of 1919 edition)

Studies of particular periods:

Wardle, Patricia. *Victorian lace.* 1968
London: Herbert Jenkins 286pp illus.
bibl.

*Report by Mr Alan Cole upon his visits to Irish
lacemaking and embroidery schools in 1897.*
1897 London: HMSO for Department of
Science and Art

Pfannschmidt, Ernst Erik. *Twentieth century
lace.* 1975 London: Mills and Boon
216pp illus.

Industrial aspects:

Felkin, William. 'The history and present
state of the machine-wrought lace trade',
JSA no 184 vol 4 1856 pp 475-485

Isemonger, Miss. 'Lace as a modern
industry', *JRSA* vol 56 May 29 1908
pp 702-716

Smith, Paul I. 'Design in the Nottingham
lace industry', *Design for Today* June 1935
pp 221-224

Whitehouse, L. 'The lace furnishing
industry. History, productions,
prospects', *Journals of the Textile Institute
Proceedings* vol 38 1947 pp 607-614

Harding, Keith. *Lace-furnishing manufacture.*
1952 London: Macmillan 198pp illus.

Local developments and studies:

Halls, Zillah. *Machine made lace in
Nottingham in the 18th and 19th century.*
1964 Nottingham City Museum and Art
Gallery 54pp illus. bibl.

Freeman, Charles. *Pillow lace in the East
Midlands.* 1958 Luton Museum and Art
Gallery 40 illus.

Horn, P. L. R. 'Pillow lacemaking in
Victorian England: the experience of
Oxfordshire', *Textile History* vol 3
December 1972 pp 100-116 bibl.

Inder, Pamela Mary. *Honiton lace.* 1971
Exeter Museum and Art Gallery 36pp
illus. bibl.

A very large bibliography:

Whiting, Gertrude. *A lace guide for makers
and collectors with bibliography and five
language nomenclature.* 1920 New York:
Dutton 415pp illus. (bibliography
pp 243-401 with 1958 entries)

Textile machinery

An understanding of some of the
mechanical developments involved in the
industrial processes is important. Useful
general surveys are:

English, Walter. *The textile industry. An
account of the early inventions of spinning,
weaving and knitting machines.* 1969
London: Longmans 242pp illus. bibl.
(basically the period 1589-1891)

Gilbert, K. R. *Textile machinery.* 1971
London: HMSO 35pp (Science Museum
illustrated booklet)

Watkins, George. *The textile mill engine vol
1. (to 1880) vol 2. (1880-1926).* 1970,
1971 Newton Abbot: David and
Charles 120pp, 112pp illus.

Brunnschweiler, David. 'Textile
machinery: competition raises standards',
Design 124 April 1959 pp 44-48

Dobson, Benjamin Palin. 'The story of
the evolution of the spinning machine',
1910 Manchester: Marsden 124pp

Urquhart, John W. 'Recent advances in
sewing machinery', *JSA* vol 35 Feb 25
1887 pp 332-346 illus.

Judkin, C. T. 'On stitching machines', *JSA*
vol 2 January 20 1854 pp 141-145

See also:

Appliances and mechanical equipment:
Sewing Machines *page 256*

4 Particular Applications

Furnishing

See also:

Interior Design *page 147*

General historical surveys:

'Furnishing fabrics', *CIBA Review* no 126 1958

Floud, Peter. 'Design review. A calendar of English furnishing textiles 1775-1905', *Architectural Review* vol 120 no 715 August 1956 pp 126-133

Dubois, Marius Joseph. *Curtains and draperies – a survey of the classic periods, translated by Violet M. Macdonald.* 1967 London: Batsford 252pp illus. (first published as *Rideaux et Draperies Classiques.* Covers period Renaissance to end of the 19th century)

Goodale, Sir Ernest. 'Furnishing fabrics of the past 200 years', *JRSA* vol 102 February 19 1954 pp 195-215 illus.

Other collections and surveys:

Templeton, J. and J. S. *Curtains and portières.* 1880 Glasgow: C. & W. Griggs (collection of chromolithographs)

Hunter, George Leland. *Decorative textiles; an illustrated book on coverings for furniture, walls and floors.* 1918 London: J. B. Lippincott 457pp 580 illus. bibl.

Walton, Allan. 'Furnishing textiles', *JRSA* vol 83 January 4 1935 pp 168-180 (a designer's point of view)

Sankey, M. and Reynolds, M. M. *Designing for printed furnishing fabrics.* 1938 London: Pitman

Merivale, Margaret. 'Furnishing fabrics. A selection of the newest Spring designs', *Studio* 117 1939 pp 116-123 13 illus.

Morton, Alastair. 'The birth of a furnishing fabric', *Art and Industry* March 1941 pp 92-98

Jackson, Holbrook. *Household fabrics, a paper read before the Royal Society of Arts on March 11 1942.* 1942 London: G. Barber 12pp (reissued from *JRSA* May 1942)

Buying for your home 1. Furnishing fabrics by Mary Shaw. 1946 London: Council of Industrial Design 32pp illus. bibl.

Goodale, E. W. 'Design in furnishing fabrics', *Journal of the Textile Institute Proceedings* vol 39 1948 pp 377-380

Maynard, Alister. 'The design policy behind "Old Glamis" fabrics', *Design* 57 September 1953 pp 22-25 (Donald Bros of Dundee)

Design for study no 8. Textiles and the consumer. A booklet about textiles for the home and personal wear. 1958 Loughborough: Education Department Cooperative Union 68pp bibl.

Smithells, Roger. *Fabrics in the home. Their place in the furnishing scheme.* 1950 London: Jenkins 239pp illus.

Taylor, Lucy D. *Know your fabrics: standard decorative textiles and their uses.* 1951 New York: Wiley 366pp illus.

Johnston, Dan. 'Surveys of Industry no 5. Furnishing fabrics', *Design* 153 September 1961 pp 42-58

Rankin, William Munn and Hildreth, E. M. *Textiles in the home.* 1966 London: Allman and Son 125pp illus.

Dress Fabrics

See also:

Costume and Fashion *page 238*

Beck, S. William. *The Draper's dictionary. A manual of textile fabrics: their history and application.* 1886 London: The Warehousemen and Draper's Journal 377pp

Ostick, Ernest (ed). *The Draper's encyclopaedia.* 1955 London: National Trade Press 523pp

Ironside, Janey. 'The materials of fashion', *Journal of the Textile Institute Proceedings* vol 51 1960 pp 507-514

Beaumont, Roberts and Hill, Walter George. *Dress, blouse and costume cloths: design and manufacture.* 1921 London: Pitman 579pp illus.

Settle, T. 'Dress fabrics', *JRSA* vol 83 December 7 1934 pp 78-88 (author editor of *Vogue* at the time)

These are just a few general references. For more specific research it is necessary to hunt through advertising and more topical and ephemeral articles at a particular time, eg:

Fraser, Grace Lovat. 'British dress fabrics for the new season', *Studio* 120 1940 pp 116-117 12 illus.

5 Carpets

See also:

Interior Design: Flooring *page 161*

Histories of British carpets and design:

Jacobs, Bertram. *The story of British carpets.* 1972 (second edition) London: Haymarket Publishing 212pp illus.

Tattershall, Creassey Edward Cecil. *A history of British carpets, from the introduction of the craft until the present day. New edition revised and enlarged by Stanley Reed.* 1966 Leigh on Sea: F. Lewis 139pp pl 176

Kendrick, A. F. 'British carpets', *JRSA* vol 67 January 24 1919 pp 136-145

Mellor, John Hanson. *The history and traditions of carpet design*. 1951 London: Wool Education Society (pamphlet)

A lot of information directly relevant to British designing is contained in the many broader histories:

Hubel, Reinhard G. *The book of carpets, translated by Katherine Watson*. 1971 London: Barrie and Jenkins 348pp illus. bibl. (translation of *Ullstein Teppichbuch*)

Farraday, Cornelia Bateman. *European and American carpets and rugs. A history of the hand-woven decorative floor coverings of Spain, France, Great Britain . . . and of the machine made carpets and rugs of modern Europe and of the United States*. 1929 Grand Rapids, Michigan: Dean Hicks 382pp pl 400

'The European carpet', *CIBA Review* no 23 1939

Kendrick, A. F. and Tattershall, C. E. C. *Handwoven carpets, Oriental and European*. 1973 (reprint) New York: Dover 388pp bibl. (first published 1922 Benn in 2 vols including 1 vol of plates)

Newton, C. S. 'History and tradition of European carpets', *Textile Institute Journal Proceedings* March 1947 P107-P117

Scobey, Joan. *Rugs and wall hangings: period designs and contemporary techniques. Original designs and illustrations by Marjorie Sablow*. 1974 New York: Dial Press 244pp illus. bibl.

Weeks, Jeanne G. and Treganowan, Donald. *Rugs and carpets of Europe and the western world*. 1969 Philadelphia: Chilton Book Company 251pp illus.

Windels, Fernand. *Le tapis; un art, une industrie*. 1935 Paris: Les Editions D'Antin 212pp illus.

Particular types of carpet:

'Machine-made carpets', *CIBA Review* 1961 issue 4

Jacobs, Bertram. *Axminster carpets (handmade) 1755-1957*. 1969 Leigh on Sea: F. Lewis 79pp pl 48

Mayorcas, Mondo J. *English needlework carpets, 16th to the 19th centuries*. 1963 Leigh on Sea: F. Lewis 62pp pl 94

Surveys of British carpet industry and design at particular times:

Dresser, Christopher. 'Carpets', in volume 6 of Bevan (ed). *British Manufacturing industries*. 1876 London 14 vols

Millar, Alexander. 'Design in modern carpets', *JSA* vol 42 April 20 1894 pp 433-451

Millar, Alexander. 'Practical carpet designing', *JSA* vol 43 March 20 1895 pp 442-462

Beaumont, Roberts. *Carpets and rugs*. 1924 London: Scott Greenwood 410pp

Mayers, Frederick J. *Carpet designs and designing*. 1934 Benfleet: F. Lewis 137pp pl 32

Tomrley, C. G. 'Contemporary British rug design', *Design for Today* April 1935 pp 135-139

Pevsner, Nikolaus. 'The designer in industry 1 Carpets', *Architectural Review* vol 79 1936 pp 185-190

Reeve, E. G. *Carpets; an enquiry into the present use of and future demand for carpets in working class households made for the Carpets working party of the Board of Trade*. 1946 London: HMSO 30pp (The Social Survey new series 82)

Robertson, Howard Robertson. 'Reconstruction and the home 8 Hangings and carpets', *Art and Industry* November 1945 pp 137-143

Tomkinson, M. W. 'Mid-century carpet design', *British Furnishing* 3 1950

Marchetti, Thomas. *About carpet design*. 1954 London: International Wool Secretariat 16pp

Ward, Neville and Austin, Frank. 'Design Review. Body carpets', *Architectural Review* vol 115 no 686 February 1954 pp 137-141

Johnston, Dan. 'A survey of British carpets', *Design* 87 March 1956 pp 26-44

Report to the Council of Industrial Design . . . on carpets. 1966 London: Council of Industrial Design 6pp

There are many shorter articles in *Studio, Architectural Review* and other illustrated journals showing selections of current or trend setting designs, eg:

'New designs for Wilton rugs by Marion V. Dorn and E. McKnight Kauffer', *Studio* vol 97 1929 pp 37-39 7 illus.

Manufacturing details and technical design:

Bartlett, J. Neville. *Carpeting the millions: the growth of Britain's carpet industry*. 1978 Edinburgh: Donald 296pp illus. bibl.

Whytock, Alexander. 'Recent improvements in carpet manufacture, their use and abuse; with a word on beauty and deformity in carpet design', *JSA* vol 4 no 170 1855 pp 240-252

Whytcock, Alexander. *Carpet manufacture and design*. 1856 Edinburgh: T. Constable 30pp

Brinton, Reginald Seymour. *Carpets*. 1919 London: Pitman 124pp illus. (Pitman's common commodities and industries series. Later editions 1939 and 1947)

Roth, A. B. 'A brief survey of carpet manufacture with special reference to the major inventions and notes on changes in design', *Journal of the Textile Institute Proceedings* vol 25 1934 P134-P143, P319-P320

Angus, G. B. 'Developments in methods of carpet manufacture', *Journal of the Textile Institute Proceedings* vol 47 1956 pp 670-684

Crossland, Arthur. *Modern carpet manufacture*. 1956 London: Columbine Press 184pp

Robinson, George. *Carpets and other textile floor coverings*. 1972 (second edition) Manchester: Textile Book Service 293pp illus. bibl. (first edition 1966)

Histories and studies of individual companies:

Benjoy, J. M. 'Design policy in industry. Carpet Trades Limited', *Design* 55 July 1953 pp 24-27 (especially postwar developments)

Sheridan, Michael. 'Experiment in carpet design', *Design* 17 May 1950 pp 5-7 (Crossley)

Stoddard, Arthur Francis & Co. *The carpet makers: one hundred years of designing and manufacturing carpets of quality*. 1962 Elderslie, Johnstone: Newman Neame 70pp illus.

Young, Fred H. *A century of carpet making 1839-1939*. 1939 Glasgow: James Templeton & Co 80pp

McKenna, Hugh. 'The problems of carpet design', *Design* 57 September 1953 pp 13-18 (Templetons)

Individual designers:

Morris, Barbara J. 'William Morris: his designs for carpets and tapestries', *Handweaver and Craftsman* Fall 1961 pp 18-21

A craft as well as an industry:

Collingwood, Peter. *The techniques of rug weaving*. 1968 London: Faber 527pp illus. bibl. (based on extensive research of old methods)

Journals that might be useful for more specific detail:

Carpet annual: yearbook and directory of the world's carpet industries and trade. 1935-1973 London: Continental Trade Press (includes colour photographs of new designs)

Carpet Review 1946- (monthly) London: British Continental Trade Press (useful historical survey 'Carpet making from Elizabeth I to Elizabeth II pp 11-21 in *Coronation Carpet Review* June 1953)

Flooring and carpet specifier: sponsoring journal of the National Flooring Centre. 1970- (monthly) London: Metcalf (continuation of *Flooring* 1956-1969)

A few interesting exhibitions:

Rugs and carpets. An international exhibition of contemporary industrial art. 1937 New York: Metropolitan Museum of Art 17pp bibl.

The British carpet exhibition. 1948 London: Carpet Manufacturers Executive Committee held at the Royal Horticultural Society's Hall

Teppiche von Arp, Bissier, Bissière, Calder, Ernst, Vieira da Silva, Klee, Laurens, Léger, Miro, Picasso. 1961 Basle: Galerie Beyeler illus. unpaginated

British carpets and designs: the modernist rug 1928-1938. 1975 Brighton: Royal Pavilion, Art Gallery and Museums

Linoleum

An important rival to the carpet that has hardly been studied at all, apart from the general introductions:

Jones, M. W. *A comprehensive account of the history and manufacture of floorcloth and linoleum; a paper read before the British section of the Society of the Chemical Industry at the Univeristy November 21 1918*. 1918 Bristol: Powell

Watson, Frederick. *The infancy and development of linoleum floorcloth*. 1925 London: Simpkin Marshall 55pp

Synopsis of the evolution of the linoleum industry n.d. Kirkcaldy: John Barry Ostlere & Shepherd Ltd

Plastics

See also:

Glass Fibre *page 225*

Textiles: Artificial Fibres *page 191*

Rubber *page 205*

'The production of plastics is one in which the technical processes are three quarters of the controlling influence in design . . . The designer should be in a position to examine with some critical ability the pronouncements of the engineer.'

H. J. Dow, head designer to British Xylonite Co Ltd. *Trend in Design in Everyday Things* no 1 1936 pp 81

General histories and surveys

Katz, Sylvia. *Plastics designs and materials.* 1978 London: Studio Vista 192pp illus. bibl.

Kaufman, Morris. *The first century of plastics. Celluloid and its sequel.* 1963 London: Plastics Institute 130pp illus.

Couzens, E. G. and Yarsley, V. E. *Plastics in the modern world. A completely revised edition of 'Plastics in the service of man'.* 1968 revised edition 356pp (first published as *Plastics* 1941. 4 editions, *Plastics in the service of man* 1956)

Imperial Chemical Industries. Plastics Division. *Landmarks in the plastics industry.* 1962 Birmingham: Imperial Chemical Industries 126pp illus.

Bawn, Cecil Edwin Henry. *Plastics: a centenary and an outlook. Sir Jesse Boot Foundation lecture 1962.* 1964 University of Nottingham 18pp

Gloag, John. 'The influence of plastics in design', *JRSA* vol 91 July 23 1943 pp 451-470 (basis of section 1 of *Plastics and Industrial Design*)

Swallow, J. C. 'The plastics industry', *JRSA* vol 99 no 4843 23 March 1951 pp 335-381 (1. Historical development, 2. Properties and fabrication, 3. The plastics industry)

Designing in plastics. 1970 London: Council of Industrial Design 25pp illus. (pp 8-21 case histories. To accompany the exhibition 'Plastics at The Design Centre')

Not forgetting America:

Dubois, John Harry. *Plastics history USA.* 1972 Boston: Cahners Books 447pp illus. bibl.

Exhibitions:

Newport, Roger. *Plastics antiques – an exhibition of plastics consumer products from the 1850s to the 1950s. Catalogue* (3 parts). 1977 London: British Institute of Plastics

Plastic as plastic, November 23 1968 to January 12 1969. 1969 New York: Museum of Contemporary Crafts. (includes a brief history of plastics)

There are also numerous technical exhibitions ranging from the International Plastics Exhibitions to individual company trade fairs/exhibitions.

Papers and surveys

Parkes, Alex. 'On the properties of parkesine and its application to the arts and manufactures', *JSA* vol 14 December 22 1865 pp 81-86

Thorp, Joseph. 'The new plastic materials', *Architectural Review* vol 73 January-June 1933 pp 259-260, pp 265-266

Landaver, Walter. 'Plastics', *Trend in Design of Everyday Things* no 2 1936 pp 75-91

Potter, H. V. 'Plastics as constructional and engineering materials', *JRSA* vol 88 June 14 1940 pp 673-693 illus.

Birrel, T. L. 'Modern plastic materials', *Art and Industry* August 1941 pp 41-46

Wornum, Grey. 'Plastic uses today and tomorrow', *Art and Industry* July 1941 pp 10-17

'Plastics survey', *Architects Journal* October 29 1942

Plastes. *Plastics and industry.* 1942 second edition London: Chapman and Hall 248pp illus. (first edition 1940)

Carr, J. Gordon. 'Plastics: characteristics and applications', *Architectural Record* June 1944

British Plastics Federation. *Plastics.* 1944 London: HMSO 47pp (Postwar Building Studies no 3)

Smith, Paul Ignatius. *Plastics for production.* 1946 (second edition) London: Chapman and Hall 216pp pl 13

Kaufman, M. 'New plastics and their application', *JRSA* vol XCIII 1945 pp 501

Sasso, John and Brown, Michael A. *Plastics in practice. A handbook of plastics applications.* 1945 London, New York: McGraw Hill 185pp illus.

Leyson, Capt. Burr W. *Plastics in the world of tomorrow.* 1947 London: Elek 95pp illus.

Doudney, E. J. 'Designing for plastics', *Art and industry* 1 January 1947 pp 22-26

Russell, R. D. 'What is wrong with plastics design?' *Art and Industry* October 1948 pp 148-153

Cooke, S. D. 'In search of better plastics', *Art and Industry* November 1948 pp 182-187

'Pitfalls and possibilities of plastics design. Comments by Paul Reilly in examples from the 1951 stock list', *Design* 17 May 1950 pp 12-15

Great Britain. Ministry of Supply. *Plastics*. 1952 HMSO for Technical Information and Documents Unit of the Dept of Scientific and Industrial Research 442pp illus. bibl.

Reilly, Paul. 'A decorative future for plastic laminates', *Design* 72 December 1954 pp 9-13

Woodfull, A. H. 'Nil desperandum', (product design service of British Industrial Plastics Ltd and its attitude to design competitions', *Art and Industry* August 1954 pp 50-53

Dunne, Gregory. 'Reinforced plastics', *Industrial Design* no 10 October 1958 pp 35-87

Allcott, Arnold. *Plastics today*. 1960 London: Oxford University Press 115pp pl 16

Edwards, Vivian. 'Surveys of Industry no 6. Plastics', *Design* 155 November 1961 pp 49-61

Southin, Shona. 'Survey. Decorative laminates', *Design* 187 July 1964 pp 34-39

'Plastics – design review', *Architectural Review* vol 141 no 844 June 1967 pp 453-456 illus.

Bradley, S. R. 'Why plastics is more than a household word', *Design* 261 September 1970 pp 30-32 (followed by examples of uses in Britain and Europe pp 33-39)

'Plastics in architecture and industry', *Design* 318 June 1975 pp 32-52

Important advances were made in Germany during the Second World War and are surveyed in:

The German plastics industry during the period 1939-1945. BIOS Surveys Report no 34 1954 HMSO

Individual company histories

Beresford-Evans, J. 'Design policy in industry. British Industrial Plastics Ltd', *Design* 60 December 1953 pp 11-17

Dingley, C. S. *The story of BIP (1894-1962)*. 1962 London: British Industrial Plastics Ltd 65pp illus.

Fielding, Thomas James. *The history of Bakelite Ltd* 1949 London: Bakelite Ltd 80pp

Merriam John. *Pioneering in plastics – the story of Xylonite*. 1976 Ipswich: East Anglian Magazine Ltd 120pp illus.

The Telecon Story 1850-1950. 1950 Telecon Ltd.

Ward-Jackson, Cyril Henry. *The 'Cellophane' story: origins of a British industrial group*. 1977 Bridgwater: British Cellophane Ltd 144pp illus.

Heyes, John. 'Getting it right first time', *Design* 217 January 1967 pp 46-53 (Ekco Plastics)

Particular types of plastics

Guides:

Brydson, J. D. *Plastics materials*. 1975 (third revised edition) London: Newnes-Butterworth 752pp (earlier edition 1966 Iliffe)

Redfarn, Cyril Aubrey. *A guide to plastics*. 1958 (second edition) London: Illiffe 150pp pl (includes useful sections on manufacturing and fabrication)

Brough, L. S. *Plastics*. 1973 London: Hutchinson 75pp

Kaufman, Morris. *Giant molecules: the technology of plastics, fibres and rubber*. 1968 London: Aldus 192pp

Penfold, Robin Charles. *A journalist's guide to plastics*. 1969 London: British Plastics Federation 28pp illus. bibl.

Smith, Paul Ignatius (comp). *Dictionary of plastics*. 1947 London: Hutchinson 168pp

Best, Alastair. 'Transparently beautiful', *Design* 239 November 1968 pp 26-31 (development of acrylic sheet)

Hirsch, Benjamin Woolf. *Nylon*. 1950 London: Plastics Institute

Kaufman, Morris. *History of PVC. Chemistry and industrial production of Polyvinyl Chloride*. 1969 London: Applied Science Publishers 204pp illus.

Teach, William Charles and Kessling, George C. *Polystyrene*. 1960 London: Chapman and Hall 176pp

Ogorkiewicz, R. M. (ed). *Thermoplastics. Properties and design*. 1974 New York: Wiley 260pp illus.

Orgorkiewicz, Richard M. *Engineering properties of thermoplastics*. 1970 New York: Wiley Interscience 328pp illus.

Fisher, Edwin George. *Extrusion of plastics*. 1958 London: Plastics Institute. (second edition 1964 London: Iliffe 271pp illus.)

Applications of plastics:

Gloag, John. *Plastics and industrial design, with a section on the different types of plastics and their uses by Grace Lovat Fraser*. 1945 London: Allen and Unwin 166pp pl 48

Newman, Thelma Rita. *Plastics as a design form*. 1972 Philadelphia: Chilton 348pp illus. bibl.

Beck, Ronald D. *Plastic product design.* 1970 New York: Van Nostrand Reinhold 480pp 400 illus.

Levy, Sidney and Dubois, J. Harry. *Plastics product design engineering handbook.* 1977 New York: Van Nostrand Reinhold 332pp

Millett, Robert. *Design and technology, plastics.* 1977 Oxford: Pergamon 102pp

Davis, Robert L. and Beck, Ronald D. *Applied plastic product design. A simplified presentation of plastic product design principles for use by engineers and students in plastics.* 1947 London: Chapman and Hall 285pp illus.

Quarmby, Arthur. *The plastics architect.* 1974 London: Pall Mall Press 224pp illus. (useful historical section)

Schools Council. Design and Craft Education Project. *Designing with plastics.* 1975 London: E. Arnold 48pp illus.

Dubois, J. H. and Pribble, W. I. *Plastics mold engineering.* 1946 New York: Van Nostrand Reinhold (1965 revised edition 450pp illus.)

Archer, L. Bruce. 'Design analysis 17. Cup and saucer in melamine', *Design* 134 February 1960 pp 44-47 (Brookes)

Hooper, Rodney. *Plastics for the home craftsman. Characteristics of the chief plastics, working them by hand and light machines, improvising equipment, original designs to make.* 1953 London: Evans 166pp (Woodworker Handbooks)

Sources of further technical information:

Yescombe, Edward Raymond. *Plastics and rubber: world sources of information.* 1976 Barking: Applied Science Publishers 547pp (earlier edition 1968)

Mark, Herman F. (ed). *Encyclopedia of polymer science and technology.* 1972 New York: Interscience 16 vols with supplement

Journals

Beetle Bulletin. House journal of the BIP Ltd. 1935- (sections on 'Plastics Antiques' 1975-1976)

British Plastics 1929-1972 London: Engineering, Chemical and Marine Press, then *Europlastics Monthly* 1972-1974, then *European Plastic News* 1974-

Modern Plastics 1925-1970, then *Modern Plastics International* 1971- McGraw Hill

Plastics 1937-July 1969 (monthly) London (incorporated in *British Plastics*)

Plastics Progress. Papers and discussions at the British Plastics Convention. 1951- London: Iliffe

RAPRA Abstracts. 1923- (bi-weekly) Shawbury: RAPRA

Materials related to plastics

See also:

Rubber *page 205*

Textiles: Artificial Fibres *page 191*

Church, Arthur Herbert. *Some minor arts; as practiced in England.* 1894 London: Seeley 82pp illus. (includes 'English work in pressed horn' by C. H. Read)

Pinto, Edward H. and Pinto, Eva. *Tunbridge and Scottish souvenir woodware, with chapters on Bois Durci and Pyrography.* 1977 London: Bell 144pp

Taylor, Wilmot. *The Sheffield horn industry.* 1927 Sheffield: J. W. Northend 72pp

Rubber

See also:

Furniture: Upholstery *page 182*

Plastics *page 202*

History

*Rubber exhibition (November 1934-April 1935).
A brief account of the history of rubber from its
source to the finished product and a descriptive
catalogue of the exhibits. Compiled by the
Rubber Growers Association.* 1934 London:
HMSO for Science Museum 43pp illus.

Institution of the Rubber Industry. *History of
the rubber industry. Edited by P. Schidrowitz
and T. R. Dawson.* 1952 Cambridge:
Heffer 406pp illus. bibl.

Geer, William C. *The reign of rubber.* 1922
London: Allen and Unwin 344pp illus.

Woodruff, William. *The rise of the British
rubber industry during the nineteenth century.*
1958 Liverpool University Press 246pp
(primarily a history of the Moulton Co of
Bradford on Avon)

Botas, Thomas. 'Cantor Lectures – second
course. India-rubber and gutta-perch
industries', *JSA* vol 28 1880 pp 753-763,
pp 773, pp 783-, pp 793-, pp 803-

Donnithorne, Audrey G. *British rubber
manufacturing. An economic study of
innovation.* 1958 London: G. Duckworth
159pp bibl.

Bauer, P. T. *The rubber industry. A study in
competition and monopoly.* 1948 London:
Longmans 404pp

An important company

Jennings, Paul. *Dunlop era. The works and
workings of the Dunlop Rubber Company.
With drawings by Edward Bawden.* 1961
Birmingham: Dunlop Rubber Co 157pp

Some technical aspects

Blow, C. M. (ed). *Rubber technology and
manufacture.* 1975 (second edition)
London: Newnes-Butterworth 552pp
illus. (1971 first edition published for the
Institution of the Rubber Industry)

'Rubber', *CIBA Review* no 87 1951

'Rubber, a review by Philip Scholberg',
Architectural Review vol 86 July-December
1939 pp 215-222

Goodyear, Charles. *Gum elastic and its
varieties, with a detailed account of its
applications and uses and of the discovery of
vulcanization.* 1853 New Haven: Yale
University Press 2 vols

Burgess, P. J. 'New uses for rubber', *JRSA*
vol 72 March 14 1924 pp 275-287 (latex,
crêpe)

Young, Dennis. 'Experiments with latex
foam', *Design* 49 January 1953 pp 20-22

Young, Dennis. *Latex foam handbook.* 1966
London: British Rubber Manufacturers
Association 21pp

Journals

Rubber and Plastics Age 1954-1969 London:
Rubber and Technical Press (monthly)
(previously *The Rubber Age* 1920-1944,
The Rubber Age and Synthetics 1945-1953)

Progress of Rubber Technology (annual)
Institute of the Rubber Industry (vol 33
1969-1970)

Rubber Developments 1948- (quarterly)
London: Natural Rubber Producers
Research Association. (Malayan Rubber
Fund Board)

Tyres

Du Cros, Arthur. *Wheels of fortune.* 1938
London: Chapman and Hall 316pp
(history of rubber tyres, especially
Dunlop)

Dunlop, J. B. *The history of the pneumatic tyre.*
1924 Dublin: Thom 103pp

Synthetic Rubber

See also:

Plastics *page 202*

Howard, Frank. *Buna rubber. The birth of an
industry.* 1947 New York: Van Nostrand
Reinhold 307pp

Not from trees alone: the story of synthetic rubber.
1968 London: British Association of
Rubber Manufacturers 51pp

Leather

See also:

Shoes *page 247*

Surveys

Concise statements of the distinctive
problems of leather design are provided by:

Waterer, John. 'The Industrial Designer
and Leather', *JRSA* vol 91 December 25
1942 pp 56-72 illus.

Waterer, John. *Leather: in Life, Art and
Industry.* 1946 London: Faber 320pp

Bembaron, Mrs D. M. 'Leather and its aesthetic possibilities', *JRSA* vol 83 December 28 1934 pp 147-161

A craft as well as an industry:

Exhibition of leathercraft through the ages: an historical survey. 1951 London: Museum of Leathercraft 68pp

Waterer, John W. 'Craftsmanship and leather', *JRSA* vol 96 March 26 1948 pp 245-260

Waterer, John. *Leather and Craftsmanship.* 1950 London: Faber 78pp 32 pl

Waterer, John. *Leather Craftsmanship.* 1968 London: Bell 121pp illus.

Francis-Lewis, Cecile. *The Art and Craft of Leatherwork.* 1928 London: Seeley Service 256pp pl 85 (interesting period piece on techniques)

Leather in the decorative arts. 1950 New York: Cooper Union Museum for the Arts of Decoration

Exhibition of ancient and modern leathercraft. 1948 London: Saddlery Manufacturers Association

Histories

The Industry and its Institutions:

Adam, Helen Pearl. *British leather: a record of achievement.* 1946 London: Batsford 82pp

Beeby, K. J. *The Wonderful Story of Leather.* n.d. London: The Leather Institute 18pp

Rimmer, W. G. 'Leeds leather industry in the nineteenth century', *Publications of the Thoresby Society* vol 46 no 108 1961 pp 119-164

Leathersellers Company. *Fine leather: the story of the British Chrome upper leather industry.* 1956

Mander, Charles Henry Waterland. *A descriptive and historical account of the Guild of Cordwainers.* 1931 London: privately published 222pp

British Leather Manufacturers Research Association. *The work of the BLMRA for the leather industry.* 1951 Egham: BLMRA 61pp

Contemporary Textbooks

Much valuable information on design problems can be followed only in contemporary accounts and textbooks of manufacturing methods:

Watt, Alexander. *Leather Manufacture: a practical handbook of tanning, currying and chrome leather dressing.* 1906 (fifth edition) London: Crosby Lockwood (first published 1885)

Proctor, Henry R. *The principles of leather manufacture.* 1922 (second edition) London: E. & F. N. Spon 696pp (first published 1903)

Moseley, G. C. *Leather goods manufacture: a practical guide to modern methods and processes.* 1947 London 334pp

Woodroffe, D. *Leather manufacture.* 1950 (second edition) Northampton 208pp (first published 1948)

'Leather industry survey', *The Times Weekly Review* 24 September 1953

Sharphouse, J. H. *The Leatherworker's handbook.* 1963 London: Leather Producers Association 234pp

Leathergoods

Surveys from the consumer's point of view:

McCullough, W. D. H. 'What men travel with', *Design for Today* August 1933 pp 140-142

Thompson, Peter and Gray, Ilse. 'A case for travel (Basic luggage design)', *Design* 239 November 1968 pp 34-39

Waterer, John. 'The Designer and his Problem. Leather and Travel Goods', *Design for Today* January 1936 pp 10-14 illus.

Waterer, John. 'Travellers' Baggage – past and present', *Art and Industry* July 1946 pp 12-19

Journals

Leather (weekly) Benn Bros

Leathergoods 1917- (monthly) London: Benn

Bibliographies

Northampton Public Libraries. *Catalogue of the Leather and Footwear Collections in the Northampton Central Reference Library and the Library of the Northampton Central College of Further Education.* 1968 Northampton County Borough 53pp

Leathers, hides and shoes; a bibliography. 1961 Washington: US Business and Defence Services Administration

Paper

Historical surveys of papermaking

Shorter, Alfred Harry. *Papermaking in the British Isles. An historical and geographical study.* 1971 Newton Abbot: David and Charles 272pp illus. bibl.

Coleman, D. C. *The British paper industry 1495-1860: a study in industrial growth.* 1958 Oxford: Clarendon Press 367pp illus. bibl. (Greenwood Press facsimile reprint 1976)

Both of these are more concerned with economic and industrial aspects while the following deal with the technical aspects:

Beadle, Clayton. 'The recent history of papermaking', *JSA* vol 46 March 18 1898 pp 405-417

Hunter, David. *Papermaking. The history and technique of an ancient craft.* 1947 New York: Knopf 421pp illus. bibl. pp 374-389

Newman, Thelma Rita. *Paper as art and craft: the complete book of the history and processes of the paper arts.* 1973 London: Allen and Unwin 308pp 755 illus.

'Paper', *CIBA Review* 72 February 1949

Machinery and techniques

Clapperton, Robert Henderson. *The paper-making machine. Its invention, evolution and development.* 1967 Oxford: Pergamon 365pp illus.

Simmonds, P. L. 'On new paper-making materials, and the progress of paper manufacture', *JSA* vol 19 January 27 1871 pp 171-179

Woolnough, C. W. 'The art of marbling', *JSA* vol 26 January 25 1878 pp 154-157

Other technical facets can also be found in some of the references on print design and bookbinding *page 114*.

Companies

Company histories can provide a useful introduction to changing uses and techniques of paper:

Evans, Joan. *The Endless Web. John Dickinson & Co Ltd. 1804-1954.* 1955 London: Cape 274pp illus.

One hundred and fifty years of papermaking. 1929 Edinburgh: Alec Cowan & Sons Ltd (includes samples)

Journals and Indexes

Paper-Maker 1880- (monthly)

Paper and Board Abstracts 1965 – Leatherhead: Printing Industry Research Association are useful for a spread of technical information. Packaging papers etc may also be detailed in the journals devised for packaging.

Bibliography

Overton, J. 'A bibliography of paper and papermaking', *The Book* no 4 1955

Uses of Paper

Dean, Frederick Ernest. *Paper.* 1966 London: Muller 124pp illus.

Paper for books. A comprehensive survey of the various types of paper used in book production. Illustrated by members of the Society of Industrial Artists. 1961 London: Robert Horne & Co 648pp

Mason, John. *Papermaking as an artistic craft.* 1960 London: Faber 96pp (reprinted 1963 Leicester: Twelve by Eight Press)

Paper and its uses. Handbook to a temporary exhibition June-December 1958 (by V. L. Morgan). 1958 Cardiff: National Museum 20pp illus.

Report on paper 1851. 1951 London: Spicers (reprint of Spicers publication of 1852)

Wallpaper

See also:

Textiles *page 184*

Interior Design: Decoration *page 159*

Histories:

Greysmith, Brenda. *Wallpaper.* 1976 London: Studio Vista 224pp illus. bibl.

Entwisle, Eric Arthur. *The book of wallpaper: a history and appreciation.* 1954 London: Barker (Kingsmead Reprint 1970) 151pp 74 illus.

Entwisle, E. A. 'Wallpaper and its history', *JRSA* vol 109 May 1961 pp 450-467

Sugden, Alan Victor and Edmondson, John Ludlam. *A history of English wallpaper 1509-1914.* 1925 London: Batsford 281pp illus. 70 col 190 bw (includes some mill records and details of designers)

Dowling, Henry G. 'Wallpaper: its history, production and possibilities', *JRSA* vol 73 May 15 1925 pp 586-604

Ackerman, Phyllis. *Wallpaper: its history, design and use.* 1923 London: Heinemann 268pp illus.

'Wall hangings', *CIBA Review* 3 November 1937

Particular periods:

Entwisle, Eric Arthur. *Wallpapers of the Victorian era.* 1964 Leigh on Sea: F. Lewis 72pp 100 illus.

Archer, Michael. 'Gothic wallpapers: an aspect of the Gothic Revival', *Apollo* August 1963 pp 109-116

Robinson, G. T. 'The Year's advance, in art manufactures no viii household decoration – wallpapers', *Art Journal* 11 1883

Jennings, Arthur Seymour. *Wallpapers and wall coverings*. 1903 London: Trade Papers Publishing Co 176pp

Jennings, Arthur Seymour. *Wallpaper decoration. A practical guide to the selection, use and hanging of wallpaper and other protable decorations.* 1907 London: Trade Papers Publishing Co

'Wallpaper. Its design and use in modern interiors by F. J. Harris', *Architectural Review* vol 86 1939 pp 253-258

'Design review. The future of wallpapers', *Architectural Review* vol 98 July 1945 pp 21-24

Mills, D. Dewar. 'Wallpapers (and Design review)', *Architectural Review* vol 112 October 1952 pp 219-226

Bendixson, T. M. P. 'Product development no 4: wallpapers', *Design* 158 1962 pp 44-48

A few designers:

Crane, Walter. 'Of wall papers', in *Arts and Crafts essays 1897*. Arts and Crafts Exhibition Society

Vallance, Aymer. 'An interview with Walter Crane. A designer of paper hangings', *Studio* vol 4 1898 pp 76-84 16 illus.

Floud, Peter. 'The wallpaper designs of William Morris', *Penrose Annual* 1960 vol 54 pp 41-45

William Morris wallpapers and chintzes, edited by Fiona Clark. 1973 London: Academy Editions 104pp 100 illus.

William Morris wallpapers and designs, edited by Andrew Melvin. 1971 London: Academy Editions 103pp

Floud, Peter. 'The wallpaper designs of C. F. A. Voysey', *Penrose Annual* 1958 vol 52

Some company histories:

A century of Sanderson 1860-1960. 1960 London: Sanderson & Sons Ltd 39pp illus. (section by Sacheverell Sitwell on wallpaper and chintz)

Carr, Richard. 'Sanderson: giant in the process of change', *Design Action DIA Yearbook* 1972 pp 13-15 illus.

Sugden, Alan Victor and Entwisle, Eric Arthur. *Potters of Darwen 1839-1939. A century of wallpaper printing by machinery.* 1939 Manchester: G. Falkner & Sons 120pp illus.

Lincrusta Walton (the Sunbury wall decoration) . . . Decorated Pattern Book. 1885 London: Frederick Walton & Co 105 col pl

Details:

Entwisle, Eric Arthur. 'Adding the finishing touches: wallpaper borders', *Country Life* 157 April 1975 pp 1006-1007

Entwisle, Eric Arthur. 'Animation and instruction; English commemorative wallpapers', *Country Life* January 17 1974 pp 92-94

Spence, T. R. 'Wall papers and stencilling', *JSA* vol 41 March 3 1893 pp 362-378 illus.

Exhibitions:

Exhibition of historical and British wallpapers, organised . . . for the British wallpaper industry (held at the) Suffolk Galleries. 1945 London: Central Institute of Art and Design 48pp

Historic wallpapers. 1972 Manchester: Whitworth Gallery (contains 'The origin and development of wallpaper' by Claire Crick)

A bibliography:

Entwisle, Eric Arthur. *A literary history of wallpaper.* 1960 London: Batsford 211pp pl 127 (year by year bibliography)

The influence of French design and techniques, both in the interwar period and through the great Exhibitions, should not be ignored:

Clouzot, Henri and Follot, Charles. *Histoire du papier peint en France.* 1935 Paris: Editions Charles Moreau 272pp pl 26

Clouzot, Henri. *Papiers peints et teintures modernes.* 1928 Paris: Editions Charles Massin 5pp pl 40

Follot, François. *Rapport du comité d'installation de la classe 68 Papiers peints à l'Exposition Universelle.* 1900 Paris

Papier mâché

As a decorative element of furniture and interior decoration, papier mâché proved quite important even into the nineteenth century:

Devoe, S. S. *English papier mâché of the Georgian and Victorian periods.* 1971 London: Barrie and Jenkins 191pp illus.

Jervis, Simon. *Nineteenth Century Papier-mâché.* 1973 London: HMSO 12pp illus. (Victoria and Albert Museum small colour book no 4)

King, Viva. 'English papier mâché', *Apollo* December 1962 pp 754-756

Riley, N. 'The top names in papier mâché', *The Antique Dealer and Collectors Guide* vol 22 no 11 June 1968 pp 80-83

Bielefeld, Charles F. *On the use of the improved papier-mâché in furniture, in the interior decoration of buildings and in works of art.* 1850 London: J. B. Nichols and Son

Bielefeld, Charles F. *Ornaments in every style of design, practically applicable to the interior of domestic and public buildings . . . manufactured in the improved papier mâché.* 1850 London: author 21pp pl 122

Aitken, W. C. 'Papier mâché manufacture', in Timmins, Samuel. *Birmingham resources and industrial history.* 1866 London

Dickinson, George. *English papier-mâché.* 1925 London: Courier Press 135pp pl 31

Ceramics

This section leans heavily towards the artistic and domestic aspects of ceramics. The literature is both accessible and plentiful, especially as this is a prime collector's area and the importance of the designer and craftsman has long been recognised. Industrial ceramics are touched on later, but are at present only accessible through an exceptionally technical literature.

General

Charleston, Robert Jesse (ed). *World ceramics: an illustrated history.* 1968 Feltham: Hamlyn 352pp illus.

Cooper, Emmanuel. *A history of pottery.* 1972 London: Longman 256pp

Hillier, Bevis. *Pottery and porcelain 1700-1914. England, Europe and North America. (The social history of decorative arts).* 1968 London: Weidenfeld and Nicolson 386pp

Litchfield, Frederick. *Pottery and porcelain.* 1963 (sixth revised edition) London: Black 356pp (first edition 1879 London: Bickers & Son 215pp)

Mitchell, Lane. *Ceramics – from Stone Age to Space Age.* 1963 New York: McGraw Hill 128pp illus. bibl.

Savage, George and Newman, Harold. *An illustrated dictionary of ceramics.* 1974 London: Thames and Hudson 320pp 599 illus.

Binns, C. F. 'The elements of beauty in ceramics', *JSA* vol 42 April 6 1894 pp 409-417

Burton, Joseph. 'Quality in pottery', *JRSA* vol 78 January 24 1930 pp 279-298

Lane, Arthur. *Style in pottery.* 1973 new edition London: Faber 80pp illus. (first edition 1948 Oxford University Press)

Wildenhain, Marguerite. *Pottery: form and expression.* 1962 New York: Reinhold for the American Craftsmen's Council 157pp illus.

Artistic and Domestic Applications

Godden, Geoffrey Arthur. *British pottery: an illustrated guide.* 1974 London: Barrie & Jenkins 452pp 607 illus.

Mankowitz, Wolf and Haggar, Reginald G. *The concise encyclopaedia of English pottery and porcelain.* 1957 London: André Deutsch 336pp illus.

Fisher, Stanley William. *English ceramics: earthenware, Delft, stoneware, cream-ware, porcelain; including a section on Welsh factories.* 1966 London: Ward Lock 256pp illus.

Godden, Geoffrey. *An illustrated encyclopedia of British pottery and porcelain.* 1966 London: Barrie and Jenkins 416pp 650 illus.

Honey, William Bowyer. *English pottery and porcelain (revised by R. J. Charleston)* 1969 (sixth edition) London: Black 285pp (Library of English Art series)

Lewis, Griselda. *Collector's history of English pottery.* 1977 (second edition) London: Barrie and Jenkins 224pp chiefly illus. (first edition 1969 Studio Vista)

Thomas, John. 'Pottery in England's industrial history', *JRSA* vol 84 March 27 1936 pp 521-546

Wills, Geoffrey. 'English pottery and porcelain', 1969 London: Guinness 404pp illus.

Particular Periods
NINETEENTH CENTURY

Wakefield, Hugh. *Victorian pottery.* 1962 London: Jenkins 208pp illus. bibl.

Godden, Geoffrey Arthur. *Jewitt's Ceramic art of Great Britain 1800-1900: being a revised and expanded edition of those parts of The ceramic art of Great Britain by Llewellyn Jewitt FSA, dealing with the nineteenth century. (revised by Geoffrey A. Godden).*

1972 London: Barrie and Jenkins 282pp illus. bibl.

Bemrose, Geoffrey. _Nineteenth century English pottery and porcelain._ 1952 London: Faber 57pp

Blacker, James F. _Nineteenth century English ceramic art . . . with over 1200 examples._ 1911 London: Stanley Paul 534pp

Haslam, Malcolm. _English art pottery 1865-1915._ 1975 Woodbridge: Antique Collectors' Club 214pp 236 illus.

Burton, William. 'Cantor Lectures 5th series. Material and design in pottery', _JSA_ vol 45 October 8 1897 pp 1127-1132; October 15 1897 pp 1139-1148; October 22 1897 pp 1157-1161

Atterbury, Paul. 'Women in late Victorian ceramics', _Antique Dealer and Collector's Guide_ August 1977 pp 72-75 illus.

Hughes, George Bernard. _Victorian pottery and porcelain._ 1959 London: Country Life 184pp

Shinn, Charles and Dorrie. _The illustrated guide to Victorian Parian china._ 1971 London: Barrie and Jenkins 125pp pl 99 bibl.

Thomas, E. Lloyd. _Victorian art pottery._ 1974 London: Guildart 238pp illus.

Church, Prof. A. H. 'Cantor Lectures 1st course. Some points of contact between the scientific and artistic aspects of pottery and porcelain', _JSA_ vol 29 December 24 1880 pp 85-88; December 31 1880 pp 95-98; anuary 1 1881 pp 105-109; January 14 1881 pp 126-129; January 21 1881 pp 140-143

Smaller periods:

Wakefield, Hugh. 'Pottery, porcelain and glass', pp 85-100 in Edwards, Ralph and Ramsey L. G. G. (eds). _The early Victorian period 1830-1860._ 1958 London: Connoisseur 180pp

TWENTIETH CENTURY

Haslam, Malcolm. 'Some Vorticist pottery', _Connoisseur_ vol 190 no 764 October 1975 pp 98-102

Europäische Keramik des Jugendstils, Modern Style, Art Nouveau. 1974 Düsseldorf: Hetjens Museum

Between the wars:

Adams, John. 'Modern British pottery', _Architectural Review_ vol 59 January-June 1926 pp 190-193 illus.

Trethowan, Harry. 'Modern industrial potters', _Studio_ vol 96 1928 pp 176-182 illus.

Maxwell, H. W. 'Modern tendencies in the Staffordshire potteries', _Studio_ vol 98 pp 566-572 illus.

Trethowan, Harry. 'Pottery and glassware', _Studio Yearbook_ 1929 pp 151-154

Stabler, Harold. 'The use and abuse of Faience', _Architectural Review_ vol 59 January-June 1926 pp 188-189

Gaunt, William. 'Design in pottery: the position of the artist', _Commercial Art_ vol 18 February 1935 pp 80

Shand, P. Morton. 'Pottery, glass, table and kitchen ware. Decoration and ornament', _Studio Yearbook_ 1931 pp 123-164

Trethowan, Harry. 'Modern British pottery design', _Studio_ vol 106 1933 pp 181-188 illus.

Victoria and Albert Museum. _English pottery old and new (Picture book of an exhibition arranged in collaboration with the Council for Art and Industry held in 1935)._ 1936 London: HMSO 56pp

Rena, Maurice. 'The English pottery industry', _Studio_ vol 112 1936 pp 266-277 illus.

Forsyth, Gordon M. 'British art in British pottery', _JRSA_ vol 83 December 14 1934 pp 104-115

Copeland, Mrs Ronald. 'Pottery and what the public wants today', _JRSA_ vol 82 July 13 1934 pp 904-918 illus.

'British designs of the thirties', _Ceramics Monthly_ 24 November 1977 pp 46-47

'British pottery of today', _Studio_ vol 102 1931 pp 366-377 illus.

Wartime and postwar:

Trethowan, Harry. 'Utility pottery', _Studio_ vol 125 1943 pp 48-50 illus.

Fraser, Grace Lovat. 'Design and decoration. The art of the potter', _Studio_ vol 122 1941 pp 104-108 illus.

Bunt, Cyril G. E. _British potters and pottery today._ 1956 Leigh-on-Sea: F. Lewis 78pp illus.

Beard, Geoffrey William. _Modern ceramics._ 1969 London: Studio Vista 167pp illus.

Birks, Tony. _Art of the modern potter._ 1976 (second revised edition) London: Country Life 208pp illus. (first edition 1967)

Cooper, Emmanuel and Lewenstein, Eileen (eds). _New ceramics._ 1974 London: Studio Vista 224pp illus. bibl.

Casson, Michael. _Pottery in Britain today._ 1967 London: Tiranti 16pp 243 illus. (Concepts in Art series)

Dalton, William Bower. _Craftmanship and design in pottery._ 1957 London: Pitman 113pp

Farr, Michael. 'The potteries. Design policy and practice', _Design_ 48 December 1952 pp 7-15

Hetteš, Karel and Rada, Pravoslav. *Modern ceramics, pottery and porcelain of the world.* 1966 London: Spring Books 205pp (University Microfilms Books in Demand)

Pottery Gazette and Glass Trade Review. *Making pottery and glassware in Britain.* Reprinted from the *Pottery Gazette and Glass Trade Review* 1954 London: Scott Greenwood 96pp

Pottery and textiles 1920-1952, made in Great Britain by artist-craftsmen. Sponsored by the Arts Department, Dartington Hall, in collaboration with the Arts Council of Great Britain. 1952 Dartington: Dartington Hall 35pp illus.

Digby, George Frederick Wingfield. *The work of the modern potter in England.* 1952 London: John Murray 110pp pl 64

Trethowan, Harry. 'Review of the Pottery Section of "Britain can make it" ', *Art and Industry* November 1946 pp 130-135

Types of Ceramics

Hamer, Frank. *The potter's dictionary of materials and techniques.* 1975 London: Pitman 350pp illus.

EARTHENWARE

Hughes, G. Bernard. *English and Scottish earthenware.* 1961 London: Lutterworth Press 238pp

Sandeman, Albert Ernest. *Notes on the manufacture of earthenware.* 1917 London: Virtue, Lockwood 371pp

Hayden, Arthur. *Chats on English earthenware.* 1919 London: T. Fisher Unwin 496pp illus.

PORCELAIN

Burton, William. *A general history of porcelain.* 1921 London: Cassell 2 vols

Burton, William. *History and description of English porcelain.* 1902 New York: Wessels Co 277pp 81 illus. (1972 EP Reprint)

Burton, William. *Porcelain. Its nature, art and manufacture.* 1906 London: Batsford 264pp pl 50

Dillon, Edward. *Porcelain.* 1904 London: Methuen 419pp 49 pl

Godden, Geoffrey A. *British porcelain: an illustrated guide.* 1974 London: Barrie and Jenkins 451pp illus.

Battie, David. *Price guide to nineteenth and twentieth century porcelain.* 1975 Woodbridge: Antique Collectors' Club 530pp illus.

Godden, Geoffrey Arthur. *Victorian porcelain.* 1961 London: Herbert Jenkins 222pp illus.

Reynolds, Ernest. *Collecting Victorian porcelain.* 1966 London: Arco 128pp

STONEWARE

Blacker, James F. *The ABC of English salt-glaze stoneware from Dwight to Doulton.* 1923 London: Stanley Paul 243pp illus.

Barber, Edwin Atlee. *Salt-glazed stoneware.* 1907 London: Hodder and Stoughton 32pp

Mountford, Arnold Robert. *The illustrated guide to Staffordshire salt-glazed stoneware.* 1971 London: Barrie and Jenkins 88pp pl 136 bibl.

The revival of salt-glaze stoneware pottery, by Ernest Marsh. 1927 London: Fine Art Society

Matthews, Maleen. 'Worth preserving – stoneware jam-jars', *Art and Antiques Weekly* September 10 1977 vol 29 no 4 pp 31-33 illus.

Finish and Decoration

DECORATION

Clarke, Harold George. *Under-glaze colour picture prints on Staffordshire pottery. (The pictorial pot lid book). An account of their origin, and a descriptive catalogue, compiled from the author's and Lambert and Jenkins collections.* 1955 London: Courier Press 293pp

Hainbach, Rudolf. *Pottery decorating: a description of all the processes for decorating pottery and porcelain, translated from the German by Charles Salter.* 1924 (second edition) London: Scott Greenwood and Son 248pp (first edition 1907)

Shaw, Kenneth. *Ceramic colours and pottery decoration: a manual for the chemist, technologist, factory manager, craftsman potter and student.* 1968 London: Maclaren 189pp pl 26 (first edition 1912)

Turner, William. *Transfer printing on enamel, porcelain and pottery. Its origin and development in the United Kingdom.* 1907 London: Chapman and Hall 175pp illus.

'Modern transfers for pottery', *Design* 68 August 1954 pp 21-23

Godden, R. 'Eric Ravilious as a designer', *Architectural Review* vol 94 December 1943 pp 155-162 illus.

'A graphic artist for pottery (Richard Guyatt)', *Design* 61 January 1954 pp 16-19

GLAZES

Burton, William. 'Crystalline glazes and their application to the decoration of pottery', *JSA* vol 52 May 27 1904 pp 595-603

Green, David. *Understanding pottery glazes.* 1963 London: Faber 128pp illus.

Shaw, Kenneth. *Ceramic glazes.* 1971 London: Elsevier 166pp illus. bibl.

Rhodes, Daniel. *Clay and glazes for the potter.* 1973 (second revised edition) London: Pitman 376pp illus. (first edition 1958)

Rix, Wilton P. 'Pottery glazes: their classification and decorative value in ceramic design', *JSA* vol 41 February 17 1893 pp 295-307 illus.

Singer, Felix and German, W. L. *Ceramic glazes.* 1960 (revised edition) London: Borax Consolidated 112pp

Chappell, James. *The potter's complete book of clay and glazes.* 1977 London: Pitman 448pp illus.

Tin glaze:

Smith, Alan Caiger. *Tin glaze pottery in Europe and the Islamic world.* 1973 London: Faber 236pp maps illus.

CREAMWARE

Towner, Donald. *Creamware.* 1978 London: Faber illus. (extensive revision of *English cream-coloured earthenware* first published 1957)

Towner, Donald C. *English cream-coloured earthenware.* 1957 London: Faber 122pp illus.

LUSTREWARE

Burton, William. 'Lustre pottery'. *JRSA* vol 55 June 7 1907 pp 756-770

Fisher, Stanley. 'English lustreware'. *Antique Dealer and Collector's Guide* July 1972 pp 63-67 illus.

Potters

Rose, Muriel. *Artist potters in England.* 1970 London: Faber 64pp illus. (previous edition 1955) (Faber monographs on pottery and porcelain)

Coysh, A. W. *British art pottery 1870-1940.* 1976 Newton Abbot: David and Charles 96pp illus. bibl.

Rothschild, Henry W. 'British potters today I and II', *Studio* vol 159 May 1960, and June 1960

Cameron, Elizabeth and Lewis, Phillippa (eds). *Potters on pottery.* 1976 London: Evans 168pp illus.

Craftsmen Potters Association. *Potters: an illustrated directory of the work of full members of the Craftsmen Potters Association of Great Britain (and) a guide to pottery training.* 1975 London: The Association 94pp illus. bibl.

English artist-potters 1913-1960. 1967 London: British Council

English artist-potters 1870-1910. 1973 Manchester: Whitworth Art Gallery

Casson, Michael. *The craft of the potter, edited by Anna Jackson.* 1977 London: BBC 128pp illus.

MICHAEL CARDEW

Cardew, Michael. *Pioneer pottery.* 1969 London: Longman 327pp illus. bibl.

Michael Cardew. A collection of essays. Edited by John Houston. 1976 London: Crafts Advisory Committee 80pp 49 illus.

Marsh, Ernest. 'Michael Ambrose Cardew, potter of Winchcombe, Gloucestershire', *Apollo* vol 37 May 1943 pp 129-131

JAMES and RALPH CLEWS

Stefano, F. Jnr. 'James and Ralph Clews, nineteenth century potters; the English experience', *Antiques* vol 105 February 1974 pp 324-328

CLARICE CLIFF

Shields, Peter Wentworth and Johnson, Kay. *Clarice Cliff.* 1976 London: private printing (L'Odeon) 81pp

'Clarice Cliff', *Art and Antiques Weekly* May 8 1976 pp 24-25

WILLIAM DE MORGAN

Clayton-Stamm, M. D. E. 'William de Morgan and his pottery', *Apollo* January 1967 pp 34-38 illus.

De Morgan, William. 'Lustre ware', *JSA* vol 40 June 24 1892 pp 756-767

Gaunt, William and Clayton-Stamm, M. D. E. *William de Morgan.* 1971 London: Studio Vista 176pp illus. bibl.

Pinkham, Roger. *Catalogue of pottery by William de Morgan.* 1973 London: HMSO 115pp illus. bibl. (Victoria and Albert Museum publication)

Sparrow, W. Shaw. 'William de Morgan and his pottery. Part 1', *Studio* vol 17 1899 pp 222-231 illus.

Stirling, Anna Maria Diana Wilhelmina. *William de Morgan and his wife.* 1922 London: Butterworth 403pp illus.

BERNARD LEACH

Leach, Bernard. *A potter's book.* 1976 new edition London: Faber 294pp illus. (first edition 1940)

Cardew, Michael. 'The pottery of Mr Bernard Leach', *Studio* vol 90 1925 pp 298-301 illus.

Leach, Bernard. *Beyond East and West.* 1978 London: Faber illus.

Leach, Bernard. *A potter's outlook.* 1929 London: New Handworkers' Gallery (Handworkers' pamphlets no 3)

Leach, Bernard. *A potter's portfolio, a selection of fine pots.* 1951 London: Lund Humphries 28pp pl 60

Leach, Bernard. *A potter's work.* 1967 London: Evelyn, Adams and Mackay 128pp illus.

Digby, G. Wingfield. 'Bernard Leach, fifty years a potter' (with bibliography), *Museums Journal* vol 60 January 1961

WILLIAM and WALTER MOORCROFT

Dennis, Richard. *William and Walter Moorcroft 1897-1973: catalogues of an exhibition of pottery at the Fine Art Society, December 4 to December 15 1973 at 148 New Bond Street, London.* 1973 London: R. Dennis 128pp 186 illus.

Moorcroft, B. 'Craftsmanship in the machine age: William Moorcroft, artist and potter', *Country Life* vol 157 January 23 1975 pp 191-193

William Moorcroft 1872-1945. 1972 London: Victoria and Albert Museum (circulation)

WILLIAM STAITE MURRAY

Marsh, Ernest, 'W. Staite Murray, studio potter of Bray, Berkshire', *Apollo* vol 39 April 1944 pp 107-109

Stoneware pottery by William Staite Murray. 1958 London: Leicester Galleries

Individual Potteries

COUNTRY

Brears, Peter C. D. *Collector's book of English country pottery.* 1974 Newton Abbot: David and Charles 207pp illus. bibl.

Brears, Peter C. D. *The English country pottery. Its history and techniques.* 1971 Newton Abbot: David and Charles 276pp illus.

Haggar, Reginald George. *English country pottery.* 1950 London: Phoenix House 160pp pl 32 bibl.

Liddell, P. C. 'The potter's art in the village (Arts and Crafts movement in Essex and Surrey)', *Treasury* May 1919 pp 141-146

BELLEEK

McCrum, S. *Belleek pottery.* 1972 Belfast: Ulster Museum

Nagel, J. D. 'Belleek porcelain', *Antiques* February 1953 pp 132-134

CASTLE HEDINGHAM POTTERY

Bradley, R. J. 'The story of Castle Hedingham pottery 1837-1905', *Connoisseur* vol 167 February-April 1968 pp 77-83, pp 152-157, pp 210-216 illus. bibl.

COALPORT AND COALBROOKDALE

Godden, Geoffrey A. *Coalport and Coalbrookdale porcelains.* 1970 London: Barrie and Jenkins 176pp illus.

DAVENPORT

Lockett, Terence A. *Davenport pottery and porcelain 1794-1887.* 1972 Newton Abbot: David and Charles 112pp illus.

DELLA ROBBIA

Rix, Wilton P. 'Modern decorative wares', *Art Journal* 1905 pp 113-118 illus. (Della Robbia pottery)

Archer, Michael. 'The Della Robbia of Liverpool', *Country Life Annual* 1968 pp 70-73

CROWN DERBY

(Crown Derby founded 1876, styled Royal Crown Derby Porcelain Company from 1890)

Gilhespy, Frank Brayshaw. *Crown Derby porcelain.* 1951 Leigh on Sea: F. Lewis 108pp illus. bibl.

Gilhespy, Frank Brayshaw. *Royal Crown Derby china from 1876 to the present day.* 1964 London: Charles Skilton 87pp illus. bibl.

Twitchett, John and Bailey, B. *Royal Crown Derby.* 1976 London: Barrie and Jenkins 224pp 200 illus.

ELTON

Ruck, P. 'A Victorian squire and his eccentric pottery', *Art and Antiques Weekly* March 27 1976 pp 18-22

Holland, William Fishley. *Fifty years a potter (an autobiography).* 1958 Tring: Pottery Quarterly 105pp illus. (describes Sir Edward Elton's pottery)

Quentin, Charles. 'Elton ware', *Art Journal* 1901 pp 374-376 illus.

GOSS

(founded 1858, closed 1940, sold by the Goss family 1929)

Emery, Norman. *William Henry Goss and Goss Heraldic china.* 1969 Stoke on Trent: Public Library 44 leaves illus. (Horace Barks Reference Library and Information Service. Occasional Paper 1)

Rees, Diana and Cawley, Marjorie G. *A pictorial encyclopaedia of Goss china.* 1970 Newport: Ceramic Book Co 29pp pl 65

LINTHORPE

Pinkham, Roger. 'A tale of three potteries (Linthorpe, Bretby and Swadlincote Art Potteries)', *Antique Dealer and Collector's Guide* September 1977 pp 80-84 illus.

Levine, J. R. A. *Linthorpe pottery: an interim report*. 1970 Middlesbrough: Teesside Museums

Linthorpe pottery. 1970 Billingham: Art Gallery

Linthorpe pottery 1879-1889: the Morris Roberts collection. 1962 Eccles: Monks Hall Museum

MARTINWARE

Beard, Charles R. *Catalogue of the collection of Martinware formed by Mr Frederick John Nettlefold, together with a short history of the firm of R. W. Martin and Brothers of Southall*. 1936 London: privately printed 252pp pl 69 bibl.

Marsh, Ernest. 'The Martin brothers, studio potters of London and Southall', *Apollo* vol 39-40. July-December 1944 pp 94-96, pp 127-129, pp 132

'Some recent developments in the pottery ware of the Martin Brothers', *Studio* vol 42 1908 pp 109-115 illus.

Ullman, Anne. 'The genius of the Martin Brothers pottery', *Art and Design* vol 2 no 3 January 1948 pp 74-78

Martin ware. 1971 London: Victoria and Albert Museum (circulation)

Paffard, Michael. 'Pottery of four dedicated brothers', *Country Life* March 23 1961 pp 652-654 illus.

Greenslade, Sidney Kyffin. *A note on the work of the Martin brothers. The salt-glazed stoneware of the Martin Brothers*. 1907 London

MASON

Godden, Geoffrey Arthur. *The illustrated guide to Mason's Patent Ironstone: the related ware – 'stone china', 'new stone', 'granite china' – and their manufacturers*. 1971 London: Barrie and Jenkins 175pp 88 pl bibl.

Haggar, Reginald George. *The Masons of Lane Delph and the origin of Masons Patent Ironstone china*. 1952 London: George L. Ashworth & Brothers 104pp

Haggar, Reginald and Adams, Elizabeth. *Mason porcelain and iron-stone 1796-1853*. 1977 London: Faber 134pp illus.

LAMBETH

Sparkes, J. 'On the further development of the fine art section of Lambeth pottery', *JSA* vol 28 March 12 1880 pp 344-357 illus.

Sparkes, John. 'On some recent inventions and applications of Lambeth stoneware, terracotta, and other pottery for internal and external decorations', *JSA* vol 22 May 1 1874 pp 557-568 illus.

Thomas, E. Lloyd. 'Forgotten artists of Lambeth Ware', *Country Life* vol 146 July 24 1969 pp 227-229 illus.

MINTON

Minton 1798-1910 (Catalogue of an exhibition . . . by Elizabeth Aslin and Paul Atterbury. 1976 London: Victoria and Albert Museum 111pp illus. bibl.

Godden, Geoffrey. 'Artists at Minton', *Apollo* December 1962 pp 797-798 illus.

Wyatt, M. Digby. 'On the influence exercised on ceramic manufacturers by the late Mr Herbert Minton', *JSA* vol 6 1858 pp 441-452

POOLE

Poole pottery. The first hundred years, edited from a script by Lucien Myers. 1973 Poole: Poole Pottery 46pp illus.

Carter, Stabler and Adams. *Poole pottery*. 1924 Poole: Poole Pottery 12pp

ROYAL DOULTON

Gosse, Sir Edmund. *Sir Henry Doulton, edited by Desmond Eyles*. 1970 London: Hutchinson 218pp illus.

Dennis, Richard. *Doulton pottery from the Lambeth and Burslem studios 1873-1939 part II: catalogue of an exhibition of pottery at the Fine Art Society 24 June to 5 July 1975*. 1975 London: R. Dennis 164pp 154 illus.

Doulton stoneware and terracotta 1870-1925 part I: catalogue of an exhibition held at Richard Dennis's shop. 1971 London: Richard Dennis 255pp illus.

Eyles, Desmond. *The Doulton Lambeth wares*. 1975 London: Hutchinson 179pp 245 illus.

Ceramics in Art and Industry 1939-1953 (nos 2-7) London: Doulton & Co

Eyles, Desmond. *Royal Doulton 1815-1965: the rise and expansion of the Royal Doulton potteries*. 1965 London: Hutchinson 208pp

'Modern British manufacturers: the Royal Doulton pottery', *Studio* vol 97 1929 pp 263-268 illus.

'Royal Doulton potteries', *Ceramics in Art and Industry* no 7 1953 (special edition)

ROYAL LANCASTRIAN

Lomax, Abraham. *Royal Lancastrian pottery 1900-1938: its achievements and makers*. 1957 Bolton: Lomax 153pp illus.

Thornton, Lynne. 'Pilkington's "Royal Lancastrian" ironstone pottery', *Connoisseur* vol 174 no 699 May 1970 pp 10-14 illus.

The new Lancastrian pottery (by Pilkingtons Ltd). Notes descriptive of the first exhibition of the new Lancastrian pottery. 1904 London: Graves Galleries

ROYAL WORCESTER

Sandon, Henry. *Royal Worcester porcelain, from 1862 to the present day.* 1975 (second edition) London: Barrie and Jenkins 294pp 237 illus. (previous edition 1963)

A collection of Worcester porcelain on loan from F. C. Dykes Esq. 1924 Manchester: City Art Gallery (Chadwyck Healey Microfiche)

Hobson, Robert Lockhart. *Worcester porcelain: a description of the ware from the Wall period to the present day.* 1910 London: Quaritch 208pp illus.

RUSKIN

Bennett, Ian. 'Ruskin pottery', *Connoisseur* vol 184 no 741 November 1973 pp 180-185

Powell, L. B. 'Chinese influence on Ruskin pottery', *Art Collection* January 1974 pp 78-80

Ruston, James H. *Ruskin pottery.* 1975 West Bromwich: Metropolitan Borough of Sandwell 59pp illus.

SPODE

Spode. Never out of fashion. Notes on the history and manufacture of Spode. 1975 Stoke on Trent: Spode Ltd illus. bibl.

200 years of Spode. 1970 London: Royal Academy of Art 91pp

Hayden, Arthur H. *Spode and his successors. A history of the Pottery, Stoke-on-Trent, 1765-1865.* 1925 London: Cassell 204pp illus.

Spode, Copeland, 1765-1965: Steingut und Porzellan. 1965 Frankfurt am Main: Museum für Kunsthandwerk

Thorpe, W. A. 'House of Spode', *Apollo* vol 17 April 1933 pp 120-129

Specimens of Spode ware, designed by Erling B. Olsen. Manufactured by W. T. Copeland and Sons Ltd. 1937 London: Brygos Gallery

WEDGWOOD

Kelly, Alison. *The story of Wedgwood.* 1975 London: Faber 144pp illus.

Kelly, Alison. *Wedgwood ware.* 1970 London: Ward Lock 96pp illus.

Lawrence, H. 'Wedgwood & Co', *Connoisseur* vol 186 June 1974 pp 110-115

Mankowitz, Wolf. *Wedgwood.* 1966 London: Batsford 284pp illus. (first edition 1953)

Lyon, Peter. 'Growth in the Wedgwood tradition', *Design* 88 April 1956 pp 36-40

Powell, Alfred. 'New Wedgwood pottery', *Studio* vol 98 1929 pp 875-880 illus.

Wedgwood bi-centenary exhibition, 1759-1959. 1959 London: Victoria and Albert Museum

Wedgwood ware, held in commemoration of the bicentenary of the birth of Josiah Wedgwood (1730-1795). 1930 London: Victoria and Albert Museum

Wedgwood, a living tradition. Catalogue by Hensleigh Wedgwood and John Meredith Graham. 1948 New York: Brooklyn Institute of Arts and Sciences 118pp

Reilly, D. R. 'Wedgwood and the two-edged sword of success', *DIA Yearbook* 1967/1968 pp 52-55

Ullstein, Gabrielle. 'Patrons of design. Josiah Wedgwood', *Design* 35 November 1951 pp 4-9 illus.

Proceedings of the Wedgwood Society 1956- London: Batsford

Wedgwood Review 1957- (3 per year) Barlaston: Wedgwood

Burton, William. *Josiah Wedgwood and his pottery.* 1922 London: Cassell & Co 195pp illus.

'Wedgwoods: pioneers in industrial art', *Art and Industry* July 1951 pp 22-27

Des Fontaines, Una. *Wedgwood fairyland lustre: the work of Daisy Makeig-Jones.* 1975 London: Sotheby Parke Bernet Pubs 300pp illus.

Barnard, Harry T. *Chats on Wedgwood ware.* 1924 London: T. Fisher Unwin 324pp 152 illus. (EP Reprint)

Honey, William Bowyer. *Wedgwood ware.* 1948 London: Faber 35pp pl 96

Kelly, Alison. *Decorative Wedgwood in architecture and furniture.* 1965 London: Country Life 146pp illus.

Gorely, Jean. *A selective bibliography of books and magazine articles on Wedgwood and other ceramics . . . a working list.* 1953 London 6pp

WEMYSS

Wemyss ware: the development of a decorative Scottish pottery c 1883-1930 (catalogue by P. H. Davis). 1971 Edinburgh: Scottish Arts Council

Scott, Amoret and Christopher. 'Wemyss pottery', *Antique Dealer and Collector's Guide* May 1972 pp 78-80 illus.

Localities

BRISTOL

Bristol porcelain bicentenary exhibition 1770-1970: commemorating the transfer of the Plymouth hard paste factory to Bristol. 1970 Bristol Museum and Art Gallery 42pp illus.

Owen, Hugh. *Two centuries of ceramic art in Bristol: being a history of the manufacture of 'the true porcelain' by Richard Champion, with an account of the Delft earthenware*

and enamel glass works. 1873
Gloucester: Bellows 420pp

STAFFORDSHIRE

Wedgwood, Josiah C. *Staffordshire pottery and its history.* 1913 London: Sampson Low, Marston & Co 229pp illus.

Wedgwood, Josiah C. and Ormsbee, T. H. *Staffordshire pottery.* 1947 London: Putnam 174pp

Sekers, David. *Popular Staffordshire pottery.* 1977 London: Joseph 48pp illus. bibl.

Rhead, George Wooliscroft and Rhead, Frederick Alfred. *Staffordshire pots and potters.* 1977 Wakefield: EP Publishing 383pp (facsimile of 1906 edition, Hutchinson)

TEESIDE

Le Vine, J. R. A. *Teeside potteries.* 1972 Teeside Museums and Art Gallery Service Research Publications 80pp illus. bibl.

Potteries of Sunderland and District, a summary of their history and products. Edited by J. T. Shaw. 1961 (second edition) Sunderland Museum and Art Gallery 48pp illus. bibl.

TYNESIDE

Bell, Robert Charles. *Tyneside pottery.* 1971 London: Studio Vista 151pp illus. bibl.

YORKSHIRE POTTERIES

Towner, Donald Chisholm. *The Leeds pottery.* 1963 London: Cory Adams and Mackay 180pp illus.

Grabham, Oxley. *Yorkshire potteries, pots and potters.* Yorkshire Philosophical Society. Annual Report 1915

Dygnas, A. F. 'The Leeds pottery and the continent', *Apollo* October 1970 pp 286-289 illus.

Marks

Cushion, John P. and Honey, William Bowyer. *Handbook of pottery and porcelain marks.* 1965 (third edition) London: Faber 477pp illus.

Cushion, John P. *Pocket book of British ceramic marks.* 1976 (third edition) London: Faber 431pp (800 marks + Index to Registered Designs 1842-1883)

Godden, Geoffrey A. *An introductory handbook to British china marks of the nineteenth century.* 1962 Worthing: author 32pp bibl.

Tableware

French, Neal. *Industrial ceramics: tableware.* 1972 London: Oxford University Press 88pp 40 illus. (Handbooks for Artists)

Tilley, Frank. *Teapots and tea.* 1958 Newport: Ceramic Book Co 135pp 260 illus.

Cushion, John P. *Pottery and porcelain tablewares.* 1976 London: Studio Vista 240pp illus.

Marshall, Betty Hayes. 'Table decoration as art', *Studio* vol 115 1938 pp 318-322 illus.

'Design Review. Tableware in Wartime', *Architectural Review* vol 97 January 1945 pp 27-28

Bryan, Arthur. 'Changes in the ceramic tableware industry', *JRSA* vol 119 February 1971 pp 171-185 illus.

Tableware 1963- Croydon (University Microfilms)

Ornaments

May, John and May, Jennifer. *Commemorative pottery 1780-1900.* 1972 Newton Abbot: David and Charles 192pp 258 illus.

Balston, Thomas. *Staffordshire portrait figures of the Victorian Age.* 1958 London: Faber 93pp

Anderson, Margaret (ed). *Victorian Fairings and their values.* 1975 Galashiels: Lyle Publications 126pp illus.

Bristowe, William C. *Victorian china fairings.* 1971 (second edition) London: Adam and Charles Black 108pp illus. (first edition 1964)

Godden, Geoffrey A. 'Victorian earthenware chimney ornaments', *Apollo* November 1965 pp 410-412 illus.

Williams-Wood, Cyril. *Staffordshire pot-lids and their potters.* 1972 London: Faber 173pp illus.

Haggar, Reginald George. *Staffordshire chimney ornaments.* 1955 London: Phoenix 158pp illus.

Pugh, Patterson David Gordon. *Staffordshire portrait figures and allied objects of the Victorian era.* 1970 London: Barrie and Jenkins 657pp 747 illus.

Mosaics

Anthony, Edgar Waterman. *A history of mosaics.* 1968 New York: Hacker Art Books 333pp pl 80 bibl.

Rossi, Ferdinando. *Mosaics. A survey of their history and techniques.* 1970 London: Pall Mall 200pp illus. (first published in Italy 1968)

Townsend, C. Harrison, 'Cantor lectures 5th course. Mosaic: its history and practice', *JSA* vol 41 June 23 1893 pp 748-756; June 30 1893 pp 772-777; July 7 1893 pp 782-788

Tiles

Barnard, Julian. *Victorian ceramic tiles.* 1972 London: Studio Vista 184pp (first edition 1968)

Barnard, Julian. 'Decorated Victorian tiles', *Antique Dealer and Collector's Guide* September 1972 pp 82-88 illus.

Berendsen, Anne and others. *Tiles. A general history.* 1967 London: Faber 285pp illus.

Colburn, Zerah. 'On the manufacture of encaustic tiles and ceramic ornamentation by machinery', *JSA* vol 13 May 19 1865 pp 445-450

Furnival, William James. *Leadless decorative tiles, faience, and mosaic, comprising notes and excerpts in the history, materials, manufacture and use of ornamental flooring tiles, ceramic mosaic and decorative tiles and faience.* 1904 Stone: W. J. Furnival 852pp

Pinkham, Roger. 'William de Morgan – tilemaker par excellence', *Antique Dealer and Collector's Guide* December 1975 pp 104-106 illus.

Ray, Anthony. *English Delftware tiles.* 1973 London: Faber 287pp illus.

Shaw, Henry. *Specimens of tile pavements drawn from existing authorities parts 1-8.* 1852-1857 London: Pickering pl 37

Thomas, Mark H. 'Tiles', *Design* 56 August 1953 pp 19-29

'Tiles (supplement), including 1. Tile work in the past, by Arthur Lane, 2. Tile work today, by William Tatton Brown', *Architectural Review* vol 85 January-June 1939 pp 261-268

Gibbons, Hinton & Co. *Catalogue. Illustrations of Majolica tiles . . . handpainted art tiles . . . slabbed surrounds . . . designs for floors . . . encaustic mosaic.* c 1910 Staffs: Gibbons, Hinton and Co. 40 col pl 15p illus.

Victoria and Albert Museum. Dept of Ceramics. *A guide to the collection of tiles, by Arthur Lane.* 1960 revised edition London: HMSO 88pp pl 49 bibl.

Sanitary Ware

Apart from early trade catalogues, most early studies of the industry are buried in technical papers

Some general material:

Shanks and Co. *Sanitary appliances.* 1907 Barrhead nr Glasgow: The Firm 275pp illus.

Beresford-Evans, J. 'Towards better ceramic sanitary ware', *Design* 70 October 1954 pp 20-25

Beresford-Evans, J. 'Design analysis. Lavatory basin (Goslett Cygnet)', *Design* 128 August 1959 pp 42-46

Adams, Alan H. 'The art of fireclay', *DIA Yearbook* 1961/1962 pp 43-45

Beresford-Evans, J. 'Surveys of industry. 1 Sanitary ware', *Design* vol 145 January 1961 pp 34-41

See also:

Interior Design: Bathrooms *page 156*

Interior Design: Services *page 167*

Industrial Applications

Chandler, Maurice Henry. *Ceramics in the modern world: man's first technology comes of age.* 1967 London: Aldus. 192pp 100 illus. (Science and Technology Series)

Singer, F. and Singer, Sonja Sibylla. *Industrial ceramics.* 1963 London: Chapman and Hall. 1455pp (Part 1 General principles. Part 2. Ceramic products bibl. 1328-)

Burton, Joseph. 'Scientific method in pottery manufacture; research and discovery', *Transactions of the English Ceramic Society* vol XV part ii 1916 pp 167-176

Wellcome Historical Medical Museum. *Medical ceramics: a catalogue of the English and Dutch collections in the Museum of the Wellcome Institute of the History of Medicine. (Edited by J. K. Crellin).* 1969 London: Wellcome Institute 304pp 486 illus.

Industrial Organisation

Searle, Alfred B. *An encyclopaedia of the ceramic industries, being a guide to the materials, methods of manufacture, means of recognition, and testing the various articles produced in the clay working and allied industry, including clays, silica, felspar, bricks, tiles, pottery, porcelain, pencils, refractory materials and many others arranged in alphabetical order for rapid reference by manufacturers, research workers, students, connoisseurs and others.* 1929 London: Benn 3 vols

Gay, P. W. and Smyth, R. L. *British pottery industry.* 1974 London: Butterworth 307pp illus. (Studies in Theoretical and Applied Economics)

Bourry, Charles Emile. *Treatise on ceramic industries. A complete manual for pottery, tile and brick workers, translated from the French by W. P. Rix.* 1901 London: Scott Greenwood 759pp (later editions 1911, 1926)

Burchill, Frank and Ross, Richard. *A history of the Potters' Union.* 1977 Hanley: Ceramic and Allied Trades Union. 292pp illus. bibl.

Ratcliffe, George. Survey. 'The potteries in transition', *Design* 177 September 1963 pp 44-51 illus.

Periodicals

British Ceramic Society Publications 1971- (8 issues per year). Stoke: British Ceramic Society. (manager of *BCS Journal* and *BCS Transactions*)

British Clayworker 1892- (monthly). (abstracts of British and overseas patents, absorbed *The Potter*)

Ceramic Digest 1947- St. Albans

Ceramic Review: the magazine of the craftsmen. 1970- (bi-monthly) London: Potters Association of Great Britain

Ceramics: the journal of the glass, pottery, clayworking, cement and silicate industries. 1947- (University Microfilms)

Journal of Ceramic History 1969- vol 1 Stafford: George St. Press

Northern Ceramic Society Journal vol 1-1972/1973 Newcastle under Lyne, Staffs: The Society

Pottery and Glass Trades Journal 1878-1879 then *Pottery Gazette and Glass Trades Journal* 1879-

Pottery Quarterly. A review of ceramic art. 1954- Tring

Tableware International: incorporating Pottery Gazette. 1970- (monthly) London: International Trade Publications. (*Pottery Gazette and Glass Trade Review* 1877-1970)

Transactions and Journal of the British Ceramic Society incorporating *British Ceramic Abstracts* 1971- (8 issues per year). (*Transactions of the British Ceramic Society* 1900-1970, *Journal of the British Ceramic Society*) Shelton: British Ceramic Society

Transactions North Staffordshire Ceramic Society 1901/1902 then *Transactions English Ceramic Society* 1903/1904-

Transactions of the English Ceramic Circle (before 1937 titled *The English Porcelain Circle*)

Bibliographies

Solon, M. L. *Ceramic literature: an analytical index to the works published in all languages on the history and the technology of the ceramic art; also to the catalogues of public museums, private collections, and of auction sales in which the description of ceramic* objects occupy an important place: and to the most important price-lists of the ancient and modern manufactories of pottery and porcelain. London, 1910 660pp (1969 Gale Reprint)

Solon, L. M. E. *List of books on the history and technology of ceramic art.* 1912 Typescript (appendix to *Ceramic literature* 1910)

Honey, William Bowyer. *Pottery and porcelain.* 1950 National Book League/Cambridge University Press 19pp (readers guide)

Emery, N. *British ceramics, their art, history and developments from medieval times to the present day: a bibliography.* 1967 FLA Thesis

A list of works on pottery and porcelain in the National Art Library including those containing references to the subject or illustrations (compiled for the use of students and visitors). 1875 London: Eyre and Spottiswode for HMSO 20pp

Abstracts

British Ceramic Abstracts in *British Ceramic Society Transactions* 1955- (all aspects, including some patents)

Glass

See also:

Ceramics *page 209*

Plastics *page 202*

General World Surveys

An old and very diverse industry

Haynes, Edward Barrington. *Glass through the ages.* 1969 Harmondsworth: Penguin 310pp illus. (first edition)

Philips, C. J. *Glass the miracle maker: its history, technology, manufacture and applications.* 1948 London: Pitman 429pp (previous edition 1941)

Vavra, Jaroslav Raimund. *5000 years of glass-making, the history of glass. (translated by I. R. Gottheimer)* 1954 Prague: Artia. 191p

Kämpfer, Fritz and Beyer, Klaus G. *Glass – a world history: the story of 4000 years of fine glass-making.* 1966 London: Studio Vista 315pp 243 illus.

Newman, Harold. *An illustrated dictionary of glass.* 1977 London: Thames and Hudson 368pp 608 illus.

Elville, E. M. *The collector's dictionary of glass.* 1961 London: Country Life 194pp illus.

The most comprehensive work on the decorative and architectural aspects of glass:

McGrath, Raymond and Frost, Albert Childerstone. *Glass in architecture and decoration.* 1937 London: Architectural Press 664pp illus. (very extensively revised 1961)

A social history:

Polak, Ada. *Glass, its makers and its public.* 1975 London: Weidenfeld and Nicolson 224pp illus.

Artistic and Domestic Applications

General studies:

Hogan, J. H. 'The development in the design of English glassware during the last one hundred years', *Transactions of the Society of Glass Technology* vol XX 1936 pp 735-740

Crompton, Sidney (ed). *English glass.* 1967 London: Ward Lock 255pp illus.

Hogan, James H. 'English design in glassware', *JRSA* vol 83 March 1935 pp 426-438

Thorpe, William Arnold. *English glass.* 1961 (third edition). London: Black 304pp pl 23 (first edition 1935, second edition 1949)

Wills, Geoffrey. *English and Irish glass.* 1968 London: Guinness Superlatives 271pp illus.

Charleston, R. J. and others (ed). *The Glass Circle 1.* 1972 Newcastle upon Tyne: Oriel Press 64pp illus.

Schrijver, Elka. *Glass and crystal. Vol 2. From the mid-nineteenth century to the present.* 1964 London: Merlin Press. 94pp illus.

Periods

NINETEENTH CENTURY

The repeal of the Glass Excise Acts in 1845 did much to stimulate developments of all sorts.

Wakefield, Hugh. *Nineteenth century British glass.* 1961 London: Faber 64pp pl 96

O'Looney, Betty. *Victorian Glass.* 1972 London: HMSO for the Victoria and Albert Museum 46pp

Lee, Ruth. *Victorian glass. Specialities of the nineteenth century.* 1945 (seventh edition) Northboro, Mass: Author 608pp

Garner, Philippe. 'Nineteenth century glassmakers. The precursors of Art Nouveau', *Antique Dealer and Collectors Guide* April 1975 pp 94-96

Lee, Ruth Webb. *Nineteenth century art glass.* 1952 New York: M. Burrows and Son 128pp illus.

Revi, Albert Christian. *Nineteenth century art glass; its genesis and development.* 1959 London: Thomas Nelson 270pp illus.

Wills, George. *Victorian glass.* 1977 London: Bell 96pp

Hughes, George Bernard. *English glass for the collector, 1660-1860.* 1958 London: Lutterworth Press 251pp pl 46

ART NOUVEAU

See also:

Art Nouveau *page 71*

Jewellery *page 234*

Grover, Ray and Lee. *Art glass nouveau.* 1967 Tokyo: Tuttle 170pp illus.

Hilschenz, Helga. *Das Glas des Jugendstils. Katalog der Sammlung Hentrich im Kunstmuseum Düsseldorf.* 1973 München: Prestel Verlag 535pp illus.

Glass designs were some of the most distinctive aspects of Art Nouveau and so it is important to note the influence of some of the key designers of this period:

O'Neal, William. 'Three Art Nouveau glass makers', *Journal of Glass Studies* vol 2 1960 pp 125-139

220

GALLE

Gros, Gabriella. 'Poetry in glass. The art of Emile Gallé', *Apollo* November 1955 pp 134-136 illus.

Frantz, Henri. 'Emile Gallé and the decorative artists of Nancy', *Studio* vol 28 1903 pp 108-117 illus.

Garner, Philippe. *Emile Gallé*. 1976 London: Academy Editions 167pp illus. bibl.

Garner, Philippe. 'Nature captured in glass: the work of Emile Gallé', *Country Life* October 4 1973 pp 1008-1009

Polak, Ada. 'Gallé glass: luxurious, cheap and imitated', *Journal of Glass Studies* vol 5 1963 pp 105-116

LALIQUE

Percy, Christopher Vane. *The glass of Lalique: a collector's guide*. 1977 London: Studio Vista 196pp illus.

McClinton, Katherine Morrison. *Lalique for collectors*. 1975 Guildford: Lutterworth Press 152pp illus. bibl.

Garner, Philippe. 'Jeweller who loved glass: the work of René Lalique', *Country Life* no 155 June 6 1974 pp 1438 ff.

Last, D. W. 'Car figureheads – the development by René Lalique of a modern field for illuminated glass', *Studio* vol 101 February 1931 pp 129-134 illus.

TIFFANY

Amaya, Mario. *Tiffany glass*. 1976 London: Studio Vista 84pp illus.

Van Tassel, Valentine. 'Louis Comfort Tiffany. 1. Favrile glass. 2. Tiffany products', *Antiques Journal* July and August 1952

Amaya, Mario. 'A taste for Tiffany', *Apollo* February 1965 pp 102-109 illus.

Louis Comfort Tiffany 1848-1933. 1958 New York: Museum of Contemporary Crafts.

Koch, Robert. *Louis C. Tiffany's glass, bronzes, lamps: a complete collector's guide*. 1971 New York: Crown 208pp illus.

Koch, Robert. *Louis C. Tiffany, rebel in glass*. 1966 (second edition) New York: Crown 246p illus. bibl. (first edition 1964)

Neustadt, Egon. *The lamps of Tiffany*. 1970 New York: Fairfield Press 224pp illus. bibl.

Tiffany, Louis Comfort. *The art work of Louis Comfort Tiffany*. 1914 Garden City: Doubleday 90pp illus.

Tiffany Glass and Decorating Company. *Tiffany favrile glass considered in its chronological relationship to other glass, as well as its usefulness in the decorative arts.* 1896 New York: Tiffany Glass

Bing, Samuel. *Artistic America, Tiffany glass and Art Nouveau, edited by R. Koch*. 1970 Cambridge, Mass 272pp illus. (reprint of essays published 1895-1903)

Waern, Cecilia. 'The industrial arts of America. The Tiffany Glass and Decorating Company', *Studio* vol 11 1897 pp 156-165 illus. vol 14 1898 pp 16-21 illus.

INTERWAR PERIOD

Powell, Harry J. 'Glassmaking before and during the war', *JRSA* vol 67 June 13 1919 pp 485-495

Janneau, Guillaume. *Modern glass, translated by J. A. Fleming*. 1931 London: Studio 184pp illus.

supplemented by:

Skelley, Leloise Davis. *Modern fine glass*. 1942 Garden City: Garden City Pub 144pp illus.

Other sources include:

Fleming, Arnold. 'Glass of today', *Studio* vol 102 1931 pp 73-93 illus.

'Decoration and craftmanship – glass', (supplement), *Architectural Review* vol 71 1932 pp 27-36

'Glass. Domestic, decorative, constructional. Decoration and craftmanship supplement' *Architectural Review* vol 73 February 1933 pp 83-94

'Fine craftmanship (glass)', *Studio* vol 106 August 1933 pp 113-122

Crankshaw, Edward. 'Glass in the home', *Design for Today* October 1934 pp 364-368 (especially P. Nash bathroom)

Robinson, J. B. Perry. 'Glass of today and how to choose it for use and decoration in the home', *Studio* vol 110 1935 pp 202-210 illus.

'Trend of design in home decoration: pottery, glass, furniture', *Studio* vol 110 September 1935 pp 169-173

Holme, C. G. 'Another aspect of glass in the art of home planning. The part it fulfils in the constructional decoration of interiors of modern homes', *Studio* vol 110 1935 pp 211-213 illus.

'New glassware: international review', *Studio* vol 113 April 1937 pp 204-211

Some important designers:

CHEESEMAN

Cheeseman, Keith. 'Designing glass for architectural and interior decorative purposes', *Art and Industry* October 1941 pp 110-117

McGRATH

'Glass in construction and decoration. A review of recent developments by Raymond McGrath', *Architectural Review* vol 85 January-July 1939 pp 99-108

MURRAY

Anderson, M. L. 'Industrial design in three materials (work of Keith Murray)', *Design for Today* August 1935 pp 318-320 (glass, pottery, silver)

Murray, Keith. 'The designer and his problem. 11. The design of table glass', *Design for Today* June 1933 p 53-56

Keith Murray. An exhibition of his ceramic and glass designs. 1976 London: Geffrye Museum

POSTWAR PERIOD

Polak, Ada. *Modern glass.* 1962 London: Faber 94pp illus. (Monographs on Glass Series, edited by R. J. Charleston)

which is usefully supplemented by the illustrations in:

Beard, Geoffrey. *Modern glass.* 1968 London: Studio Vista 160pp illus. (Dutton picture book no 31)

Trethowan, Harry. 'Domestic glass and its postwar uses', *Art and Industry* September 1941 pp 71-77

Hollowood, Albert Bernard. *Pottery and glass.* 1947 Harmondsworth: Penguin 63pp (Things we see series)

Studio Glassworking

As well as these industrial developments, the craft of studio glass has made an important contribution to general developments in glass design:

Flavell, Ray and Smale, Claude. *Studio glassmaking.* 1974 New York: Van Nostrand Reinhold 96pp illus. (looks at historical developments)

Grover, Ray and Grover, Lee. *Contemporary art glass.* 1975 New York: Crown Publishers 208pp illus. bibl.

Grover, Ray and Grover, Lee. *Carved and decorated European art glass.* 1970 Tokyo: Tuttle 244pp illus.

Stennett-Willson, Ronald. *The beauty of modern glass.* 1958 London: Studio 128pp illus.

Stennett-Willson, Ronald. *Modern glass.* 1975 London: Studio Vista 160pp illus. (picture book)

Crystal

Farr, Michael. 'English crystal glass design', *Design* 54 June 1953 pp 24-29

Wolfenden, Ian. *English 'rock crystal' glass 1878-1925.* 1976 Dudley Art Gallery

Steuben Glass. *British artists in crystal.* 1954 New York: Steuben Glass

Colour

Davis, Derek Cecil and Middlemas, Robert Keith. *Coloured glass. Photographs by Michael Plomer.* 1968 London: Herbert Jenkins 119pp

Weyl, Woldemar Anatol. *Coloured glasses.* 1951 Sheffield: Society of Glass Technology 541pp illus. (Monographs on Glass Technology)

Cut and Engraved

English and Irish cut glass 1750-1950. 1953 London: Country Life 95pp

Cut and flowered: two centuries of British glass decoration. 1974 Manchester: Whitworth Art Gallery 16pp

Beard, Geoffrey William. *Nineteenth century cameo glass.* 1956 Newport: Ceramic Book Company 149pp illus.

Webb, Thomas and Sons. *A descriptive booklet illustrating the art of making 'Webb's' hand made crystal tableware.* n.d.

Norman, Barbara. *Engraving and decorating glass.* 1972 Newton Abbot: David and Charles 200pp illus.

Piper, John. 'Fully licensed (Engraved glass in public houses)', *Architectural Review* vol 87 pp 87-100; pp 142-146 illus.

Whistler, Laurence. *The engraved glass of Laurence Whistler.* 1952 Hitchin: Cupid Press 47pp pl 82

Whistler, Laurence. *Engraved glass 1952-1958.* 1959 London: Hart-Davis 38pp pl 88

Whistler, Laurence. 'Some engraved glass by David Peace', *Connoisseur* vol 168 no 677 July 1968 pp 175-177

Collections

Brierley Hill Public Library. *The collections of glass at Brierley Hill Public Library. Handlist compiled by W. A. Thorpe.* 1949 Brierley Hill: Libraries and Arts Committee 48pp

Buckley, Wilfred. *The art of glass. Illustrated from the Wilfred Buckley Collection in the Victoria and Albert Museum.* 1939 London: Allen and Unwin 285pp

Crellin, J. K. and Scott, J. R. *Glass and British Pharmacy. A survey and guide to the Wellcome Collection of British glass.* 1972 London: Wellcome Institute of the History of Medicine 72pp illus.

London. Science Museum. *Descriptive catalogue of the collection illustrating glass technology by S. E. Janson.* 1969 London: HMSO 55pp pl 16

Victoria and Albert Museum. *Glass. A handbook for the study of glass vessels of all periods and countries and a guide to the Museum collection by W. B. Honey.* 1946 London: HMSO 169pp

Nesbitt, Alexander. *Glass. A descriptive catalogue of the glass vessels in the South Kensington Museum.* 1878 London: Chapman and Hall (South Kensington Museum Handbook)

Exhibitions

Stourbridge Glass Manufacturers. *Detailed catalogue of the exhibits of a loan exhibition of Stourbridge glass . . . held at Stourbridge 18 to 30 June 1951*

An exhibition of glass: or glass making as a creative art through the ages, held 6 October to 12 November 1961. (Introduction by Robert Charleston). 1961 Leeds: Temple Newsam House

Circle of Glass Collectors: commemorative exhibition 1937-1962. Catalogue edited by R. J. Charleston. 1962 London: Victoria and Albert Museum 72pp illus.

Innovations in glass: Scottish Arts Council Exhibition. 1973 Edinburgh: Scottish Arts Council (set of 15 cards)

Glass Tableware

See also:

Ceramic Tableware *page 216*

GENERAL

Elville, E. M. *English tableglass.* 1951 London: Country Life 274pp illus.

Angus-Butterworth, L. M. *British table and ornamental glass.* 1976 London: Howard Baker 120pp illus. (previous edition 1956 Leonard Hill)

Victoria and Albert Museum. *Glass tableware.* 1952 London: HMSO 32pp (Small picture book Series)

PERIOD

Morris, Barbara. *Victorian table glass and ornaments.* 1978 (July) London: Barrie and Jenkins 162pp illus.

'Craftsman's Portfolio. Modern table glass', *Architectural Review* vol 62 July-December 1927 pp 88-90 illus.

Kershaw, Kathleen. 'Art and the table', *Studio* vol 102 1931 pp 267-271 illus.

Connolly, Cyril. 'Household glass', *Architectural Review* vol 73 January-June 1933 pp 86

'Fine craftmanship. Table appointments', *Studio* vol 107 1934 pp 210-214 illus.

'Art of the table: designs in the public eye', *Studio* vol 110 August 1935 pp 88-90, pp 93-95

Board of Trade. *Handblown domestic glassware.* 1947 London: HMSO 143pp

Council of Industrial Design. *Report to the Council of Industrial Design . . . on tableware.* 1966 London: CoID 19pp

Mirrors

Roche, Serge. *Mirrors; with 294 plates by Pierre Devinoy and translated by Colin Duckworth.* 1957 London: Duckworth 38pp illus.

Schweig, Bruno. *Mirrors. A guide to the manufacture of mirrors and reflecting surfaces.* 1973 London: Pelham 264pp illus.

Other Objects

Churchill, Arthur Ltd. *History in glass. A Coronation exhibition of Royal, historical, political and social glasses commemorating eighteenth and nineteenth century events in English history, April 26-May 28 1937* 1937 London: Arthur Churchill Ltd 42pp 44 pl

Lukins, Jocelyn. 'Glass rolling pins', *Antique Dealer and Collector's Guide* May 1970 pp 65-68 illus.

Paperweights

Cloak, Evelyn Campbell. *Glass paperweights.* 1969 London: Studio Vista 196pp illus. bibl. pp 172-190

Elville, E. M. *Paperweights and other glass curiosities.* 1954 London: Country Life 116pp pl 16

Mackay, James. *Glass paperweights.* 1973 London: Ward Lock 136pp illus.

Hollister, Paul Jnr. (ed.) *The encyclopaedia of glass paperweights.* 1969 London: W. H. Allen 344pp illus. bibl.

Containers

Moody, Brian. *Packaging in glass.* 1977 revised edition London: Hutchinson Benham 383pp illus. (first edition 1963)

Wyatt, Victor. *From sand-core to automation: a history of glass containers.* 1966 London: Glass Manufacturers Federation 23pp

Toulouse, Julian Harrison. *Fruit jars.* 1969 London: Nelson 542pp

Bottles

The current enthusiasm for bottle collecting has spawned a number of detailed studies:

Morgan, Roy. *Sealed bottles: their history and evolution (1630-1930)*. 1977 Burton on Trent: Midlands Antique Bottle Publishing 120pp illus. bibl.

Fletcher, Edward. *The best of British bottles*. 1975 Braintree: Bottles and Relics Pubs. 100pp illus. (Bottle collectors' library series no 3)

Brise, Sheelah Maud Emily Ruggles. *Sealed bottles*. 1949 London: Country Life 175pp illus.

Adams, Tony and Payne, Audrey. *The bottle collectors' dictionary, containing an illustrated identification aid and price guide*. 1976 Southampton: Southern Collectors Publications 46pp illus.

Davis, Derek C. *English bottles and decanters 1650-1900*. 1972 New York: World Publishing Co 80pp illus.

Meigh, Edward. 'Notes on the design of glass bottles', *Journal of the Society of Glass Technology* 1934 pp 122-127

Meigh, Edward. *The story of the glass bottle*. 1972 Stoke on Trent: C. E. Ramsden and Co 88pp illus.

Morgan, Roy. *Mainly Codd's wallop: the story of the great British pop bottle*. 1977 (revised edition) Wellingborough: Kollectarama (first edition 1974) 24pp illus.

Shand, P. Morton. 'Wine bottles and wine glasses', *Design for Today* October 1934 pp 373-377

Wills, Geoffrey. *English glass bottles 1650-1950 for the collector*. 1974 Edinburgh: J. Bartholomew 82pp illus.

Wills, Geoffrey. *The bottle collector's guide*. 1978 Edinburgh: John Bartholomew 128pp illus.

Meigh, Edward. 'The development of the automatic bottle machine', *Glass Technology* vol 1 1960 pp 25-50

Scent Bottles

Matthews, Leslie G. *The antiques of perfume*. 1977 London: Bell 100pp

Foster, Kate. *Scent bottles*. 1966 London: Connoisseur-Michael Joseph 111pp illus. (*Connoisseur* monograph)

Windows

Crittall, W. F. 'The window', *Design for Today* March 1934 pp 89-95

Pilkington Technical Advisory Service. *Window glass design guide, edited by Denis Philip Turner*. 1977 London: Architectural Press 111pp

Short, Audrey. 'Workers under glass in 1851', *Victorian Studies* vol X December 1966 pp 193-202 (expected and actual behaviour of workers under glass at the Great Exhibition)

Stained Glass

Armitage, Edward Liddall. *Stained glass: history, technology and practice*. 1959 London: L. Hill 216pp pl 117

British Society of Master Glass Painters. *A directory of stained glass windows executed within the past twenty years*. 1955 London: The Society (various editions 1930-)

Modern stained glass 1960-1961 (catalogue of an exhibition). 1960 London: Arts Council of Great Britain 12pp pl 8

Piper, John. *Stained glass: art or anti-art*. 1968 London: Studio Vista 98pp

Englefield, William Alexander Devereux. *The history of the Paint-Stainers Company of London*. 1923 London: Chapman and Dodd 248pp illus.

TECHNIQUE

Winston, Charles. *Memoirs illustrative of the art of glass-painting . . . illustrated with engravings from the author's original drawings by P. H. Delamotte*. 1865 London: John Murray

Day, Lewis Foreman. 'Stained glass windows as they were, are and should be', *JSA* vol 30 February 3 1882 pp 292-306

Day, Lewis Foreman. 'The making of a stained glass window', *JSA* vol 46 March 25 1898 pp 421-430

Day, Lewis Foreman. *Windows; a book about stained and painted glass*. 1909 (third revised edition) London: Batsford 420pp (first edition 1897, second 1902) (Oxford Microfilm Edition)

Holiday, Henry. *Stained glass as an art*. 1896 London: Macmillan 173pp

Voysey, C. F. A. 'Unfamiliar uses for stained glass', *Apollo* vol 17 April 1933 pp 153-154

Hogan, James H. 'Stained glass', *JRSA* vol 88 May 3 1940 pp 569-585 illus.

Reyntiens, Patrick. *The technique of stained glass*. 1967 London: Batsford 192pp illus. bibl.

Sowers, Robert. *Stained glass: an architectural art*. 1965 London: Zwemmer 128pp illus. bibl.

PERIODS

Harrison, Martin. 'Victorian stained glass', *Connoisseur* vol 182 no 734 April 1973 pp 251-254

Sewter, A. C. 'Victorian stained glass', *Apollo* December 1962 pp 760-765 illus.

Bumpus, T. F. 'Stained glass in England since the Gothic revival: with some account of the churches referred to', *The Architect* – serially vols LXII-LXVI 1899-1901

Drake, Maurice. 'War memorial windows', *Architectural Review* vol 52 July-December 1922 pp 116-121

'Modern stained glass', *Architectural Review* vol 59 January-June 1926 pp 200-202 illus.

'Craftsman's Portfolio. XVII Modern stained glass', *Architectural Review* vol 62 July-December 1927 pp 124-126 illus.

COMPANIES

Chance, James Frederick. *A history of the firm of Chance Bros. and Co, glass and alkali manufacturers.* 1919 London: Spottiswode, Ballantyne & Co 302pp

INDIVIDUALS

Sewter, Albert Charles. *The stained glass of William Morris and circle.* 1974 Yale University Press for the Paul Mellon Centre for Studies in British Art 2 vols text + illus.

Sewter, A. C. 'William Morris's designs for stained glass', *Architectural Review* vol 127 no 757 pp 196-200 illus.

Vallance, Aymer. 'Sir Edward Burne-Jones's designs for painted glass', *Studio* vol 51 1911 pp 91-103 23 illus.

'The work of Selwyn Image', *Studio* vol 14 1898 pp 3-10 illus. Part 1. Stained glass

Stained glass by the artists of the Whitefriars Studios (James Powell & Sons): chief designer, E. Liddell Armitage. 1956 London: Walker's Gallery

Windows for Coventry. 1956 London: Victoria and Albert Museum

Organisations

L'Association internationale pour l'histoire du verre based on Le Musée du Verre de la Ville de Liège published:

Annales des congrès des Journées internationales du verre.

International Congress on Glass, eighth London 1968. *Studies in glass history and design.* 1970 Society of Glass Technology 135pp

International Congress on Glass. Committee B concerns itself with glass history:

Eighth International Congress 1968 London, edited by R. J. Charleston (history), Wendy Evans (design), A. E. Werner (scientific aspects)

Howard, Alexander Liddon (ed). *The Worshipful Company of Glass-Sellers of London, from its inception to the present day.* 1940 London: Rawlinson 152pp illus.

Manufacture

Angus-Butterworth, Lionel Milner. *The manufacture of glass.* 1948 London: Pitman 274pp illus.

Marson, Percival. *Glass and glass manufacture, revised and enlarged by L. M. Angus-Butterworth.* 1949 (fourth edition) London: Pitman 143pp (first edition 1918)

Haggar, Reginald George. *Glass and glass makers.* 1961 London: Methuen 80pp (Methuen's outlines)

Tooley, Fay. *Handbook of glass manufacture.* 2 vols 1953-1960 New York: Ogden

Powell, Harry James. *Glassmaking in England.* 1935 Cambridge 183pp (first edition 1923). (last chapter Adam to present)

Hogan, James H. 'Design and form as applied to the manufacture of glassware', *JRSA* vol 81 March 3 1933 pp 364-383 illus.

Speight, Sadie. 'Glass – new methods with an old material', *Art and Industry* April 1944 pp 98-108

Kitt, Michael. 'Glass. Survey of an industry', *Design* 215 November 1966 pp 26-47

Turner, William Ernest Stephen. *Twenty-one years – a professor looks out on the glass industry.* 1937 Sheffield: Society of Glass Technology 70pp

Stourbridge and West Midlands

Guttery, David Reginald. *From broad-glass to cut crystal: a history of the Stourbridge glass industry.* 1956 London: Hill 161pp pl 69

Haden, Harry Jack. *Notes on the Stourbridge glass trade.* 1949 Brierley Hill: Libraries and Arts Committee 37pp (latest edition 1969)

Haden, Harry Jack. *The Stourbridge glass industry in the nineteenth century.* 1971 Stourbridge: Black Country Society 38pp

Sims, R. *Contributions towards a history of glassmaking and glassmakers in Staffordshire . . . by R. S.* 1894 Wolverhampton: Whitehead Bros

Factories

Barker, Theodore Cardwell. *The glassmakers: Pilkington: the rise of an international company 1826-1976.* 1977 London: Weidenfeld and Nicolson 557pp pl 32

(Chapters 1-11 based on *Pilkington Brothers and the glass industry* 1960)

'The glass age', *Architectural Review* February 1939 (special supplement on the Pilkington Brothers)

'Design in relation to the problem: handmade glass, James Powell & Sons (Whitefriars)', *Commercial Art* vol 13 August 1932 pp 53-68

Northwood, John, the Younger. *John Northwood: his contribution to the Stourbridge flint glass industry 1850-1902*. 1958 Stourbridge: Mark and Moody Ind. 134pp

Weyman, John. 'Design policy. Mass produced glassware (post 1945 United Glass Bottles)', *Design* 46 October 1952 pp 7-9

Materials and Technology

Maloney, F. J. Terence. *Glass in the modern world: a study in materials development*. 1967 London: Aldus 192pp illus.

Beadle, J. D. (ed). *Glass – an engineering material*. 1969 West Wickham: Morgan Grampian 76pp

Evans, Wendy. *Glass history*. 1969 London: Glass Manufacturers Federation 24pp

McMillan, P. W. *Glass ceramics*. 1964 London: Academic Press 229pp

Stanworth, John Edwin. *The physical properties of glass*. 1950 Oxford: Clarendon Press 224pp

Volf, Milos Bohuslav. *Technical glasses*. (English translation by Sylvia E. Myhre and K. Fink). 1961 London: Pitman 465pp

Process

Powell, Harry James, Chance, H. and Harris, H. G. *The principles of glass making . . . together with treatises on crown and sheet glass by H. Chance and plate glass by H. G. Harris*. 1883 London: G. Bell and Sons 186pp illus.

Phillips, Charles J. *Glass, its industrial applications*. 1960 London: Chapman and Hall 260pp illus.

Powell, H. J. 'The manufacture of glass for decorative purposes', *JSA* vol 29 May 13 1881 pp 546-551 illus.

Scoville, Warren Chandler. *Revolution in glass making. Entrepreneurship and technological change in the American industry 1880-1920*. 1948 Cambridge, Mass: Harvard University Press 398pp illus.

Glass making elsewhere in Europe

150 Jahre Österreichisches Glaskunst: Lobmeyr 1823-1973 (exhibition catalogue) 1973 Vienna

Schmidt, Robert. *100 Jahr Österreichische Glaskunst. Lobmeyr 1823-1923*. 1925 Vienna: Schroll 115pp illus.

Glass Fibre

See also:

Plastics *page 202*

Blake, John E. 'Glass fibre: current developments and future possibilities', *Design* 98 February 1957 pp 24-29

Davies, A. Hudson. 'The development and use of glass fibres', *JRSA* vol 105 26 April 1957 pp 437-455 illus.

Morgan, Phillip (ed). *Glass reinforced plastics*. 1954 London: Iliffe and Sons 248pp illus.

Blake, H. V. 'Glass fibre: a new medium for designers', *Design* 60 December 1953 pp 28-32

Ashford, F. C. 'Glass fibre in use', *Design* vol 76 April 1955 pp 30-39 bibl.

Brawne, Michael. 'Skill. Polyester fibreglass', *Architectural Review* vol 126 no 754 December 1959 pp 359-362

Hutton, Geoffrey. 'About glass fibre', *DIA Yearbook* 1963-1964 pp 57-64

Parkyn, Brian (ed). *Glass reinforced plastics*. 1970 London: Iliffe 350pp (small history section)

Journals

Glass 1923- (monthly) London: Fuel and Metallurgical Journals. (University Microfilms)

Glass Age: architectural, application, design, construction. 1958- (quarterly) London: Blandford Press

The Glass Circle vol 1 1972 Newcastle upon Tyne: Glass Circle (collectors' association founded in 1937)

Glass Technology 1960- (monthly) Sheffield: Society of Glass Technology (continuation of Journal of the Society of Glass Technology 1919-1959)

Journal of Glass Studies 1959- (annual) New York: Corning Museum of Glass (international)

Bibliographies

Duncan, George Sang. *Bibliography of glass (from the earliest records to 1940)*. 1960 London: Dawsons of Pall Mall for the Society of Glass Technology 544pp

Brierley Hill Public Libraries. *Glass and glass making: a check list.* 1962 Brierley Hill Public Libraries

Glass manufacture: a bibliography of pertinent articles in periodicals and other literature issued in 1938. 1940 Pittsburgh: Carnegie Institute of Technology 251pp

Klaarenbeek, F. W. and Stevels, J. M. (eds). *Bibliography of glass literature, under the aegis of the International Commission on Glass.* 1964 Bussum, Holland: Grafisch Bedrijf T. Hamers 117pp

A list of books and pamphlets in the National Art Library of the South Kensington Museum, illustrating glass. 1887 London: Eyre and Spottiswode 48pp

Solon, Louis Marc Emmanuel. 'Contribution towards a bibliography of the art of glass Part I. Glass making and technology. Part II. Glass painting (a) Technology (b) Stained and painted glass: description and reproduction', *Transactions of the Ceramic Society* 1912-1913 vol 12 pp 65-77, pp 285-324

Metals

A lot of the most interesting writing on design techniques in metal is very specialised and tucked away in the technical press. What follows is a selection of the more generally available works that can be approached without the benefit of detailed technical knowledge. Unfortunately many of the engineering aspects are very limited in applications and have had to be excluded from this general survey. The section is in three main parts:

1 General studies – historical surveys, individual designers and developments

2 Particular metals

3 Some applications – cutlery, jewellery, coins

Machinery, eg domestic appliances, machine tools, cars will be found under its more specific heading in other sections, eg Transport: Road.

1 General Studies

History of metals:

Aitchison, Leslie. *A history of metals.* 1960 London: Macdonald and Evans 2 vols 647pp illus. bibl.

Slade, Edward. *Metals in the modern world: study in materials development.* 1967 London: Aldus 192pp illus.

Alexander, William and Street, Arthur. *Metals in the service of man.* 1976 Harmondsworth: Penguin 346pp illus. (first published 1956. Many other editions)

Dennis, William Herbert. *A hundred years of metallurgy.* 1963 London: Duckworth 342pp illus. (period 1850-1950)

Design:

Haedeke, Hanns-Ulrich, *Metalwork, translated from the German by Vivienne Menkes.* 1970 London: Weidenfeld and Nicolson 227pp pl 128 bibl. (The Social History of the Decorative Arts series)

Braun-Feldweg, Wilhelm. *Metal: design and technique, translated by F. Bradley.* 1975 London: Batsford 296pp 481 illus. (first published as *Metall* 1950)

With the engineer in mind:

Williams, E. H. *Designing in metal.* 1968 London: Iliffe 232pp 75 illus.

Horger, Oscar J. *Metals engineering design handbook.* 1965 New York: McGraw Hill 619pp (first published 1953 American Society of Mechanical Engineers Handbook)

With the craftsman (particularly decorative) in view:

Lister, Raymond. *The craftsman in metal.* 1966 London: Bell 208pp bibl.

Stoddard, H. W. *Art metalcrafts: design and decorative processes.* 1951 London: Dent 102pp

Scott, Peter. *The Thames and Hudson manual of metalworking.* 1978 London: Thames and Hudson

Wider-ranging historical studies:

Lueer, Herman and Creutz, May. *Geschichte der Metallkunst.* 1904-1909 Stuttgart: F. Enke 2 vols 660pp 462pp

Smith, Cyril Stanley. 'Metallurgical footnotes to the history of art', *Proceedings of the American Philosophical Society* 116 1972 pp 97-135

A particular application:

Goodwin-Smith, R. *English domestic metalwork*. 1937 Leigh on Sea: F. Lewis 101pp pl 139 (earliest times to present)

One of the richest collections of pattern books:

Goodison, Nicholas. 'The Victoria and Albert Museum's collection of metalwork pattern books', *Furniture History* vol 11 1975

with:

Hall, Ivan. 'Metalwork pattern books – an addendum', *Furniture History* vol 12 1976

Surveys of metalwork at particular periods:

Melton, James. 'Domestic metalwork', pp 101-112 in Edwards, Ralph and Ramsey, L. G. G. (eds). *The early Victorian period 1830-1860*. 1958 London: Connoisseur 180pp

Tylor, Alfred. *Paris Universal Exhibition. Report on general metal work*. 1857 London: HMSO 2 vols in 1 (supplementary report)

'Gothic metal work', *Art Journal* 1861 pp 335-

Yapp, George Wagstaffe. *Art industry: metal-work, illustrating the chief processes of art-work applied by the goldsmith, silversmith, jeweller, brass, copper, iron and steel worker, bronzist etc.* 1878 London: Virtue pl 1200

Saunders, A. F. 'Influence of style on the art metalwork of modern times', *Metal Industry* February-October 1914, March-October 1915, May 1916 pp 64-66, pp 417-418; pp 80-81, pp 321-322; pp 149-150

Gilbert, Walter. 'The essentials of good craftsmanship in metalwork', *Architectural Review* vol 59 1926 pp 147-159

'Metals. Decoration and craftsmanship supplement', *Architectural Review* vol 75 June 1934 pp 217-226

'Metals – special issue', *Architectural Review* vol 81 June 1937 pp 251-300 (includes useful bibliography pp 300)

Weaver, Lawrence. *Tradition and modernity in metalwork*. 1929 Birmingham: Birmingham Guild 30pp illus. (reprinted from *Architectural Review*)

Glenister, Sydney Haywood and Larkman, Brian. *Contemporary design in metalwork*. 1963 London: Murray 119pp illus.

Larkman, Brian. *Metalwork designs of today*. 1969 London: Murray 88pp illus.

Some individual designers and companies:

Bury, Shirley. 'The Liberty metalwork venture'. *Architectural Review* vol 133 no 792 February 1963 pp 108-111

reprinted in Richards, J. M. and Pevsner, Nikolaus (eds). *The Anti-Rationalists*. 1973 London: Architectural Press

Tilbrook, A. J. *The designs of Archibald Knox for Liberty and Co.* 1976 London: Ornament Press 290pp 290 illus.

Mackintosh, Charles Rennie. *Some examples of ironwork and metalwork by Charles Rennie Mackintosh at the Glasgow School of Art, selected and described by H. Jefferson Barnes*. 1969 Glasgow School of Art 73pp illus.

Metalwork for presents, chosen from recent designs carried out at the Dryad works. 1914 Leicester: Dryad

'Modern British craftsman – Mr J. Starkie Gardner', *Architectural Review* vol 45 1919 pp 39-42

Mills, K. S. 'William Bainbridge Reynolds (1855-1935) craftsman in metals', *Transactions of the Ecclesiological Society* new series vol 3 1954 pp 77-85

A tradition of fine craftsmanship. 1959 Cambridge: George Lister and Sons Ltd 16pp

In all consideration of designing in metals it is vital to realise that we are on the edge of a very complex technology. A few more general works to help introduce something of these issues:

Smith, Cyril Stanley. *A history of metallography. The development of ideas on the structure of metals before 1890*. 1960 Chicago: University of Chicago Press 291pp

Smith, Cyril Stanley (ed). *History of metallurgy. Sorby Centennial Symposium*. 1966 London: Gordon and Breach 562pp illus.

Hadfield, Sir Robert Abbott. *Metallurgy and its influence on modern progress*. 1925 London: Chapman and Hall 388pp pl 70

Untracht, Oppi. *Metal techniques for the craftsman*. 1969 London: Hale 500pp illus.

Sharman, John Charles. *Drop, press and machine forging*. 1954 Brighton: Machinery Publishing Company 163pp (Machinery's Standard Reference series)

Aitken, W. C. 'On progress made in ornamental processed connected with metallic and other industries', *JSA* vol 22 April 24 1874 pp 513-522

Roberts-Austen, W. C. 'The use of alloys in art metal-work', *JSA* vol 38 June 13 1890 pp 689-701

2 Particular Metals

Iron and Steel

General studies of iron and steel are essential to an understanding of diversity of activities involved:

Gale, Walter Keith Vernon. *The British iron and steel industry: a technical history.* 1970 Newton Abbot: David and Charles 198pp illus.

Burnham, Thomas Hall and Hoskins, George Owen. *Iron and steel in Britain 1870-1930.* 1943 London: Allen and Unwin 352pp

Gale, Walter Keith Vernon. *The Black Country iron industry: a technical history.* 1966 London: Iron and Steel Institute 192pp

Stones, Frank. *The British ferrous wire industry 1882-1962.* 1977 Sheffield: Northend 418pp illus.

Osborne, Alice Katherine (comp). *An encyclopedia of the iron and steel industry.* 1956 London: Technical Press 558pp illus. bibl.

More specifically concerned with design:

Ironwork by J. Starkie Gardner. Part III A complete survey of artistic working of iron in Great Britain from the earliest times. 1922 London: Victoria and Albert Museum, printed under the authority of the Board of Education

Zimelli, Umberto and Vergerio, Giovanni. *Decorative ironwork.* 1969 Feltham: Hamlyn 159pp (first published 1966 as *Il ferro battuto*)

Decorative ironwork: some aspects of design and technique. 1962 London: Rural Industries Bureau 79pp illus.

A particularly important designer was the Frenchman, Edgar Brandt:

Mourey, Gabriel. 'Edgar Brandt, the French ironworker', *Studio* vol 91 1926 pp 330-335

Clouzot, Henri. *Modern French ironwork.* 1928 London: Tiranti 5pp pl 36

Clouzot, Henri. *La ferronerie moderne, presenté par H. Clouzot.* 1925-1936 Paris: Charles Moreau 5 vols

WROUGHT IRON

Histories and surveys of design:

Lister, Raymond. *Decorative wrought ironwork in Great Britain.* 1970 Newton Abbot: David and Charles 267pp illus. bibl. (first published 1957)

Ayrton, Maxwell and Silcock, Arnold. *Wrought iron and its decorative use.* 1929 London: Country Life 194pp illus. bibl.

English wrought-iron work. 1950 London: Victoria and Albert Museum

Gardner, J. Starkie. 'Wrought ironwork', *JSA* vol 35 February 25 1887 pp 313-332

Stevenson, J. A. R. 'The craft of the decorative iron worker', *JRSA* vol 80 1932 pp 464-483

Kühn, Fritz. *Decorative work in wrought iron and other materials, translated from the German by Gillian Brett.* 1967 London: Harrap 152pp 225 illus.

More specific historical studies:

Stephens, J. E. 'Wrought iron's nineteenth century revival', *Country Life* May 19 1966 pp 1277-1280

Spencer, Edward and Spencer, Walter. 'Wrought iron work', *Studio* vol 46 1909 pp 207-210 (chronicles nineteenth century decline and the activities of their own Artificers Guild)

Underwood, Austin. *Creative wrought ironwork.* 1965 London: Batsford 96pp

More technical considerations:

Lillico, J. W. *Blacksmith's manual illustrated. A practical treatise on modern methods of production.* 1930 London: Crosby Lockwood 211pp

Kühn, Fritz. *Wrought iron, translated from 10th German edition by Charles B. Johnson.* 1965 London: Harrap 120pp 191 illus.

Meyer, Franz Sales. *A handbook of art-smithing, translated from the second German edition with an introduction by J. Starkie Gardner.* 1897 London: Batsford 207pp

CAST IRON

Histories and surveys:

Lister, Raymond. *Decorative cast ironwork in Great Britain.* 1968 London: Bell 258pp

Tripp, B. 'The story of iron casting: as old uses vanish, new ones arise', *Ironmonger* (Centenary number) May 1959 pp 197-199 (traces developments in ironfounding 1859-1959)

Robertson, E. Graeme and Robertson, Joan. *Cast iron decoration. A world survey.* 1977 London: Thames and Hudson 336pp illus. bibl.

A very important aspect of nineteenth century design:

Owen, Michael. *Antique cast iron.* 1977 Poole: Blandford 127pp illus.

Margaretson, Stella. 'London's cast iron elegance', *Country Life* 154 October 25 1973 pp 1286-1287

Lethaby, W. R. 'Cast iron and its treatment for artistic purposes', *JSA* vol 38 February 14 1890 pp 272-284

Ashbee, C. R. 'An experiment in cast iron work', *Studio* vol 14 1898 pp 254-256 (a fireplace for Falkirk Ironworks)

Some important companies:

Campbell, R. H. *Carron Company.* 1961 Edinburgh: Oliver and Boyd 346pp illus.

Carvell, J. L. *The Coltness Iron Company; a study in private enterprise.* 1948 Edinburgh: Constable 199pp illus.

Tripp, Basil Howard. *Grand Alliance. A chapter of industrial history.* 1951 London: Chantry Publications 56pp pl 31 (the history of Allied Ironfounders Ltd pp 26ff – covers post 1851 period)

More recent technical applications:

Sheppard, Richard. *Cast iron in building.* 1945 London: Allen and Unwin 98pp pl 48

Pearce, J. G. 'Cast iron in contemporary building and engineering', *JRSA* vol 94 August 2 1946 pp 540-550

Hallett, M. M. 'Cooperation between designer and foundryman', *British Cast Iron Research Association Journal* vol 6 1955-1957 pp 530-545 (Report no 458)

Goyns, H. G. 'Design of cast components', *Engineer and Foundryman* vol 23 July 1958 pp 54-64 (general principles)

Carmichael, C. 'Casting's role in modern designs', *Foundry* vol 87 December 1959 pp 65-67

Caine, J. B. 'How to design reliable castings', *Foundry* vol 90 March 1962 pp 70-73

McIntyre, J. B. 'The design of castings for production', *British Cast Iron Research Association Journal* vol 8 1960 pp 393-397 (Report no 547)

Tinplate:

Minchinton, W. E. *The British tinplate industry.* 1957 Oxford: Clarendon Press 286pp

Cox, Ralph. *Victorian tinware with notes on a nineteenth century catalogue.* 1970 Stamford: Stamford Properties 96pp (76pp of illustrations from facsimile of an 1862 priced catalogue)

Gould, Mary Earle. *Antique tin and toleware: its history and romance.* 1958 Rutland, Vermont: Tuttle 136pp (American)

The Worshipful company of tin plate workers. Report of the . . . deputation in South Wales and Cornwall. 1914. 1925 London: Rixon and Arnold 16pp

Finally, a bookseller's catalogue that also makes a useful bibliography:

The use of iron in construction and decoration, with a supplement of trade catalogues for

foundries and ironmongers. 1967 London: Weinreb and Breman Ltd

STEEL

Histories:

Carr, J. C. and Taplin, W. *History of the British steel industry.* 1952 Cambridge, Mass: Harvard University Press 632pp

Brearley, Harry. *Steel-makers.* 1933 London: Longman 156pp

Wilson, James. 'On the manufacture of articles from steel, particularly cutlery', *JSA* vol 4 1856 pp 357-366

Stainless steel:

Spark, Robert. 'Materials. Fifty years of stainless steel', *Design* 181 January 1964 pp 26-33

Wells, E. Hargord. 'The battle of stainless steel', *Art and Industry* November 1958 pp 172-177

See also:

Cutlery *page 233*

Razor blades:

Coster, Ian. *The sharpest edge in the world: the story of the rise of a great industry.* 1948 London: Gillette Industries Ltd 86pp

A design manual amongst many:

A practical guide to the design of steel castings. 1958 Sheffield: British Steel Castings Research Association 52pp

Pewter and Britannia Metal

Peal, Christopher A. *British pewter and Britannia metal.* 1971 London: Gifford

Unfortunately most other surveys of pewter have little on the pewter of the period:

Cotterell, H. H. *Pewter down the ages from mediaeval times to the present day.* 1932 159 illus. (includes a short list history of British pewterers and their marks)

Michaelis, R. F. *British pewter.* 1969 London: Ward Lock

Hatcher, John and Barker, Theodore C. *A history of British pewter.* 1974 London: Longman 363pp illus. bibl.

Massé, H. J. L. 'Pewter: some of its uses', *Architectural Review* vol 6 1899 pp 131-138

A short history of the Worshipful company of Pewterers of London, and a catalogue of pewterware in its possession. 1968 London: Pewterers Company 103pp bibl.

Smith, Frederick Richard. *Pewter work.* 1930 London: Pitman 113pp

On the nineteenth century:

Peal, Christopher A. *Let's collect pewter.* 1978 Norwich: Jarrolds 40pp illus.

Peal, Christopher A. '19th century, pure and simple', *Antique Dealer and Collectors Guide* September 1973

Peal, Christopher A. 'Britannia metal is pewter', *Antique Finder* October 1971

Peal, Christopher A. 'Rule Britannia', *Antique Dealer and Collectors Guide* January 1975

Its revival at the end of the century:

Liberty, Arthur Lasenby. 'Pewter and the revival of its use', *JSA* vol 52 June 10 1904 pp 626-644

Gardner, J. Starkie. 'Pewter', *JSA* vol 42 June 1 1894 pp 627-647

Art Nouveau pewter. 1968 London: Victoria and Albert Museum (circulating exhibition)

More recent pewter:

Contemporary pewter. 1936 London: International Tin Research and Development Council

Pewter of today. Catalogue of the international exhibition June 10-30 1955 London: Tin Research Institute 66pp

The manufacture of pewter:

Englefield, Elsie. *A treatise on pewter and its manufacture.* 1933 London: Priory Press 85pp

Engelfield, Elsie. *A discourse . . . delivered at a conversazione given by the Worshipful Company of Pewterers . . . 1934.* 1935 London: Priory Press 34pp

Osburn, B. N. and Wilber, G. O. *Pewter: spun, wrought and cast.* 1939 Scranton: International Text Book Co 151pp

Sheffield Plate

Although superceded by the beginning of the period, production did continue for a time and so it may be helpful to look at its historical roots:

Bradbury, Frederick. *History of old Sheffield plate.* 1912 London: Macmillan

Wyler, Seymour B. *The book of Sheffield plate.* 1949 New York: Crown 188pp

Brass and Copper

Wills, Geoffrey. *The book of copper and brass.* 1968 Feltham: Hamlyn 96pp illus.

Wills, Geoffrey. *Collecting copper and brass.* 1962 London: Mayflower 160pp illus.

Hamilton, H. *The English brass and copper industries.* 1926 London: Longmans 388pp

Aitken, W. C. 'Brass and brass manufacture', pp 225-380 in Timmins, Samuel (ed). *The resources, products and industrial history of Birmingham and the Midland hardware district.* 1866 London: Robert Hardwicke

Hull, Daniel R. *Casting of brass and bronze.* 1950 Cleveland: American Society of Metals 186pp (covers developments from 1900 to the present)

Lindsay, John Seymour. *Iron and brass implements of the English house.* 1927

Aluminium

Smithells, Colin J. 'Three Cantor lectures on the manufacture, properties and applications of aluminium and its alloys. 1. Production of aluminium, 2. Aluminium and its alloys, 3. Applications of aluminium', *JRSA* vol 98 August 25 1950 pp 822-863

Frary, F. C. and Edwards, J. D. '50 years of a new product development', (aluminium), *Chemical and Metallurgical Engineering* 43 February 1936 pp 6-7, pp 64-67

Barman, Christian. 'Light new world', *Art and Industry* September 1941 pp 62-67

Friese-Grene, G. H. 'The aluminium industry and the importance of design and craftsmanship in its development', *Art and Industry* June 1946 pp 162-185

Early papers:

Addenbrooke, G. L. 'Uses and applications of aluminium', *JSA* vol 40 May 13 1892 pp 661-668

Wilson, Sir Ernest. 'Aluminium', *JSA* vol 50 December 13 1901 pp 54-62

More technical applications and considerations:

A symposium on aluminium packaging. 1958 London: Aluminium Development Association

Light Metals Bulletin 1939- (bi-weekly) London: British Aluminium Company

Lead

A survey:

Weaver, Lawrence. *English leadwork. Its art and history.* 1909 London: Batsford 268pp illus. bibl (Reprinted by Blom 1970. Contains 'A first attempt at a bibliography of publications relating to the history of English leadwork' pp 251-257)

Lethaby, W. R. 'Leadwork', *JSA* vol 45 April 9 1897 pp 452-459

Smaller studies:

Burges, William. 'Ornamental leadwork', *Ecclesiologist* 1857

Radford, Ernest. 'Mr G. P. Bankart's leadwork', *Studio* vol 28 1906 pp 90-93

Vallance, Aymer. 'Recent leadwork by Mr G. P. Bankart', *Studio* vol 28 1906 pp 194-

Weaver, Lawrence. 'Modern leadwork, 1. Larger uses, 2. Rainwater heads, 3. Cisterns, fonts, vases', *Architectural Review* vol 22 1907 vol 23 1908 pp 221-, pp 268-; pp 84-89

'Mr F. E. Osborne's cast lead work', *Studio* vol 89 1925 pp 145-147

'Craftsman's portfolio. Decorative leadwork', *Architectural Review* vol 66 1929 pp 311-312

For more technical material:

Lead abstracts: a review of recent technical literature on the uses of lead and its products. 1958- (6 per year) London: Lead Development Association

Other Metals

Betteridge, Walter. *Nickel and its alloys.* 1977 Plymouth: Macdonald and Evans 146pp illus. (Industrial metals series)

Howard-White, F. B. *Nickel: an historical review.* 1963 London: Methuen 350pp (1750 to present)

Charleton, A. G. 'Nickel: its history, uses and distribution', *JSA* vol 42 May 4 1894 pp 496-513

McDonald, Donald. *A history of platinum.* 1960 London: Johnson, Matthey and Co 254pp illus.

Hedges, E. S. *Tin in social and economic history.* 1964 London: E. Arnold

Tin through the ages in arts, crafts and industry. 1941 Cardiff: National Museum of Wales

Randolph, Denys. 'From rapiers to razor blades: the development of the light metals industry', *JRSA* vol 122 May 1974 pp 338-355

Two abstracting services:

BNF Abstracts 1921- (monthly) (formerly *British Non-Ferrous metals Association Bulletin*)

Zinc Abstracts: a review of recent technical literature on the uses of zinc and its products. 1943- (bi-monthly) London: Zinc Development Association

Electrometallurgy, particularly electroplate

Bury, Shirley. *Victorian electroplate.* 1971 Feltham: Hamlyn 63pp illus.

Catalogue of art manufacturers exhibited by Elkington and Company at the Great Exhibition, London 1851. 1851 London

Coles, Sherard Cowper. 'Sheffield plate and electroplate', *JSA* vol 55 July 12 1907 pp 853-866, pp 873-886 (historical sketches of the replacement of one by the other with a bibliography)

Silver

Three particularly useful studies of nineteenth century silver:

Culme, John. *Nineteenth century silver.* 1977 London: Hamlyn 232pp illus. bibl.

Wardle, Patricia. *Victorian silver and silver plate.* 1963 London: Herbert Jenkins 238pp illus.

Harris, Ian. *Price guide to Victorian silver.* 1971 Woodbridge: Antique Collectors Club 276pp 290 illus.

and for more recent work:

Hughes, Graham. *Modern silver throughout the world 1880-1967.* 1967 London: Studio Vista 256pp illus. bibl.

As it is the main collected metal there are very many more general books on silver. A few of the more useful are:

Lever, Christopher. *Goldsmiths and silversmiths of England.* 1975 London: Hutchinson 256pp illus. (covers period c 1690-1972)

Clayton, Michael. *The collector's dictionary of silver and gold.* 1971 London: Country Life 351pp illus. bibl.

Fletcher, Lucinda. *Silver.* 1973 London: Orbis 64pp 101 illus.

Delieb, Eric. *Silver boxes.* 1968 London: Jenkins 119pp illus.

Hackenbroch, Y. *English and other silver in the Irwin Untermeyer collection.* 1964 London: Thames and Hudson 96pp pl 200

Oman, Charles. *English engraved silver 1150-1900.* 1978 London: Faber

Taylor, Gerald. *Art in silver and gold.* 1964 London: Studio Vista 160pp illus.

Taylor, Gerald. *Silver.* 1964 (second edition) Harmondsworth: Penguin 301pp pl 64 (first edition 1963)

Hallmarks:

Wilkinson, Wynyard Russell T. *A history of hallmarks.* 1975 (revised edition) London: Queen Anne Press 160pp illus.

Bradbury, Frederick. *Bradbury's book of hallmarks: a guide to marks of origin on British and Irish silver, gold and platinum and on foreign imported silver and gold plate, 1544-1975.* 1975 (revised edition) Sheffield: Northend 112pp illus.

Technique:

Goodden, Robert and Popham, Philip. *Silversmithing.* 1971 Oxford University Press 128pp illus.

Maryon, Herbert. *Metalwork and enamelling: a practical treatise on gold and silversmiths work and their allied crafts.* 1971 (revised edition) New York: Dover (first edition 1912, third edition 1954) 335pp illus.

Studies of particular periods:

Bury, Shirley. 'Silver and silver plate', pp 69-84 in Edwards, Ralph and Ramsey, L. G. G. (eds). *The early Victorian period 1830-1860.* 1958 London: Connoisseur

Banister, J. 'Silver of 1874', *Connoisseur* 185 January 1974. pp 49-54

Freeman, Larry. *Victorian silver: plated and sterling, hollow and flatware.* 1967 Watkins Glen, New York: Century House 400pp illus. bibl. (American but wide ranging and detailed)

Illustrated catalogue of silver plate. 1854 Birmingham: Elkington, Mason and Company

Hughes, Therle. *Tommorow's treasure. The work of Edwardian silversmiths.* Country Life 156 October 24 1974 pp 126, pp 128

Holbrook, John Swift. *Silver for the dining room.* 1912 Cambridge University Press 119pp illus.

Ramsden, Omar. 'English silver and its future', *JRSA* vol 77 November 30 1928 pp 51-71

Weaver, Sir Lawrence. *Art in industry and salesmanship, with special reference to the work of the silversmith. Being a lecture delivered at Goldsmith's Hall.* 1929 London: Curwen Press 25pp

Holme, Charles Geoffrey. 'British silverware today', *Studio* vol 104 October 1932 pp 214-219

Benson, Oscar. 'The trend of design in silverware', *Studio* vol 107 June 1934 pp 323-325

Murphy, H. G. 'British silver today', *Studio* vol 111 1936 pp 36-42

'The design of British silverware. A criticism', *Studio* vol 116 1938 pp 212-213

Wallis, W. Cyril. *Scottish enterprise: silver, glass and pottery.* 1947 Glasgow: Council of Industrial Design Scottish Committee 16pp

Goodden, R. Y. 'Modern English silversmithing', *JRSA* vol 114 October 1966 pp 890-903

Lyon, Peter. 'Modern jewellery as works of art', *Apollo* January 1971 pp 54-57

Exhibitions of silver are many but often very particular. The most valuable to the historian are those commemorating centenaries or even bicentenaries, eg:

Sheffield silver 1773-1973: an exhibition to mark the bicentenary of the Sheffield Assay office. 1973 Sheffield City Museum 107pp illus. bibl.

Birmingham gold and silver 1773-1973: an exhibition celebrating the bicentenary of the Assay office. Catalogue of the exhibition 28 July-16 September. 1973 Birmingham City Museum and Art Gallery 288pp illus.

The Goldsmiths Company London has exercised an extremely powerful influence on the development of design through its exhibitions and other forms of patronage:

The Worshipful Company of Goldsmiths as patrons of their craft 1919-1953 by George Ravensworth Hughes. 1965 London: Worshipful Company of Goldsmiths 2 vols (Part 1. Company and their craft. Part 2. Catalogue)

Hughes, Graham. 'Goldsmiths Company: its role as patron and collector', *Museums Journal* 74 December 1974 pp 121-124

The scientific and technical factors of production of gold and silverwork . . . lectures held at Goldsmith's Hall. 1935-1936 London: Curwen Press 86pp

Exhibition of silverwork by craftsmen of the present day . . . lent from the collection of the Worshipful Company of Goldsmiths. 1936 London: Courtauld Institute

Exhibition of modern silverwork. 1938 London: Goldsmiths Company

English silverwork including ceremonial plate by contemporary craftsmen. 1951 London: Goldsmiths Company 20pp

Modern silver. 1954 London: Goldsmiths Company 24pp

Modern silver: a review of modern British gold and sterling silver. 1959 London: Goldsmiths Company

Topham trophy competition, 1962. (Selected designs from the 1962 . . . competition, with the winning trophies of the years 1950-1962). 1962 London: Goldsmiths Company

Modern British silver: a picture book of gold and sterling silver by British designers. 1963 London: Goldsmiths Company

New gold, silver and jewels commissioned by industry: an exhibition organised for the Institute of Directors. 1965 London: Goldsmiths Company

The Goldsmith today. Acquisitions of new silver and jewels since 1953 by the Worshipful Company of Goldsmiths. 1967 London: Goldsmiths Company

Unfortunately there is not the space to detail any more than a few individual designers. A useful introduction to some of the better known is provided by:

Honour, Hugh. *Goldsmiths and silversmiths.* 1971 London: Weidenfeld and Nicolson 320pp illus. bibl.

A selection of interesting studies:

Ashbee, Charles Robert. *Modern English silverwork. A new edition with introductory essays by Alan Crawford and Shirley Bury.* 1974 London: Weinreb (first edition 1909 Essex House Press)

Bury, Shirley. 'An Arts and Crafts experiment; the silverwork of C. R. Ashbee', *Victoria and Albert Museum Bulletin* vol III no 1 January 1967 (reprinted as a pamphlet by HMSO 1967)

Bury, Shirley. 'The silver designs of Dr Christopher Dresser', *Apollo* December 1962 pp 766-770

Wood, T. Martin. 'Alexander Fisher and his silver work: a maker of beautiful things', *Studio* vol 31 1904 pp 224-226

Cymric silver designs. 1900 London: Liberty pl 53

Omar Ramsden 1873-1939: centenary exhibition of silver. 1973 Birmingham Museum and Art Gallery 80pp 60 illus.

Robert Welch, design in a Cotswold workshop. Introduction by Alan Crawford. Edited by Colin Forbes. 1973 London: Lund Humphries 64pp illus.

Wilson, Henry. *Silverwork and jewellery.* 1978 London: Pitman 528pp illus. (first edition 1912)

Gold

Sutherland, Carol Humphrey Vivian. *Gold. Its beauty, power and allure.* 1959 London: Thames and Hudson 196pp illus. (general history)

Jackson, Sir Charles James. *English goldsmiths and their marks.* 1905 (second edition) London: Macmillan 696pp (other editions 1921, 1949)

An old bibliography that is useful for earlier materials:

Science and Art Department of the Committee on Education. *A list of works on gold and silversmiths work and jewellery in the National Art Library (compiled for the use of students and visitors).* 1882 London: Eyre and Spottiswode for HMSO 61pp

3 Some Applications

Cutlery

General histories and surveys:

Pagé, Camille. *La coutellerie depuis l'origine jusqu'à nos jours.* 1896 Paris: Chatellerault, H. Rivière 6 vols (Standard history – vol 2 contains part 3: Modern cutlery, vols 5 & 6 contain part 5: foreign cutlery ie foreign to France)

Garlick, P. C. 'Cutlery progress over 250 years: notes on the history of Sheffield cutlery and allied trades since 1700', *International Cutler* vol 1 pp 14-16, vol 2 no 1 pp 10-13, vol 2 no 2 pp 12-15, vol 2 no 3 pp 10-15, vol 2 no 5 pp 12-13, vol 3 no 1 pp 24-25. 1951-1953 (based on a thesis)

Himsworth, J. B. *The story of cutlery: from flint to stainless steel.* 1953 London: Benn 208pp illus. (originally 16 articles in *The Hardware Trade Journal* 3 March 1950 to 12 January 1951)

Hayward, J. F. *English cutlery.* 1956 London: HMSO for Victoria and Albert Museum

Lloyd, G. I. H. *The cutlery trades: an historical essay in the economics of small scale production.* 1913 London: Longmans Green 493pp

Knife, fork, spoon: the story of our primary eating implements and the development of their form. 1951 Minneapolis: Walker Art Center 64pp

Girtin, Tom. *Mark of the sword: a narrative history of the Cutler's Company 1189-1975.* 1975 London: Hutchinson 488pp illus.

Cutlery. A bibliography. 1960 Sheffield Libraries, Art Galleries and Museums Committee 30pp

Singleton, H. Raymond. *A chronology of cutlery.* 1973 Sheffield City Museum 8pp pl 5

SPOONS

Rainwater, Dorothy T. and Felger, Donna H. *A collector's guide to spoons around the world.* 1976 New York: Everybodys Press Inc 406pp illus. bibl.

Belden, Gail and Snodin, Michael. *Spoons.* 1976 Radnor: Chilton 112pp

Snodin, Michael. *English silver spoons*. 1974
London: Charles Letts 79pp illus. bibl.

Selected details:

Postgate, Richmond. 'The tools of the table',
Design for Today January 1934 pp 14-17

Knives, spoons forks: a design folio. 1950
London: Council of Industrial Design
6pp pl 12

Gregson, Tom 'Cutlery and flatware.
Mechanisation and modern design in
Sheffield', *Design* 84 December 1955
pp 26-29

Holmes, Rathbone. 'Implements of the
table', *Art and Industry* vol 63 October
1957 pp 122-127

Beresford-Evans, J. and Archer, L. Bruce.
'Design analysis 8. Stainless steel cutlery
and flatware', *Design* 114 June 1958
pp 39-44

Jewellery

The collector's literature par excellence.
Some general studies:

Black, J. Anderson. *A history of jewels*. 1974
London: Orbis 400pp illus. bibl.

Hughes, Graham. *The art of jewellery*. 1972
London: Studio Vista 248pp illus.

Armstrong, Nancy. *Jewellery: an historical
survey of British styles and jewels*. 1973
London: Lutterworth Press 304pp illus.

Evans, Joan. *A history of jewellery 1100-1870*.
1973 (third edition) London: Faber
224pp illus. (first edition 1953)

Lyon, Peter. *Design in Jewellery*. 1956
London: Peter Owen 188pp

Hughes, Graham. *Jewellery*. 1966 New
York: Dutton 167pp illus.

Hinks, Peter. *Jewellery, illustrated by Martin
Battersby*. 1969 Feltham: Hamlyn 160pp
illus.

Earlier studies:

Davenport, Cyril James Humphries.
Jewellery. 1905 London: Methuen 166pp
pl 25

Smith, H. Clifford. *Jewellery*. 1973 East
Ardsley: EP 457pp illus. (facsimile
reprint of 1908 edition)

A dictionary:

Mason, Anita and Packer, Diane (eds). *An
illustrated dictionary of jewellery*. 1973
Reading: Osprey 400pp illus.

The great interest and now value of
Victorian jewellery has helped to create a
large body of fairly recent literature:

Armstrong, Nancy. *Victorian jewelry*. 1977
London: Studio 160pp 136 illus.

Bradford, Ernle. *English Victorian jewellery*.
1967 London: Spring Books 141pp
illus. (first edition 1959)

Flower, Margaret. *Victorian jewellery*. 1967
(revised edition) London: Cassell
271pp illus. (first edition 1951)

Flower, Margaret. *Jewellery 1837-1901*. 1968
London: Cassell 64pp illus. (Collectors
pieces 15)

Hinks, Peter. *Nineteenth century jewellery*.
1975 London: Faber 200pp illus. (Faber
collectors library)

Janson, Dora Jane. *From slave to siren. The
Victorian woman and her jewelry. From
neoclassic to Art Nouveau*. 1971 Durham,
North Carolina: Duke University Museum
of Art 111pp 183 illus.

Gere, Charlotte. *European and American
jewellery 1830-1914*. 1975 London:
Heinemann 240pp illus. bibl.

Gere, Charlotte. *Victorian jewellery design*.
1972 London: William Kimber 285pp
illus. bibl.

Gere, Charlotte. 'Victorian jewellery',
Connoisseur June 1976 pp 146-151

Grundy, Anne Hall. 'Victorian jewellery',
Apollo February 1961 pp 40-44

O'Day, Deidre. *Victorian jewellery*. 1974
London: Charles Letts 80pp illus. bibl.

Peter, Mary. *Collecting Victorian jewellery*.
1970 London: MacGibbon and Kee
100pp illus.

Particular types of jewellery:

Cooper, Diana and Batterhill, Noreen.
Victorian sentimental jewellery. 1972
Newton Abbot: David and Charles 127pp
illus. bibl.

Lewis, M. D. S. *Antique paste jewellery*. 1970
London: Faber 80pp illus. (first edition
1957)

Banister, Judith. 'Victorian jewellery –
changing fashions in an era of change and
mourning jewellery', *Antique Dealer and
Collector's Guide* December 1970
pp 100-107

Regrettably there is no work of such scale
and detail covering English jewellery as
there is French:

Vever, Henri. *La bijouterie Française au XIXe
siècle*. 1908 Paris: H. Floury 3 vols
(reprint by Studio per Edizione Scelte,
Florence)

Turn of the century:

See also:

Glass: Art Nouveau *page 219*

Art Nouveau *page 71*

Mourey, Gabriel and Vallance, Aymer. *Art nouveau jewellery and fans*. 1974 New York: Dover 159pp illus.

Holme, Charles (ed.) *Modern designs in jewellery and fans*. 1901/1902 London: Studio special Winter number 44pp illus.

Melville, Robert. 'The soft jewellery of art nouveau', pp 143-151 in Richards, J. M. and Pevsner, J. M. (eds). *The Anti-Rationalists*. 1973 London: Architectural Press

Hughes, Graham. 'Art nouveau jewellery', in Wilson, P. C. *Antiques International* 1966 London: Joseph 368pp

La Revue de la Bijouterie, la Joaillerie, et l'Orfevrerie 1900-

Developments later in the twentieth century:

Hadaway, Mrs. 'Developments in the art of jewellery', *JRSA* vol 56 February 7 1908 pp 287-297

Heming, George B. 'Art education in the jewellery, goldsmithing and allied trades', *JRSA* vol 59 March 1910 pp 497-510

'Some examples of modern English jewellery', *Studio* vol 60 1914 pp 265-272

Worsley, Cyril. 'British craftsmanship: modern jewellery by the Goldsmiths and Silversmiths company', *Studio* vol 97 1929 pp 314-317

Zinkeisen, A. K. 'Suggestions for the design of modern jewellery', *Studio* vol 109 March 1935 pp 149-151

Instone, Bernard. 'The art of the jeweller. A review of modern design in precious stones and metals', *Studio* vol 116 1938 pp 280-287

Postwar:

Hughes, Graham. *Modern Jewelry: an international survey*. 1968 London: Studio Vista 256pp illus. bibl. (previous editions 1963, 1964)

Turner, Ralph. *Contemporary jewelry. A critical assessment 1945-1975*. 1976 London: Studio Vista 208pp illus. bibl.

Bradford, Ernle S. *Contemporary jewellery and silver design*. 1950 London: Heywood 134pp illus.

Von Neumann, Robert. *The design and creation of jewelry*. 1962 London: Pitman 228pp illus. bibl.

Brynner, Irene. *Modern jewelry: design and technique*. 1968 New York: Van Nostrand Reinhold 95pp

Davenport, Tarby. 'Craftsmen in modern jewellery', *Design* December 1967 pp 33-37

Morton, Philip. *Contemporary jewelry*. 1970 New York: Holt Rinehart and Winston 308pp illus. bibl.

Journals and organisations (apart from the Goldsmiths Company):

Bulletin of the Design and Research Centre for the Gold, Silver and Jewellery Industries 1948- London: (not published June 1953-November 1957. Bulletin for members only)

Gemmologist 1931-1962 (incorporated with Horologial Journal. From 1937 to 1946 published as supplement to *Goldsmiths Journal*)

Gemmological Association of Great Britain. *History (1908-1951), constitution and byelaws*. 1952 London 36pp (earlier edition 1948)

The jeweller and metalworker: fortnightly review of watchmaking and gold and silversmith trades. 1894-1965 London

Journal of Gemmology and Proceedings of the Gemmological Association of Great Britain 1947-

Particular types of jewellery
CAMEOS

Davenport, Cyril James Humphreys. *Cameos*. 1900 London: Portfolio 74pp (Portfolio monographs 41)

Marsh, J. B. 'Cameo cutting as an occupation', *JSA* vol 35 January 21 1887 pp 148-155

COSTUME JEWELLERY

Oved, Sali. *The book of necklaces*. 1953 London: Barker 110pp illus.

Banister, Judith. 'Changing fashions in memorial jewellery', *Antique Dealer and Collector's Guide* November 1967 pp 53-56

Becker, Vivienne. 'Pendants at the turn of the century', *Art and Antiques Weekly* September 17 1977 pp 22-25

Hinks, Peter. 'Jewellery which was made to be worn', *Antique Jewellery and Collectors Guide* May 1975 pp 74-78

DIAMONDS

Tolansky, S. *The history and use of diamond*. 1962 London: Methuen 166pp illus. bibl.

Bruton, Eric. *Diamonds*. 1970 London: NAG Press 372pp illus.

Emanuel, Harry. *Diamonds and precious stones: their history, value and distinguishing characteristics*. 1867 London: J. C. Holten 266pp illus. bibl. (first edition 1865)

Church, A. H. 'The discrimination and artistic use of precious stones', *JSA* vol 29 April 8 1881 pp 440-448

RINGS

Kunz, George Frederick. *Rings for the finger.* 1973 London: Constable 512pp 290 illus.

McCarthy, James Remington. *Rings through the ages. An informal history.* 1945 New York: Harper 202pp (University Microfilms)

Oman, Charles. *British rings 800-1914.* 1974 London: Batsford 146pp illus. bibl.

WHITBY JET

Bamford, Joan. 'Whitby jet set', *Art and Antiques Weekly* vol 5 March 4 1972 pp 18-19

Kendall, Hugh P. *The story of Whitby jet, its workers from earliest times.* 1936 Whitby: privately printed 12pp

Bower, John A. 'On Whitby jet and its manufacture', *JSA* vol 22 December 1873 pp 80-87

OTHER DETAILS

Clifford, Anne. *Cut steel and Berlin iron jewellery.* 1971 Bath: Adams and Dart 96pp illus.

Dent, H. C. *Piqué: a beautiful minor art.* 1923 London 32pp pl 36

Larkins, W. G. 'On trinkets and their manufacture', *JSA* vol 20 March 1 1872 pp 285-292

Sykes, Marjorie. 'Fishing for pearls – British pearls', *History Today* October 1976 pp 678-682

Exhibitions

Of the hundreds, a few wide-ranging examples:

International exhibition of modern jewellery, 1890-1961. Exhibition organised . . . in association with the Victoria and Albert Museum. 1961 London: Goldsmiths Company 2 vols in 1

Nineteenth century jewelry from the first Empire to the first world war. 1955 New York: Cooper Union Museum for the Arts of Decoration 23pp

Le bijou 1900: modern style-juwelen. 1965 Brussels: Hotel Solvay 102pp illus.

Jewellery and jewellery design 1850-1930, and John Paul Cooper 1869-1933 (An exhibition arranged in association with the Adelaide Festival of Arts and John Jesse. 1975 Uxbridge: Hillingdon Press

Pendulum to atom. Centenary exhibition catalogue. 1958 London: Goldsmiths Company

The ageless diamond: an exhibition sponsored by Christies and De Beers Consolidated Mines. 1959 London: Christie's illus.

Individuals

A very small selection of important figures:

Hughes, Graham. 'Contemporary British craftsman: Gerda Flockinger', *Connoisseur* vol 155 no 624 February 1964 pp 109-113

Jewellery by Bruno Martinazzi. 1965 London: Goldsmiths Company

FABERGE

Snowman, Abraham Kenneth. *The art of Carl Fabergé.* 1964 London: Faber 186pp illus. (first edition 1953)

Bainbridge, Henry Charles. *Peter Carl Fabergé, goldsmith and jeweller to the Russian Imperial Court.* 1966 London: Spring Books 167pp pl 128

Fabergé and his contemporaries; the India Early Minshall collection of the Cleveland Museum of Art by Henry Hawley. 1967 Ohio: Cleveland Museum of Art 139pp illus. bibl.

Fabergé. 1977 London: Victoria and Albert Museum

Ross, Marvin Chauncey. *The art of Karl Fabergé and his contemporaries.* 1965 Norman: University of Oklahoma Press 238pp

Enamel

Surveys:

Enamel: an historic survey to the present day. 1954 New York: Cooper Union Museum for the Arts of Decoration 26pp

Barsali, Isa Belli. *European enamels, translated by Raymond Rudorff.* 1969 Feltham: Hamlyn 158pp illus. (first published as *Lo Smalto in Europa*)

Cunynghame, Henry H. *European enamels.* 1906 London: Methuen 188pp illus.

Day, Lewis F. *Enamelling, a comparative account of the development and practice of the art.* 1907 London: Batsford 222pp

Hughes, Therle and Hughes, George Bernard. *English painted enamels.* 1951 London: Country Life 156pp

Technique:

Gardner, J. Starkie. 'Enamels and enamelling', *JSA* vol 39 March 20 1891 pp 331-345

Heaton, Clement. 'The use of cloisonné for decoration in ancient and modern times', *JSA* vol 39 April 3 1891 pp 375-389

'Fred Miller. An enameller and his work',
Studio vol 8 1897 pp 149-156

Cunynghame, Henry. *On the theory and
practice of art-enamelling upon metals.* 1899
London: Constable 135pp illus.

Fisher, Alexander. 'The art of true
enamelling upon metals', *Studio* vol 22,
vol 23 1901, vol 25 1902 pp 242-254,
pp 88-92; pp 108-118

Miller, Fred. 'The art of the enameller and
of Mr Alex Fisher in particular', *Art
Journal* 1898 pp 263-267

Murray, H. 'Enamelling in relief: Mr Henry
Holiday's interesting invention', *Studio*
vol 34 1905 pp 304-306

Smith, Hamilton T. 'Harold Stabler, worker
in metals and enamels', *Studio* vol 64 1915
pp 34-40

Bates. *Enamelling. Principle and practice.*
1951 London: Constable 208pp illus.

Rothenberg, Polly. *Metal enamelling.* 1970
London: Allan and Unwin 211pp illus.
bibl.

Church plate

See also:

Interior Design: Churches *page 162*

*Copy or creation: Victorian treasures from
English churches. Exhibition organised by the
Worshipful Company of Goldsmiths and the
Victorian Society. Catalogue by Shirley Bury.*
1967 London: Goldsmiths Company
48pp pl 4 bibl. refs.

Gilchrist, James. *Anglican church plate.* 1967
London: Joseph 122pp

Hughes, Graham. 'Modern British church
plate', pp 58-63 in *The Care of churches:
16th Annual review of the Council for the
Care of Churches.* 1962 London: Church
Information Office

Burges, William. 'Altar plate', *Ecclesiologist*
1858 221pp

Modern church plate. 1965 Manchester City
Art Gallery

Coins

Linecar, Howard. *British coin designs and
designers.* 1978 London: Bell 144pp

Brooke, George C. *English coins from the
seventh century to the present day.* 1976 (third
edition) London: Spink 300pp illus.

There is a vast range of more specialised
literature for the collector but it clearly lies
beyond the scope of the present work.

Costume and fashion

See also:

Textiles *page 184*

The literature spanning the history of fashion and costume is large and various with numerous specialised groups. What follows is only a brief introduction to be filled out by information available from the Costume Society and other bodies publishing and listing in this area.

General Surveys

Black, J. Anderson and Garland, Madge. *A history of fashion*. 1975 London: Orbis 400pp illus. bibl.

Pistolese, Rosana and Horsting, R. *History of fashions*. 1970 New York: Wiley. 340pp illus. bibl.

Assailly, Gisele d'. *Ages of elegance: five thousand years of fashion and frivolity*. 1968 London: Macdonald. (translation of *Les Quinze Révolutions de la Mode* 1968). 251pp illus.

Lister, Margot. *Costume: an illustrated survey from ancient times to the twentieth century*. 1967 London: Barrie and Jenkins. 360pp 252 illus.

Laver, James. *A concise history of costume*. 1969 London: Thames and Hudson. 288pp illus.

Wilcox, R. Turner. *The mode in costume. (History of costume throughout the ages)*. 1949 New York: Scribner. 419pp

Braun-Ronsdorf, Margarete. *The wheel of fashion: costume since the French Revolution 1789-1929*. 1964 London: Thames and Hudson. 270pp illus. (translated from the German by Oliver Coburn)

Dorner, Jane. *Fashion: the changing shape of fashion through the years*. 1974 London: Octopus. 128pp illus. bibl.

Garland, Madge. *The changing form of fashion*. 1970 London: Dent 130pp illus.

Brogden, J. *Fashion design*. 1971 London: Studio Vista 96pp. (long chapter on 'The great fashion designers')

Hill, Margot H. and Bucknell, P. *Evolution of fashion: pattern and cut from 1066-1930*. 1967 London: Batsford 225pp illus.

Taylor, John. *It's a small, medium and outsize world*. 1966 London: Evelyn 132pp illus. (1800-1965)

Settle, A. 'Fashion and trade', *JRSA* vol 118 1970 pp 94-107. (from the eighteenth century to the present)

Laver, James. *Dress: how and why fashions in men's and women's clothes have changed during the past hundred years*. 1966 (second edition) London: John Murray 47pp (first published 1950)

Laver, James. *Taste and fashion from the French Revolution to the present day*. 1945 (second edition) London: Harrap 232pp pl 12 (first published 1937)

Moore, Doris Langley. *The woman in fashion*. 1949 London: Batsford 184pp

Bradfield, Nancy. *Costume in detail: women's dress 1730-1930*. 1968 London: Harrap 391pp

Dictionaries and Encyclopaedias

Kybalova, Ludmila and others. *The pictorial encyclopedia of fashion*. 1968 London: Hamlyn 608pp

Leloir, Maurice. *Dictionnaire du costume et ses accessoires*. 1949 Paris: Grund 435pp

Picken, Mary Brooks. *The fashion dictionary. Fabric, sewing and dress as expressed in the language of fashion*. 1957 New York: Funk & Wagnalls 397pp illus. (first published 1939)

Wilcox, R. Turner. *The dictionary of costume*. 1971 London: Batsford 406pp illus.

English Costume/Fashion

Bradfield, Nancy. *Historical costume of England 1066-1968*. 1970 London: Harrap 200pp bibl.

Brooke, Iris. *The history of English costume*. 1968 (third edition reprinted) London: Eyre Methuen 300pp (original third edition 1949)

Cunnington, Cecil Willett. *The art of English costume*. 1948 London: Collins

Cunnington, Cecil Willett and others. *A dictionary of English costume, 900-1900*. 1960 London: Black 281pp illus.

Cunnington, Cecil Willett and Cunnington, Phillis. *Picture history of English costume*. 1960 London: Vista 160pp

Fashion: an anthology by Cecil Beaton. Exhibition October 1971 to January 1972. Catalogue compiled by Madeleine Ginsburg. 1971-72 London: HMSO for the Victorian and Albert Museum

Gough, Barbara Worsley. *Fashions in London*. 1952 London: Allan Wingate 118p illus.

Hansen, Henry Harold. *Costume cavalcade*. 1956 London: Methuen 160pp

Hartnell, Norman. *Royal courts of fashion*. 1971 London: Cassells. 192pp illus. bibl. (to 1919)

Laver, James. 'Fashion – the English contribution', *Studio* vol 108 1934 pp 247-252

London Museum. *Costume guide.* 1953

Mackenzie, M. 'Jaeger: health gospel of 1884, fashion movement of 1937', *Art and Industry* 23 August 1937 pp 42-57

Manchester City Art Gallery. Gallery of English Costume. *Picture books. 1. A brief view. 4. 1835-70 Women's costume. 1951. 5. 1870-1900 Women's costume. 1953. 6. 1900-1930 Women's costume. 7. Children's costume. 8. Costume for sport*

Yarwood, Doreen. *English costume from the second century BC to 1960.* 1972 (fourth edition) London: Batsford 320pp illus. bibl.

Technical Historical Surveys

Houston, Mary Galway. *A technical history of costume.* 1954 (second edition) London: Adam and Charles Black

Arnold, Janet. *Patterns of fashion: Englishwomen's dresses and their construction vol 1 1660-1860.* 1964 London: Wace 72pp. Vol 2:1860-1940 1972 London: Macmillan 88pp

Hughes, Talbot. *Dress design. An account of costume for artists and dressmakers.* 1926 London: Pitman 362pp illus. (Arts and Crafts series edited by W. R. Lethaby)

Patterns of fashion. 1971 Dunfermline: Carnegie United Kingdom Trust

Tilke, Max. *Costume patterns and designs: a survey of costume patterns and designs of all periods and nations from antiquity to modern times.* 1956 London: Zwemmer 177pp illus.

Waugh, Norah. *The cut of women's clothes 1600-1930.* 1968 London: Faber 336pp

Fashion Plates/Photos

Holland, Vyvyan. *Hand coloured fashion plates 1770-1899.* 1955 London: Batsford 200pp pl 5

Laver, James. *Fashion and fashion plates 1800-1900.* 1943 London: Penguin 30pp pl 16

Laver, James. *Costume illustration, the nineteenth century.* 1947 London: HMSO for Victoria and Albert Museum (Large picture book no 2) 8pp pl 100

Monro, I. S. and Cook, D. F. (eds). *Costume index. A subject index to plates and to illustrated text.* 1937 New York: H. W. Wilson. (with supplement 1957)

Moore, Doris Langley. *Fashion through fashion plates 1771-1970.* 1971 London: Ward Lock 192pp

Traphagen, Ethel. *Costume design and illustration.* 1932 (second edition) New York: Wiley 248pp (first published 1918)

Periods

Nineteenth Century

Brooke, Iris. *English costume in the nineteenth century.* 1929 London: A & C Black

Boehn, Max von and Fischel, Oskar. *Modes and manners of the nineteenth century.* 1976 New York: Arno 4 vols in 2 vols. (facsimile of 1927 edition)

Buck, Anne. *Victorian costume and costume accessories.* 1961 London: Barrie and Jenkins 215pp illus. (Victorian Collector series)

Cunnington, Cecil Willett. *English women's clothing in the nineteenth century.* 1937 London: Faber 460pp illus.

Cunnington, Cecil Willett. *Feminine attitudes in the nineteenth century.* 1935 London: Heinemann 314pp illus.

Cunnington, Cecil Willett and Cunnington, Phillis. *Handbook of English costume in the nineteenth century.* 1970 (third edition) London: Faber 617pp illus. (previous editions 1959, 1966)

Cunnington, Cecil Willett. *The perfect lady.* 1948 London: Max Parrish 71pp illus. (1815-1914)

The declaration of the artists of the nineteenth century on the influence of costume and fashion upon high art. With supplementary observations by some amateurs. 1862 London: Emily Faithfull 16pp

Gernsheim, Alison. *Fashion and reality 1840-1914.* 1963 London: Faber 104pp

Gibbs-Smith, Charles Harvard. *The fashionable lady in the nineteenth century.* 1960 London: Victoria and Albert Museum 184pp

Holden, Angus W. E. *Elegant modes in the nineteenth century: from high waist to bustle.* 1936 London: Allen and Unwin 123pp pl 12

Norris, Herbert and Curtis, Oswald. *Costume and fashion. Vol 6. The nineteenth century.* 1933 London: Dent 264pp

Sichel, Marion. *Costume reference: 6 The Victorians.* 1978 London: Batsford

Starvridi, Margaret. *The Hugh Evelyn history of costume. 1. The nineteenth century.* 1966 London: Evelyn 48pp

Wilson, Anne. *Women's clothing in the nineteenth century.* 1973 Belfast: Ulster Museum pl 12

1800 to 1860

Costume Society. *Early Victorian costume 1830-1860. Proceedings of the Third Annual Conference of the Costume Society 1969.* 1969 London: published for the Sociey 46pp

Buck, Anne M. 'Costume', pp 129-142 in Edwards, Ralph and Ramsey, L. G. G. (eds). *The early Victorian period 1830-1860.* 1958 London: Connoisseur 180pp

1860 to 1890

Costume Society. *2nd Annual Conference. Leicester. 1968. High Victorian costume 1860-1890.* 1969 London: Costume Society

Blum, Stella. *Victorian fashions and costumes from Harper's Bazaar 1867-1898.* 1974 New York: Dover 303pp illus.

Haweis, Mary Eliza. *The art of beauty.* 1878 London: Chatto and Windus 127pp (ABC Reprint)

Ormond, Leonee. 'Female costume in the aesthetic movement of the 1870s and 1880s, *Costume* no 2 1968 pp 33-38

Ashdown, D. M. (ed). *Over the teacups.* 1971 London: Cornmarket Reprint 236pp. (gossipy anthology of 1890s women's articles on fashion trends)

Dress reformers:

Newton, Stella Mary. *Health, art and reason: dress reformers of the nineteenth century.* 1974 London: J. Murray 200pp illus.

Aglaia. Journal of the Healthy and Artistic Dress Union. 1893-94 London 3 vols

Ballin, Ada S. *The science of dress in theory and practice.* 1885 London: S. Low 273pp

Rational Dress Association. *Exhibition catalogue.* 1883 London 68pp illus. (ABC Reprint)

Rational Dress Association. *Gazette.* 1888-1889 London 60pp (ABC Reprint)

'to promote the adoption, according to individual taste and convenience, of a style of dress based upon consideration of health, comfort, and beauty, and to deprecate constant changes in fashion that cannot be recommended on any of these grounds'

1890 to 1914

Costume Society. *La Belle Epoque. Costume 1890-1914. Proceedings of the First Annual Conference of the Costume Society, April 1967.* 1968 London: HMSO 65pp

Gattey, Charles Neilson. *The bloomer girls.* 1967 London: Femina 192pp

Twentieth Century

GENERAL

Brooke, Iris. *English costume 1900-1950.* 1951 London: Methuen 96pp

Caffrey, Kate. *The 1900s lady.* 1976 London: Gordon and Cremmesi 176pp

Burgelin, O. 'L'etiquette de la modernité', *Traverses* May 1976 pp 74-85 (twentieth century parallel of architectural functionalism and 'spontaneous vestimentary functionalism')

Carter, Ernestine. *The changing world of fashion. 1900 to the present.* 1977 London: Weidenfeld & Nicolson 256pp illus.' bibl.

Carter, Ernestine. *Twentieth century fashion: a scrapbook 1910 to today.* 1975 London: Eyre Methuen 128pp illus. (mostly photographs ranged year by year)

Cunnington, Cecil Willett. *English women's clothing in the present century.* 1952 London: Faber 312pp illus.

Ewing, Elizabeth. *History of twentieth century fashion.* 1974 London: Batsford 256pp illus.

Fashion 1900-1939. 1975 London: Idea Books International in association with the Scottish Arts Council and the Victoria and Albert Museum 78pp illus.

Mansfield, Alan and Cunnington, Phillis. *Handbook of English costume in the twentieth century. 1900-1950.* 1973 London: Faber 371pp illus.

Torrens, Deborah. *Fashion illustrated: a review of women's dress 1920-1950.* 1974 London: Studio Vista 288pp 278 illus.

BETWEEN THE WARS

Dorner, Jane. *Fashion in the twenties and thirties.* 1973 London: I. Allan 130pp

Laver, James. *Women's dress in the Jazz Age.* 1964 London: H. Hamilton 63pp

Robinson, Julian. *The golden age of style. Art Deco fashion illustration.* 1976 London: Orbis 126pp 100 colour illus. bibl.

The twenties: female fashion 1920 to 1929. 1969 London: Victoria and Albert Museum

Garland, Madge. *The indecisive decade: the world of fashion and entertainment in the thirties.* 1968 London: Macdonald 254pp

Symonds, Edward H. 'The power of fashion', *JRSA* vol 81 April 21 1933 pp 529-545. (discusses fashion as a trade factor. By the President of the British Fashions and Fabrics Bureau)

1940s

Dorner, Jane. *Fashion in the forties and fifties.* 1975 London: Allan 160pp illus.

Robinson, Julian. *Fashion in the forties. and fifties.* 1976 London: Academy Editions 103pp illus.

Laver, James. 'Fashion and War', *JRSA* vol 92 May 26 1944 pp 303-311 illus.

Withers, Audrey. 'Utility and haute couture', *Architectural Review* vol 93 Jan-June 1943 pp 114-116 illus.

1950 AND 1960s

Adburgham, Alison. '1953 to 1973 – a journalist's view', *Costume* vol 8 1974 pp 4-12

Amies, Hardy. *Just so far.* 1954 London: Collins 255pp

Baynes, Ken and Kate. 'Behind the scene, (Carnaby Street)', *Design* 212 August 1966 pp 18-29 illus.

Salter, Tom. *Carnaby Street.* 1970 Walton on Thames: Margaret and Jack Hobbs 71pp illus.

Hill, Patricia. *Reflections on wool fashions since World War II. 1959 Lecture to the Royal Society of Arts.* London: International Wool Secretariat 23pp illus.

Ironside, Janey. *A Fashion alphabet.* 1968 London: Michael Joseph. (postwar terminology)

HOLLYWOOD

An important influence in the twentieth century on many aspects of the development of fashion):

Chierichetti, David. *Hollywood costume design.* 1976 London: Studio Vista 192pp illus.

Leese, Elizabeth. *Costume design in the movies.* 1976 Bembridge, Isle of Wight: B C W Publishing Ltd. 160pp 200 illus.

Regan, Michael. *Hollywood film costume.* 1977 Manchester: Whitworth Art Gallery 48pp (exhibition catalogue)

Individual Viewpoints

A very small selection:

Chase, Edna Woolman and Chase, Ilka. *Always in Vogue.* 1954 London: Gollancz 343pp illus.

Howell, Georgina (ed). *In Vogue: six decades of fashion.* 1975 London: Allen Lane 352pp 1000 illus.

Peacock, John. *Fashion sketchbook: 1920-1960.* 1977 London: Thames and Hudson 128pp illus.

Hawes, Elizabeth. *Fashion is spinach.* 1933 New York: Random House 336pp

Hartnell, Norman. *Silver and gold.* 1955 London: Evans

Ironside, Janey. *Janey.* 1973 London: Michael Joseph

Quant, Mary. *Quant by Quant.* 1974 Bath: Chivers Reprint 232pp illus. (first published 1966 Cassell)

Adburgham, Alison. *View of fashion: drawings by Haro.* 1966 London: Allen and Unwin

Amies, Hardy. 'What makes fashion?', *JRSA* vol 112 pp 473

Beaton, Cecil. *The glass of fashion.* 1954 London: Weidenfeld and Nicolson 343pp

Beaton, Cecil and Buckland, Gail. *The magic image.* 1975 London: Weidenfeld and Nicolson 304pp illus.

Industrial Developments

Beazley, Alison. 'The "heavy" and "light" clothing industries 1850-1920', *Costume* 7 1973 pp 55-59

Wray, Margaret. *The women's outerwear industry.* 1957 London: Duckworth 318pp

National Union of Tailors and Garment Workers. *The needle is threaded. The history of an industry.* 1964 London: Heinemann 241pp illus.

Dobbs, S. P. *The clothing workers of Great Britain.* 1928 London: Routledge & Kegan Paul 216pp bibl.

Psychological/Social Factors

Bell, Quentin. *On human finery.* 1976 (revised edition) London: Hogarth Press 224pp illus.

Binder, Pearl. *Muffs and morals. (An account of dress and fashion related to moral standards).* 1953 London: Harrap 256pp illus.

Cunnington, Cecil Willett. *Why women wear clothes.* 1941 London: Faber 261pp

Flugel, J. G. *The psychology of clothes.* 1950 London: Hogarth Press 258pp. (first published 1930)

Hurlock, Elizabeth. *The psychology of dress: an analysis of fashion and its motive.* 1976 New York: Arno (facsimile reprint of 1929 edition) 224pp

König, René. *The restless image: a sociology of fashion.* 1973 London: Allen & Unwin

Langner, Lawrence. *The importance of wearing clothes.* 1960 London: Constable 349pp

Polhemus, Ted and Procter, Lynn. *Fashion and anti-fashion. An anthropology of clothing and adornment.* 1978 London: Thames and Hudson 186 illus.

Roach, Mary Ellen and Eicher, Joanne
Bubolz. *Dress, adornment and the social
order.* 1970 New York: Wiley 446pp.
(first published 1965)

Design Factors

Audsley, George Ashdown. *Colour in dress.
A manual for ladies in all matters connected
with the proper selection and harmonious
combination of colours suitable for the
various complexions. Based on the
indisputable phenomenon of colour.* 1912
London: Sampson Low 132pp illus.

Brockman, Helen Lewis. *The theory of
fashion design.* 1965 New York: Wiley
332pp

Farr, Michael. 'Ergonomic clothing', *DIA
Yearbook 1968/9* pp 34-38

French Fashion

French fashion has always been very
important and so must not be overlooked
in any listing of works in British fashion.

General

Lynam, Ruth (ed). *Paris fashion: the great
designers and their creations.* 1972
London: Michael Joseph 256pp illus.

Uzanne, Octave. *Fashion in Paris: the
various phases of feminine taste and aesthetics
from 1797 to 1897.* 1898 London:
Heinemann

Latour, Anny. *Kings of fashion.* 1958
London: Weidenfeld and Nicolson
270pp

Particular Periods

Battersby, Martin. *Art Deco fashion: French
designers 1908-1925.* 1974 London:
Academy Editions 112pp 118 illus. (20
colour)

Robinson, Julian. *Grand chic: fashion
1910-1925.* 1976 London: Studio Vista
192pp (three reconstructed *Gazettes* –
1910-1918, 1919-1922, 1922-1925)

*Inventive Paris clothes: 1909-1939.
Photographic essay by Irving Penn.
Introduction and captions by Diana Vreeland.*
1977 London: Thames and Hudson

Mode des années folles 1919-1929.
1970/1971 Paris: Musée du Costume

Dars, Celestine. *A fashion parade.* 1978
London: Blond and Briggs 128pp
(Seiberger photos of Paris 1905-1950.)

Bertin, Celia. *Paris à la mode. A voyage of
discovery.* 1956 London: Gollancz.
(translation of *Haute Couture – Terre
Inconnue* 1956)

Individuals

Spencer, Charles. *Leon Bakst.* 1973
London: Academy Editions 250pp 277
illus. (30 colour)

Balmain, Pierre. *My years and seasons.* 1964
London: Cassell 181pp

Charles-Roux, Edmonde. *Chanel: her life,
her world and the woman behind the legend
she herself created. Translated by Nancy
Amphoux.* 1976 London: Cape 416pp.
(translation of *L'Irregulière* 1974
Grasset)

Baillen, Claude. *Chanel solitaire.* 1973
London: Collins

Haedrich, Marcel. *Coco Chanel – (her life,
her secrets). Translated by C. L. Markham.*
1972 London: Hale 320pp illus.

Kochno, Boris. *Diaghilev and the Ballet
Russes.* 1971 London: Allen Lane
293pp illus.

Dior, Christian. *Dior by Dior.* 1957
London: Weidenfeld and Nicolson
218pp pl 16. (translation of *Christian
Dior et Moi* 1956)

Dior, Christian. *Talking about fashion.* 1954
London: Hutchinson 100pp illus.
(translation of *Je suis Couturier* 1951)

'Erté' Fashions. 1972 London: Academy
Editions 112pp 180 illus.

Erté. *Things I remember: an autobiography.*
1975 London: Peter Owen 208pp
77 illus.

Erté. *Designs by Erté: fashion drawings and
illustrations from 'Harper's Bazaar' selected
with introduction by Stella Blum.* 1976
London: Constable 129pp illus.

Spencer, Charles. *Erté.* 1970 London:
Studio Vista 198pp illus. bibl.

Forbes-Robertson, Diana. *Maxine.* 1964
London: Hamish Hamilton 266pp illus.
(life of Maxine Elliott)

Iribe, Paul. *Les robes Paul Poiret.* 1908
Paris: Societe Générale d'Impression,
for Paul Poiret

Poiret, Paul. *My first fifty years.* 1931
London: Gollancz 327pp

White, Palmer. *Poiret.* 1973 London:
Studio Vista 192pp illus. bibl.

Saunders, Edith. *The age of Worth.* 1954
London: Longmans 218pp

Schiaparelli, Elsa. *Shocking life.* 1954
London: Dent. (translation of *Shocking*
1954)

*Vingt-cinq ans d'élégance à Paris
(1925-1950). Album composed at the request
of Marcel Rochas.* 1951 Paris: Tisné
111pp illus.

Men's Fashion

Most general works on fashion/costume tend to concentrate on women's costume, and so there now follows a section on men's wear to cover the more neglected area:

'Men's dress', *CIBA Review* no 124 January 1958

Schoeffler, O. E. and Gale, W. *'Esquire's encyclopaedia of twentieth century men's fashions.* 1973 New York: McGraw Hill 720pp illus.

Waugh, Norah. *The cut of men's clothes 1600-1900.* 1964 London: Faber 160pp 1 col. 40bw 42 cutting diags 27 patterns

Amies, Hardy. *ABC of men's fashion.* 1964 London: Newnes 128pp

Of men only: a review of men's and boys' fashions 1750-1975. Exhibition 18 Sept. 1975 – 18 Jan. 1976. Catalogue by Elizabeth Ann Coleman. 1975 New York: Brooklyn Museum 32pp

Simonson, Lee. 'Colour and the English male', *Studio* 108 1934 pp 252-257 7 illus.

Bennett-England, Rodney. *Dress optional: the revolution of menswear.* 1967 London: Peter Owen 240pp illus.

Cohn, N. K. *Today there are no gentlemen: the changes in Englishmen's clothes since the war.* 1971 London: Weidenfeld and Nicolson 180pp illus.

Conspicuous waist: waistcoats and waistcoat designs 1700-1952. 1952 New York: Cooper Union Museum of the Arts of Decoration 11pp bibl.

Men's Wear. 1902- (weekly). London: Textile Trade Publications

Company Histories

Tute, Warren Stanley. *The grey top hat. The story of Moss Bros of Covent Garden.* 1961 London: Cassell 163pp illus.

Burton, Montague Ltd. *Ideals in industry. Being the story of Montague Burton Ltd 1900-1950. Golden Jubilee issue compiled and edited by Ronald Redmayne.* 1951 Leeds: M. Burton 481pp

Design Texts

Chaudry, Abdul Ghani. *Advanced practical designing for men's clothing.* 1970 London: Tailor and Cutter 131pp

Chaudry, Abdul Ghani. *Designing and cutting modern leisure and cotton garments for men.* 1964 London: Tailor and Cutter 115pp

Industrial Production

British factory production of men's clothes. 1950 London: Clarke and Cockeran 326pp illus.

Annual Survey of the British Menswear Industry. 1951- London: National Trade Press

Children's Fashion

Brooke, Iris. *English children's costume since 1775.* 1930 London: A and C Black 86pp

Cunnington, Phillis and Buck, Anne. *Children's costume in England: from the fourteenth to the end of the nineteenth century.* 1965 London: Black 236pp illus. bibl. pl 32

'Children's dress', *CIBA Review* no 32 1940 illus.

Moore, Doris Langley. *The child in fashion.* 1953 London: Batsford pl 51. (1760 to the present century. Many of the costumes described are now in the Museum of Costume, Bath)

Toller, Jane. 'Children's dress through the age', *Antique Dealer and Collectors' Guide.* November 1973

Laver, James. *Children's fashions in the nineteenth century.* 1951 London: Batsford 16pp pp 116

Ballin, A. S. *Children's dress.* 1884 London: International Health Education Exhibition 28pp. Lecture

Guppy, Alice. *Children's clothes 1939-1970. The advent of fashion.* 1978 Poole: Blandford 320pp illus.

Work/Protective

Protective

Protective clothing can only be studied in detail in relation to the work involved and the prevailing British Standards and safety regulations. Useful introductions are provided by:

Freeman, Nelson Thomas. *Protective clothing and devices. A guide to the selection, use and legal requirements relating to all types of protective equipment for individual workers.* 1962 London: United Trade Press 193pp

Bettenson, Anne. 'Industrial protective clothing and equipment', *Costume* 8 1974 pp 46-50

'Work clothing', *CIBA Review* vol 12 no 138 June 1960. (from clothes to protective clothes to safety clothing pp 18-33 including bibl. by R. Schramm)

Occupational Costume

Many organisations evolved complex and detailed liveries or uniforms that can be studied through their own printed manuals or regulations. Nevertheless there are now some useful general introductions in:

Cunnington, Phillis and Lucas, Catherine. *Occupational costume in England: from the eleventh century to 1914.* 1967 London: Black 427pp illus.

Lister, Margot. *Costumes of everyday life: an illustrated history of working clothes from 900 to 1910.* 1972 London: Barrie and Jenkins 178pp 252 illus.

Lansdell, Avril. *Occupational costume and working clothes 1776-1976.* 1977 Aylesbury: Shire Publications 33pp illus. bibl. pp 33

Lansdell, Avril. 'A guide to the study of occupational costumes in the museums of England and Wales', in *Strata of Society. Costume Society Conference, Newcastle 1973.* 1974 London: Costume Society pp 41-55. (based on a survey)

Cunnington, Phillis. *Costume of household servants: from the Middle Ages to 1900.* 1974 London: A and C Black 176pp illus.

Ewing, Elizabeth. *Women in uniform: through the centuries.* 1975 London: Batsford 160pp

Lansdell, Avril. *The clothes of the cut: a history of canal costume.* 1975 British Waterways Board 36pp

Oakes, Alma and Hill, Margot Hamilton. *Rural costume: its origin and development in Western Europe and the British Isles.* 1970 London: Batsford 256pp 378 illus.

'The story of industrial uniforms', *American Fabrics* no 26 Summer 1953 pp 111-115

Woollcombe, Joan. 'Work and clothes', *Design for Today* August 1934 pp 308-311

Types of Dress

Occasions

ACADEMIC AND CEREMONIAL

Baker, J. H. 'History of the gowns worn at the English Bar', *Costume* no 9 1975 pp 15-21

Franklin, afterwards Franklyn, Charles Aubrey H. *Academical dress from the Middle Ages to the present day, including Lambeth degrees.* 1970 Hassocks: private 254pp illus.

Shaw, George Wenham. *Academical dress of British universities.* 1966 Cambridge: Heffer 120pp

Lockmiller, David Alexander. *Scholars on parade: college and university costume and degrees.* 1969 London: Collier Macmillan 290pp

Norris, Herbert. *Church vestments: their origin and development.* 1949 London: Dent 190pp pl 16

Smith, Hugh H. *Academic dress and insignia of the world.* 3 vols 1977 Cape Town: A. A. Balkema 1843pp vol 1: British Commonwealth, Eire and S. Africa

BRIDAL

‚ Stevenson, Pauline. *Bridal fashions.* 1978 Shepperton: I. Allan 128pp illus.

Clarke, Judith. *Wedding dresses 1760-1976. (Catalogue of exhibition). Carlisle Museum, Aug-Sept 1976.* 1976 Carlisle Museum and Art Gallery 22pp

Wedding dresses 1735-1970. 1977 Manchester Gallery of English Costume

Brides 1934- (6 per year). New York: Condé Nast (previously *Bride's Magazine*)

Cunnington, Phillis and Lucas, Catherine. *Costume for births, marriages and deaths.* 1972 London: A and C Black 331pp

MATERNITY

Shonfield, Zuzanna. 'The expectant Victorian (late 19th century maternity clothes)', *Costume* no 7 1972 pp 36-42

Sport

Cunnington, Phillis and Mansfield, Alan. *English costume for sports and outdoor recreation from the sixteenth to the nineteenth centuries.* 1969 London: Black 288pp illus.

'Sportswear', *CIBA Review* 1965-1974

Costume for sport. 1963 Manchester: City Art Gallery. (Gallery of English Costume Picture Book no 8)

Foster, Irene. 'The development of riding costume c 1880-1920', *Costume* no 3 1969 pp 55-60. (for ladies)

Kerr, Diana Rait. 'The costume of the cricketer', *Costume* no 7 1973 pp 50-54

Tinling, Teddy. *White ladies.* 1963 London: S Paul 190pp

Underwear

Cunnington, Cecil Willett and Cunnington, Phillis. *The history of underclothes.* 1951 London: M. Joseph 266pp

Saint-Laurent, Cecil. *A history of ladies' underwear.* 1968 London: Michael Joseph 221pp

Ewing, Elizabeth. *Fashion in underwear.* 1971 London: Batsford 160pp illus.

'Crinoline and bustle', *CIBA Review* no 46. May 1943. (series of articles by W. Born)

Lord, William Barry. *The corset and the crinoline.* 1868 London: Ward Lock and Taylor 227pp illus. (University Microfilms)

Mactaggart, P. and R. A., 'Half a century of corset making: Mrs Turner's recollections', *Costume* no 11 1977 pp 123-132

Page, Chris. 'The Symington Collection of period corsetry', *Costume Society Conference 'High Victorian'* 1968 pp 42-48

Waugh, Norah. *Corsets and crinolines.* 1970 (second edition) London: Batsford 176pp pl 116 text diags bibl. (first published 1954)

Reyburn, Wallace. *Bust-up: the uplifting tale of Otto Titzling and the development of the bra.* 1971 London: Macdonald 112pp

Corsetry and Underwear 1935- (monthly) London

Parts of Dress

'The shirt', *CIBA Review* no 122 September 1957

Mansfield, Alan. 'Blazers', *Costume* no 5 1971 pp 25-28

'The stocking', *CIBA Review* no 106 October 1954

Love, D. M. 'The silken ladder'. *DIA Yearbook 1968/69* pp 39-42. (stockings)

See also:

Textiles: Hosiery *page 197*

Accessories

See also:

Jewellery *page 234*

Each aspect has a vast and specialised literature. The following are a few more general works:

Boehn, Max von. *Ornaments: lace, fans, walking sticks, parasols, jewelry and trinkets* (Mode and Manners supplement). 1976 New York: Arno (facsimile reprint of 1929 edition) 293pp illus.

D'Allemagne, Henry René. *Les accessoires du costume et du mobilier.* 1970 New York: Hacker 507pp pl 393 3000 illus.

Fur

Wilcox, Ruth Turner. *The mode in furs. The history of furred costume of the world from the earliest times to the present.* 1951 New York: Scribner 257pp illus.

Links, Joseph Gluckstein. *The book of fur.* 1956 London: James Barrie 185pp illus.

Chiffon

Pritchard, Mrs Eric. *The cult of chiffon.* 1902 New York: Grant Richards 212pp illus.

Bags

Double, Walter Charles. *Design and construction of handbags.* 1960 Oxford University Press 244pp

Fastenings

Hughes, Therle. 'Caught in a clasp: a history of buckles', *Country Life* 157 May 29 1975 pp 1398-1400

Manchester, Herbert. *The evolution of fastening devices, from the bone pin to the Koh-i-nor Kover-Zip.* 1938 (enlarged edition) Long Island, NY: Waldes Koh-I-Nor Inc.

BUTTONS

Epstein, Diana. *Buttons.* 1968 London: Studio Vista 84pp

Peacock, Primrose. *Buttons for the collector.* 1972 Newton Abbot: David and Charles 128pp illus.

Squire, Gwen. *Buttons: a guide for the collector.* 1972 London: Muller 228pp 100 photo plates

Perry, E. *Metal Buttons.* Concise Encyclopaedia of Antiques vol 3 pp 265

Buttons; the journal of the British button industry. 1949- (monthly). London

Fans

Rhead, George Woolliscroft. *The history of the fan.* 1910 London: Kegan Paul 311pp fol.

Armstrong, Nancy. *Collectors history of fans.* 1974 London: Studio Vista 208pp illus.

Green, Bertha de Vere. *A Collector's guide to fans over the ages.* 1975 London: Muller 380pp 172 illus.

Gostelow, Mary. *The fan.* 1976 London: Gill & Macmillan 151pp illus.

Schreiber, Lady Charlotte. *Fans and fanleaves. 1. English, collected and described by Lady Charlotte. 2. Foreign.* 1888-1890 London: John Murray 161 illus. 153 illus.

Maciver, Percival. *The fan book.* 1920 London: T. Fisher Unwin bibl.

Fans in fashion 1975. Catalogue by Emmeline Levy. Leeds: Temple Newsam House 24pp c. 1700-1930

Waddell, Madeline C. 'Rise and fall of the fan', *Antiques Collector* vol 37 no 6 December 1966-January 1967 pp 245-250

Gostelow, Mary. 'English 19th century fans', *Antique dealer and Collectors Guide* December 1974 pp 115-119

Gloves and Muffs

Beck, S. *Gloves, their annals and associations. A chapter of trade and social history.* 1883 London: Hamilton Adams & Co. 263pp

'Gloves', *CIBA Review* no 61 October 1947

Leyland, N. L. and Troughton, J. E. *Glovemaking in West Oxfordshire: the craft and its history.* 1974 Oxford City and County Museum (Publication no 4) 45pp illus. bibl.

The handkerchief

Braun-Ronsdorf, Margarete. *The history of the handkerchief.* 1960 Leigh on Sea: F. Lewis 40pp 105 illus.

'The handkerchief', *CIBA Review* no 89

Hats

Harrison, Michael. *The history of the hat.* 1960 London: H. Jenkins 188pp bibl.

'The hat', *CIBA Review* no 35 September 1940

Amphlett, Hilda. *Hats: a history of fashion in headgear.* 1974 Chalfont St. Giles: R. Sadler 237pp illus.

Wilcox, R. Turner. *The mode in hats and headdress including hair styles, cosmetics and jewelry.* 1959 New York: Scribner's 348pp illus. bibl.

Dony, John George. *A history of the straw hat industry.* 1942 Luton: Gibbs Bamforth 219pp

Inwards, Harry. *Straw hats: their history and manufacture.* 1922 London: Pitman 125pp illus.

Dony, J. G. 'Straw hats. A selective bibliography', *Costume* 1 1967 pp 14-16

British Millinery 1939-1963 continued as *Millinery and Boutique* 1963-

The Hatter's Gazette 1877-1957. (Dony recommends this journal as a most reliable source of information on hats generally)

HATPINS

Peacock, Primrose. 'Decorative hatpins', *Costume* 9 1975 pp 60-67. (principally Edwardian)

Shawls

Whyte, Dorothy. 'Paisley shawls and others', *Costume* 4 1970 pp 32-36 illus. bibl.

Irwin, John. *Shawls.* 1955 London: HMSO (Victoria and Albert Museum monograph no 9)

Rock, C. *Paisley shawls: a chapter of the Industrial Revolution.* 1966 Paisley: Museum and Art Gallery

Stewart, A. M. *The history and romance of the Paisley shawl.* 1946 Paisley

Blair, Matthew. *The Paisley shawl and the men who produced it. A record of an interesting epoch in the history of the town.* 1904 Paisley: Alexander Gardner 84pp

Hunter, James. 'Paisley shawls', *Discovering Antiques* Part 59 1971 pp 1410-1412 illus. brief bibl.

Whyte, D. 'Some Edinburgh shawls', *Scottish Costume Society Bulletin* no xiii Spring 1974

Irwin, John. *The Kashmir shawl.* 1973 London: HMSO (Victoria and Albert Museum monograph no 29)

Hair

Courtais, Georgine de. *Women's headdress and hairstyles in England from AD 600 to the present day.* 1973 London: Batsford 184pp 400 illus.

Corson, Richard. *Fashions in hair: the first five thousand years.* 1965 London: Peter Owen 701pp 3500 illus.

Cooper, Wendy. *Hair: sex, society and symbolism.* 1971 London: Aldus

Asser, Joyce. *Historic hairdressing.* 1966 London: Pitman 134pp

Keyes, Jean. *A history of women's hairstyles.* 1967 London: Methuen 86pp

Cox, James Stevens. *Illustrated dictionary of hairdressing and wigmaking.* 1971 Jersey: Toucan Press 384pp 664 illus. (first published 1966 by the Hairdressing Council)

Hair and Beauty 1866- (monthly). London: Park Lane Pubs. (previously *Hairdressers Chronicle*)

Woodforde, John. *The strange story of false hair.* 1971 London: Routledge 144pp 50 illus.

Spectacles

Black, Sam. 'Design for sight', *Design* 55 July 1953 pp 28-31

Corson, Richard. *Fashions in eyeglasses.* 1967 London: P. Owen 280pp illus.

Ties

Colle, Doreice. *Collars, stocks, cravats: a history and costume dating guide to civilian men's neckpieces 1655-1900.* 1974 London: White Lion 212pp illus.

'Neckties', *CIBA Review* no 38 March 1941

Laver, James. *The book of ties.* 1968 London: Seeley Service 96pp illus.

The umbrella

Crawford, T. S. *A history of the umbrella.* 1970 Newton Abbot: David and Charles 219pp illus.

Field, June. 'The flattering parasol – an accessory in the game of love', *Antique Dealer and Collector's Guide* April 1972, pp 77-79 illus.

'The umbrella', *CIBA Review* no 42
February 1942

Shoes

See also:

Leather *page 205*

Plastics *page 202*

Rubber *page 205*

Historical Studies

Wilson, Eunice. *A history of shoe fashions: a study of shoe design in relation to costume for shoe designers, pattern cutters, manufacturers, fashion students and dress designers.* 1969 London: Pitman 334pp

Brooke, Iris. *Footwear: a short history of European and American shoes.* 1972 London: Pitman 136pp illus. (first published 1949 as *A history of English footwear*)

Born, W. 'The development of footwear', *CIBA Review* no 34 June 1940 pp 1206-1244

Wilcox, R. Turner. *The mode in footwear (from antiquity to the present day).* 1948 New York: Charles Scribner's Sons 190pp

Wright, Thomas. *The romance of the shoe: being the history of shoemaking in all ages, and especially in England and Scotland.* 1968 Detroit: Singing Tree Press 323pp illus. (reissue of first edition 1922)

Bordoli, Ernest. *Footwear down the ages.* 1933 Northampton: Mercury Co. 68pp

British United Shoe Machinery Company Ltd. *Historical survey of shoemaking.* 1932 Leicester: BUSMC Ltd.

Sulser, Wilhelm. *A brief history of the shoe.* 1958 Felsgarten: Bally. (reprint from *Fashion in Human Society*) 14pp

White, Claude V. 'The evolution of the shoe', *Connoisseur* vol 39 no 155 July 1914 pp 173-179

Swallow, A. W. 'Footwear through the ages', *Chiropodist* vol 15 no 3 March 1960 pp 84-93

The history of shoe fashions. 1976 Northampton: Northampton Museum

Survey

Bordoli, Ernest (ed). *The boot and shoe maker. A complete survey and guide.* 1935 London: Gresham Pub. Co. 4 vols. (Part 1 includes an outline of the history of footwear 335pp, 316pp, 315pp, 341pp)

Catalogues of Collections

Catalogue of the Bally Shoe Museum, Felsgarten, Schoenenwerd, Switzerland (by W. Sulzer). 1948 226pp

Northampton's boot and shoe collection. (Catalogue by Reginald W. Brown). 1929 Northampton Museum 18pp

Local Studies

Adcock, Arthur. *The Northampton shoe.* 1931 Northampton: Archer & Goodman 58pp

Mounfield, P. R. 'The shoe industry in Staffordshire, 1767 to 1951, *North Staffordshire Journal of Field Studies* vol 5 1965 pp 74-80

Sparks, W. L. *The story of shoemaking in Norwich.* 1949 Northampton 119pp

Studies of Details

Vigeon, Evelyn. 'Clogs or wooden soled shoes', *Costume* 11 1977 pp 1-27

Mould, P. 'Changing shoe buckles', *Art and Antiques Weekly* January 8 1977 pp 38-41

Contemporary Thoughts and Texts

The boot and shoemaker's assistant. Illustrated with engravings and pattern plates. Preceded by a history of feet costume, with illustrations of the fashions of the Ancient Egyptians . . . and in England . . . down to the present time. By one who has worked on the seat and at the cutting board. 1853 London 104pp pl 60

Dowie, James. *The foot and its covering with Dr Camper's work 'On the best form of Shoe'.* 1871 (second edition) London: Hardwicke 287pp (first published 1861)

Meyer, Hermann. *Why the shoe pinches: a contribution to applied anatomy.* 1874 (second edition) Edinburgh 55pp (first published 1860)

Peck, J. L. *Dress and care of the feet.* 1872 London 157pp

Swaysland, Edward J. C. *Boot and shoe design and manufacture.* 1905 Northampton: Tebbutt 244pp pl 118 supp. vol

Patrick, H. J. *Modern pattern cutting and design.* 1962 Kettering 134pp

Thornton, J. H. (ed). *Textbook of footwear manufacture.* 1964 (third edition) Heywood: National Trade Press 627pp. Part 1 on Shoe design (first published 1953)

Rossi, William A. *The sex life of the foot and shoe.* 1977 London: Allen and Unwin 272pp illus.

Machinery

Kestell, T. A. 'Evolution and design of machinery primarily used in the manufacture of boots and shoes,

Proceedings of the Institute of Mechanical Engineers vol 178 part 1 no 24 1963/64 pp 625-683

Wilkinson, C. R. 'Last development and design', *Journal of the British Boot and Shoe Institution* 3 1948 pp 472

Company Studies

Manufacturers' histories and sources of particular changes:

Fowler, Eric. *Buckinghams: a hundred years in the shoe trade 1862-1962*. 1962 Norwich: Buckinghams 31pp

Clark's of Street 1829-1950. 1950 Street: Clark's 177pp

Hudson, Kenneth. *Towards precision shoemaking: C & J Clark Limited and the development of the British shoe industry*. 1968 Newton Abbot: David and Charles 109pp

History of Messrs Mansfield & Sons Ltd.

Mobbs & Lewis Ltd. *Seventy five years of progress 1885-1960*. 1960 Kettering 22pp

Weldon, F. W. *A Norvic century and the man who made it 1846-1946*. 1946 Norwich: Norvic 160pp

Stead and Simpson Ltd. *A hundred years in the boot and shoe trade*. 1934 Leicester: Stead and Simpson 32pp

Timpson, David J. *William Timpson Limited: a century of service 1865-1965*. 1965 Kettering: Timpson 67pp

Developments of Bodies within the industry

Bradley, Henry, *SATRA: its inception and first four years 1919-23*. 1969 Kettering: Shoe and Allied Trades Research Association 31pp

Fitch, Charles. *The history of the Worshipful company of pattenmakers*. 1926 Bungay: R. Clay 141pp

Fox, Alan. *A history of the National Union of Boot and Shoe Operatives 1874-1957*. 1958 Oxford: Blackwell 684pp (useful for information on conditions within the industry)

Journals

Shoe and Leather News 1925- (weekly) (previously *Shoe Trades Journal* 1915-1925, *Boot and Shoe Trades Journal* 1880-1915, *Boot and Shoe Maker* 1878-1879, *St Crispin* 1869-1878)

British Boot and Shoe Institution Journal vol 1 no 1 April 1930- (bi-monthly) previously *National Institution of the Boot and Shoe Industry (Incorporated) Journal*

Footwear Weekly 1963-1974 (incorporating *Footwear* 1917-, *British Shoeman* 1921-)

replaced by *Footwear World* 1975- (monthly)

SATRA Bulletin 1952- (previously *Monthly Bulletin of the British Boot, Shoe and Allied Trades Research Association*)

Shoe and Leather News 1916- (weekly) (incorporating *Shoe and Leather Record* 1886-)

Bibliography

Shoe and Leather bibliography. 1965 Northampton County Borough Museum and Art Gallery 8pp (spanning the whole field of costume and fashion)

Journals

In this section are included trade journals and women's magazines that can be potentially rich sources of visual material and historical documentation.

Fashion Magazines 1799-1975: an exhibition. 1975 Manchester Polytechnic Library

Art, Goût, Beauté. 1920-1932 Godde, Bedin, Mondon et Cie, Paris later *Voici la Mode, Art, Goût, Beauté. Journal des Dames* 1933-1936

Clothing Institute Journal 1952- (bi-monthly) London

Costume. The Journal of the Costume Society 1967- (annual) London

Costume Society of Scotland Bulletin. 1966- Edinburgh

Elle. 1945- (weekly) Paris

Falbalas et Fanfreluches 1922-1926 Paris: Editions Meynial

Femina 1874- (weekly) Copenhagen

Femme Chic 1911- (quarterly) Paris: Publications Lonchel

Feuillets D'Art: division De La Mode. 1919-1922 Paris: Lucien Vogel. Chadwyck Healey Microfiche

Gazette du Bon Ton. Art-mode et frivolités. Later *Art-mode-chroniques* 1913-1925 (suspended during World War One) Paris: Ed Lucien Vogel later Jean Labuquiere. (Chadwyck Healey Michrofiche)

La Guirlande des Mois 1917-1921 Paris: Librairie Emile Jean-Fontaine et Jules Meynial

Harpers & Queen 1929- (monthly) London. Incorporating *Queen* (University Microfilm)

Harper's Bazaar 1867- (monthly) New York: Hearst

Le Jardin des Modes (supplement to *L'Illustration*) 1922- (previously *L'Illustration des Modes*)

Journal des Dames et des Modes 1912-1914
Paris: Bureau d'Abonnement

The Ladies Cabinet of Fashion, Music and Romance 1832-1870

La Mode Illustrée: Journal de la Famille 1860-1899

Mademoiselle 1935- (monthly) New York: Condé Nast

Modes et manières d'Aujourd'hui 1912-1922 Paris: Pierre Corrard

Officiel de la Couture et de la Mode de Paris 1921- (10 per year) Paris

Styl 1922-1924 Berlin: Otto v Holten

La Vie Parisienne 1863-

Vogue
Note the different editions:
(USA) 1892- (monthly); (Britain) 1916- (16 per year); (France) 1921- (10 per year); (Italy) 1950- (13 per year) incorporating *Vanity Fair*

Vogue Patterns 1934- (bi-monthly) London: Condé Nast

Weldon's Home Dressmaker 1895-

Weldon's Home Milliner 1895-1928

Weldon's Illustrated Dressmaker 1880-1935, then *Weldon's Good Taste* 1935-1939, then *Good Taste* 1939-

Weldon's Ladies Journal of Dress Fashion, Needlework, Literature and Art 1879-

Weldon's Ladies Journal Portfolio of Fashions

Woman 1937- (weekly) London: IPC

Woman's Journal 1927- (monthly) London: IPC

Woman's Own 1932- (weekly) London: IPC

La Grande Revue 1888-1893

Tailor and Cutter 1866- Cloth and Clothes

Bibliographies

Anthony, Pegaret and Arnold, Janet. *Costume. A general bibliography revised and enlarged edition prepared by Janet Arnold.* 1974 London: Costume Society. (Costume Society Bibliography no 1) 42pp

Colas, René. *Bibliographie générale du costume et de la mode.* 1969 New York: Hacker Art Books 2 vols 1411+73pp index (first published 1933 Paris)

Hiler, Hilaire and Hiler, Meyer. *Bibliography of costume. A dictionary catalogue of about 8000 books and pamphlets.* 1939 (reprinted 1967) New York: Benjamin Blom 951pp

Laver, James. *The literature of fashion. Exhibition catalogue of books on costume held at the National Book League November 2*

1947-January 1948. 1947 Cambridge University Press

Reade, Brian. 'Books on European costume, (bibliographical notes)'. *British Book News* 180 1955 pp 1147-1151

Snowden, James. *Readers Guide to books on costume.* 1972 (second edition) London: Library Association. Public Libraries Group 30pp

Directories

Prime sources of further information

Arnold, Janet. *A handbook of costume.* 1973 London: Macmillan 336pp illus.

Centro Internazionale delle Arte e del Costume, Palazzo Grassi, Venice. *Guida internazionale ai musei e alle collezione pubbliche di costumi e di tessuti.* 1970 Venice: Centro Internazionale (international guide to collections based on information supplied by themselves)

Davies, M. S. T. and others (eds). *Directory of clothing research.* 1968 Manchester: Textile Institute, Society of Dyers and Colourists and the Clothing Institute 136pp

Huenefield, Irene Pennington. *International directory of historical clothing.* 1967 Metuchen, New Jersey: Scarecrow Press 175pp

Lambert, Eleanor. *World of fashion: people, places, resources.* 1976 New York: Bowker 361pp

Watkins, Josephine (comp). *Who's who in fashion.* 1975 New York: Fairchild Books

Appliances and mechanical equipment

Tools

See also:

Textiles *page 184*

Furniture *page 173*

for tools relating to these specific activities.

General

Lilley, Samuel. *Men, Machines and history: the story of tools and machines in relation to social progress.* 1966 (second edition) London: Lawrence and Wishart 352pp

Surveys and reports of tools and machinery exhibited at the great international exhibitions can also act as useful introductions to the technical progress at a particular period, eg:

Clark, Daniel Kinnear. *The exhibited machinery of 1862: a cyclopaedia of machinery represented at the International Exhibition.* 1864 London: Day 104pp (with 140 figures of machine tools)

Hand Tools

Hogg, Gary. *Hammer and tongs.* 1964 London: Hutchinson 160pp

Winterthur portfolio II English tools in America. 1965 Winterthur, Delaware: Du Pont Museum

Particular types of tools:

Preston, Frank. *Man makes hole. A brief history of the development of boring tools.* n.d. Sheffield: Stanley 8pp illus.

Williams, Peter. *More to a hammer than meets the eye.* 1964 Sheffield: Stanley 8pp illus.

'At close range: hammerheads, photographed by F. Bruguière', *Architectural Review* vol 75 February 1934 pp 60a

'30 years of saws', *Design* 83 November 1955 pp 39 (James Neill & Co hacksaws)

Periodically *Design* has published useful analyses of individual appliances which now may have historical value:

'Case history. Smoothing plane', (David Pye's plane), *Design* 68 August 1954 pp 15-17

Beresford-Evans, J. 'Power tools for amateurs', *Design* 117 September 1958 pp 41-48

Carr, Richard. 'Design analysis: electric drill', (Wolf Sapphire), *Design* 203 November 1965 pp 58-65

'Designing a miniature soldering iron', *Design* 11 November 1949 pp 19-20

Machine Tools

General studies:

Bradley, Ian. *A history of machine tools.* 1972 Hemel Hempstead: Model and Allied Publications Ltd. 224pp illus.

Roe, Joseph Wickham. *English and American tool builders.* 1916 London: Oxford University Press 315pp illus. (reprint 1926 by McGraw Hill)

Rolt, Lionel T. C. *Tools for the job. A short history of machine tools.* 1965 London: Batsford 256pp illus.

Rolt, Lionel T. C. 'The development of machine tools', *History Today* May 1971

Steeds, W. *History of machine tools 1700-1910.* 1969 London: Oxford University Press 204pp 153 illus.

Gilbert, K. R. *The machine tool collection (Science Museum). Catalogue of exhibits with historical introduction.* 1966 London: HMSO for Science Museum 111pp pl 32

Useful general introductions to particular periods are provided by:

'Early days of machine tools', *British Machine Tool Engineering* vol 30 no 154 October-December 1948 pp 145-151, pp 176

'Some machine tools of the past century', *Machinery* August 1935 pp 733-737

Burgess, Frank and Sizer, Harold. 'Industrial design and the machine tool', *Design* no 26 February 1951 pp 8-12

Habicht, Frank Henry. *Modern machine tools.* 1963 New York: Van Nostrand 259pp illus.

More detailed technical information can be sought in:

International Machine Tool Engineering vol 1 1918-

International Machine Tool Exhibition official catalogue. 1952- London: Machine Tool Trades Association

International Machine Tool Design and Research Conference. 1959- (with published annual advances/proceedings)

Detailed studies of the machine tool industry are beginning to emerge and these can cast a useful light on developments:

Floud, Roderick. *The British machine tool industry 1850-1914.* 1976 Cambridge University Press 217pp

Rosenberg, Nathan. 'Technological change in the machine tool industry 1840-1910', *Journal of Economic History* vol 23 December 1963 pp 414-446

The influence on the machine tool industry of the development of materials. 1974 Macclesfield: Machine Tool Research Association 69pp illus.

Many extremely complicated issues are involved in machine tool design. The following standard works raise many of these basic issues:

Steeds, W. *Engineering materials, machine tools and processes.* 1964 (fourth edition) London: Longman 430pp

Holtzapffel, Charles. *Turning and mechanical manipulation.* 1846-1884 London: Holtzapffel 5 vols

TYPES OF MACHINE TOOL

Northcott, W. Henry. *Examples of lathes, apparatus and work.* 1889 London

Northcott, W. Henry. *A treatise on lathes and turning, simple, mechanical and ornamental.* 1868 London

Holtzapffel, John Jacob. *Principles and practice of ornamental or complex turning.* 1974 New York: Dover 683pp 600 illus. (facsimile of 1893 edition)

Shelley, C. P. B. *Workshop appliances.* 1873 London: Longmans Green 312pp 209 figs

Tweddle, Norman. 'The rose-engine lathe. Its history, development and modern use', *Bulletin of the Society of Ornamental Turners* (supplement) 1950-1954

Thread grinding. An interesting part of its history and development. 1947 Coventry Gauge and Tool Company Ltd. 44pp illus.

Woodbury, Robert S. *History of the gear-cutting machine.* 1958 Cambridge, Massachusetts: MIT Press 135pp illus. bibl.

Woodbury, Robert S. *History of the grinding machine.* 1959 Cambridge, Massachusetts: MIT Press 191pp illus. bibl.

Woodbury, Robert S. *History of the lathe to 1850.* 1960 Cambridge, Massachusetts: MIT Press 107pp illus. bibl.

Woodbury, Robert S. *History of the milling machine.* 1960 Cambridge, Massachusetts: MIT Press 107pp illus. bibl.

These studies have been condensed into one volume in:

Woodbury, Robert S. *Studies in the history of machine tools.* 1973 Cambridge, Massachusetts: MIT Press 557pp illus. bibl.

A small selection of case histories/design analyses:

'Case history. 400 ton hydraulic press', *Design* no 84 December 1955 pp 30-31

'Design development of a spot welder', (Metrovik) *Design* no 53 May 1953 pp 30-32

Carr, Richard, Ashford, Fred and Easterby, Ron. 'Development. A lathe for world markets', (Colchester Mascot 1600), *Design* no 204 December 1965 pp 44-53

'Evolution in machine design. Scottish firm's part in the development of envelope-making machinery, *Design* no 33 September 1951 pp 26-27

King, David I. 'Case history. Heat treatment furnaces', *Design* no 73 January 1955 pp 25-27

Mayall, W. H. 'Vertical milling machine', *Design* no 142 October 1960 pp 58-63

Stafford, Jack. 'Case history. Oxy-acetylene cutting tools', *Design* no 67 July 1954 pp 28-30

JOURNALS

Amongst the many technical journals the following now include detail that can be useful to the student of the development of machine tools:

Design Engineering (incorporating Sub-assembly component fastening and fluid power international) 1964- (monthly) London: Morgan-Grampian

International Journal of Machine Tool Design and Research 1961- (quarterly) Oxford: Pergamon

Machinery and Production Engineering (previously *Machinery* 1912-1965) 1965- (weekly) Brighton: Machinery Publishing Company

Bulletin of the Society of Ornamental Turners 1949- (twice a year)

BIBLIOGRAPHIES

There are many very specialised lists but two quite helpful and wide ranging works are:

Abell, Sydney George, Leggat, John and Ogden, Warren Greene Jnr (comps). *A bibliography of the art of turning and lathe and machine tool industry.* 1956 (reprinted 1970) Rustington: Society of Ornamental Turners 89pp. (first edition 1950)

Bostan, Orlan W. *A bibliography on cutting of metals 1864-1943.* 1945 New York: American Society of Mechanical Engineers 547pp

Agricultural Equipment

See also:

Transport: Steam *page 265*

General:

Fussell, George Edwin. *The farmer's tools 1500-1900. The history of British farm implements, tools and machinery before the tractor came.* 1952 London: Andrew Melrose 246pp pl 111 bibl.

Fussell, George Edwin. *Farming technique from prehistoric to modern times.* 1966 Oxford: Pergamon 269pp illus. bibl. pp 255-264

Partridge, Michael. *Farm tools through the ages.* 1973 Reading: Osprey 240pp bibl.

Jenkins, Geraint J. *The English farm wagon: origins and structure.* 1961 Lingfield: Oakwood Press for the University of Reading 248pp illus. bibl.

Arnold, James. *Farm waggons and carts.* 1977 Newton Abbot: David and Charles

Jenkins, J. Geraint. *English farm wagon.* 1977 Newton Abbot: David and Charles

Cashmore, W. H. 'Power on the land. The developments of farm machinery in Britain', *Design* 28 April 1951 pp 2-7 illus.

G. E. Fussell. *A bibliography of his writings on agricultural history.* 1967 Reading: Museum of English Rural Life 34pp

Collins, Edwin John T. *Sickle to combine: a review of harvest techniques from 1800 to the present day.* 1969 Reading: Museum of English Rural Life 47pp illus.

Courtney, Frank Stuart. 'Agricultural machinery', *JRSA* vol 66 May 10 1918 pp 403-415

Fussell, George Edwin. 'The development of agricultural machinery in England', *Engineering* vol 138 August 10, 1934 pp 134-136; August 17, 1934 pp 161-162

Science Museum. *Handbook of the collections illustrating agricultural implements and machinery . . . by A. J. Spence.* 1930 London: HMSO 94pp

Matthews, J. *Ergonomics in agricultural equipment design.* 1971 Silsoe: National Institute of Agricultural Engineering 61pp

Steam cultivation:

Spence, Clark C. *God speed the plow: the coming of steam cultivation to Great Britain.* 1960 Urbana: University of Illinois Press 183pp illus. bibl. pp 167-172

Fowler, John Jnr. 'On cultivation by steam; its past history and probable prospects', *JSA* vol 4 no 167 1855 pp 163-178

Williams, Michael. *Steam power in agriculture.* 1977 London: Blandford 160pp 60pp in colour

Situation at particular periods:

Jewell, C. A. *Victorian farming, a sourcebook.* 1975 Winchester: Barry Sherlock 138pp (illustrations based on Henry Styles *The Book of the Farm*)

Wright, S. J. 'Recent improvements in agricultural machinery: and their bearing on the home production of food, *JRSA* vol 87 April 28 1939 pp 606-626 illus.

Floyd, W. F. 'Men and machines on the farm', *Design* 220 April 1967 pp 56-63

Tools and Tillage 1968- (a journal that surveys all periods of agriculture and will eventually include relevant material for the period of this book)

The plough:

Bentzien, Ulrich. 'International bibliography of plough literature, preliminary report and practical examples', *Tools and Tillage* vol 1 no 1 1968 pp 28-32 (plans to include all references to the history of the plough)

Bonnett, Harold. *Saga of the steam plough.* 1972 Newton Abbot: David and Charles 208pp illus.

Tractors:

Cawood, C. L. 'The history, and development of farm tractors, Part 1 and Part 2: 1918-1951, *Industrial Archaeology* 1970 vol 7 no 3: Part 1 pp 264-292; no 4: Part 2 pp 397-423

Wright, Philip. *Old Farm tractors.* 1972 Newton Abbot: David and Charles 77pp illus. (first published 1962)

Williams, Michael. *Farm tractors in colour.* 1974 London: Blandford 183pp illus. bibl.

Davis, Alec. 'Designing the new Fordson Major', *Design* 38 February 1952 pp 27-29

Product design and development

See also:

Theories of design and craftsmanship *page 52* for discussion of technique and general historical surveys.

Design has conducted a number of design analyses of particular products that may now have historical interest in their discussion of particular features and techniques. Some of these will be found in the sections that follow.

Domestic Equipment

See also:

Interior Design: Domestic *page 147*

Harrison, Molly. *Home inventions*. 1975 London: Usborne Pubs. 48pp illus.

Adamson, Gareth. *Machines at home*. 1969 London: Lutterworth Press 48pp

Brooke, Sheena. *Hearth and home: a short history of domestic equipment*. 1973 London: Mills and Boon 176pp

De Haan, David. *Antique household gadgets and appliances 1860-1930*. 1977 Poole: Blandford 160pp illus.

Darling, C. R. 'Modern domestic scientific appliances', *JRSA* vol 79 January 2 1931 pp 163-176; January 9 1931 pp 185-198; January 16 1931 pp 205-216

Harden, Leslie. 'The design of domestic equipment', *Art and Industry* June 1948 pp 213-217

Household things. 1920 London: Whitechapel Art Gallery

Howe, Jack. 'Domestic equipment – a survey of modern home appliances', *Design* 103 July 1957 pp 20-26

'Interior house equipment; illustrated catalogue of well designed objects', *Architectural Review* vol 78 no 469 December 1935 pp 225-304

Novy, Priscilla. *Housework without tears*. 1945 London: Pilot Press 124pp

Peet, Louise Jenison and Thye, Lenore Esteline. *Household equipment*. 1955 fourth edition London: Chapman and Hall 444pp (first edition 1940)

Phillips, R. Randall, *The servantless house*. 1923 (second edition) London: Country Life 159pp (first edition 1920)

Wheatcroft, Mildred. 'Industry and domestic appliances', *The Manager* January 1951

COOKING

See also:

Interior Design: Kitchens *page 156*

Norwak, Mary. *Kitchen antiques*. 1975 London: Ward Lock 136pp illus.

Curtis, Tony (comp). *Kitchen equipment*. 1977 Galashiels: Lyle Publications 126pp illus.

Marshall, Jo. *Kitchenware*. 1976 London: Pitman 112pp illus. (Collecting for tomorrow series)

Brett, Gerard. *Dinner is served: a history of dining in England, 1400-1900*. 1968 London: Rupert Hart-Davis 144p

Period interest:

Cottington-Taylor, D. D. 'Domestic equipment: 25 years progress in cooking equipment, *JRSA* vol 83 April 26th 1935 pp 516-534

Department of Scientific and Industrial Research Fuel Board. *Special Report no 4. Tests on ranges and cooking appliances*. 1922

Cadman, H. G. *Kitchen design and equipment*. 1928

British Electrical Development Association. *Electric kitchen design for small houses*. 1947

Altherr, A. 'Die Küche in ihrem Heim', *Bauen und Wohnen* no 2 1948

Ward, Mary. 'Design review. Kitchen thermics', *Architectural Review* vol 114 no 681 September 1953 pp 195

'Surveys of industry: major kitchen equipment', *Design* 151 July 1961 pp 42-54

STOVES

See also:

Gas *page 255*

Solid Fuel *page 255*

Electricity *page 255*

Dye, Frederick William. *The cooking range: its failings and remedies*. 1888 London: E. & F. N. Spon 52pp

'Design development. The changing shape of the electric cooker', *Design* 34 october 1951 pp 22-23

'Fifty years of cooker design', *Design* 199 July 1965 pp 52-59 illus.

Particular examples:

The story of Belling 1912-1962. 1963 Enfield: Belling and Co.

'Design analysis 11: electric cooker', (Creda Mercury), *Design* 120 December 1958 pp 30-34

Stafford, Jack. 'Case history. Gas cooker', *Design* 65 May 1954 pp 16-19

The best source of accurate information remains the catalogues and publicity material put out by the manufacturer concerned, eg:

Ideal Standard Ltd. (National Radiator Co. Ltd. 1911-1930). *Trade catalogues*

Parkinson Stove Co. Ltd., Birmingham. *Trade catalogues*

The saga of Aga. Aga Heat Ltd.

KITCHEN UTENSILS

Gray, John. 'Catering for cooks', *Design* 73 January 1955 pp 15-19. (Skyline tools)

MIXERS

'Design review. Food preparation equipment', *Architectural Review* vol 121 no 725 June 1957 pp 461-463

Archer, L. Bruce. 'Electric food mixers', *Design* 125 May 1959 pp 36-45

Brookes, Malcolm J. 'Product development no 2. Domestic food mixer'. (Kenwood), *Design* 148 April 1961 pp 64-68

TOASTERS

Brookes, Malcolm J. 'Design analysis no 23. Toaster', (Morphy Richards TO S), *Design* 157 January 1962 pp 44-49

REFRIGERATORS

Woolrich, William Raymond. 'The history of refrigeration; 220 years of mechanical and chemical cold 1748-1968', *American Society of Heating, Refrigeration and Airconditioning Engineers* July 1969 pp 31-39

Woolrich, William Raymond. *The men who created cold: a history of refrigeration.* 1967 New York: Exposition Press 212pp bibl. pp 205-212

Gosney, W. B. 'Modern refrigeration', *JRSA* vol 116 May 1968 pp 448-505

Smith, Edgar C. 'Some pioneers of refrigerations', *Transactions of the Newcomen Society* vol 23 1942/1943 pp 99-107

Van Doren, Harold. 'Streamlining: fad or function', *Design* 10 October 1949 pp 2-5 (examples of fridge evolution)

For more technical detail:

The proceedings of the Institute of Refrigeration 1900- Wallington: Institute of Refrigeration

Refrigeration and Air conditioning. 1898- (monthly) Croydon: MacLaren

Analysis of particular examples:

Beresford-Evans, J. and Archer, L. Bruce. 'Design analysis 9. Domestic refrigerator', (Prestcold), *Design* 116 August 1958 pp 24-28

Archer, L. Bruce. 'Design analysis 25', (Prestcold DP 101), *Design* 163 July 1962 pp 32-37

CLEANING

Laundry and washing:

For details of technical advances there are the abstracts of patents published in:

Laundry and Cleaning 1889- (fortnightly) (formerly *Laundry Record and Journal*)

Most of the general articles are very sketchy:

'100 years of wringer design', *Design* 5 May 1949 pp 12-13
or concentrate on particular machines:

Stafford, Jack. 'Case history. Domestic washing machine', *Design* 75 March 1955 pp 17-20 (Parkinson)

Ward, Mary. 'Techniques. Washing machines and boilers', *Architectural Review* vol 120 no 718 November 1956 pp 341-344

Ward, Mary. 'Techniques. Clothes drying', *Architectural Review* vol 121 no 722 March 1957 pp 210-214

Thirlwell, John and Meade, Dorothy. 'Design analysis 12. Washing machine', (Hotpoint Countess), *Design* 122 February 1959 pp 34-38

Brookes, Malcolm J. 'Design analysis 22. Washing machine', (Radiant Parnell), *Design* 151 July 1961 pp 61-70

Hill, Oliver. ' "Automatic" washing machine', *Design* May 1966 pp 46-47

VACUUM CLEANERS

Giedion, S. Vacuum in the home', *Technology Review* January 1947 pp 157-160 (to supplement sections in the author's book *Mechanisation takes command.* 1947 Oxford University Press)

IRONS AND PRESSING

Glissman, A. H. *The evolution of the sad iron.* 1970 Carlsbad, Oceanside California: MB Printing 282pp illus.

Kalecki, E. 'Historical outline of developments in ironing and pressing', *Clothing Institute Journal* vol 20 no 6 November-December 1972

Jewell, Brian. 'Smoothing irons. A history and collector's guide', 1977 Tunbridge Wells: Midas Books 71pp illus.

Archer, L. Bruce. 'Ironing: an enquiry into the efficiency of current appliances', *Design* 111 March 1958 pp 32-37 (review of over 10 irons)

HEATING APPLIANCES

A popular introduction:

Wright, Lawrence. *Home fires burning. The history of domestic heating and cooking.* 1964 London: Routledge and Kegan Paul 219pp illus.

Reflections and surveys at different times:

Darling, Charles R. 'Methods of economising heat . . . the heating of rooms and buildings', *JRSA* vol 61 January 17 1913 191 pp 219-230

Barker, Arthur Henry. 'Methods of radiant heating', *JRSA* vol 76 February 24 1928 pp 356-377

Yorke, F. R. S. 'Modern heating and ventilation', *Architectural Review* vol 81 1932 pp 160-168

Gunn, Edwin. 'Heating systems', *Designs for Today* November 1933 pp 251-256 (preceded by 'evolution of the grate in England')

Veasey, Christine. 'Decorative heating equipment', *Studio* vol 108 1934 pp 298-300

Ward, Neville. 'Design review: space heaters. A survey of gas, oil and electric units', *Architectural Review* vol 113 May 1953 pp 311-315

Beresford-Evans, J. 'Domestic boilers', *Design* 97 January 1957 pp 26-32

Shaw, W. F. B. (ed). *Domestic heating. A guide to all forms of space heating and hot water supply systems for the home.* 1960 London: Temple Press 194pp

Appliances based on particular energy sources

GAS

Gas at your service. 1951 London: Gas Council (survey 1812-1951)

Surveys at different times:

'The modern gas fire', *Architectural Review* vol 39 1916 pp 113-116

Weaver, Sir Lawrence. *Gas fires and their settings.* 1929 London: Fanfare Press 68pp illus.

Weaver, Sir Lawrence. 'Tradition and modernity in craftsmanship V. The design of gas fires and their settings', *Architectural Review* vol 65 1929 pp 99-101

'The Gas fire. Decoration and craftsmanship supplement', *Architectural Review* vol 75 March 1934 pp 99-110 (includes an article by T. W. Coghlin on the rise of the gas fire)

Masterman, C. A. *The future of gas appliance design.* 1937 London: Institution of Gas Engineers paper no 158

Evans, J. Beresford. 'Design in the gas industry', *Art and Industry* vol 25 July 1938 pp 2-10

'Design review: gas appliances', *Architectural Review* vol 100 August 1946 pp 51-53

Hardern, Leslie. 'Design of gas and coke appliances', *Art and Industry* November 1946 pp 140-148

Abbot, Mrs G. E. 'Gas in the home', *JRSA* vol 95 August 15 1947 pp 627-639

Hardern, Leslie. 'Radiused corners, better finishes in new gas and coke appliances. A review of post-war design trends in an important field of domestic equipment', *Design* 18 June 1950 pp 20-22

Stafford, Jack. 'Design development of a gas boiler', *Design* 59 November 1953 pp 22-24

For detail the best sources are clearly the many technical manuals, eg:

Knights, Charles Cromwell. *The Gas Council's sales training manual.* 1957 London: Gas Council 335pp illus.

SOLID FUEL

Pinckheard, John. 'Domestic solid fuel appliances 1900-1950', *Architect and Building News* 19 January 1951

Shaw, W. F. B. 'The history of the development of domestic solid fuel appliances', *The Coal Merchant and Shipper* vol 108 nos 2788, 2793 vol 109 nos 2797, 2802, 2806, 2810, 2815, 2819, May 1, June 5, July 3, August 7, September 4, October 2, November 6, December 4, 1954 pp 375-380, pp 481-487, pp 9-13, pp 109-115, pp 189-194, pp 271-275, pp 369-374, pp 453-459 (reprinted as an offprint)

Low, Archibald Montgomery. *The romance of the fire.* 1941 London: Gifford 238pp

Peirce, Josephine Halvarson. *Fire on the hearth; the evolution and romance of the heating stove.* 1951 Springfield, Massachusetts: Pond-Ekberg Co 254pp illus. bibl.

Austin, Frank. 'Design review. Solid Fuel', *Architectural Review* vol 113 June 1953 pp 391-394

'Case history. Continuous burning fire', *Design* 66 June 1954 pp 9-12 (historical developments since 1946)

Beresford-Evans, J. 'The place of the fire', *Design* 73 January 1955 pp 33-40 (recent smokeless fuel appliances)

See also:

Interior Design: Fireplaces *page 161*

ELECTRICITY

See also:

Interior Design: Lighting *page 167*

General studies:

Hennessey, R. A. S. *The Electric revolution.* 1972 London: Oriel Press 190pp (c 1880-1930)

Forty, Adrian. 'The electric home. A case study of the domestic revolution of the interwar years', pp 40-62 in Newman, Geoffrey and Forty, Adrian. *British Design.* 1975 Milton Keynes: Open University Press (History of Architecture and Design 1890-1939 course)

Forty, Adrian. 'Electrical appliances 1900-1960', pp 104-107 in *Design 1900-1960 Studies in Design and Popular Culture in the 20th Century, edited by T. Faulkner.* 1976 Newcastle upon Tyne Polytechnic

Journals are probably the richest source of detail:

Electrical Review 1872- (weekly) London: IPC (October issues review new electrical household equipment marketed during the year)

Electrical World 1874- (monthly) New York: McGraw Hill

Introductions to early developments:

Crompton, R. E. 'The use of electricity for cooking and heating', *JSA* vol 43 April 26 1895 pp 511-520

Lancaster, Maud. *Electric cooking, heating, cleaning etc., being a manual of electricity in the service of the home.* 1914 London: Constable 338pp

Solomon, Henry George. *Domestic electric heating.* 1927 London: Crosby Lockwood 116pp

Pevsner, Nikolaus. 'Designer in industry; gas and electric fittings', *Architectural Review* vol 80 July 1936 pp 45-48

'Electrical apparatus: some recent developments', *JRIBA* vol 45 February 7 1938 pp 349-352

'Electric fire design, sponsored by GEC: prizewinning designs and judges reports', *Art and Industry* June 1948 pp 220-225

Whitaker, A. 'Designing a radiant electric heater. A case history', *Design* 10 October 1949 pp 13-15

'Evolution of the thermovent', *Design* 60 December 1953 pp 18-19

'Switches, plugs and sockets', *Design* 107 November 1957 pp 47-61

An important interwar development was the Electrical Association for Women and its encouragement of improved electrical designs:

Scott, Peggy. *An electrical adventure.* 1934 London: J. Truscott 119pp. ('The historic part which the Electrical Association for Women has played in the modern development of things electrical')

Randell, Wilfrid L. *Electricity and women. 21 years of progress.* 1945 London: Electrical Association for Women 86pp

The Electrical Age 1932- (previously *The Electrical Age for Women. The Official Journal of the Electrical Association for Women* June 1926- January 1932)

The electrical handbook for women, edited by C. Haslett. 1934 London: Hodder and Stoughton 416pp (many later editions)

The show house at Bristol:

'Domestic uses of electricity; the demonstration house built at Stoke Bishop, Bristol, by the Electrical Association for Women', *JRIBA* vol 43 1935 pp 88-92

Pheysey, M. E. 'An all-electric house in Bristol', *Design for Today* January 1936 pp 5-8

Other domestic equipment

SEWING MACHINES

See also:

Textile Machinery *page 198*

Needlework Tools *page 196*

A short introduction:

Gilbert, K. R. *Sewing machines.* 1970 London: HMSO for Science Museum 36pp illus.

For more detail:

Ewers, William and Baylor, H. W. *Sincere's history of the sewing machine.* 1970 Phoenix, Arizona: Sincere Press 256pp illus. bibl.

Cooper, Grace Rogers. *The invention of the sewing machine.* 1968 Washington: Government Printing Office 156pp 137 illus.

Alexander, Edwin P. 'On the sewing machine: its history and progress', *JSA* vol 11 April 10 1863 pp 358-370

Antiques:

Jewell, Brian. *Veteran sewing machines. A collector's guide.* 1975 Newton Abbot: David and Charles 172pp illus. bibl.

Periodicals:

Sewing Machine Times: news and views for progressive sewing machine dealers. 1939- (bi-monthly) London

Sewing machines and pram gazette 1937- (previously *Sewing Machine Gazette* 1874-1881 then *Journal of Domestic Appliances and Sewing Machines Gazette* 1881-1936 then *Domestic Appliances*)

Industrial applications:

Bibliography of sewing machines. Attachments, seams, seaming and sewing. March 1968 London: Furniture Development Council 13pp

LOCKS AND KEYS

General histories:

Eras, Vincent J. M. *Locks and keys throughout the ages.* 1974 Folkestone: Bailey and Swinfen 176pp illus. (first published 1957)

Hogg, Gary. *Safe bind, safe find; the story of locks, bolts and bars.* 1968 New York:

Criterion 158pp illus. (reissue of 1961 London edition)

Monk, Eric. *Keys: their history and collection.* 1974 Aylesbury: Shire 64pp illus. bibl.

Chubb, George C. H. 'Security offered by locks and safes', *JRSA* vol 100 May 30 1952 pp 475-488

Some earlier studies:

Chatwood, Samuel. 'Locks and safes', *JSA* vol 36 May 11 1888 pp 704-718

Chubb, Harry W. 'The construction of locks and safes', *JSA* vol 41 April 14 1893 pp 510-528 (includes bibliography of books and articles)

Butter, Francis J. *Locks and lockmaking.* 1931 London: Pitman 132pp (first edition 1926)

Giedion, S. 'Complicated craft is mechanized; development of the pin-tumbler cylinder lock by Linus Yale Jnr', *Technology Review* 46 November 30 1943 pp 26-31

CLOCKS

There is a very large collector's literature, even though the past hundred years has been studied in a very selective way.

General surveys:

'About time: clocks, watches, calendars and other devices which rule our lives: their development, uses and abuses', *Design* 299 November 1973 pp 54-79

Shenton, Alan and Shenton, Rita. *The price guide to clocks 1840-1940.* 1977 Woodbridge: Antique Collectors Club 540pp illus. bibl.

Symonds, Robert Wemyss. *A history of English clocks.* 1947 Harmondsworth: Penguin 79pp pl 72

Robertson, J. Drummond. *The evolution of clockwork . . . together with a comprehensive bibliography of horology.* 1931 London: Cassell 358pp illus.

A few of the many popular surveys:

Ullyett, Kenneth. *Clocks and watches; illustrated by Martin Battersby.* 1971 Feltham: Hamlyn 159pp illus. bibl.

Bruton, Eric. *Clocks and watches.* 1968 Feltham: Hamlyn 140pp illus.

Jagger, Cedric. *Clocks.* 1973 London: Orbis 64pp illus.

Joy, Edward Thomas. *The Country Life book of clocks.* 1967 London: Country Life 96pp illus. bibl.

Some earlier work:

Wyatt, Sir Matthew Digby. *The history of the manufacture of clocks.* 1868 London: privately published 32pp (reprinted from *Clerkenwell News*)

Cescinsky, Herbert and Webster, Malcolm R. *English domestic clocks.* 1914 London: Routledge 353pp illus. (later editions)

Lloyd, Herbert Alan. *English domestic clock. Its evolution and history. A brief guide to the essential details for dating a clock.* 1938 London: author 28pp

Dictionaries and lists of makers:

Baillie, Grenville Hugh. *Watchmakers and clockmakers of the world.* 1966 London: Methuen 388pp illus. (first edition 1929)

Britten, Frederick James. *Old clocks and watches and their makers.* 1973 (eighth edition) London: Eyre Methuen 586pp (first edition 1899. Many later editions and reprints)

Britten, Frederick James. *The watch and clockmakers handbook, dictionary and guide.* 1884 London: Spon (15th edition 1955, 1976 Barron reprint of 1915 edition)

De Carle, Donald. *Watchmakers and clockmakers encyclopaedic dictionary.* 1950 London: NAG Press 252pp

Collections of examples:

Lloyd, Herbert Alan. *Some outstanding clocks over seven hundred years 1250-1950.* 1958 London: L. Hill 160pp (pp 137-153 1851 to 1950)

Baillie, Grenville Hugh. *Clocks and watches. An historical bibliography.* 1951 London: NAG Press 414pp illus.

Types of clocks:

Allix, Charles. *Carriage clocks: their history and development.* 1974 Woodbridge: Antique Collectors Club 484pp 500 illus.

Edwardes, Ernest L. *The grandfather clock. An historical and descriptive treatise on the English long case clock.* 1971 (third edition) Altrincham: Sherratt 270pp illus. (first published 1949)

Howe, B. 'Chronometers for the Victorian deck', *Country Life* January 1973 pp 161-163

Watches:

Chapuis, Alfred and Jaquet, Eugene. *The history of the self-winding watch 1770-1931. English adaptation by R. Savare Grandvoinet.* 1956 London: Batsford 246pp 154 illus.

Clutton, Cecil and Daniels, George. *Watches of Europe and America.* 1965 London: Batsford 159pp

Cuss, Theodore Patrick Camerer. *The Country Life book of watches.* 1967 London: Country Life 128pp illus.

Cuss, Theodore Patrick Camerer. *The story of watches.* 1952 London: MacGibbon and Kee 172pp illus.

Gray, John. 'Growing a new industry', (British watches since 1945), *Design* 85 January 1956 pp 13-19

Baillie, Grenville Hugh. *Watches; their history decoration and mechanism.* 1929 London: Connoisseur 383pp pl 75

Pipe, Robert William. *The automatic watch.* 1952 London: Heywood 156pp illus.

Saunier, Claudius. *The watchmaker's handbook, translated by Tripplin and Rigg.* 1945 London: Technical Press 498pp illus. (first edition 1881)

Electrical clocks:

Shenton, R. K. 'Early electric clocks', *Art and Antiques Weekly* 5 February 1977 pp 24-25

Philpott, Stuart Field. *Modern electric clocks.* 1935 (second edition) London: Pitman 214pp

Hope-Jones, Frank. *Electric timekeeping.* 1949 (second edition) London: NAG Press 279pp illus. (first edition 1940)

Wise, S. J. *Electrical clocks. Principles, construction, operation, installation and repair of mains and battery operated clocks for domestic and industrial purposes.* 1951 (second edition) London: Heywood 150pp 137 illus. (first edition 1948)

Individual companies:

Cole, John Francis and Cuss, Theodore Patrick Camerer. *A watchmaking centenary: Usher & Cole 1861-1961.* 1961 London: Camerer Cuss 18pp illus.

Benoy, J. M. 'Design policy in industry. Smiths English Clocks Ltd', *Design* 50 February 1953 pp 14-19

Museum collections:

Daniels, George and Clutton, Cecil. *Clocks and watches. The collection of the Worshipful Company of Clockmakers.* 1977 London: Sotheby Parke Bernet 160pp illus. (oldest and most comprehensive collection on horology)

Maddision, F. R. and Turner, A. J. *Oxford Museum of the History of Science. Catalogue 2. Watches.* 1973 Oxford Museum of the History of Science 91pp illus. bibl.

BAROMETERS

Middleton, William Edgar Knowles. *The history of the barometer.* 1964 Baltimore: Johns Hopkins University Press 489pp illus.

Goodison, Nicholas. *English barometers 1680-1860.* 1977 (revised edition) Woodbridge: Antique Collectors Club 300pp illus. (first edition 1969 Cassell)

WRITING EQUIPMENT

Whalley, Joyce Irene. *Writing implements and accessories from the Roman stylus to the typewriter.* 1975 Newton Abbot: David and Charles 144pp illus. bibl.

Pens:

Bore, Henry. *The story of the invention of steel pens. With a description of the manufacturing processes by which they are produced.* 1892 London: Perry 67pp (first edition 1886)

MacGuinness, James. 'Reservoir and stylographic pens', *JSA* vol 53 1904 pp 1125-1145, 1168, 1194, 1195

Desk furniture:

Rivera, Betty and Rivera, Ted. *Inkstands and inkwells: a collector's guide.* 1973 New York: Crown 216pp illus. bibl.

Gloag, John. 'Victorian desk furniture', *Connoisseur* vol 188 April 1975 pp 274-276

Typewriters:

General histories:

Beeching, Wilfred A. *Century of the typewriter.* 1974 London: Heinemann 276pp illus. bibl.

Adler, Michael H. *The writing machine.* 1973 London: Allen and Unwin 318pp 328 illus. (detailed technical history to about 1930)

Current, Richard Nelson. *The typewriter and the men who made it.* 1954 Urbana: University of Illinois Press 149pp illus.

Alfieri, B. 'Mightier than the pen? Development in typewriters', *Country Life* 155 May 2 1974 pp 1088-1089

Historical developments:

Rigg, Rev. Arthur. 'On type-printing machinery and suggestions thereon', *JSA* vol 22 February 13 1874 pp 238-245

Harrison, John. 'Type-writers and type-writing', *JSA* vol 36 February 17 1888 pp 345-355

Jenkins, Henry Charles. 'Typewriting machines', *JSA* vol 42 September 21 September 28 1894 pp 839-853, pp 855-868 (concentrates on evolution)

Morton, Arthur E. 'Modern typewriters and accessories', *JRSA* vol 55 March 1 1907 pp 428-442

Gould, R. T. 'The modern typewriter and its probable future development', *JRSA* vol 76 May 25 1928 pp 717-738

An early bibliography:

Gamble, William Burt (comp). *List of work relating to the development and manufacture of typewriting machines.* 1913 New York Public Library 18pp

An introduction to an important public collection:

The history and development of typewriters by G. Tilghman Richards. 1964 London: HMSO for Science Museum 56pp (earlier editions 1948, 1955)

Particular firms and models:

Archer, L. Bruce. 'A new British typewriter', (Byron), *Design* 79 July 1955 pp 26-29

Olivetti, formes et recherche . . . 19 novembre-1 janvier 1970. Textes de Giovanni Giudici. 1969 Paris: Musée des Arts Decoratifs

Instruments

A small selection of histories and analyses from an enormous field. Scientific and precision instruments:

Calculations, machines and instruments. Catalogue of the collection in the Science Museum. Originally compiled by D. Baxandall. Revised and updated by Jane Pugh. 1976 London: Science Museum

Wynter, Harriet and Turner, Anthony. *Scientific instruments.* 1975 London: Studio Vista 240pp 260 illus. bibl. (astronomy, navigation, sundials, surveying, optics)

Cooper, Herbert John (ed). *Scientific instruments.* 1946, 1948 London: Hutchinson 2 vols

Michel, Henri. *Scientific instruments in art and history, translated by R. E. W. Maddison and Francis R. Maddison.* 1967 London: Barrie and Rockliff 108pp pl 103

Bryden, D. J. *Scottish scientific instrument makers 1600-1900.* 1975 Edinburgh: Royal Scottish Museum 59pp illus.

Fischbacher, Ronald E. 'Designing for man in an automated world', *Design* 214 October 1966 pp 58-63 (on 50th anniversary of Scientific Instrument Makers Association)

Stock, John T. *Development of the chemical balance.* 1969 London: HMSO for Science Museum 50pp illus. bibl.

Middleton, William E. K. *A history of the thermometer and its use in meteorology.* 1966 Baltimore: Johns Hopkins University Press 249pp illus.

Middleton, William E. K. and Spilhaus, Athelstan F. *Meteorological instruments.* 1960 Toronto University Press 286pp illus.

Optical instruments:

Disney, Alfred N. and others. *Origins and development of the microscope.* 1928 London: Royal Microscopical Society 303pp illus. large bibl.

Palmer, F. and Sahiar, A. B. *Microscopes. To the end of the 19th century.* 1971 London: HMSO for Science Museum 50pp illus.

King, Henry C. *The history of the telescope.* 1955 London: Griffin 456pp

Lockyer, J. Norman. 'Some new optical instruments', *JSA* vol 32 October 31 November 7 1884 pp 1109-1114, pp 1120-1128 (especially telescopes)

Weighing machines:

Sanders, L. *A short history of weighing.* 1947 Birmingham: W & T Avery 59pp

Kisch, Bruno. *Scales and weights.* 1965 New Haven: Yale University Press 297pp illus.

Dickinson, H. W. 'Bicentenary of the platform weighing machine', *Engineer* 178 December 29 1944 pp 504-506

Benoy, J. M. 'Design policy in industry. W & T Avery', *Design* 53 May 1953 pp 8-15

Ashford, F. C. 'Design in the balance', *Design* 72 December 1954 pp 26-33 (criticism of contemporary British designs)

Draughtsmen's equipment:

Dickinson, H. W. 'A brief history of draughtsmen's instruments', *Transactions of the Newcomen Society* vol 27 1949/1951 pp 73-84

Watnaby, J. *Surveying instruments and methods.* 1968 London: Science Museum 32pp illus.

Dunnett, H. McG. 'Design for the drawing office', *Design* 60 December 1953 pp 22-27

Archer, L. Bruce. 'The designers equipment', *Design* 122 February 1959 pp 50-53

Materials testing equipment:

Gibbons, Chester H. 'History of testing machines for materials', *Transactions of the Newcomen Society* vol 15 1934/1934 pp 169-184

Gibbons, Chester H. *Materials testing machines.* 1935 Pittsburg: Instruments Publishing Company 90pp illus.

Urwin, W. C. 'Machines for testing materials, especially iron and steel', *JSA* vol 35 July 8, July 15, July 22 1887 pp 790-798, pp 803-811, pp 813-821

Amusement machines

Fairground and arcade:

Murphy, Thomas. 'The evolution of amusement machines', *JRSA* vol 99 September 7 1951 pp 791-806

Jones, Barbara. *The unsophisticated arts.* 1951
London: Agricultural Press 192pp illus.
(decorative art of fairground,
amusement arcade, seaside . . .)

Colmer, Michael. *Pinball: an illustrated
history.* 1976 London: Pierrot 120pp

Music boxes:

Ord-Hume, A. W. J. G. *Clockwork music; an
illustrated history of mechanical musical
instruments from the musical box to the
pianola, from automaton lady virginal players
to orchestrions.* 1973 London: Allen and
Unwin 334pp illus.

Clarke, John E. T. *Musical boxes: a history and
appreciation.* 1961 (third edition)
London: Allen and Unwin 264pp (first
published 1948)

The Music Box: journal of the Musical Box
Society of Great Britain.
1962/1963- (quarterly) Edenbridge: the
Society

Telecommunications Equipment

General studies:

*From semaphore to satellite . . . on the occasion of
the centenary of the International
Telecommunications Union (1865-1965).*
1965 Geneva: International
Telecommunications Union 343pp illus.
bibl.

Harlow, Alvin Fay. *Old wires and new waves.
The history of telegraph, telephone and
wireless.* 1936 London and New York:
Appleton Century 548pp illus. bibl.

The Post Office and its role:

Robinson, Howard. *The British Post Office. A
history.* 1948 New Jersey: Princeton
University Press 467pp illus.

Robinson, Howard. *Britain's Post Office. A
history of development from the beginnings to
the present day.* 1953 Oxford University
Press 299pp illus.

Wainwright, David. 'G.P.O. A design policy
for the Post Office', *Design* 173 May 1963
pp 33-35

Telegraphy:

Kieve, Jeffrey L. *The electric telegraph: a social
and economic history.* 1973 Newton Abbot:
David and Charles 310pp illus. bibl.

Marland, Edward Allen. *Early electrical
communications.* 1964 London and New
York: Abelard Schumann 220pp

Blake, George Gascoigne. *History of radio
telegraphy and telephony.* 1926 London:
Radio Press 424pp illus. large bibl.
(facsimile Arno Reprint 1976)

Wilson, Geoffrey. *The old telegraphs.* 1976
Chichester: Phillimore 252pp bibl.

Bain, Alexander. 'Automatic telegraphy',
JSA vol 14 January 19 1866 pp 138-146

Durham, John Francis Langton. *Telegraphs
in Victorian London.* 1959 Cambridge:
Golden Head Press 30pp

Carr, Richard. 'Olivetti's teleprinter', *Design*
231 March 1968 pp 32-37 (case history of
a recent design)

Telephone:

Robertson, J. H. *The story of the telephone. A
history of the telecommunications industry of
Britain.* 1947 London: Pitman 299pp

Kingsbury, John E. *The telephone and
telephone exchanges: their invention and
development.* 1972 New York: Arno
558pp illus. bibl. refs. (facsimile reprint
of 1915 edition)

Baldwin, Francis George C. *The history of the
telephone in the United Kingdom.* 1925
London: Chapman and Hall 728pp illus.
(later edition 1938)

Bell, Alexander Graham. 'The telephone',
JSA vol 26 November 30 1877 pp 17-24

Preece, Sir William Henry and Maier,
Julius. *The telephone.* 1889 London:
Whitaker and G. Bell 498pp

Cooke, Conrad W. 'On Edison's
electro-chemical or loud-speaking
telephone', *JSA* vol 27 May 23 1879
pp 558-569

Gray, John. 'G.P.O. telephone', *Design* 115
July 1958 pp 38-41 (on the introduction
of a new design range)

Cronin, G. 'You may telephone from here',
Carron Cupola vol 9 July 1958 pp 3-6 (on
changes in telephone boxes made of cast
iron since 1900)

Brookes, Malcolm J. 'Product development
6. Switchboard', *Design* 165 September
1962 pp 54-56

Gramophones

General histories:

Gelatt, Roland. *The fabulous phonograph
1877-1977.* 1977 (second edition)
London: Cassell 349pp illus. (first edition
1955)

Chew, V. K. *Talking machines 1877-1914:
some aspects of the early history of the
gramophone.* 1967 London: HMSO for
Science Museum 81pp illus. bibl.

Read, Oliver and Welch, Walter L. *From tin
foil to stereo: evolution of the phonograph.*
1959 Indianapolis: H. W. Sams 524pp
illus. bibl.

Cain, John. *Talking machines.* 1961 London:
Methuen 80pp illus.

Exhibitions and collections:

*Phonographs and gramophones: a
commemorative catalogue of the exhibition held
at the Royal Scottish Museum from 2nd
July-2nd October 1977 to celebrate the
centenary of Thomas Edison's invention . . .*

compiled by Alistair G. Thompson. 1977
Edinburgh: Royal Scottish Museum 24pp
pl 32

*Phonographs and gramophones: a symposium
organised by the Royal Scottish Museum in
connection with the exhibition . . . held . . .
Saturday 2nd July 1977.* 1977 Edinburgh:
Royal Scottish Museum 141pp illus. bibl.

EMI Collection. *Catalogue.* 1973 (reprinted
1977) London: EMI illus.

Historical developments:

Voskuil, J. 'The speaking machine through
the ages', *Transactions of the Newcomen
Society* vol 26 1948/1949 pp 259-267

Preece, W. H. 'The phonograph', *JSA* vol 26
May 10 1878 pp 534-538

Gouraud, Col. 'The phonograph', *JSA* vol
37 November 30 1888 pp 23-33

Reddie, Lovell N. 'The gramophone, and
the mechanical recording and
reproduction of musical sounds', *JSA* vol
56 May 8 1908 pp 633-649

Ford, Peter. 'History of sound recording'
(series) *Recorded Sound* nos 7, 8, 9,
10/11, 12, 13 1962-1964 pp 221-227,
pp 266-267, pp 115-123, pp 146-150,
pp 181-188

Hi-Fi News and Record Review
1956- (monthly) Croydon: Link (also
carries historical material, such as a
further 36 articles published by Peter
Ford January 1960-July 1963)

Radio

General design histories:

Hill, Jonathan. *The Cat's whisker. 50 years of
wireless design.* 1978 London: Oresko
Books

Littmann, Frederic. 'The evolution of the
wireless receiver and its use in the home',
Design for Today March 1936 pp 95-100

*The wireless show! 130 classic radio receivers
1920s to 1950s. A loan exhibition presented by
the Museum in association with the British
Vintage Wireless Society.* 1977 London:
Victoria and Albert Museum 16pp illus.

A vital social and general history:

Briggs, Asa. *The history of broadcasting in the
United Kingdom.* 1961-1970 Oxford
University Press 3 vols

More technical history:

Geddes, Keith. *Broadcasting in Britain
1922-1972.* 1972 London: HMSO for
Science Museum 64pp

Pawley, Edward. *BBC Engineering
1922-1972.* 1972 London: BBC
Publications 572pp illus.

Busby, Gordon. *Vintage crystal sets
1922-1927.* 1976 London: IPC/Wireless
World 100pp illus.

Geddes, Keith. *Guglielmo Marconi
1874-1937.* 1974 London: HMSO for
Science Museum 64pp illus.

Science Museum. *Handbook of the collections
illustrating radio communications; its history
and development, by W. T. O'Dea.* 1949
(revised edition) London: HMSO for
Science Museum 94pp (first edition
1934)

Studies of the industry and its products:

Maclaurin, William Rupert. *Invention and
innovation in the radio industry . . . with the
technical assistance of R. Joyce Harman.*
1949 New York: Macmillan 304pp illus.
bibl.

Moggridge, G. E. 'Product development
no 1. Television and radio receivers',
Design 146 February 1961 pp 26-31

Sharp, Peter E. M. 'Surveys of industry no
7. Radio and T.V.', *Design* 157 January
1962 pp 34-42

There are many popular encyclopaedias for
the technically minded enthusiast:

Harmsworth's Wireless Encyclopaedia.
1923/1924 London: Harmsworth
Encyclopaedias 3 vols

The design of radio cabinets and bodies has
long been a popular subject:

Pevsner, Nikolaus. 'Broadcasting comes of
age. The radio cabinet 1919-1940',
Architectural Review vol 87 1940 pp 189-90

Forty, Adrian. 'Wireless style. Symbolic
design and the English radio cabinet
1928-1933', *Architectural Association
Quarterly* vol 4 April-June 1972 pp 23-31

Van Dyck, A. 'Dynamic symmetry in radio
design', *Proceedings of the Institute of Radio
Engineers* September 1932 pp 1481-1511

Russell, Gordon. 'The designer and his
problem 1. Designing a radio cabinet',
Design for Today May 1933 pp 17-19

Wells, Percy A. *Radio and gramophone
cabinets.* 1934 London: Studio 64pp

'Fine craftsmanship. Design in radio sets',
Studio vol 107 1934 pp 41-44

McGrath, Raymond. 'Bodywork for radio',
Commercial Art vol 19 August 1935
pp 38-43

Fejer, George. 'Housing the radio family',
Art and Industry February 1949 pp 60-66

'Recent uses of plastics in radio cabinets',
Design 16 April 1950 pp 14-15

White, J. K. 'Radio and television cabinets,
a practical approach', *Design* 37 January
1952 pp 12-15

Sharp, Peter E. M. 'Radio cabinets 1952',
Design 46 October 1952 pp 24-26

Lambert, Sam. 'Developing design for
radio cabinets', *Design* 74 February 1955
pp 36-37

Evans, J. Beresford and Archer, L. Bruce.
'Design analysis 6. Portable radio', *Design*
110 February 1958 pp 24-28

The contribution of R. D. Russell:

Pritchard, J. C. 'R. D. Russell RDI, FSIA
The man, his work and his influence on
cabinet design', *Art and Industry* May
1949 pp 172-177

Russell, R. D. 'Gramophone, radio and
television', pp 101-103 in *Design '46*
1946 London: Council of Industrial
Design

'Design Review. The industrial designer in
practice', (R. D. Russell and Murphy)
Architectural Review vol 98 November
1945 pp 144-146

Casson, C. R. 'Building trust in Murphy
radio', *Art and Industry* November 1949
pp 168-173

Some of the longest-lived journals are now
prime historical sources:

Wireless World: electronics, television, radio.
1913- (monthly) London: IPC (called
The Marconigraph 1911-1912)

Electrical and Electronic Trader
1925- (weekly) London: IPC (previously
titled *Wireless and Electrical Trader*)

Television

*History of television: vol 1. First 40 years by
A. Davies, vol 2. The News by A. Davis, vol
3. How it works by P. Fairley.* 1976
London: Independent Television
Books/Severn House 160pp, 144pp,
160pp

Mitchell, W. G. W. 'Developments in
television', *JRSA* vol 79 May 22 1931
pp 616-642

Garratt, Gerald R. M. *Television, an account
of the development and general principles of
television as illustrated by a special exhibition
held at the Science Museum June-September
1937.* 1937 London: HMSO for Science
Museum

Puckle, O. S. 'Television cabinet design.
The engineer's point of view', *Art and
Industry* September 1949 pp 106-111

Sharp, Peter E. M. 'The trend in television
cabinets', *Design* 59 November 1953
pp 18-19

Computers

It is still perhaps too soon for a definitive
history of computer design but there is a
growing range of general studies:

Goldstine, Herman H. *The computer from
Pascal to Von Neumann.* 1972 New Jersey:
Princeton University Press 378pp illus.

Harmon, Margaret. *Stretching man's mind: a
history of Data Processing.* 1975 New York:
Mason/Charter 239pp illus. bibl.

Hollingdale, S. H. and Toothill, G. C.
Electronic computers. 1965
Harmondsworth: Penguin 336pp
(concentrates on British developments.
Over one third historical, especially
analogue computers)

Lavington, S. H. *A history of Manchester
computers.* 1975 Manchester: National
Computing Centre 45pp illus.

Wilkes, M. V. 'How Babbage's dream came
true', *Nature* 257 1975 pp 541-544
(followed by a computer supplement
pp 541-560)

Rodgers, William. *Think. A biography of the
Watsons and IBM.* 1970 London:
Weidenfeld and Nicolson 320pp illus.
bibl.

Developments:

Rosenberg, Jerry Martin. *The computer
prophets.* 1969 New York: Macmillan
192pp illus.

Morrison, Philip and Morrison, Emily
(eds). *Charles Babbage and his calculating
machines. Selected writings by Charles Babbage
and others.* 1961 New York: Dover
400pp illus.

Boys, C. V. 'Calculating machines', *JSA*
vol 34 March 5 1886 pp 376-389
(developments to that time)

Wilkes, M. V. 'Automatic calculating
machines', *JRSA* vol 100 December 14
1951 pp 56-90

Howe, Jack. 'Case history. Automatic
accounting', *Design* 77 May 1955
pp 34-37 (British Tabulating Machine Co
1885-)

Flores, Ivan. *Computer design.* 1967
Englewood Cliffs: Prentice Hall 465pp
illus.

Carr, Richard. 'Updating the computer',
Design 247 July 1969 pp 60-63
(development of ICL 1900 series)

Advances in Computers vol 1. 1960 New York:
Academic Press

Van Cleemput, W. M. *Computer aided design
of digital systems. A bibliography.* 1977
London: Pitman 2 vols 388pp, 300pp
(vol 1 Developments to December 1974,
vol 2 January 1975 to May 1976)

For more detail:

Ralston, Anthony and Meek, Chester L.
Encyclopaedia of Computer Science. 1976
London: Input Two Nine 1523pp

Transport

General

With the exception of broad historical surveys:

Jackman, W. T. *The development of transportation in modern England.* 1962 London: Cass 820pp (first published 1916 Cambridge University Press. Added bibl. pp 750-811)

general discussions of transport design tend to be very general indeed:

Barman, Christian. 'Design in modern transport'. *JRSA* vol 93 September 28 1945 pp 549-559

Barman, Christian. *Public Transport.* 1949 Harmondsworth: Penguin 64pp illus. (Things we see series no 5)

Hughes-Stanton, Corin. *Transport design.* 1967 London: Studio Vista 96pp illus.

Faulks, R. W. *Principles of transport.* 1973 London: Ian Allan 232pp illus. (previously *Elements of Transport* 1964)

Encyclopedias and well researched visual publications can have a value even if the text is very general eg:

Encyclopedia of transport, edited by Donald Clarke. 1976 London: Marshall Cavendish 248pp 220 illus. (first published in *How it works*)

There are some very useful studies of the economic development of transport:

Aldcroft, Derek. *British transport since 1914; an economic history.* 1975 Newton Abbot: David and Charles 336pp illus. bibl.

Dyos, H. J. and Aldcroft, D. H. *British transport, an economic survey from the seventeenth century to the twentieth.* 1969 Leicester University Press 473pp maps, tables (to 1939)

General guides to the many transport collections:

Simmons, Jack. *Transport museums in Britain and Western Europe.* 1970 London: Allen and Unwin 300pp illus.

Historical transport guide: transport museums, ships, aircraft, minor railways and other displays of historical transport in Great Britain and Ireland. London: IPC Transport Press for Transport Trust (annual)

Guides to individual types of transport collections are introduced in the following more specific pages.

Although most of the journals specialising in historical and general studies of transport tend to emphasise economic history much of their information will be valuable to the design historian:

Transport History 1968-1973 (published by David and Charles), 1974 (published by Bratton), 1977- (published by Graphmitre) (generally 3 per year)

Journal of Transport History first series 1953-1966, second series 1971– (2 per year) Leicester University Press

Modern Transport 1919-1968 London (University Microfilms)

Journal of the Institute of Transport 1923- London

Studies of transport systems have been popular, particularly London Transport:

Pick, Frank. 'The organisation of transport, with special reference to the London Passenger Transport Board'. *JRSA* vol 84 January 3 1936 pp 207-221

Barker, Theodore Cardwell and Robbins, Michael. *A history of London Transport: passenger travel and the development of the metropolis.* London: Allen and Unwin vol 1. *The nineteenth century.* 1975 (revised edition) vol 2 *The twentieth century to 1970.* 1976 (revised edition)

Dutton, Norbert. 'Living design – London Transport'. *Art and Industry* October 1946 pp 98-123

Sekon, G. A. *Locomotion in Victorian London.* 1937 London: Oxford University Press 211pp

Barker, T. D. 'Passenger transport in nineteenth century London'. *Journal of Transport History* vol 6 May 1964 pp 166-174

For more detailed study the many publications of the national bodies can be very useful eg British Transport Commission which held its first design conference 4-8 July 1960. Most have design panels generating vast amounts of technical information.

Road

Carriages and engineless vehicles

See also:

Agricultural Equipment *page 251*

General histories:

Ellis, C. Hamilton. *Popular carriages. Two centuries of carriage design for road and rail.* 1962 London: British Transport Design 36pp illus. (first edition 1954)

Ingram, Arthur. *Horse-drawn vehicles since 1760.* 1977 London: Blandford 160pp, 80pp colour

Reid, James (comp). *The evolution of horse-drawn vehicles, with historical notes chronologically arranged and compiled by James Reid*. 1933 London: Institute of British Carriage and Automobile Manufacturers 109pp

Chancellor, Albert. 'Origin and history of carriages'. *JSA* vol 50 May 9 1902 pp 554-567

MacCausland, Hugh. *The English carriage*. 1948 London: Batchworth 144pp bibl.

Sparkes, Ivan. *Stage coaches and carriages. An illustrated history of coaches and coaching*. 1975 Bourne End: Spur Books 160pp illus.

Straus, Ralph. *Carriages and coaches. Their history and evolution*. 1912 London: Martin Secker 310pp illus.

Tyrwhitt-Drake, Sir Garrard. 'Carriages and their history'. *JRSA* vol 100 January 25 1952 pp 167-180 illus.

Watney, Marylian. *The elegant carriage. The history of horse-drawn carriages . . . Coachmen's liveries . . . The Coachbuilders*. 1961 London: J. A. Allen 88pp bibl.

Nockolds, Harold (ed). *The coachmakers: a history of the Worshipful Company of Coachmakers and Coach Harness Makers 1677-1977*. 1977 London: J. A. Allen 239pp illus. bibl. pp 228-229

Coachbuilding surveys:

Thrupp, G. A. 'Cantor lectures – The history of the art of coachbuilding. Lectures 1, 2, 3, 4, 5'. *JSA* vol 25 December 29 1876 pp 99-104; January 5 1877 pp 109-118; January 12 1877 pp 125-132; January 19 1877 pp 152-158; January 26 1877 pp 176-183

Thrupp, G. A. *History of the art of coachbuilding*. 1877 London: Kirby and Endean 152pp (Chapter 4 especially on nineteenth-century design)

Papers read before the Institution of British Carriage Manufacturers 1883-1901

Horse-drawn trade vehicles: a source book (selected) by John Thompson. 1977 Fleet (Hants): J. Thompson 60pp (basically the catalogue of the Bristol Wagon and Carriage Works Company Limited of 1894)

Period developments:

Hooper, George N. 'On the construction of private carriages in England; and on the carriage department of the Paris Exhibition of 1855', *JSA* vol 4 no 159 1855 pp 29-40

Hooper, George N. 'Carriage building and street traffic in England and France', *JSA* vol 38 March 28 1890 pp 460-484 (especially development since 1851)

Philipson, John. *The art and craft of coachbuilding*. 1897 London: Bell 191pp

Gilbey, Sir Walter. *Modern carriages*. 1903 London: Vinton 136pp illus.

An assemblage of nineteenth century horses and carriages from the original sketches by the late William Francis Freelove, written by Jennifer Lang. 1971 Farnham: Perpetua Press 72pp illus.

Sumner, Philip. *Carriages to the end of the nineteenth century*. 1970 London: Science Museum 44pp illus.

Carriage Journal vol 1 no 1 June 1963-

Types of vehicle:

Lee, Charles Edward. *The horse bus as a vehicle*. 1962 London Transport 32pp

Moore, Henry Charles. *Omnibuses and cabs: their origin and history*. 1902 London: Chapman and Hall 282pp illus.

CARAVANS

Whiteman, W. M. *The history of the caravan*. 1973 London: Blandford 295pp illus. good bibl.

Boumphrey, G. M. 'The evolution of the caravan', *Design for Today* June 1933 pp 57-59 illus.

Blake, John E. 'Design for caravans. The problems of a new industry', *Design* 62 February 1954 pp 24-30, *Design* 64 April 1954 pp 22-26, *Design* 66 June 1954 pp 22-26

Cheetham, Dennis. 'The vans that trail behind', *Design* 149 May 1961 pp 52-53

BICYCLES

History:

Alderson, Frederick, *Bicycling – a history*. 1972 Newton Abbot: David and Charles 214pp illus.

Woodforde, John. *The story of the bicycle*. 1970 London: Routledge and Kegan Paul 175pp illus.

Caunter, C. F. *History and development of cycles, as illustrated by the collections of cycles in the Science Museum*. 1955 London: HMSO for the Science Museum. (Pt 1 History and development. 1955 70pp, Pt 2 Descriptive catalogue 1958 75pp)

Wilkinson-Latham, Robert. *Cycles in colour*. 1978 Poole: Blandford 160pp

Design studies:

Sharp, Archibald. 'Cantor lectures third course. Cycle construction and design', *JSA* vol 47 August 18 1899 pp 755-764; August 25 1899 pp 767-774; September 1 1899 pp 779-790; September 8 1899 pp 791-800

Carr, R. 'Design Analysis: Bicycle', *Design* 176 August 1963 pp 43-47

Whitt, Frank Rowland and Wilson, David Gordon. *Bicycling science. Ergonomics and mechanics.* 1974 London: MIT Press 248pp illus.

Starley, J. K. 'The evolution of the cycle', *JSA* vol 46 May 20 1898 pp 601-616

Griffin, Harry Hewitt. *Bicycles and tricycles of the year 1886.* 1971 Otley: Olicana Books Ltd. 190pp 103 illus. (facsimile reprint)

Hillier, George Lacy. 'Cycling: historical and practical', *JSA* vol 45 April 2 1897 pp 440-448

Sumner, Philip Lawton. *Early bicycles.* 1966 London: Evelyn 13pp pl 12

Bowden, Gregory Hunston. *The story of the Raleigh cycle.* 1975 London: W. H. Allen 216pp illus.

Boys, C. V. 'Bicycles and tricycles', *JSA* vol 32 May 9 1884 pp 622-635

Boys, C. V. 'International Inventions Exhibition. Bicycles and tricycles', *JSA* vol 33 September 4 1885 pp 989-992

PRAMS

Sewell, Samuel J. 'The history of children's and invalids' carriages', *JRSA* vol 71 September 7 1923 pp 716-728

King, C. E. 'Forerunners of the pram', *Art and Antiques Weekly* July 9 1977 pp 44-47

Mason, Carola. 'Zero 12345', *Design* 160 April 1962 pp 58-64. (prams and pushchairs review)

INVALID CARRIAGES

Rayner, Claire. 'Wheelchairs', *Design* 164 August 1962 pp 30-39

Powered Transport

Kidner, Roger Wakely. *A short history of mechanical traction and travel.* 1946/1947 Chislehurst: Oakwood Press. In 2 vols.

Pt 1. The early history of the motor car 1769-1897. 1946 59pp

Pt 2. The development of road motors 1890-1946. 1946 pp 64-138

Pt 3. The early history of the railway locomotive 1804-1879. 1946 38pp

Pt 4. The development of the railway locomotive 1880-1946. 1946 pp 40-81

Pt 5. A short history of the railway carriage 1825-1946. 1946 pp 81-104

Pt 6. Multiple unit trains, rail motors and tramcars 1829-1947 pp 107-150

Steam

See also:

Agricultural Equipment *page 251*

Technical Developments *page 106*

Traction engines:

Hughes, William Jesse. *A century of traction engines: being an historical account of the rise and decline of an industry.* 1970 Newton Abbot: David and Charles 262pp bibl. (first published 1959 London: Percival Marshall)

Beaumont, Anthony. *Traction engines past and present.* 1974 Newton Abbot: David and Charles 96pp illus.

Johnson, Brian. *Steam traction engines, wagons and rollers in colour.* 1971 London: Blandford 166pp

Wilkes, Peter. *An illustrated history of traction engines.* 1977 Bourne End: Spur Books 144pp illus.

Wright, Philip A. *Traction engines.* 1959 London: A. & C. Black 89pp illus.

Russell, James Harry. *Painted engines; first series of colour photographs of steam traction engines, their histories and specifications.* 1965 London: Allen and Unwin 94pp illus.

Technical history:

Clark, Ronald H. *The development of the English steam wagon.* 1963 Norwich: Goose 237pp illus. (1895-1915)

Clark, Ronald H. *The development of the English traction engine.* 1960 Norwich: Goose 390pp 582 illus.

Fletcher, William. *English and American steam carriages and traction engines.* 1973 Newton Abbot: David and Charles Reprints 428pp illus. (first published 1904)

Fletcher, William. *Steam on common roads.* 1971 Newton Abbot: David and Charles Reprints 307pp illus. (first published as *The history and development of steam locomotives on common roads* 1891)

Public transport:

Davison, C. St. C. B. *History of steam road vehicles mainly for passenger transport.* 1953 London: HMSO 60pp illus.

Clarkson, Thomas. 'Steam cars for public service', *JSA* vol 52 February 5 1904 pp 233-244

Cossons, Neil. 'The Grenville steam carriage', *Transport History* vol 1 no 3 1968 pp 277-284

Lee, Charles E. 'Rise and decline of the steam driven omnibus', *Transactions of the Newcomen Society* vol XXVII 1949/1951 pp 181-198

Particular types:

Beaumont, Anthony. *Ransome's steam engines: an illustrated history.* 1972 Newton Abbot: David and Charles 110pp illus. (picture book)

Hughes, W. J. (ed). *Fowler steam road vehicles – catalogues and working instructions.* 1970 Newton Abbot: David and Charles 134pp illus.

Kelly, Maurice A. *The Overtype steam road waggon.* 1971 Norwich: Goose and Son 147pp illus. (1880s-1930s)

Kelly, Maurice Anthony. *The Undertype steam road waggon.* 1975 Cambridge: Goose 242pp illus.

Internal Combustion Motor Vehicles

Automobiles

General:

Rolt, L. T. C. *Horseless carriage: history of the motor car in England.* 1950 London: Constable 204pp illus.

Bird, Anthony. *The motor car 1765-1914.* 1963 London: Batsford 256pp illus.

Georgano, G. N. (ed). *The complete encyclopaedia of motor cars 1885-1968.* 1968 London: Ebury Press 640pp 1974 photos (pl 60, colour) (later editions)

Hammond, Maurice. *Motorcade: a dictionary of motoring history 1769-1965.* 1970 London: Bell 256pp illus.

Wise, David Burgess. *Classics of the road.* 1978 London: Orbis 128pp 450 photos

Wherry, Joseph H. *Automobiles of the world: the story of the development of the automobile with many rare illustrations from a score of nations.* 1968 Philadelphia: Chilton 713pp illus.

Crompton, R. E. 'The motor car: its birth, its present and its future', *JRSA* vol 73 November 21 1924 pp 3-26

A few picture histories:

Rolt, Lionel Thomas Caswell. *A picture history of motoring.* 1956 London: Hulton 159pp illus.

Brockbank, Russell. *Motoring through Punch 1900-1970.* 1972 Newton Abbot: David and Charles 160pp 230 illus.

Wise, David Burgess. *The motor car: an illustrated international history . . . special photography by J. Spencer Smith.* 1977 London: Orbis Books 316pp illus.

Lists of cars:

Culshaw, David and Horrobin, Peter. *The complete catalogue of British cars.* 1974 London: Macmillan 511pp illus. (excludes racing and commercial vehicles)

Doyle, G. R. *The world's automobiles 1862-1962. A record of one hundred years of car building, rev. by G. N. Georgano.* 1963 London: Temple Press 180pp (A-Z list of manufacturers and dates)

Museums:

Nicholson, T. R. *The world's motor museums.* 1970 London: Dent 143pp illus.

Design histories:

Barker, Ronald and Harding, Anthony. *Automobile design: great designers and their work.* 1970 Newton Abbot: David and Charles 374pp illus.

Setright, L. J. K. *The designers.* 1976 London: Weidenfeld and Nicolson 199pp illus. (70 motor car designers)

Richards, J. M. 'Man in a hot tin box', *Architectural Review* vol. 123 no 736 May 1958 pp 299-302

Mills, D. Dewar. 'Design review: carriage tradition versus wind tunnel', *Architectural Review* vol 111 no 662 February 1953 pp 125-127

Frostick, Michael. *The cars that got away: ideas, experiments and prototypes.* 1968 London: Cassell 104pp illus.

Caunter, C. F. *The light car. A technical history of cars with engines of less than 1600cc capacity.* 1970 London: HMSO: Science Museum

Beaumont, W. Morby. 'Modern motor car design. Some criticisms and some suggestions', *JRSA* vol 76 July 13 1928 pp 862-878

Carr, Richard. 'In search of the town car', *Design* 211 July 1966 pp 28-37

SOME DESIGN FACTORS

Coker, A. J. (ed). *Automobile engineer's reference book. A comprehensive work of reference providing a summary of the latest practice in all branches of automobile engineering.* 1959 (third edition) London: Newnes (first published 1956)

Donkin, Charles Thomas Brodie. *Elements of motor vehicle design. A textbook for students and draughtsmen.* 1935 London: Oxford University Press 289pp illus. (first edition 1926)

Ergonomics:

Black, Stephen. *Man and motor cars: an ergonomic study.* 1966 London: Secker and Warburg 373pp

Shackel, Brian and others. 'Ergonomics versus styling in cars', *Design* 115 July 1958 pp 29-35 (especially safety aspects)

Safety:

Unsafe at any speed. The designed-in dangers of the American automobile. 1965 New York: Grossman 365pp (including a section on *The stylists*)

Gissane, William. 'The safety aspects of motor car design', *JRSA* vol 114 1966 pp 254ff

Legislation:

Plowden, William. *The motor car and politics 1896-1970*. 1971 London: Bodley Head 469pp

Economics:

Sherman, Roger and Hoffer, George. 'Does automobile style change pay off?', *Applied Economics* vol 3 1971 pp 153-165

Bodies:

McLellan, John. *Bodies beautiful: A history of car styling and craftsmanship*. 1975 Newton Abbot: David and Charles 192pp illus.

'Body Engineering. A symposium arranged by the Automobile Division of the Institute of Mechanical Engineers and the Advanced School of Automobile Engineering', *Institution of Mechanical Engineers Proceedings* 1969-1970 vol 184 Part 3M (including *Towards the all-plastics motorcar* by G. O. Gurney and *The structural design of buses* by G. H. Tidbury

Pawlowski, Janusz. *Vehicle body engineering, edited by Guy Tidbury*. 1969 London: Business Books 300pp (translation of 1964 Polish book *Nadwozia samochodowe*)

Everett, Leslie Albert. *The shape of the motor car*. 1958 London: Hutchinson 182pp

Oliver, George A. *A history of coachbuilding*. 1962 London: Cassell 216pp

Scibor-Rylski, Adam Julius. *Road vehicle aerodynamics*. 1975 London: Pentech Press 213pp illus. bibl.

'The shape of the Postwar motorcar – as foreseen by H. Connolly the motor artist', *Art and Industry* October 1943 pp 108-112

Hosking, Herbert. 'Theory of evolution applied to radiator shells of automobiles', *Automotive Industries* September 6th 1930

Foxlee, Henry J. 'The artist designer and the motor car', *Art and Industry* March 1945 pp 74-81

Engines:

Wankel, Felix. *Rotary piston engines. Classification of design principles for engines, pumps and compressors, translated and edited by R. F. Ansdale*. 1965 London: Iliffe 64pp (taxonomy of designs 1800 – present)

Williams, D. S. D. *The modern diesel. Development and design*. 1972 (14th edition) London: Butterworths 248pp (first edition 1932 Iliffe)

Faith, Nicholas. *The Wankel engine*. 1977 London: Allen and Unwin 234pp illus.

Parts:

See also:

Rubber: Tyres *page 205*

Nockolds, Harold. *Lucas: the first hundred years. Vol 1: The King of the road. Vol 2: 1939 to today*. 1977 Newton Abbot: David and Charles

The Ferodo story. Sixty years of safety 1897-1957. 1957 Chapel en le Frith: Ferodo 62pp illus.

Parsons, R. Clerc. 'Improvements in resilient wheels for vehicles', *JRSA* vol 58 December 3rd 1909 pp 44-62

Fitments:

Nicholson, Timothy Robin. *Car badges of the world*. 1970 London: Cassell & Co. 137pp illus.

Sirignano, Guiseppe di and Sulzberger, David. *Car mascots. An enthusiast's guide*. 1977 London: Macdonald and Jane's 120pp illus. bibl.

JOURNALS

The richest and most accessible sources of motor vehicle design information are the many journals:

Autocar 1895- (weekly) London: Iliffe (University Microfilms) (road tests)

Automobile Quarterly. The commuter's magazine of motoring today, yesterday and tomorrow. 1962-

Automotive Design Engineering. Vol 1 no 1 September 1962- (monthly). London: Rowse Muir Publications

The Light Car 1912-1956 London (weekly) (known as *Cyclecar* 1912-1913, *Light Car and Cycle car* 1913-1933)

The Motor 1903- (weekly) London: Temple Press (road tests)

Motor Car Journal 1899-1912 London

Car Illustrated

Motor Sport 1924- (1924-25 known as *The Brooklands Gazette*. Organisation of motor and motor cycle sport)

Motor Transport 1905-London (University Microfilms) (1905-1920 known as *Motor Traction*. Dealing with motor vehicles for business purposes)

'Motor' Road Test Annual 1949-

EARLY DEVELOPMENTS

Beaumont, W. Worby. 'Cantor lectures. First course. Mechanical road carriages', *JSA* vol 44 December 27 1895 pp 87-102; January 3 1896 pp 130-144; January 10 1896 pp 150-165 illus.

Beaumont, W. Worby. 'Mechanical road carriages', *JSA* vol 51 October 16 1903 pp 894-902; October 23 1903 pp 903-916; October 30 1903 pp 919-930; November 6 1903 pp 932-946 illus.

Beaumont, W. Worby. 'Recent developments in mechanical road carriages', *JSA* vol 45 November 27 1896 pp 17-37 illus.

Cunynghame, H. H. 'Locomotive carriages for common roads', *JSA* vol 44 November 29 1895 pp 23-32, pp 55-63

Johnson, Claude. 'The horseless carriage 1885-1905', *JSA* vol 54 February 16 1906 pp 358-378

Salomons, Sir David. 'Motor traffic: technical considerations', *JSA* vol 45 May 14 1897 pp 581-602

A short history of the Institute of British Carriage and Automobile Manufacturers. 1961 London: The Institute 12pp

Nagle, Elizabeth. *Veterans of the road. The history of veteran cars and the Veteran Car Club of Great Britain.* 1955 London: Arco 239pp illus.

O'Gorman, Mervin. 'Popular motor cars', *JSA* vol 52 April 22 1904 pp 478-485

Posthumus, Cyril. *The story of veteran and vintage cars.* 1977 London: Hamlyn 128pp illus. (first appeared as *First Cars*)

Veteran and Vintage Magazine 1956- (monthly). Beaulieu: Pioneer Publications. (previously 1953- (monthly) *The Vintage and Thoroughbred Car.*)

Veteran Car 1938- (quarterly). Haywards Heath: Veteran Car Club.

VEHICLES OF PARTICULAR PERIODS

Moncrieff, D. Scott. *Victorian and Edwardian motor cars.* 1955 London: Batsford 256pp illus.

Nicholson, T. R. *Passenger cars 1863-1904.* 1970 London: Blandford 160pp

Nicholson, T. R. *Passenger cars 1905-1912.* 1971 London: Blandford 166pp

Nicholson, T. R. *Passenger cars 1913-1923.* 1972 London: Macmillan 157pp

Davis, Alec. 'The car as vehicle', *Design for Today* June 1934 pp 226-229

Dow, George. 'Streamline. The influence of speed on form', *Design for Today* August 1934 pp 281-288

Hudson, Bruce. *British light cars 1930-1939.* 1975 Yeovil: Foulis 334pp illus. bibl.

Sedgwick, Michael. *Cars of the 1930s.* 1970 London: Barsford 384pp

Sedgwick, Michael. *Passenger cars 1924-1942.* 1975 Poole: Blandford 176pp

Vanderveen, Bart H. *British cars of the early thirties 1930-1934.* 1973 London: F. Warne 80pp illus.

Vanderveen, Bart H. *British cars of the late thirties 1935-1939.* 1973 London: F. Warne 80pp illus.

Vanderveen, Bart H. *British cars of the early forties 1940-1946.* 1974 London: F. Warne 64pp illus.

Vanderveen, Bart H. *British cars of the late forties 1946-1949.* 1974 London: F. Warne 64pp illus.

Vanderveen, Bart H. (ed). *British cars of the early fifties 1950-1954.* 1976 London: F. Warne 64pp illus.

Vanderveen, Bart H. (ed). *British cars of the late fifties 1955-59.* 1975 London: F. Warne 64pp illus.

Ware, Michael E. *Making of the motor car 1895-1930.* 1976 Buxton: Moorland Publishing Co. 112pp 159 illus.

Kearley, N. F. 'Style or design? Commentary on London's Motor Show', *Art and Industry* March 1949 pp 90-95

Robson, Graham. *The postwar touring car.* 1977 Yeovil: Haynes 129pp

THE MOTOR INDUSTRY

McLeay, P. 'The Wolverhampton motor car industry 1896-1937', *West Midlands Regional Studies Journal* vol 3 1969

Richardson, Kenneth. *The British motor industry 1896-1939.* 1977 London: Macmillan

MAKES – A SELECTION

Harding, Anthony (ed). *Classic car profiles.* Nos 1-24, 1966, nos 25-60, 1967. Leatherhead: Profile Publications Ltd.

The same publishers have produced other series:

Luxury and Thoroughbred Cars in Profile. 1967 Windsor: Profile Publications

Veteran and Vintage Cars in Profile. 1967 Windsor: Profile Publications

Cars in Profile 1972- (monthly). (Classic Cars in Profile) Windsor: Profile Publications

Thoroughbred and Classic Cars. Vol 2 no 1 – October 1974- (monthly) (continues *Classic Car*)

Day, K. R. *The Alvis car 1920-1966.* 1966 New Malden: Day 170pp illus.

Hull, Peter and Johnson, Norma. *The vintage Alvis.* 1967 London: Macdonald 400pp illus.

Stafford, Jack. 'Racing into design (Aston Martin)', *Design* 61 January 1954 pp 25-30

The Aston Martin: a collection of contemporary road tests (compiled by Adrian M. Feather.) Vol 1: 1921-1942; vol 2: Competition cars 1977, 1975, Leigh on Sea: Feather 80pp 90pp illus.

Lambert, Z. E. and Wyatt, R. J. *Lord Austin: the man*. 1968 London: Sidgwick and Jackson 187pp illus.

Wyatt, Robert John. *The Austin Seven: a pictorial tribute*. 1975 Croydon: Motor Racing Publications 80pp illus. bibl.

Pomeroy, Laurence. *The Mini story*. 1964 London: Temple Press 176pp

Setright, Leonard J. K. *Bristol cars and engines*. 1974 Croydon: Motor Racing Publications 159pp illus.

Nixon, St. John C. *Daimler 1896-1946*. 1946 London: Foulis 232pp illus.

Ford in Europe: the first seventy years. 1975 London: IPC Transport Press 85pp

Blake, John E. 'Refinement in three stages. Ford cars since 1951', *Design* 92 August 1956 pp 16-22

Thirlby, David. *The chain-driven Frazer Nash*. 1965 London: Macdonald 237pp illus.

Harvey, Chris. *The big Healey*. 1978 Oxford Illustrated Press 256pp

Montagu, Edward John Barrington. *Jaguar, a biography. Research by Michael Sedgwick*. 1967 (third revised edition) London: Cassell 300pp illus.

Skilleter, Paul. *Jaguar sports cars*. 1975 Yeovil: Foulis 360pp 104pp of plates bibl.

Harvey, Chris. *E type: end of an era*. 1977 Oxford: Oxford Illustrated Press 236pp illus.

Browning, Peter and Blumsden, John. *The Jensen Healey stories*. 1974 Croydon: Motor Racing 160pp illus.

Bird, A. and Hutton-Scott, F. *Lanchester motor cars*. 1965 London: Cassell 240pp

Robson, Graham. *The Land-Rover: workhorse of the world*. 1976 Newton Abbot: David and Charles 148pp illus.

More Morgan: a pictorial history of the Morgan sports car (compiled by), Gregory Houston Bowden. 1976 London: Wilton House Gentry 223pp illus.

Righyni, S. L. 'Small man's car; how Morris motors put Britain on the mass-production map', *Art and Industry* vol 23 November 1937 pp 178-187

Wherry, Joseph H. *The M.G. story; the story of every M.G. from 'Old No 1' in 1923 to the most modern, with specifications and photos*. 1967 Philadelphia: Chilton Books 205pp illus.

Birmingham, Anthony T. *Riley: the production and competition history of the pre 1939 Riley motor cars*. 1965 London: Foulis 248pp illus. 1 (1974 second edition 272pp)

Bennett, Martin. *Rolls-Royce; the history of the car*. 1974 Oxford: Oxford Illustrated Press 179pp illus.

Bird, Anthony and Hallows, Ian. *The Rolls-Royce motor car*. 1972 (third edition). London: Batsford 328pp illus.

Robson, Graham. *The Rover story*. 1977 Cambridge: Stephens

Oliver, George. *The Rover*. 1971 London: Cassell 220pp illus.

Panofsky, Erwin. 'The ideological antecedents of the Rolls-Royce radiator', *Proceedings of the American Philosophical Society* vol 107 no 4 August 1963

Dalton, Lawrence. *Coachwork on Rolls-Royce, 1906-1939*. 1975 London: Watson 448pp mostly illus.

Robson, Graham. *Story of Triumph sports cars*. 1973 Croydon: Motor Racing Publications 192pp 105 illus.

TYPES OF CAR

Racing cars:

Campbell, Colin. *Design of racing sports cars*. 1973 London: Chapman and Hall 257pp illus.

Clutton, Cecil and others. *The racing car: development and design*. 1962 London: Batsford 247pp illus. (first edition 1956)

Costin, Michael and Phipps, David. *Racing and sports car chassis design*. 1965 London: Batsford 192pp illus.

Nicholson, T. R. *Racing cars and record breakers 1898-1921*. 1971 London: Blandford Press 169pp illus.

Posthumus, Cyril. *Classic racing cars*. 1977 London: Hamlyn 160pp illus.

Terry, Len and Baker, Alan. *Racing car design and development*. 1973 Croydon: Motor Racing Publications 256pp illus.

Sports cars:

Campbell, Colin. *The sports car: its design and performance*. 1969 third edition London: Chapman and Hall 336pp illus.

Georgano, George Nicolaus. *A history of sports cars*. 1970 London: Nelson 320pp

Stanford, John. *The sports car: development and design*. 1957 London: Batsford 224pp illus.

Watkins, Martyn. *British sports cars since the war*. 1974 London: Batsford 208pp illus.

Electric cars:

Bentley, Walter Owen. *An illustrated history of the battery car 1919-1931*. 1964 London: Allen and Unwin 192pp

Marshall, Charles William. *Electric vehicles*. 1925 London: Chapman and Hall 170pp (University Microfilms)

Taxis:

Warren, Philip and Linskey, Malcolm. *Taxicabs: a photographic history.* 1976 London: Almark Publishing 96pp illus. bibl.

Georgano, George Nicolas. *A history of the London taxicab.* 1972 Newton Abbot: David and Charles 180pp illus.

BIBLIOGRAPHIES

The printed catalogue of a very large library collection:

The Automotive history collection of the Detroit Public Library: a simplified guide to its holdings. 1966 Boston: G. K. Hall 2 vols

The National Library of Motoring, Beaulieu is probably the richest British collection and if its catalogue is ever published will make the most useful single bibliography.

ABSTRACTS

This part of the bibliography has deliberately avoided many of the technical papers and studies that are particularly important in such a high technology industry. A useful point of entry to this potentially difficult area is provided by:

MIRA Abstracts: a monthly survey of automobile research and development 1972-Nuneaton: Motor Industry Research Association (previously titled *MIRA Abstracts* 1946-1954, *MIRA Monthly Summary* 1955-1967, *Automobile Abstracts* 1968-1971)

There is the earlier service:

Automotive Abstracts 1923/1924-1934 Cleveland, Ohio. (absorbed into *Automotive Industry*)

Motor Cycles

General studies:

Caunter, C. F. *Motor cycles. A technical history.* 1978 London: HMSO for Science Museum

Tragatsch, Erwin. *The world's motorcycles 1894-1963; a record of 70 years of motorcycle production.* 1964 London: Temple 192pp (an alphabetical listing)

Hough, Richard Alexander and Setright, L. J. K. *A history of the world's motorcycles.* 1966 London: Allen and Unwin 192pp (reissued 1972)

Setright, Leonard, J. K. *Motorcycles.* 1976 London: Weidenfeld and Nicolson 159pp illus.

Sumner, Philip Lawton. *Motorcycles.* 1972 London: HMSO for Science Museum 47pp illus.

Clew, Jeff. *British racing motor cycles.* 1976 Yeovil: Foulis 183pp illus.

Thompson, Eric E. *Motor cycles in colour.* 1974 London: Blandford 192pp

Willoughby, Vic. *Classic motorcycles.* 1975 Feltham: Hamlyn 176pp illus.

The classic motorcycles, edited by Harry Louis and Bob Currie. 1977 Cambridge: Stephens 126pp illus.

Ixion. *Motor cycle cavalcade.* 1971 East Ardsley: S. R. Publishers 272pp illus.

Munro, David. 'Style on two wheels. A review of progress in motor cycle design', *Design* 25 January 1951 pp 14-17

Crowley, Terence Eldon. *Discovering old motorcycles.* 1977 (second edition) Aylesbury: Shire 54pp illus. bibl. (1884-1960)

Particular periods:

Sheldon, James. *Veteran and vintage motorcycles.* 1974 Brentford: Transport Bookman Publications 208pp illus. (first published 1961 Batsford)

Partridge, Michael. *Motorcycle pioneers: the men, the machines, the events 1860-1930.* 1976 Newton Abbot: David and Charles 112pp illus. bibl.

Vanderveen, Bart H. (ed). *Motorcycles to 1945.* 1975 London: Warne 64pp illus.

Vanderveen, Bart H. (ed). *Motorcycles and scooters from 1945.* 1976 London: Warne 64pp illus.

A few makes:

Clark, Ronald Harry. *Brough Superior, the Rolls-Royce of motor cycles.* 1974 (second edition) Norwich: Goose 176pp illus. (first published 1964)

Clew, Jeff. *The best twin: the story of the Douglas motor cycle.* 1974 Norwich: Goose 224pp illus.

Holliday, Bob. *The story of BSA motor cycles.* 1978 Cambridge: Stephens 128pp

Louis, Harry and Currie, Bob. *The story of Triumph Motor Cycles.* 1975 Cambridge: Stephens 128pp illus.

Masters, Dave. *Velocette 1905-1971: an illustrated reference.* 1976 London: Transport Bookman Publications 187pp illus.

Journals:

Motor Cycle 1903- (weekly) London: IPC (incorporating *Motor Cycling* 1909-1967)

Motor Cycle and Cycle Trader 1895- (bi-weekly) Watford: Wheatland Journals

Technical:

Bacon, Roy H. and many others. *The motor cycle manual.* 1976 London: Butterworth 128pp

Commercial Vehicles
LORRIES
General studies:

Georgano, G. N. *The world's commercial vehicles, 1830-1964: a record of 134 years of commercial vehicle production.* 1965 London: Temple Press 122pp illus. (basically an alphabetical list of manufacturers)

Marshall, Prince and Bishop, Denis. *Lorries, trucks and vans 1897-1927.* 1972 London: Blandford 160pp illus.

Ingram, Arthur. *Lorries, trucks and vans 1927-1973.* 1975 London: Blandford 182pp illus.

Klapper, C. F. *British lorries 1900-1945.* 1973 Shepperton: I. Allan 159pp illus.

Stevens-Stratton, S. W. *British lorries 1945-1970.* 1978 Shepperton: I. Allan 192pp illus.

Gibbins, Eric. *The story of trucks.* 1978 London: Orbis 144pp illus.

Cornwell, E. L. *Commercial road vehicles.* 1960 London: Batsford 288pp illus.

Commercial vehicles in collections:

Jenkinson, Keith Anthony. *Preserved lorries.* 1977 Shepperton: I. Allan 352pp illus.

Journals:

Commercial Motor 1905-(weekly) London: IPC Transport Press (University Microfilms)

Vintage Commercial vol 1 nos 1-9 1962-1963 London: North London Artists

A few companies:

The first 50 years 1913-1963. 1969 (revised edition) Bristol: Bristol Commercial Vehicles Ltd.

Forty years of achievement. 1965 Guy Motors Ltd.

Some points of detail:

Nicholl, J. S. 'The development of goods transport by road', *JRSA* vol 89 January 24 1941 pp 119-133 (regulations, controls and designs)

Davis, Alec Edward. 'New shapes on wartime roads', *Architectural Review* vol 94 1943 pp 51-52

Davey, J. B. 'Designed for safety', *Design* 139 July 1960 pp 42-47 (lorry cab design)

Falconer, Peter. 'The container revolution', *Architectural Review* vol 142 December 1967 pp 477-484

BUSES
General surveys:

Booth, Gavin. *The British motor bus: an illustrated history.* 1977 Shepperton: I. Allan 112pp illus.

Hibbs, John (ed). *The Omnibus: readings in the history of road passenger transport.* 1971 Newton Abbot: David and Charles 215pp illus. (collection of papers published by the Omnibus Society)

Dunbar, Charles Stuart. *Buses, trolleys and trams.* 1967 Feltham: Hamlyn 141pp 200 illus.

Hilditch, G. *Looking at buses.* 1978 Shepperton: I. Allan

Hibbs, John 'A history of the motor bus industry: a bibliographical survey', *Journal of Transport History* new series vol 2 1973/1974 pp 41-55

Particular periods:

Lee, Charles Edward. *The early motor bus.* 1962 London Transport Board 40pp illus.

Montagu of Beaulieu, Lord. 'Motor omnibuses', *JRSA* vol 55 February 15 1907 pp 374-385

Vanderveen, Bart H. *Passenger vehicles 1893-1940.* 1973 London: F. Warne 64pp illus.

Kaye, David. *Buses and trolley buses 1919 to 1945.* 1970 London: Blandford Press 191pp illus.

Vanderveen, Bart H. *Buses and coaches from 1940.* 1974 London: F. Warne 64pp illus.

Kaye, David. *Buses and trolleybuses since 1945.* 1968 London: Blandford Press 184pp illus.

Cornwell, E. L. and Parke, John. *Britain's buses in the forties.* 1977 Shepperton: I. Allan 80pp illus.

Morrissey, Charles B. *Modern buses and coaches.* 1952 London: Temple 86pp pl 14

Particular types and makes:

Jack, Doug. *The Leyland bus.* 1977 Glossop: Transport Publishing Co. 440pp illus.

Wagstaff, J. S. *The London 'Routemaster' bus.* 1975 Tarrant Hinton, Dorset: Oakwood Press 48pp (Locomotion papers no 83. Standard London Transport bus 1950-1968)

Williams, George. 'Motor coaches 1952', *Design* 47 November 1952 pp 29-31

London General: the story of the London bus 1856-1956. 1956 London Transport 72pp illus.

Martin, Gavin. *Development of the London Bus 1929-1933.* 1973 London: West Farthing Garage 56pp illus.

Gray, John A. *London buses in camera 1933-1969.* 1971 Shepperton: I. Allan 144pp

Buses conserved in museums and other collections:

Jenkinson, Keith. *Preserved buses.* 1978 Shepperton: I. Allan 264pp illus.

Journals:

Buses 1968- (monthly) Shepperton: I. Allan (incorporating *Passenger Transport* 1898-1967 and *Buses Illustrated* 1949-1967)

Omnibus Magazine 1929- (bi-monthly) London: Omnibus Society

Detail:

Gill, Dennis. 'Improving bus design', *Design* 130 October 1959 pp 48-51

Carr, Richard. 'Luxury coach facelift', *Design* 237 September 1968 pp 54-57

Trolleybuses:

Owen, Nicholas. *History of the British trolleybus.* 1974 Newton Abbot: David and Charles 188pp illus. bibl.

Symons, R. D. H. and Creswell, P. R. *British trolleybuses.* 1967 Shepperton: I. Allan 80pp illus.

Crosley, A. S. 'Early development of the railless electric trolleybus . . . up to 1924', *Transactions of the Newcomen Society* vol 33 1960/1961 pp 93-111

Trolleybus Magazine: journal of the National Trolleybus Association 1966 – (bi-monthly) London

Special Types of Road Transport

Vanderveen, Bart H. (ed). *Earthmoving vehicles.* 1972 London: Warne 64pp illus.

Vanderveen, Bart H. (ed). *Fairground and circus transport . . . research by Dennis N. Miller.* 1973 London: Warne 64pp illus.

Gilbert, K. R. *Fire engines and other fire fighting appliances.* 1969 (new edition) London: HMSO for Science Museum 21pp illus.

Ingram, Arthur. *Fire engines in colour.* 1973 Blandford 235pp illus. bibl.

Vanderveen, Bart H. (ed). *Fire fighting vehicles 1840-1950.* 1972 London: Warne 80pp illus.

Vanderveen, Bart H. (ed). *Fire and crash vehicles from 1950.* 1976 London: Warne 72pp illus.

Vanderveen, Bart H. (ed). *The Jeep.* 1976 London: Warne 64pp illus.

Whitehead, R. A. *A century of steam-rolling.* 1975 Shepperton: I. Allan 192pp illus. bibl.

Vanderveen, Bart H. (ed). *Wreckers and recovery vehicles.* 1972 London: Warne 72pp illus.

'Case history. Fork lift truck', *Design* 62 February 1954 pp 7-10 (Stacatruc by Industrial Truck Development Ltd)

Railways

Three useful introductions to an enormous literature:

Bryant, Eric Thomas. *Railways. A readers guide.* 1968 London: Clive Bingley 249pp (mostly post-1945 literature, excluding technical matter)

Ottley, George. *A bibliography of British railway history.* 1965 London: Allen and Unwin 683pp

Ottley, George. *Railway history: a guide to sixty-one collections in libraries and archives in Great Britain.* (Subject Guide to Library Resources no 1) 1973 London: Library Association 80pp

A few general historical surveys:

Ellis, Cuthbert H. *British railway history* vol 1. 1830-1876, vol 2. 1877-1947. 1954, 1959 London: Allen and Unwin

Haresnape, Brian. *Railway design 1830-1914.* 1968 Shepperton: I. Allan 128pp illus.

Hawke, G. R. *Railways and economic growth in England and Wales 1840-1870.* 1970 Oxford University Press 421pp

Ferneyhough, Frank. *History of railways in Britain.* 1975 London: Osprey 288pp illus.

Nock, Oswald Stevens. *Railways then and now. A world history.* 1975 London: Elek 214pp 324 illus.

Pollins, Harold. *Britain's railways: an industrial history.* 1971 Newton Abbot: David and Charles 223pp illus.

Simmons, Jack. *The railways of Britain: an historical introduction.* 1968 (second edition) London: Macmillan 276pp pl 17 bibl. pp 244-263

Simmons, Jack (ed). *Rail 150 The Stockton and Darlington Railway and what followed.* 1975 London: Eyre Methuen 208pp illus.

Some early works:

Foxwell, E. and Farrer, T. D. *Express trains, English and foreign.* 1964 Shepperton: I. Allan (reprint of classic first published 1889)

Williams, Frederick S. *Our iron roads, their history, construction and administration.* 1968 London: F. Cass 514pp illus. (new impression of second edition of 1883)

There are a very great number of local and regional studies, some of which contain useful design detail eg:

Young, John N. *Great Northern Suburban.* 1977 Newton Abbot: David and Charles 168pp illus.

Davis, Alec. 'Modernising British Transport. Glasgow Suburban Railway', *Design* 131 November 1959 pp 40-43

Dow, George. 'Design for trains (LNER)', *Design for Today* November 1935 pp 441-446

Some more technical discussion:

Allen, Cecil J. *Modern railways: their engineering, equipment and operation.* 1959 London: Faber 307pp illus.

Snell, J. B. *Mechanical engineering: railways.* 1971 London: Longman 177pp illus. bibl.

'Railways – special issue', *Design* 81 September 1955

'British Railways special issue', *Design* 171 March 1963

Mann, Paul B. 'Problems for the Designer: railways', *Art and Industry* November 1943 pp 146-151

A guide to collections and societies:

Body, Geoffrey (ed). *Railway Enthusiasts Handbook 1970-1971.* 1970 (third edition) Newton Abbot: David and Charles 176pp

Railway decoration:

Ellis, C. Hamilton. 'Colours for British trains', *Architectural Review* vol 103 May 1948 pp 215-216

Dow, George. *Railway heraldry.* 1973 Newton Abbot: David and Charles 269pp illus.

Journals:

Journal of the Railway and Canal Historical Society 1955- (quarterly) Caterham: Railway and Canal Historical Society

Locomotive, Railway Carriage and Wagon Review 1921-1959 London

Modern Railways 1961- (monthly) Shepperton: I. Allan (incorporating *Trains Illustrated* 1945, *Locomotive Magazine* 1897-. University Microfilms)

The Railway Engineer 1880- January 1935 (absorbed by *Railway Gazette*)

Railway Gazette International 1905- (monthly) London: IPC Business Press. (title varies back to *Railway Magazine* 1835- *Bradshaws Railway Gazette* 1846-1872, *Transport* 1892-1904)

Railway World 1952- (monthly) Shepperton: I. Allan (*Railways* 1939-1952)

Indexes and abstracts:

Bulletin of the International Railway Congress Association 1896- (monthly index of journal articles)

Selection of International Railway Documentation. 1965- (monthly) Paris and Brussels: International Union of Railways and International Congress Association (four language editions)

Railway Engineering Abstracts 1946-1962 London: Institute of Civil Engineers

Monthly Review of Technical Literature 1950- Derby: British Railways Research Department (information abstracts)

For the enthusiasts there are the many publications of groups such as the Railway Correspondence and Travel Society and the Stephenson Locomotive Society.

Locomotives

A general study:

Glover, Graham. *British locomotive design 1825-1920.* 1967 London: Allen and Unwin 113pp illus.

Collections and museums:

Casserley, H. C. *Preserved locomotives.* 1977 (fourth edition) Shepperton: I. Allan 368pp illus.

Steam

Jones, Kevin P. *Steam locomotive development. An analytical guide to the literature on British steam locomotive development 1923-1962.* 1969 London: Library Association 413pp

Ahrons, Ernest Leopold. *The British steam railway locomotive 1825-1925.* 1927 London: Locomotive Publishing Co 391pp illus. (facsimile reprint 1963 Ian Allan)

Nock, Oswald Stevens. *The British steam railway locomotive vol 2. 1925-1965.* 1966 Shepperton: I. Allan 276pp illus.

Nock, Oswald Stevens. *Steam locomotion: the unfinished story of steam locomotives and steam locomotive men on the railways of Great Britain.* 1968 (second edition) London: Allen and Unwin 273pp pl 33

Ahrons, Ernest Leopold. *Development of British locomotive design.* 1914 London: Locomotive Publishing Company 229pp

Cox, Ernest Stewart. *British Railways standard steam locomotives.* 1966 Shepperton: I. Allan 218pp illus.

Davies, B. R. 'Design and technique in British locomotive development', *Art and Industry* June 1947 pp 162-173

Fenton, William. *Nineteenth century locomotive engravings.* 1964 London: Hugh Evelyn (20 engravings and description)

Ellis, Cuthbert Hamilton. *Some classic locomotives.* 1949 London: Allen and Unwin 173pp illus.

Reed, Brian. *150 years of British steam locomotives.* 1975 Newton Abbot: David and Charles 128pp illus.

Cox, E. S. *World steam in the twentieth century.* 1969 Shepperton: I. Allan 191pp illus.

Allen, Cecil John. *Locomotive practice and performance in the twentieth century.* 1949 Cambridge: Heffer 302pp illus.

Poultney, Edward Cecil. *British express locomotive development 1896-1948.* 1952 London: Allen and Unwin 175pp illus.

Ransome-Wallis, P. *The last steam locomotives of British railways.* 1974 Shepperton: I. Allan 192pp illus.

Tuplin, William Alfred. *The steam locomotive: its form and function.* 1974 Bath: Adams and Dart 158pp illus.

Industrial Locomotive Society. *Steam locomotives in industry.* 1967 Newton Abbot: David and Charles 112pp 154 illus.

Fox, M. J. and King, G. D. *Industrial steam album.* 1970 Shepperton: I. Allan 144pp

Brutton, E. D. *British steam 1948-1955.* 1977 Shepperton: I. Allan 128pp illus.

A few locomotives designed for particular regions:

Armstrong, Jim. *LNER locomotive development between 1911 and 1947: with a brief history of developments from 1850 to 1911.* 1974 Seaton: Peco 93pp illus. bibli.

Casserley, Henry Cecil. *LNER locomotives 1923-1948.* 1977 Truro: Barton 96pp illus.

Clay, J. F. and Cliffe, J. *The LNER 2-8-2 and 2-6-2 classes.* 1977 Shepperton: I. Allan 144pp illus,

Clay, J. F. and Cliffe, J. *The LNER 4-6-0 classes.* 1975 Shepperton: I. Allan 240pp illus.

British Locomotive Catalogue 1825-1923. 1977 Buxton: Moorland Publishing vol 1. Summary, vol 2. LNWR and constituents edited by D. Baxter.

Some of the many detailed studies of particular types of locomotives:

Clay, J. F. and Cliffe, J. *The West coast Pacifics.* 1976 Shepperton: I. Allan 240pp illus.

Allen, Cecil J. *British Atlantic locomotives, revised by G. F. Allen.* 1976 Shepperton: I. Allan 184pp illus.

Allen, C. J. *British Pacific locomotives.* 1971 Shepperton: I. Allan 240pp illus.

Bulleid locomotives: a pictorial history (compiled) by Brian Haresnape. 1977 Shepperton: I. Allan 112pp

Bulleid, H. A. V. *Bulleid of the Southern.* 1977 Shepperton: I. Allan 240pp illus.

Allen, Cecil J. and Townroe, Stephen C. *Bulleid Pacifics of the Southern.* 1977 Shepperton: I. Allan 56pp illus.

Haresnape, Brian and Swain, Alec (comps). *Churchward locomotives: a pictorial history.* 1976 Shepperton: I. Allan 112pp illus.

Allen, Cecil J. and others. *The Deltics: a symposium.* 1977 (second edition) Shepperton: I. Allan 80pp illus.

Abbott, Roland A. S. *The Fairlie locomotive.* 1970 Newton Abbot: David and Charles 103pp illus.

Durrant, A. E. *The Garratt locomotive.* 1969 Newton Abbot: David and Charles 144pp illus.

Nock, Oswald S. *The locomotives of Sir Nigel Gresley.* 1945 London: Longman 180pp

Bellwood, John and Jenkinson, David. *Gresley and Stanier. A centenary tribute.* 1976: HMSO for Science Museum 103pp illus.

Haresnape, Brian. *Ivatt and Riddles locomotives.* 1977 Shepperton: I. Allan 112pp illus.

Nock, Oswald S. *The 'Kings' and 'Castles' of the GWR.* 1977 Shepperton: I. Allan 96pp illus. (first published 1949)

Haresnape, Brian (comp). *Maunsell locomotives: a pictorial history.* 1977 Shepperton: I. Allan 128pp

Nock, Oswald S. *The locomotives of R. E. L. Maunsell 1911-1937.* 1954 Bristol: Edward Everard 192pp

Atkins, C. P. *The Scottish 4-6-0 classes.* 1976 Shepperton: I. Allan 128pp illus.

Haresnape, Brian. *Stanier locomotives.* 1970 Shepperton: I. Allan 128pp illus.

Nock, Oswald S. *William Stanier.* 1975 Shepperton: Allan 190pp illus.

Warren, J. G. H. *A century of locomotive building by Robert Stephenson & Co 1823-1923.* 1970 Newton Abbot: David and Charles 461pp illus. (first published 1923)

Designers:

Marshall, John. *A biographical dictionary of railway engineers.* 1978 Newton Abbot: David and Charles 252pp bibl. notes

Cox, E. S. *Speaking of steam.* 1971 Shepperton: I. Allan 127pp illus. (extracts from statements of locomotive engineers on trends in design)

Rogers, H. C. B. *G. J. Churchward: a locomotive biography.* 1975 London: Allen and Unwin 216pp illus.

Rogers, H. C. B. *The last steam locomotive engineer: R. A. Riddles CBE.* 1970 London: Allen and Unwin 215pp

Cornwell, H. J. Campbell. *William Stroudley, craftsman of steam.* 1968 Newton Abbot: David and Charles 263pp illus. bibl.

Loewy, Raymond. *The Locomotive.* 1937 London: Studio 108pp illus.

Compressed Air

Beaumont, F. 'The Beaumont compressed air locomotive', *JSA* vol 29 March 18 1881 pp 384-394

Hadfield, C. *Atmospheric railways, a Victorian venture in silent speed.* 1967 Newton Abbot: David and Charles 240pp

Diesel/Internal Combustion

Webb, Brian. *British internal combustion locomotive 1894-1940.* 1973 Newton Abbot: David and Charles 120pp illus.

Tayler, A. J. H. *The Brush class 47 diesels.* 1977 Shepperton: I. Allan 128pp illus. (largest and best known diesel with BR)

Electric

Haut, Frederick J. G. *The history of the electric locomotive.* 1969 London: Allen and Unwin 148pp pl 258 bibl.

Haut, Frederick J. G. 'The early history of the electric locomotive', *Transactions of the Newcomen Society* vol 27 1949/1951 pp 153-162

Haut, Frederick J. G. *Electric locomotives of the world.* 1977 Truro: Barton 96pp illus.

Journals

Journal of the Stephenson Locomotive Society 1909- (monthly) Birmingham

The Locomotive 1897- London

Locomotives in Profile 1970- (monthly) Windsor: Profile Publications

Journal of the Institution of Locomotive Engineers 1911-

Locomotives Illustrated 1975- (quarterly) Shepperton: I. Allan (each issue concentrates on a different loco class)

Rolling Stock

A general survey 1930-1950:

Sinclair, F. W. M. 'Rolling stock design and construction', *Times Review of Industry* December 1950

Carriages and coaches:

Ellis, C. Hamilton. 'The room on wheels', *Architectural Review* vol 109 January 1951 pp 29-37 (a general history)

Ellis, Cuthbert Hamilton. *Railway carriages in the British Isles from 1830 to 1914.* 1965 London: Allen and Unwin 279pp illus.

Ellis, Cuthbert Hamilton. *Nineteenth century railway carriages in the British Isles from the 1830s to the 1900s.* 1949 London: Modern Transport Publishing Company 176pp illus.

Dow, George. 'Railway coach design innovations on tourist trains', *Design for Today* March 1934 pp 110-113

Colquhoun, Ian. 'Design for railways', *Design* 47 November 1952 pp 15-19

Mallabrand, P. and Bowles, L. J. *The coaching stock of British Railways: classifications, allocations, formations, detail variations.* 1974 Kenilworth: Railway Correspondence and Travel Society 132pp

Particular types of coach:

Jones, Barbara. 'Royal transport', *Architectural Review* vol 113 January 1953 pp 49-57

Harris, Michael. *Gresley's coaches.* 1973 Newton Abbot: David and Charles 160pp illus. (Great Northern and LNER)

Russell, J. M. *A pictorial record of Great Western coaches* vol 1: 1838-1903, vol 2. 1913-1948. 1972-1973 Oxford Publishing Company

Esserey, R. J. and Jenkinson, D. *The LMS coach 1923-1957.* 1971 Shepperton: I. Allan 134pp

A history of the Gloucester Railway Carriage and Wagon Company. 1960 London: Weidenfeld and Nicolson 64pp illus.

Bruce, J. Graeme. *Steam to silver: an illustrated history of London Transport railway surface rolling stock.* 1975 London Transport 170pp (first published 1970)

Spark, Robert. 'Modernising British transport no 4 Pullman express', *Design* 140 August 1960 pp 36-41

Details of collections and museums:

Harris, Michael. *Preserved railway coaches.* 1977 Shepperton: I. Allan 208pp illus.

Goods wagons:

Essery, R. J., Rowland, D. P. and Steel, W. O. *British goods wagons, from 1887 to the present day.* 1970 Newton Abbot: David and Charles 144pp illus.

Atkins, A. G. *A history of GWR goods wagons vol 1. general.* 1975 Newton Abbot: David and Charles 95pp illus.

Cranes:

Brownlie, John Stewart. *Railway steam crane: a survey of progress since 1875.* 1973 Glasgow: author, distributed by Holmes McDougall 369pp illus.

Signalling

Nock, Oswald S. *British railway signalling. A survey of fifty years progress.* 1969 London: Allen and Unwin 180pp illus.

Hamilton, Paul. 'The power signal box', *Architectural Review* vol 138 no 825 1961 pp 333-337

Trams

General histories:

Buckley, R. J. *History of tramways.* 1975 Newton Abbot: David and Charles 192pp illus.

Rush, Robert William. *British electric tramcar designs 1885-1950.* 1976 Oxford Publishing 122pp illus. bibl.

Wilson, Frank Edward. *The British tram.* 1961 London: Percival Marshall 87pp illus.

Joyce, J. *Trams in colour since 1945.* 1970 London: Blandford Press 160pp

Jackson-Stevens, E. *British electric tramways.* 1971 Newton Abbot: David and Charles 112pp illus. (mostly pictures)

Klapper, Charles E. *The Golden age of tramways.* 1974 (second edition) Newton Abbot: David and Charles 344pp illus.

Wilson, Geoffrey. *London United Tramways. A history 1894-1933.* 1971 London: Allen and Unwin 240pp illus.

Thompson, Julian. *British trams in camera.* 1978 Shepperton: I. Allan 128pp illus.

Some early works:

Adams, W. Bridges. 'Tramways and their structure, vehicles, haulage and uses', *JSA* December 1 1971 pp 41-50

Clark, Daniel Kinnear. *Tramways: their construction and working.* 1894 (second edition) London: Crosby Lockwood 758pp illus. (first edition 1878)

Journals:

Bulletin of the Tramway and Light Railway Society. 1956 – (quarterly) London

Modern Tramway and Light Railway Review: official organ of the Light Railway Transport League. 1937-(monthly) London

Underground Railways

The London Underground has been extensively studied:

Day, John Robert. *The story of London's Underground.* 1972 (revised edition) London Transport 200pp illus. (earlier edition 1968)

Lindsey, C. F. *Underground railways in London: a select bibliography.* 1973 London: author 12pp

Bruce, J. Graeme. *Tube trains under London.* 1968 London: Transport 114pp illus.

Howson, H. F. *London's underground.* 1967 (fourth edition) Shepperton: I. Allan 142pp illus. (first edition 1951)

Lee, Charles Edward. *Sixty years of the Piccadilly.* 1966 London Transport 25pp pl 12

Prigmore, B. J. and Atkinson, F. G. B. *London Underground tubestock 1900-1920: an analysis.* 1958 London: Electric Railway Society

Prigmore, B. J. *London Transport tube stock 1923-1934: an analysis.* 1957 London: Electric Railway Society

Prigmore, B. J. *London Transport tube stock till 1939.* 1960 London: Electric Railway Society

Prigmore, B. J. *Tube stock to 1951.* 1967 (revised edition) London: Electric Railway Society 32pp

Shand, P. Morton. 'The underground', *Architectural Review* vol 66 1929 pp 217-224

The Glasgow underground:

Kelly, Paul J. and Willsher, M. J. D. *Glasgow Subway 1896-1977.* 1977 London: Light Railway Transport League 28pp illus.

Other Forms of Land Transport

Tough, John M. and O'Flaherty, Coleman A. *Passenger conveyers. An innovatory form of communal transport.* 1971 Shepperton: I. Allan 176pp illus. bibl. (includes historical survey)

Air

Powered Flight

General histories:

Gibbs-Smith, Charles H. *Aviation. An historical survey from its origins to the end of World War II*. 1970 London: HMSO illus. bibl. pp 269-275 (previously published as *The Aeroplane: an historical survey* 1960)

Gibbs, Charles H. *The invention of the aeroplane (1799-1909)*. 1966 London: Faber 360pp

Gibbs-Smith, Charles H. *A history of flying*. 1953 London: Batsford 304pp illus.

' "A Centenary of British Aeronautics" – centenary issue', *Royal Aeronautical Society Journal* vol 70 January 1966 302pp (many short historical articles)

'The aeroplane (Cantor lectures) 1. The birth of the aeroplane by C. H. Gibbs-Smith, 2. The development of the aeroplane by Peter W. Brooks, 3. The future of the aeroplane by Eric Mensforth', *JRSA* vol 107 1958 pp 78-140

Taylor, John W. R. and Munson, Kenneth (eds). *History of Aviation*. 1978 (new edition) London: New English Library 511pp illus.

Taylor, John W. R. *The lore of flight*. 1975 London: Nelson 426pp illus. (very useful encyclopaedic index)

Hudson, Kenneth. *Air travel. A social history*. 1972 Bath: Adams and Dart 174pp illus.

Technical histories:

Miller, Ronald and Sawers, David. *The technical development of modern aviation*. 1968 London: Routledge and Kegan Paul 351pp pl 20 bibl. pp 317-338 (useful information on the economic factors of airliners)

Nayler, J. L. and Ower, E. *Aviation: its technical development*. 1965 London: P. Owen and Vision Press 306pp illus.

Brooks, P. W. 'The development of the aeroplane (Evolution of engineering series)', *Chartered Mechanical Engineer* vol 11 April 1964 pp 194-201

Stevens, James Henry. *The shape of the aeroplane*. 1953 London: Hutchinson 302pp illus.

Andrews, Allen. *Back to the drawing board. The evolution of flying machines*. 1977 Newton Abbot: David and Charles 168pp 138 illus.

Reflections on particular periods:

Bruce, Eric Stuart. 'Mechanical flight', *JRSA* vol 57 December 4 1908 pp 49-60

Walker, Percy Brooksbank. *Early aviation at Farnborough: the history of the Royal Aircraft Establishment*. 1972-1974 London: Macdonald and Jane's *vol 1. Balloons, kites and airships, vol 2. The first aeroplanes*

Jones, Lewis R. 'Design for aeroplanes', *Design for Today* December 1935 pp 470-474

Macaulay, R. H. H. 'Problems for the designer: airways. Design for the coming air age', *Art and Industry* September 1943 pp 75-82

Worcester, R. G. 'The influence of art on aircraft design', *Art and Industry* February 1946 pp 34-40

Worcester, R. G. 'Towards the new aircraft', *Art and Industry* April 1947 pp 98-103 (anticipates the development of the jet)

Nayler, Joseph Lawrence. *Modern aircraft design*. 1950 London: Temple Press 122pp illus.

Hildred, William P. 'From subsonic to supersonic', *JRSA* vol 109 1965 pp 782ff

Wood, Derek. *Project cancelled: a searching criticism of the abandonment of Britain's advanced aircraft projects*. 1975 London: Macdonald and Jane's 251pp illus.

Surveys of aircraft:

Jane's All the World's Aircraft 1909/1910- (annual). London: Macdonald and Jane's

Gibbs-Smith, Charles H. *A directory and nomenclature of the first aeroplanes, 1809 to 1909*. 1966 London: HMSO for Science Museum 120pp pl 88

Lewis, Peter M. H. *British aircraft 1809-1915*. 1968 New York: Funk & Wagnalls 576pp illus.

Dickson, Bonner W. A. *Aircraft from airship to jet propulsion 1908-1948*. 1948 London: Naldwell Press for Vickers Armstrong 78pp illus.

Stroud, John. *The world's civil marine aircraft*. 1975 London: Putnam 128pp illus.

Le Corbusier. *Aircraft*. 1935 London: Studio 16pp illus. ('the symbol of the New Age . . . advance guard of the conquering armies of the New Age, the airplane arouses our energies and our faith')

Rice, Michael S. (comp). *Guide to pre-1930 aircraft engines*. 1972 Milwaukee: Aviation 57pp illus.

Guides to collections and relics:

Ellis, Ken and Butler, Phil. *British museum aircraft: 39 museums and the histories of their exhibits*. 1977 Liverpool: Mersey Aviation Society Ltd. 166pp illus. bibl. pp 158-160

Robertson, Bruce. _Aviation archaeology: a collector's guide to aeronautical relics._ 1977 Cambridge: Stephens 152pp illus.

Civil Aircraft

See also:

Interior Design: Aircraft _page 167_

Jackson, Aubrey Joseph. _British Civil aircraft since 1919._ 1959, 1960, 1974 London: Putnam (includes details, specifications and illustration of each aircraft):
1 A.B.C. Robin to Chilton D.W.1. 567pp
2 Christen CH 3 Au to Hawker Siddeley HS 650 Argosy. 560pp
3 Hawker Siddeley H.S. 748 to Youngman-Baynes High Lift monoplane. 636pp

Airliners and freight:

Munson, Kenneth. _Airliners between the wars 1919-1939._ 1972 Poole: Blandford 186pp illus.

Munson, Kenneth. _Airliners since 1946._ 1976 (second edition) Poole: Blandford 172pp illus.

Stroud, John. _European transport aircraft since 1910._ 1966 London: Putnam 680pp illus.

Stroud, John Hector. _Annals of British and Commonwealth air transport, 1919-1960._ 1962 London: Putnam 675pp illus.

Brooks, Peter Wright. _The modern airliner: its origins and development._ 1961 London: Putnam 176pp illus.

Miles, F. G. 'British civil air transports', _Art and Industry_ September 1946 pp 66-72

Munson, Kenneth. _Pictorial history of BOAC and Imperial Airways._ 1970 London: I. Allan 96pp illus.

Munson, Kenneth. _Flying boats and seaplanes since 1910._ 1971 Poole: Blandford 64pp illus.

Light aircraft:

Boughton, Terence B. A. _The story of the British light aeroplane._ 1963 London: John Murray 321pp illus.

Lewis, Peter. _British racing and record-breaking aircraft._ 1977 London: Putnam 496pp 470 illus.

Aircraft developed by particular companies:

Tapper, Oliver. _Armstrong Whitworth aircraft since 1913._ 1973 London: Putnam 398pp 385 illus.

Jackson, Aubrey Joseph. _Avro aircraft since 1908._ 1965 London: Putnam 470pp illus.

Jackson, Aubrey Joseph. _Blackburn aircraft since 1909._ 1968 London: Putnam 555pp illus.

Barnes, C. H. _Bristol aircraft since 1910._ 1964 London: Putnam 415pp illus.

Sharp, Cecil Martin. _D.H.: an outline of De Havilland history._ 1960 London: Faber 419pp illus.

Jackson, Aubrey Joseph. _De Havilland aircraft since 1909._ 1978 (second edition) London: Putnam 542pp illus (first edition 1962)

Taylor, Harold Anthony. _Fairey aircraft since 1915._ 1974 London: Putnam 450pp illus.

James, Derek N. _Gloster aircraft since 1917._ 1971 London: Putnam 456pp illus.

Clayton, Donald C. _Handley Page: an aircraft album._ 1970 Shepperton: I. Allan 126pp illus.

Barnes, Christopher Henry. _Hadley Page aircraft since 1907._ 1976 (revised edition) London: Putnam 664pp illus.

Mason, F. K. _Hawker aircraft since 1920._ 1971 (second edition) London: Putnam 495pp illus.

Brown, Don Lambert. _Miles aircraft since 1925._ 1970 London: Putnam 430pp illus.

Andrews, C. F. _Vickers aircraft since 1908._ 1969 London: Putnam 576pp illus.

Particular aircraft:

Harvey, Derek. _Famous airliners._ 1958 London: Cassell 4 vols:
1 The Viscount
2 The Britannia
3 The seven seas: DC 1 – DC 7C
4 The Comet

Dempster, Derek David. _The tale of the Comet._ 1959 London: Wingate 218pp illus.

Bramson, Alan and Birch, Neville. _The Tiger Moth story._ 1964 London: Cassell 256pp illus.

Carr, Richard. 'Pup, up and away', _Design_ 239 November 1968 pp 44-47

Ellis, Ken (ed). _A history of the Short SC-7 Skyvan._ 1975 Liverpool: Merseyside Aviation Society and Ulster Aviation Society 31pp illus.

Turner, P. St. John. _Handbook of the Vickers Viscount._ 1968 Shepperton: I. Allan 170pp illus.

Journals and Bibliographies

Journals:

The Aeronautical Journal 1897- (monthly) London: Royal Aeronautical Society (previously _Journal of the Royal Aeronautical Society_ 1923-1968)

Aeroplane 1911-1959 (later the *Aeroplane and Astronautics* 1959-1962 then *The Aeroplane and Commercial Aviation News* 1962-1966, then *Aeroplane. The International Air Transport Journal* 1966-1968, then incorporated with *Flight International*)

Aircraft Illustrated 1968- (monthly) Shepperton: I. Allan

Aircraft in Profile 1965- (monthly) Windsor: Profile Publications

Air Enthusiast 1971- (monthly) London: Fine Scroll (mostly historical material. Title changed to *Air International* 1974)

Aerospace Historian 1954- (quarterly) Kansas State University (formerly *Airpower Historian*)

Aircraft Engineering 1929- (monthly) London: Bunhill

Aviation Week and Space Technology 1916- (weekly) New York: McGraw Hill (previous title *Aviation*)

Flight International 1967- (weekly) London: IPC (titled *Flight* 1909-1967)

Bibliographies:

Gibbs-Smith, Charles H. *History of Flying. Readers Guide.* 1957 London: National Book League 32pp

History of Aeronautics and Astronautics. A preliminary bibliography compiled by Katherine Murphy Dickson. 1968 Washington: National Aeronautics and Space Administration 420pp (annotated with some detail on vehicles)

Gamble, William B. (comp). *History of Aeronautics. A selected list to material in the New York Public Library.* 1938 (reprinted 1971) New York Public Library/Arno Press Inc 325pp

Hovercraft

Hayward, Leslie H. *History of Air cushion vehicles.* 1963 London: Kalerghi-McLeary 45pp

Hovercraft Craft and Hydrofoil 1961- (monthly) London: Kalerghi Pubs.

Helicopters

Munson, Kenneth. *Helicopters and other rotorcraft since 1907.* 1973 (second edition) Poole: Blandford 176pp illus.

Gregory, Hollingsworth Franklin. *The helicopter.* 1976 London: Yoseloff 223pp illus. (first published 1944 as *Anything a horse can do*)

Lambermont, Paul M. and Pirie, Anthony. *Helicopters and autogyros of the world.* 1970 (revised edition) London: Cassell 446pp illus. (first edition 1958)

Airships

Jane's pocket book of airship development, compiled by Lord Ventry and Eugène M. Kolesnik. 1976 London: Macdonald and Jane's 244pp illus. bibl.

Higham, Robin. *The British rigid airship 1908-1931.* 1962 London: Foulis 426pp illus.

Collier, Basil. *The airship: a history.* 1974 London: Hart Davis MacGibbon 271pp illus. bibl.

Hartcup, Guy. *The achievement of the airship: a history of the development of rigid, semi-rigid and non-rigid airships.* 1974 Newton Abbot: David and Charles 296pp illus. bibl.

Rolt, Lionel T. C. *The Aeronauts: a history of Ballooning 1783-1903.* 1966 London: Longman 267pp pl 32 bibl. (includes a chronology)

Payne, Lee. *Lighter than air.* 1978 London: Yoseloff/Tantivy

Ege, Lennart. *Balloons and airships in colour, edited by K. Munson.* 1973 Poole: Blandford 208pp

Jackson, Robert. *Airships in peace and war.* 1971 London: Cassell 277pp illus. bibl.

Toland, John. *Great Dirigibles. Their triumphs and disasters.* 1973 (revised edition) London: Dover 352pp illus.

Gliders

Ellison, Norman. *British gliders and sailplanes 1922-1970.* 1971 London: A and C Black 296pp illus. bibl.

Welch, Lorne and Welch, Ann. *The story of gliding.* 1965 London: Murray 211pp

Water

Sea Transport

General introductions to the whole area:

Landström, Bjorn. *The ship. A survey of the history of the ship from the primitive raft to the nuclear powered submarine.* 1961 London: Allen and Unwin 309pp illus. bibl.

Kemp, Peter K. (ed). *Oxford Companion to ships and the sea.* 1976 Oxford University Press 976pp 417 illus.

Motor powered shipping

Surveys:

Baker, William A. *From paddle steamer to nuclear ship: a history of the engine-powered vessel.* 1966 London: Watts 268pp illus.

Deeson, Arthur F. L. *An illustrated history of steamships.* 1976 Bourne End: Spurbooks 158pp illus.

Isherwood, J. H. *Steamers of the past.* 1968 Liverpool: Journal of Commerce and Shipping Telegraph Ltd 115pp illus. (reprints of material first published in *Mariners Mirror*)

Technical developments:

Guthrie, J. *A short history of Marine Engineering.* 1971 London: Hutchinson 294pp illus.

Smith, Edgar Charles. *A short history of Naval and Marine Engineering.* 1938 Cambridge University Press 376pp pl 16

British Ship Research Association Journal 1946- (monthly) Wallsend

Hunter, N. M. 'Changes in ship construction methods 1850-1950', *Engineering* 173 June 6 1952 pp 730-731

Barnaby, K. C. *The Institution of Naval Architects 1860-1960.* 1960 London: Royal Institution of Naval Architects 645pp (review of *Transactions* year by year with table of contents 1860-1960)

Duff, Peter. *British ships and shipping: a survey of modern ship design and shipping practice.* 1949 London: Harrap 240pp illus.

Barr, G. E. 'History and development of machinery for paddle steamers', *Transactions of the Institute of Engineers and Shipbuilders in Scotland.* 1951/1952 pp 101ff

Spratt, H. Philip. *The birth of the steamboat.* 1958 London: Charles Griffin 149pp illus.

Hardy, A. C. *History of motorshipping. The story of fifty years of progress which have had a profound influence upon the development of sea transport during the twentieth century.* 1955 London: Whitehall Technical Press 390pp illus.

Gray, Thomas. 'On modern legislation in regard to the construction and equipment of steamships', *JSA* vol 14 February 23 1866 pp 239-254

Lenaghan, James. 'The design of ships in Scotland', *Design* 57 September 1953 pp 8-12 (especially postwar developments)

Symonds, T. E. 'On the construction of twinscrew steamships', *JSA* vol 11 April 24 1863 pp 391-398

Somake, Ellis E. 'The design of ships today', *JRSA* vol 106 1957 pp 269ff

Propulsion:

Burgh, N. P. 'On marine engines from 1851 to the present time', *JSA* vol 13 March 17 1865 pp 291-301

Henning, Graydon R. 'Britain and the motorship: a case of the delay and adoption of new technology', *Journal of Economic History* 35 June 1975 pp 353-385 (on the power of the coal lobby)

Hindliffe, R. 'Fifty years of progress in propulsion efficiency', *Transactions of the North East Coast Institution of Engineers and Shipbuilders* vol 63 1947 pp 183ff

FREIGHTERS

Baker, George Stephen. *The merchant ship: design, past and present.* 1948 London: Sigma Books 159pp pl 16

Bathe, B. W. *Merchant ships to 1880.* 1969 London: HMSO for Science Museum 47pp illus.

Bathe, B. W. *Merchant ships from 1880.* 1973 London: HMSO for Science Museum 47pp illus.

Spratt, H. P. *Merchant steamers and motor ship. Descriptive catalogue.* 1970 (new edition) London: HMSO for Science Museum 154pp illus.

Dunn, Laurence. *Merchant ships of the world in colour 1910-1929.* 1973 Poole: Blandford 200pp illus.

Hunter, G. B. and Rusett, E. W. de. 'Sixty years of merchant shipbuilding on the North East coast', *Transactions of the Institution of Engineers and Shipbuilders in Scotland* 1908/1909 pp 323ff

Murray, J. M. 'Merchant ships 1860-1960. Paper presented at the centenary meeting May 1960', *Transactions of the Royal Institution of Naval Architects* 1960

Robertson, J C and Hagan, H. H. 'A century of coaster design and operation', *Transactions of the Institution of Engineers and Shipbuilders in Scotland* 1953/1954 pp 204ff

Sawyer, L. A. and Mitchell, W. H. *The Liberty ships: the history of the emergency type cargo ships constructed in the United States during World War II.* 1970 Newton Abbot: David and Charles 224pp illus.

LINERS

See also:

Interior Design: Ship interiors *page 166*

Gibbs, Charles R. Vernon. *British passenger liners of the five oceans, a record of the British passenger lines and their liners from 1838 to the present.* 1963 London: Putnam 560pp illus.

Coleman, Terry. *The liners.* 1976 London: Allen Lane 240pp illus.

Transatlantic liners:

Phillips-Birt, Douglas. *When luxury went to sea.* 1971 Newton Abbot: David and Charles 96pp illus. (particularly 1890s)

Gibbs, Charles Robert Vernon. *Passenger liners of the Western Ocean. A record of the North Atlantic steam and motor passenger vessels from 1838 to the present day.* 1952 London: Staples Press 352pp illus.

Spratt, Hereward Philip. *One hundred years of transatlantic steam navigation 1838-1938; a brief outline of the history and development of the Atlantic ferry since the advent of the steamship.* 1938 London: HMSO for Science Museum 23pp illus.

Ransome-Wallis, Patrick. *North Atlantic panorama 1900-1976.* 1977 Shepperton: I. Allan 192pp illus. bibl.

Bonsor, N. R. P. *North Atlantic seaway. An illustrated history of passenger services linking the old world with the new.* 1975 (revised edition) Newton Abbot: David and Charles 480pp illus. (first published 1955 with supplement 1960)

Cairis, N. T. *North Atlantic passenger liners since 1900.* 1972 Shepperton: I. Allan 224pp illus.

Spratt, Hereward Philip. *Transatlantic paddle steamers.* 1968 (second edition) Glasgow: Brown, Son and Ferguson 92pp illus. bibl. (first edition 1951)

Cunard and the Queens:

Hyde, Francis Edwin. *Cunard and the North Atlantic 1840-1973: a history of shipping and financial management.* 1975 London: Macmillan 382pp illus. bibl. refs.

Lacey, Robert. *Queens of the North Atlantic.* 1973 London: Sidgwick and Jackson 128pp 80 illus.

Knell, K. A. 'Q4: her ancestry and heritage', *Cambridge University Engineering Society Journal* 36 1966 pp 56-68

Dunn, Laurence (ed). *Famous liners of the past Belfast built.* 1964 London: Adlard Coles 238pp illus.

FERRIES

Duckworth, C. L. and Langmuir, G. E. *Railway and other steamers.* 1968 Preston: T. Stephenson & Sons 432pp illus.

Strange, Lt Col A. 'Ships for the Channel passage', *JSA* vol 21 February 7 1873 pp 198-205, pp 218-224 (problems of design)

Salmon, Geoffrey. 'Modernising British transport no 2 Cross Channel ferry', *Design* 133 January 1960 pp 44-47

Ransome-Wallis, P. *Train ferries of Western Europe.* 1968 Shepperton: I. Allan 289pp illus.

LIFEBOATS

Fry, Eric C. *Lifeboat design and development.* 1975 Newton Abbot: David and Charles 128pp illus.

Some earlier papers:

Henderson, Andrew. 'The past and present position of lifeboats', *JSA* vol 3 June 1 1855 pp 510-517

Green, J. F. 'Steam lifeboats', *JSA* vol 39 January 16 1891 pp 127-137

INDIVIDUALS

Shipbuilders:

Scott, John Dick. *Vickers. A history.* 1962 London: Weidenfeld and Nicolson 416pp

Two hundred and fifty years of shipbuilding by Scotts at Greenock. 1961 (fourth edition) Glasgow: Scotts 280pp illus.

Borthwick, Alastair. *Yarrow and Company Limited. The first hundred years 1865-1965.* 1965 Glasgow: Yarrow 135pp illus.

Two early designers:

Russell, John Scott. *The modern system of naval architecture.* 1864-1865 London: Day and Son 3 vols

Emmerson, George S. *John Scott Russell. A great Victorian engineer and naval architect.* 1977 London: John Murray 342pp illus.

Fairbairn, William. 'On the application of iron for the purposes of naval construction', *JSA* vol 13 November 25 1864 pp 20-33

Fairbairn, William. *Treatise on iron ship building: its history and progress as comprised in a series of experimental researches in the laws of strain; the strength, forms and other conditions of the material.* 1865 London: Longmans Green 313pp illus.

A few ships:

Corlett, E. C. B. *The Iron ship: history and significance of Brunel's Great Britain.* 1975 Bradford on Avon: Moonraker Press 253pp 149 illus.

Corlett, E. C. B. 'The steamship "Great Britain" ', *Transactions of the Royal Institution of Naval Architects* vol 113 1971 pp 411-437

Beaver, Patrick. *The big ship: Brunel's 'Great Eastern' – a pictorial history.* 1969 London: Hugh Evelyn 136pp illus.

Dugan, James. *The great iron ship. The story of the 'Great Eastern'.* 1953 London: Hamilton 224pp

The Cunard White Star Quadruple-screw liner Queen Mary. 1973 Cambridge: Patrick Stephens (reprint of June 1936 souvenir number of *The Shipbuilder and Marine Engine-Builder*)

Watt, David S. and Birt, R. *The Queen Elizabeth. The world's greatest ship.* 1947 London: Winchester Publications 148pp illus.

Sailing ships

General surveys:

Folkard, Henry Coleman. *The sailing boat. A treatise on sailing boats and small yachts their varieties of type, sails, rig etc.* 1973 Wakefield: EP 381pp (facsimile of fourth edition 1870. Five editions 1854-1901)

Chapelle, Howard I. *The search for speed under sail 1700-1855.* 1968 London: Allen and Unwin 453pp illus.

Chatterton, Edward Keble. *Fore and aft. The story of the fore and aft rig from the earliest times to the present day.* 1912 London: Seeley Service 347pp

Victorian and Edwardian sailing ships from old photographs, compiled by Basil Greenhill and Ann Giffard. 1976 London: Batsford 144pp

Merchant vessels:

Macgregor, David R. *Fast sailing ships. Their design and construction 1775-1875.* 1973 Lymington: Nautical Publishing Company 314pp 259 illus. large bibl.

McCutchan, Philip. *Tall ships: the golden age of sail.* 1976 London: Weidenfeld and Nicolson 160pp illus.

Greenhill, Basil and Giffard, Ann. *The merchant sailing ship: a photographic history.* 1970 Newton Abbot: David and Charles 112pp 127 photos (based on National Maritime Museum collections)

Macgregor, David R. *The tea clippers.* 1972 (revised edition) London: Conway Marine 272pp illus. (first published 1952)

Greenhill, Basil. *The merchant schooners, a portrait of a vanished industry, being a survey in two volumes of the history of the small fore and after rigged sailing ships of England and Wales in the years 1870-1940 with something*

of their previous history and subsequent fate. 1968 (revised edition) Newton Abbot: David and Charles 2 vols 264pp, 259pp illus.

Course, A. G. *The wheel's kick and the wind's song.* 1968 (third edition) Newton Abbot: David and Charles 266pp pl 17 (history and technical detail of the last merchant sailing ship fleet – John Stewart & Co of London 1877-1928)

Coastal vessels:

March, Edgar J. *Inshore craft of Britain in the days of sail and oar.* 1970 Newton Abbot 2 vols 276pp, 309pp illus.

Carr, Frank G. G. *Vanishing craft. British coastal types in the last days of sail.* 1934 London: Country Life 108pp illus. bibl.

Slade, W. J. and Greenhill, Basil. *West country coasting ketches.* 1974 London: Conway Maritime 136pp illus. bibl.

Barges:

Davis, Dennis J. *The Thames sailing barge: her gear and rigging.* 1970 Newton Abbot: David and Charles 94pp illus.

Yachts:

Phillips-Birt, Douglas. *Fore and aft sailing craft and the development of the modern yacht.* 1962 London: Seeley Service 286pp

Phillips-Birt, Douglas. *History of yachting.* 1974 London: Hamilton 288pp 152 illus.

Heaton, Peter S. *Yachting. A history.* 1955 London: Batsford 280pp illus. bibl.

Baader, Juan. *The sailing yacht: how it developed – how it works, translated from the German by James and Ingeborg Moore.* 1965 New York: Norton 336pp illus.

Cannell, David and Leather, John. *Modern development in yacht design.* 1976 London: Coles 152pp illus. bibl.

Chappelle. *Yacht designing and planning for yachtsmen, students and amateurs.* 1936 London: Putnam 319pp illus. bibl.

Fox, Uffa. 'Designing, building and sailing yachts and boats', *JRSA* vol 108 1959 pp 133ff

Phillips-Birt, Douglas. *Sailing yacht design.* 1976 (third edition) London: Coles 360pp illus. (earlier edition 1966)

Journals

Containing historical surveys:

Maritime History 1971- (2 per year) Tavistock: Bratton

The Mariner's Mirror 1911-(quarterly) London: Society for Nautical Research (Index 1-35 (1911-1949) compiled by R. C. Anderson 1955 183pp Index 36-55

(1950-1969) compiled by Elizabeth
Rolfe 1974 188pp)

Sea Breezes: the magazine of ships and the
sea. 1919- (monthly) Liverpool: Journal
of Commerce and Shipping Telegraph

A few of the many technical journals:

*Transactions of the Royal Institution of Naval
Architects.* 1860- (annual) London

The Naval Architect: journal of the Royal
Institution of Naval Architects
1971- (quarterly) London

Shipping World and Shipbuilder
1883- (monthly) London: Benn
(incorporating *World Shipbuilding* 1951-,
Ship Builder and Marine Engine Builder
1906-, *Syren and Shipping International*
1967-)

Motor Ship 1920- (monthly) London: IPC

Marine Engineer and Naval Architect 1876
London

*Transactions of Institution of Engineers and
Shipbuilders in Scotland* 1857- (monthly)
Glasgow

*Transactions of North East Coast Institution of
Engineers and Shipbuilders* 1884-(6 per
year) Newcastle upon Tyne

*Shipbuilding and Marine Engineering
International* 1958- (monthly)

Abstracts:

Journal of Abstracts 1968- (monthly)
Wallsend: British Ship Research
Association (*Journal of the British Ship
Research Association* 1962-1968, *Journal of
the British Shipbuilding Research Association*
1946-1962)

A bibliography:

Sanderson, Michael. *Development of the boat.
A select bibliography.* 1974 London:
National Maritime Museum 120pp

Canals and Inland Waterways Transport

Chaplin, Thomas William. *A short history of
the narrow boat.* 1967 Norwich: Dibb
48pp illus.

Chaplin, Tom. *The narrow boat book.* 1978
Salisbury: Michael Russell 128pp illus.

'Canals – special issue', *Architectural Review*
vol 106 July 1949 (includes chronology
and bibliography)

Smith, Peter. *Waterways heritage.* 1971 Luton
Museum 68pp illus.

Smith, Donald John. *Canal boats and boaters.*
1976 London: Evelyn 132pp illus.

Journals

The periodicals set out below relate to the broader aspects of design. Journals related to more specific activities are listed under these activities elsewhere in this book.

General

Design 1949- (monthly) London: Design Council

Art and Industry 1936-1958 London (titled *Commercial Art and Industry* 1927-1935. Changed to *Design for Industry* 1959 and died)

Design for Today 1933-1936 London: Week End Publications

Idea international design annual 1953-

A useful source of current information on developments in design history is:

Design History Society Newsletter 1978- Wolverhampton: Design History Society

Architectural Periodicals

Perhaps the richest source of detail:

Architectural Review 1897- (monthly) London: Architectural Press (University Microfilms)

Architectural Design 1930- (monthly) London

Architect and Building News 1929- (weekly) London (previously *The Architect* 1869-1929. Title changed back to *The Architect* in 1972)

Architectural Association Journal 1905-1968 London

Architectural Association Quarterly 1969- London

L'Architecture d'Aujourd'hui 1930- (6 issues per year) Boulogne

L'Architecture Vivante 1923-1933 (reprinted 1976 by Trewin Copplestone Publishing Ltd)

The Builder 1842- (weekly) London (title changed to *Building* 1966-)

Domus 1928- (monthly) Milan (a historical survey of *Domis* from 1928 to 1973 is to be found in 'Domus: 45 ans d'architecture, design, art', in *Domus* no 522 May 1973 pp i-viii)

Focus 1-4 1938-1939 London: Lund Humphries

Lotus no 1 1965- (annual) Milan: Industrie Grafiche Editoriale SpA (*Lotus* 12 September 1976 Industrial Architectural Review)

Perspecta: the Yale architectural journal. 1952- (annual) New Haven, Connecticut

Journal of the Royal Institute of British Architects 1894- (monthly) (previously *Journal of Proceedings* . . . 1885-1893, *Proceedings* 1834-1884. University Microfilms)

RIBA Transactions 1835-1892 (University Microfilms)

There are many many others.

Engineering Journals

The general engineering journals, especially those aimed at the design engineer, will become increasingly valuable for technical details of design history:

Design Engineering 1964- (monthly) London: Morgan Grampian

Design Methods and Theories 1966- (4 per year) Berkeley, California: Design Methods Group, University of California (previously *DMG-DRS Journal: Design Research and Methods*)

Design News: the design engineers idea magazine 1946- (fortnightly) Boston: Cahners

Engineering 1866- (monthly) London: Design Council (other publishers previously)

The Engineering Designer 1950- (monthly) London: Institute of Engineering Designers

General Art Periodicals

Of particular value:

Art Journal 1839-1912 London: Virtue

Its history and influence:

The Art Journal. A short history follows of a monthly publication that has been issued continuously since 1839 . . . 1906 London: Virtue 40pp

The Studio 1893-1964 (monthly) (later *Studio International* 1965-)

Its influence:

Johnson, Diane Chalmers. 'The *Studio:* a contribution to the 90's', *Apollo* March 1970 pp 198-203

Gaunt, William. 'The Studio 1893-1928
Retrospect and prospect', Studio vol 95
1928 pp 3-11

Holme, C. G. 'Nation endorses The Studio's
foresight', Studio vol 105 February 1933
pp 71-73

Holme, C. G. 'Studio's leadership, its
post-war campaign for improved
industrial design vindicated', Studio
vol 105 March 1933 pp 139-141

Levetus, Amelia S. 'The European
influence of The Studio', Studio vol 105
1933 pp 257-259

The Studio Yearbook of Decorative Art
1906-1925 London (Decorative Art
1926-1960/1961, Decorative Art in Modern
Interiors 1961-1962-1974-1975)

Other magazines aimed more at the
collector and connoisseur:

Apollo 1925- (monthly) London: Financial
Times (ABC reprint 1925-1969)

Burlington Magazine 1903- (monthly)
London

The Connoisseur 1901- (monthly) London
(Microcards Editions 1901-1962)

Country Life 1897- (weekly) London: IPC
(cumulative index vols 1-152, 1897-1972
Town and Country Houses)

Victoria and Albert Museum Bulletin 1965-
(irregular)

Consumer Journals

Journals published by consumers
organisations can be useful for details of
particular products, especially:

Which? 1957- (monthly) London:
Consumers Association

European and American Journals

A small selection:

France

Design Industrie 1952- (bi-monthly) Paris:
(after 1964 includes short English
translation of many articles. Earlier
called Esthétique Industrielle)

superseding:

Art Présent no 1-13 1947-1950 Paris

Art et Industrie 1925-1936 Paris

L'Amour de l'Art 1945- Paris (previously
L'Amour de l'Art 1920-1938, Promethée
1939-1940)

Art et Décoration 1897-1938 Paris

Art International Aujourd'hui 1929-1930
nos 1-17, 19 Paris: Moreau
(Chadwyck-Healey microfiche)

L'Art Vivant. Peinture, sculpture, le livre, arts
décoratifs et appliqués. Revue
bi-mensuelle des amateurs et des artistes.
nos 1-234 January 1925-July 1939 Paris
(Chadwyck-Healey microfiche)

Cimaise, revue de l'art actuel. no 1 1953-
(bi-monthly) Paris (Chadwyck-Healey
microfiche)

Connaissance des Arts 1952- (monthly) Paris:
Société d'Etudes et de Publications
Artistiques

Gazette des Beaux Arts. 1859- (10 per year)

Germany

Form. Internationale Revue 1957-1965 (1966-
Form: Zeitschrift für Gestaltung)

Ulm. 1958-1968 Ulm: Hochschule für
Gestaltung (trilingual)

Design Report Darmstadt: Rat für
Formgebung

Dekorative Kunst 1897-1929 Munich

Deutscher Kunst und Dekoration 1897-1934
Darmstadt

United States

Industrial Design; designing for industry.
February 1954- (6 per year) New York:
Billboard Pubs. (1954-1974 University
Microfilms)

Design: the magazine of creative art, for
teachers, artists and craftsmen. 1899-
(bi-monthly) Indianapolis (ABC
Microfilm) (especially handcrafts)

Industrial Design in America 1949-1950-
(annual) New York: Farrar, Straus and
Young (edited by the Society of Industrial
Designers)

Design Quarterly 1946- (quarterly)
Minneapolis: Walker Art Center (ABC
Microfilm)

Metropolitan Museum of Art Bulletin 1942-
(quarterly) New York

Museum of Modern Art Bulletin 1933- New
York (ABC Reprint)

Product Design and Development 1946-
(monthly) Radnor, Pennsylvania:
Chilton Company

Italy

Stile Industria 1954-1963 Milan

Casabella 1928- Milan

Austria

Kunst und Kunsthandwerk 1898-1921 Vienna

Netherlands

Vorm 1952- (10 per year) Beurs: Design
Council of the Netherlands

Functie en Vorm 1956- Bussum: Monsadelt
(text in Dutch, French and English)

Norway

Nye Bonytt-Design for Living; Norsk
    spesialblad for hus, hjemog
    boliginnredning 1941- (formerly called
    Bonytt)

Sweden

Form. Svenska Slöjdforeningens Tidskrift.
    1905- Stockholm: Svenska
    Slöjdforeningens (Chadwyck-Healey
    microfiche. English summaries of
    articles)

Kontur: Swedish Design Annual 1950-
    (annual) Stockholm: Svenska
    Slöjdforeningen

Switzerland

Das Werk. Schweizer Monatsschrift für
    Architektur, Kunstgewerbe und
    Kunstlerisches Gewerbe. 1915-
    Winterthur: Bund Schweizer Architekten
    und Schweizer Werkbund

Bibliographies, indexes, abstracts and catalogues

Earlier sections have detailed some of the bibliographical works that have evolved to serve the needs of particular areas. The purpose of this section is to draw attention to some of the more general works. As might be expected of a subject in its infancy, Design History is patchily served by a motley selection of works created very largely to serve other subjects and purposes.

Bibliographies

Tentative introductions to the whole area are provided by:

Karpel, Bernard. 'The Idea of Design. A suggestive bibliography', pp 137-157 in *Idea 55 International Design Annual*. 1955 Stuttgart: Hatje

the modified version:

Karpel, Bernard. 'The language of art: a bibliography', in McCurdy, Charles (ed). *Modern art: a pictorial anthology*. 1958 New York: Macmillan

Poole, Mary Elizabeth. *'History' references from the 'Industrial Arts Index' 1913-1957*. 1958 Raleigh, North Carolina: D. H. Hill Library, North Carolina State College 119pp (University Microfilms facsimile reprint 1973)

Booksellers' catalogues can also be very useful:

Catalogue 29. The Arts Applied. 1975 London: B. Weinreb

Art and the Decorative Arts:

Ehresmann, Donald L. *Applied and decorative arts: a bibliographic guide to basic reference works, histories and handbooks.* 1977 Littleton, Colorado: Libraries Unlimited

Universal catalogue of books on art. Compiled for the use of the National Art Library and the Schools of Art in the United Kingdom. By order of the Lords of the Committee of the Council on Education, edited by J. H. Pollen. 1870-1877 London: Chapman and Hall 3 vols with supplements 1887, 1888

Lietzmann, Hilda. *Bibliographie zur Kunstgeschichte des 19 Jahrhunderts, Publikationer der Jahre 1940-1966.* 1968 Munich: Prestel 234pp illus.

Industry and technology:

Josephson, Aksel G. S. *A list of books on the history of industry and the industrial arts.* 1915-1916 Chicago: John Crerar Library 2 vols with supplement

Perhaps the most useful general bibliographies are provided by the printed catalogues of libraries rich in design history material:

National Art Library Catalogue, Victoria and Albert Museum. *Author Catalogue.* 1972 Boston: G. K. Hall 10 vols and *Catalogue of Exhibition Catalogues.* 1972 Boston: G. K. Hall 1 vol

Dictionary Catalog of the Art and Architecture division, the Research Libraries of the New York Public Library. 1975 Boston: G. K. Hall 30 vols

with supplements:

Bibliographic guide to Art and Architecture. 1975- (annual) 1976- Boston: G. K. Hall (first supplement 766pp)

Catalog of the Library of the Graduate School of Design, Harvard University. 1968 Boston: G. K. Hall 44 vols with supplements

Catalog of the Library of the Museum of Modern Art, New York. 1976 Boston: G. K. Hall 14 vols

Library Catalog, Metropolitan Museum of Art New York. 1960 Boston: G. K. Hall 25 vols with supplements

Catalog of the Avery Memorial Architectural Library, Columbia University, New York. 1968 (second edition) Boston: G. K. Hall 19 vols with supplements

Abstracts

The task is daunting, but a start has been made in a small way by:

Design Abstracts International 1977- (quarterly) Paris: ICSID (previously *ICSID Information Bulletin,* earlier *Design Bibliography* 1966-1974)

Abstracting services designed primarily for the art historian do help reveal some fairly accessible material in:

Art Bibliographies Modern 1971- Oxford: ABC Clio

Art Bibliographies Current Titles 1972- Oxford: ABC Clio

RILA: Repertoire international de la littérature de l'art 1973, 1975-

Repertoire d'Art et Archéologie (de l'époque
paléochrétienne à 1939) Paris: Centre
de Documentation Sciences Humaines

Art and Archaeology Technical Abstracts 1955-
New York: Institute of Fine Art
(formerly IIC Abstracts. Primarily
concerned with conservation)

In practice the coverage of most aspects
of design is very scanty.

The Council of Industrial Design did start
a series of mimeographed *Industrial Design
Abstracts* in the late 1940s and this feature
was transferred to *Design*, but the effort
very soon expired.

The range of more technical abstracts is
wider but less accessible to the
non-specialist:

Electrical and Electronics Abstracts 1966-
(monthly) London: Institute of
Electrical Engineers (previously *Electrical
Engineering Abstracts* 1898-1966)

'Abstracts and references' in *Electronics and
radio Engineer* 1957- (previously in
Wireless Engineer 1924-1956)

Indexes

The two commonest British general
indexes:

British Humanities Index 1962- (quarterly)
London: Library Association

and:

British Technology Index 1962- (monthly)
London: Library Association

divide Design amongst themselves in a
way that their predecessor – *Subject Index
to Periodicals* 1915-1961 – deliberately and
successfully did not.

The newest index is yet to prove itself:

Arts and Humanities Citation Index 1978-
Philadelphia: ISI

Apart from these general works there is
some coverage in the main art indexes:

Art Index 1929- (quarterly) New York:
Wilson

Art Design Photo 1972- (annual) Hemel
Hempstead: Alex Davis Publications
(particularly strong on the graphic
aspects. Previously named *LOMA:
Literature on Modern Art*)

*Catalogue d'articles de Périodiques – Arts
décoratifs et Beaux-Arts (Catalog of
periodical articles – Decorative and Fine
Arts), Bibliotheque Forney.* 1972 Boston:
G. K. Hall 4 vols

*Index to Art periodicals compiled in the Ryerson
Library, Art Institute of Chicago.* 1962
Boston: G. K. Hall 11 vols

More useful for technical material are the
architectural indexes:

Architectural Periodicals Index 1973-
(quarterly) London: RIBA (previously
Sir Bannister Fletcher Library Bulletin and
RIBA Annual Review of Periodical Articles.
The *Comprehensive Index to Architectural
Periodicals* 1956-1972 is available on
World Microfilms)

Architectural Index 1950- (annual)
Boulder, Colorado

Avery index to architectural periodicals. 1973
(second edition) Boston: G. K. Hall
15 vols with supplements

Avery obituary index of architects and artists,
Columbia University. 1963 Boston:
G. K. Hall 338pp

Some of the more general technological
indexes include quite a lot of useful design
references but they can be difficult to
extract:

Applied Science and Technology Index: a
cumulative subject index to English
language periodicals in the fields of
aeronautics and space science,
automation, chemistry, construction,
earth sciences, electricity and electronics
etc. 1958- (monthly except July) New
York: H. W. Wilson (previously *Industrial
Arts Index* 1913-1957)

Informationsdienst geschicte der technik 1961-
(annual) Dresden: Technische
Universitat Sektion Philosophie und
Kulturwissenschaften

*Bulletin Signaletique. Part 522: Histoire des
Sciences et des Techniques.* 1961-
(quarterly) Paris: Centre National de
la Recherche Scientifique

Engineering Index; abstracting and indexing
services covering sources of the world's
engineering literature. 1906- (annual,
post-1962 monthly with annual
cumulation) New York: Engineering
Index (superseded *Engineering Index*
1884-1891 – 1901-1905 published in 4
vols by *Engineering Magazine*)

*Design in Industry. The industrialist is an
artist.* May 1930-April 1931 Newark, New
Jersey: Newark Public Library

Exhibition and museum publications often
present great problems and tend to
become fugitive materials. Perhaps the new
annual:

*Bibliography of Museum and Art Gallery
Publications and Audiovisual aids in Great
Britain and Ireland.* 1978 Cambridge:
Chadwyck-Healey

may help although the best single guide to
older materials is still the one volume

based on the holdings of the National Art Library:

Catalogue of exhibition catalogues. 1972
   Boston: G. K. Hall

Dissertations and Unpublished Material

Although this bibliography has deliberately tried to exclude unpublished material it is important to know about the keys to research:

Dissertation Abstracts International

   Section A: *Humanities and Social Sciences*

   Section B: *Physical Sciences and Technology*

   Section C: *European dissertations*

   1938- (monthly) Ann Arbor
   (previously *Dissertations Abstracts*)

Comprehensive Dissertation Index. 1973
   London: University Microfilms 32 subject vols, 5 author volumes with annual supplements (doctoral theses USA and Canada. On Datrix II computer base)

Index for theses accepted for higher degrees in the universities of Great Britain and Ireland. 1950/1951- (annual) London: ASLIB

Some deposits of unpublished material and archives are noted in:

Architectural History and the Fine Arts and Applied Arts: sources in the National Register of Archives. 1969- (annual) London: National Register of Archives

Subject finder

What follows is an index to the sections and major subjects of the bibliography, not an index to all the authors and subjects it includes or touches upon. Entries are repeated where necessary to avoid cross references.